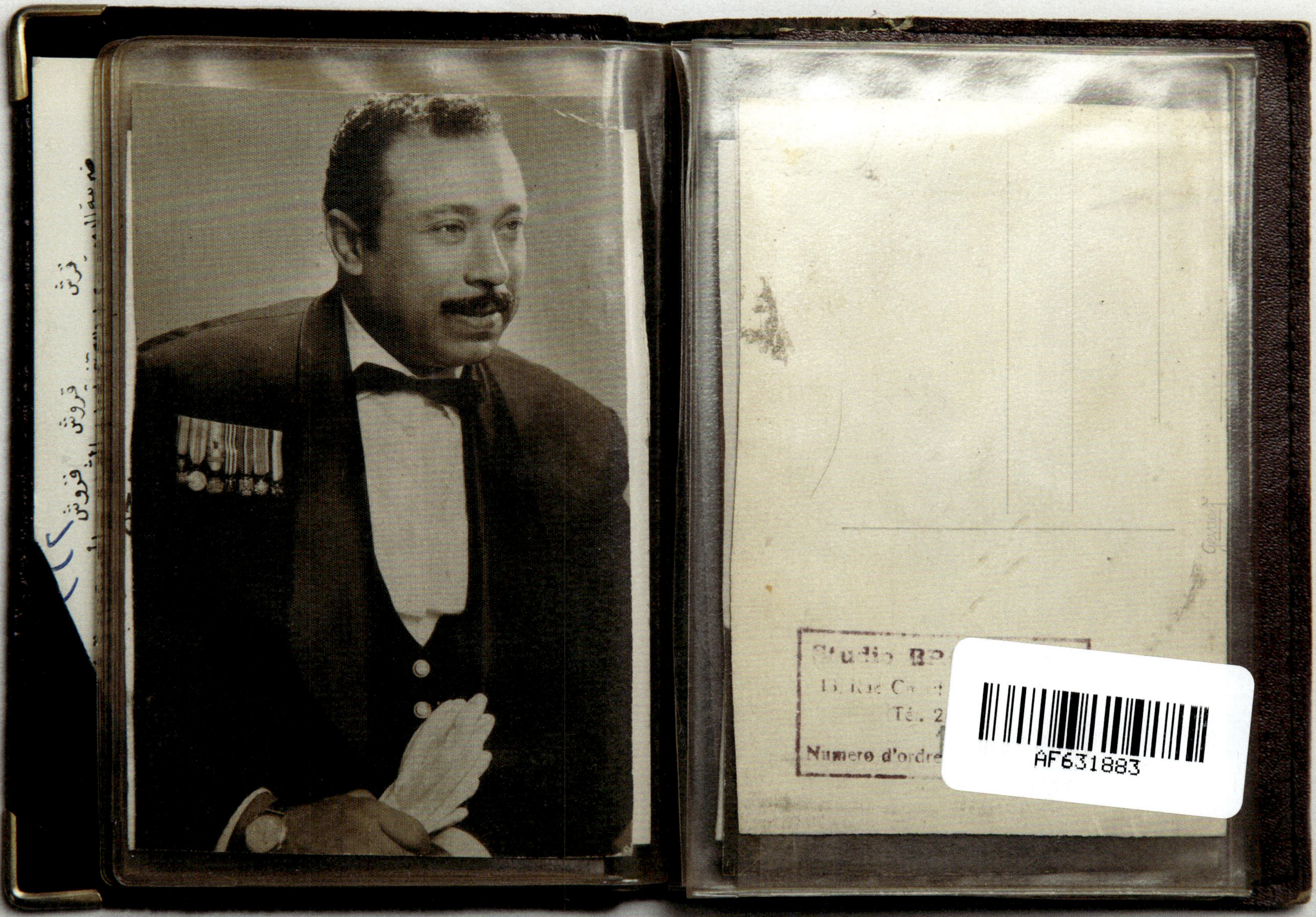

1 Heba Farid, *"General" Louis Ibrahim Album* from the series / aus der Serie *Making Heroes – Photograph Albums from Egyptian Military and Police Officers*, from the collection of / aus der Sammlung von Amgad Naguib /

هبة فريد- ألبوم "الجنرال" لويس إبراهيم -من سلسلة صناعة الأبطال- ألبومات لأفراد من الجيش و الشرطة المصرية. من مقتنيات أمجد نجيب

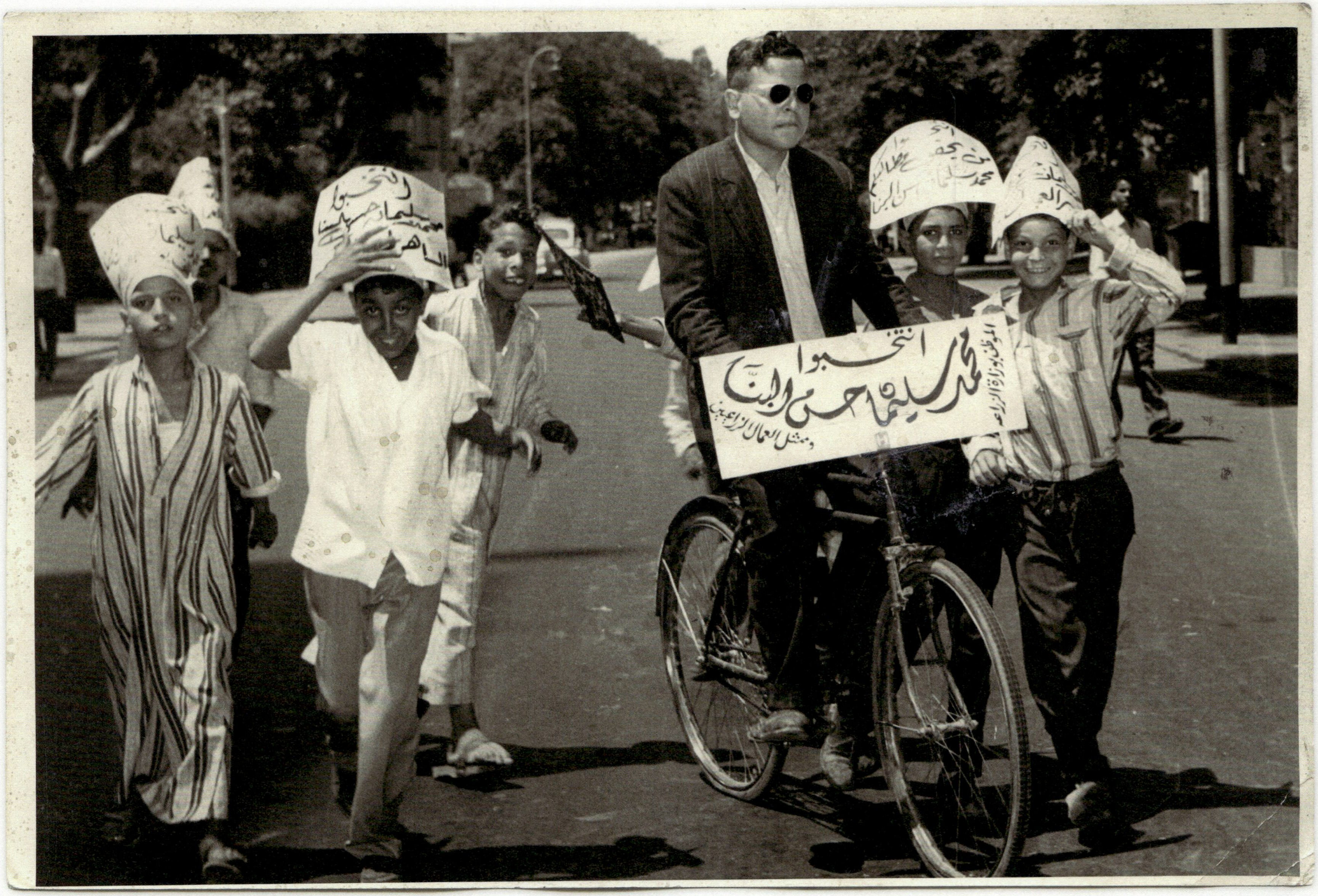

2 Heba Farid, from the series / aus der Serie *Testimonies, Protests, and Photojournalism*, from the collection of / aus der Sammlung von Amgad Naguib / هبة فريد، شهادات، المظاهرات والصحافة المصورة؛ من مقتنيات: أمجد نجيب.

Election campaign for Mohamed Hassan El-Banna; June 19, 1959, unknown location / Wahlkampagne für Mohammed Hassan El-Banna; 19. Juni 1959, Ort unbekannt, photographer / Fotograf: Ibrahim Omar / الحملة الانتخابية لمحمد حسن البنا؛ 19 يونيو 1959، المكان غير معروف، المصور: إبراهيم عمر

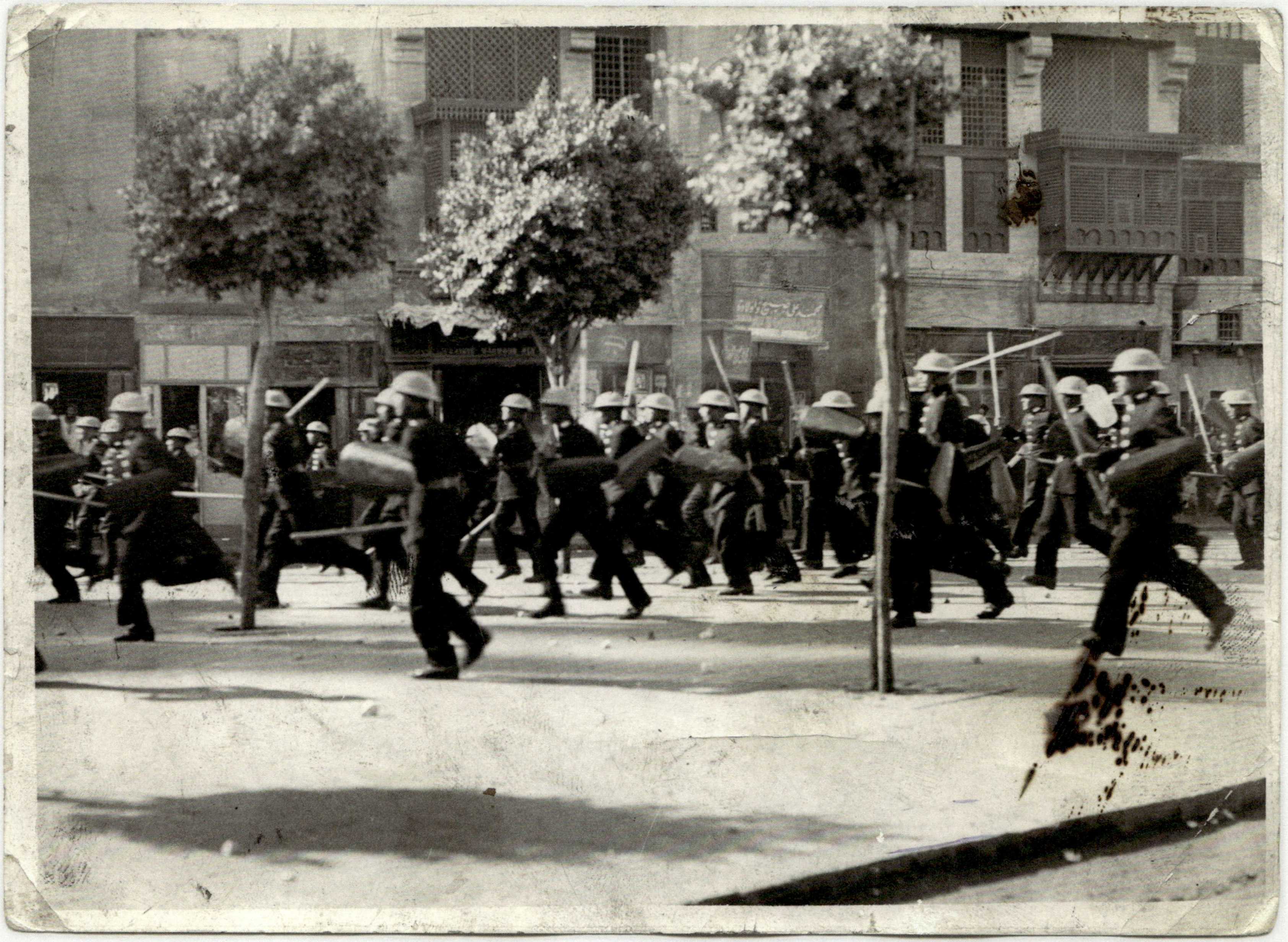

3 Heba Farid, from the series / aus der Serie *Testimonies, Protests, and Photojournalism*, from the collection of / aus der Sammlung von Amgad Naguib / هبة فريد، شهادات، المظاهرات والصحافة المصورة؛ من مقتنيات: أمجد نجيب.

Protests and riot Police, after 1948, Azhar Street, Cairo, photographer unknown / Proteste und Bereitschaftspolizei, nach 1948, Azhar-Straße, Kairo, Fotograf unbekannt / المظاهرات والأمن المركزي، بعد 1948، شارع الأزهر، القاهرة. المصور: غير معروف

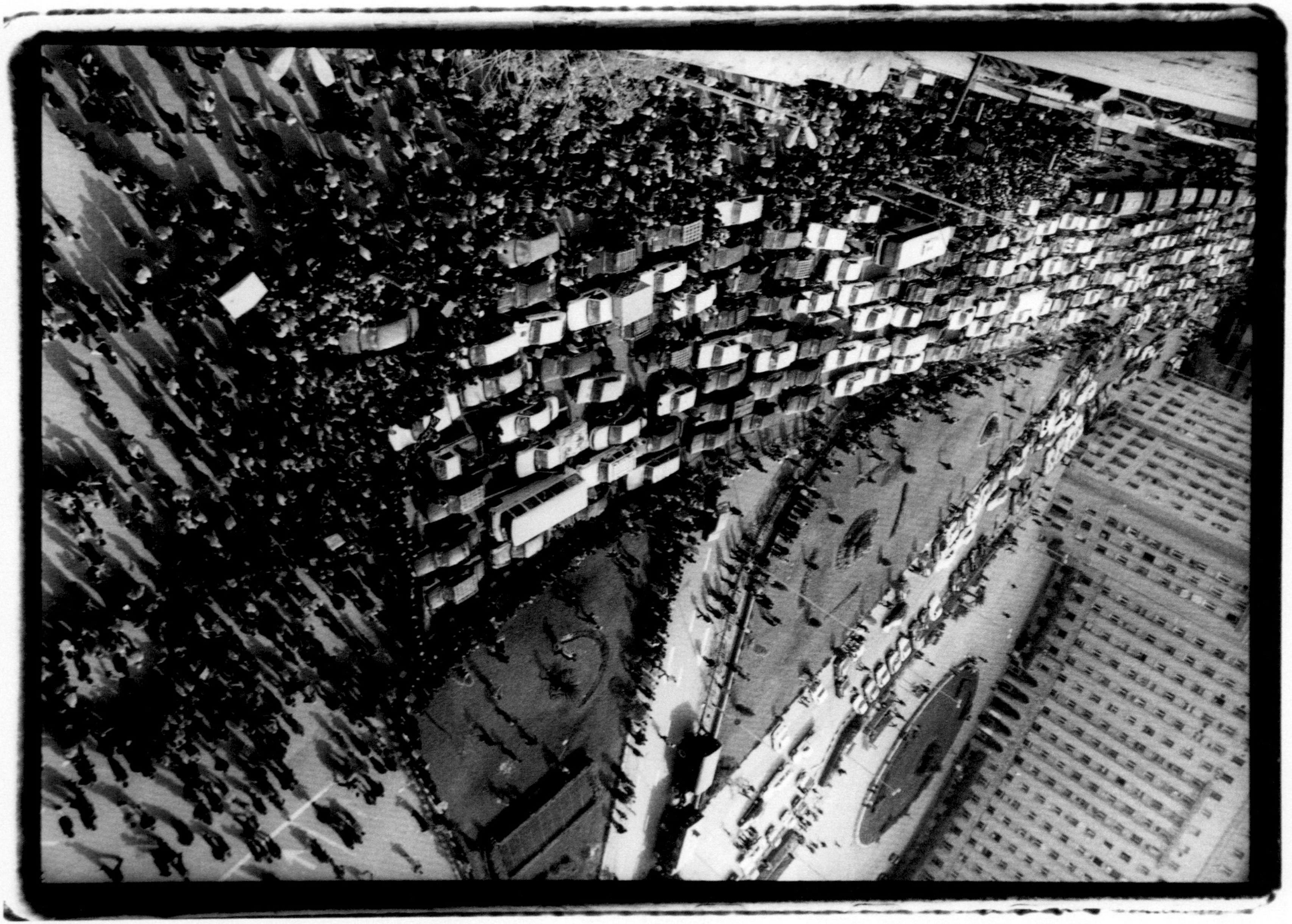

4 Randa Shaath, from the series / aus der Serie *Under the Same Sky: Cairo,* 2003/
2003 ,رندا شعث، من سلسلة تحت نفس السماء: القاهرة

Cairo. Open City / Kairo. Offene Stadt

New Testimonies from an Ongoing Revolution /

Neue Bilder einer andauernden Revolution

With photographs, videos, drawings, and texts by /
Mit Fotografien, Videos, Zeichnungen und Texten von

Khalid Abdalla, Myriam Abdelaziz, Ahmed Abdellatif, Peter van Agtmael, Amira El Ahl, Roger Anis, Kim Badawi, Mostafa Bahgat, Mirette Bakir, Lara Baladi, Ahmed Basiony, Kaya Behkalam, Taha Belal, Eva Bertram, Sarah Carr, Denis Dailleux, Osama Dawod, Johanna Domke & Marouan Omara, Heba Khalifa, Heba el Kholy, Hala Elkoussy, Hossam el-Hamalawy, Mohamed El Maymony, Shady El Noshokaty, Mosa'ab Elshamy, Rowan El Shimi, Fadi Ezzat, Mohamed Ezz, Heba Farid, Nermine Hammam, Thomas Hartwell, Aly Hazza'a, Tarek Hefny, Eman Helal, Gigi Ibrahim, Magdy Ibrahim, Ahmed Kamel, Sabry Khaled, Heba Khalifa, Nadine Khan & Mariam Mekiwi, Maha Maamoun, Alex Majoli, Jasmina Metwaly, Chris Michalski & Sebastian Stumpf, George Mohsen, Samuel Mohsen, Amira Mortada, Jihan Nasr, Nasser Nouri, Alex Nunns, Ivor Prickett, Jonathan Rashad, Philip Rizk, Ibrahim Saad, Randa Shaath, Rafi Shaker, Lobna Tarek, Lilian Wagdy, Sally Zohney, and various anonymous photographers / und einigen anonymen Fotografen

This book takes a constellation of images, texts, and documents, and proposes a way of locating them within a constant stream of news reports and political flux. It marks the end of a cooperative process of exchange and dialogue, of looking and listening.

The work of editing the material was completed in mid-July 2013, at which point it was already apparent that the political and social changes taking place in Egypt were part of an ongoing and inherently painful process. We are aware that our choice of images will one day be read in a very different light from how we see them today. /
Dieses Buch macht einen Vorschlag für eine Konstellation von Bildern, Texten und Dokumenten, für eine feste Anordnung innerhalb eines unaufhörlichen Flusses von Nachrichten und politischen Veränderungen. Es steht am Ende eines kollegialen Prozesses des Austauschs und des Dialogs, des Hinschauens und Zuhörens.

Die redaktionelle Arbeit endete Mitte Juli 2013, als sich bereits abzeichnete, dass der politische und soziale Wandel in Ägypten ein schmerzhafter Prozess werden wird. Wir sind uns bewusst, dass auch die Auswahl der Bilder eines Tages anders gelesen wird, als wir es heute tun.

Edited by / herausgegeben von Florian Ebner and / und Constanze Wicke

Funded by / Gefördert durch

KULTURSTIFTUNG DES BUNDES — GOETHE INSTITUT — Stiftung Presse-Haus NRZ

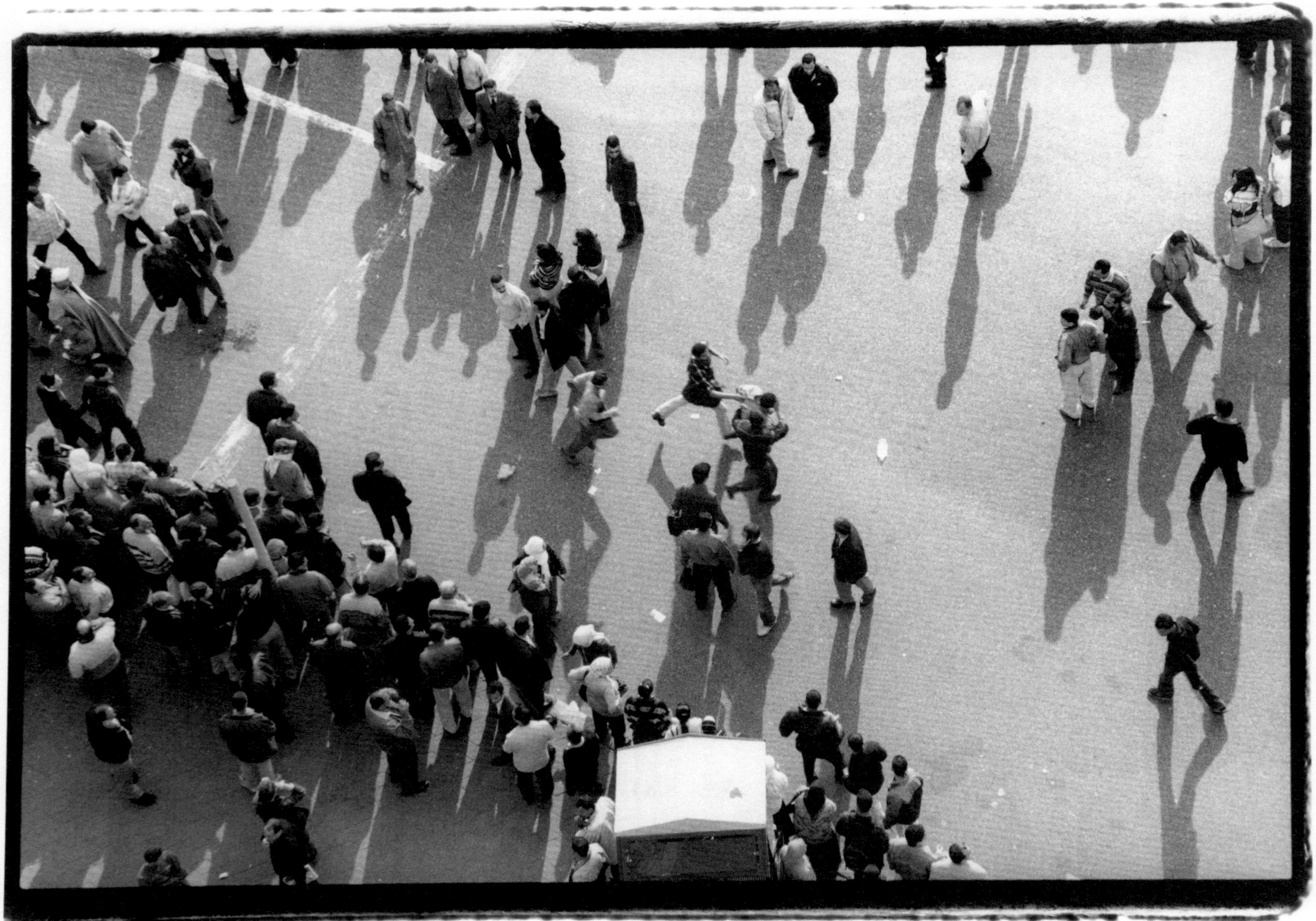

5 Randa Shaath, from the series / aus der Serie *Under the Same Sky: Cairo*, 2003
رندا شعث، من سلسلة تحت نفس السماء: القاهرة، 2003

Cairo. Open City. New Testimonies from an Ongoing Revolution is an experiment, a project in flux and constantly transforming, a local dialogue that is taken up a thousand miles away. As an exhibition, it takes on concrete form at a specific moment in time, governed by the physical space and political context it occupies. We hope that this project will also be visible one day in Cairo. / *Kairo. Offene Stadt. Neue Bilder einer andauernden Revolution* ist ein Experiment, ein Projekt im Fluss, in ständiger Metamorphose, ein Dialog vor Ort und über tausende Kilometer hinweg. Als Ausstellung gewinnt sie zu einem bestimmten Moment eine konkrete Form, je nach räumlicher Situation und politischem Kontext. Wir hoffen, dass die Ausstellung eines Tages auch in Kairo zu sehen sein wird.

Exhibition / Ausstellung

Exhibition concept / Ausstellungskonzept: Florian Ebner, Constanze Wicke
In cooperation with / In Zusammenarbeit mit: Lara Baladi, Osama Dawod, Rowan El Shimi, Heba Farid, Thomas Hartwell, Tarek Hefny, Ahmed Kamel, Jasmina Metwaly, Alex Nunns, Philip Rizk

---

September 28 – December 23, 2012
Museum für Photographie Braunschweig / 267 Quartiere für zeitgenössische Kunst und Fotografie
Hamburger Str. 267
D-38 114 Braunschweig

Technical design and production / Technische Konzeption und Produktion: Manuel Reinartz, Martin Salzer, Thomas Steen
Architecture / Architektur: Bernhard Tatter, denkenbauenwohnen architekten
Installation team / Aufbauteam: Kristleifur Björnsson, Günter Cosmann, Stefan Dau, Simon Kraus, Matthias Ludt, David Gaupp-Maier, Jasmin Meinold, Max Neumann, Ulrike & Dieter Rixe
Interns / PraktikantInnen: Kira Hüllenkremer, Sabine Niemczyk, Stefan Saalmüller

Project management and PR / Projektmanagement und Öffentlichkeitsarbeit: Svea Kellner
Administration / Verwaltung: Andrea Herrmann

Executive Board / Vorstand
Chairman / 1. Vorsitzender: Michael Schwarz; *Vice-chairman / 2. Vorsitzender:* Uwe Brodmann; *Vice-chairman / 3. Vorsitzender:* Karl-Christian Amme
Secretary / Schriftführer: Hauke Hagena; *Treasurer / Schatzmeister:* Andreas Janßen

---

March 2 – May 5, 2013
Museum Folkwang
Museumsplatz 1
D-45 128 Essen

Director / Direktor: Tobia Bezzola

Photographic Collection / Fotografische Sammlung
Head / Leiter: Florian Ebner
Management of the collection / Sammlungsverwaltung: Petra Steinhardt
Administration / Ausstellungssekretariat: Christina Buschmann, Annegret Küppers
Technical design and production / Technische Konzeption und Produktion: Manuel Reinartz, Oliver Sieber
Architecture / Architektur: Bernhard Tatter, denkenbauenwohnen architekten
Restoration / Restaurierung: Christiane Schneider
Interns / Praktikantinnen: Donja Nasserie, Barbara Werr

Museum administration / Verwaltung
Head / Leiter: Holger Peters
Financial controlling / Controlling und Finanzen: Fabian Klemt, Michael Kleinert
Registrars / Registrarinnen: Susanne Brüning, Alexandra Seese
Organization of exhibition installation / Organisation des Aufbaus: Alexandra Klein, Daniel Wimmer
Installation team / Aufbauteam: Reiner Baldau, Daniela Friebel, Simon Kraus, David Gaupp-Maier, Anatoli Marcin, Jasmin Meinold, Max Neumann, Michael Peters, Klaus Schlüter, Frank Sternberg, Gerd Ufer, Till Wellner, Stephan Zmudzinski

Education and communication / Bildung und Vermittlung: Heike Kropff
PR and marketing / Öffentlichkeitsarbeit und Marketing: Doerthe Ramin
Press officer / Pressereferentin: Anna Sophie Littmann
PR assistant / Assistenz der Öffentlichkeitsarbeit: Ineke Klosterkemper

---

October 19 – November 25, 2012
5th European Month of Photography Berlin / 5. Europäischer Monat der Fotografie Berlin
Formerly The Kennedys Museum / Ehemaliges Kennedy-Museum
Pariser Platz 4A
D-10 117 Berlin

Curator Month of Photography / Kuratorin Monat der Fotografie: Katia Reich
Project manager / Projektmanger: Oliver Bätz
Project assistant / Projektassistenz: Marte Kräher
Project support team / Mitarbeit Projektassistenz: Charlotte Finke, Gabriele Zöllner, Birte Hoffmann, Annekathrin Müller
Media relations / Medienarbeit: Achim Klapp
Technical design and production / Technische Konzeption und Produktion: Manuel Reinartz
Installation / Aufbau: RT Ausstellungstechnik, Berlin

August 16 – November 17, 2013
Museum für Kunst und Gewerbe Hamburg
Steintorplatz
D-20 099 Hamburg

Director / Direktorin: Sabine Schulze
Commercial director / Kaufmännischer Geschäftsführer: Udo Goerke

Head of photography and new media department / Leiterin der Sammlung Fotografie und neue Medien: Esther Ruelfs
Exhibition designer / Ausstellungsarchitektur: René Hillebrand, Hamburg
Exhibition project management / Projektmanagement Ausstellungen: Frank Hildebrandt
Interns / PraktikantInnen: Annika Sellmann, Ariane Batou-To Van, Victoria Haseler, Nathalie Klinck

Head of technical services / Technische Leitung: Thomas Frey
Technical production / Technische Produktion: Manuel Reinartz
Installation team / Aufbauteam: Alberto Polo-Pallares, Egon Busch, Damian Kowalczyk, Grigori Medvedev, Mike Meier
Management of the collection / Sammlungsverwalter: Harald Dubau

Registrar / Registrarin: Annika Pohl-Ozawa
Marketing / Marketing: Silke Oldenburg, Ulrike Blauth
PR / Öffentlichkeitsarbeit: Michaela Hille
Interpretation of art and design / Kunst- und Designvermittlung: Silke Oldenburg, Manuela van Rossem, Friederike Fankhänel

Catalogue / Katalog

Editors / Herausgeber: Florian Ebner, Constanze Wicke
Picture editors / Bildredaktion: Florian Ebner, Ahmed Kamel
Text editors / Redaktion: Florian Ebner, Constanze Wicke
Copy editor, German texts / Lektorat der deutschen Texte: Tanja Milewsky
Proofreader, German texts / Korrektorat der deutschen Texte: Nina Köller
Copy editor and proofreader, English texts / Lektorat und Korrektorat der englischen Texte: Simon Cowper
Proofreader, Arabic texts / Korrektorat der arabischen Texte: Dona Abboud, Mirette Bakir

Design concept and design / Gestaltungskonzept und Gestaltung: Ahmed Kamel, Andrej Loll, Nicola Reiter
Arabic typesetting / Arabischer Satz: Dona Abboud
Image processing / Bildbearbeitung: Sylvia Doebelt, Manuel Reinartz
Production / Gesamtherstellung: Druckerei zu Altenburg GmbH

Translations / Übersetzungen
from German into English / aus dem Deutschen ins Englische: Simon Cowper
from English into German / aus dem Englischen ins Deutsche: Daniela Friebel, Heike Geißler, Barbara Werr
from German into Arabic / aus dem Deutschen ins Arabische: Ebtihal Shedid

First edition 2013 / Erste Auflage 2013

ISBN 978-3-940064-70-7

Spector Books
Harkortstrasse 10
D-04 107 Leipzig
www.spectorbooks.com

Auslieferung Deutschland, Österreich:
GVA Gemeinsame Verlagsauslieferung Göttingen GmbH & Co. KG
www.gva-verlage.de

Auslieferung Schweiz:
AVA Verlagsauslieferung AG
www.ava.ch

Distribution in the UK, France, Japan:
Anagram Books Ltd
www.anagrambooks.com

Distribution in the US:
RAM Publications + Distribution Inc.
www.rampub.com

Thanks to / Dank an

We would like to thank all those who have taken part in this process. This project has been shaped by their work, suggestions, and critical input. / Wir danken all denjenigen, die an diesem Projekt teilgenommen haben. Durch ihre Arbeit, ihre Anregung und Kritik haben sie diesem Ausstellungsprojekt Gestalt gegeben.

In particular we would like to thank / Insbesondere gilt dies: Lara Baladi, Osama Dawod, Rowan El Shimi, Heba Farid, Thomas Hartwell, Tarek Hefny, Ahmed Kamel, Jasmina Metwaly, Alex Nunns, Philip Rizk

Our thanks go to the authors and the participating curators and cultural producers in Cairo / Wir danken den Autorinnen und Autoren, den beteiligten Kuratorinnen und Kuratoren sowie Kulturschaffenden in Kairo: Khalid Abdalla, Edgar Blume, Günther Hasenkamp (Goethe-Institut Kairo), Ghada El-Sherbiny (Goethe-Institut Kairo), Dina Kafafi (Townhouse Gallery, Cairo), Mia Jankowicz (CIC, Contemporary Image Collective, Cairo), Silvia Mollicchi (CIC), Yara Salah (Goethe-Institut Kairo), Tamer El Said, Amira El Ahl, Alexandra Stock (Townhouse Gallery, Cairo), William Wells (Townhouse Gallery, Cairo)

We also thank the artists for their cooperation and trust / Und ebenso gilt unser Dank den KünstlerInnen und FotografInnen für die vertrauensvolle Zusammenarbeit: Myriam Abdelaziz, Ahmed Abdellatif, Peter van Agtmael, Roger Anis, Kim Badawi, Mostafa Bahgat, Kaya Behkalam, Taha Belal, Eva Bertram, Sarah Carr, Denis Dailleux, Johanna Domke & Marouan Omara, Heba Khalifa, Heba el Kholy, Hala Elkoussy, Hossam el-Hamalawy, Mohamed El Maymony, Shady El Noshokaty, Mosa'ab Elshamy, Mohamed El Sheshtawy, Fadi Ezzat, Mohamed Ezz, Nermine Hammam, Aly Hazza'a, Eman Helal, Gigi Ibrahim, Magdy Ibrahim, Sabry Khaled, Heba Khalifa, Nadine Khan & Mariam Mekiwi, Maha Maamoun, Alex Majoli, Chris Michalski & Sebastian Stumpf, George Mohsen, Samuel Mohsen, Osama Abdel Moneim, Amira Mortada, Jihan Nasr, Mohammad Nouhan, Nasser Nouri, Maggie Osama, Susanne Pomrehn, Ivor Prickett, Jonathan Rashad, Ibrahim Saad, Randa Shaath, Rafi Shaker, Lobna Tarek, Lilian Wagdy, Sally Zohney

Workshop participants / TeilnehmerInnen des Workshops Braunschweig – Cairo – Nîmes: Hesham Amin, Sabrina Asche, Brigitte Bauer & Jean-Marc Cerino, Kai Behrendt, Hauke Burghart, Pauline Chappet, Lisa Domin, Dörte Eißfeldt, Mario Fam, Arnold Fuad, Colin G., Morgane Gille, Sophia Hamann, Sabiha Keyif, Manuel Klotz, Marcelina Kwiatkowski, Bettina Lockemann, Enas El-Komsan, David Maher, Nadia Mounier T., Omneia Naguib, Doreen Schwarz, Lauren Scott, Robert Stürzl, Sarah Vialle

In Kooperation mit / In cooperation with

MUSEUM FÜR PHOTOGRAPHIE BRAUNSCHWEIG
Museum Folkwang
MK&G MUSEUM FÜR KUNST UND GEWERBE HAMBURG
Townhouse

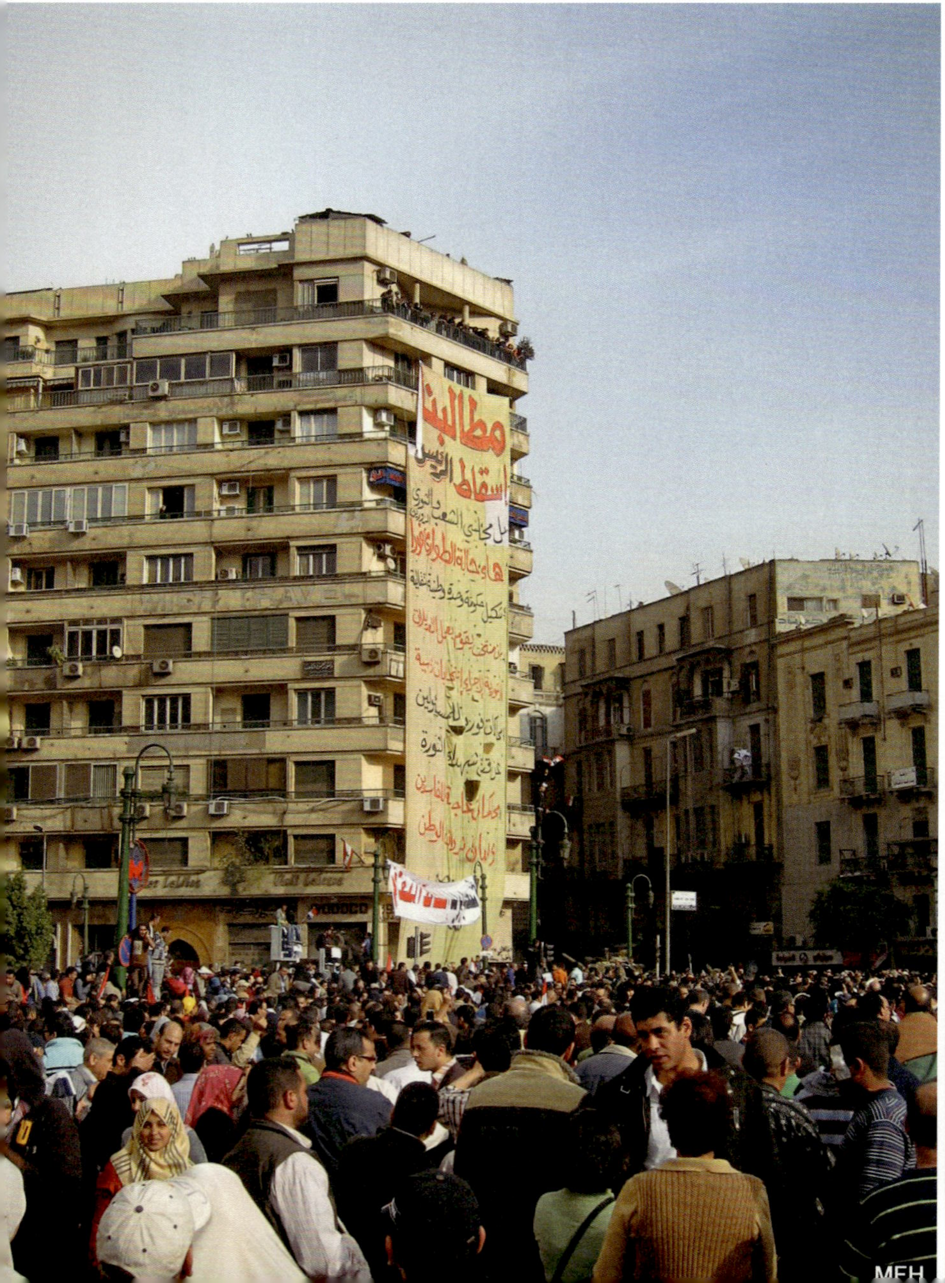

8 User205 (ThawraMedia), May 4, 2011 / 2011 المستخدم رقم 205 (ثورة ميديا)، 4 مايو

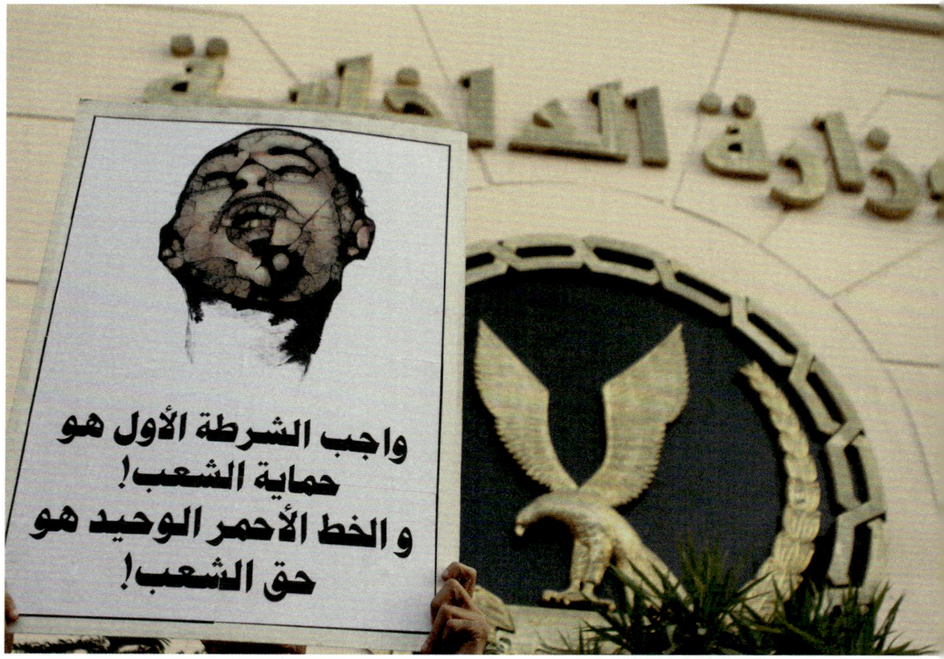

6 Sarah Carr, *Khaled Said, One Year Later*, June 6, 2011 / 2011 سارة كار، من ألبوم خالد سعيد بعد مرور عام، 6 يونيو

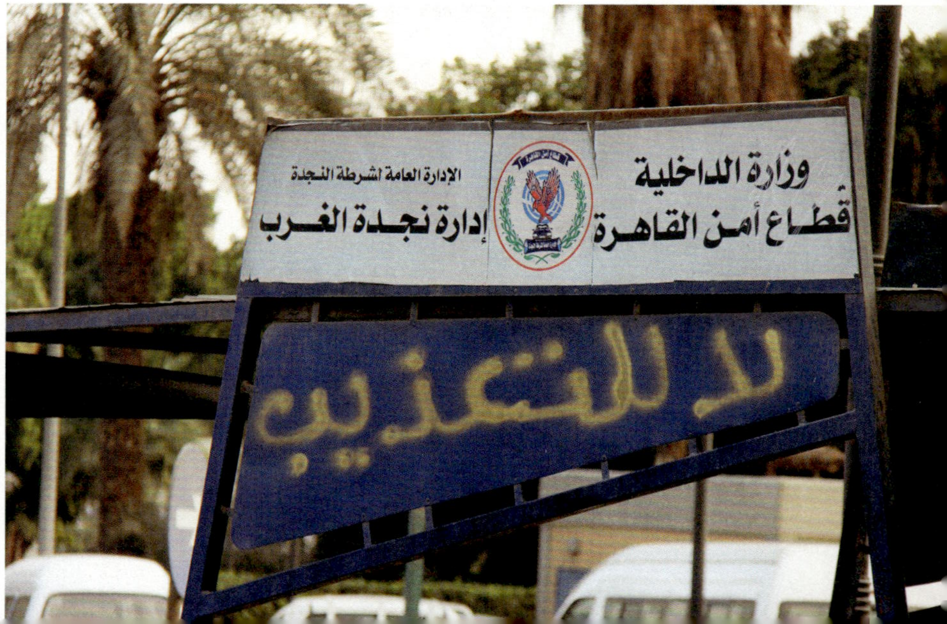

7 User18 (ThawraMedia), Jan. 30, 2011 / 2011 المستخدم رقم 18 (ثورة ميديا)، 30 يناير

9 Sarah Carr, *1st Anniversary*, Jan. 25, 2012/2012 سارة كار، العيد الأول للثورة، 25 يناير
10 User204 (ThawraMedia), Feb. 7, 2011/2011 المستخدم رقم 204 (ثورة ميديا)، 7 فبراير
11 Sarah Carr, *Tahrir, Day 17*, Feb. 10, 2011/2011 سارة كار، التحرير، اليوم السابع عشر، 10 فبراير
12 Fadi Ezzat, *Cairo University, Mar. 20, 2011/2011* فادي عزت، جامعة القاهرة، 20 مارس

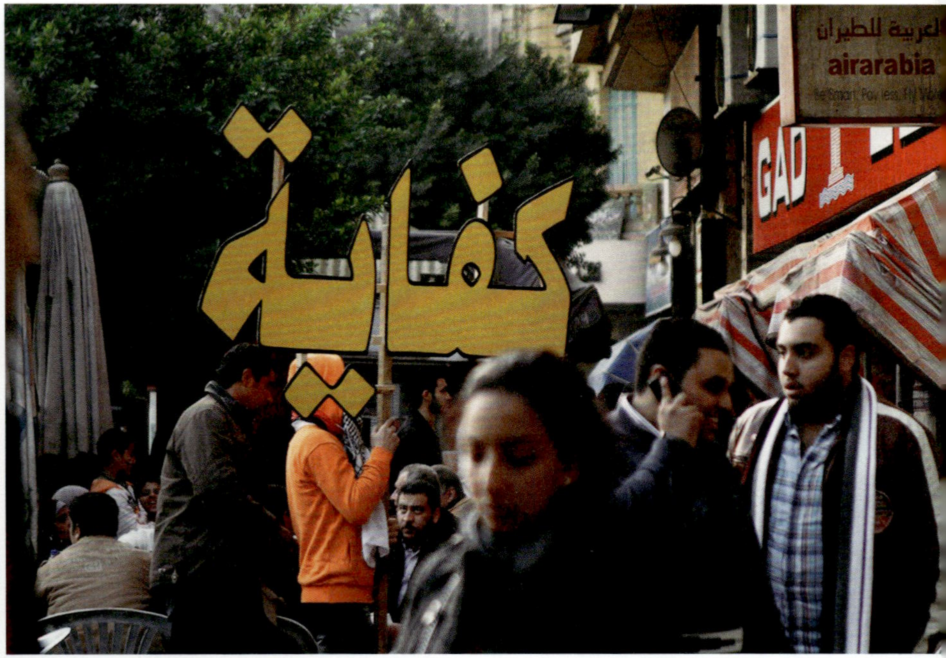

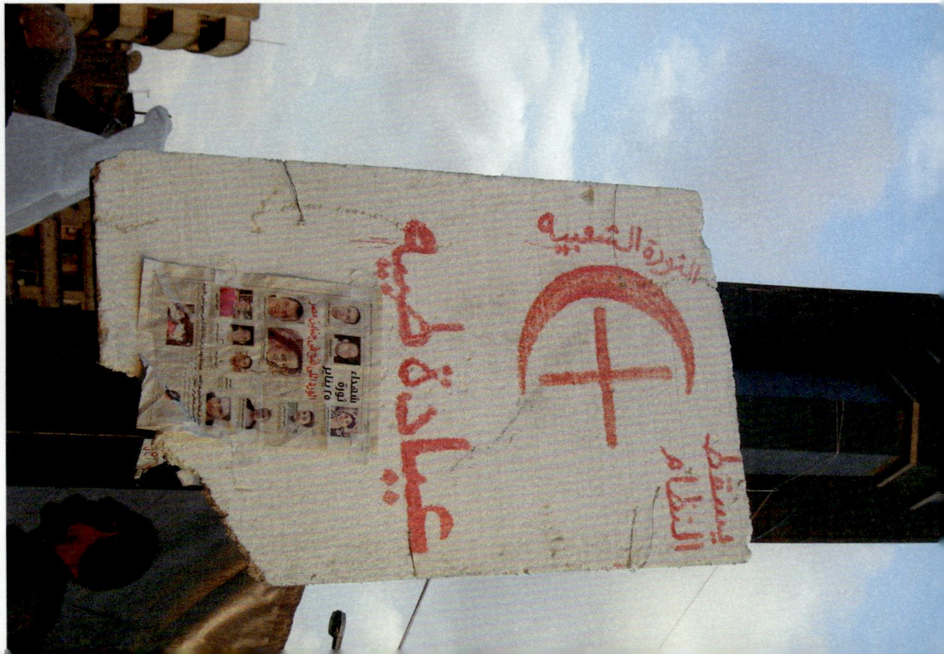

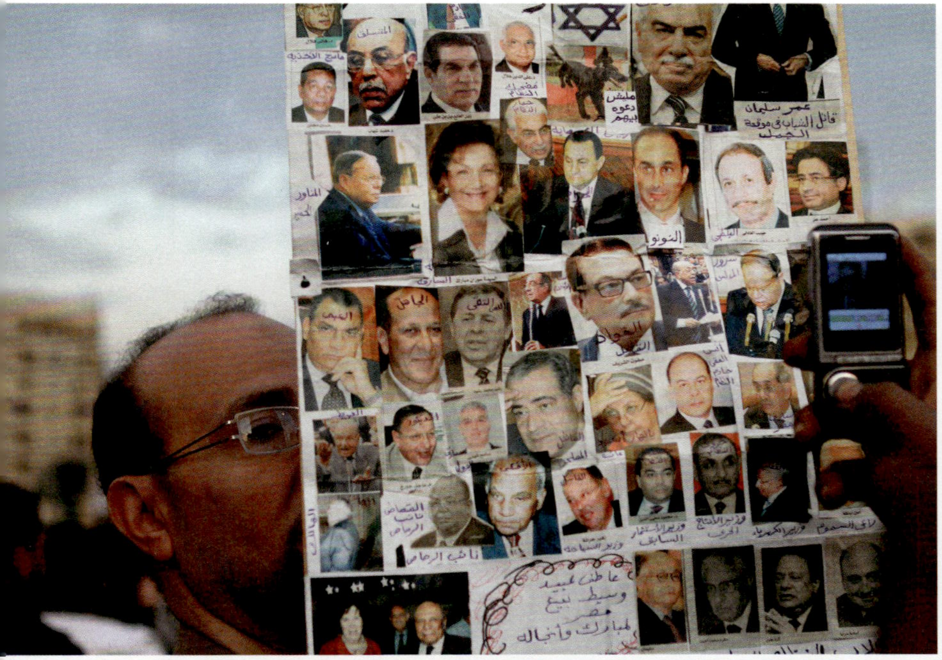

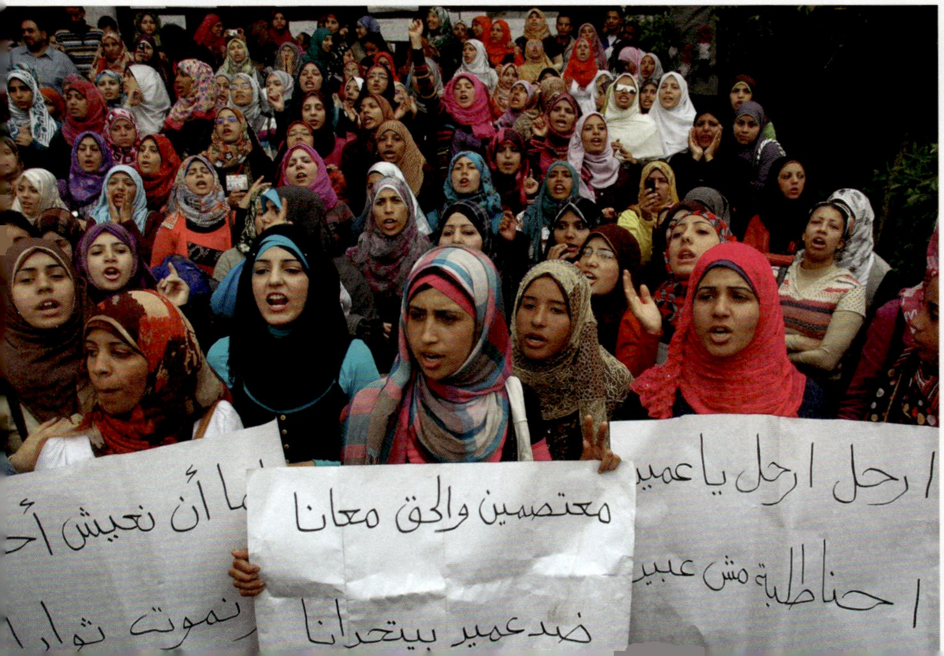

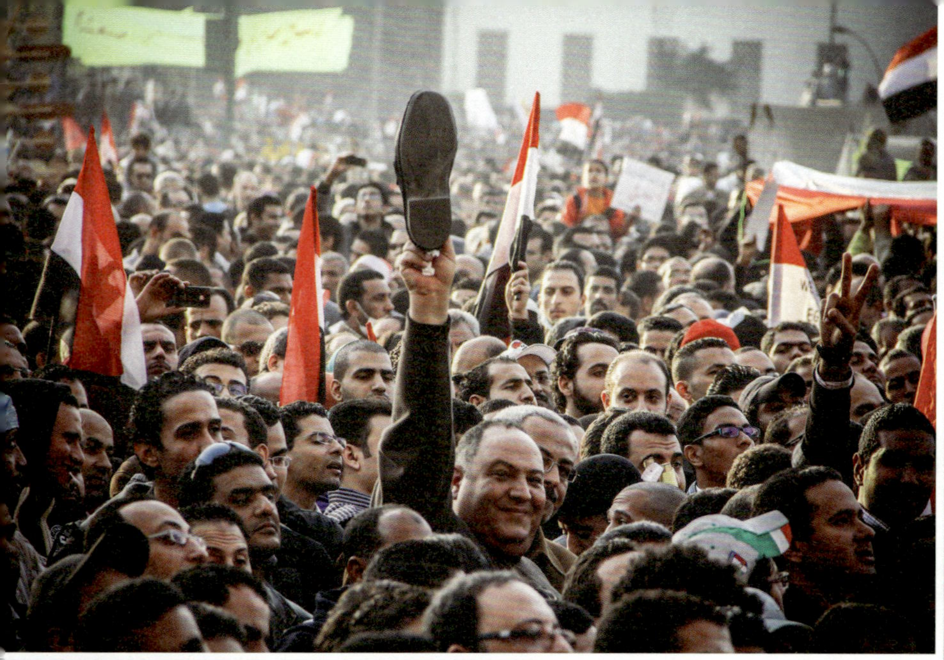

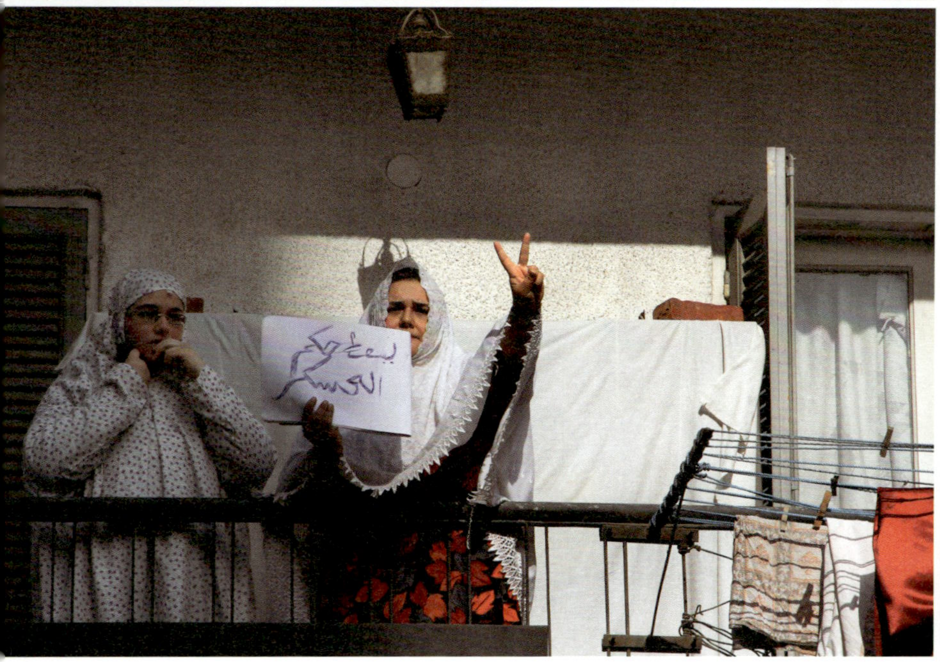

14 Mosa'ab Elshamy, *Revolution's 2nd Anniversary*, Jan. 25, 2013/ مصعب الشامي، العيد الثاني للثورة، 25 يناير 2013

15 Roger Anis, *Mohandeseen, Cairo, Jan. 25, 2012*/2012 روجر أنيس، المهندسين القاهرة، 25 يناير 2012

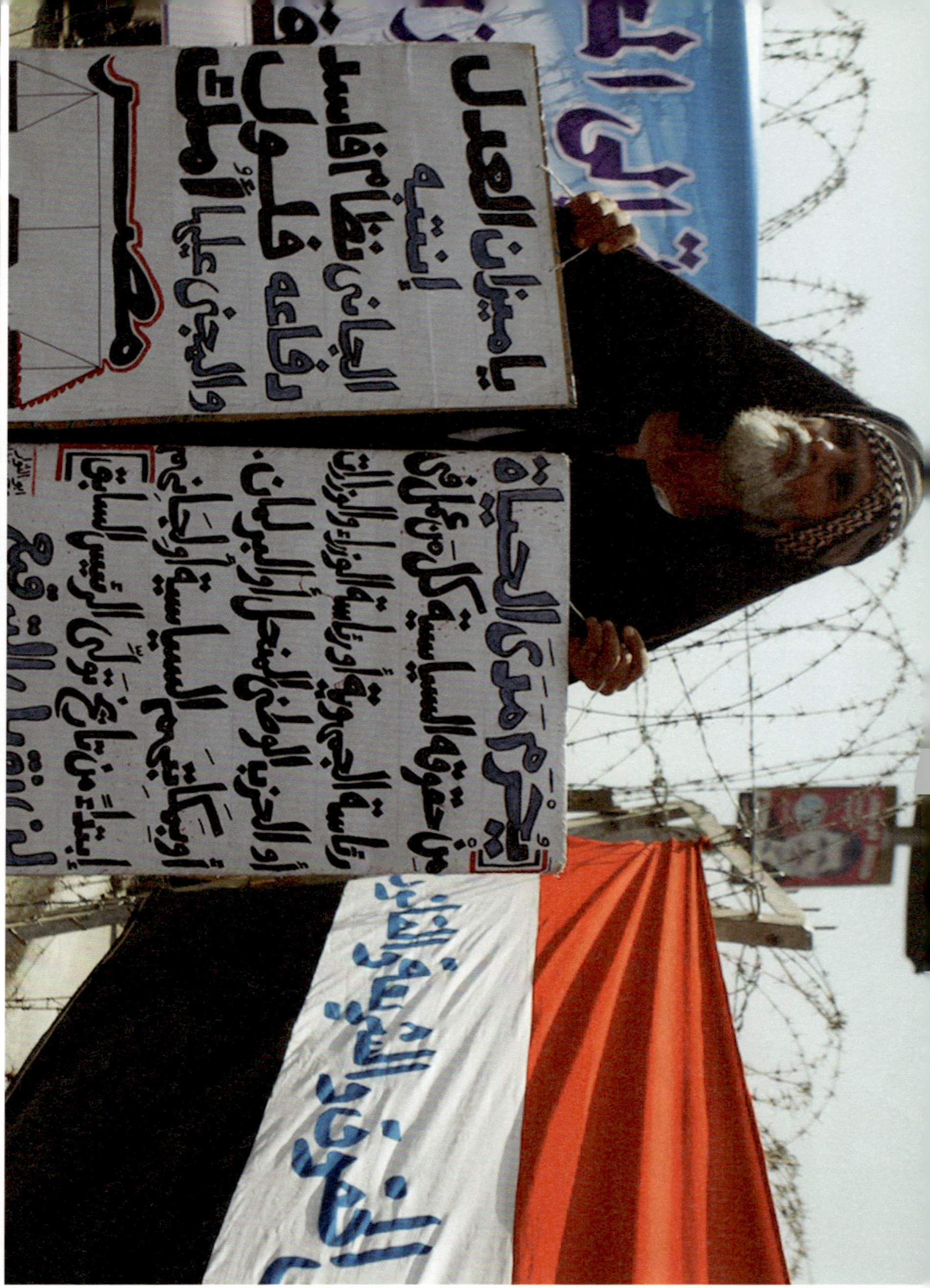

13 Sarah Carr, *SCC*, June 14, 2012/2012 سارة كار من ألبوم *SCC*، 14 يونيو 2012

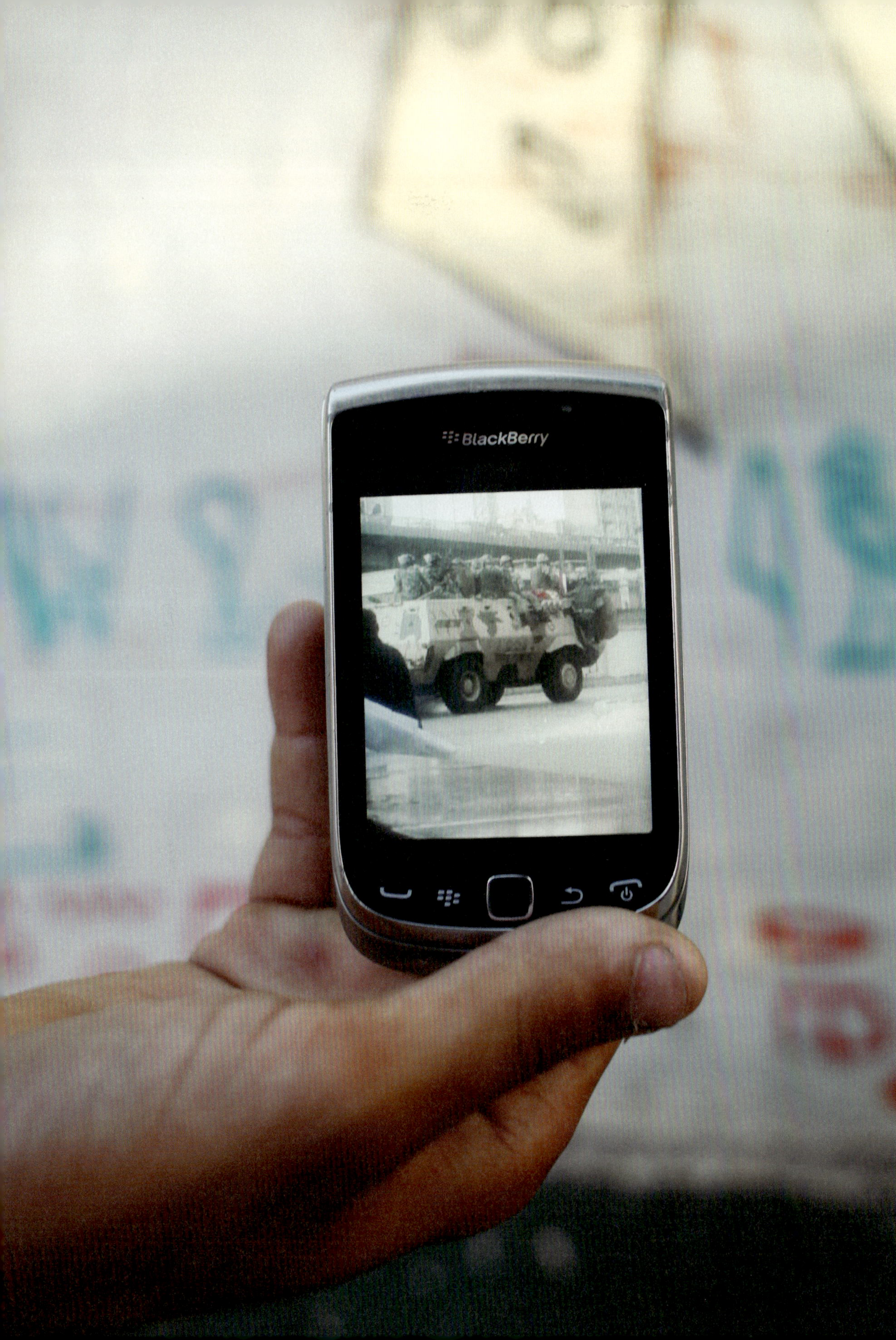

16 Myriam Abdelaziz, from the series / aus der Serie *Cell Phone Stories*, 2012 / مريم عبد العزيز من
سلسلة حكايات المحمول، 2012

ThawraMedia – Internet Archive by Citizen Journalists / Internetarchiv von Bürgerjournalisten / ثـورة ميديـا- مبادرة لبناء أرشيف إلكتروني أسسه صحفيون من مجال الصحافة الشعبية

18 User 204, Jan. 28, 2011 / 2011 المستخدم رقم 204، 28 يناير

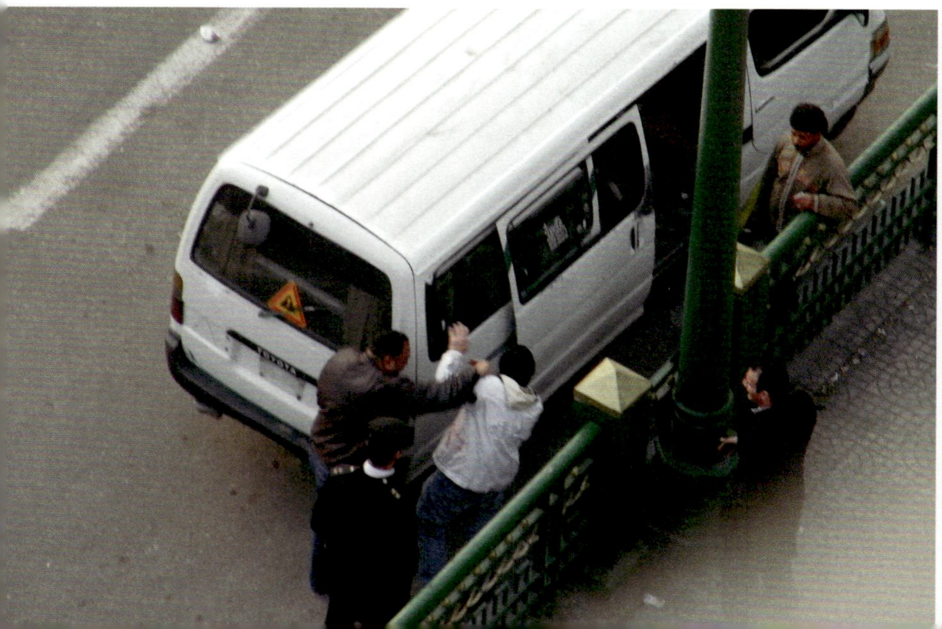

17 User 57, Jan. 28, 2011 / 2011 المستخدم رقم 57، 28 يناير

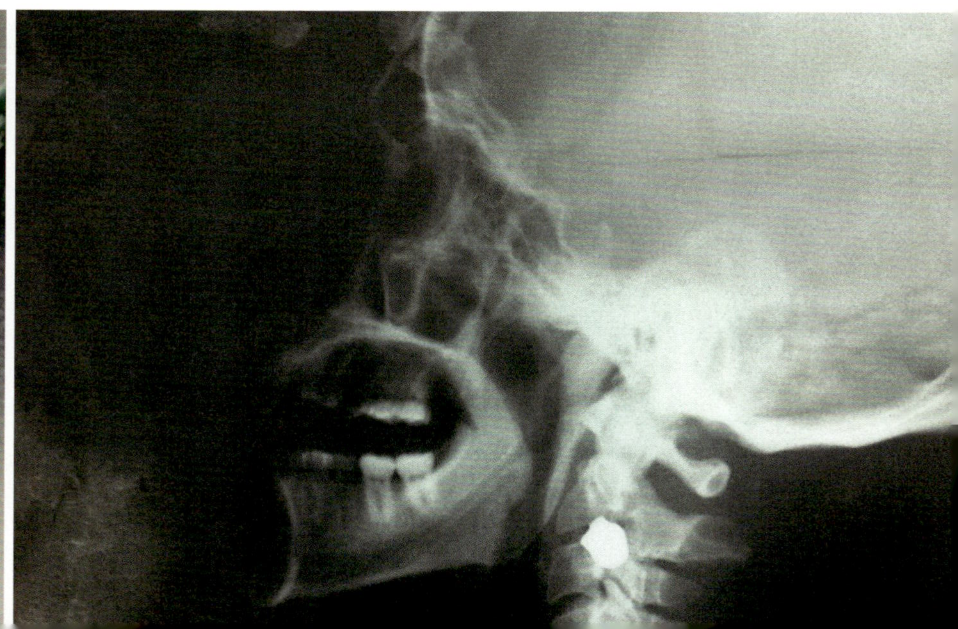

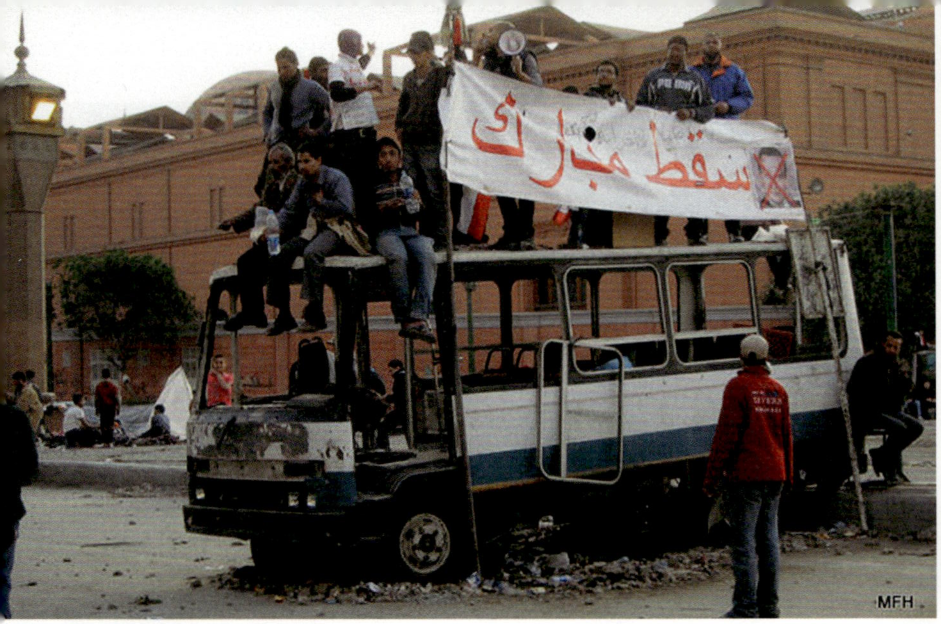

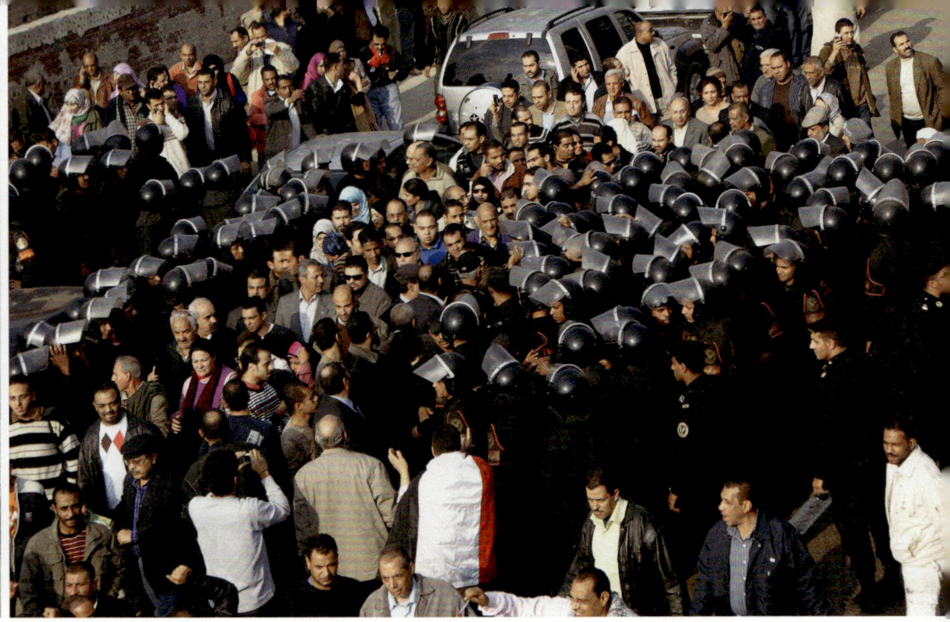

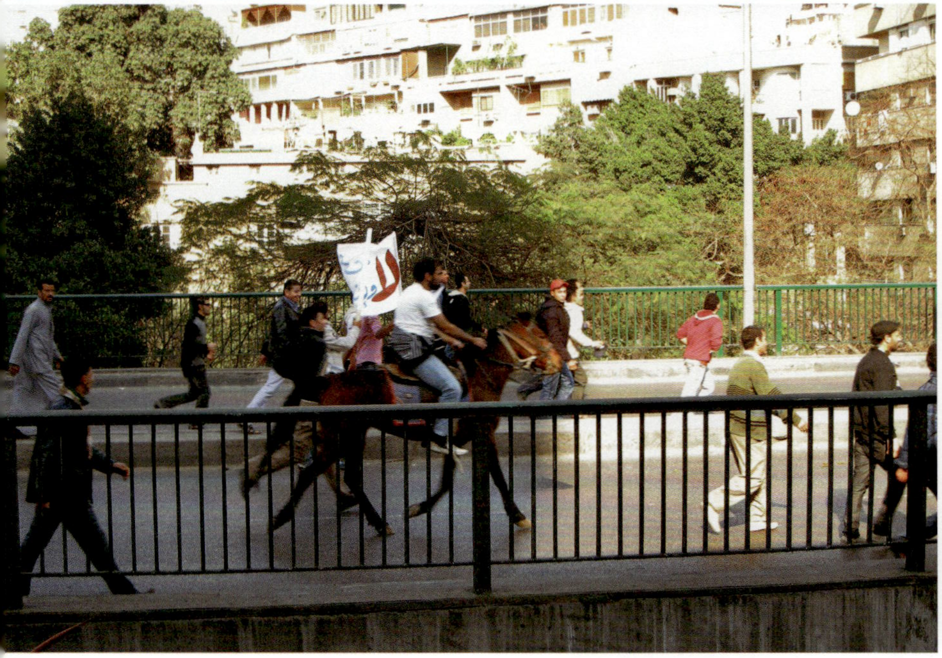

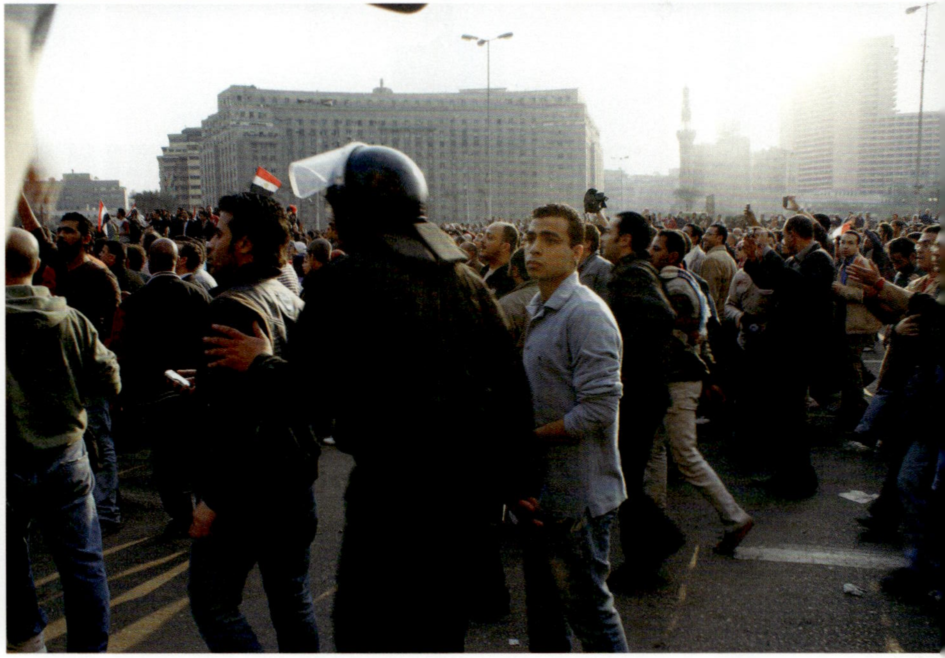

21 User2, Feb. 8, 2011/2011 المستخـدم رقـــم 2، 8 فبراير
22 User210, Feb. 2, 2011/2011 المستخدم رقم 210، 2 فبراير

19+20 User203, Jan. 24, 2011/2011 المستخدم رقم 203، 24 يناير

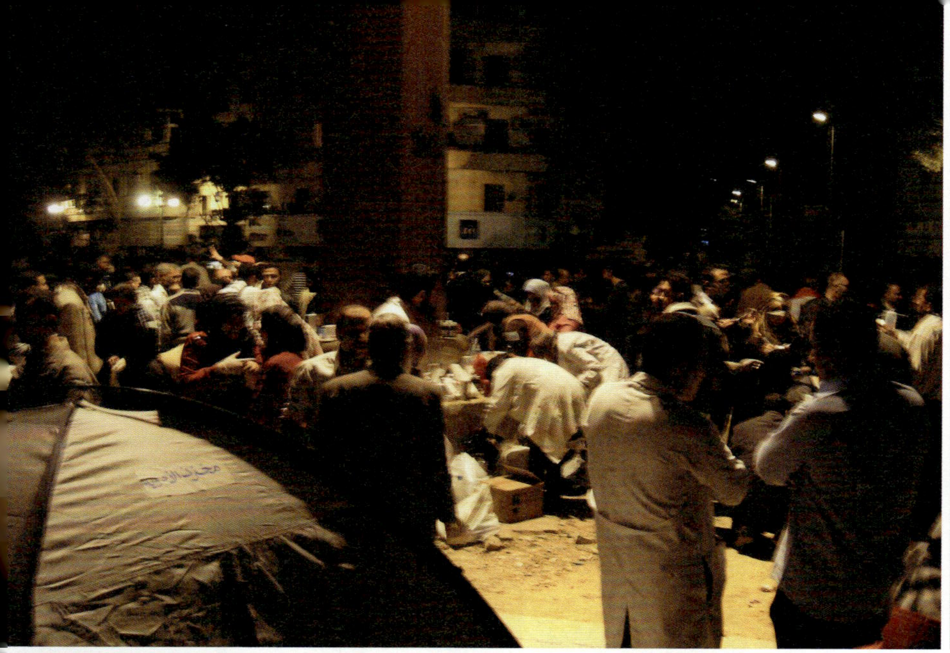

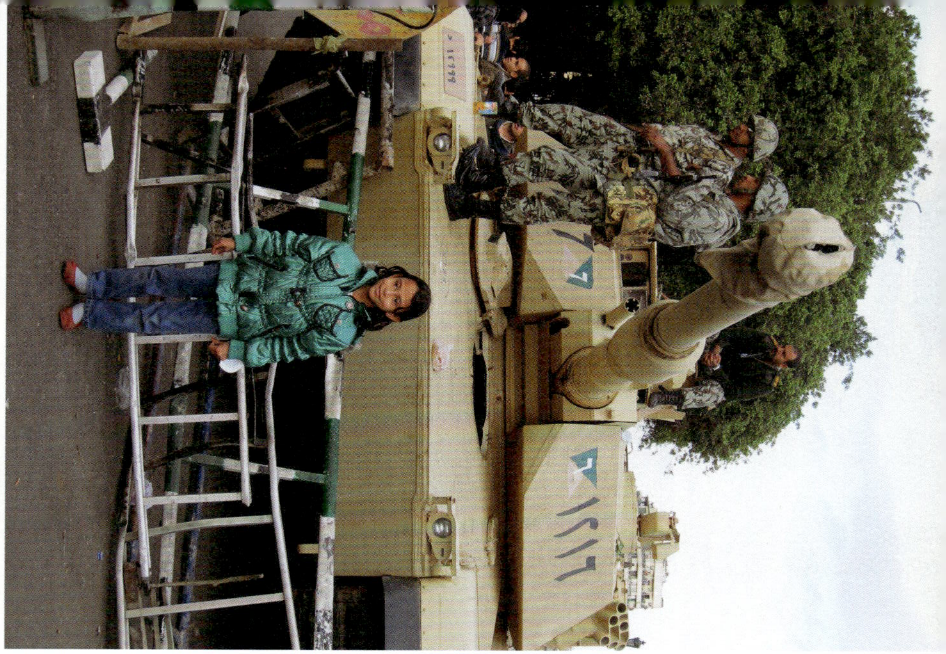

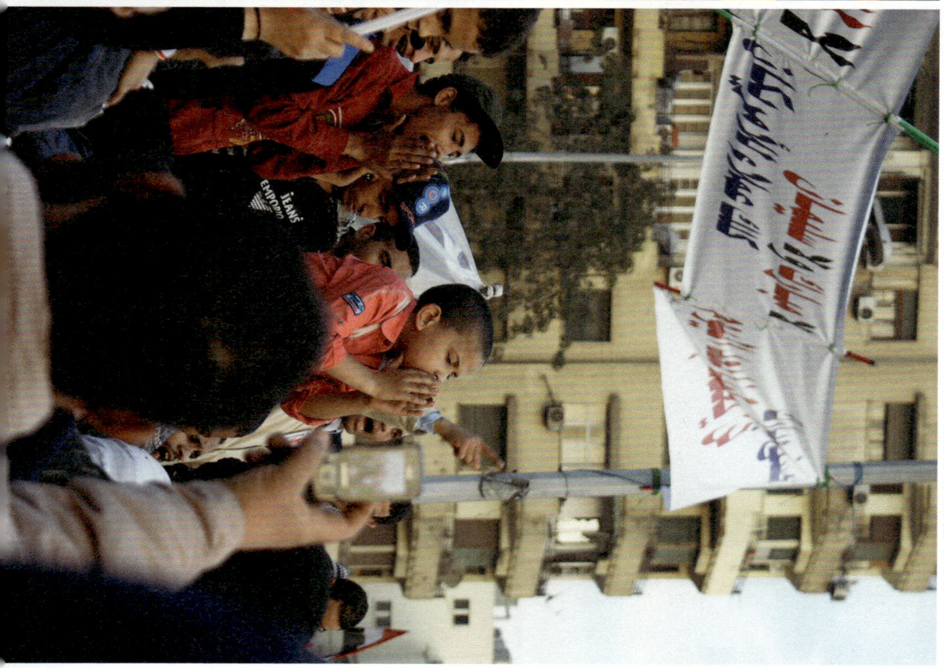

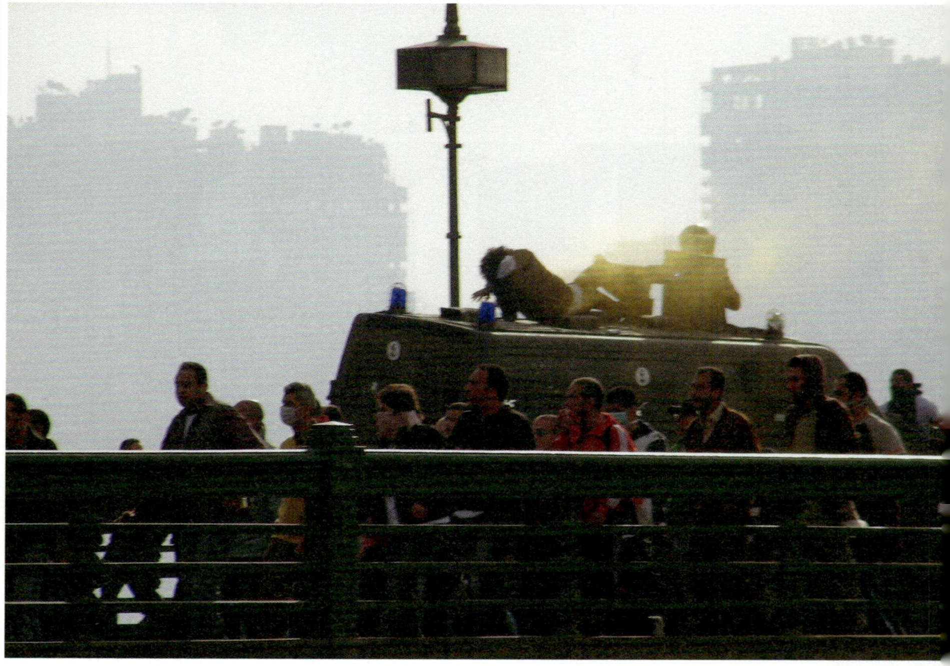

23 User210, Jan. 31, 2011/2011 المستخدم رقم 210، 31 يناير
24 User204, Jan. 28, 2011/2011 المستخدم رقم 204، 28 يناير

25 User217, Feb. 3, 2011/2011 المستخدم رقم 217، 3 فبراير
26 User203, Feb. 6, 2011/2011 المستخدم رقم 203، 6 فبراير

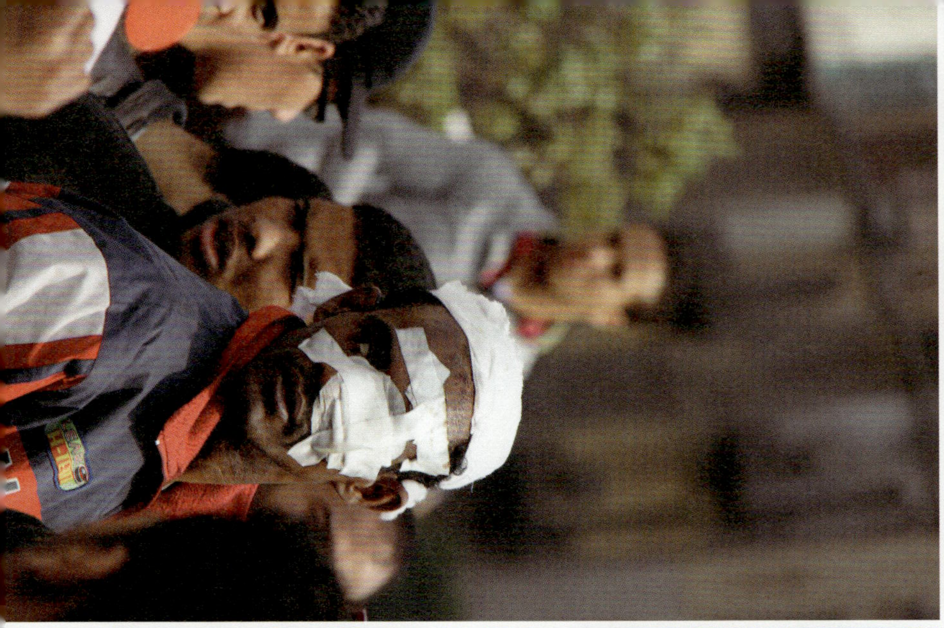

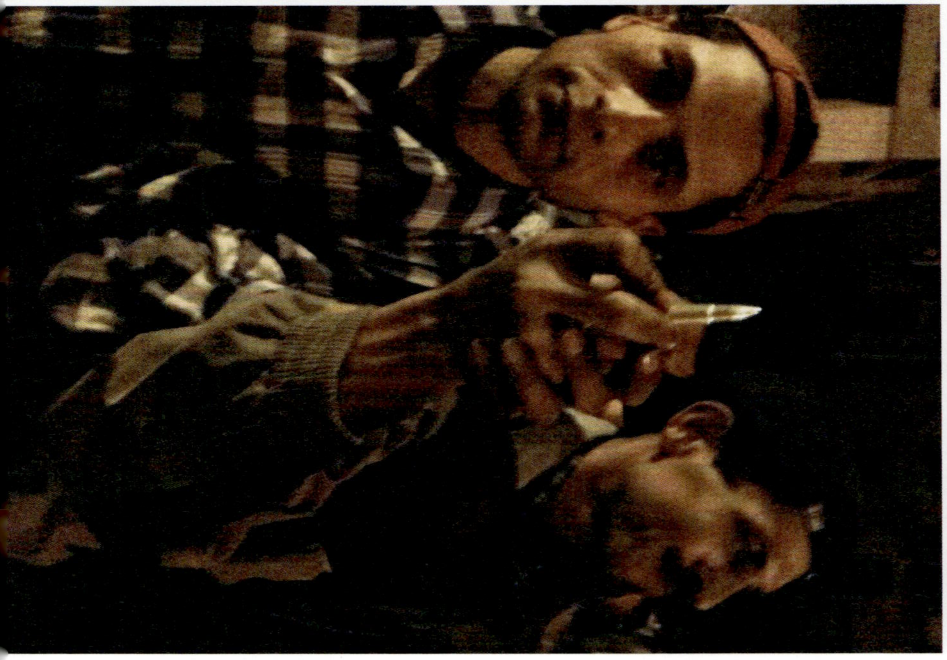

29 User18, Jan. 30, 2011 / 2011 المستخدم رقم 18، 30 يونيو
30 User57, Jan. 29, 2011 / 2011 المستخدم رقم 57، 29 يناير

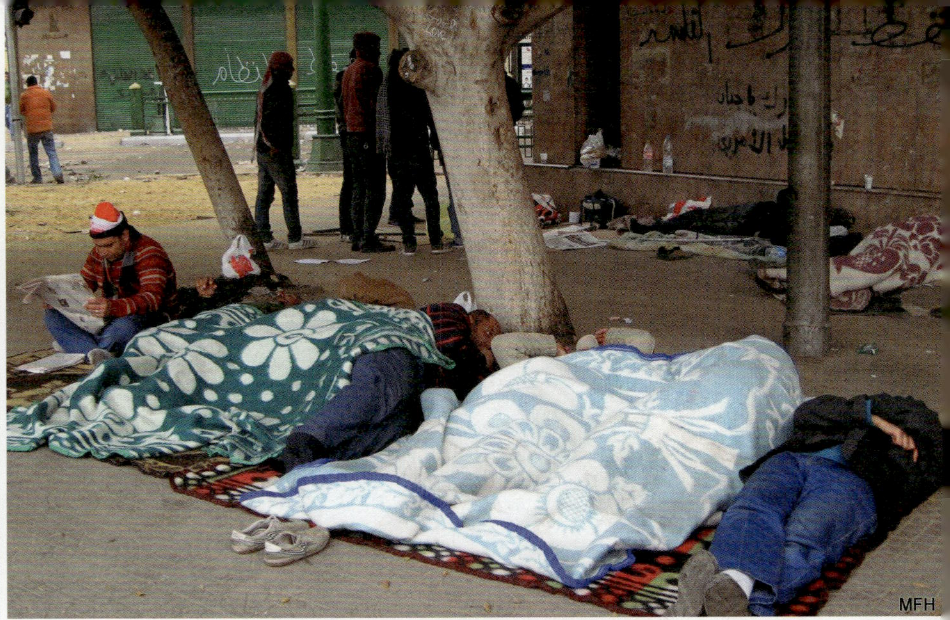

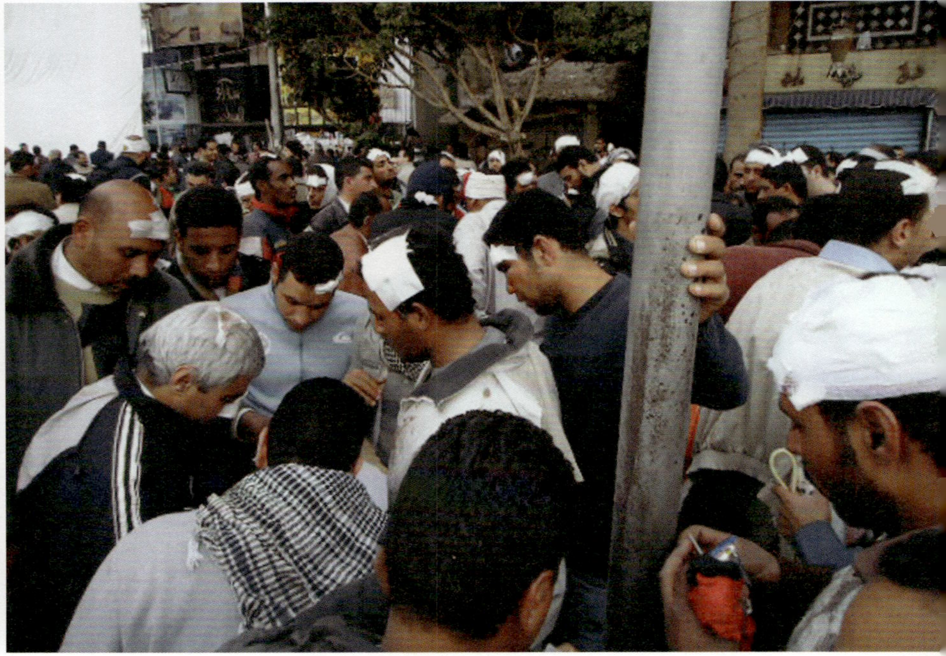

27 User205, Feb. 5, 2011 / 2011 المستخدم رقم 205، 5 فبراير،
28 User216, Feb. 2, 2011 / 2011 المستخدم رقم 216، 2 فبراير،

31

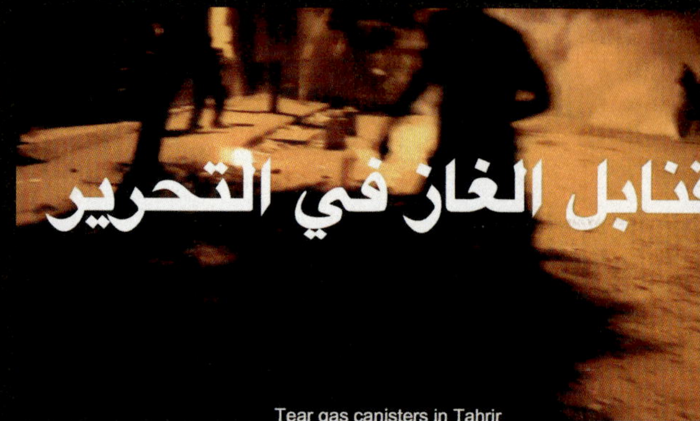

Teargas in Tahrir / Tränengas auf dem Tahrir-Platz /
قنابل الغاز في التحرير
Uploaded on Nov. 23, 2011

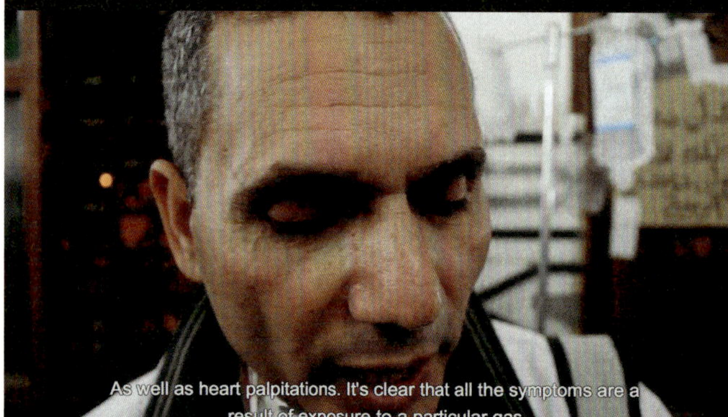

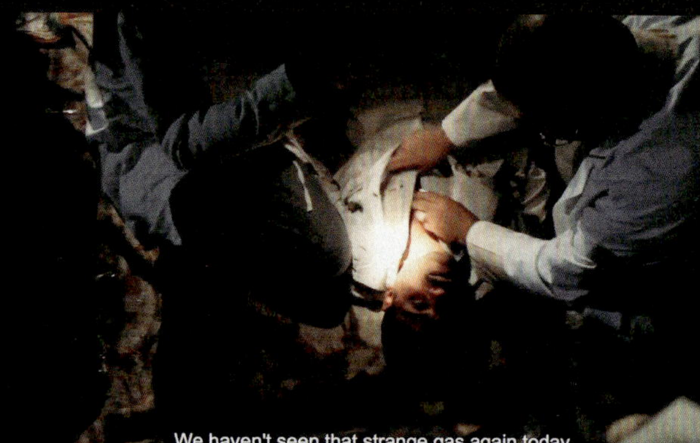

32

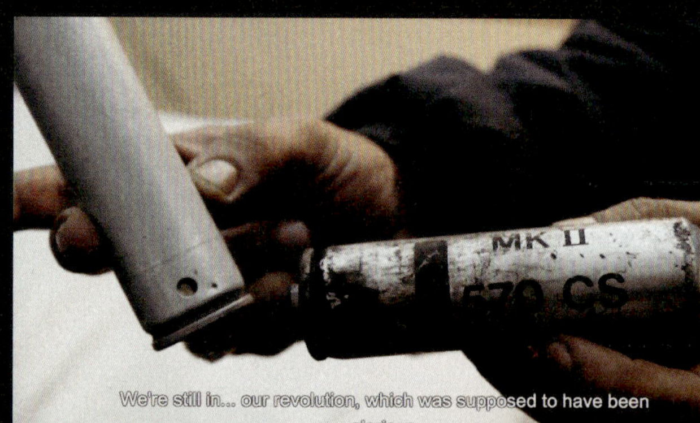

The Heroes of Tahrir / Die Helden des Tahrir-Platzes /
أبطال شارع محمد محمود
Uploaded on Dec. 2, 2011

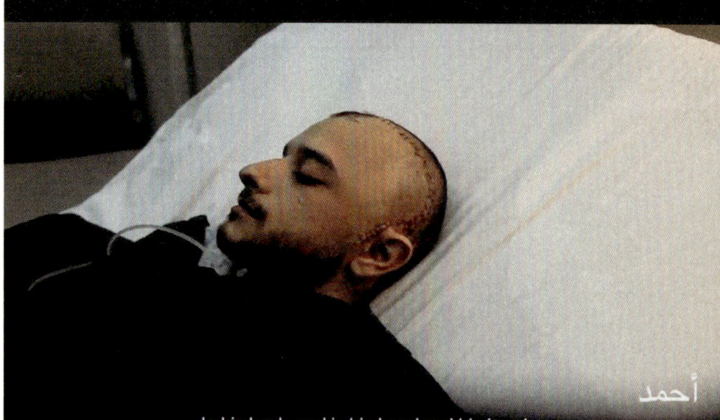

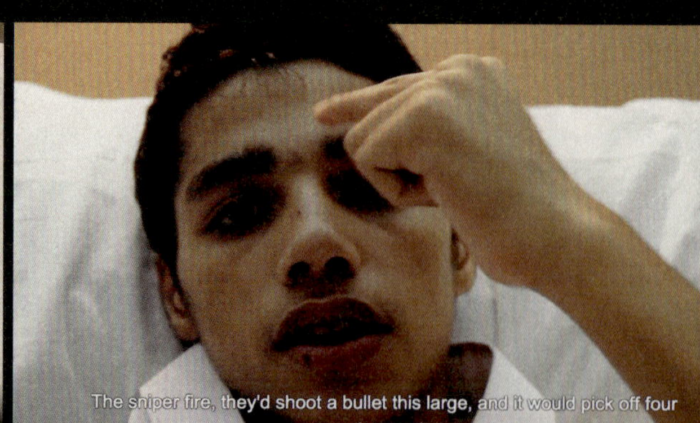

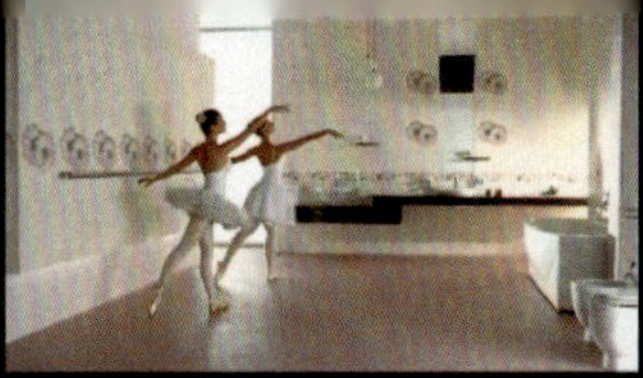

The Strike of the Ceramica Cleopatra Workers / Streik der Arbeiter bei Ceramica Cleopatra / إضراب عمال سيراميكا كليوباترا ضد ممول موقعة الجمل
Uploaded on Mar. 17, 2012

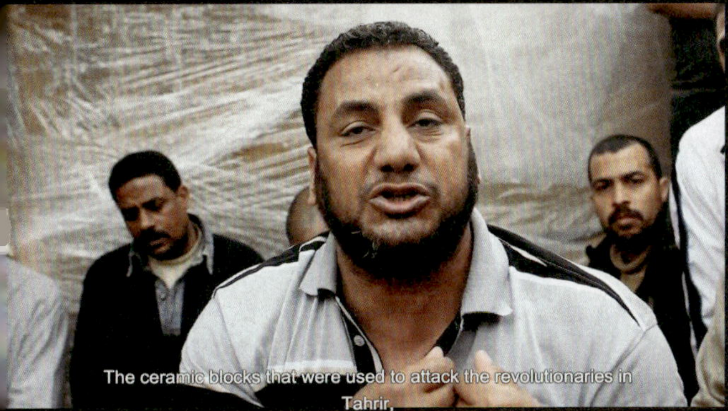

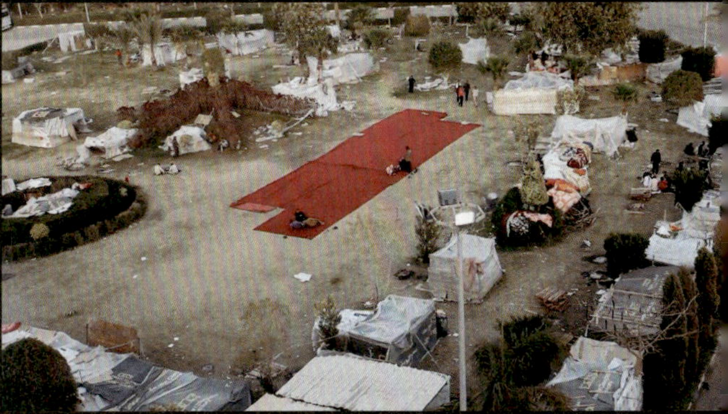

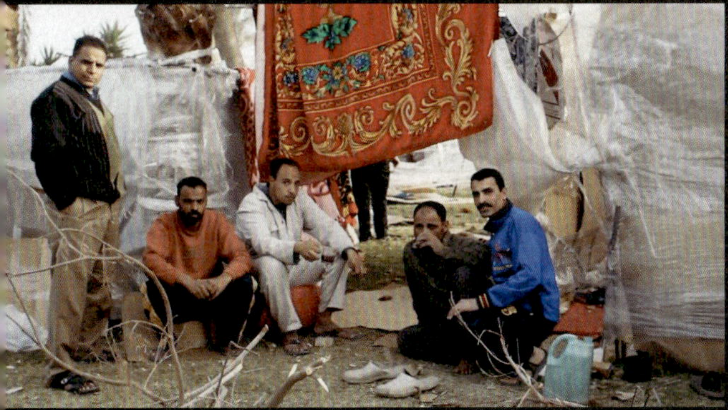

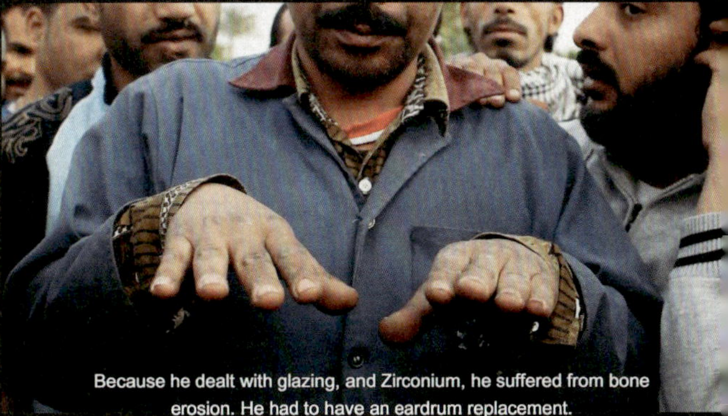

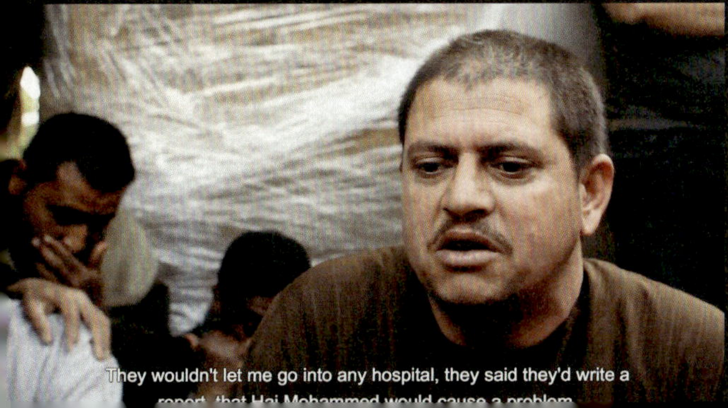

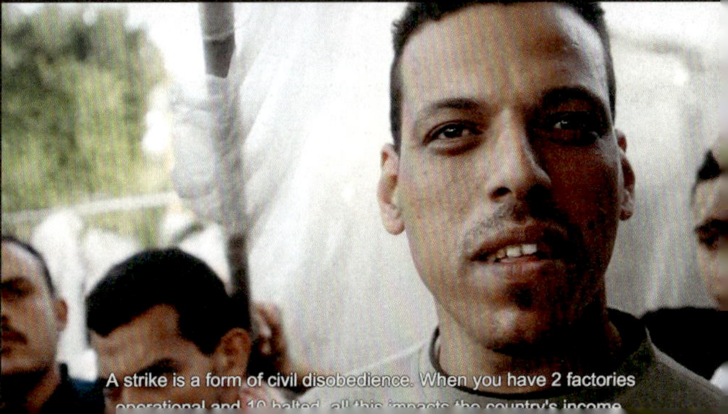

Videos documenting Ittihadiya Palace clashes / Videos zu den Zusammenstößen vor dem Präsidentenpalast, Dec. 2012 / فيديو يوثق الاصطدامات أمام القصر الرئاسي، ديسمبر 2012

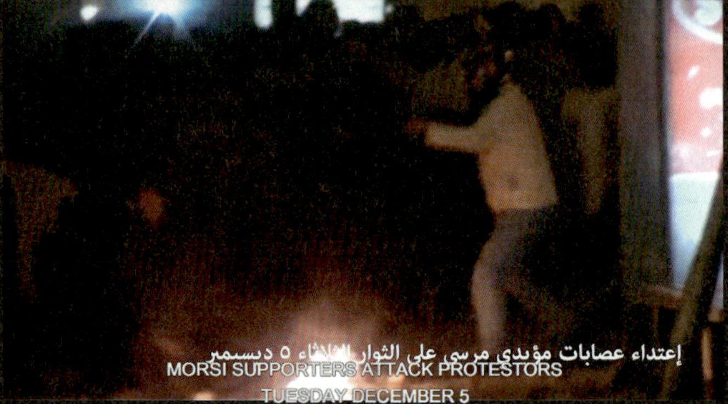

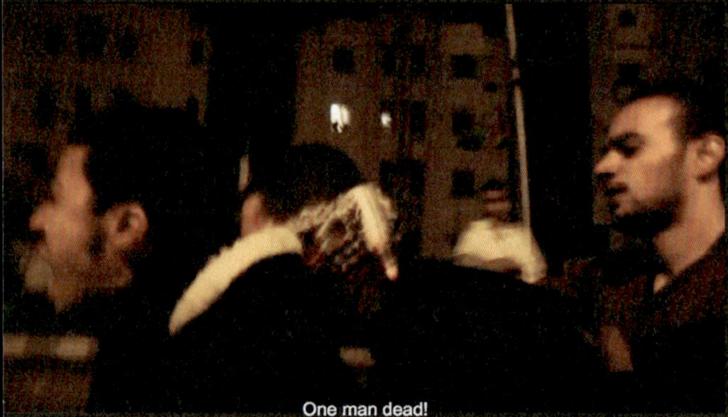

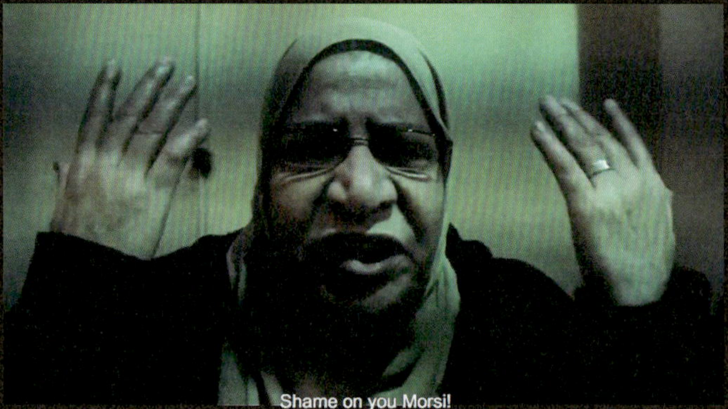

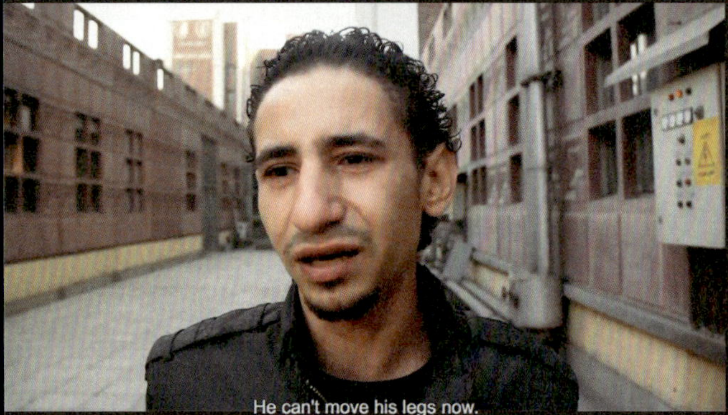

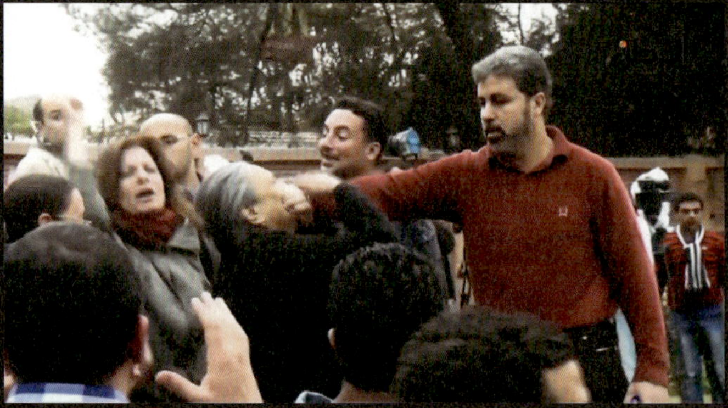

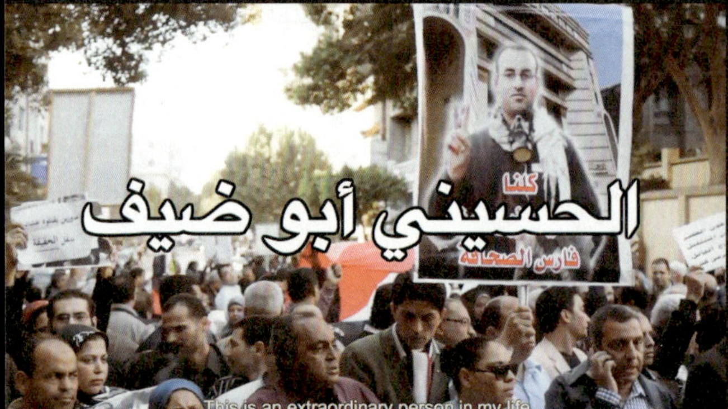

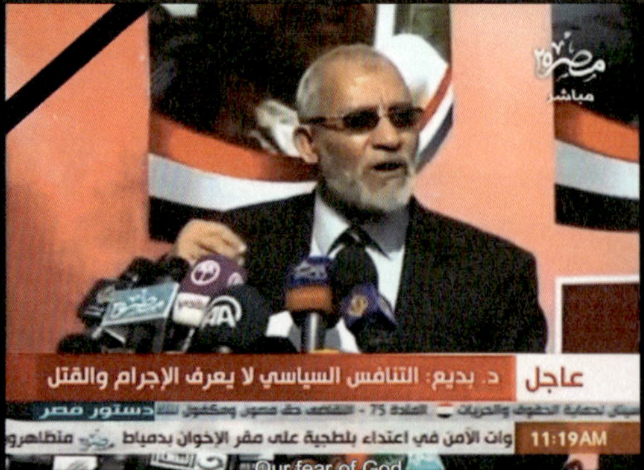

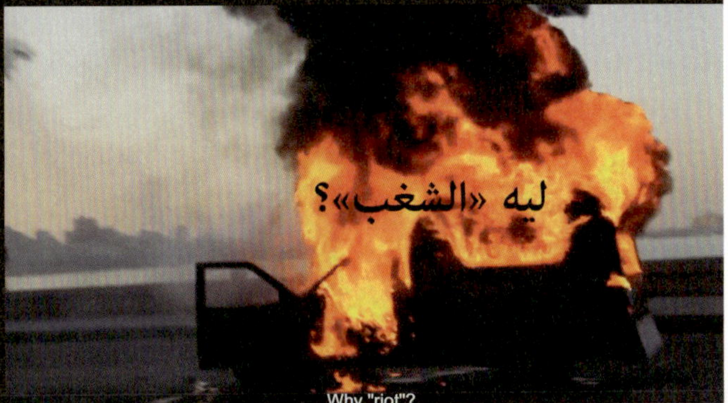

Why Riot? / Warum der Aufstand? / ليه الشعب؟
Uploaded on Mar. 18, 2013

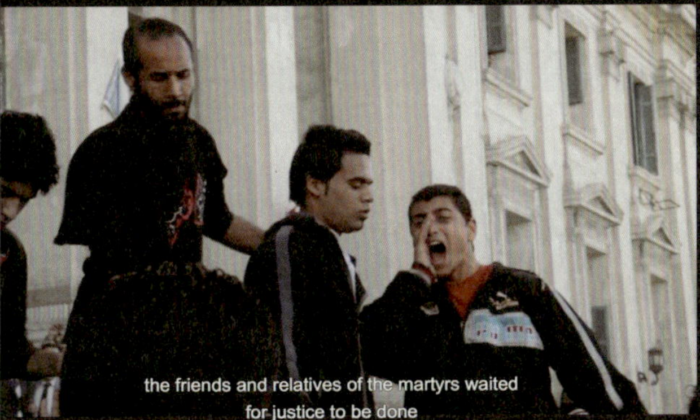

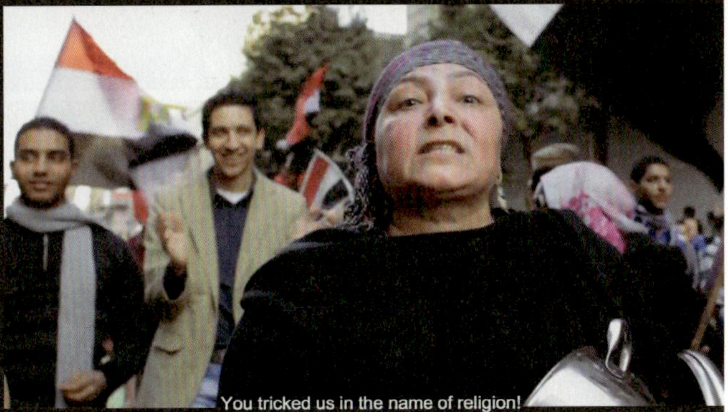

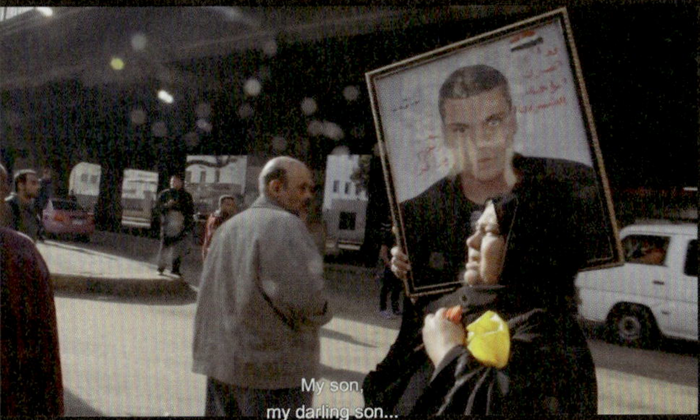

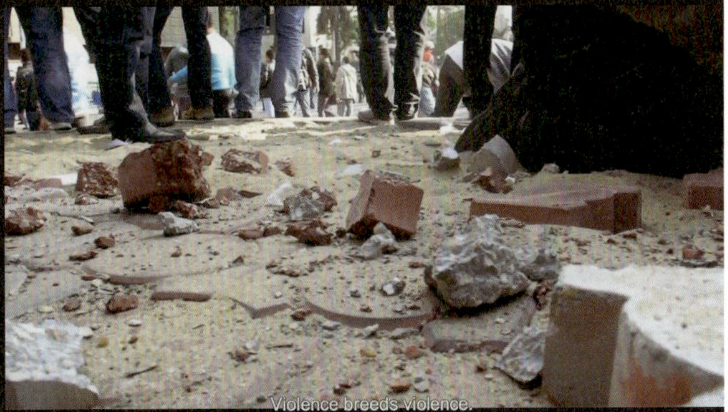

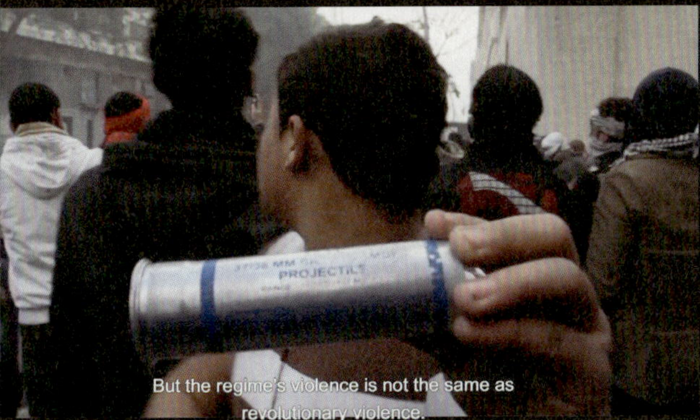

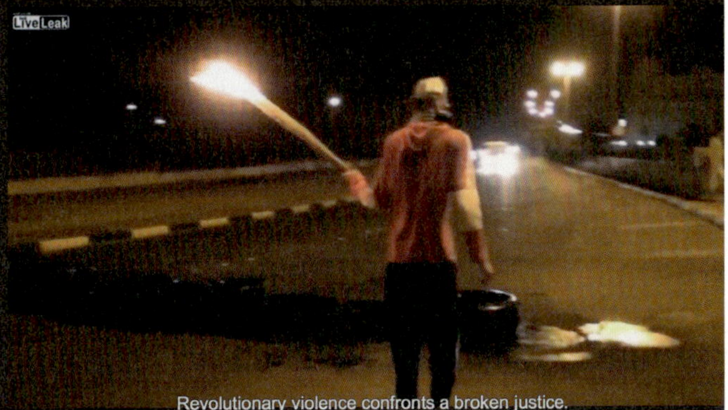

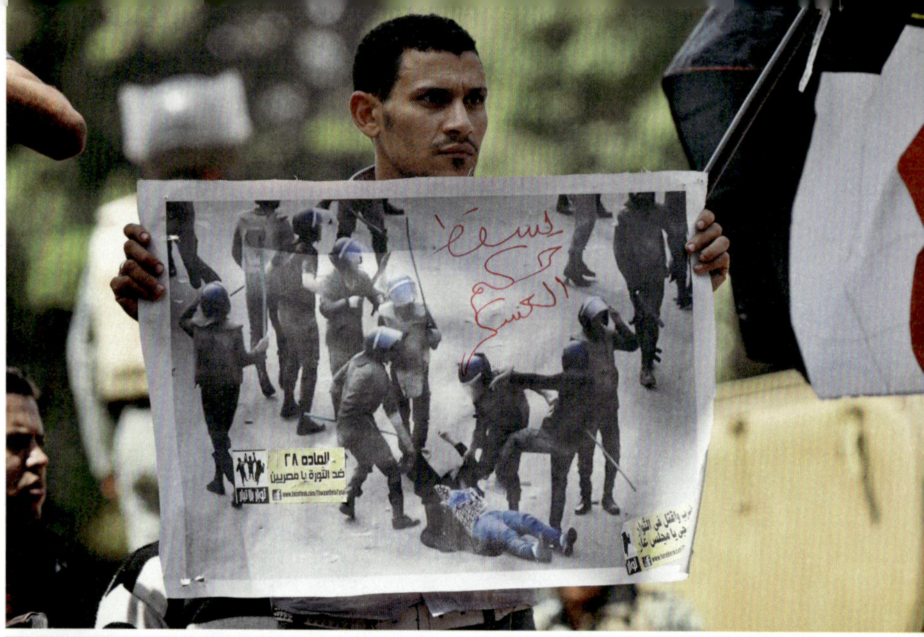

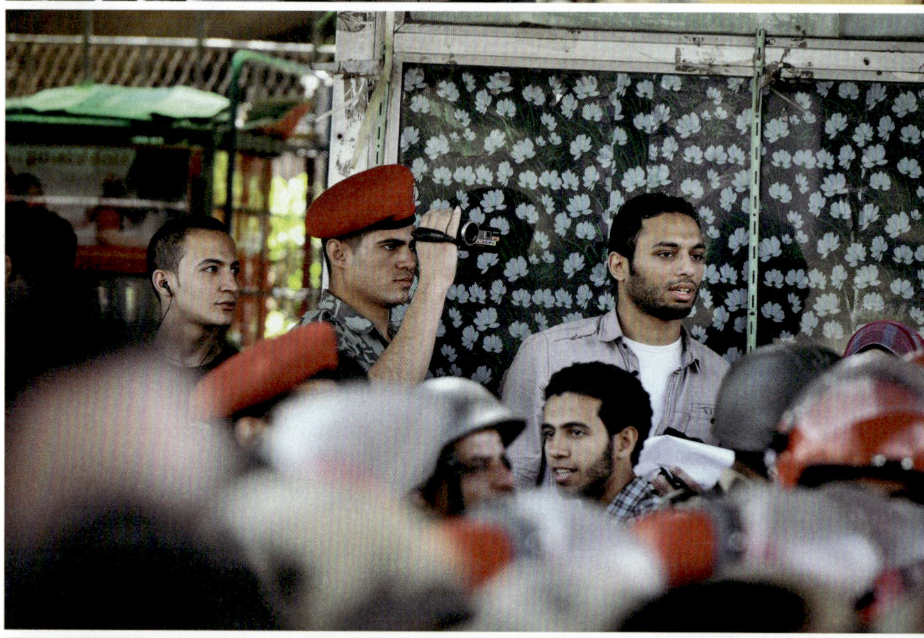

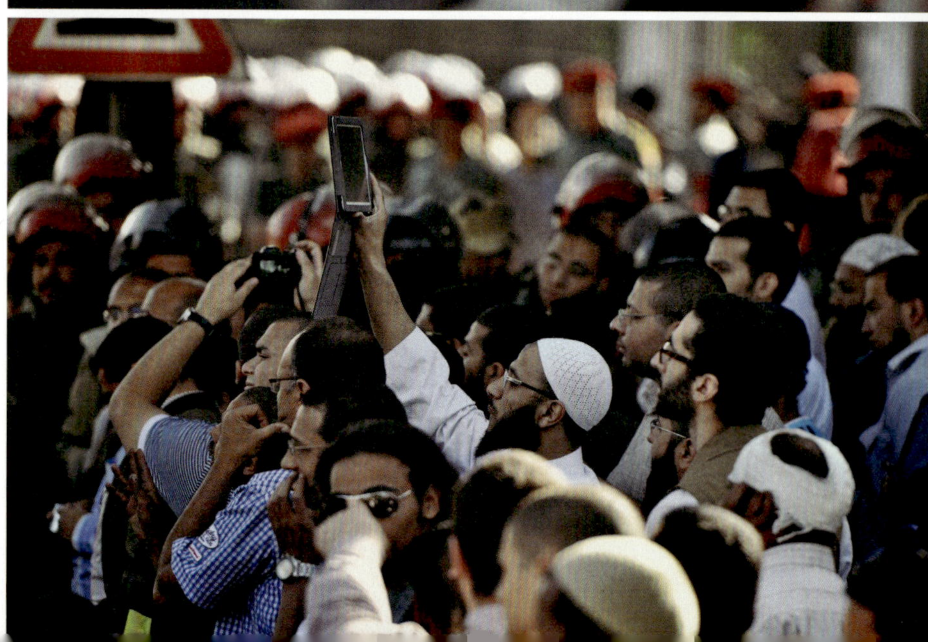

Two Albums on Flickr/Zwei Alben bei Flickr/ألبومان من فليكر

36 – 38 Jonathan Rashad, from the Flickr album / aus dem Flickr-Album *Egypt Clashes – May 2012* / جوناثان رشاد، من ألبوم اشتباكات مصرية- مايو 2012

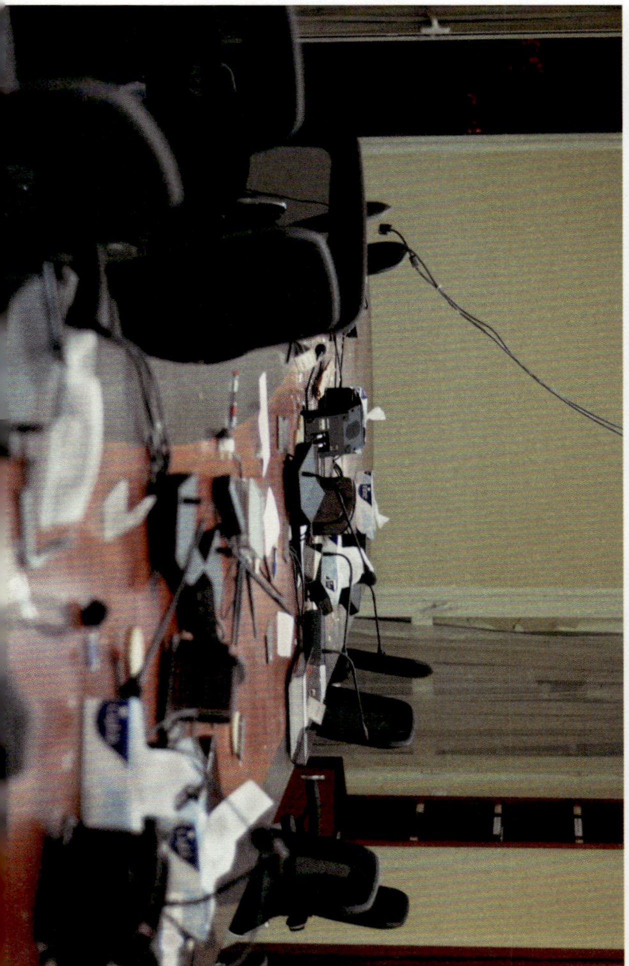

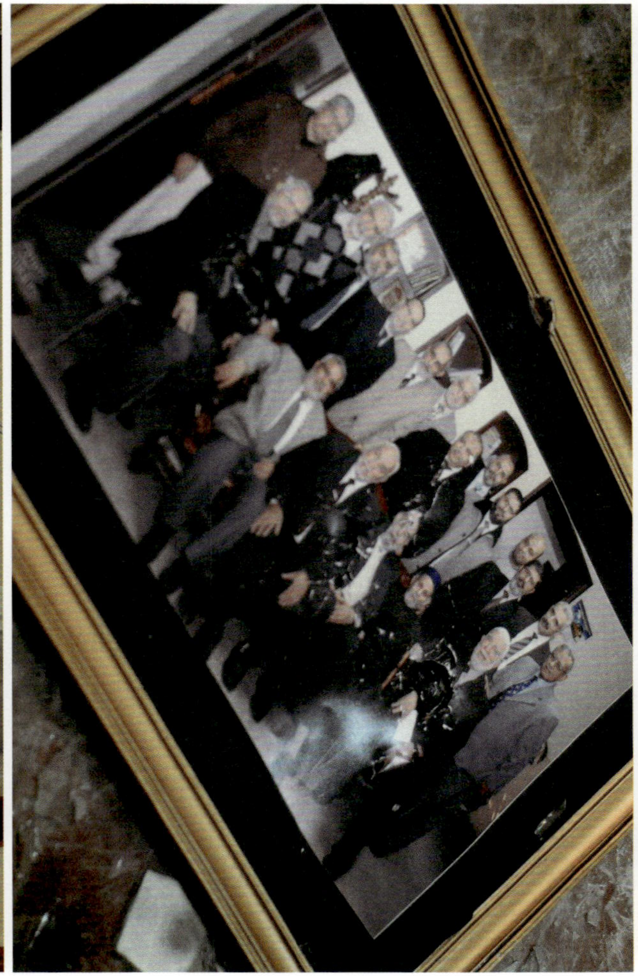

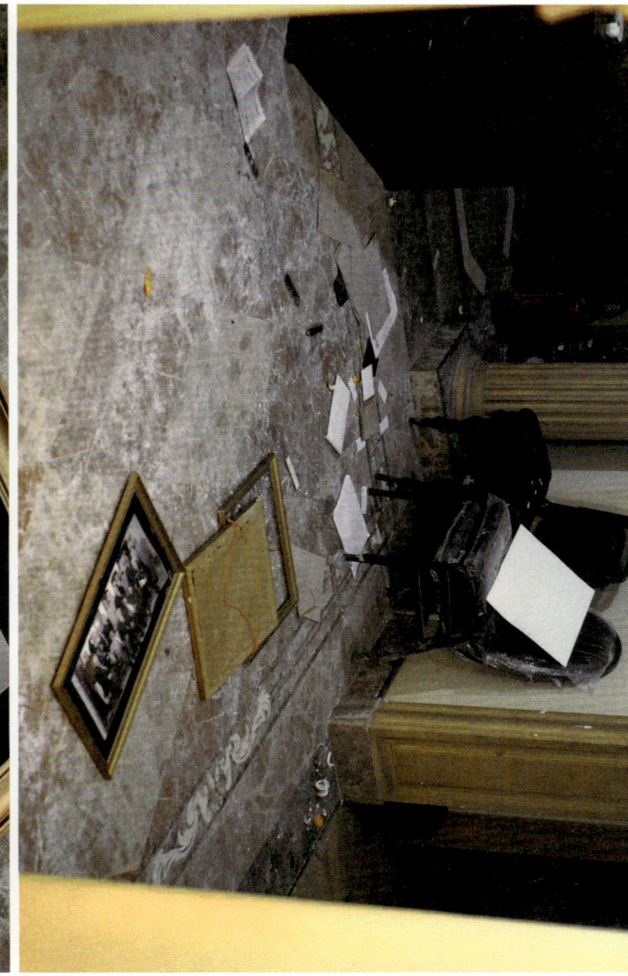

39 – 41 Jonathan Rashad, from the Flickr album / aus dem Flickr-Album *Brotherhood's Headquarters Stormed,* Dec. 7, 2012 / جوناثان رشاد، من ألبوم المقر الرئيسي للإخوان بعد اقتحامه من قبل متظاهرين معارضين لمرسي على موقع فليكر، 7 ديسمبر 2012

42 Sarah Carr, *SCC*, June 14, 2012/2012 سارة كار من ألبوم *SCC*، 14 يونيو 2012

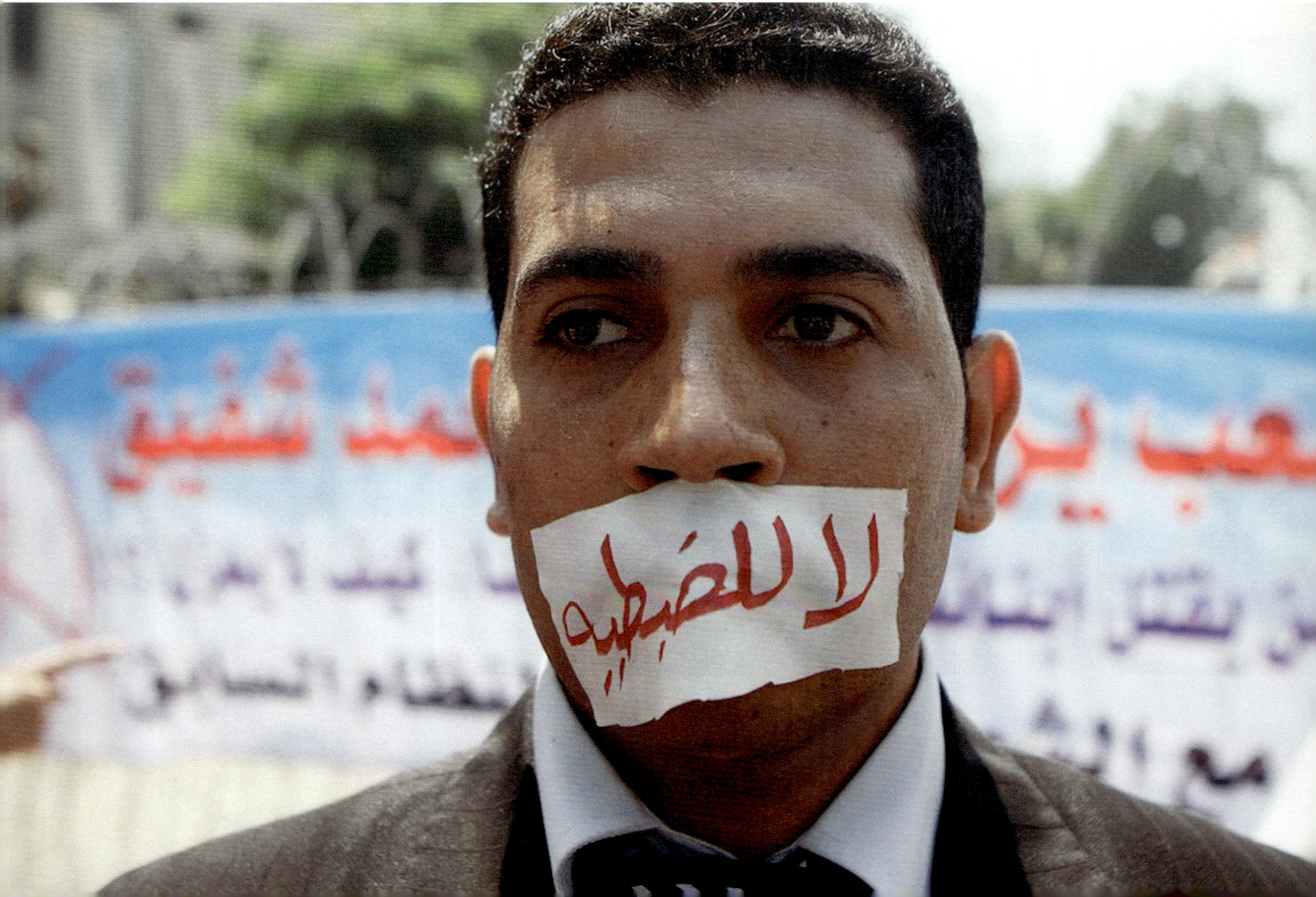

45 Sarah Carr, *Port Said Clashes, Day 2*, Feb. 3, 2012/2012 اشتباكات بورسعيد اليوم الثاني، 3 فبراير
46 Sarah Carr, *November 23*, Nov. 23, 2011/2011 نوفمبر 23، 23 نوفمبر

43 Sarah Carr, *Cabinet Sit-In Attack Protests*, Dec. 18, 2011/مظاهرات ضرب اعتصام مجلس الوزراء، 18 ديسمبر 2011
44 Sarah Carr, *Port Said Clashes, Day 2*, Feb. 3, 2012/2012 اشتباكات بورسعيد اليوم الثاني، 3 فبراير

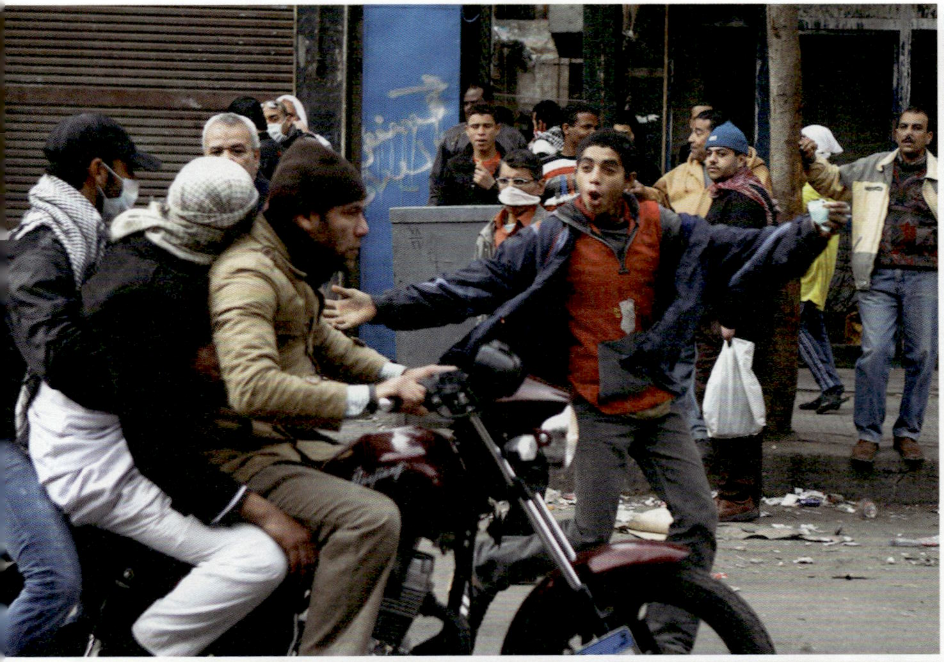

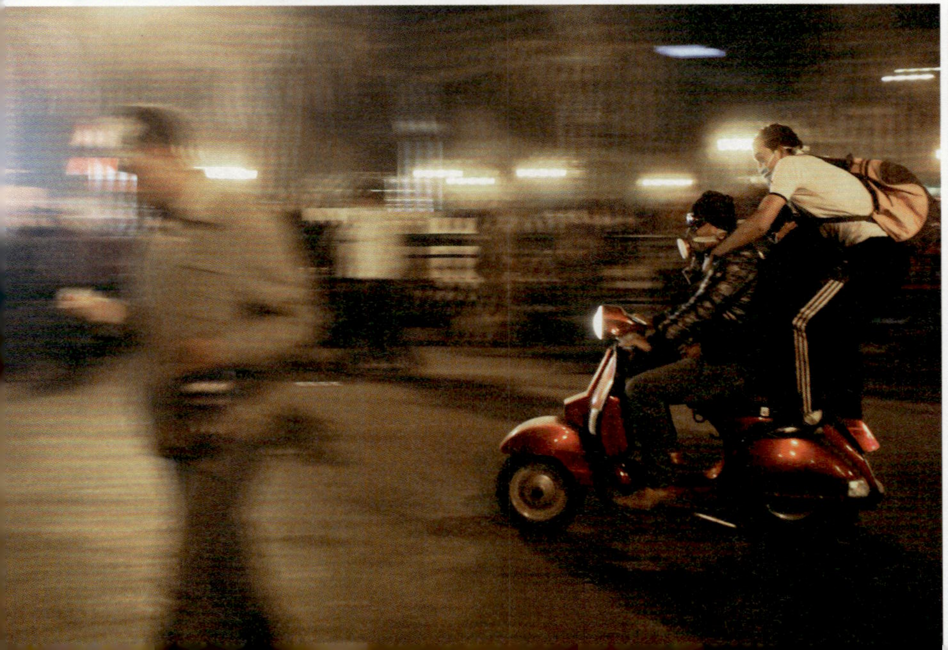

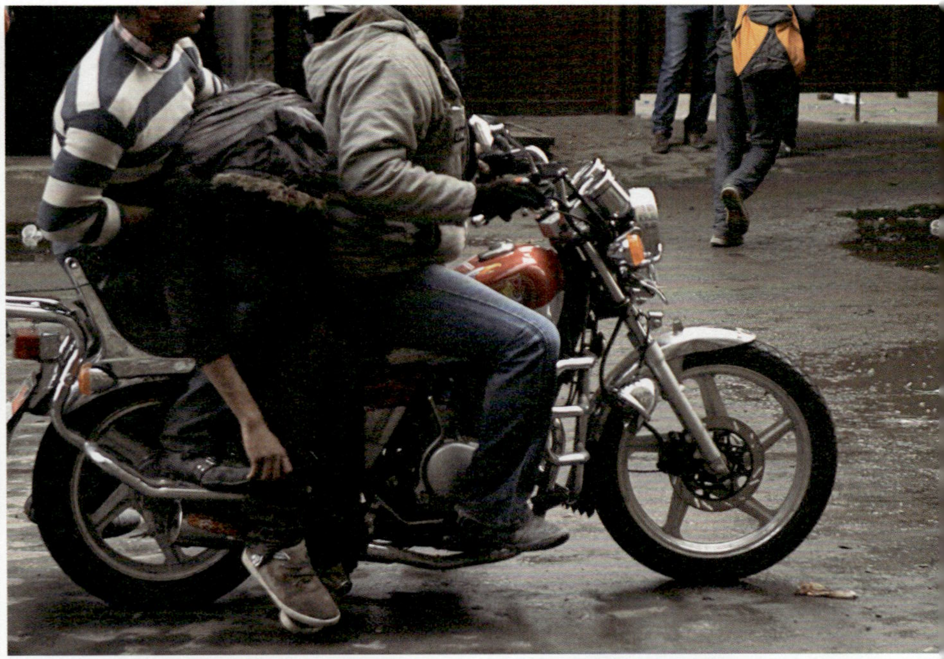

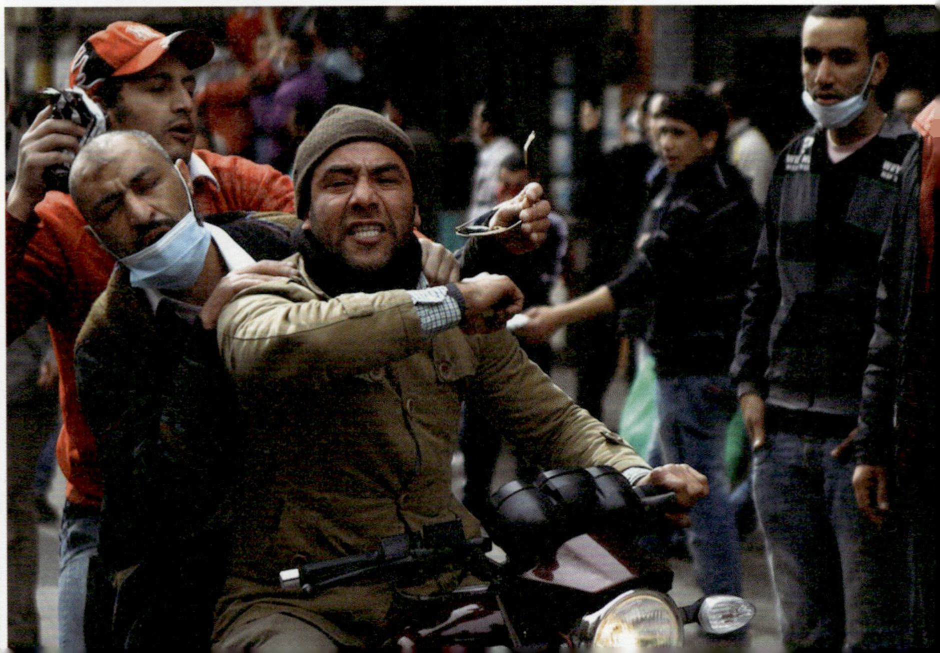

47 Heba Khalifa, *Cairo, Dec. 1, 2011* / هبة خليفة، القاهرة، 1 ديسمبر، 2011
48 Fadi Ezzat, *Mohammed Mahmoud St., Cairo, Nov. 23, 2011* / فادي عزت، شارع محمد محمود، القاهرة، 23 نوفمبر 2011

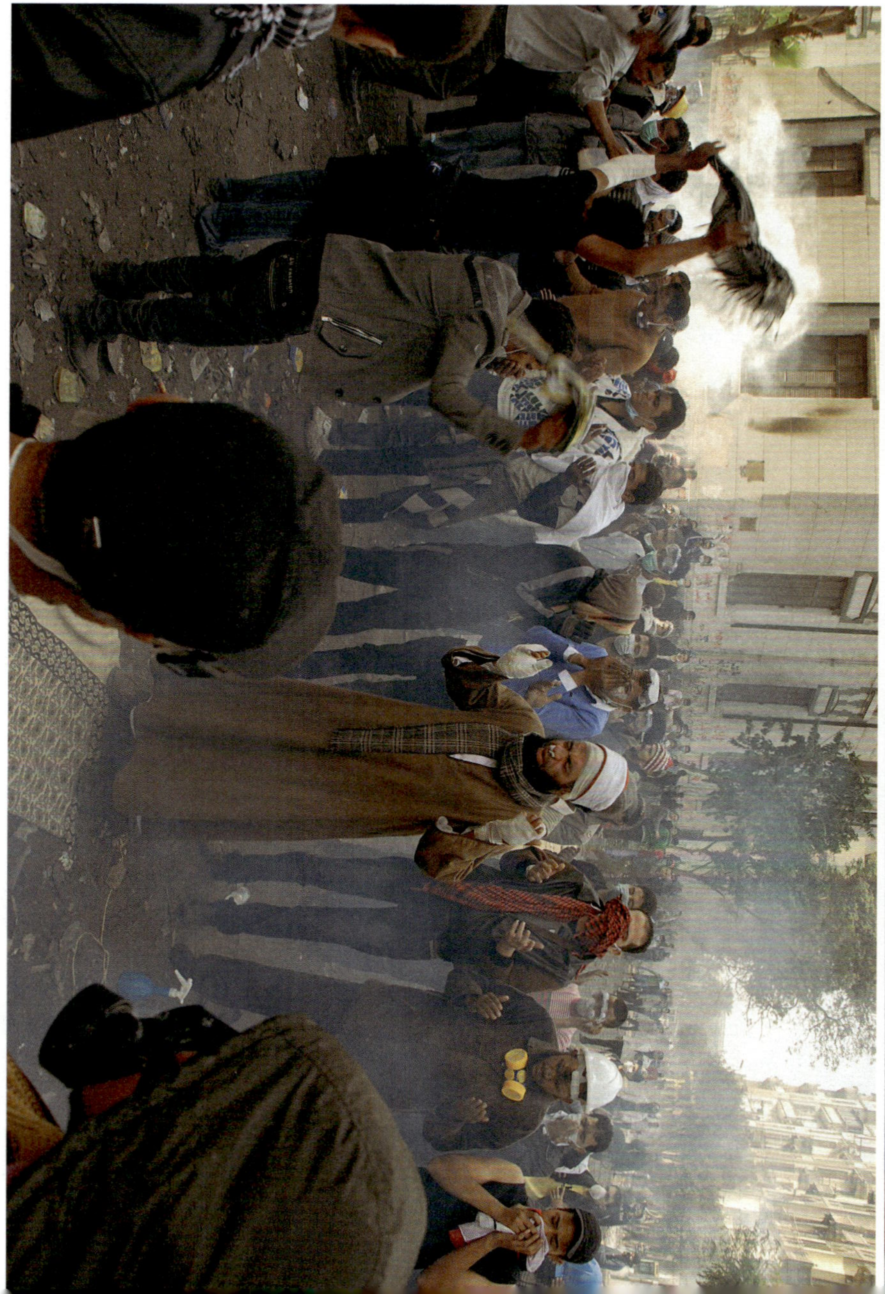

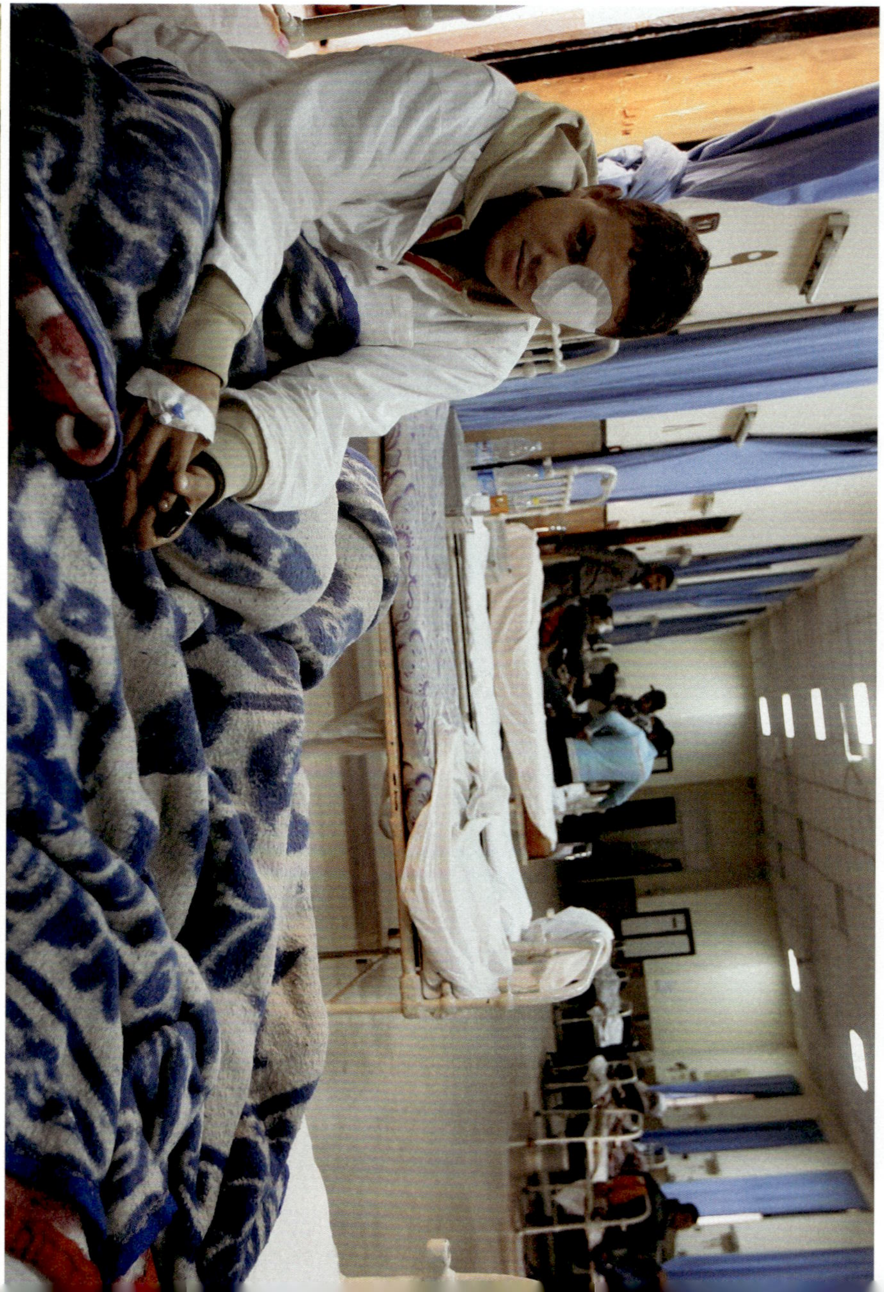

50 Ahmed Abdellatif, *Suez, Jan. 26, 2013* / أحمد عبد اللطيف، السويس، 26 يناير 2013

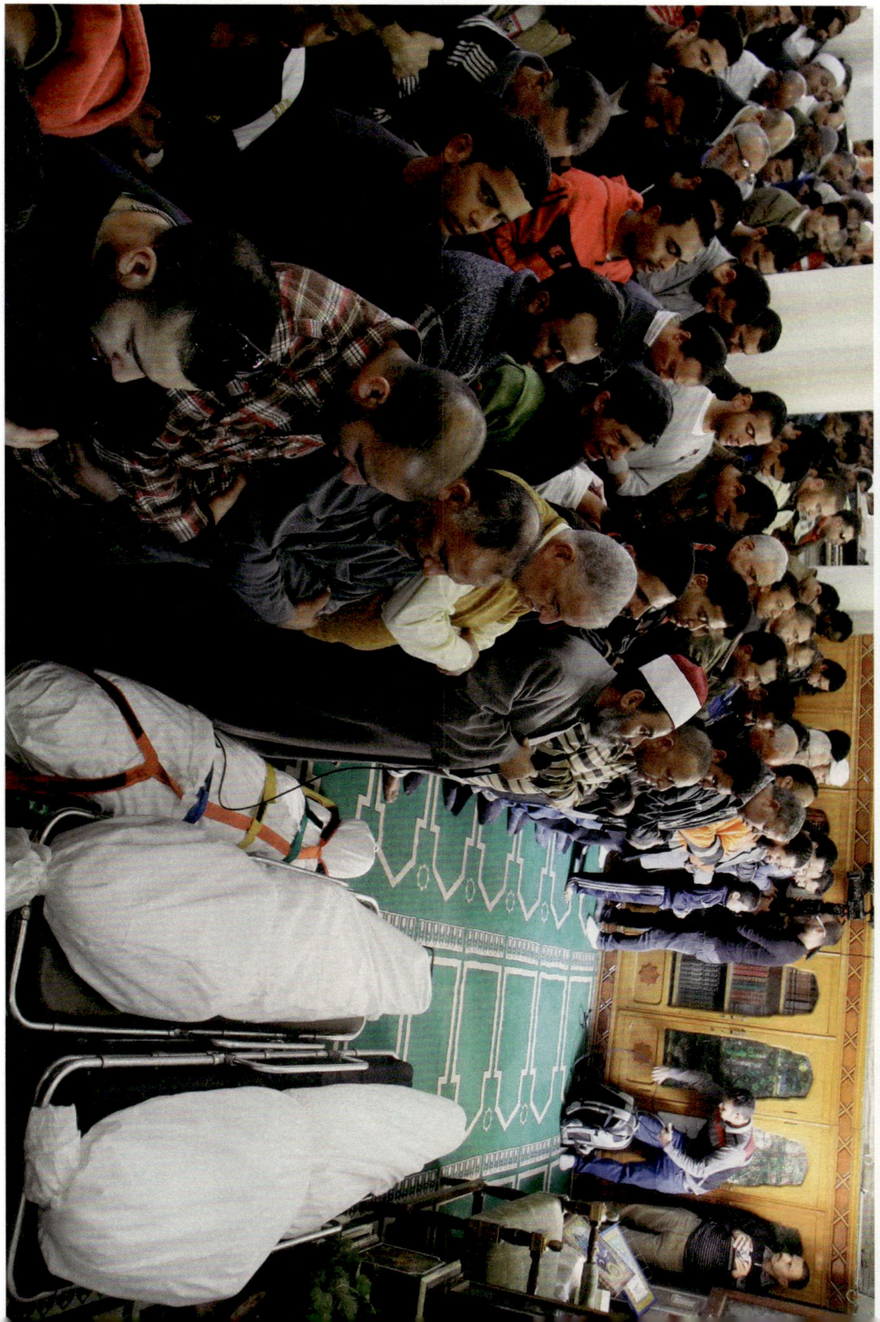

49 Jihan Nasr, *Tahrir, Cairo, Feb. 12, 2011* / جيهان نصر، التحرير، القاهرة، 12 فبراير 2011

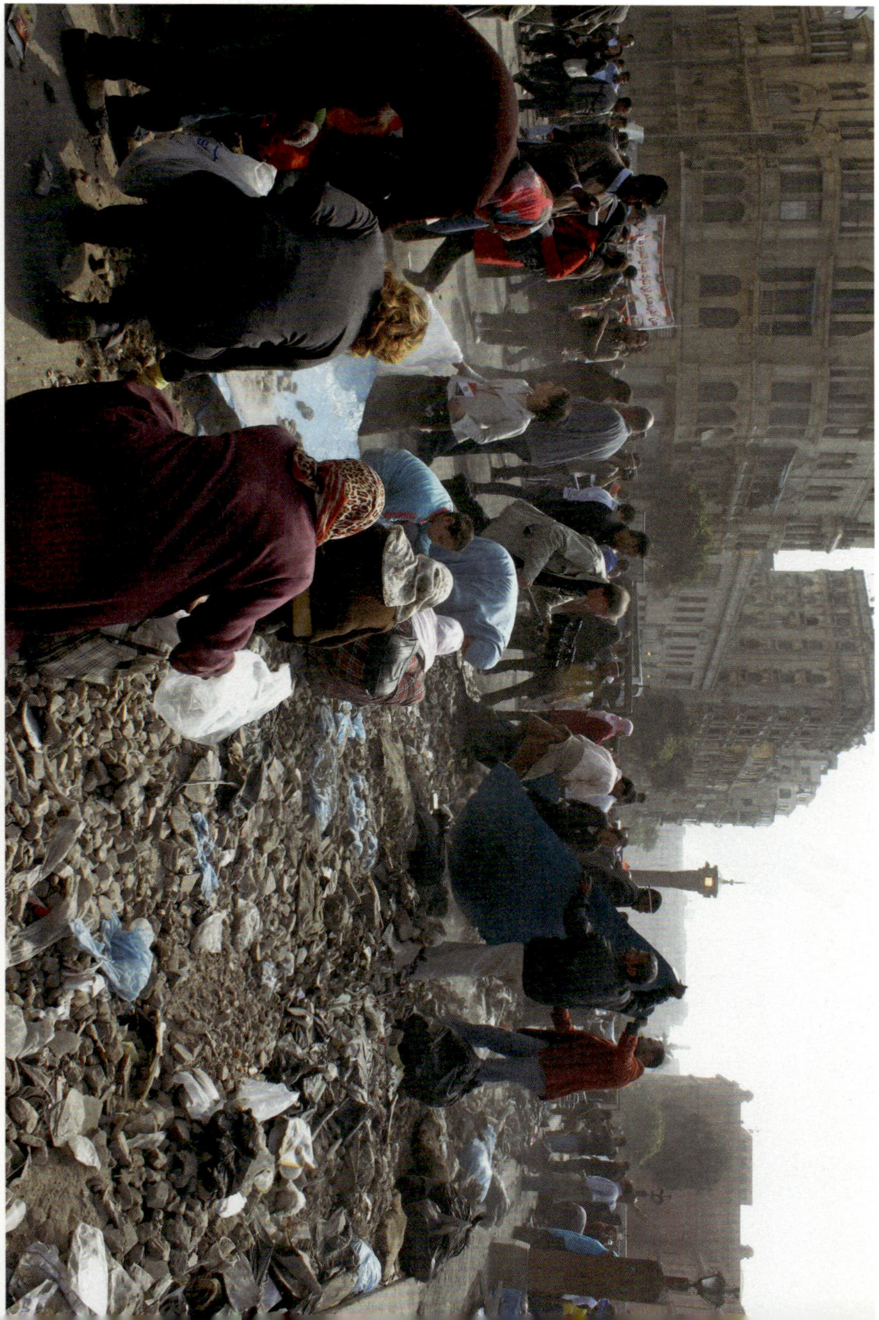

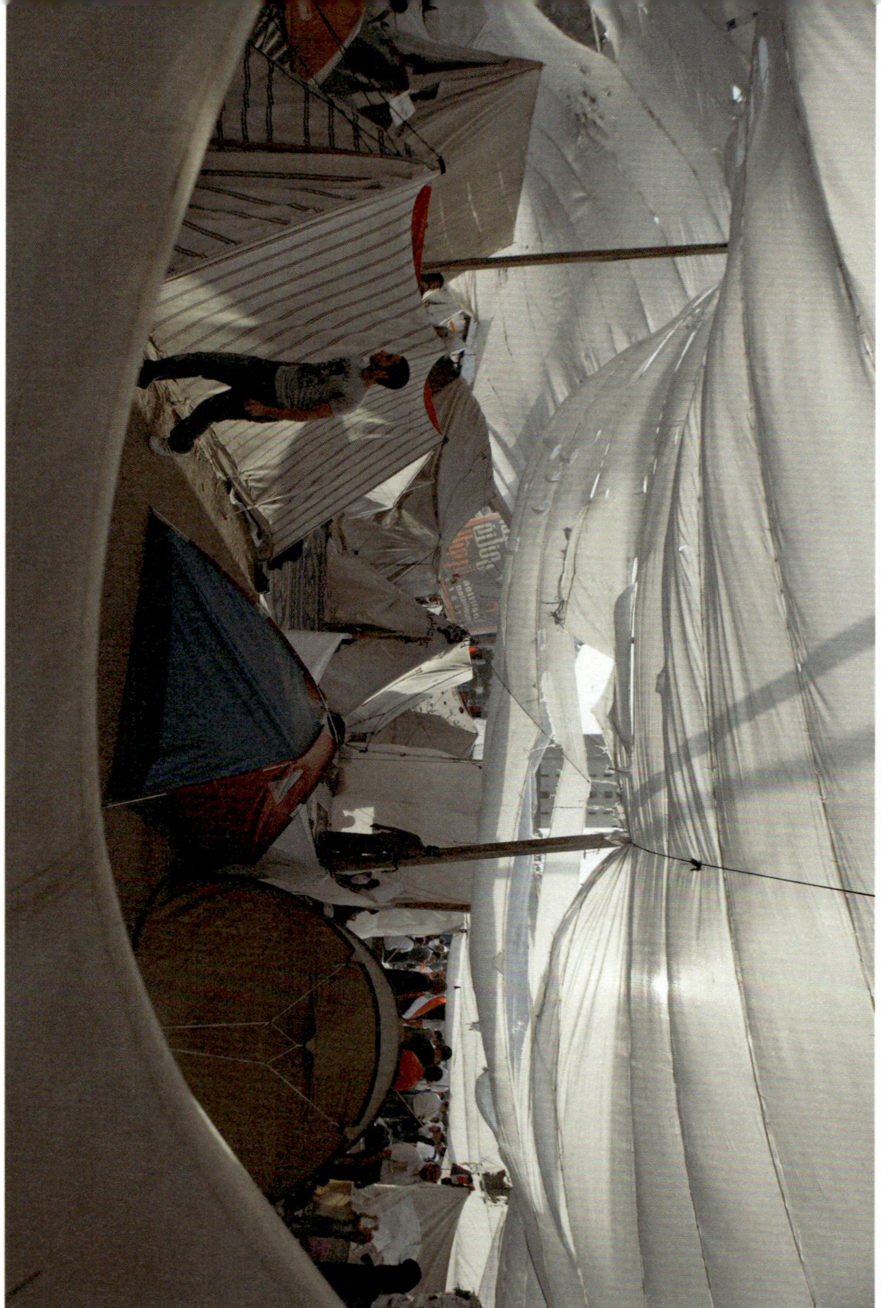

52 Thomas Hartwell, *Tahrir, Cairo, July 15, 2011* / *2011* توماس هارتويل، التحرير، القاهرة، *15 يوليو*

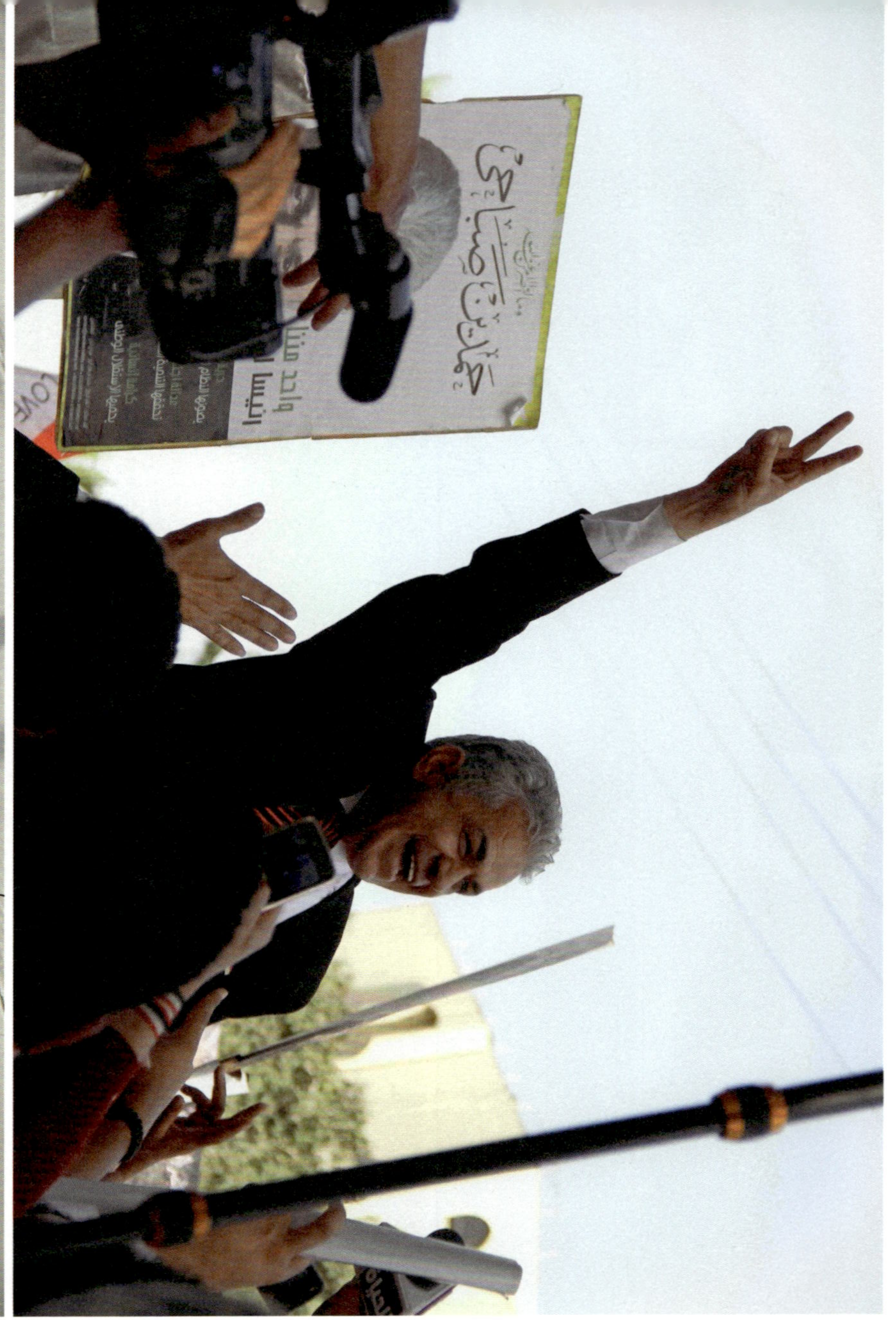

51 Lobna Tarek, *Heliopolis, Cairo, Apr. 6, 2012* / *2012* لبنى طارق، مصر الجديدة، القاهرة، *6 أبريل*

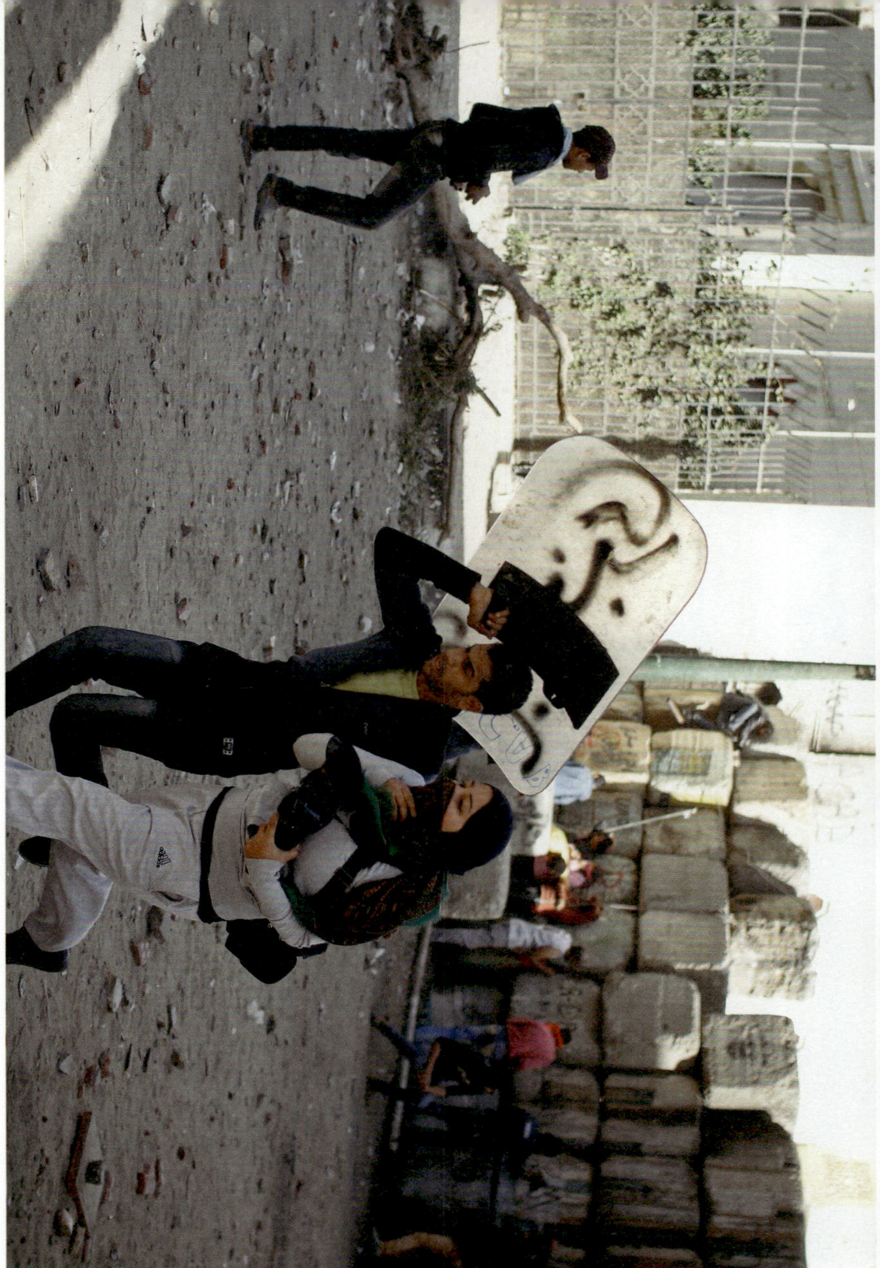

54 Aly Hazza'a, *El Kasr El Aini, Jan. 25, 2013* / 2013 على هزاع، القصر العيني، 25 يناير

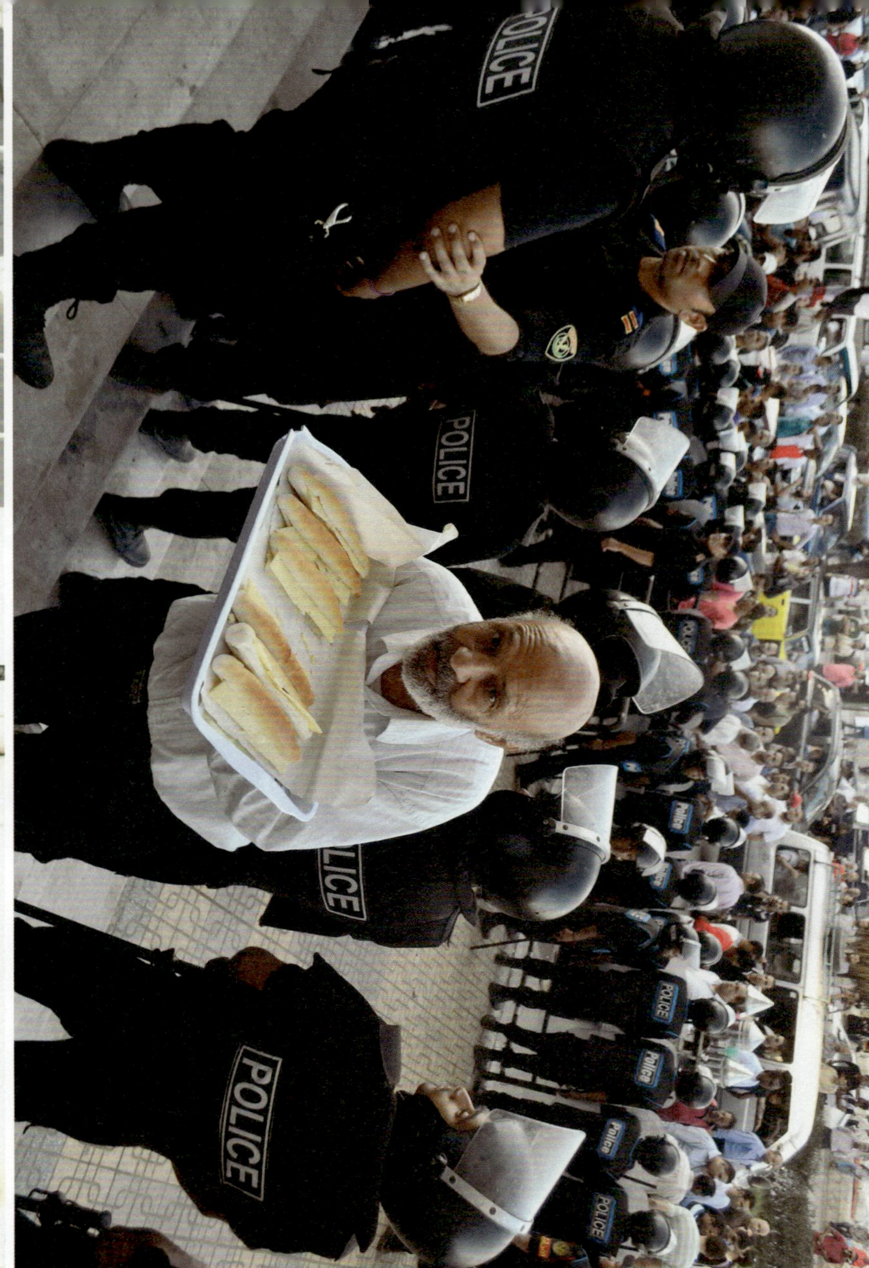

53 Amira Mortada, *Alexandria, Feb. 21, 2013* / 2013 أميرة مرتضى، الإسكندرية، 21 فبراير

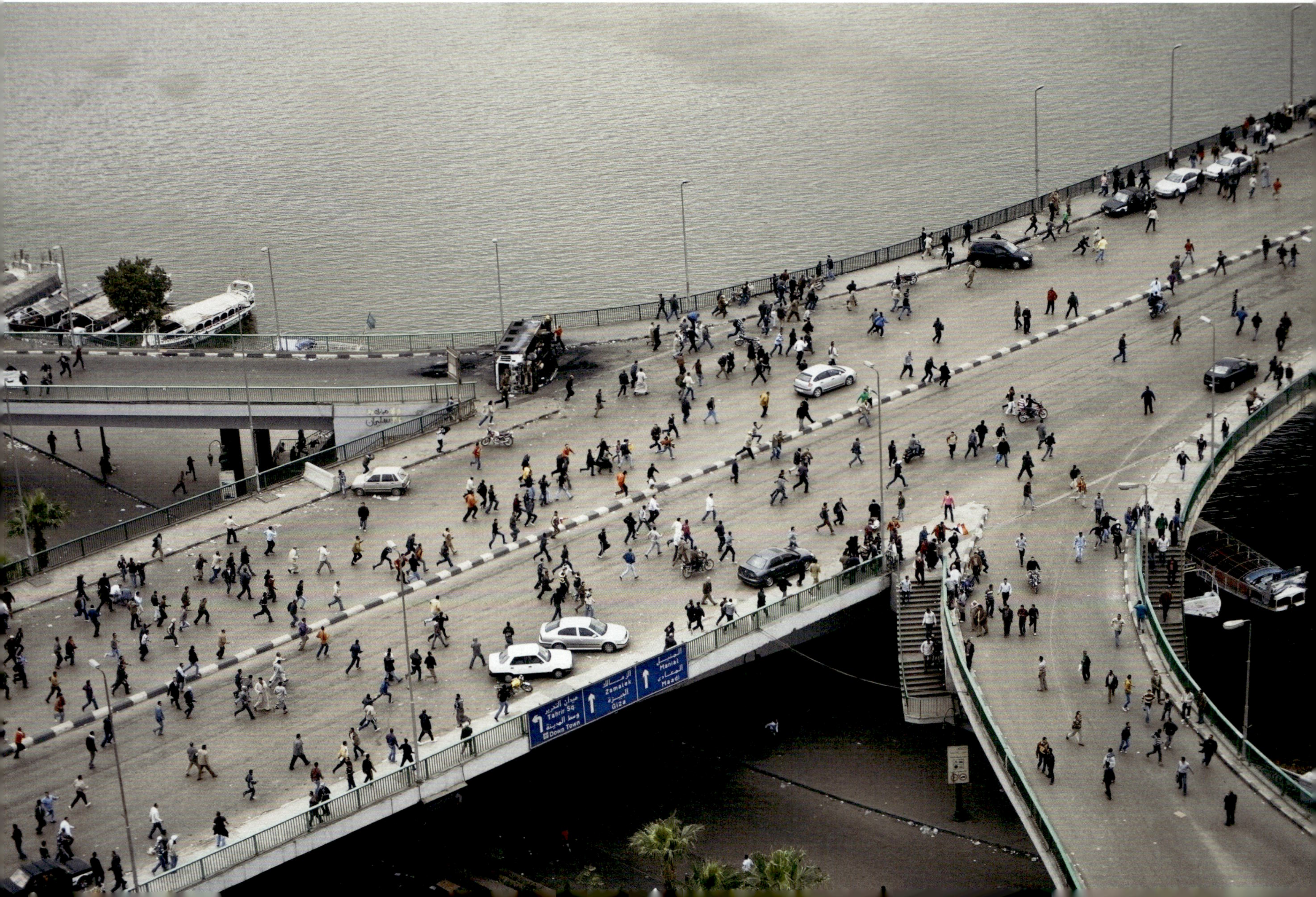
ميدان التحرير
Tahrir Sq
وسط المدينة
Down Town
الزمالك
Zamalek
الجيزة
Giza
المنيل
Manial
المعادي
Maadi

55 + 56 Peter van Agtmael, *Egypt. Cairo. Feb. 3, 2011* / بيتر فون أجتميل، مصر، القاهرة، 3 فبراير 2011

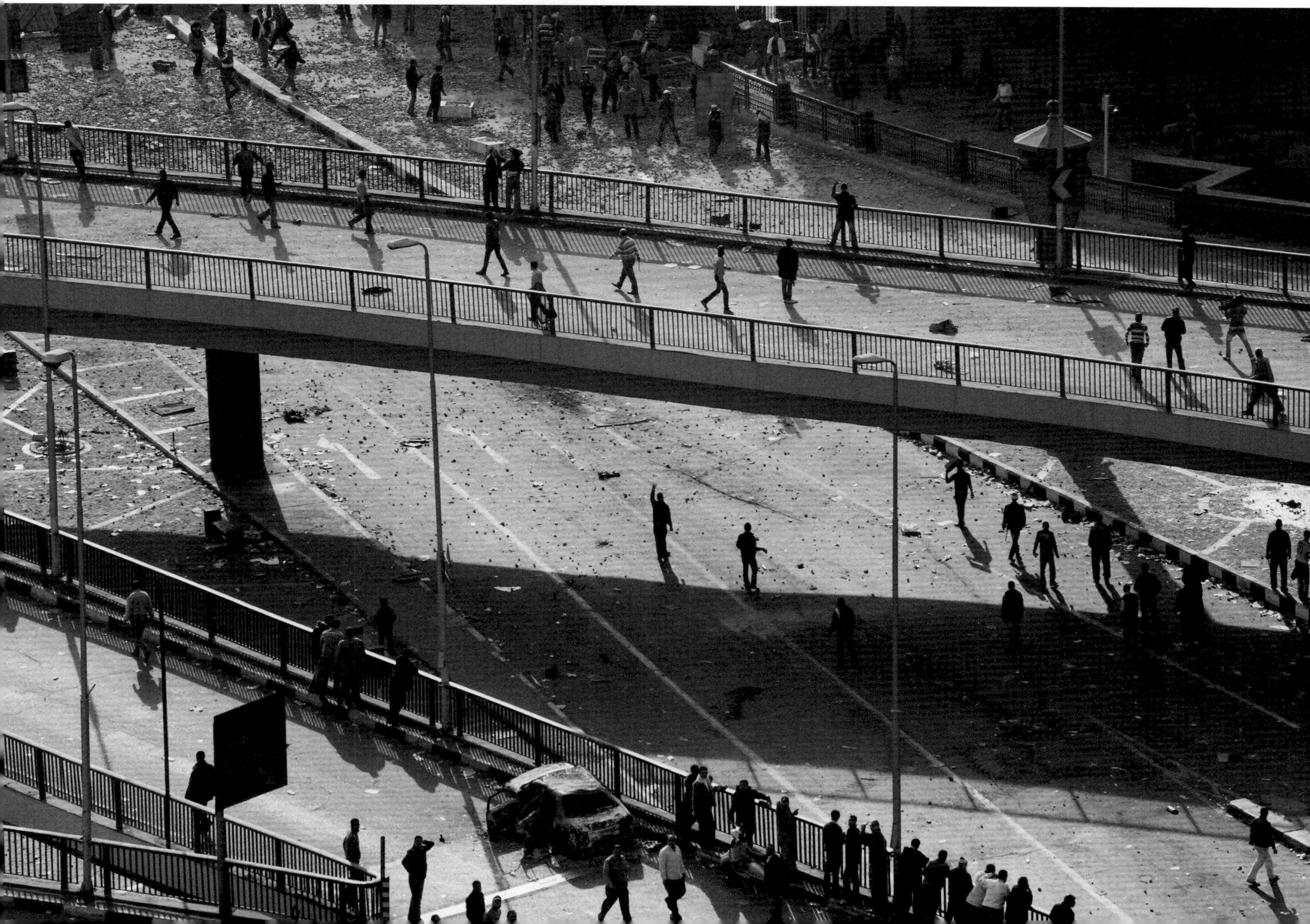

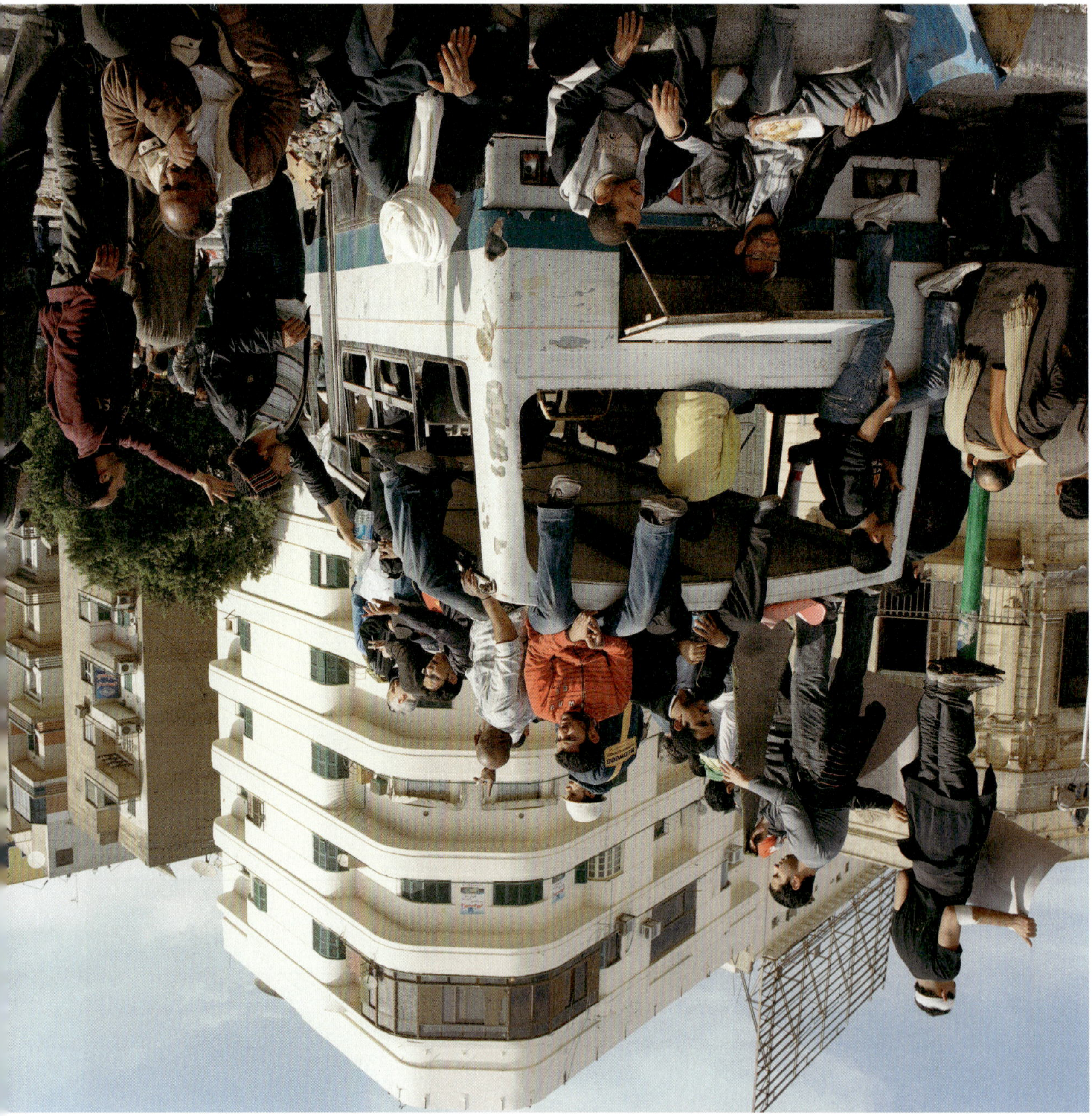

57 + 58 Ivor Prickett, from the series / aus der Serie *Days of Anger*, 2011 /
أيفور بريكيت، من سلسلة أيام الخطر، 2011

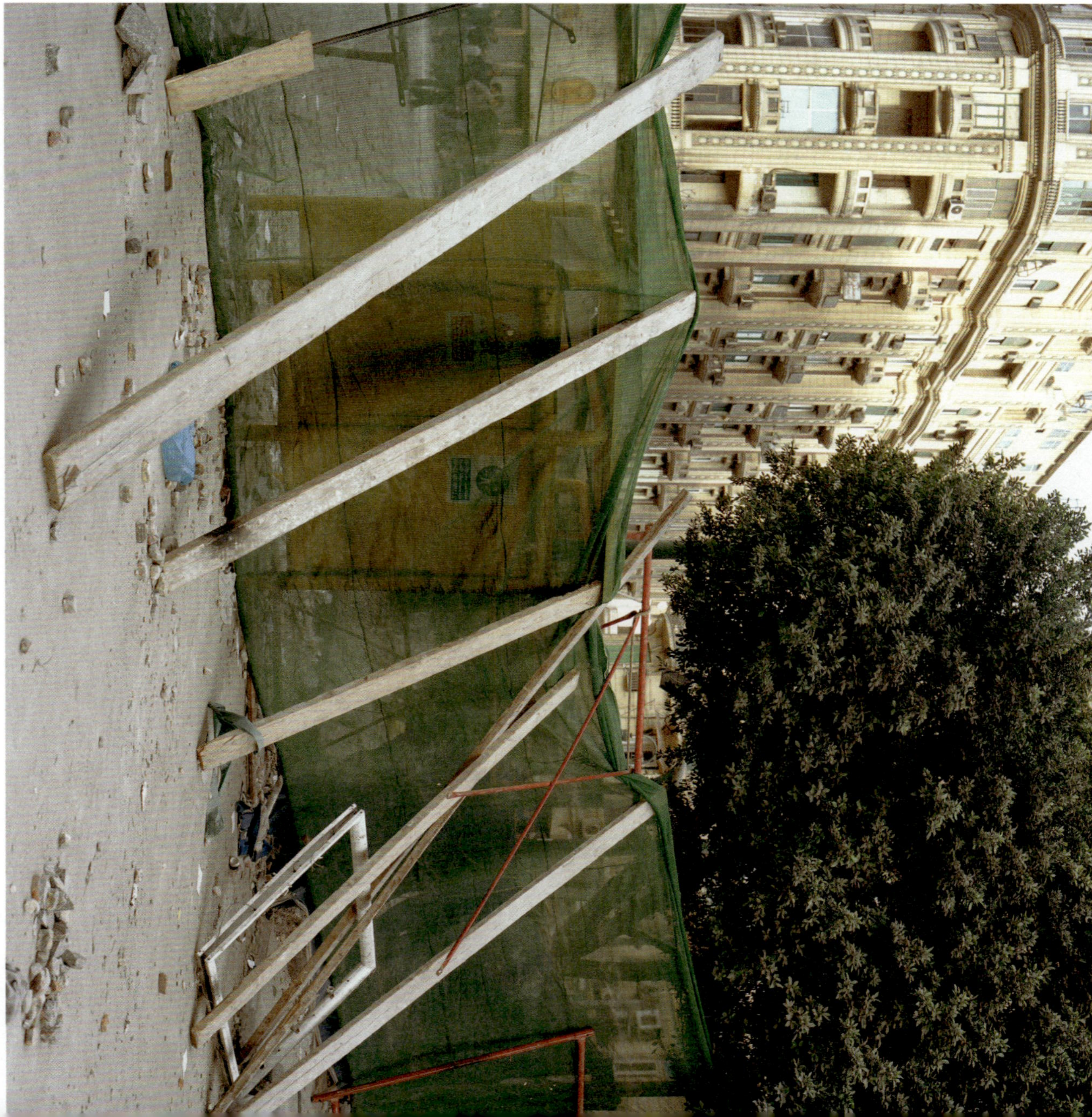

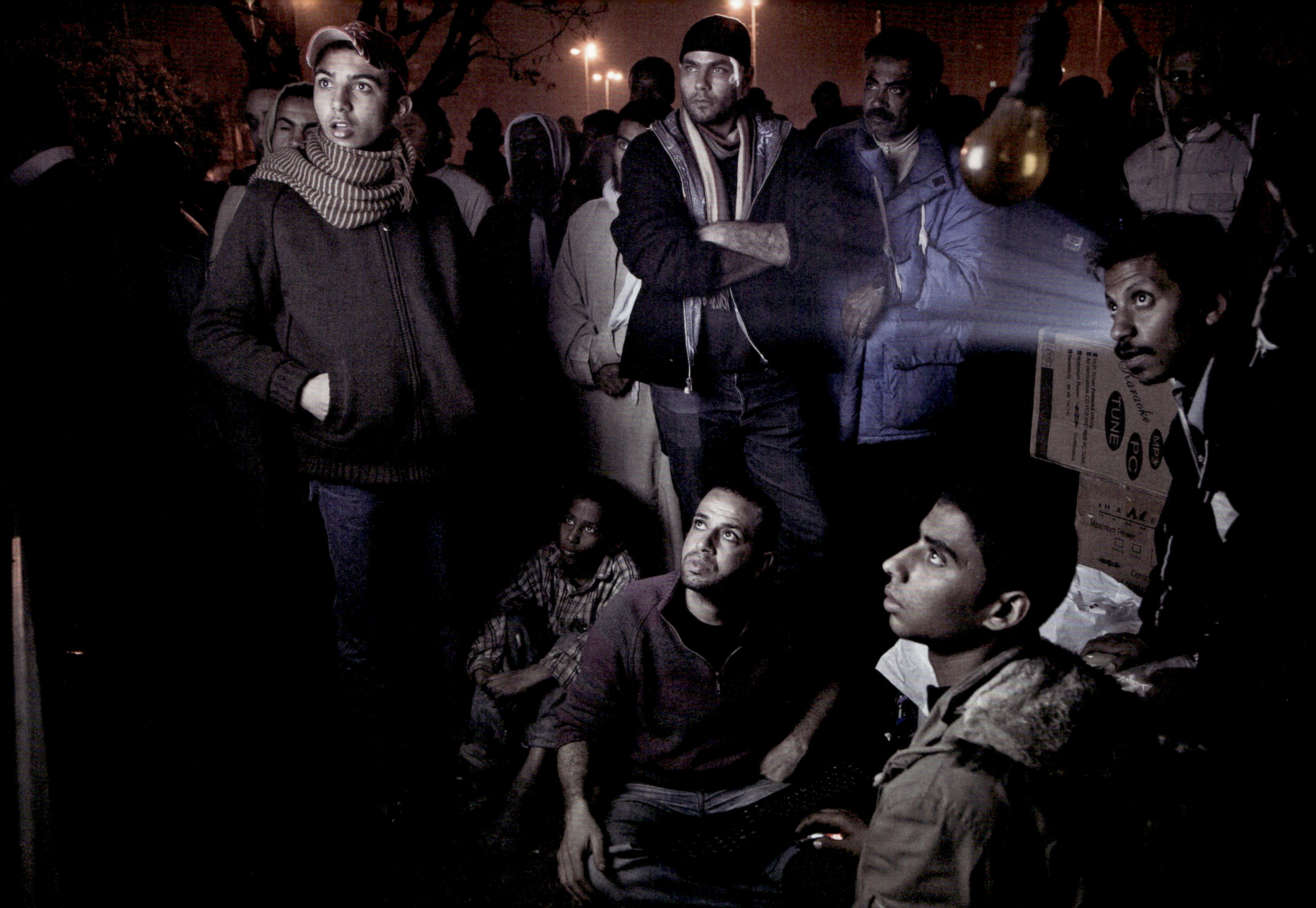

View of an Egyptian Photographer Living Abroad / Blick eines im Ausland lebenden ägyptischen Fotografen / رؤية مصور مصري مقيم في الخارج

59 Kim Badawi (Reportage by Getty), *Tahrir Square, Cairo*, Feb. 6, 2011 / كيم بدوي (موقع ريبورتاج باي جيتي)، ميدان التحرير، القاهرة، 6 فبراير 2011.

Content / Inhalt

The project *Cairo. Open City. New Testimonies from an Ongoing Revolution* is in one sense very close to present-day political events in Egypt, yet at the same time far removed: some 2,000 miles from the Museum für Photographie in Braunschweig, which spawned this initiative, and from the Folkwang Museum in Essen, which the pictures from this exhibition have now moved on to, brought up to date and complemented by new images of a political process whose outcome remains open-ended.

Proximity in time married with physical separation—this constellation leaves considerable scope for misinterpretation. Many of the images that the Western media have portrayed as "the Arab Spring" are the product of gross oversimplification, misplaced emphasis, or unreliable sources. For this reason, one of the tasks of this project is to review and augment our image of the Egyptian Revolution. At first sight, it may seem surprising that this task should be performed by museums of all places—because, in the context of this project, there is absolutely no place for the museum.

It is all about work: about the work of the eye and of the mind in determining how the Egyptian Revolution is perceived, who is in the vanguard of it, who its representatives are, and the revolutionary role photography plays in it. As is emphasized in the text accompanying this diverse body of work, what is at stake is no less than "a new chapter in photography in the Arab world"—and, by extension, "a new chapter in the history of images."

Contemporary political history and the history of images are interdependent. What is more, it is political events that bring new applications for photography into being: as political testimony in digital form, capable of being produced and distributed by anyone in a matter of seconds, and of being fed as a form of instant evidence straight back into the political process, and thereby shaping public opinion.

The speed at which this happens—and the fact that, in today's world, anyone with a cell phone has the technical wherewithal immediately at their disposal to become a citizen journalist with links to multiple networks—represents a qualitative leap forward in photography's ability to have a social impact. It is only natural then that this project pays particular attention to that broad category of "image actors" who produced the visual material for this (photographic) revolution in Cairo. This includes not only the young English-speaking interpreters of the revolution that Western news correspondents have liked to put in front of their cameras and microphones, but also the filmmakers, bloggers, artists, professional journalists, and photographers who became documentarians by using their cameras or cell phones to record the political upheavals. And what is special about this exhibition is that we also get to know some of these actors, whose activities extend beyond the current events in Tahrir Square and who have been at work to reflect on the social situation in Egypt for many years, long before the Arab Spring was proclaimed. At the same time, the array of different images shows how varied their role, intention, and function is, from testimony and observation to acts of remembrance.

The German Federal Cultural Foundation is delighted to have been able to fund this project. We would like to thank Florian Ebner and Constanze Wicke for developing the idea for this exhibition and inviting Egyptian photographers, artists, activists, and journalists to help translate it into reality and curate the main sections of the exhibition. Our thanks too to Lara Baladi, Osamạ Dawod, Rowan El Shimi, Heba Farid, Thomas Hartwell, Ahmed Kamel, Jasmina Metwaly, Alex Nunns, Philip Rizk, and Tarek Hefny, who provide their own accounts of the revolution.

Hortensia Völckers, Executive Board / Artistic Director
Alexander Farenholtz, Executive Board / Administrative Director

Das Projekt *Kairo. Offene Stadt. Neue Bilder einer andauernden Revolution* ist einerseits sehr nah dran an den politischen Ereignissen im Ägypten der Gegenwart, andererseits ist es weit weg: etwa 3.000 Flugkilometer vom Museum für Photographie in Braunschweig, wo diese Initiative ihren Ausgang nahm, oder zum Folkwang Museum in Essen, wohin die Bilder dieser Ausstellung weiter gereist sind – aktualisiert und ergänzt um neue Bilder eines politischen Prozesses, dessen Ausgang offen ist.

Zeitliche Nähe bei gleichzeitiger räumlicher Distanz – diese Konstellation bietet Raum für Missverständnisse. Manches von dem Bild, das westliche Medien als „Arabischer Frühling" gezeichnet haben, ist das Ergebnis grober Vereinfachungen, falscher Zuspitzungen oder ungenügender Quellen. Deswegen besteht eine der Aufgaben des Projektes darin, unser Bild von der Revolution in Ägypten zu überprüfen und zu ergänzen. Dass diese Aufgabe ausgerechnet von Museen geleistet wird, mag auf den ersten Blick überraschen. Denn „museal" ist an diesem Projekt gleich gar nichts.

Es geht um Arbeit: Um die Augen- und Gedankenarbeit daran, wie sich die Revolution in Ägypten verstehen lässt, wer sie vorantreibt, wer sie repräsentiert und welche revolutionäre Rolle die Fotografie hierbei spielt. Wie der begleitende Text zu dieser Konstellation von Arbeiten hervorhebt, soll es dabei um nicht weniger als „ein neues Kapitel der Fotografie in der arabischen Welt" gehen. Und hiermit verbunden um „ein neues Kapitel in der Geschichte der Bilder."

Beide, politische Zeitgeschichte und die Geschichte der Bilder, sind aufeinander angewiesen. Mehr noch, es sind die politischen Ereignisse, die eine neue Verwendung der Fotografie hervorbringen: als digitale politische Zeugnisse, die in Sekundenschnelle von jedermann und jeder Frau produziert und distribuiert werden und als eine Art augenblicklicher Beweise sofort wieder in den politischen Prozess und in den Prozess der Meinungsbildung eingespeist werden können.

Das Tempo, in dem dies geschieht – und die Tatsache, dass jeder, der heute ein Mobiltelefon besitzt, technisch sofort in der Lage ist, zu einem vielfach vernetzten Bürgerjournalisten zu werden – markiert einen qualitativen Sprung in der sozialen Wirksamkeit von Fotografie. Von daher ist folgerichtig, dass dieses Projekt vor allem jenes breite Feld an „Bild-Akteuren" in den Fokus rückt, die das visuelle Material dieser (fotografischen) Revolution in Kairo produziert haben. Dazu zählen nicht nur jene jungen englischsprachigen Revolutionsinterpreten, denen westliche Nachrichtenkorrespondenten bevorzugt Kamera und Mikrofon vor das Gesicht halten. Sondern auch die Filmemacher, Blogger, Künstler, professionellen Journalisten und Fotografen, die mit Kamera oder Mobiltelefon zu Dokumentaristen der politischen Umbrüche werden.

Und das Besondere dieser Ausstellung besteht wohl darin, dass wir zudem einige derjenigen Akteure kennen lernen, die jenseits der aktuellen Geschehnisse auf dem Tahrir-Platz aktiv sind, die schon seit vielen Jahren, lange, bevor der „Arabische Frühling" ausgerufen worden ist, in ihren Arbeiten die soziale Situation Ägyptens reflektieren. Zum anderen zeigt die Konstellation der unterschiedlichen Bilder, wie vielfältig deren Rolle, Intention und Funktion ist, von der Zeugenschaft, über die Überwachung bis hin zur Erinnerung. Die Kulturstiftung des Bundes ist sehr froh, dieses Projekt fördern zu können. Wir danken Florian Ebner und Constanze Wicke dafür, dass sie die Idee zu dieser Ausstellung entwickelt und dass sie für ihre Umsetzung ägyptische Fotografen und Künstler, Aktivisten und Journalisten eingeladen haben, damit diese zentrale Kapitel der Ausstellung kuratieren. Unser weiterer Dank geht daher an Lara Baladi, Osama Dawod, Rowan El Shimi, Heba Farid, Thomas Hartwell, Ahmed Kamel, Jasmina Metwaly, Alex Nunns, Philip Rizk und Tarek Hefny. Sie erzählen ihre eigene Geschichte von der Revolution.

Hortensia Völckers, Vorstand / Künstlerische Direktorin
Alexander Farenholtz, Vorstand / Verwaltungsdirektor

The Arab revolutions have challenged every cultural institution with an international focus to rethink its current practices of international cultural exchange. In the wake of the uprisings, it has become more important than ever—in addition to our own cooperative activities in the host countries—to send information back to Germany and Europe about what motivates people at the local level and what factors act as social drivers.

When the initial research for the exhibition project *Cairo. Open City. New Testimonies from an Ongoing Revolution* was first undertaken in the Egyptian capital, the motivation and overall intention of this project was to convey a tangible sense of the reality there—to let the actors themselves have their say. During their time in Cairo, the curators, Florian Ebner and Constanze Wicke, committed themselves to creating a network of partnerships, which were then built into the cooperative structure of the project. This soon won them the appreciation of those on the cultural scene.

The images, film sequences, and installations can now be seen in a number of German museums. It is all but impossible to escape their current relevance and sheer visual power, or the tremendous emotional intensity of many of the exhibits. Indeed, in the world of cultural exchange, images are more potent than any verbally articulated story line. This exhibition project thus has the potential to reveal new ways of exploring one of Europe's most important regional neighbors—the Arab world of today.

Gabriele Becker and Günther Hasenkamp
Goethe-Institut Cairo

Die arabischen Revolutionen haben alle internationalen Kultureinrichtungen herausgefordert, ihre bisherige Praxis des internationalen Kulturaustausches zu überdenken. Mehr als zuvor kommt es seither darauf an, neben unseren eigenen Kooperationen im Gastland auch nach Deutschland und Europa zurück zu vermitteln, was vor Ort die Menschen bewegt und die Gesellschaften in Bewegung hält.

Als die ersten Recherchen zum Ausstellungsprojekt *Kairo. Offene Stadt. Neue Bilder einer andauernden Revolution* in der ägyptischen Hauptstadt begannen, war die Motivation und Zielrichtung eines solchen Vorhabens mit Händen zu greifen – die Akteure selbst sollten das Wort haben. Die Kuratoren Florian Ebner und Constanze Wicke haben, bei ihren Aufenthalten in Kairo, mit großer Partnerschaftlichkeit ihre Projektkooperationen aufgebaut, was ihnen schnell die Anerkennung der Kulturszenen einbrachte.

Nun sind die Bilder, Filmsequenzen und Installationen in deutschen Museen zu sehen. Ihrer aktuellen Relevanz, ihrer puren Visualität sowie der enormen emotionalen Intensität vieler Exponate entzieht man sich nicht so leicht. Gerade im Kulturaustausch sind Bilder mächtiger als jede verbale Handlung. So hat dieses Ausstellungsprojekt das Potenzial, neue Wege zu eröffnen für die Erkundung einer großen europäischen Nachbarregion – der arabischen Welt heute.

Gabriele Becker und Günther Hasenkamp
Goethe-Institut Kairo

Florian Ebner
Constanze Wicke

Intervening Images: Towards a Mapping of a Revolution in Pictures

A Witness at the Outset

From amongst the images of the Egyptian Revolution, one face initially draws the eye of the viewer: the video testimony *The Politics of Bread*[1] (→ fig. 31)—uploaded to YouTube on December 1, 2011 by the Mosireen Media Collective—tells the story of the arrest, interrogation, and torture of the young casual laborer Mohamed Mounir. In the video, the young man describes what prompted him to go out on the streets to demonstrate. He is not political by nature—"My politics is the politics of bread"—but, like many other people, he was scandalized by the short videos put up on the Internet by activists and later shown on television. These included the scene in which a dead body was dragged onto a rubbish heap by soldiers, following an attack by soldiers in the area around Tahrir Square (→ fig. 32). Mohamed was arrested at a protest rally and beaten unconscious. Once he had regained his senses, he was interrogated. It must have been one of the officers who interrogated him that filmed him and then uploaded the video on YouTube. In the course of questioning him, the security forces pretended to pull money from his pocket that was probably simply taken out of one of their own pockets off camera. This supposedly damning footage was put up on the Internet in an attempt to discredit the protest movement by proving the presence in its midst of paid agent provocateurs like Mohamed.

The Politics of Bread operates on two levels: on the one hand, there is the dialogue with Mohamed, where the camera empathically focuses in on his face; on the other, there is the spliced-in material, the activists' videos recording the brutal actions of the security forces, and the interrogation sequence, with the signs of torture plain to see on Mohamed's face. This sequence was downloaded from the Internet and then inserted into the film along with the other material. In the video we can see how images take on various functions and work on different levels: as personal testimony, certainly, but also as a means of agitation—in either case, a claim staked to another truth. *The Politics of Bread* is not simply a denunciation of torture and abuse: as a film it directs the viewer's attention to the way images are used.

From the Empathic to the Empiric

This project started out as a gesture of possibly rather naive empathy—a fascination, fueled by the many reports and feature articles that in spring 2011 helped lead to the Facebook Revolution or Revolution 2.0, spearheaded by Tunisian and Egyptian youth using the digital media and social networks to galvanize protest. A sense of democracy would appear to be a media pledge written into digital culture, the early promise of photography now picked up on and carried forward by the digital channels and communication media. But this gives rise to certain questions: Did the democratic dimension take on real concrete form in the Arab Spring? What is the complexion of the images and news reports circulating worldwide on these channels? How are we to understand their function and the intentions of their authors? These were our initial concerns, but the *Cairo. Open City. New Testimonies from an Ongoing Revolution* project expanded on these questions in its various phases—this book is an attempt to document the process that took place.

We went to Cairo for the first time at the end of summer 2011, our aim being to learn more about the images we had seen of the revolution, the background to which we could only really understand by "going local." Prior to this visit, we were, of course, part of a group of media spectators—the "onlookers" addressed by Philip Rizk in his open letter, which is published as part of this book—more of those Western observers whose primary attention was on the supposed protagonists of this uprising, with whom we could all identify, an Internet-savvy generation, using their cameras and mobile phones like Kalashnikovs, an image depicted in countless illustrations and pieces of graffiti.

But our stay in Cairo and our conversations with the photographers and artists, activists and journalists, filmmakers and curators we met there changed our perspective. Some things could only really be grasped by the fact of being there: that representation does not take precedence over reality, that images can skew one's view of the actuality they reference, and that the time for such considerations may not yet be ripe. And if our view is already focused on the pictures, then the image culture of this uprising is made up of much more than simply the new recordings of events that consigned old-style photojournalism to the wilderness. This book is a response to what we learned from the people we encountered on our trip and the many things they showed us; it is their viewpoints and attitudes that are represented here, and their contributions and input were crucial in determining the way the material was selected.

This book is not intended as a premature commemorative volume in celebration of the revolution—there have been plenty of those published already; nor is it a historical account of the events that took place, and it makes no pretense of offering an exhaustive analysis of the role played by images. Rather it attempts to render a kind of typological cross-section of the images produced by the revolution, a cartography delineating the various usages to which images are put, a kind of photo album of this complex process of social and political upheaval, which is still going on and has no end in sight. It includes the images of young Egyptian photojournalists, as well as the agency pictures of foreign reporters; the myriad visual forms assumed by so-called "citizen journalism"; the young Tahrir Square photographers who post their pictures on Flickr; the videos made by activists and the websites they use to generate an alternative public version of events to counter the official reports; the street art of a globalized youth and other urban grassroots movements; the actions of artists who eschew a direct representation of what happened; and, last but not least, historical photos and artistic works that preceded events and which also give an idea of the extent to which photojournalism, the photos used in news reports, and photography itself are in a state of upheaval.

The Image You Make Is the Image You Have

This book approaches its subject by taking a synoptic view as its key mode of exposition; using a simple method of comparison, it reveals how images change, something that is evident at first glance as we see the material substance of the pictures changing. The synoptic approach sensitizes the eye to the variances in photographic quality. We may be looking at an image taken by a professional photojournalist, where the photographer seeks to condense the essence of an event into a picture, or at a photo shot by an amateur with a mobile phone, where the image has its own "reality effect" and a powerful sense of drama, despite the lack of polish in its visual language. Moreover, this approach offers insights into the viewpoint or attitude the photographer has in relation to the event being recorded. Is it seen with the eye of a participant, "from within" as it were, or "from without," at one remove, a distanced perspective? In its formal contextualization—how and where these images are to be seen—this synoptic view also allows us to make inferences about the various places the pictures were taken, about their new virtual existence on the Internet, on blogs, websites, and photo communities, or their more classical role occupying the pages of newspapers and magazines. If nothing else, it allows us to see how pictures migrate, to follow the paths they take as they register in the physical space of the city, moving from websites to banners, placards, and graffiti. It may be that this is a special moment in the history of the camera, with the coexistence of an extraordinary variety of image forms, analogue and digital, public and private, all mutually dependent on one another. Perhaps this coexistence is particularly visible in the production of images portraying a society in upheaval, as in Egypt, where the thrust towards modernization has encountered social fault lines in bloody fashion.

These pictures serve multiple functions, as a call to arms, as a recording of events, as a legitimization of one's own violence, as a means to analyze the manipulative use of images, as a memorial to the victims of the violence, and as a way to remember what happened. Among these, it is possible to draw out a general motif that might be termed "testimony." There are many different kinds of testimony to be seen here: they range from video close-ups of people describing what they have seen, to Twitter messages posted by eyewitnesses on the street, and the solitary figure alone in the urban space silently holding up a picture or a text.

The New Digital City and the Old Revolutionary Street

Our fascination with the Facebook and Twitter revolution caused us to lose sight of the importance of the city's physical space as a public environment. At first, it seemed that it was only the new invisible city that could hold our attention, YouTube as the virtual "agora," a complementary counterpart to the television screen, which, during the first eighteen days of the revolution, brought home to us the mass of numbers gathered on Cairo's Tahrir Square, offering us a kind of bird's-eye perspective of them, the view from the hotel roofs. Yet for all that, a good many of the photographs in this book represent images that have appeared as a form of protest in the real-world city.[2]

Among these documents, one form of image stands out, and it also seems to be part of a tradition in Egypt. People on Tahrir Square and other streets and squares in Cairo carry pictures in their hands or placards with hand-written messages, addressed to people walking by, to passing cars, or to the cameras belonging to countless eyewitnesses and reporters (←fig. 6–16, →fig. 14–6). Reproduced on a massive scale, these images now reach a worldwide audience. Silent, indignant, determined, and proud, the protesters stand there and hold out to us a blown-up laser print or a piece of cardboard with writing on it. The messages have changed over the last two-and-a-half years. The jibes at Hosni Mubarak were followed by protests against military rule and rebellion against Mohamed Morsi, who now, since the fall of the Muslim Brothers, has been progressively iconized as a political martyr. These forms of visual protest are many and various, from the pictures of fallen boys held up by mothers dressed all in black, to teenage martyrs and scenes from the Internet, like the picture of the humiliated "Woman in the Blue Bra." The pictures unmistakably signify a clear political stance, and for this reason, if for no other, the images and the people carrying them have become the most frequently photographed motifs to be seen in news reports.

"The image of pictures being carried in people's hands is a reference to the fabricated nature and function of the photograph. As a news picture, it generates a gap, setting it apart from the pictures that we see people carrying and holding: an über-image, a meta-image. But the success of this type of image may be due far more to the fact that it credibly documents the power that images have over people, or, to put it another way, the way that images and people interact."[3]

A Society of Images

New images emerge from the meeting of the new digital city and the physical street, in the interaction between pictures and people. Cairo, December 17, 2011: soldiers have beaten and kicked a young woman so brutally that she is lying on the street with her torso exposed, changed in an instant from a simple demonstrator to the "Woman in the Blue Bra." The pictures of her not only convey this egregious scene of barbarism to a worldwide audience and provoke the largest women's protest march the Arab world has seen, they also transform this incident into an iconic moment of indictment.

This act of gross violence and humiliation caught on camera can now be seen again as printed screenshots and newspaper pages in the hands of countless demonstrators, both male and female, as a motif used by street artists, as a graffitied pop-culture Supergirl sprayed on the walls of the city, or as a prominent image on banners at solidarity marches. The scene of the "Woman in the Blue Bra" surrounded by soldiers has thus morphed into many different shapes, developing both its own iconic existence[4]—an immediately identifiable visual—and an abstract, symbolic quality.

There is a particular sense in which the function of the artistic works in this book seems to be to examine the diverse ways in which images "migrate." The construction of social identity plays no small part in this. A *Hypothetical Society* looks back at us from Ahmed Kamel's drawings, whose heavily schematized figures are taken from group photos posted on Egyptian Facebook pages; they convey the vague outlines of a sense of identity promised by a form of social communication that is still in its infancy. In contrast to this, the artist Heba Farid trains her eye on Facebook's predecessor, the photo album, a dying form, an outmoded means of storing photographs and telling stories in pictures. How do the privileged members of the military present themselves in these albums? What importance did the army have for the identity of the young Egyptian nation in the twentieth century? Denis Dailleux's triptychs in turn confront us with the families and homes of the martyrs who lost their lives in the course of the revolution. Their portraits now stand on domestic altars, occupying the place left vacant by the sons that have disappeared.

Last but not least, Lara Baladi's archive *Alone, Together... In Media Res* shows us the society of images, the juxtaposition and proximity of snapshots, video clips, and testimonies on the Internet. There is an extreme immediacy about the way the Internet gives birth to the iconic analogy, the historical reference. The man standing alone in front of a tank in Cairo becomes a close relative of the 1989 "Tank Man" on Beijing's Tiananmen Square, and the medium itself is turned into an imaginary museum of revolutionary iconography.

Intervening Images

As a complement to her artistic work, Lara Baladi has also contributed to this book the essay *When Seeing Is Belonging*, at the end of which she asks questions about the function of the pictures taken by the people in Tahrir Square. Behind the sheer volume of images Baladi detects the fear of death that people experienced. She also makes reference to Susan Sontag's celebrated book *On Photography*, quoting her as the only author to express the particular form of uneasiness with regard to photography that for more than thirty years has shaped the cultural critique of the medium.[5] According to Sontag, photography fosters a voyeuristic attitude to the world, in which intervention is replaced by mere recording.

The synoptic view of the images in this book may also allow us to revise Sontag's criticism of photography, which has degenerated into a rhetorical refrain. Even if we factor in the use of images for economic interests and propaganda purposes, and notwithstanding the fact that the picture community on Facebook, Flickr, or YouTube is full of visual noise and trashy images, many of these photos do achieve one thing, and that is empathy—something which they had seemingly lost the capacity for after years of being criticized. We find it in every picture that spurs someone to go out and demonstrate, in every picture that is held aloft hour after hour as a protest message. Thus the images do not have a distancing effect and they are not mere depictions of the event they represent; rather they are already a part of the political process, an act of intervention. This does not mean that we should naively believe in the good of images, that they should replace the arguments of political dispute, but that, by engendering emotional identification, they represent a key instrument of political participation.

1 *The Politics of Bread*: www.youtube.com/watch?v=qv8esL-lgvc
2 On the tradition of street politics in Egypt, see: Asef Bayat, *Life as Politics: How Ordinary People Change the Middle East*, Cairo: The American University in Cairo Press, 2009
3 Tom Holert, "Massenmedien-Akte II. Über visuelle Programmierungen des politischen Raums: Tragebilder und Bilderträger" [Mass media acts: On the visual programming of political space], in: *Camera Austria* 89, 2005, p. 72 [translated]
4 Cf. Clément Chéroux, *L'image photographique à l'ère des médias globalisés: Essais sur le 11 septembre 2001* [Diplopia: The image politics of 11 September], Cherbourg: Le Point du Jour, 2009
5 Susan Sontag, *On Photography*, New York: Farrar, Straus, and Giroux, 1977. See also Susie Linfield: *The Cruel Radiance: Photography and Political Violence*, Chicago: University of Chicago Press, 2010

Florian Ebner
Constanze Wicke

Intervenierende Bilder: Für eine Kartografie der Aufnahmen einer Revolution

Ein Zeuge zu Beginn

Der Blick auf die Bilder der ägyptischen Revolution fällt zunächst auf ein Gesicht: Das Video-Testimony *The Politics of Bread*[1] (→Abb. 31), am 1. Dezember 2011 vom Videokollektiv Mosireen auf YouTube hochgeladen, erzählt die Geschichte der Verhaftung, des Verhörs und der Folter des jungen Arbeiters Mohamed Mounir. Der junge Mann schildert darin seine Motivation, an den Demonstrationen und Protestaktionen auf den Kairoer Straßen teilzunehmen. Er sei kein politischer Mensch, seine Politik sei die des Brotes. Aber ihn hätten, wie viele andere Menschen auch, die Videos empört, die Aktivisten ins Internet gestellt haben und die später im Fernsehen zu sehen waren, etwa die Szene, in der Soldaten nach einer Auseinandersetzung nahe des Tahrir-Platzes einen toten Körper in den Müll zogen (→Abb. 32). Er selbst wurde bei einer Protestkundgebung festgenommen und bewusstlos geschlagen. Wieder bei Bewusstsein, wurde er verhört. Ein Offizier muss die Szene mit einem Handy gefilmt haben. Darin meint man zu sehen, wie die Sicherheitskräfte Geld aus seiner Tasche ziehen (was jedoch außerhalb der Kameraeinstellung passierte und aus ihren Taschen stammte). Diese kurzen Aufnahmen sollten als Beweis dienen, um Mohamed Mounir als bezahlten Agent provocateur zu überführen, und wurden auf YouTube hochgeladen, um die Protestbewegung zu diskreditieren.

The Politics of Bread besteht aus zwei Ebenen, zum einen das Gespräch mit Mohamed Mounir und die empathisch auf sein Gesicht gehaltene Kamera, zum anderen das einmontierte Material, die erwähnten Videos der Aktivisten, die das brutale Vorgehen der Sicherheitskräfte festhalten, aber auch die Verhörsequenz des Offiziers, das geschundene Gesicht, aus dem Internet heruntergeladen und ebenfalls einmontiert. So zeigt das Video die unterschiedlichen Funktionen und Ebenen der Bilder, die des Zeugnis-Ablegens, aber auch die der Agitation, wenn die Bilder eine jeweils andere Wahrheit für sich beanspruchen. *The Politics of Bread* ist nicht nur eine Anklage gegen Folter und Misshandlung, als Film lenkt es den Blick ebenso auf die Gebrauchsweisen der Bilder.

Von der Empathie zur Empirie

Eine vielleicht naive Empathie stand am Anfang des vorliegenden Projekts. Eine Faszination, die von den vielen Berichten und Feuilletonartikeln genährt wurde, wonach der tunesischen und ägyptischen Jugend im Frühjahr 2011 mithilfe der digitalen Medien und sozialen Netzwerke eine „Revolution 2.0“ oder eine „Facebook-Revolution“ gelungen sei. Konkretisierte sich im Arabischen Frühling die demokratische Dimension, welche der digitalen Kultur eingeschrieben zu sein scheint, ein mediales Versprechen, das schon in den Kinderschuhen der Fotografie zu stecken schien und nun in den digitalen Kanälen und Kommunikationsmedien seine Fortsetzung findet? Wie sehen die Bilder und Nachrichten aus, die innerhalb dieser Kanäle weltweit zirkulieren, welche Funktionen nehmen sie ein und welche Intentionen haben ihre Autoren? So lauteten unsere ersten Fragen, doch während der unterschiedlichen Entwicklungsphasen des Projekts *Kairo. Offene Stadt. Neue Bilder einer andauernden Revolution* wurden es weitaus mehr Fragen, die das vorliegende Buch jetzt zu dokumentieren versucht.

Gewiss gehörten wir zu den medialen „Zaungästen“, zu den „Onlookers“, an die Philip Rizk seinen in diesem Buch abgedruckten Brief adressiert hat, bevor wir im Spätsommer 2011 zum ersten Mal nach Kairo fuhren, um mehr über die Bilder einer Revolution zu erfahren, deren Hintergründe wir erst vor Ort verstehen sollten. Gewiss waren wir Teil jener westlichen Beobachter, deren Augenmerk zunächst auf den vermeintlichen Protagonisten dieses Aufstands lag, mit denen wir uns identifizieren konnten, auf einer *internet savy generation*, ihrer Verwendung von Kameras und Mobiltelefonen als Kalaschnikow, wie zahlreiche Graffiti und Illustrationen es zeigen.

Doch im Laufe der Aufenthalte in Kairo und nach den Gesprächen mit Fotografen und Künstlerinnen, Aktivistinnen und Journalisten, Filmemachern und Kuratorinnen, veränderte sich die Perspektive. Dass die Repräsentation nicht wichtiger ist als die Realität, dass die Bilder auch den Blick auf das verstellen können, worauf sie eigentlich verweisen, dass die Zeit vielleicht noch nicht reif ist für diese Fragen – dies waren Dinge, die wir vor Ort begriffen. Und wenn der Blick schon den Bildern gilt, so besteht die Bildkultur dieses Aufstands eben aus viel mehr als nur den neuen Aufnahmen, die den alten Fotojournalismus ins Abseits stellten. Dieses Buch ist eine Reaktion auf das, was uns die Protagonisten vor Ort, die zu kritischen Begleitern wurden, gezeigt und worauf sie hingewiesen haben, es ist eine Sammlung von Sichtweisen und Haltungen, deren Auswahl sie getroffen haben.

So versteht sich dieses Buch nicht als Jubelbuch zur Revolution, derer so viele erschienen sind; es ist kein Band, der die Ereignisse beleuchtet, und gibt genauso wenig vor, eine erschöpfende Analyse der Rolle der Bilder zu leisten. Vielmehr versucht es, eine Art typologischen Querschnitt durch die Bildproduktion dieser Revolution zu liefern, eine Kartografie, welche die unterschiedlichen Gebrauchsweisen der Bilder absteckt, eine Art Fotoalbum dieses komplexen sozialen und politischen Umbruchprozesses, der noch im Gange und dessen Ende unabsehbar ist. Das Buch umfasst Aufnahmen junger ägyptischer Fotojournalisten ebenso wie Agenturbilder ausländischer Fotoreporter, die vielfältigen visuellen Formen des sogenannten Bürgerjournalismus, die Bilder vom Tahrir-Platz, welche junge Fotografen auf Flickr posten, die Videos von Aktivisten und die Internetplattformen, mit denen sie Raum für Gegendarstellungen zur offiziellen Berichterstattung schaffen, die Street Art einer globalisierten Jugend und anderer Urban-Grassroots-Bewegungen, die Aktionen von Künstlerinnen und Künstlern, die sich einer direkten Repräsentation des Geschehens entziehen, und nicht zuletzt historische Aufnahmen und künstlerische Arbeiten, die dem Geschehen vorausgegangen sind und zudem eine Vorstellung davon vermitteln, in welchem Maß das berichtende Bild und die Fotografie an sich im Umbruch sind.

Die Einstellung ist die Einstellung

Die zentrale Methode dieses Buches ist der synoptische Blick, er offenbart mit den simplen Mitteln des Vergleichs den Wandel der Bilder, der bereits auf den ersten Blick am Wandel der materiellen Substanz ablesbar ist. Die Zusammenschau sensibilisiert das Auge für die unterschiedliche fotografische Qualität, ob es sich um eine fotojournalistische Aufnahme handelt, die den Kern des Geschehens in einem Foto zu verdichten versucht, oder um die amateurhafte, aber nicht weniger dramatische Sprache eines Handybildes mit seinen ganzen eigenen „Realitätseffekten". Sie erlaubt darüber hinaus auch Rückschlüsse auf den Standpunkt oder die Haltung der Fotografin oder des Fotografen zum Geschehen. Ist es ein teilnehmender Blick „von innen" oder eine distanzierte Perspektive „von außen"? Über ihre formale Kontextualisierung – wie und wo sind diese Bilder zu sehen – versucht diese Zusammenschau auch Rückschlüsse über die unterschiedlichen Orte der Bilder zu ermöglichen, über ihre neue virtuelle Existenz auf Webseiten, Blogs und Photo-Communities im Internet oder ihre klassische Rolle in Zeitungen und Magazinen. Nicht zuletzt macht sie die Migration von Bildern sichtbar, ihre Wege von den Webseiten auf die Banner, Plakate und Graffiti im physischen Raum der Stadt. Vielleicht ist dieser Moment der Koexistenz verschiedenster Bildformen, analoger und digitaler, öffentlicher und privater, die sich gegenseitig bedingen, ein besonderer in der Geschichte der Kamerabilder. Und vielleicht wird diese Koexistenz in der Bildproduktion einer Gesellschaft im Umbruch, wie es die ägyptische ist, besonders sichtbar, in der die Modernisierungsschübe und sozialen Verwerfungen auf blutige Weise aufeinandertreffen.

Unter den vielen Funktionen, die diese Bilder innehaben – zum Widerstand aufrufen, das Geschehen festhalten, die eigene Verwendung von Gewalt legitimieren, den manipulativen Gebrauch von Bildern analysieren, der Opfer gedenken und Bilder für die Erinnerung schaffen –, ist ein wiederkehrendes Motiv herauszustellen, das sich im Englischen mit dem Begriff *testimony* bezeichnen und ins Deutsche nur unzureichend mit „Zeugnis-Ablegen" oder „Zeugenschaft" übersetzen lässt. Die *testimonies* sind vielfältiger Natur, sie beginnen bei den Videogroßaufnahmen von Gesichtern, die erzählen, was sie gesehen haben, reichen über die Twitter-Nachricht der Augenzeugen auf der Straße bis hin zur einsamen Figur im Stadtraum, die schweigend ein Bild oder eine sprachliche Botschaft in die Höhe hält.

Die neue digitale Stadt und die alte revolutionäre Straße

Mit unserer Faszination für die Facebook- und Twitter-Revolution haben wir die Bedeutung des öffentlichen und physischen Raums der Stadt aus den Augen verloren. Zunächst schien es, als wollte uns nur noch die neue unsichtbare Stadt interessieren, YouTube als die virtuelle Agora, das komplementäre Gegenstück zu den Fernsehbildern, die uns während der ersten achtzehn Tage der Revolution die Menschenmassen auf dem Kairoer Tahrir-Platz aus der Vogelperspektive der Hoteldächer ins Wohnzimmer brachten. Doch nicht wenige Fotografien in diesem Buch zeigen den Auftritt der Bilder als Form des Protests im realen Stadtraum.[2]

Hier sticht eine Bildform heraus, die in Ägypten Tradition zu haben scheint und nun massenhaft reproduziert ein weltweites Publikum erreicht: Menschen auf dem Tahrir-Platz und anderen Straßen und Plätzen in Kairo halten Bilder oder Plakate mit handgeschriebenen Botschaften in den Händen, adressiert an Passanten, vorbeifahrende Autos oder an die Kameras der zahllosen Augenzeugen und Berichterstatter. Schweigend, empört, entschlossen, stolz stehen sie da und halten uns einen großformatigen Laserdrucker-Print oder ein beschriebenes Stück Pappe entgegen (⟵ Abb. 6–16, ⟶ Abb. 14–6). Die Botschaften veränderten sich im Laufe der vergangenen zweieinhalb Jahre, auf die Verhöhnung Husni Mubaraks folgte der Protest gegen die Militärherrschaft, dann die Auflehnung gegen Mohammed Mursi und – seit dem Sturz des Muslimbruders – seine fortschreitende Ikonisierung als politischer Märtyrer. Vielfältig sind diese Formen des visuellen Protests: von den Porträts der gefallenen Söhne in den Händen der schwarz gekleideten Mütter über die Bilder der jugendlichen Märtyrer bis zu Szenen aus dem Internet, sind die unverwechselbaren Signaturen einer politischen Haltung, nicht zuletzt deshalb sind sie und die Personen, die sie tragen, die am häufigsten fotografierten Motive der Berichterstattung: „Im Bild des getragenen Bildes zitiert die Fotografie die eigene Gemachtheit und Funktion und schafft – als Nachrichtenbild – eine Differenz, die es von den getragenen und gehaltenen Bildern abhebt: als Bild-über-Bilder, als Meta-Image. Doch möglicherweise ist weit mehr für den Erfolg dieses Bildtyps die Tatsache verantwortlich, dass er zuverlässig dokumentiert, welche Macht Bilder auf Menschen ausüben oder, anders ausgedrückt: wie Bilder und Menschen interagieren.“[3]

Die Gesellschaft der Bilder

Im Zusammentreffen der neuen digitalen Stadt und der physischen Straße, in der Interaktion von Menschen und Bildern entstehen neue Bilder. Als am 17. Dezember 2011 eine junge Frau in Kairo von Soldaten derart geschlagen und mit Füßen getreten wird, dass sie entblößt auf der Straße liegt und sich von einer anonymen Demonstrantin in „The Woman in the Blue Bra“ verwandelt, sind es Bilder, die diese ungeheure Szene der Grausamkeit nicht nur in die Welt tragen und den bis dahin größten Protestmarsch von Frauen im arabischen Raum provozieren, sondern die diesen Moment auch in einen ikonischen Moment der Anklage verwandeln.

Die von einer Kamera festgehaltene Szene größter Demütigung und Gewalt findet sich als ausgedruckter Screenshot oder Zeitungsausschnitt in den Händen unzähliger demonstrierender Männer und Frauen wieder, auf den Bannern von Solidaritätsumzügen, als Motiv von Straßenmalereien, als Supergirl-Motiv der Pop-Graffiti-Kultur an den Mauern der Städte. Die Szene der entblößten Frau im blauen BH, umgeben von Soldaten, erfährt somit die vielfältigsten Metamorphosen, sie entwickelt eine eigene ikonische Existenz[4], eine sofort identifizierbare bildliche Gestalt, aber auch eine abstrakte, zeichenhafte Qualität.

Es scheint in besonderer Weise die Funktion der künstlerischen Arbeiten in diesem Buch zu sein, die Migrationen der Bilder herauszuarbeiten. Keine geringe Rolle spielt dabei die Konstruktion sozialer Identität. Eine *Hypothetische Gesellschaft* blickt uns aus Ahmed Kamels Zeichnungen entgegen, deren stark schematisierende Figuren aus fotografischen Gruppenporträts von ägyptischen Facebook-Seiten entnommen wurden und die unscharfen Identitätsversprechen einer noch jungen sozialen Kommunikationsform zum Ausdruck bringen. Das Interesse der Künstlerin Heba Farid gilt den Vorgängern von Facebook, den Fotoalben, aussterbenden Speichern und Erzählformen des Fotografischen. Wie präsentieren sich die privilegierten Mitglieder des Militärs in solchen Alben, welche Bedeutung hatte das Militär für die Identität der jungen ägyptischen Nation im zwanzigsten Jahrhundert? In den Triptychen von Denis Dailleux treten uns die Familien und Wohnorte der Märtyrer entgegen, die im Laufe der Revolution ihr Leben verloren haben. Ihre Porträts nehmen nun auf den heimischen Altären den Platz der verschwundenen Söhne ein.

Nicht zuletzt zeigt uns Lara Baladis Archiv *Alone, Together... In Media Res* die Gesellschaft der Bilder, das Nebeneinander und die Nachbarschaft der Schnappschüsse, Videomitschnitte und *testimonies* im Internet. In höchster Unmittelbarkeit gebiert das Internet die ikonische Analogie, die historische Referenz. Der einsame Mann vor dem Panzer in Kairo wird zum Verwandten des Tank Man auf dem Pekinger Tiananmen-Platz von 1989 und das Medium selbst zum imaginären Museum der Revolutionsikonografie.

Intervenierende Bilder

Neben ihrer künstlerischen Arbeit hat Lara Baladi auch das Essay *Wenn sehen heißt dazuzugehören* zu diesem Buch beigesteuert, in dem sie zuletzt die Frage nach der Funktion der Bilder stellt, die die Menschen auf dem Tahrir-Platz aufgenommen haben. Hinter der schieren Masse an Bildern entdeckt sie die Angst des Menschen vor dem Tod. Hierbei verweist sie auch auf Susan Sontags berühmten Band *Über Fotografie* und nennt dabei jene Autorin, die wie keine andere eine bestimmte Form des Unbehagens der Fotografie gegenüber zum Ausdruck gebracht hat, das für mehr als dreißig Jahre auch die Kulturkritik der Fotografie prägte.[5] Demnach fördere die Fotografie eine voyeuristische Haltung zur Welt, in der das reine Aufzeichnen die Intervention ersetze.

Vielleicht erlaubt die Zusammenschau der Bilder in diesem Buch auch die zu einem rhetorischen Muster verkommene Kritik Sontags an der Fotografie zu revidieren. Auch wenn wir darunter die Verwendung von Bildern für ökonomische Interessen und zu propagandistischen Zwecken finden, auch wenn die Nachbarschaft der Bilder auf Facebook, Flickr oder YouTube voll visuellen Lärms und Mülls ist, so bewirken viele dieser Bilder doch eines, was sie scheinbar in den langen Jahren der Kritik an ihnen verloren haben: Empathie. Jedes Bild, das die Menschen dazu bringt, auf die Straße zu gehen, jedes Bild, das sie als Botschaft stundenlang in die Höhe heben. Somit halten die Bilder nicht das Ereignis von uns fern, sie bilden es nicht nur ab, sie sind selbst bereits

Teil des politischen Prozesses und der Intervention. Dies bedeutet nicht, dass wir auf eine naive Weise an das Gute der Bilder glauben, dass sie die Argumente der politischen Auseinandersetzung ersetzen, aber dass sie doch mit ihren emotionalen Mitteln der Identifikation wichtige Instrumente politischer Teilhabe sind.

1 *The Politics of Bread*: www.youtube.com/watch?v=qv8esL-lgvc
2 Siehe zur Tradition der politischen Straße in Ägypten: Asef Bayat, *Life as Politics. How Ordinary People Change the Middle East*, Cairo: The American University in Cairo Press, 2009
3 Tom Holert, „Massenmedien-Akte II: Über visuelle Programmierungen des politischen Raums, Tragebilder und Bilderträger", in: *Camera Austria* 89, 2005, S. 72
4 Siehe hierzu: Clément Chéroux, *Diplopie. Bildpolitik des 11. September*, Konstanz: Konstanz University Press, 2011
5 Susan Sontag, *Über Fotografie* (*On Photography*, 1977), München: Hanser, 1978. Siehe hierzu: Susie Linfield, *The Cruel Radiance: Photography and Political Violence*, Chicago: University of Chicago Press, 2010

Philip Rizk

2011 Is Not 1968: An Open Letter to an Onlooker

On January 28, 2011, Egyptians started marching through the streets of their country's cities in a powerful show of protest. As onlookers, you gazed at the spectacle developing before your eyes, on your TV screens, across various international news channels. A fixation, a sense of intrigue emerged in relation to the images that were projected, particularly from one site: *Midan al-Tahrir* – Liberation Square. The fascination with the constant stream of images stimulated your imaginations, which then ran wild. Egyptians had been inspired, as well as shamed, into action by their North African neighbors in Tunisia. Our uprising in turn helped trigger movements in your cities around the world, from the Take The Square movement in Europe, to a city center occupation in Madison, Wisconsin, and the Occupy movement, not to mention an array of uprisings around the region that are still ongoing today in Bahrain, Syria, and Sudan, to name but a few.

To make sense of the unfolding scenes, media outlets turned to a group of individuals who, for many, have come to represent the revolution. These news agencies interviewed political commentators and activists—increasingly becoming celebrities in their own right—in an attempt to decipher the actions behind the images that were seen. Interpretation and then meaning were layered onto the images, causing significant distortion to the acts taking place behind the scenes. Non-Arabic-language media outlets relied primarily on English-speaking activists—many of us middle class, many of us already politicized before January 25. Arabic-language news stations similarly turned frequently to middle-class activists to speak on behalf of the revolution, each of whom interpreted every moment according to their respective ideological perspectives. Thus, we became the translators of a collective uprising we were far from representative of. Our faces reflected your own. Our voices were comprehensible. We served to make this revolution seem accessible. The intonation in our words gave meaning to what was, for you, unfamiliar territory. Our explanations also satisfied the practical requirements and standards of a media industry with a target audience accustomed to an interlocutor with a particular profile using a specific political discourse. This process drowned out the voices of the majority. No matter how hard we tried to argue otherwise, we fit the part—middle-class, Internet-savvy, young, and thus revolutionary.

Did you hear the voices of the underclass? Did you see the family members of the martyrs clad in black and mourning in their homes? Did you see images of unnamed civilians gunned down by snipers on the roofs of police stations? Did you see police officers opening prison doors in order to undermine this revolutionary moment and wreak havoc on nearby communities? Did you see protesters storming police stations on January 28, seeking vengeance for years of unaccounted-for torture, violence, and psychological domination? Did you see the Molotov cocktails prepared by women and lowered from their balconies to avenge the maiming of their sons and neighbors? This was not non-violent. Only the fixation of certain images seen in daylight through the lens of a camera on Tahrir Square could appease you with that impression. Other industries soon followed suit: hard on the heels of the journalists came academics, filmmakers, the world of art, and NGOs, all relying on us as the ideal interpreter of the extraordinary. They all eventually bought into and further fueled the hyper-glorification of the individual, the actor, the youth subject, the revolutionary artist, the woman, the non-violent protestor, the Internet user. All this took place in the undercurrent of an unrelenting need to identify, validate, and valorize the role of the familiar. Revolution became unimaginable without the imagery of a model demonstrator, who protected you from the potential of being faced with the unknown: a collectivist uprising against a global system of domination within which there is no place for an onlooker.

The Internet helped create the aura that all this was familiar. By channeling the outrage on the streets through a medium that you recognized, the narrative presented on news channels diluted the mystery within the events and chained your imagination to what was familiar. The layers of interpretation painted over the images diminished your fear of the unknown. "This is only an act against dictatorship." "This is the individual cry for freedom." "This is a demonstration for democracy." "This revolution is non-violent." The Internet replaced the Kalashnikov. These discourses silenced the structural dimensions of injustice and concealed the role of neoliberal policies, promoted by the likes of the IMF, the EU, and the USA, in deepening the stratification between poor and rich. They made you forget that it is out of these structures of injustice that the desire for social justice is born in the first place. These dominating narratives—the narratives of domination—localized the problematic, for instance, to that of a homegrown dictatorship. By isolating the crime, and highlighting the corruption of individuals, these accounts helped set the neocolonial stage for the now empty shells of the old regime to be replaced by another that maintains the same logic of governance.

It is no surprise that the owners of these images are commercial news agencies run by corporations that support or are supported by the very systems of domination against which we revolted. The images taken by the cameras of the BBC, the CNN, or Al Jazeera become the private property of these institutions, which then use them to tell their narratives, to celebrate what they desire to promote, and silence what they want to suppress. The framing and broadcasting of an image is a practice of power. These images circulate in the name of freedom, but by utilizing the captured images for the ends of a profit-driven enterprise, the dominance of the narrative provided has the potential to misinterpret and ultimately undermine the very acts of resistance.

Youth activists were by no means representative of the protests, but they were the dominant voice presented. We were but a handful of individuals amongst a cacophony of shouts calling for change, each person with their own concerns, complaints, desires, motives for action, and reason for revenge. Throughout the upsurge in protests, there was a strong horizontal inclination, a non-centralized decision-making process, a leaderless movement that could not be represented to a centralized, individual-focused media apparatus through a penned article, a particular speech, an authored art work, or a character-driven documentary film. Such a process of representation falsifies reality.

In this letter I too fall into this same logic.

2011 Is Not 1968

The 1960s were pregnant with the political: battles for racial equality, Vietnam, the Cold War, the final throws of overt imperialism. Nineteen sixty-eight arose out of this moment, a young generation confronted with distant scenes of occupation and colonization, a student generation, zealous with ideology and radicalized by the social and political reality of the times. Over forty years later, the effects of imperialism through the cloak of postcolonialism provoked people yet again into mass protest. Under these new conditions, as Frantz Fanon recounted so clearly, the former colonizers succeeded in hiding their economic interests behind partnerships with the ruling elites of postcolonial states.

Thus, 2011 is not 1968. The events of 2011 were an uprising of discontent against the political reality within the neocolonial condition. There was no intellectual revolution in 2011, no burgeoning of ideas. In Egypt, no radicalization of the population had taken place, nor was the nation tangled up in a cross-border conflict. There was no ideology but the ideology of desperation, the unbearable weight of hypocrisy, and the limits of a people living in denial of it. The rising militancy amongst organized workers and the growing opposition through small middle-class movements like Kefaya (Enough) and the April 6 Youth Movement, as well as through Internet-based groups like Kolina Khaled Said (We Are All Khaled Said) came about as a direct reaction to the political ruling class's ongoing repression of an entire population. By 1968, conflict had spread everywhere, whereas, in the run-up to 2011, the seeds of revolt had only just become ready to sprout. In Egypt there wasn't a movement, but there was movement, and there was momentum, an undefined force that was much more powerful than any organization could be. Under Mubarak's regime, the repression of even the seedling opposition groupings had meant that there was hardly a "left" to speak of. The universities were, and still are, a place for the theft of public funds, not a place of critical thought. The year 2011 witnessed fast-track political radicalization in the face of years of fast-track neoliberalization. The street was the academy, where we exchanged rocks for gunfire with the regime's security forces and military personnel, while exchanging ideas amongst ourselves.

This is how radical politicization occurred amongst the Egyptians that carried the revolution. The uprising that began in Egypt in the early days of 2011 was given impetus by an unprecedented number of protesters. Similar to the uprising in Argentina in 2001, street protests in Egypt were marked by widespread participation that crossed class, generational, and gender lines. As in 1968, students and workers both participated, although in Egypt, not as students and workers per se, but rather as part of a collective, popular movement. Significantly, the protests remained leaderless; we confronted a repressive hierarchical and hegemonic state apparatus using horizontal tactics. It was the vast numbers of protesters that, even if only temporarily, brought the centralized state structure to its knees.

The demonstrators had a wide variety of demands, and there is no one reason why people started flooding streets and public squares across Egypt on January 28 as different people rejected different faces of the same system of power that dominated our everyday lives. As observers, it was your obsession with comprehending the uprising that fed the media industry's raison d'être, which sought to quench those desires. It was your gaze with its dominant Western standpoint that excited references to the common, to the familiar, to what you already knew, making 2011 seem as if it was akin to 1968.

But 2011 is not 1968. The revolution of 2011 was not the "classic" revolution of the socialists: students and workers taking to the street to replace one regime with another of their own. No matter how hard people tried, there were no political parties with a revolutionary blueprint prior to January 25, and none have emerged since. A united voice that rang loud and clear from the start—"The people want the downfall of the system"—entailed a cacophony of dissent that translated into a desire to put an end to the status quo: change was necessary, some kind of change, but how that change looked was uncertain. This was not a sign of weakness within the uprising but testifies rather to a global crisis in the ability to imagine other forms of social organization that might offer an alternative to the neoliberal state with its self-perpetuating, self-destructive stratification. Furthermore, this leaderless form of protest, free of prepackaged ideology, allowed for the emergence of ideas in process, a process of resistance that is only beginning.

Workers and Revolution

A significant moment that made the January 25 Revolution thinkable was the rising wave of worker protests that started in 2006. The 27,000 textile workers that went on strike in the industrial city of El-Mahalla El-Kubra in Egypt's Nile Delta in December 2006 enabled countless Egyptians that caught a glimpse of that mighty act, or of the multitude of protests that followed, to begin to imagine revolution. Inevitably, strikes and demonstrations started spreading across the country. On April 6, 2008, the independent worker leaders of the same public-sector textile mill called for another strike, but this time the government succeeded in deterring the action by settling with a select group of workers ahead of time. The demand for increased wages was tied to rising food prices, and as almost every home in Mahalla has a family member employed at the massive textile factory, the strike was anticipated by more than just the workers. On that day, Mahalla's citizens were expecting a confrontation, and the insults of a police officer directed to an elderly woman on the street sparked an uprising.

April 6 was significant in that the protest moved beyond the geographical lines of one industrial site and was carried out by an entire community. In 2006, workers had broken the social rules of conduct through their public protest. In 2008, the boundaries of possible resistance were pushed further still, beyond the limits set by the ruling class. The government used all their wit and force, and managed to prevent April 6, 2008, from turning into what became January 25, 2011. In 2008, the government succeeded in preventing the spread of dissent from one industrial town to the rest of the region—let alone the country—by ordering security forces from across six governorates to descend on the city. In April 2008, the conditions were not yet ripe for what would emerge less than three years later. On January 28, 2011, demonstrators, spread all over the country, prevailed over those same security forces in a matter of hours. Again, at this juncture there is a need to emphasize that 2011 is not 1968. Nineteen sixty-eight would have been impossible without the waves of worker strikes and factory occupations in parallel with student protests. In the case of the January 25 Revolution, while participants spanned all social classes, bringing together the middle class, the unemployed, workers, and farmers, it was precarious workers, and not Egypt's traditional working class, that acted as the radicalizing factor of the revolution. This may sound like a trivial differentiation, but it is at the crux of the distinction between 2011 and 1968.

From 2006 until January 25, 2011, and in the period since then, workers from organized workspaces never stopped demonstrating for better wages, and against privatization, corruption, and injustice. The wave of protests that began on January 25 included a vast number of precarious workers primarily from Egypt's many *eshwa'eyat*, or informal neighborhoods. This needs some clarification. Starting in 2006, workers protested against the effects of the intense neoliberalization process that Mubarak's final government was exercising. Workers reacted directly—even if the reaction was rarely articulated in these specific terms—to the implementation of the Western economic paradigm of neoliberalism. This had seen the government easing the entry of foreign capitalists into Egyptian industry, privatizing factories and public sector enterprises, and reducing subsidies, while strongly encouraging production for export markets. Backed by international financial institutions, this system enabled foreign investors to access Egypt's natural resources with fewer restrictions and to exploit its working class with more freedom. This process included the intense downsizing of the traditional workforce. It forced workers into what is sometimes termed casualized work, or the "informal sector," which meant working without contracts, without guarantees, and without social protection, thus making the working conditions of the traditional working class precarious. Those most suppressed, most exploited, and most desperate under the former regime's political system were the underclass who lacked the luxury of being able to obtain an education, had no fixed jobs, and were thus vulnerable to the reality that police officers and employers existed above the law.

Precarious workers often maintain two or three jobs in order to make ends meet. Compared to them, Egypt's traditional working class lives in more secure conditions. In spite of the usually pitiful pay, the outrageous hours in the private sector, poor working conditions, and minimal benefits, the traditional working class has fixed contracts and steady incomes, which gives them a luxury standing within a working-class milieu with few guarantees. Consequently, the working class begin to mimic the middle class's cautious lifestyle, making them unwilling to risk losing their jobs. While the working class will fight for better work conditions and speak out against corruption and abuse in the workplace, their struggles are limited to this because they are not willing—and understandably so—to take their battles beyond the boundaries of their workplaces. Participating in the street battles of the revolution meant taking to the streets and risking giving their employers the justification to fire them for being "troublemakers." The lines of the unemployed ready to take their jobs, were they to be fired, limited their participation in the revolution. Losing the luxury of employment was a risk many contracted workers were usually unwilling to take.

The implementation of new economic paradigms since 1968 has further concentrated capital in the hands of the rich while reducing the livelihoods of everyone else. These policies have brought about the conditions whereby the "lumpenprecariat" have become the radical element within the revolutionary struggle, having proven themselves to be a force to be reckoned with. The embedding of deep economic stratification in this neoliberal era has provoked new forms of resistance; it is this condition that brought Egyptians to the brink of revolution, and it is this condition that will continue to determine future lines of protest.

On Saturday, June 19, 2012, a group of Mubarak supporters gathered outside a military hospital on the shores of the Nile after reports of the former dictator's death emerged. One of the demonstrators held a sign for drivers-by to see: "January 25 Revolution: History Will Judge."

You must decide how January 25 goes down in your annals of history. Is it another 1968, a revolution to your liking? Or is it a movement that goes beyond the meaning you've given to the few images you've seen, that may one day soon confront you at your front door?

This essay was written especially for this book in August 2012.

Philip Rizk lives in Cairo, where he makes films, protests, and writes.
He is a member of the Mosireen Media Collective (mosireen.org).
Follow him on Twitter: @tabulagaza

Philip Rizk

2011 ist nicht 1968: Offener Brief an einen Zuschauer

Am 28. Januar 2011 fanden sich Millionen von Ägyptern in einem gewaltigen Akt des Protests auf den Straßen ihres Landes zusammen. Du hast diesem Schauspiel zugeschaut, wie es sich vor Deinen Augen auf Deinem Bildschirm und in verschiedensten internationalen Nachrichtensendern entwickelte. Als Folge einer Fixierung oder gar einer Intrige konzentrierte sich die Aufmerksamkeit auf die Übertragung der Bilder eines ganz bestimmten Platzes: *Midan al-Tahrir* – Tahrir-Platz, der Platz der Befreiung. Deine Begeisterung für diese nicht abreißende Bilderflut beflügelte Deine Fantasie. Deinem Vorstellungsvermögen wurde freier Lauf gelassen. Von den nordafrikanischen Nachbarn in Tunesien zugleich beschämt und zur Auflehnung inspiriert, begannen wir Ägypter zu protestieren. Unser Aufstand wiederum hat Bewegungen in verschiedenen Städten auf der ganzen Welt ausgelöst: von der *Take The Square*-Bewegung über die Besetzung des Stadtzentrums in Madison, Wisconsin, bis hin zur *Occupy*-Bewegung und nicht zu vergessen die Reihe von Aufständen in unserer Region, die bis heute unter anderem in Bahrain, Syrien und dem Sudan andauern.

Um die Bedeutung der sich überstürzenden Ereignisse richtig verstehen und analysieren zu können, wandten sich die Medien an eine Gruppe von Individuen, die mittlerweile für viele zu Repräsentanten der Revolution geworden sind. Verschiedene Nachrichtenagenturen interviewten politische Analytiker oder Aktivisten (welche so zunehmend selbst einen gewissen Berühmtheitsstatus erlangten), um die den übertragenen Bildern zugrunde liegenden Tatsachen zu entschlüsseln. Indem die Interpretationen und anschließenden Deutungen wie Schichten auf die Bilder aufgebracht wurden, kam es zu erheblichen Verfälschungen. Die nicht-arabischsprachigen Medien beriefen sich hauptsächlich auf englischsprachige Aktivisten – viele von uns entstammen der Mittelschicht und waren schon vor dem 25. Januar 2011 politisiert. Auch arabischsprachige Nachrichtensender wandten sich zum Großteil Aktivisten aus der Mittelschicht zu, um diese im Namen der Revolution sprechen zu lassen; jeder interpretierte die Ereignisse im Sinne seines eigenen ideologischen Standpunktes. Auf diese Weise wurden wir zu

Übersetzern eines Volksaufstandes, dessen typische Repräsentanten wir bei Weitem nicht waren. In unseren Gesichtern spiegelte sich Dein Gesicht. Was wir sagten, war verständlich. Dank uns bekam jeder einen Zugang zu dieser Revolution. Der Klang unserer Worte hat Dir ein bis dahin unbekanntes Gelände erschlossen. Unsere Erklärungen entsprachen zudem den konkreten Anforderungen der internationalen Medienindustrie und deren an einen bestimmten politischen Diskurs bestimmter Korrespondenten gewöhntes Zielpublikum. Dieser Vorgang übertönte die Stimmen der Mehrheit. Egal, wie sehr wir versuchten, anders zu argumentieren, wir passten (und passen) genau in das Raster – zur Mittelschicht gehörend, internetversiert, jung und demzufolge revolutionär.

Aber lass mich Dich fragen: Hast Du die Stimmen aus der Unterschicht vernommen? Hast Du die schwarz gekleideten Familien der Märtyrer in ihren Häusern trauern sehen? Hast Du Bilder der zahl- und namenlosen Zivilisten gesehen, die hinterhältig von den Dächern der Polizeiwachen aus von Scharfschützen erschossen wurden? Hast Du gesehen, wie Polizisten die Revolution untergruben, indem sie die Gefängnistüren öffneten und schließlich in Stadtteilen und Wohngebieten der Umgebung organisierte Verwüstungen geschehen ließen? Hast Du gesehen, wie Demonstranten am 28. Januar 2011 Polizeiwachen stürmten und Vergeltung suchten für Jahre nicht eingestandener Folter, der Gewalt und psychologischer Peinigung? Hast Du die Molotowcocktails gesehen, die von Frauen vorbereitet und von den Balkonen zu den Demonstranten hinuntergelassen wurden, um damit die Verstümmelungen ihrer Nachbarn und Söhne rächen zu können? Das war nicht gewaltlos. Nur der fixierte Blick durch die Kamera auf den Tahrir-Platz im Tageslicht konnte Dich von einer solchen Annahme überzeugen. Andere Branchen folgten dem Beispiel des Journalismus: Die akademische Welt, Kunst, Kultur und Kino, private und öffentliche NGOs verließen sich auf uns ideale Interpreten dieser außergewöhnlichen Ereignisse. Sie alle schenkten dem Schauspieler, dem Jugendlichen, dem revolutionären Künstler, der Frau, dem gewaltlosen Demonstranten und dem Internetnutzer Glauben und schürten so die Überglorifizierung des Einzelnen. All das war geprägt vom unerbittlichen Bedürfnis nach Identifizierung, dem unbedingten Wunsch nach Wiedererkennung. Für Dich wurde die Revolution unvorstellbar ohne das symbolische Bild eines Demonstranten, der Dich von einer möglichen Konfrontation mit dem Unbekannten verschonte: dem kollektiven Aufstand gegen ein globales Herrschaftssystem, in welchem es keinen Raum für Zaungäste gibt.

Das Internet half, den Ereignissen den Anschein des Vertrauten zu verleihen. Indem der Zorn der Straße durch ein Dir bekanntes Medium übertragen wurde, verwässerten die von den Nachrichtensendern ausgestrahlten Erzählungen das Undurchschaubare und Fremde der

Ereignisse und ketteten Dein Vorstellungsvermögen an das, was Dir vertraut war. Die Deutungen, die sich wie Schlieren in Schichten über die Bilder legten, schmälerten Deine Angst vor dem Unbekannten. „Das hier ist nur ein Akt gegen die Diktatur." „Das ist der Ruf des Einzelnen nach Freiheit." „Das ist eine Demonstration im Namen der Demokratie." „Diese Revolution ist gewaltlos." Das Internet ersetzte die Kalaschnikow. Diese Diskurse ignorierten die strukturellen Dimensionen der Ungerechtigkeit und kaschierten die Rolle, welche die durch den Internationalen Währungsfonds (IWF), die EU, die USA und andere geförderte neoliberale Politik bei der Vertiefung der Kluft zwischen Arm und Reich gespielt hatte. Sie ließen Dich vergessen, dass der Wunsch nach sozialer Gerechtigkeit überhaupt erst aus diesen Mechanismen der Ungerechtigkeit entsteht. Der vorherrschende Diskurs – der Diskurs der Machthaber – verortete diese Probleme beispielsweise in einer hausgemachten Diktatur. Indem das Verbrechen eingegrenzt und korrupte Einzelpersonen präsentiert wurden, war die neokoloniale Bühne vorbereitet, so dass das ausgehöhlte, alte Regime durch eines ersetzt werden konnte, das im Grunde nur der gleichen Logik folgte.

Es ist nicht überraschend, dass die Inhaber dieser Bilder kommerzielle Nachrichtenagenturen sind, Unternehmen, die genau diejenigen Herrschaftssysteme, gegen die wir uns aufgelehnt haben, unterstützen oder von ihnen unterstützt werden. Die von den Kameras der Fernsehanstalten BBC, des CNN oder Al Jazeera öffentlich – und kostenlos – aufgenommenen Bilder sind zum Privateigentum dieser Institutionen geworden und werden von ihnen benutzt, um ihren Diskurs zu verbreiten, um das, was sie zu fördern gedenken, zu zelebrieren und das, was sie unterdrücken möchten, zum Schweigen zu bringen. Übertragung und thematische oder deutende Einbettung eines Bildes sind Akte der Machtausübung. Diese Bilder wurden im Namen der Freiheit aufgenommen und öffentlich gemacht, aber indem sie für die Zwecke eines profitorientierten Unternehmens genutzt werden, kann die Vorherrschaft der von den Unternehmen zur Verfügung gestellten deutenden Narrationen bewirken, dass jene Handlungen des Widerstands falsch ausgelegt und letztendlich untergraben werden.

Junge Aktivisten waren keineswegs repräsentative Stellvertreter der Protestierenden, aber doch wurde, was sie sagten, als vorherrschende Meinung präsentiert. Wir waren nur eine Handvoll Individuen inmitten einer kakophonen Vielzahl von Rufern nach Wandel; jeder erschien mit seinen eigenen Bedenken, Beschwerden, Wünschen, Motivationen und Anlässen zur Rache am Regime. Während der Welle von Protesten gab es eine starke horizontale Ausrichtung, dezentralisierte Entscheidungsprozesse, eine führerlose Bewegung, die in einem zentralisierten, auf Individuen abgestimmten Medienapparat oder durch einen verfassten Artikel, in einer gehaltenen Rede, einem konkreten Kunstwerk oder einem auf Personen und deren innere Entwicklung ausgerichteten Dokumentarfilm einfach keine Entsprechung finden konnte. Mit derlei Darstellungen wird die Realität verfälscht.

Mit diesem Brief erliege auch ich diesem Schema.

2011 ist nicht 1968

Die 1960er Jahre gingen mit dem Politischen schwanger: Ziel der Kämpfe waren die Rassengleichheit, Vietnam, der Kalte Krieg und die letzten Verwerfungen des offenen Imperialismus. 1968 ist aus diesem Moment entstanden. Zudem wurde 1968 von einer jungen Generation getragen, die sich von den in großer räumlicher Entfernung zu ihr abspielenden Szenen von Besatzung und Kolonialisierung konfrontiert sah, eine Studentengeneration, die sprühend vor Ideologie durch die soziale und politische Realität jener Zeit radikalisiert worden war. Über vierzig Jahre später provozierten die Auswirkungen des Imperialismus durch die Kloake des Postkolonialismus erneut Massenproteste. Unter diesen neuen Bedingungen, wie Frantz Fanon so klar herausgestellt hat, gelang es früheren Kolonialisten, ihre ökonomischen Interessen hinter Partnerschaften mit den regierenden Eliten der postkolonialen Staaten zu verbergen. Demzufolge ist 2011 nicht 1968. 2011 war ein Aufstand aus Unzufriedenheit mit der politischen Realität unter neokolonialen Bedingungen. 2011 war keine intellektuelle Revolution, es gab kein breites Aufkeimen unterschiedlicher Ideen und Theorien. Weder hatte in Ägypten vor 2011 unter der allgemeinen Bevölkerung ein Radikalisierungsprozess stattgefunden noch war die Nation zum Zeitpunkt der Revolution in einen grenzüberschreitenden Konflikt verwickelt. Es gab keine Ideologie außer der Ideologie der Verzweiflung, das unerträgliche Gewicht der Scheinheiligkeit und die Grenzen eines Volkes, das diese Lage zu lange verleugnet hatte. Ansteigende Militanz unter organisierten Arbeitergruppen und wachsende Opposition durch kleinere Bewegungen aus der Mittelschicht, wie zum Beispiel die Kefaya (Genug-Bewegung), die 6. April-Bewegung und die im Internet entstandenen Gruppen, wie Kolina Khaled Said (Wir sind alle Khaled Said) waren eine direkte Reaktion auf die nicht enden wollende Unterdrückung der gesamten Bevölkerung durch die politische Elite. Im Fall von 1968 hatten sich die verschiedenen Konflikte langsam aber stetig auf allen Ebenen bis zum besagten Jahr hin intensiviert und ausgebreitet, während in Ägypten in der Zeit vor 2011 die Samen der Revolution erst kurz vor dem Keimen waren. In Ägypten gab es nicht *eine Bewegung*, sondern es gab Bewegung, es gab einen Impuls, eine unbestimmte Kraft, die viel mächtiger war als eine Organisation es je sein könnte. Da unter Mubaraks Regime selbst die Anfänge einer Opposition sofort im Keim erstickt worden waren, gab es in Ägypten kaum etwas, was man

„links" hätte nennen können. Das Jahr 2011 war Zeuge einer rasanten politischen Radikalisierung angesichts jahrelanger ebenso rasanter Neoliberalisierungsprozesse. Die Universitäten hier waren und sind kein Ort kritischer Reflexion, sondern reines Alibi für den Diebstahl öffentlicher Gelder. Die Straßen waren die Hörsäle, wo wir mit den Sicherheitskräften der Regierung und dem Militär Steine gegen Feuer tauschten und untereinander Ideen und Gedanken. Auf diese Weise wurden die revoltierenden Ägypter radikal politisiert. Der Aufstand, der wenige Tage nach Anbruch des Jahres 2011 begann, wurde von einer zuvor niemals dagewesenen Masse von Demonstranten vorangetrieben. Ähnlich dem Aufstand in Argentinien 2001 waren die Proteste in Ägypten von einer klassen-, generationen- und geschlechterübergreifenden Teilnahme geprägt. Genau wie 1968 protestierten sowohl Studenten als auch Arbeiter in Ägypten, allerdings nicht als Zugehörige zu einer Einzelkategorie „Student" oder „Arbeiter", sondern vielmehr als Teil einer kollektiven, aus dem Volk gewachsenen Massenbewegung. Die Proteste blieben ohne einen eindeutigen Anführer; stattdessen haben wir die repressiven Hierarchien und den hegemonialen Staatsapparat mit unseren horizontalen Taktiken angegriffen. Es war die schiere Anzahl der Demonstranten, die, wenn auch nur temporär, die zentralistische Staatsstruktur in die Knie zwang. Dabei waren Forderungen der Demonstranten zahlreich und vielfältig, es gab nicht einen einstimmigen Grund, aus dem die Menschen in ganz Ägypten am 28. Januar 2011 auf die Straßen und Plätze strömten. Jeder Demonstrant hatte eigene Forderungen und Beweggründe, das den Alltag beherrschende Machtsystem abzulehnen. Dein Drang, diese Ereignisse als Zuschauer zu begreifen, hatte zur Folge, dass die Raison d'Être der Medienindustrie bestätigt und gefördert wurde, um Dein Bedürfnis zu befriedigen. Vom alles bestimmenden westlichen Standpunkt aus warfst Du einen Blick auf die Dinge, der den Vergleich mit dem Alltäglichen, dem Vertrauten, mit dem, was Du schon kanntest, heranzog und der 2011 so erscheinen ließ, als ähnelte es 1968.

2011 ist nicht 1968. 2011 war nicht die „klassische" Revolution der Sozialisten: demonstrierende Studenten und Arbeiter, die ein Regime durch ihr eigenes ersetzen wollten. So sehr es von den Ägyptern auch erwünscht ist – weder vor noch nach dem 25. Januar 2011 gab es in diesem Land eine ausgereifte Opposition, politische Parteien mit einem revolutionären Plan. Die Forderung, die von Anfang an laut und deutlich vernehmbar war – „Das Volk fordert den Fall des Regimes" – zog ein Stimmengewirr widersprüchlicher Meinungen nach sich, deren kleinster gemeinsamer Nenner die Forderung nach dem Ende des Status quo war: Wandel war notwendig, irgendeine Art von Wandel, aber wie dieser Wandel aussehen sollte, das war ungewiss. Diese Ungewissheit darf den Aufständen nicht als Schwäche angelastet werden, sondern sie bezeugt vielmehr jene globale Krise, sich gesellschaftliche Organisationen als alternative Formen zum neoliberalen Staat mit seinen sich selbst erneuernden, selbstzerstörerischen Hierarchien auszumalen. Darüber hinaus ließ dieser Protest ohne Anführer und vorgefertigte Ideologien es zu, dass Ideen entstehen und kontinuierlich weiterentwickelt werden konnten – das ist eine Entwicklung des Widerstands, die gerade erst beginnt.

Arbeiter und Revolution

Ein entscheidender Prozess, der die Revolution des 25. Januar überhaupt erst vorstellbar machte, war die seit 2006 ansteigende Welle von Arbeiterprotesten. Die 27.000 Textilarbeiter, die im Dezember 2006 in der Industriestadt El-Mahalla El-Kubra im ägyptischen Nildelta mit ihrem Massenstreik begannen, eröffneten unzähligen Ägyptern, die von diesem eindrucksvollen Akt oder auch der Vielzahl der darauffolgenden Proteste Kenntnis nahmen, die Möglichkeit einer Revolution. Unaufhaltsam breiteten sich Streiks und Demonstrationen im ganzen Land aus. Am 6. April 2008 riefen unabhängige Arbeiterführer dieser staatlichen Textilfabrik erneut zu einem weiteren Streik auf, der allerdings aufgrund vorab geführter Verhandlungen zwischen der Regierung und einer ausgewählten Gruppe von Arbeitern abgebrochen wurde. Die Forderung nach höheren Löhnen basierte auf den stetig steigenden Lebensmittelpreisen, und da in Mahalla beinahe jeder Haushalt von der riesigen Textilfabrik Masr abhängig ist, knüpften nicht nur die Arbeiter Erwartungen an diesen Streik. Am Tag des 6. April 2008 rechneten die Einwohner Mahallas mit einer Konfrontation. Auslöser des Aufstands war schließlich die öffentliche Beleidigung einer älteren Frau durch einen Polizisten. Der 6. April 2008 war einmalig, da sich die Mahalla-Proteste erstmals jenseits der geografischen Grenzen eines Industriegeländes ausbreiteten und dadurch von einer ganzen Gemeinde getragen wurden. Es waren jene Arbeiter in El-Mahalla El-Kubra, die durch ihren öffentlichen Protest zum ersten Mal die Regeln für sozial normiertes Verhalten brechen konnten. 2008 wurden die Grenzen des möglichen Widerstandes weit über die von der Regierung vorgegebenen Normen hinaus verschoben. Die Regierung bot all ihren Verstand und ihre Kraft auf und konnte nur knapp verhindern, dass der 6. April 2008 zum 25. Januar 2011 wurde. 2008 konnte die Regierung abwenden, dass der Protest aus einer Industriestadt auf das ganze Land – ganz zu schweigen auf die gesamte Region – überschwappte, indem sie aus sechs Regierungsgebieten Sicherheitskräfte orderte. Vom heutigen Standpunkt aus scheint es klar, dass die Zeit im April 2008 noch nicht reif war für das, was weniger als drei Jahre später aufkommen sollte. Am 28. Januar 2011 gewannen Demonstranten im ganzen Land innerhalb weniger Stunden über genau jene Sicherheitskräfte die Oberhand. An diesem Punkt muss wieder unterstrichen werden, dass 2011 nicht 1968 ist. 1968 wäre ohne Arbeiterstreikwellen und Fabrikbesetzungen, die parallel zu Studentenprotesten stattfanden, nicht möglich gewesen. Im Fall der Revolution vom 25. Januar kamen die Akteure aus allen Gesellschaftsschichten, sie brachten die Mittelschicht mit den Erwerbslosen, den Arbeitern und den Bauern zusammen, aber es waren die Menschen aus dem Arbeiterprekariat und nicht Ägyptens traditionelle Arbeiterklasse, die als das radikalisierende Element der Revolution agierten. Diese Abgrenzung mag trivial erscheinen, ist jedoch einer der Dreh- und Angelpunkte der Unterschiede zwischen 2011 und 1968.

Von 2006 zum 25. Januar 2011 und bis zum heutigen Tag haben Arbeiter aus geregelten Arbeitsverhältnissen unaufhörlich für bessere Löhne und gegen Privatisierung, Korruption und Ungerechtigkeit demonstriert und gestreikt. An den am 25. Januar 2011 beginnenden Protestwellen beteiligte sich eine große Anzahl Arbeiter aus dem Prekariat, hauptsächlich aus Ägyptens unzähligen *eshwa'eyat*, den provisorischen, inoffiziellen Siedlungen. Dies bedarf einer genaueren Erläuterung. Ab 2006 begannen Ägyptens Arbeiter gegen die Auswirkungen des unter Mubaraks letzter Regierung beschleunigten neoliberalen Prozesses zu protestieren. Die Arbeiter haben direkt – auch wenn sie es nicht in dieser Konsequenz formulierten – auf die Implementierung des westlichen ökonomischen Paradigmas des Neoliberalismus reagiert. Indem sie Betriebe und Unternehmen des Öffentlichkeitssektors privatisierte, Subventionen kürzte und die Produktion für den Export förderte, hatte Mubaraks Regierung ausländischen kapitalistischen Unternehmen den Einstieg in die ägyptische Industrie erleichtert. Mit dem Rückhalt internationaler Finanzinstitutionen und durch weniger Restriktionen hat dieses System ausländischen Investoren den Zugang zu Ägyptens natürlichen Ressourcen ermöglicht, was die Ausbeutung der hiesigen Arbeiterklasse zur Folge hatte. Dieser Prozess führte zu einer enormen Umwandlung der traditionellen Arbeiterschicht. Arbeiter sahen sich gezwungen, die so genannten Gelegenheitsjobs auf dem informellen Arbeitsmarkt anzunehmen, wobei es sich um Arbeit ohne Verträge, ohne Garantien und ohne soziale Absicherung handelte, was ihre sowieso schon prekären Arbeitsbedingungen weiter verschlimmerte. Sie müssen oft zwei oder drei Jobs parallel ausüben, um über die Runden zu kommen. Eine Ausbildung ist unerreichbarer Luxus. Diese am untersten Rand der Gesellschaft stehenden Arbeiter hatten am meisten unter der Unterdrückung und Ausbeutung des vorigen Regimes zu leiden. Gerade diese Unterklasse war Opfer des Umstands, dass Polizisten und Arbeitgeber jenseits der Gesetze standen. Verglichen mit dem Prekariat lebt die traditionelle Arbeiterklasse unter gesicherteren Bedingungen. Trotz des zumeist kargen Lohns, der skandalösen Arbeitszeiten im privaten Sektor, der schlechten Arbeitsbedingungen und der geringen Zuschüsse, hat die traditionelle Arbeiterklasse mit ihren festen Verträgen und dem geregelten Einkommen eine privilegierte Stellung in einer Arbeitswelt mit wenigen Garantien. Um den Verlust des Jobs nicht zu riskieren, begann die Arbeiterklasse, den Lebensstil der auf Sicherheit bedachten Mittelklasse nachzuahmen. Auch wenn die Arbeiterklasse sich für bessere Arbeitsbedingungen einsetzt und sich gegen Korruption und Missbrauch am Arbeitsplatz ausspricht, beschränken sich ihre Anstrengungen doch genau auf diese Forderungen, weil sie – verständlicherweise – nicht willens ist, ihre Kämpfe jenseits des Arbeitsplatzes auszutragen. Die Teilnahme an der Revolution bedeutete auf die Straße zu gehen und war mit dem Risiko verbunden, dem Arbeitgeber durch „Unruhestiftung“ einen Kündigungsgrund zu liefern. Das Heer der Arbeitslosen, die sofort in jeden freien Job drängten, minderte die Bereitschaft zum Protest. Das Risiko, ein so wertvolles Gut wie eine Festanstellung zu verlieren, wollte kaum ein festangestellter Arbeiter eingehen.

Die Umsetzung der neuen ökonomischen Paradigmen seit 1968 hat weiterhin das Kapital in den Händen der Reichen konzentriert und die Existenzgrundlage für alle anderen reduziert. Diese politische Ausrichtung trug dazu bei, dass das „Lumpenprekariat“ zum radikalen Element innerhalb des revolutionären Kampfes wurde und sich selbst bewies, dass mit ihm gerechnet werden muss. Die Zunahme komplexer ökonomischer Verflechtungen der neoliberalen Ära hat neue Formen des Widerstands hervorgebracht. Das sind die Bedingungen, welche die Ägypter an den Rand der Revolution gebracht haben, und es sind diese Bedingungen, welche die zukünftigen Protestbewegungen kennzeichnen werden.

Nachdem Berichte von Mubaraks Tod aufgetaucht waren, versammelte sich am Samstag, den 19. Juni 2012, eine Gruppe seiner Unterstützer vor einem Militärhospital am Ufer des Nils. Einer der Demonstranten hielt für die Vorbeifahrenden ein Schild in die Luft: „Die Revolution des 25. Januar: Die Geschichte wird urteilen.“

Du entscheidest, wie der 25. Januar 2011 in Deine eigene Geschichtsschreibung eingeht. Ist er ein zweites 1968, eine Revolution nach Deinem Geschmack? Oder ist er eine Bewegung, die die wenigen von Dir gesehenen Bilder und deren Bedeutungen übersteigt und die Dir eines Tages an Deiner Haustür gegenüberstehen könnte?

Dieser Essay wurde im August 2012 für das vorliegende Buch geschrieben.

Philip Rizk ist ein in Kairo lebender Filmemacher und Autor. Er ist Mitglied des Mosireen Medienkollektivs (mosireen.org). Folge ihm auf Twitter: @tabulagaza

Lara Baladi

When Seeing Is Belonging: The Photography of Tahrir

Photographs of Tahrir Square (*Midan al-Tahrir*—Liberation Square) taken on the "Friday of Victory," a week after a popular uprising forced President Hosni Mubarak to relinquish power, represent a better tomorrow and the birth of a new Egypt. These images portray Liberation Square as an oasis of peace and justice, a paradise regained, and an icon of freedom and renewed Egyptian identity. While in French the word *cliché* still means "photograph," for the rest of the world it refers to a stereotype with associations that, while familiar, conceal more truths than they reveal. Have these images of Tahrir Square replaced the pyramids as the ultimate Egyptian cliché?

When Napoleon Bonaparte addressed his army before the Battle of the Pyramids, he said, "Soldiers! Forty centuries behold you!" In August 1990, hordes of Kuwaitis sought refuge in Egypt. These tourists-in-spite-of-themselves flocked to the pyramids every day. My debut in photography coincided with this, Saddam Hussein's first invasion of Kuwait. I too was there on the Giza Plateau, photographing the pyramids.

That winter, Operation Desert Storm became the first war to be broadcast live on television. The perversity of how things were represented affirmed once more Guy Debord's *La Société du Spectacle* and took his ideas beyond mere theory. The dark image on the convex screen was filled with occasional explosions in the night sky of an obscure city, with CNN's big fat logo ever-present in the lower left corner. This "clean," "bloodless" war—mediated instantaneously, minute by minute, to the world—the speed at which events unfolded, America's overwhelming military response, and the new elaborate surveillance technology were all subject to much criticism and analysis. Jean Baudrillard, in his controversial and oft-cited text on that period, went so far as to suggest that "the Gulf War did not take place."[1] And indeed, many of the images that saturated our TV screens inspired a whole new market of video games, where soldiers, tinged with the green glow of infrared, crawled through the night.

A decade later, in 2001, this "casualty-free" representation of the Gulf War, achieved in 1991 by CNN, was turned on its head by a new generation of documentary photographers and filmmakers—citizen journalism was born. The 9/11 attacks were the first major historical twenty-first-century event to be documented by hundreds of people with digital cameras, more thoroughly and effectively, as it happened, than by the mainstream media. Beyond recording the horror of people jumping out of windows, others covered in ashes running in the debris, some carrying the wounded, and some trying to escape hell, those who witnessed and photographed the attack on the World Trade Center in New York contributed to breaking the long-established monopoly of power held by the media over the representation of reality.

In a little corner shop, the image of a plane exploding into the twin towers flashed on TV. While gathering up my groceries, I asked the shopkeeper sitting under the screen what this was. She glanced at it fleetingly over her shoulder and said with a shrug, "It must be a film." Never in the history of cinema had a scene of this amplitude been shot. Action movies have been trying, and failing, to catch up ever since. Reality surpassing fiction.

If, for so many, the Gulf War turned warfare into a computer game,[2] the photo and film amateurs on the ground, documenting the 110-story towers collapsing, rehumanized reality.

The first step toward the democratization of photography was the invention by Kodak of the Brownie camera. In 1888, with the slogan "You press the button, we do the rest," George Eastman transformed a cumbersome and complicated procedure, until then only affordable for an elite, into something easy and obtainable. Photography became even more accessible when, in 1975, another Eastman Kodak engineer, Steven Sasson, came up with a further major invention, the digital camera. By 2001, most people in the West had one. Snapping photos was no longer the hobby of amateurs but a fully integrated aspect of most people's daily life.

Another decade later—with the Internet frenzy, cameras in mobile phones (smart or not), webcams, and social media—the democratization of photography took on a new dimension as it became globalized. The mass media lost even more ground in the distribution of information with the appearance of social media. This new media form, in which the user could participate in the process of selecting and distributing information and make images instantaneously available worldwide, replaced visual media, thus further sharing the power of knowledge by shifting the hands holding it. In the Middle East, when Israel attacked Southern Lebanon in 2006, Lebanese online activists and bloggers attracted enough of the world's attention to put pressure on the international community and stop the war. Short-lived but devastatingly destructive, this war lasted long enough to spark the beginning of a new trend of online political activism in the whole Arab region. "The power of letters and the power of pictures distribute themselves and evaporate into the social media such that it becomes possible for everyone to act instead of simply being represented," observed Peter Weibel in a recent article, "Power to the People: Images by the People."[3]

On January 25, 2011, I was at home with a few friends. None of us knew, beyond the eerie silence in the street, how unprecedented the protests were. To distract ourselves from the growing tension outside, we played a game of Memory, illustrated with black-and-white photographs from the archive of the Arab Image Foundation (AIF). As I played with these past images from the Arab world, little did I know that the history of the region, of Arab photography, and photography in general was about to take a quantum leap.

Complicit as societies become under dictatorship, Egyptians had for generations bowed to routine police humiliation in broad daylight, and worse brutality in the darkness of their torture chambers. Very few images of these crimes had gone public. After the 2008 Mahalla protests, the notion that we had a right to see and be seen began to revive. Egyptian activist Arabawy blogged, "The revolution will be flickrised," pointing to the need to document and disseminate the regime's torture procedures; seeing would mean believing and revolting for those blinded by the national media, which persistently concealed the reality of the power that had been in place for thirty years.

This was never more true than in Tahrir Square. Here, and in the whole region during the Arab uprisings, the act of taking photographs became not only an act of seeing and recording, it was fully participatory. At the core of the Egyptian uprising, taking photographs was a political act, equal in importance to demonstrating, civil disobedience, and defiance to the regime. In Egypt, taking photographs was prohibited in many areas during the Mubarak era; I was arrested no fewer than seven times over fifteen years for taking pictures in various parts of the country. Fearmongering propaganda made people paranoid, feeding an ever-present and general suspicion of the camera, and, by extension, of the "other."

In the midst of the emergency, all theories about the subjectivity of photography suddenly became irrelevant. During the eighteen days, people in the square took photos because they felt the social responsibility to do so. Photography became objective; photography showed the truth—yes, a "truth" made up of as many truths as there were protestors in the square, but nonetheless one that had urgently to be revealed at this turning point in history. The camera became a nonviolent weapon aimed directly at the state, denouncing it. By consequence, taking photographs, a stand against the regime, was a way of reconquering territory and ultimately the country. Taking photographs meant belonging.

In his classic television series *Ways of Seeing*, John Berger tells us: "The images come to you. You do not go to them. The days of pilgrimage are over." Today, in the digital age, Slavoj Žižek argues further, "I think that a much more interesting notion, crucial to understanding what goes on today, is not 'virtual reality' but the 'reality of the virtual.'"[4] A media revolution also took place in Tahrir, when that reality met the one on the street. Images were not just coming to us through our screens, they were "reality."

Except in China, whose government banned the word "Egypt" from its Google search engine, images of Tahrir Square spilled out into everyone's living spaces, transcending computers, televisions screens, and other virtual channels, inexorably spreading the energy of the square around the world. As Žižek said when interviewed about the Arab revolutions: "It was a genuine universal event, immediately understandable. . . . It is every true universality, the universality of struggle." Unlike during the other conflicts that provoked a media shift—namely, the Gulf War and 9/11—people all over the world identified with the protesters in the square. Tahrir became everyone's revolution. Occupy movements followed in a chain reaction, proving for the history of photography that image-making can change the world.

Thousands of people moved, took photographs, and stood together in solidarity with each other against totalitarianism. By day, protesters held signs and slogans in their hands above their heads, and when night came, the blue glowing lights of electronic devices—from mobile phones, iPads, and even computers. While signifying the demand for social justice and freedom, these devices were not only emanating a light of hope reminiscent of the dancing flames during the protests of the sixties, they were simultaneously absorbing the ambient light, thus recording life in Tahrir Square from every possible angle, in every possible quality and format.

The mainstream international media grabbed the event and sucked everything it could out of it. While it supported the crowds in Tahrir, it also destroyed the revolution's momentum by referring to it in the past tense after the eighteen days and moving on to other news, thus confirming Marshall McLuhan's theory that "you can actually dissipate a situation by giving it maximal coverage."[5] At this point, the power of images had been embraced by ordinary people to such an extent that the media, often way behind the news on the ground, referred to the Internet for information, broadcasting videos shot by amateurs or activists that had already gone viral on the web. Never since the invention of the camera had a historical event been so widely documented, with more videos and photos than there were protesters in the square.

The new economy brought about by digital photography (anyone who owns a camera can produce limitless images for free) has exponentially amplified photography's intrinsic factory-like quality—both its great promise and its greatest threat. Images are distributed at tremendous speed and there follows a lack of critical distance over their reading—for example, photoshopped images are mostly taken at face value in such a context. The lack of morality and ethics that this allows for contributes to a general desensitization to reality. Vilém Flusser in his book *Towards a Philosophy of Photography* rightly warns us of the dangers of this hyper-democratization of photography in the digital age: "Anyone who takes snaps has to adhere to the instructions for use—becoming simpler and simpler—that are programmed to control the output end of the camera. This is democracy in the post-industrial society. Therefore people taking snaps are unable to decode photographs: they think photographs are an automatic reflection of the world."[6]

During the Arab uprisings, a great number of shaky and blurry cell-phone videos, shot in Syria, Libya, and Bahrain, and uploaded every day onto the Internet, were not "decodable." Many battle scenes, highly pixelated and graphic, resembled each other, yet nothing in them was clearly definable or, in itself, recognizable—confusing at best, and often downright misleading. Their title was the only thing that gave them content. Viewers easily disengaged from following or attempting to understand how these uprisings were evolving, and if they did, once again they referred to and relied on the mainstream media, thus handing the power back all over again.

The other burning question in this digital democratization of image-making is: How long will the biggest multivoiced documentary ever made, this extraordinary and unedited portrait of Egyptians in *Midan al-Tahrir*, survive in the virtual archive that is the Internet? In his article "Ephemeral to Enduring: The Internet Archive and Its Role in Preserving Digital Media," Eli Edwards writes, "Just as the Internet, particularly the World Wide Web, is noted for its growing capacity and diversity of material, it is also notorious for its impermanence."[7] With most of the images of the eighteen days vanishing into the bottomless pit of Google's PageRank algorithm, will the vision of a possible new world people had in the square also die with them?

Although the endless proliferation of images in Tahrir was produced for our own national consumption rather than for that of a Western audience, images from the square almost instantly turned old established clichés of Egypt on their heads. The angry Arab terrorist became a dignified peace warrior. "Egypt Help Us. One World One Pain", read banners in the protests that erupted in Wisconsin in the US, three weeks after the Egyptian uprising. The once "dirty Arab" had transformed into the perfect politically and socially conscious citizen. U.S. President Barack Obama even declared in a television speech he gave after the Camel Attack[8] in the midst of the eighteen days: "We should raise our children to be like Egyptian youth."

The most enduring orientalist Egyptian cliché of them all, the Giza Pyramids, imprinted in our collective consciousness since the beginning of history, has been upstaged by the bird's-eye picture of a million people in Tahrir. People circulating around the tents in the center of the square resonated at times with images of people praying around the

Kaaba in Mecca. In the last two years, Tahrir itself has become a pilgrimage site for revolution tourists.

The oldest debate in photography is its relationship with death: "Photographs are a way of imprisoning reality. . . . One can't possess reality, one can possess . . . images," writes Susan Sontag in *On Photography*. "One can't possess the present but one can possess the past."[9] The fear of death and the fear that the vision born in Tahrir would vanish soon after the eighteen days may have been what pushed people incessantly to make images there. Ultimately, perhaps, taking photographs in Tahrir was an act of faith. As if recording the ecstatic reality of the present would remind us, in the future, of the square's utopian promise and help us to keep hope when the real battle would start.

This essay was written especially for this book in March 2013.

1 Jean Baudrillard, *The Gulf War Did Not Take Place*, trans. Paul Patton, Bloomington, IN: Indiana University Press, 1995
2 In the Wikipedia entry for "Gulf War," the second sentence reads: "'Operation Desert Storm' redirects here. For the video game, see Operation: Desert Storm (video game)." en.wikipedia.org/wiki/Gulf_War
3 blog.zkm.de/en/editorial/power-people-images-people/
4 www.youtube.com/watch?v=RnTQhIRcrno
5 "Only puny secrets need protection. Big secrets are protected by public incredulity. You can actually dissipate a situation by giving it maximal coverage. As to alarming people, that's done by rumours, not by coverage." Marshall McLuhan and Barrington Nevitt, *Take Today: The Executive as Drop Out*, New York: Harcourt Brace Jovanovich, 1972, p. 92
6 Vilém Flusser, *Towards a Philosophy of Photography*, trans. Anthony Mathews, London: Reaktion, 2000, p. 54
7 Eli Edwards, "Ephemeral to Enduring: The Internet Archive and Its Role in Preserving Digital Media", in *Information Technology and Libraries* 23, no. 1 (March 2004), pp. 3–8, here: p. 3 http://www.madlibrarian.net/wp-content/uploads/archive.pdf
8 This refers to the attack on demonstrators by armed loyalist groups, who charged into Tahrir Square mounted on camels on February 1, 2011.
9 Susan Sontag, *On Photography*, New York: Farrar, Straus, and Grioux, 1977

Lara Baladi

Wenn sehen heißt dazuzugehören: Die Bilder vom Tahrir-Platz

Fotos vom Tahrir-Platz, die am „Freitag des Sieges“, also eine Woche nach einem Volksaufstand gemacht wurden, der Präsident Husni Mubarak gezwungen hatte, seine Macht abzugeben, zeigen eine bessere Zukunft, die Geburt eines neuen Ägypten. Diese Bilder porträtieren den Tahrir-Platz, den Platz der Befreiung, als eine Oase des Friedens und der Gerechtigkeit. Wenngleich das Wort *cliché* auf Französisch noch immer *Fotografie* bedeutet, bezieht es sich für den Rest der Welt auf ein Stereotyp, das Assoziationen hervorruft, die trotz ihrer Geläufigkeit mehr Wahrheiten verbergen als sie enthüllen. Haben diese Bilder vom Tahrir-Platz (mittlerweile) die Pyramiden als maßgebliches ägyptisches Klischee ersetzt?

Als Napoleon Bonaparte sich vor der Schlacht bei den Pyramiden an seine Armee richtete, sagte er: „Denkt daran, dass von diesen Monumenten 40 Jahrhunderte auf euch herabblicken.“ Im August 1990 suchten Scharen von Kuwaitis Zuflucht in Ägypten. Diese „Touristen wider Willen“ versammelten sich jeden Tag bei den Pyramiden. Mein Einstieg in die Fotografie fiel damit zusammen: mit Saddam Husseins erster Invasion in Kuwait. Auch ich war da auf dem Gizeh-Plateau und fotografierte die Pyramiden.

In jenem Winter wurde die „Operation Wüstensturm“ zum ersten jemals live im Fernsehen übertragenen Krieg. Die Perversität der Art, wie alles gezeigt wurde, bestätigte jenseits aller Theorie Guy Debords *Gesellschaft des Spektakels*. Das dunkle Bild auf dem Bildschirm wurde von gelegentlichen Explosionen am Nachthimmel einer obskuren Stadt erleuchtet. CNNs aufgeblasenes Logo dabei allgegenwärtig in der unteren linken Ecke. Dieser „saubere“, „blutlose“ Krieg, Minute um Minute sofort in die Welt übertragen, die Geschwindigkeit, mit der sich die Ereignisse offenbarten, Amerikas überwältigende militärische Antwort und die neue ausgeklügelte Überwachungstechnologie waren allesamt Gegenstand zahlreicher Kritik und Analysen. Jean Baudrillard ging in seinem kontroversen und zu dieser Zeit oft zitierten Text so weit zu sagen: „Der Golfkrieg hat nicht stattgefunden.“[1] Und tatsächlich, viele der Bilder, die unsere sich nach außen wölbenden[, betagten] Fernsehbildschirme tränkten, regten einen komplett neuen Markt von Videospielen an, in welchen Soldaten, gefärbt vom grünen Schein aus ihren Infrarotgeräten, durch die Nacht krochen.

Ein Jahrzehnt später, 2001, wurde diese opferlose Darstellung des Golfkriegs, 1991 vollbracht von CNN, durch eine neue Generation von Dokumentarfotografen und Filmemachern auf den Kopf gestellt – der Bürgerjournalismus entstand. Der 11. September 2001, 9/11, war das erste historische Großereignis des einundzwanzigsten Jahrhunderts, das von hunderten Menschen mit Digitalkameras in dem Moment, da es geschah, dokumentiert wurde; gründlicher und effektiver, als von den gängigen Massenmedien. Darüber hinausgehend, den Horror von aus den Fenstern springenden Menschen aufzunehmen oder den Horror derer, die mit Asche bedeckt durch die Trümmer liefen oder Verwundete trugen und anderer, die versuchten, der Hölle zu entkommen – dazu, das lange Zeit etablierte Machtmonopol der Medien über die Darstellung der Wirklichkeit zu brechen, trugen jene bei, die Zeugen des Angriffs auf das World Trade Center in New York waren und ihn fotografierten.

In einem kleinen Eckladen flackerte im Fernseher das Bild eines in die Twin Towers hinein explodierenden Flugzeugs auf. Während ich meine Lebensmittel zusammenklaubte, fragte ich die Geschäftsinhaberin, die unter dem Bildschirm saß, was das wohl sei. Sie warf einen flüchtigen Blick über ihre Schulter und sagte mit einem Schulterzucken „Das muss ein Film sein“. Noch nie in der Geschichte des Kinos war eine Szene solcher Komplexität gedreht worden. Actionfilme haben es probiert und versagt und versagen weiterhin darin, gleichzuziehen. Die Realität übertrifft die Fiktion.

Insofern der Golfkrieg die Kriegsführung für so viele in ein Computerspiel[2] verwandelte, vermenschlichten die Foto- und Filmamateure am Boden der Geschehnisse die Realität wieder, indem sie den Einsturz der einhundertzehngeschossigen Türme dokumentierten.

Der erste Schritt in Richtung der Demokratisierung der Fotografie war die Erfindung der Brownie-Kamera von Kodak. Im Jahr 1888, begleitet von dem Slogan „Sie drücken den Auslöser – wir machen den Rest“, verwandelte George Eastman ein umständliches und kompliziertes Verfahren, das bis dahin nur für eine Elite erschwinglich gewesen war, in etwas Einfaches und Erreichbares. Fotografie wurde noch zugänglicher, als 1975 Steven Sasson, ein anderer Ingenieur der Eastman Kodak Company (Kodak), eine weitere bedeutende Erfindung machte: die Digitalkamera. Im Jahr 2001 hatten die meisten Bewohner der westlichen Welt eine solche. Fotos zu machen war nicht länger das Hobby von Amateuren, sondern ein voll integrierter Bestandteil des Lebens der meisten Menschen.

Eine weiteres Jahrzehnt später, mit dem Internet-Rausch, den Kameras in Mobiltelefonen (smart oder auch nicht), mit Webcams und den Social

Media, nimmt die Demokratisierung der Fotografie im Rahmen ihrer Globalisierung eine neue Dimension an. Mit dem Aufkommen der Social Media verloren die Massenmedien bezüglich der Informationsverteilung weiter an Boden. Social Media, in welchen der Nutzer am Prozess der Auswahl und Verteilung von Informationen teilnehmen und Bilder ohne Verzögerung weltweit verfügbar machen kann, ersetzten die visuellen Medien. Die Macht wurde weiter aufgeteilt, indem die Hände, in denen sie lag, ausgewechselt wurden. Als Israel 2006 den Libanon angriff, zogen libanesische Online-Aktivisten und Blogger im Nahen Osten ausreichend Aufmerksamkeit der Welt an, um international Druck auszuüben und den Krieg zu beenden. Von kurzer Dauer, verheerend und zerstörerisch, währte dieser Krieg doch lange genug, um einen neuen Trend von politischem Online-Aktivismus in der ganzen arabischen Region auszulösen. „Die Macht der Buchstaben und die Macht der Bilder verteilen sich und verdampfen in den sozialen Medien, in denen alle handeln können, anstatt nur repräsentiert zu werden“, beobachtete Peter Weibel in einem neueren Artikel: „Power to the People: Images by the People.“[3]

Am 25. Januar 2011 war ich mit ein paar Freunden zuhause. Abgesehen von der unheimlichen und ungewöhnlichen Stille in den Straßen, fanden wir keine Anzeichen für die Beispiellosigkeit der Proteste. Um uns von der wachsenden Anspannung draußen abzulenken, spielten wir Memory, illustriert mit Schwarzweiß-Fotografien aus den Archiven der Arab Image Foundation (AIF). Während ich mit diesen älteren Bildern aus der arabischen Welt spielte, ahnte ich nicht, dass die Geschichte der Region, der arabischen Fotografie und die Fotografie im Ganzen dabei waren, einen Quantensprung zu vollziehen.

Die Ägypter hatten sich, mitverantwortlich geworden, wie es Gesellschaften in Diktaturen passiert, über Generationen hinweg den routinemäßigen Demütigungen durch die Polizei am helllichten Tag und der schlimmeren Brutalität in der Dunkelheit derer Folterkammern gebeugt. Nur sehr wenige Bilder dieser Verbrechen gelangten an die Öffentlichkeit. Nach den Mahalla-Protesten 2008 begann die Ansicht, dass wir ein Recht zum Sehen und Gesehenwerden hatten, wieder aufzuleben. Der ägyptische Aktivist Arabawy bloggte damals „Die Revolution wird flickrisiert werden“ und wies damit auf die Notwendigkeit hin, die vom Regime ausgeübte Gewalt zu dokumentieren und öffentlich zu machen und darauf, wie für jene, die von den nationalen Medien verblendet wurden, welche kontinuierlich dreißig Jahre lang das Wirklichsein der vorhandenen Kräfte verschleiert hatten, zu sehen bedeuten würde, glauben und revoltieren zu können.

Das traf insbesondere auf den Tahrir-Platz zu. Während der arabischen Aufstände wurde der Akt des Fotografierens hier und in der ganzen Region nicht nur zu einer Handlung des Sehens und Aufzeichnens, sondern zu einem Akt kompletter Partizipation. Im Kern der ägyptischen

Aufstände war das Fotografieren eine politische Handlung, bezüglich ihrer Relevanz dem Demonstrieren gleichgestellt: ziviler Ungehorsam und Missachtung des Regimes. Während der Mubarak-Ära war das Fotografieren in vielen Gegenden verboten. Ich wurde innerhalb von fünfzehn Jahren nicht weniger als siebenmal verhaftet, weil ich in verschiedenen Regionen des Landes Bilder gemacht hatte. Die Propaganda der Angstmacherei machte die Menschen paranoid, nährte einen immer gegenwärtigen Generalverdacht gegen die Kamera und infolgedessen gegen das „Andersartige".

Auf dem Höhepunkt der Ereignisse wurden alle Theorien zur Subjektivität der Fotografie plötzlich irrelevant. Während der achtzehn Tage machten die Menschen auf dem Platz Fotos, weil sie die gesellschaftliche Verantwortung dazu verspürten. Die Fotografie wurde objektiv; Fotografie zeigte die Wahrheit – jawohl, eine Wahrheit geformt aus ebenso vielen Wahrheiten wie da Protestierende auf dem Platz waren, aber dennoch eine, die dringend an diesem Wendepunkt der Geschichte enthüllt werden musste. Die Kamera wurde eine friedliche, direkt auf den Staat gerichtete, den Staat denunzierende Waffe. Das Fotografieren, eine regimekritische Haltung, wurde in der Konsequenz zu einer Möglichkeit, zuerst Territorium und schließlich das Land zurückzuerobern. Zu fotografieren hieß dazuzugehören.

In seiner bekannten Fernsehserie *Ways of Seeing* teilt uns John Berger mit: „Die Bilder kommen zu dir. Du gehst nicht zu ihnen. Die Tage der Pilgerschaft sind vorbei." Heute, im digitalen Zeitalter, führt Slavoj Žižek aus: „Ich denke, dass eine viel interessantere Vorstellung, wesentlich, um zu verstehen, was heute vor sich geht, nicht die 'virtuelle Realität' ist, sondern die 'Realität des Virtuellen'"[4]. Eine Revolution der Medien fand auch auf dem Tahrir-Platz statt, als diese Realität auf die der Straße traf. Bilder kamen nicht einfach nur über unsere Bildschirme zu uns, sie waren Wirklichkeit.

Abgesehen von China, dessen Regierung das Wort „Ägypten" aus seinen Google-Suchmaschinen verbannen ließ, schwappten die Bilder vom Platz in jedermanns Wohnraum, überwanden die Grenzen der Computer, Fernsehbildschirme und anderer virtueller Kanäle, verbreiteten die Energie vom Platz unaufhaltsam auf der Welt. Wie Žižek sagte, als er zur arabischen Revolution interviewt wurde: „Es war ein wirkliches universales Ereignis, sofort verständlich... Es ist jede wahre Universalität, die Allgemeinheit des Kampfes." Abweichend von den anderen Konflikten, namentlich Golfkrieg und 11. September 2011, die einen Wandel der Medien auslösten, identifizierten sich Menschen auf der ganzen Welt mit den Demonstranten auf dem Platz. Der Tahrir-Platz wurde zu jedermanns Revolution. Die *Occupy*-Bewegungen folgten in einer Kettenreaktion und bewiesen der Fotografiegeschichte, dass das Bildermachen die Welt verändern kann.

Tausende von Menschen bewegten sich, fotografierten, standen solidarisch miteinander gegen den Totalitarismus zusammen. Am Tag hielten die Protestierenden Zeichen und Slogans über ihre Köpfe, und wenn es Nacht wurde die blau leuchtenden Lichter elektronischer Geräte – von Mobiltelefonen, iPads und auch von Computern. Während sie die Forderung nach gesellschaftlicher Gerechtigkeit und Freiheit bedeuteten, entströmte diesen Geräten nicht nur ein Licht der Hoffnung, das an die tanzenden Flammen der Proteste in den 1960er Jahren erinnerte, sie saugten im gleichen Moment das sie umgebende Licht auf, nahmen so aus jedem möglichen Winkel, in jeder möglichen Qualität und jedem möglichen Format das Leben auf dem Tahrir-Platz auf.

Die internationalen Massenmedien schnappten sich das Ereignis und zogen alles, was sie konnten, daraus. Wenngleich das die Menschen auf dem Tahrir-Platz unterstützte, zerstörte es auch die Wucht der Revolution, denn nach den achtzehn Tagen wurde in Vergangenheitsform über sie berichtet und sich dann anderen Nachrichten gewidmet, womit Marshall McLuhans These, dass man eine Situation tatsächlich auflösen kann, lässt man ihr nur ein Maximum an Berichterstattung angedeihen[5], bestätigt wurde. In diesem Moment wurde die Kraft der Bilder in einem solchen Ausmaß von gewöhnlichen Menschen vereinnahmt, dass die Medien – oft weit hinter den Nachrichten von der Basis herhinkend – sich für ihre Informationen des Internets bedienten und von Amateuren oder von rasend schnell im Netz bekannt gewordenen Aktivisten aufgenommene Videos ausstrahlten. Seit der Erfindung der Kamera ist kein historisches Ereignis so umfassend dokumentiert worden – mit mehr Videos und Fotos als Protestierende auf dem Platz zugegen waren.

Die neue Effizienz, die die digitale Fotografie mit sich brachte (jeder, der eine Kamera besitzt, kann unbegrenzt und kostenlos Bilder herstellen) hat in exponentiellem Maß die der Fotografie immanenten fabrikähnlichen Eigenschaften verstärkt: sowohl ihr großes Versprechen als auch die von ihr ausgehende größte Bedrohung. Bilder werden in rasender Geschwindigkeit verbreitet und anschließend mit fehlender Distanz gedeutet – zum Beispiel werden mit Photoshop bearbeitete Bilder für bare Münze genommen. Der Mangel an Moral und Ethik, der dies ermöglicht, führt zu einer allgemeinen Desensibilisierung gegenüber der Wirklichkeit. Vilém Flusser warnt uns in seinem Essay *Für eine Philosophie der Fotografie* zu Recht vor den Gefahren der Überdemokratisierung der Fotografie im digitalen Zeitalter: „Wer knipst, muß sich an die immer einfacher werdenden Gebrauchsanweisungen halten, die auf der Outputseite des Apparats programmiert sind. Das ist Demokratie in der nachindustriellen Gesellschaft. Darum ist der Knipser unfähig, Fotos zu entziffern: Er hält die Fotos für automatisch abgebildete Welt.“[6] Während der arabischen Aufstände waren viele der jeden Tag ins Internet hochgeladenen, verwackelten und unscharfen Mobiltelefon-videos, aufgenommen in Syrien, Libyen und Bahrain, nicht „entzifferbar". Viele Kampfszenen, stark pixelig und grafisch, ähnelten einander und doch war nichts in ihnen definierbar oder an sich erkennbar – bestenfalls verwirrend und oft geradewegs in die Irre führend. Ihr Titel war das einzige, was ihnen Inhalt gab. Die Betrachter entbanden sich mühelos vom Versuch zu folgen oder zu verstehen, wie diese Aufstände sich entwickelten. Versuchten sie es doch, bezogen sie sich erneut auf die Massenmedien und verließen sich auf diese und reichten auf diese Art alle Macht zurück.

Die andere brennende Frage in dieser digitalen Demokratisierung des Bildermachens ist: Wie lange wird diese längste und vielstimmigste Dokumentation, die je entstand, dieses „außergewöhnliche" und unbearbeitete Porträt der Ägypter auf dem Tahrir-Platz in diesem virtuellen Archiv, dem Internet, überstehen? In seinem Artikel *Vom Vergänglichen zum Beständigen: Das Internetarchiv und seine Rolle in der Bewahrung digitaler Medien*[7] schreibt Eli Edwards: „So, wie das Internet, genauer das World Wide Web, für seine wachsende Kapazität und die Vielfalt des Materials berühmt ist, ist es berüchtigt für seine Vergänglichkeit." Wird die Vision einer möglichen neuen Welt, die die Menschen auf dem Platz hatten, so verblassen, wie die Bilder der achtzehn Tage im bodenlosen, von Googles PageRank-Algorithmus bereiteten Loch verschwinden?

Wenngleich die endlos wuchernde Menge von Bildern vom Tahrir-Platz eher für unseren eigenen nationalen Bedarf als für den der Zuschauer in der westlichen Welt produziert worden war, wurden die Bilder vom Platz in deren Köpfen nahezu sofort zu altbekannten Klischees von Ägypten. Aus dem wütenden arabischen Terroristen wurde der würdevolle Friedenskämpfer. „Ägypten hilf uns. Eine Welt Ein Schmerz" stand drei Wochen nach den Aufständen in Ägypten auf Transparenten bei in Wisconsin, USA, aufgekommenen Protesten zu lesen. Der zuvor „schmutzige Araber" hatte sich zu einem in politischer und gesellschaftlicher Hinsicht perfekten Bürger entwickelt. US-Präsident Barack Obama erklärte sogar in einer Fernsehansprache, die er nach der Kamelschlacht[8] in der Mitte der achtzehn Tage gab: „Wir sollten unsere Kinder aufziehen, wie die ägyptische Jugend zu sein".

Das beständigste orientalistisch-ägyptische Klischee von allen, die Pyramiden von Gizeh, eingeprägt im kollektiven Bewusstsein seit dem Anfang der Geschichte, wurde von dem eine Million Menschen auf dem Tahrir-Platz zeigenden Vogelperspektiven-Bild in den Hintergrund gedrängt: Menschen, die um die Zelte in der Mitte des Platzes gehen, erinnern manchmal an die Bilder Betender um die Kaaba in Mekka. In den letzten beiden Jahren ist der Tahrir-Platz selbst zu einem Pilgerort für Revolutionstouristen geworden.

Die älteste Debatte der Fotografie ist jene über das Verhältnis der Fotografie zum Tod: „Das Fotografieren ist eine Methode zum Einfangen einer [...] Realität. [...] Realität kann man nicht besitzen, aber Bilder kann man besitzen, […] so wie man nicht die Gegenwart, wohl aber die Vergangenheit besitzen kann“[9], schreibt Susan Sontag in *Über Fotografie*. Die Angst vor dem Tod und die Angst, dass die auf dem Tahrir-Platz geborene Vision alsbald nach den achtzehn Tagen verschwinden könnten, waren es wohl, was die Menschen antrieb, dort unablässig Fotos zu machen. Letztendlich war das Fotografieren auf dem Tahrir-Platz vielleicht ein Akt des Glaubens. So, als ob die Aufzeichnung der ekstatischen Wirklichkeit der Gegenwart uns in der Zukunft an das utopische Versprechen des Platzes erinnern und uns helfen würde, dann die Hoffnung zu bewahren, wenn die wirkliche Schlacht beginnt.

Dieser Essay wurde im März 2013 für das vorliegende Buch geschrieben.

1 Jean Baudrillard, *La Guerre du Golfe n'a pas eu lieu*, Paris: Édition Galilée, 1991
2 Im englischen Wikipedia-Eintrag für „Golfkrieg“ lautet der zweite Satz: „Umgeleitet von ‚Operation Desert Storm‘. Für das Videospiel siehe: Operation: Desert Storm (Videospiel).“
3 blog.zkm.de/blog/editorial/peter_weibel/power-to-the-people-images-by-the-people/
4 www.youtube.com/watch?v=RnTQhIRcrno
5 „Only puny secrets need protection. Big secrets are protected by public incredulity. You can actually dissipate a situation by giving it maximal coverage. As to alarming people, that's done by rumours, not by coverage.“ Vgl., Marshall McLuhan und Barrington Nevitt: *Take Today: The Executive as Drop Out*, New York: Harcourt Brace Jovanovich, 1972, S. 92
6 Villém Flusser: *Für eine Philosophie der Fotografie*, Göttingen: European Photography, 1983, S. 54
7 Eli Edwards, "Ephemeral to Enduring: The Internet Archive and Its Role in Preserving Digital Media", in *Information Technology and Libraries* 23, 2004, S. 3 www.madlibrarian.net/wp-content/uploads/archive.pdf
8 Gemeint ist hier der Angriff auf die Demonstranten durch bewaffnete, regierungstreue Gruppen, die den Tahrir-Platz am 1. Februar 2011 auf Kamelen reitend stürmten. (d. ÜS)
9 Susan Sontag, *Über Fotografie* (*On Photography*, 1977), München: Hanser, 1978

From a Certain Distance: Works by Artists Reflecting or Anticipating the Political Changes/

Aus einer bestimmten Distanz: Künstlerische Arbeiten, die den politischen Wandel reflektieren oder vorwegnehmen/

من مسافة معينة: أعمال لفنانين تعكس أو تستبق التغيير السياسي

Many of the photographs and video stills in this book share an immediate quality of testimony. The following chapter sets up a contrast to this. The artistic works presented here maintain a certain distance to events, and indeed some of them were produced on the eve of the revolution. What links them is their refusal to take a euphoric view of what happened. Instead they examine the new forms of images in circulation, their ubiquity on YouTube and the social networks, and their shifting materiality and mediality. Some of the works address the significance of the military for the country's sense of social identity or reflect the developments that have taken place in press photography. Others attempt to create new forms of witnessing, beyond the realms of journalistic narrative./
Viele Fotografien und Videostills in diesem Buch teilen eine unmittelbare Augenzeugenschaft. Das folgende Kapitel versteht sich als Kontrast hierzu. Die vorgestellten künstlerischen Arbeiten wahren eine gewisse Distanz zum Geschehen, einige sind schon am Vorabend der Revolution entstanden. Was sie gemeinsam haben, ist die Verweigerung einer euphorischen Darstellung der Ereignisse. Vielmehr analysieren sie die neuen Formen der Bilder, ihre Omnipräsenz auf YouTube und in den sozialen Netzwerken sowie ihre sich wandelnde Materialität und Medialität. Einige Arbeiten thematisieren die Bedeutung des Militärs für das soziale Selbstverständnis des Landes oder reflektieren die Entwicklungen in der Pressefotografie. Wieder andere versuchen, neue Zeugnisse zu schaffen, jenseits der journalistischen Erzählung./
تعرض لنا الكثير من الصور و مقاطع الفيديـو في هذا الكتاب، شهادة مباشرة. و تشكل الصفحات السابقة تناقض لهذه الشهادة. فالأعمال الفنيـة المقدمة فيه تقف على مسافة من الأحداث، بعض من هذه الأعمال نشأ قبل الثورة بيـوم. وما يجمعها، هو رفض رؤيـة الأحداث المباشرة التي تحدث الآن بشكل مبهج. ولكنها تحلل أشكال الصـور وحضورها الأبـدي على اليوتيوب وفي مواقع التواصل الإجتماعي وتغيـر شكلها ووسيطها الدائم. وتنـاقش أعمـال أخرى أهمية الجيش لفهم المجتمع لنفسه أو أيضـاً التصوير الصحفي المتغيـر. مرة أخرى يحاول آخرون عرض الشهادات بعيـداً عن الكلام الصحفي.

"Many of those who are driven to this life are desperately searching for those pockets of silence where we can root and grow. We must all hope we find them."

Mark Rothko, in: Simon Schama, *Power of Art: Rothko* (BBC Two, Dec. 12, 2006) /
مارك روثـكو، مقتبس من: سيمون شما *Power of Art: Rothko*. بي بي سي اثنان، *12* ديسمبـر *2006*

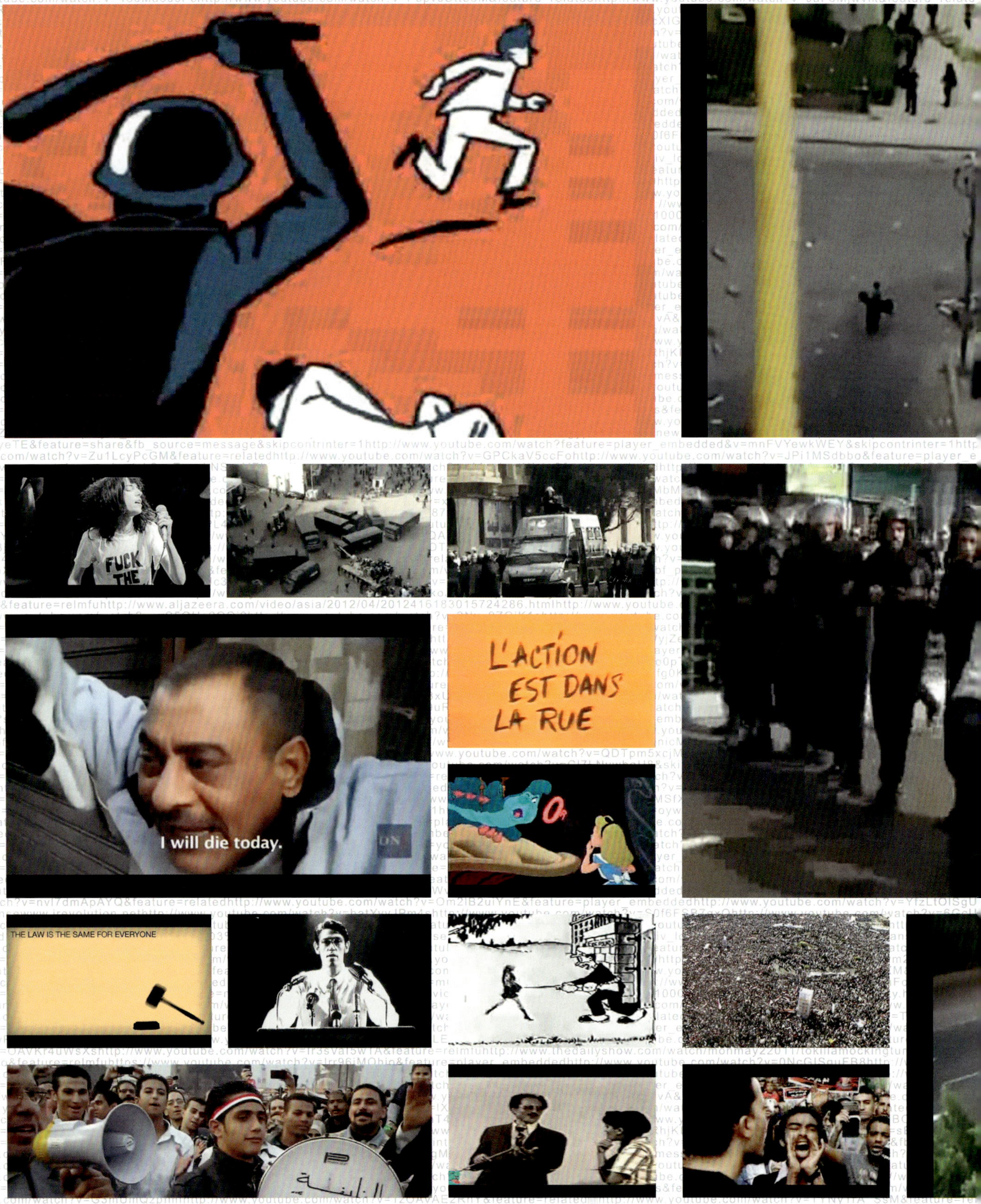

Lara Baladi / لارا بلدي, *Alone, Together… In Media Res*, 2012
Three-channel video installation / Drei-Kanal-Videoinstallation, 42:00 min. / عرض فيديو ثلاثي القنوات، 42:00 دقيقة → p. / S. 130 / ص.٥٣

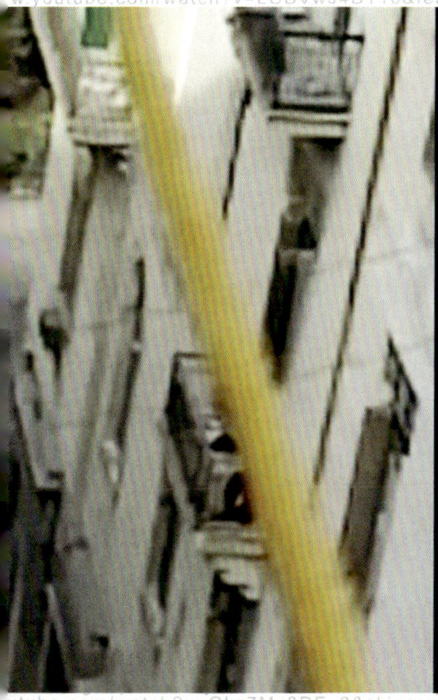

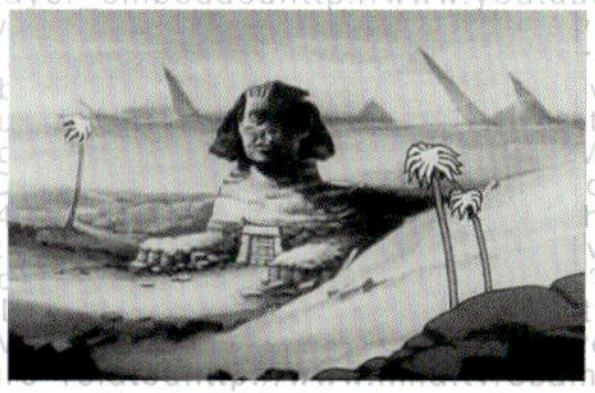

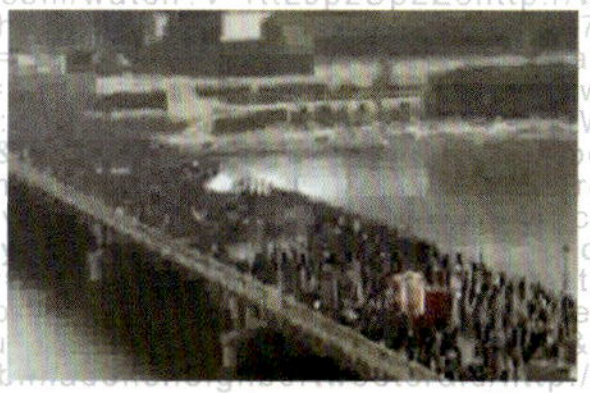

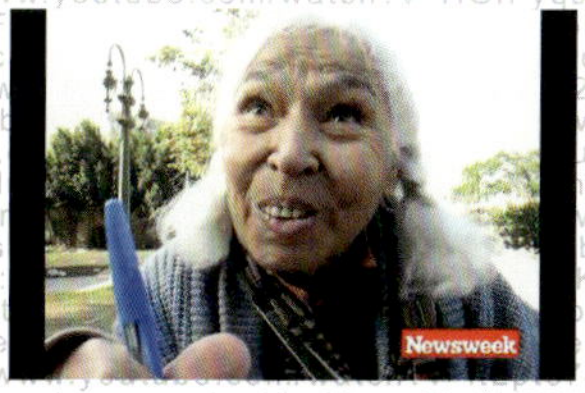
Newsweek

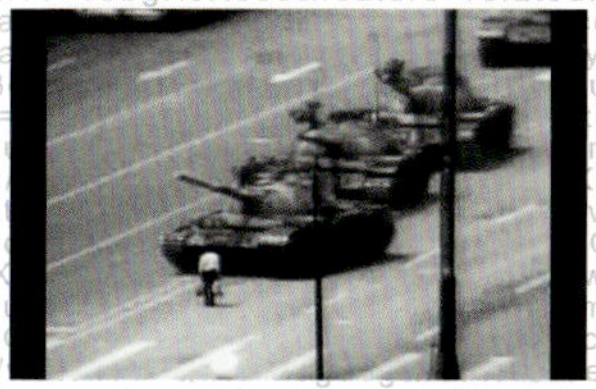

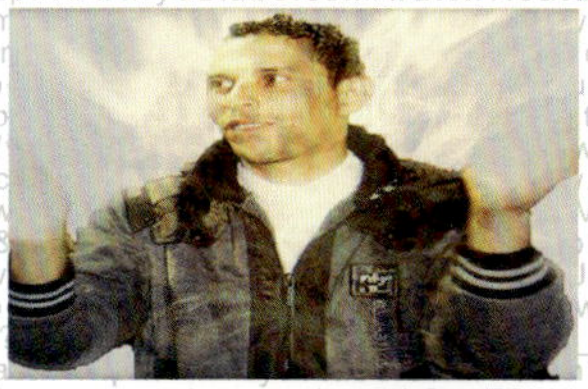

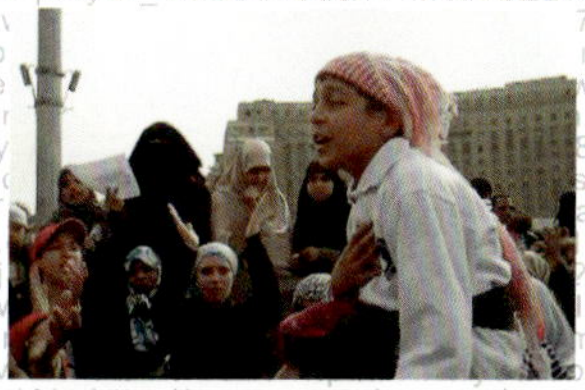

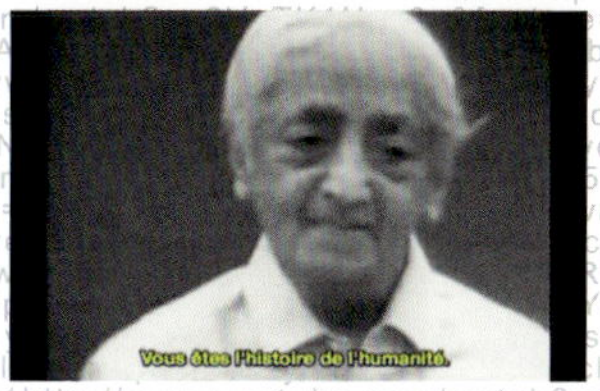
Vous êtes l'histoire de l'humanité.

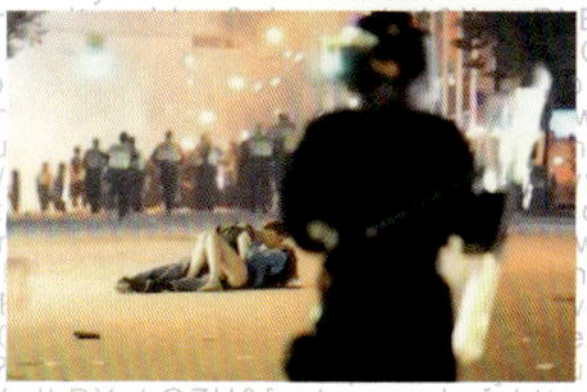

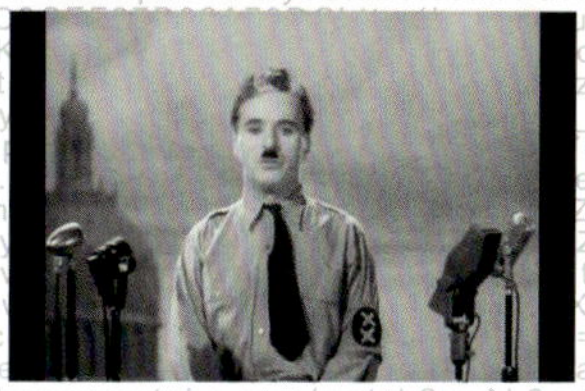

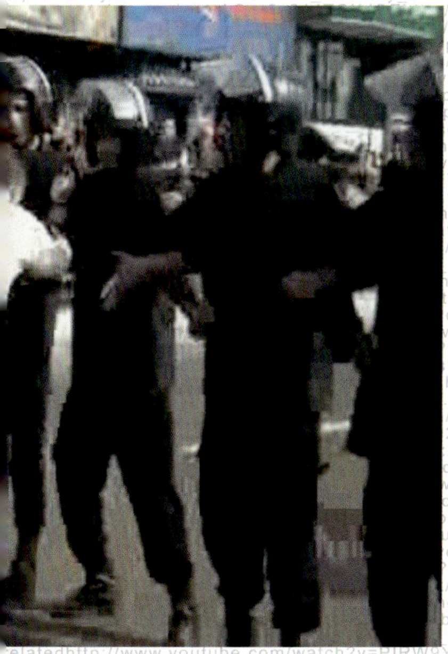

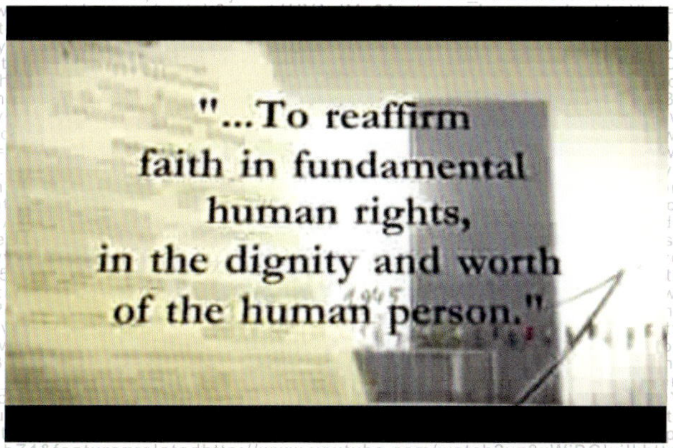
"...To reaffirm
faith in fundamental
human rights,
in the dignity and worth
of the human person."

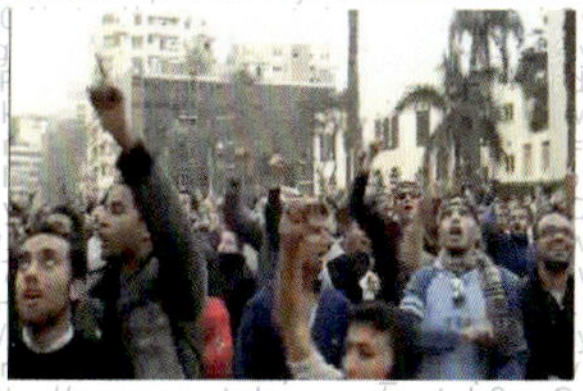

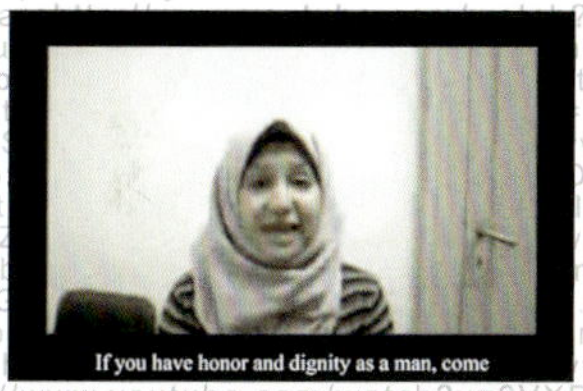
If you have honor and dignity as a man, come

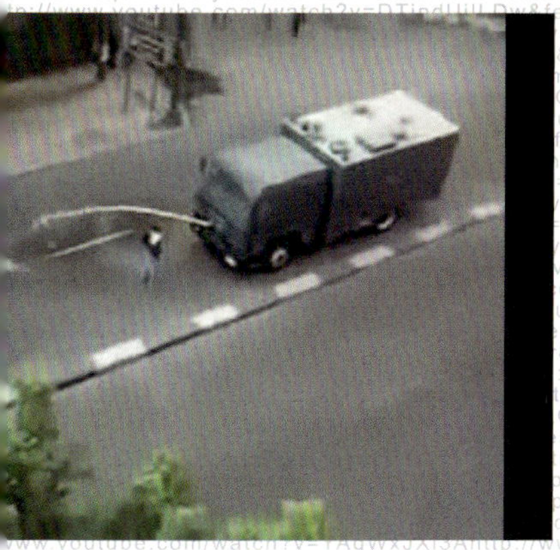

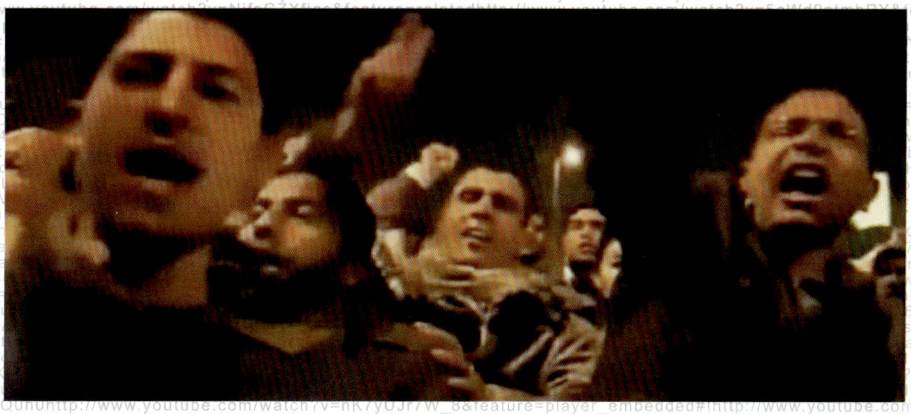

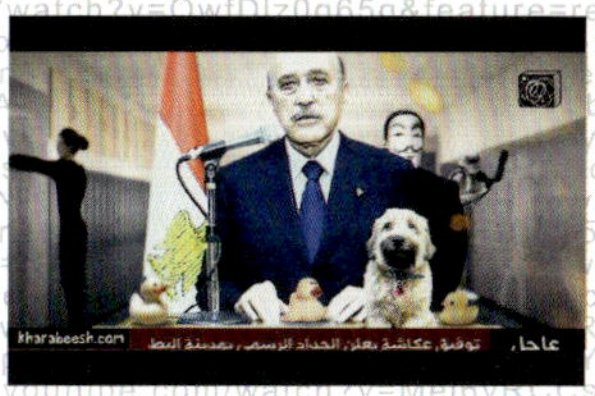
kharabeesh.com

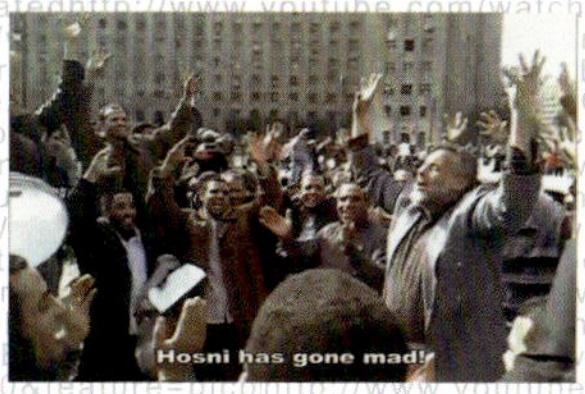
Hosni has gone mad!

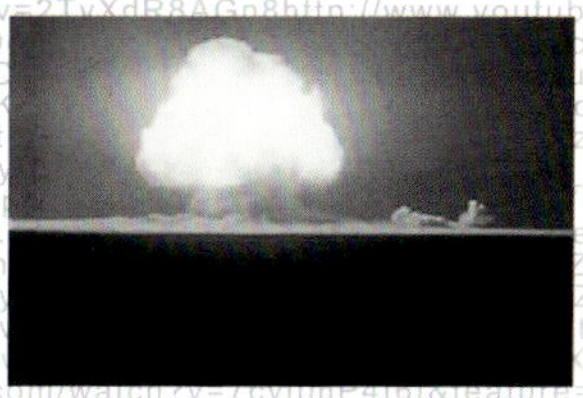

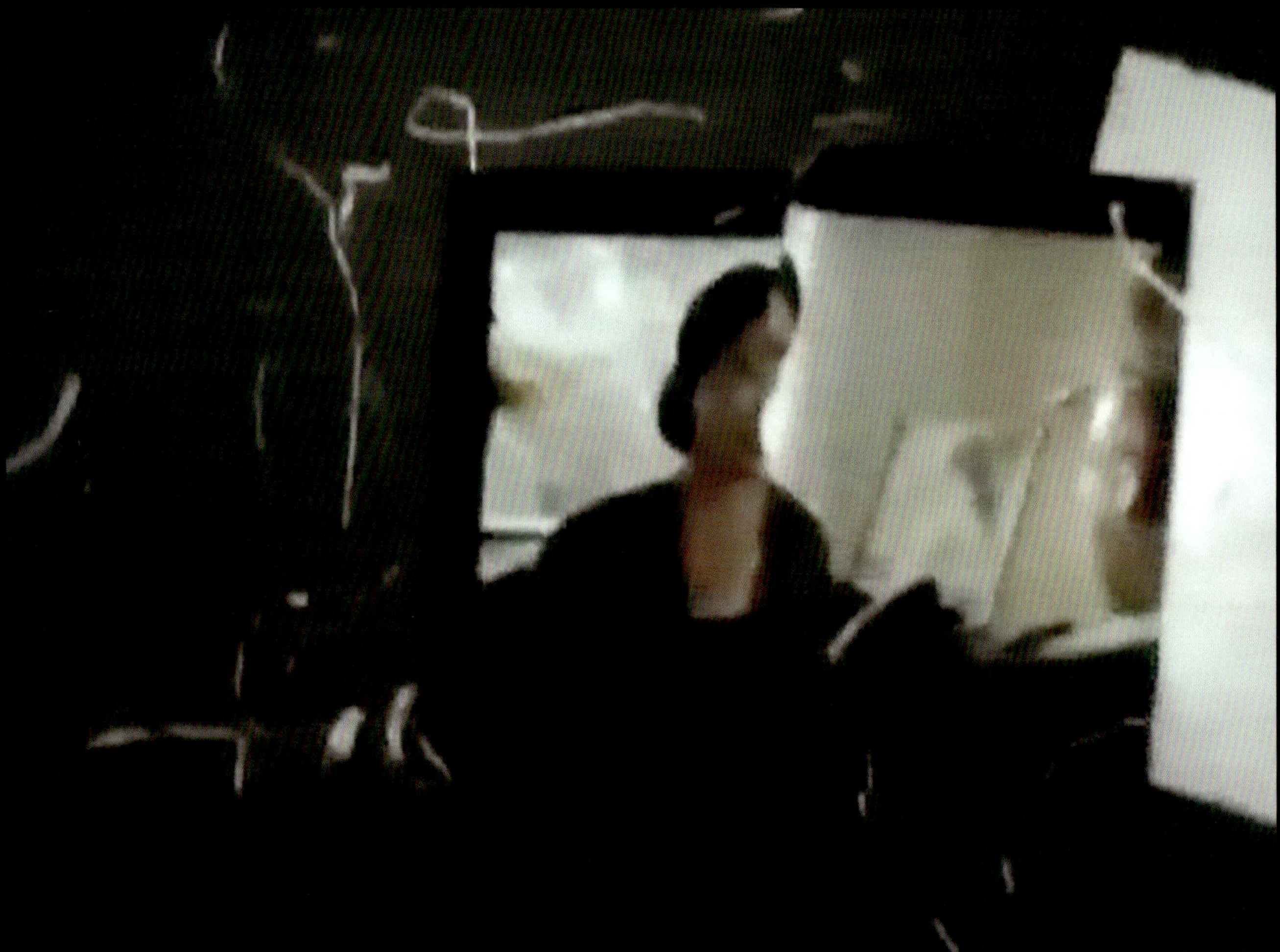

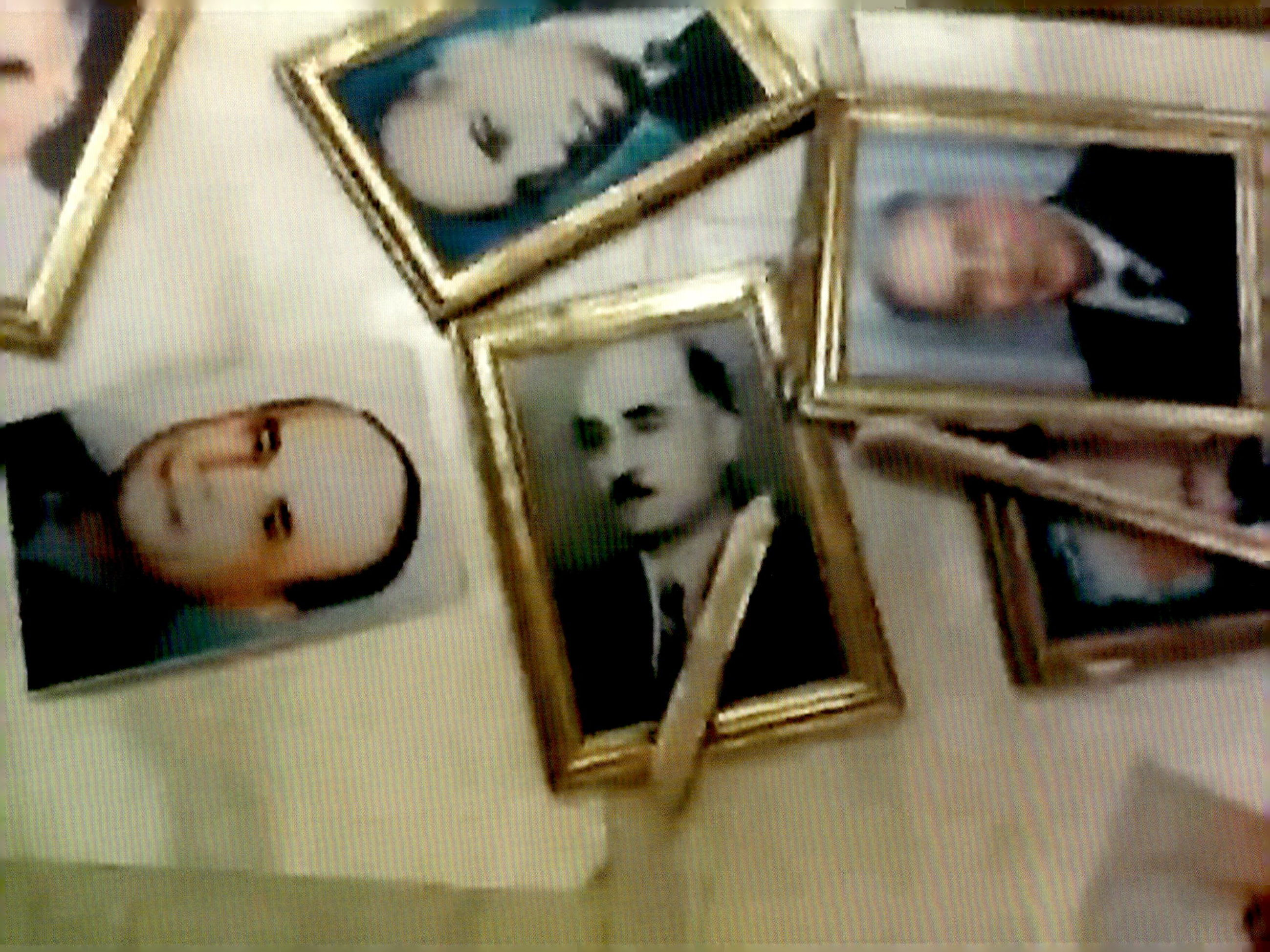

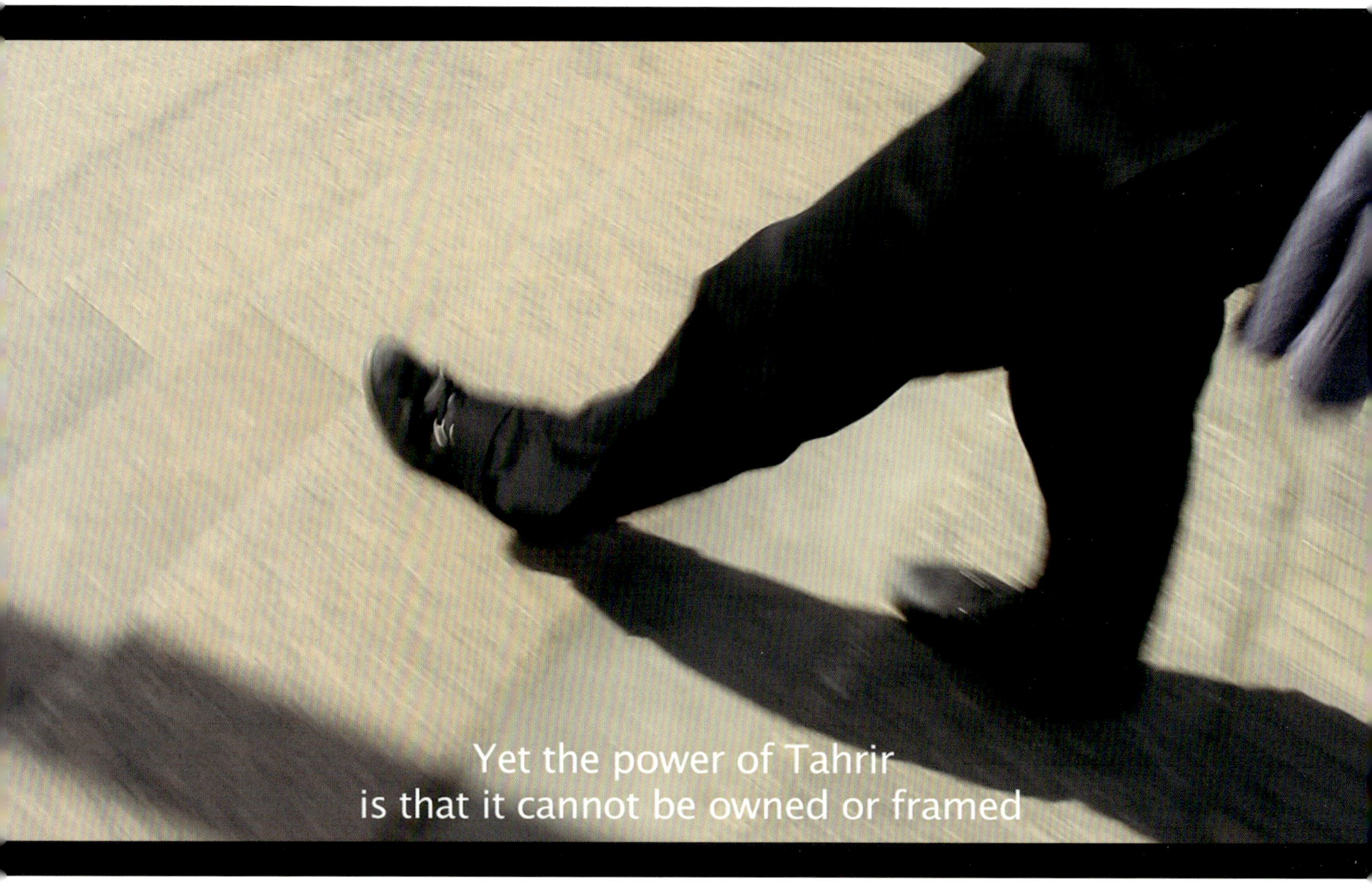

بس قوة الميـدان إنه ملوش ملكة، ملوش إطار يتحط فيه

Nadine Khan / نادين خان & Mariam Mekiwi / مريم مكيوي, *I Will Speak of the Revolution*, 2011
HD video, 1:07 min. / فيديو عالي الدقة، 1:07 دقيقة → p. / S. 137 / ص.٥٣

انتصار فردي أوجماعي أو في وجهة نظر عامة أو في حكاية عسكري أو شاب أو حجرة أو شعار أو صوت أو شهيد أو دمعة أو أو أو

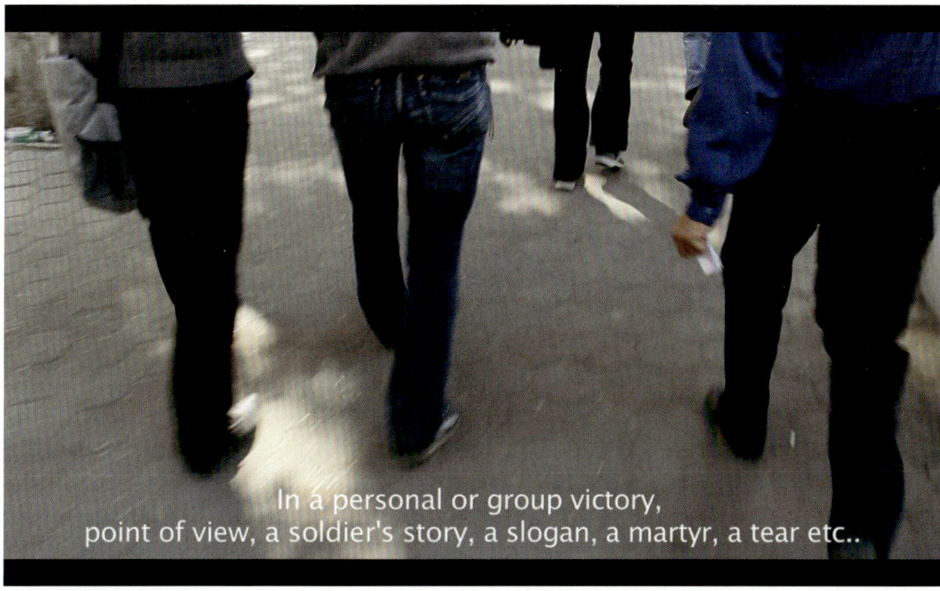

كلها قصص جميلة وملهمة هتطلع بس في الوقت المناسب وقت ماحس إن في وسط فرصة التغير اللي عندي دلوقتي مبقتش فرصة بقت حقيقة

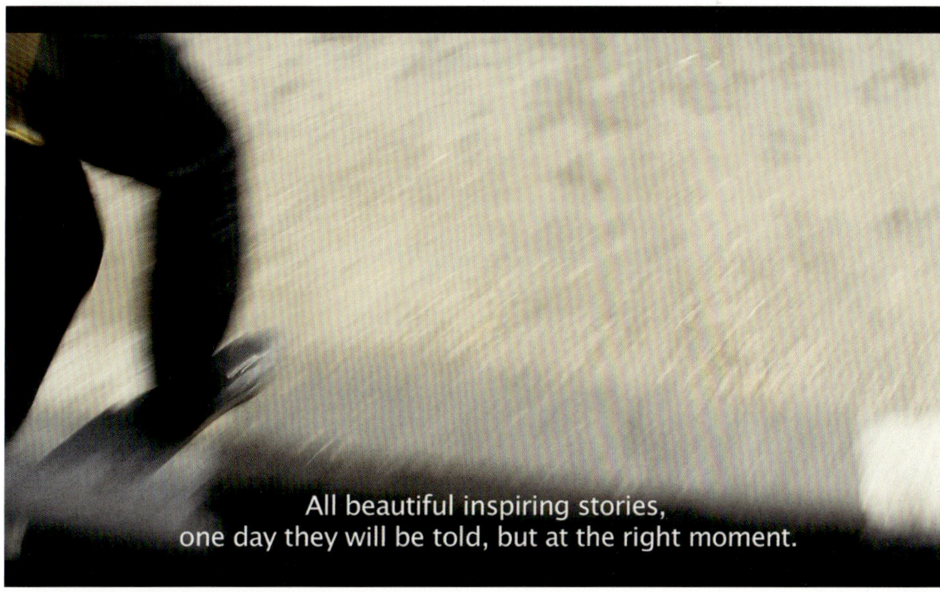

متهيألي إني متكلمش عن الثورة دلوقتي أحسن

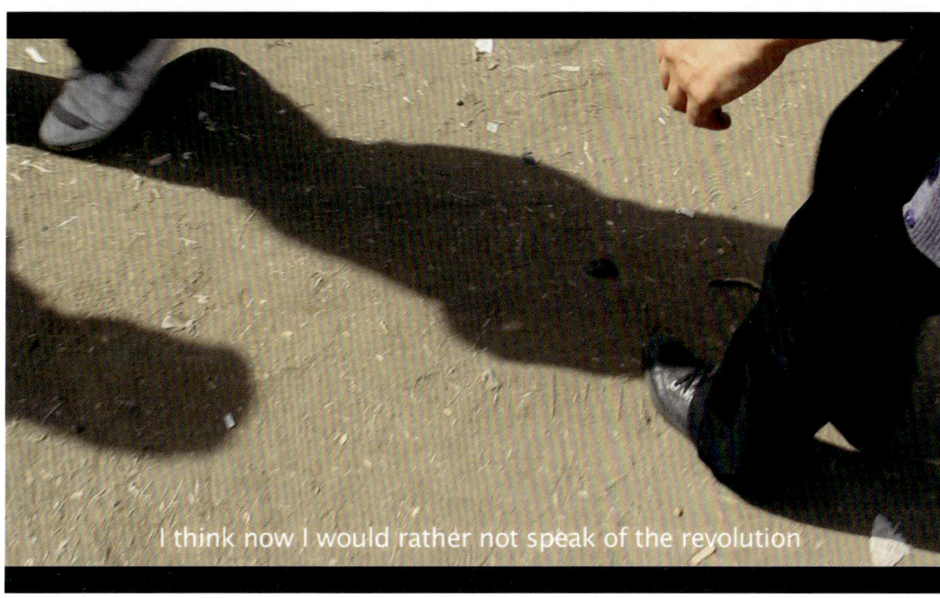

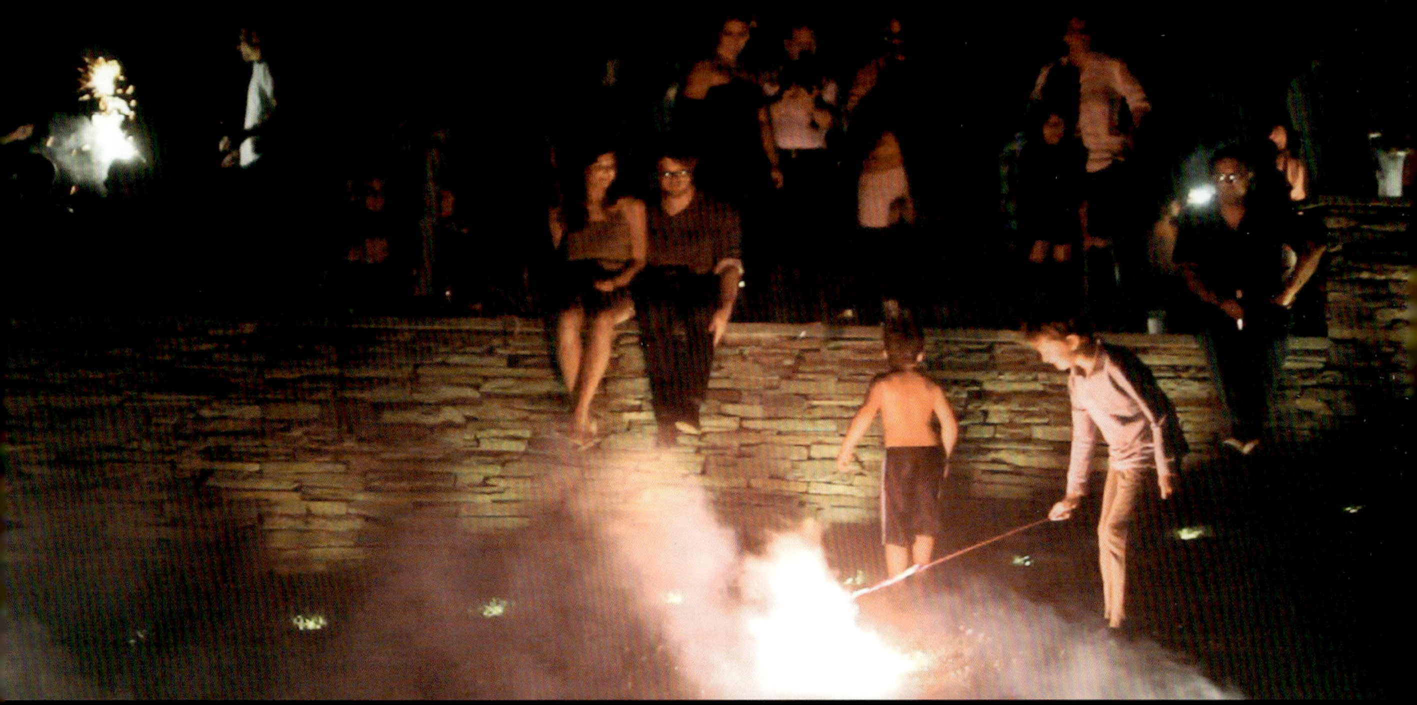

Jasmina Metwaly / ياسمينة متولي, *Play Time*, 2012
Installation based on a video projection (5:00 min.) and a slide projection (20 video stills transferred on to slide transparencies) / Installation aus Videoprojektion (5:00 min.) und Diaprojektion (20 Videostills,transferiert auf Diafilm) / عمل فني مجمع من عرض فيديو (5:00 دقائق) وعروض صور سلايد (20 صورة ثابتة من الفيديو منقولة إلى صور سلايد)
→ pp. / S. 137–138 / ص. ٥٥

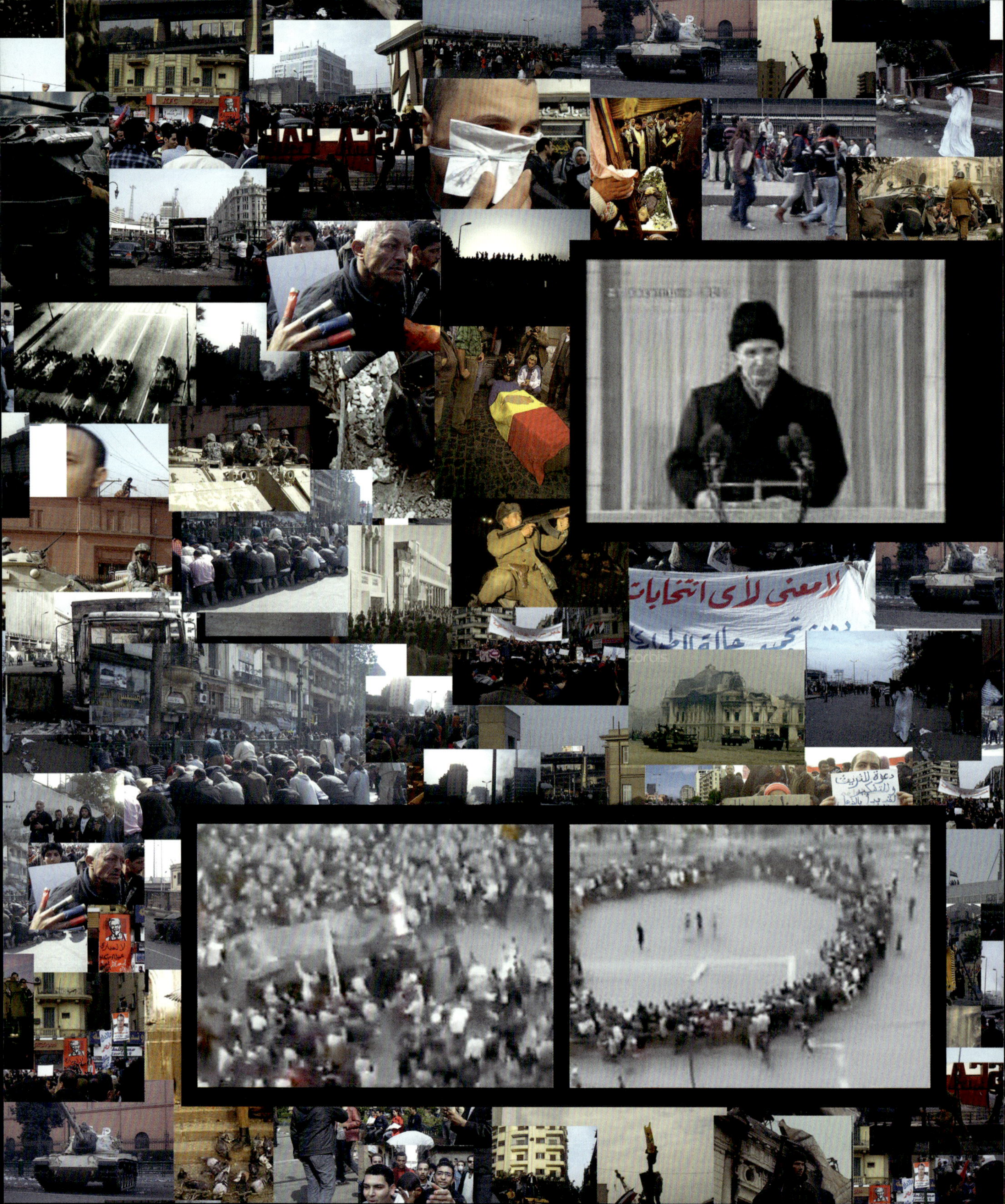
لامعنى لأى انتخابات

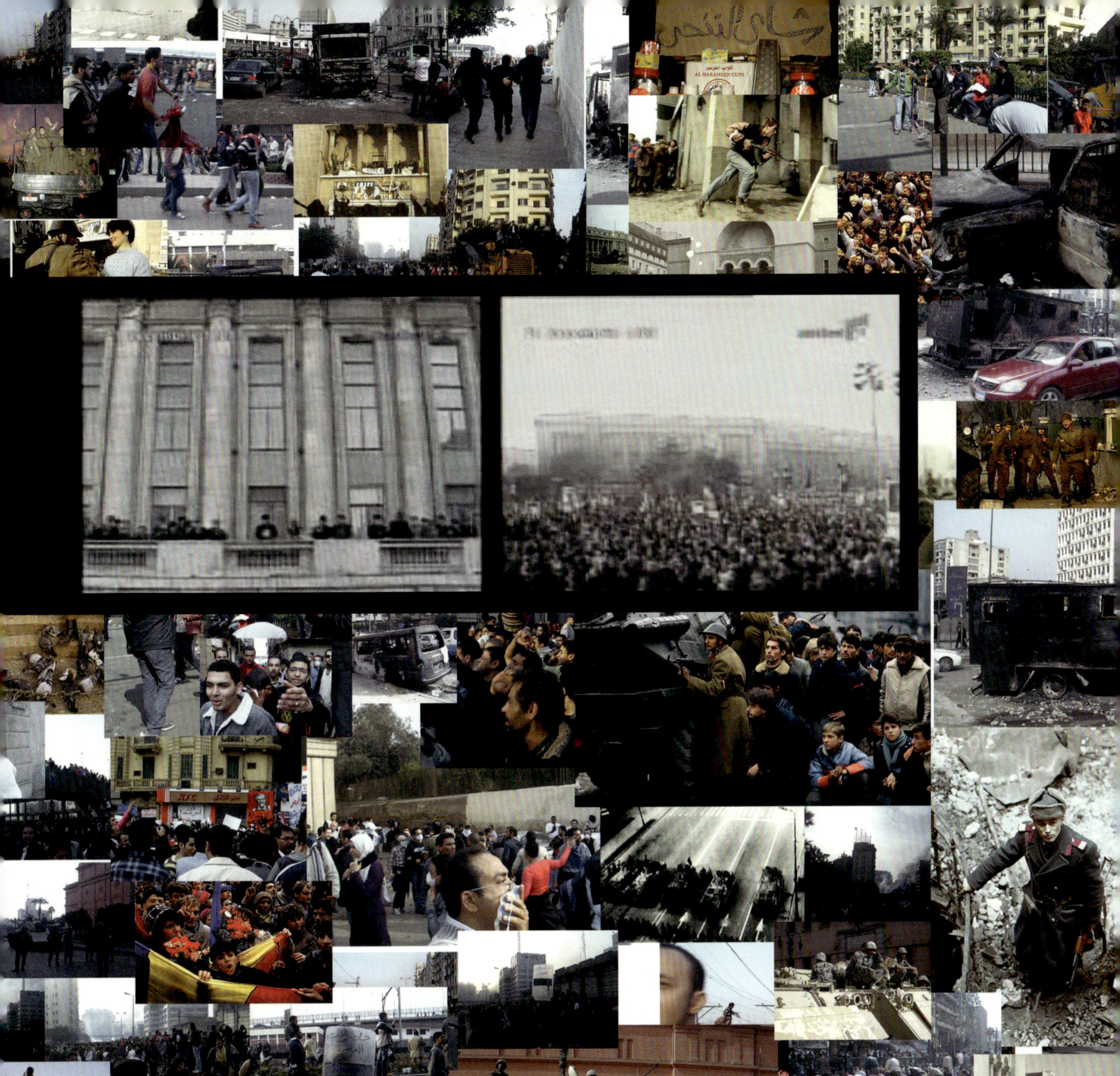

Ibrahim Saad / إبراهيم سعد, *The House of the Republic*, 2012
Installation with large-scale photomontage and two-channel video presentation /
Installation aus großflächiger Fotomontage und Zwei-Kanal-Videopräsentation, 10:06 min. /
p. / S. 139 /

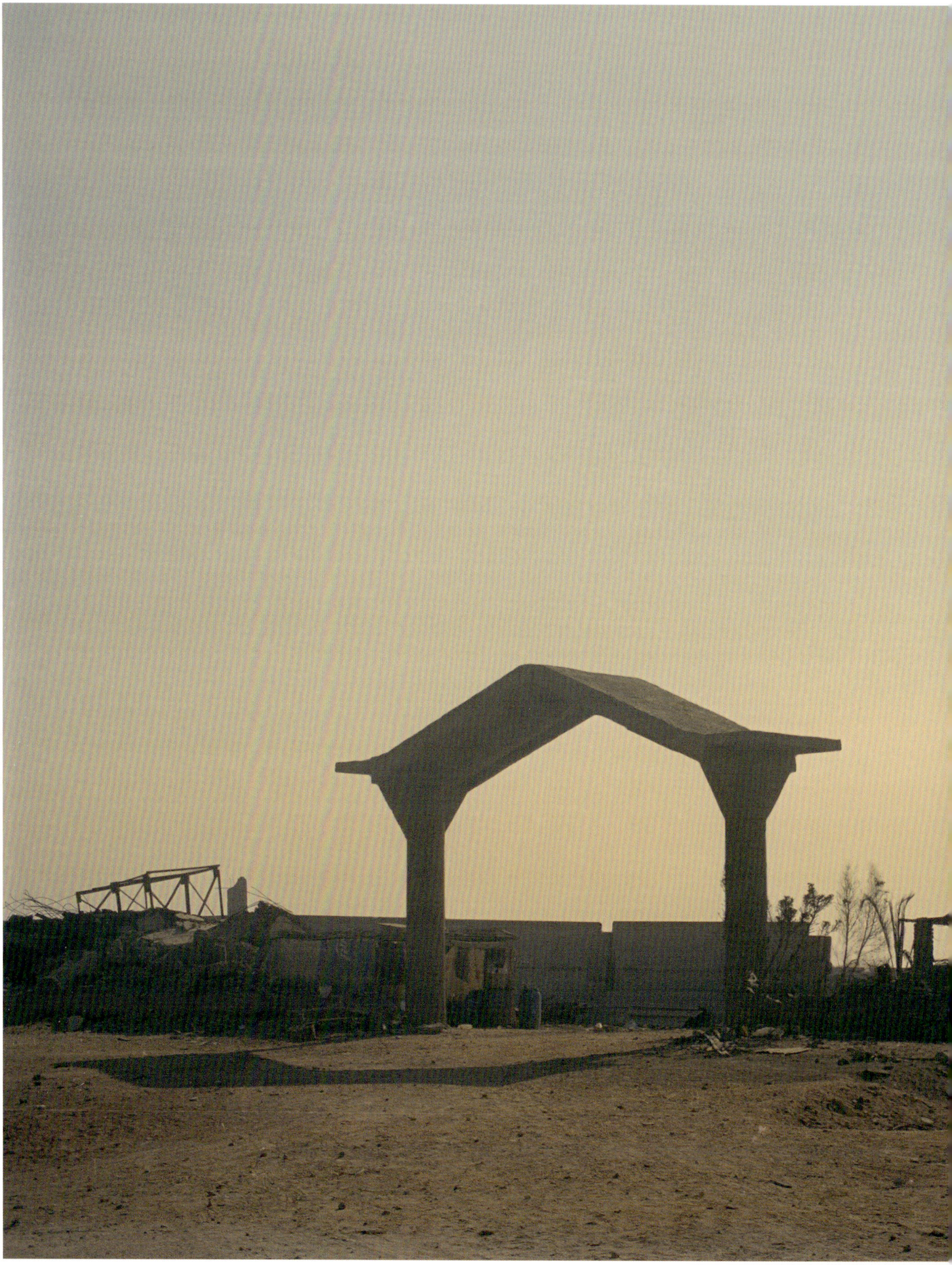

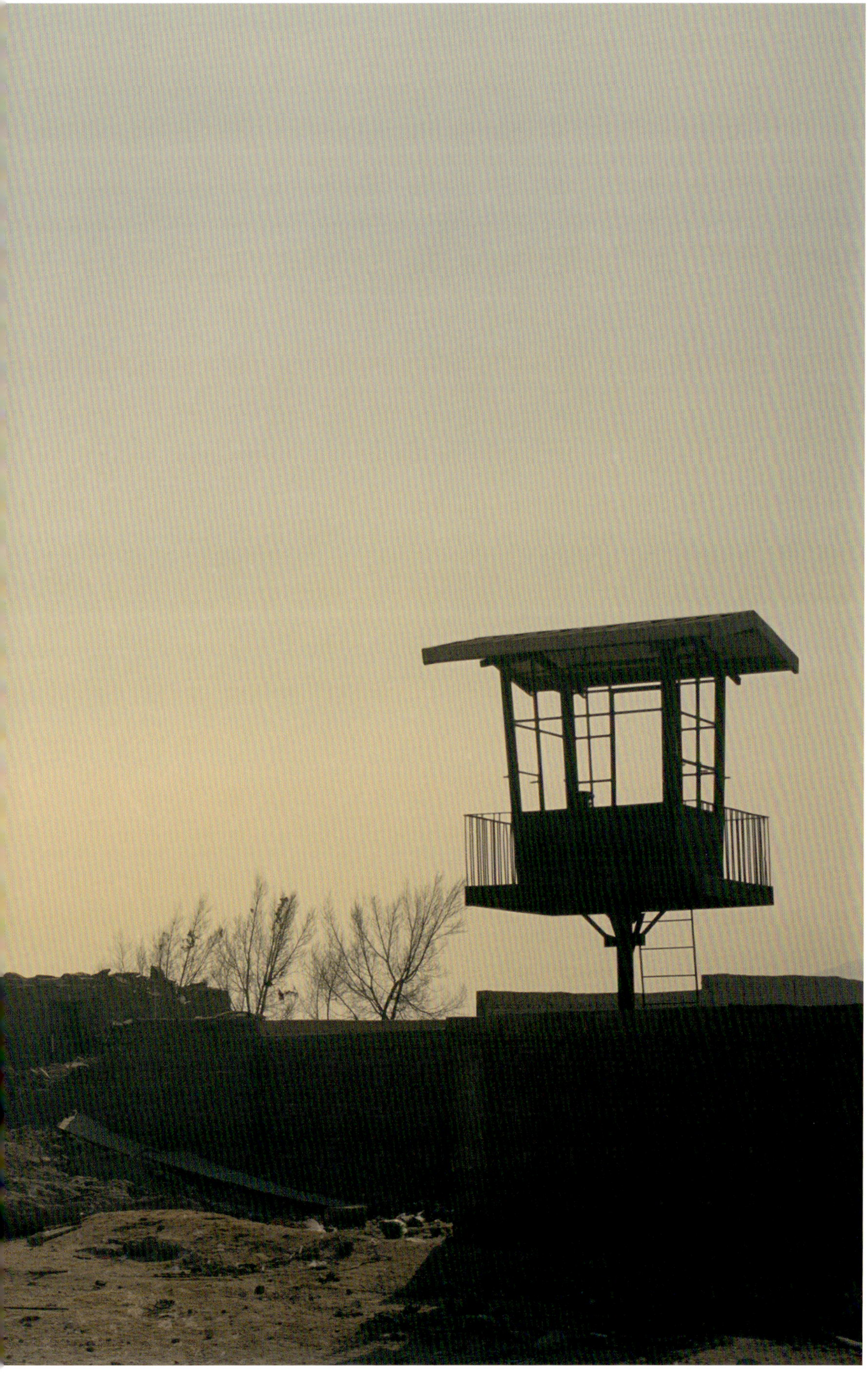

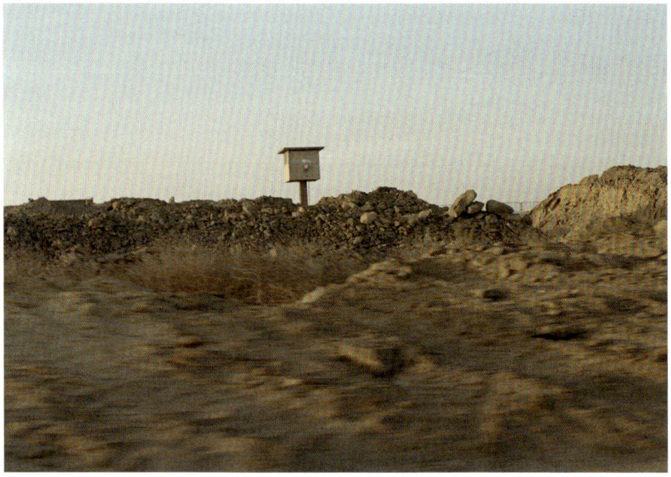

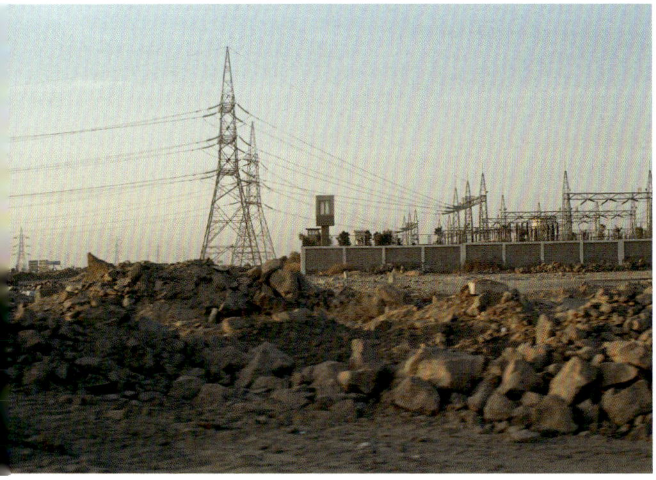

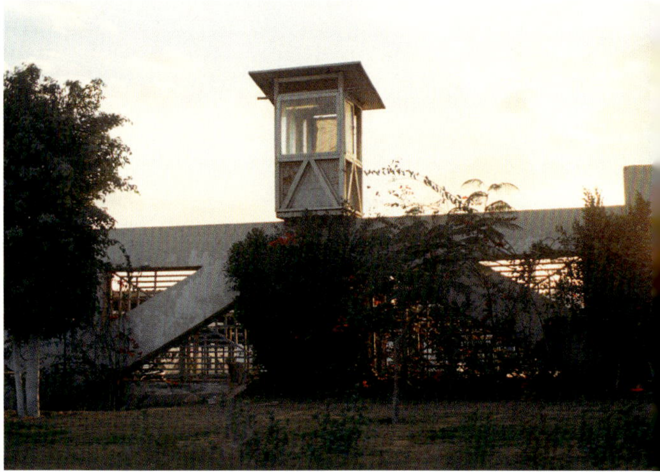

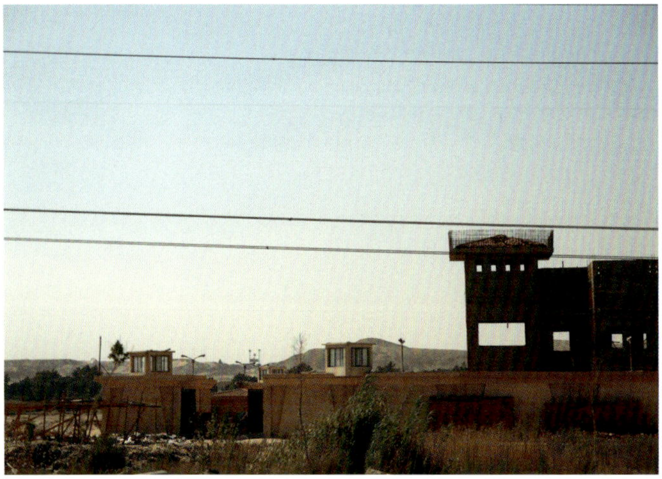

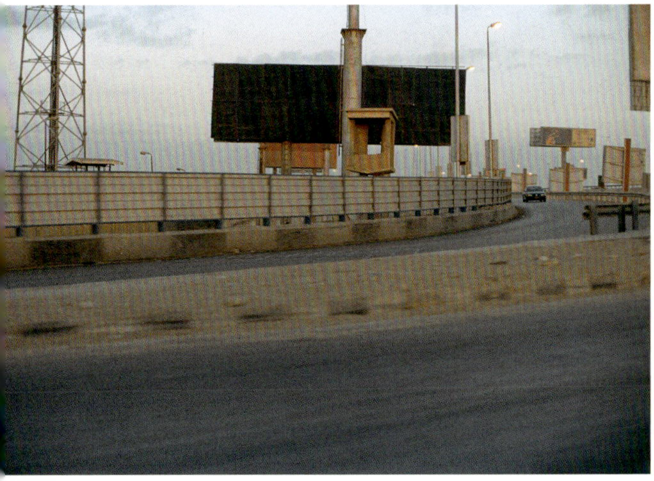

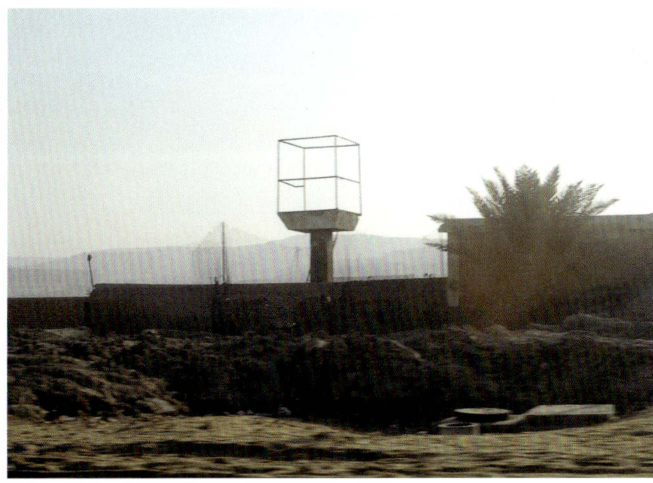

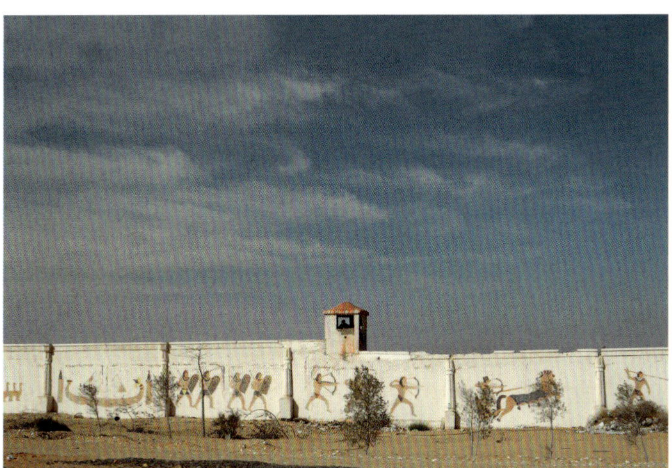

Eva Bertram / إيفا بيرترام, *High Seats*, 2008–2012
C-prints, 20 × 30 cm / مطبوعات صور ملونة / → p. / S. 131 / ص.٥٣

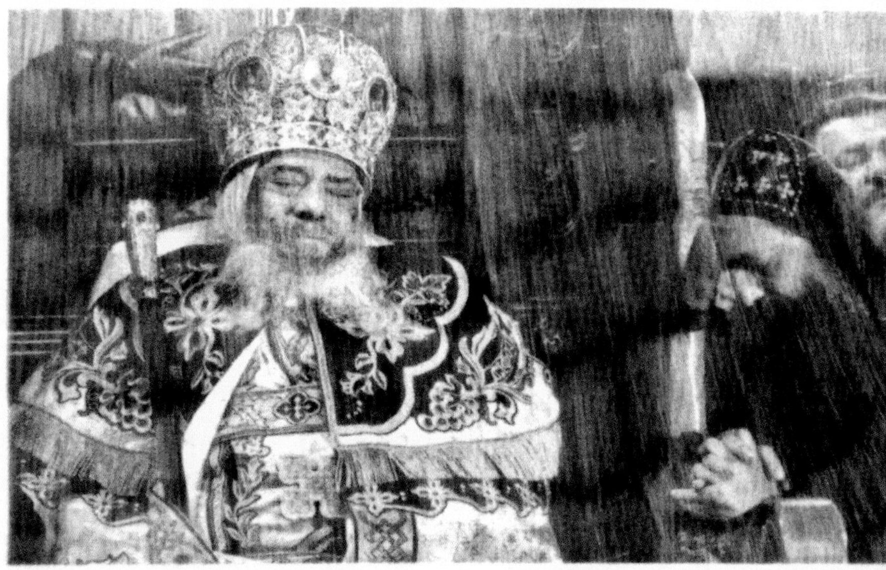

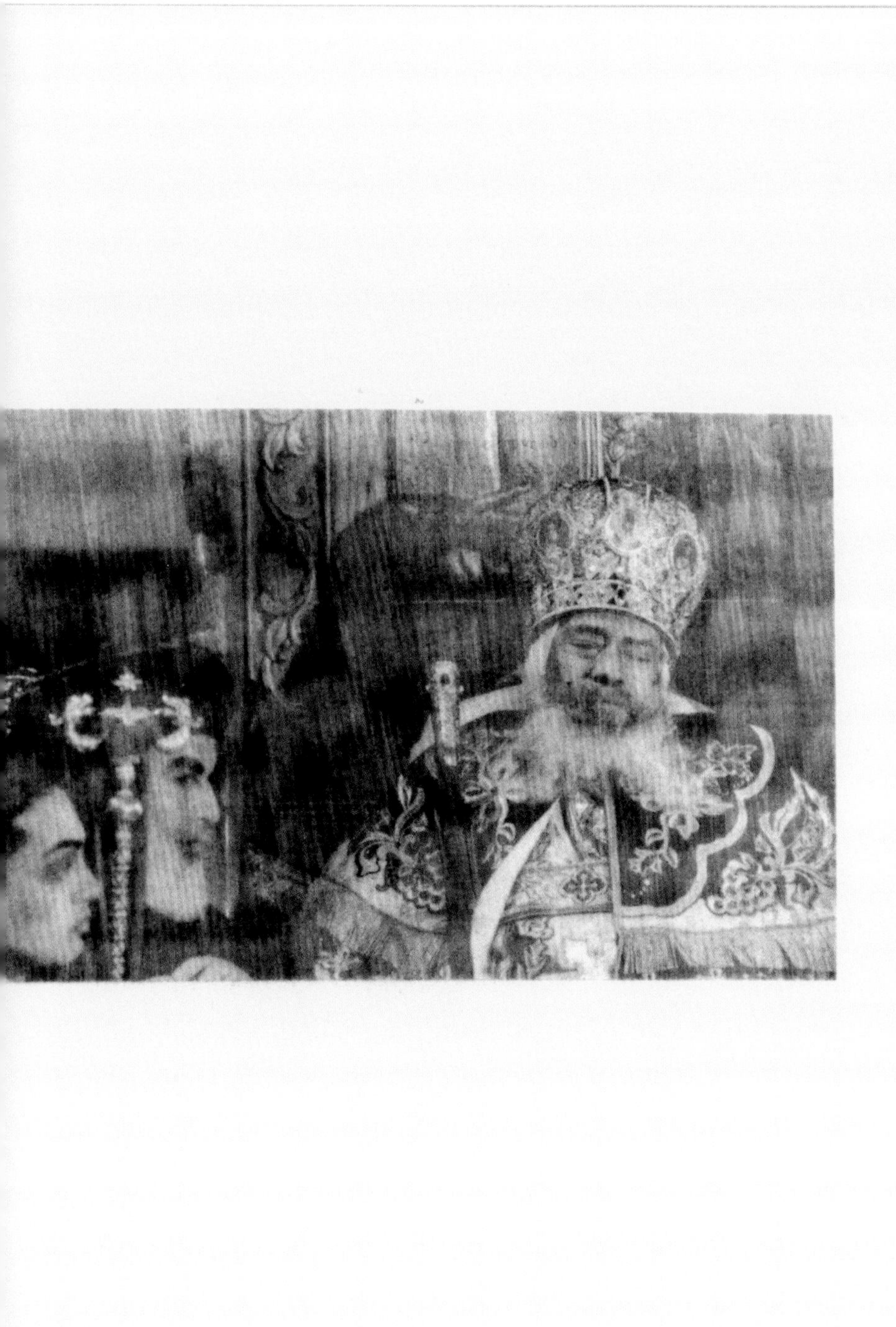

Taha Belal / طه بلال, *The Death of Pope Shenouda*, 2012
Newspaper transfer on paper / Zeitung auf Papier übertragen, 29.7×42 cm / ورق جرائد منقول و
ملصق على ورق → p. / S. 131 / ص.٥٣

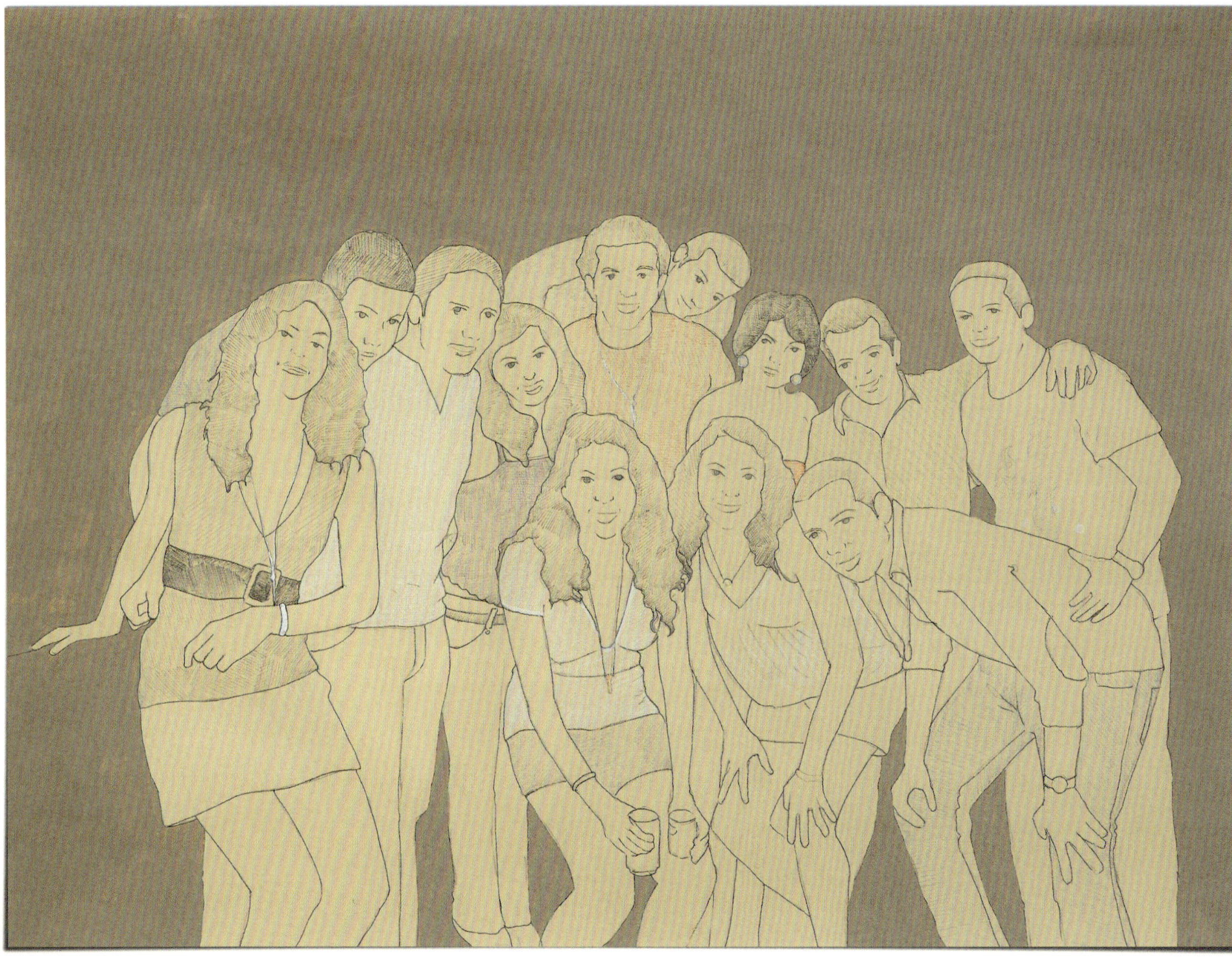

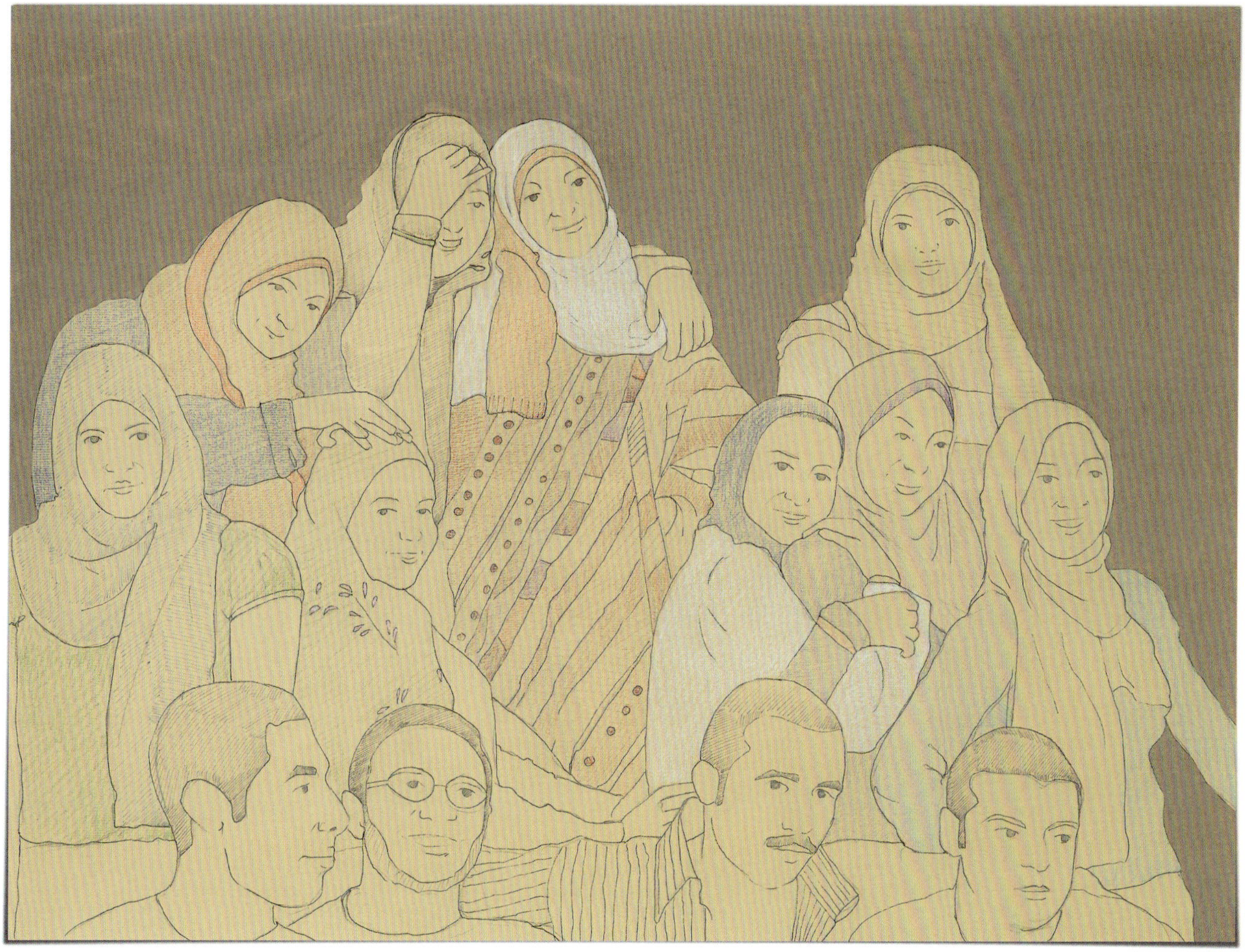

Ahmed Kamel / أحمد كامل, *Hypothetical Society*, 2009
Drawings on paper / Zeichnungen auf Papier, 49.5 × 56 cm, 32 × 50 cm / رسومات على ورق
→ pp. / S. 136–137 / ص. ٥٥

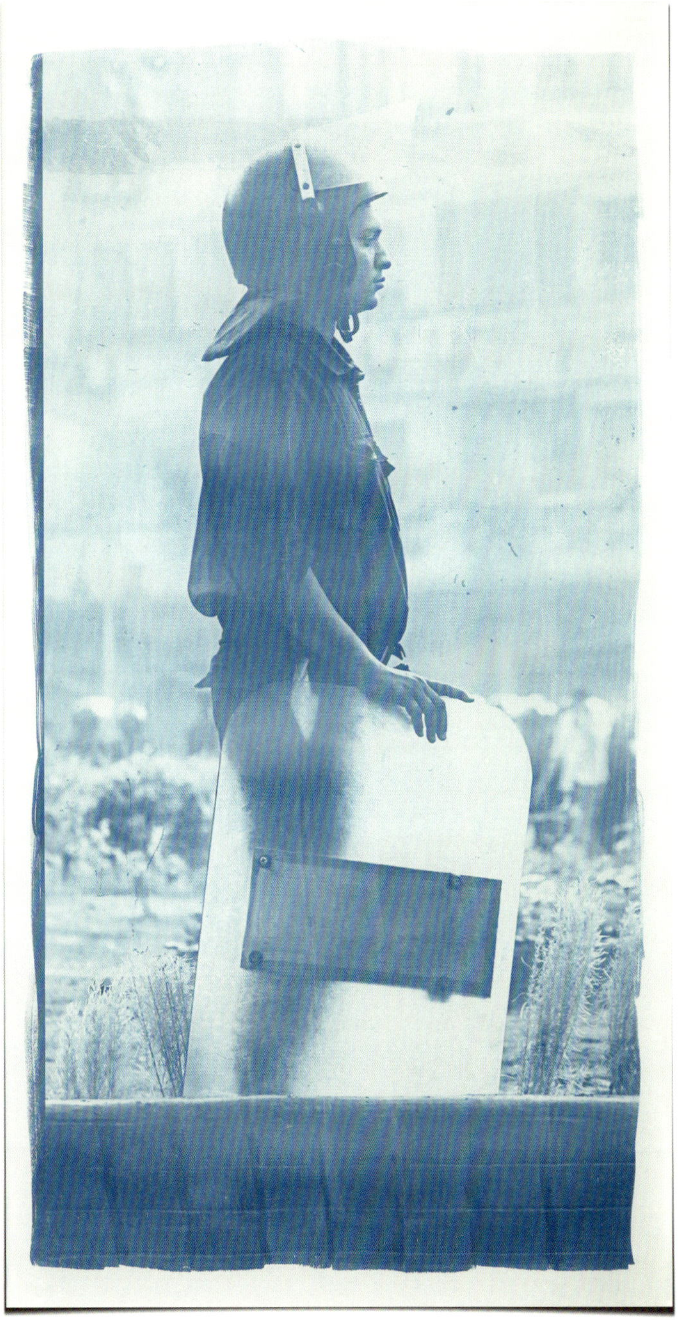

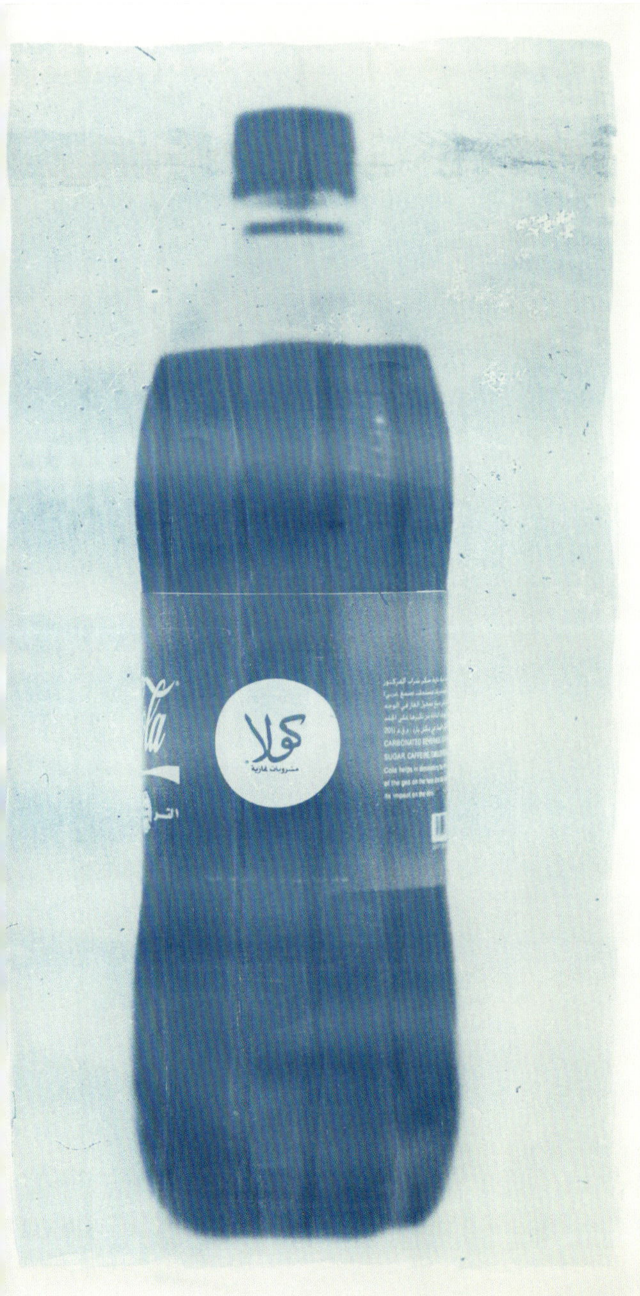

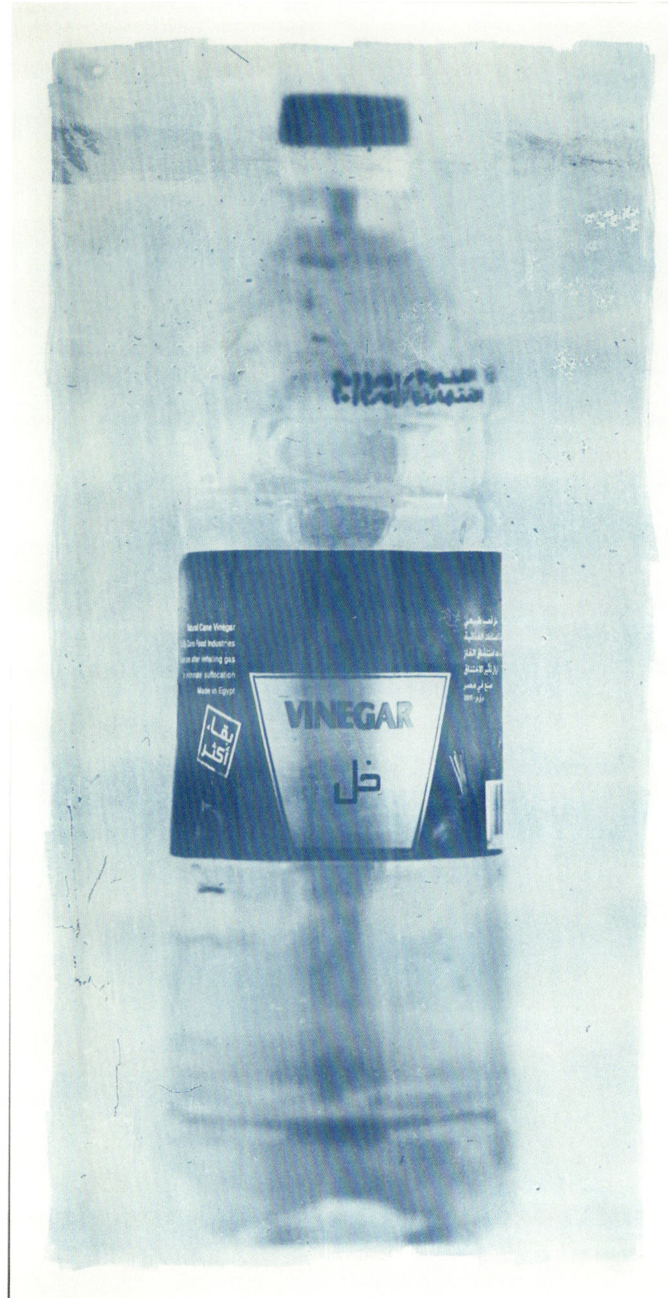

Mohamed Ezz / محمد عز, *Vinegar .. Soldier .. Coke*, 2011
Cyanotype prints on cotton paper / Cyanotypie-Drucke auf Baumwollpapier, 120 × 60 cm /
طباعة زرقاء على ورق قطني ⟶ p. / S. 134 / ص. ٥٤

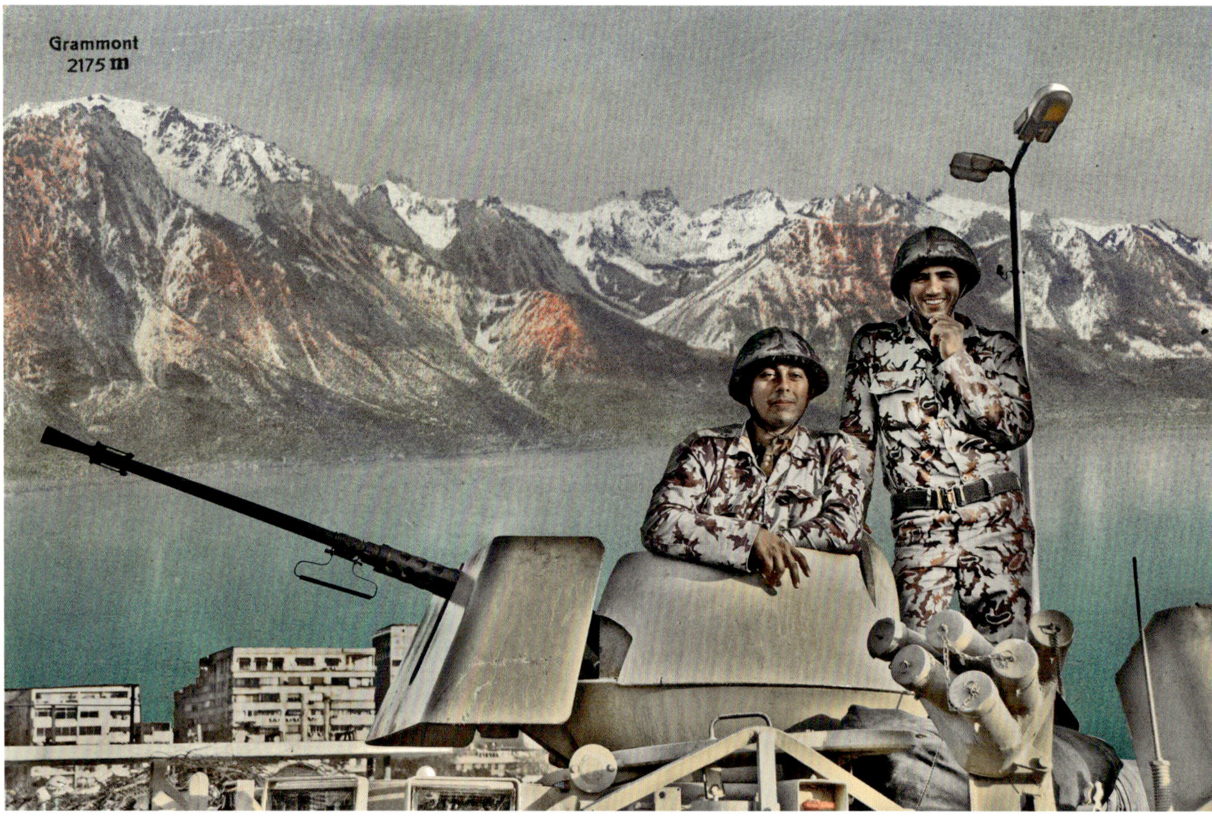
Grammont
2175 m

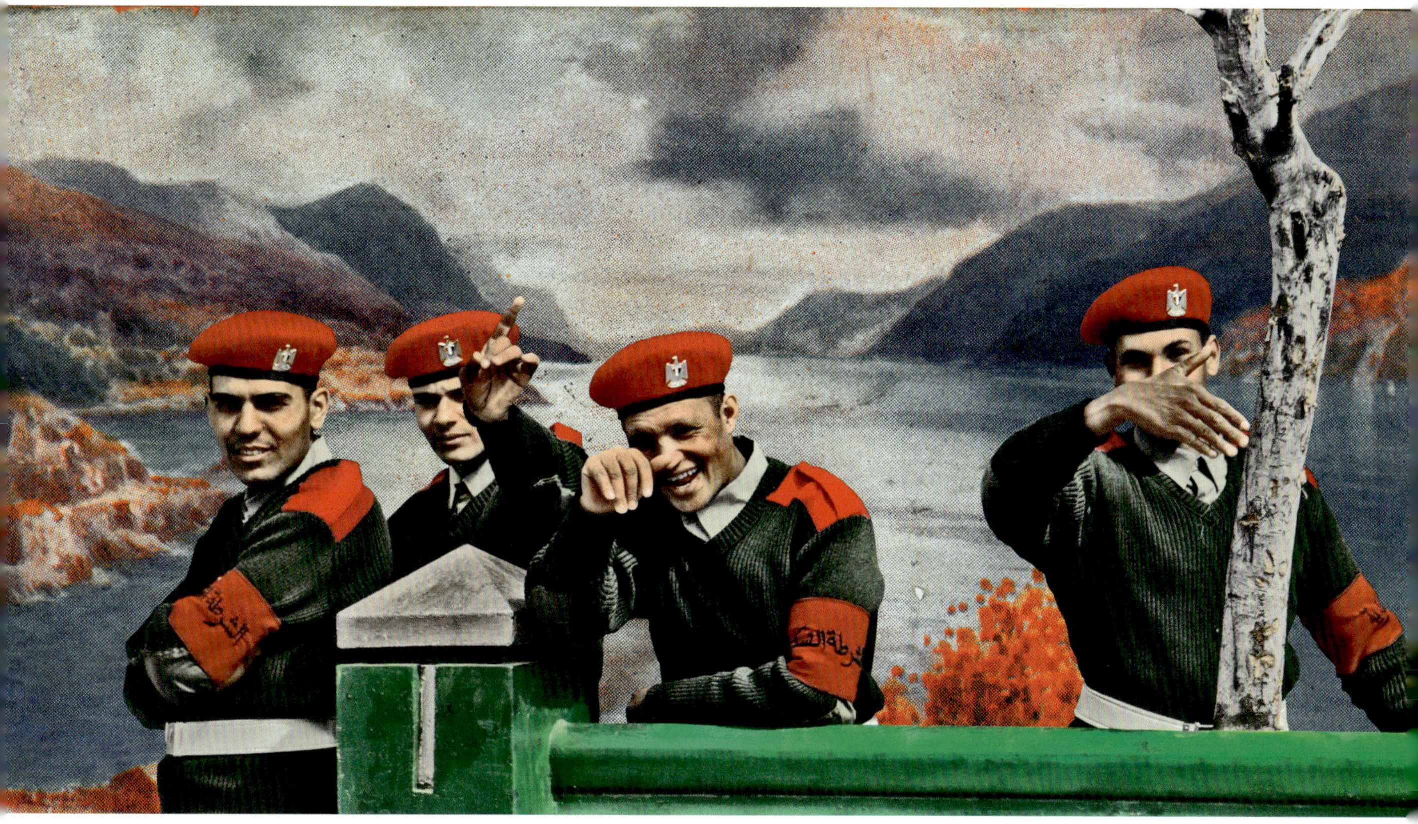

Nermine Hammam / نرمين همام, from the series / aus der Serie / من سلسلة *Upekkha*, 2011
Inkjet prints, 60 × 90 cm, 50 × 90 cm / مطبوعات حبر سائل ⟶ p. / S. 136 / ص. ٥٥

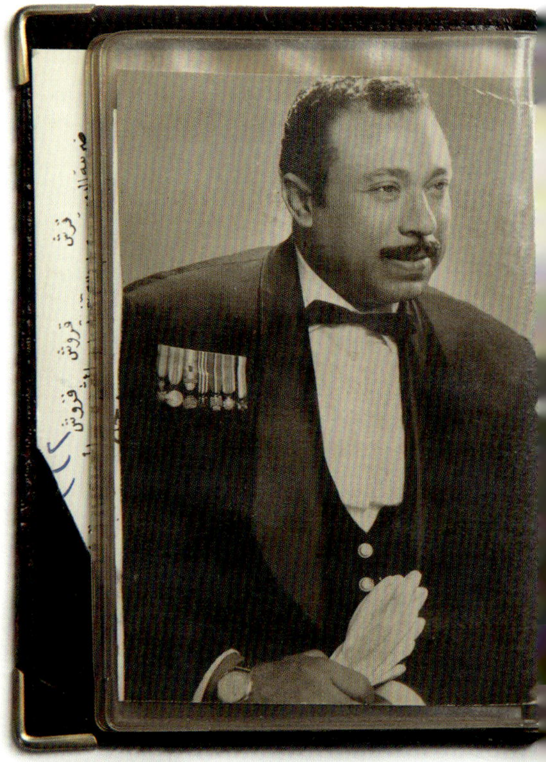

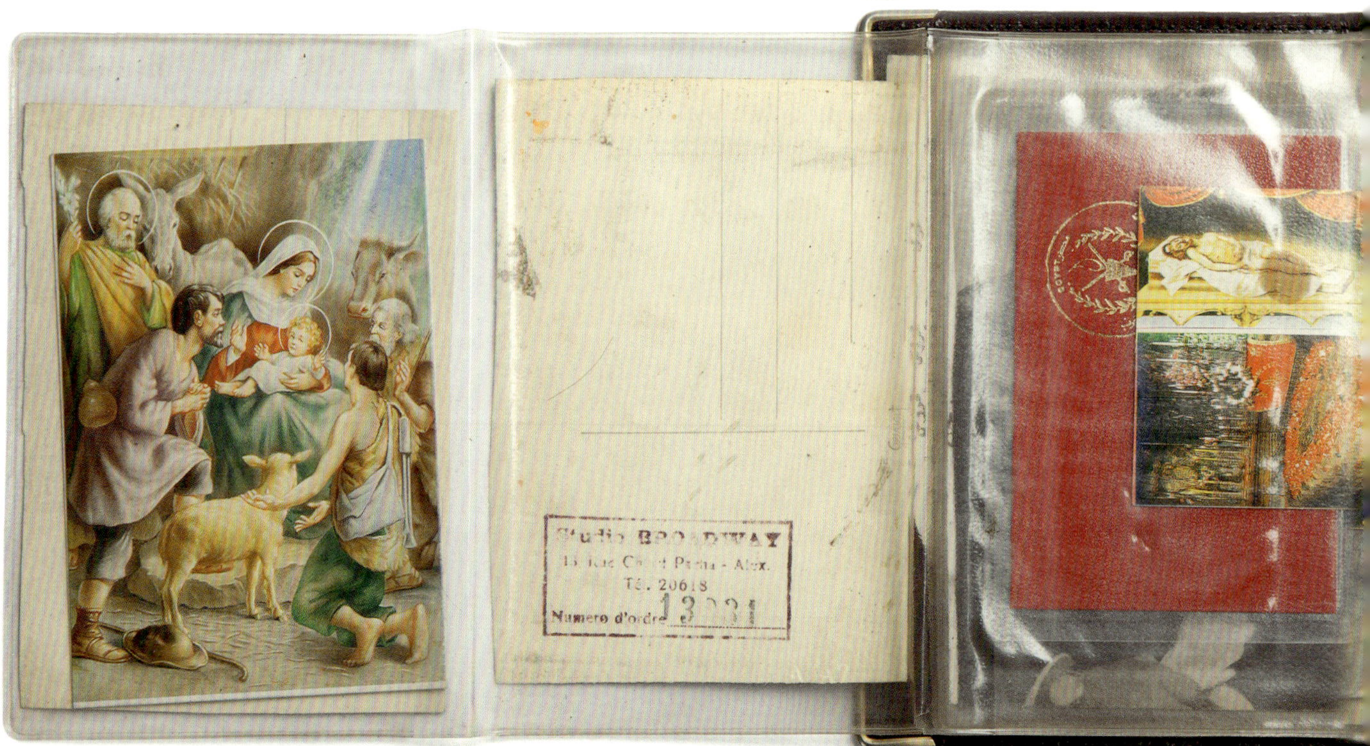
BROADWAY
Alex.
Numero d'ordre

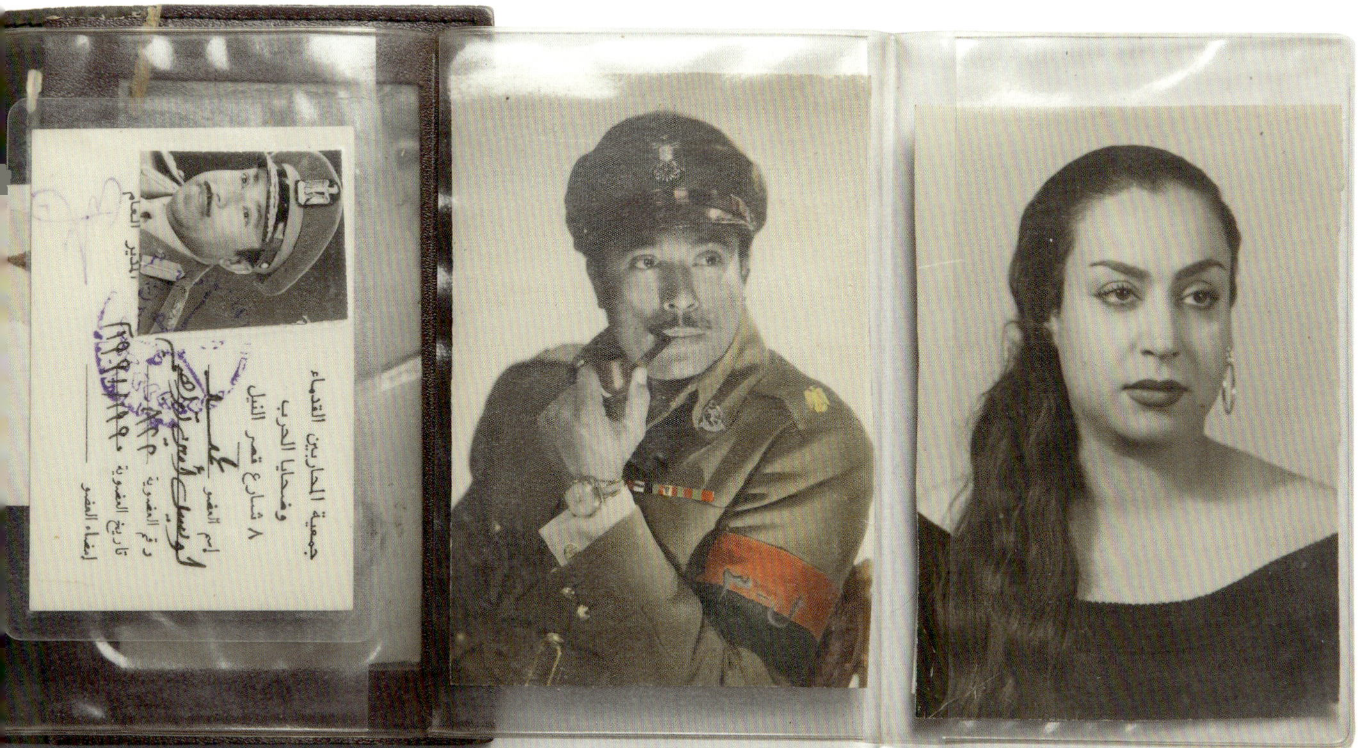
جمعية المحاربين القدماء
وضحايا الحرب
٨ شارع قصر النيل
إسم العضو
رقم العضوية
تاريخ العضوية
إمضاء العضو
المدير العام

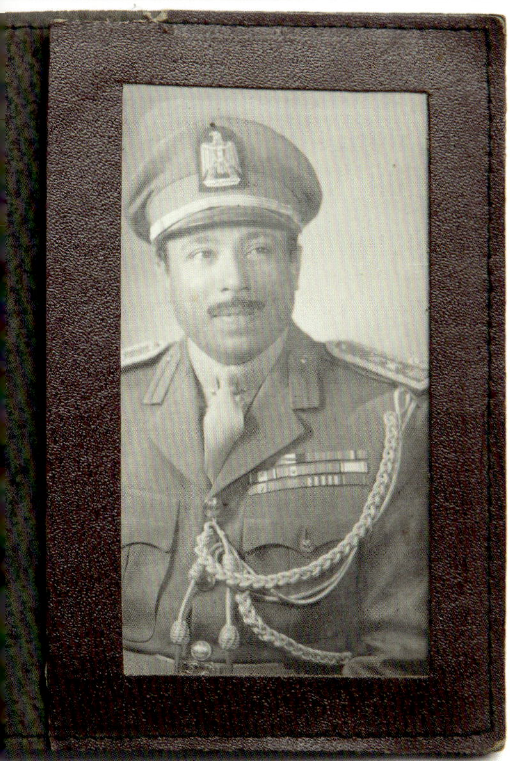

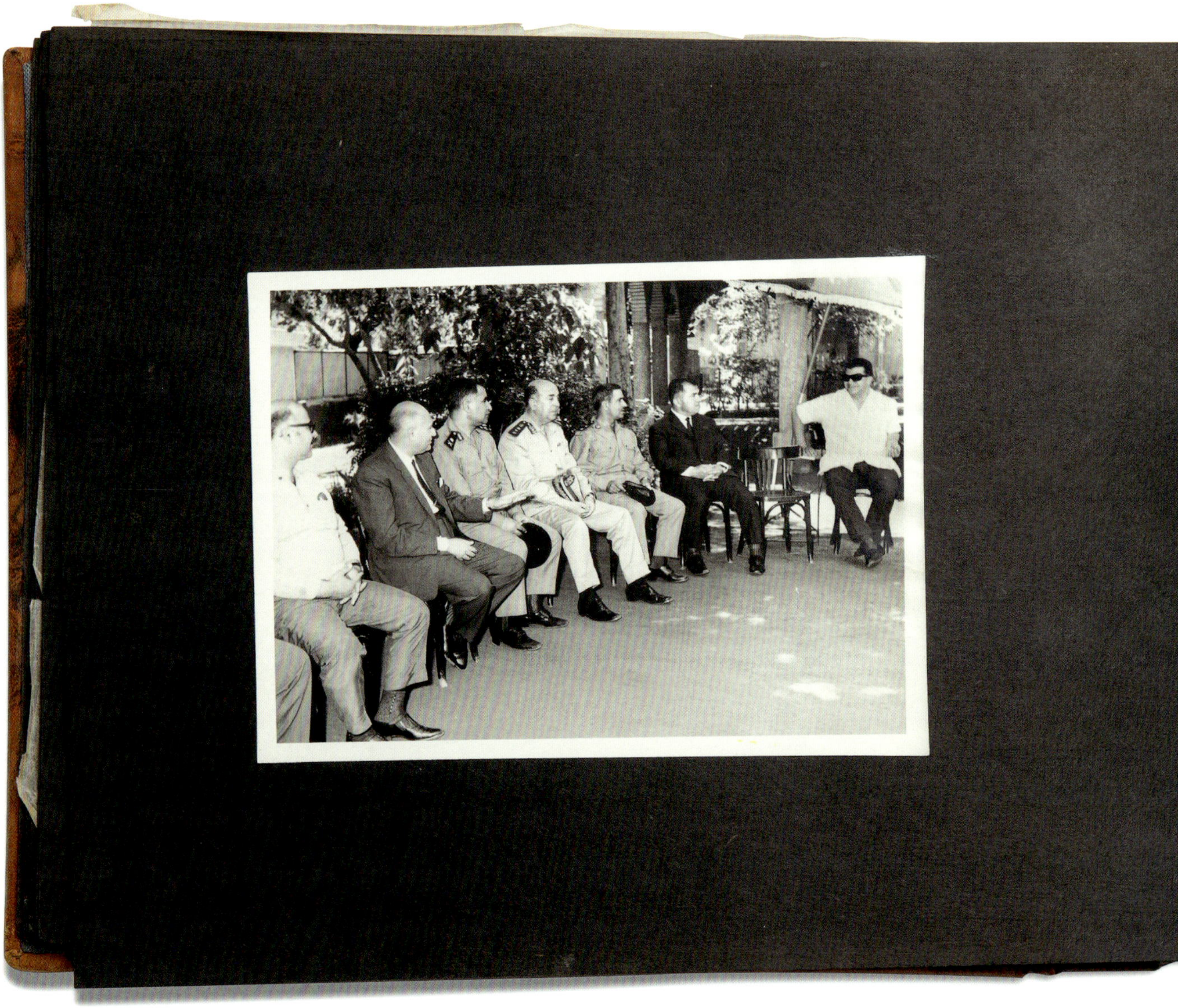

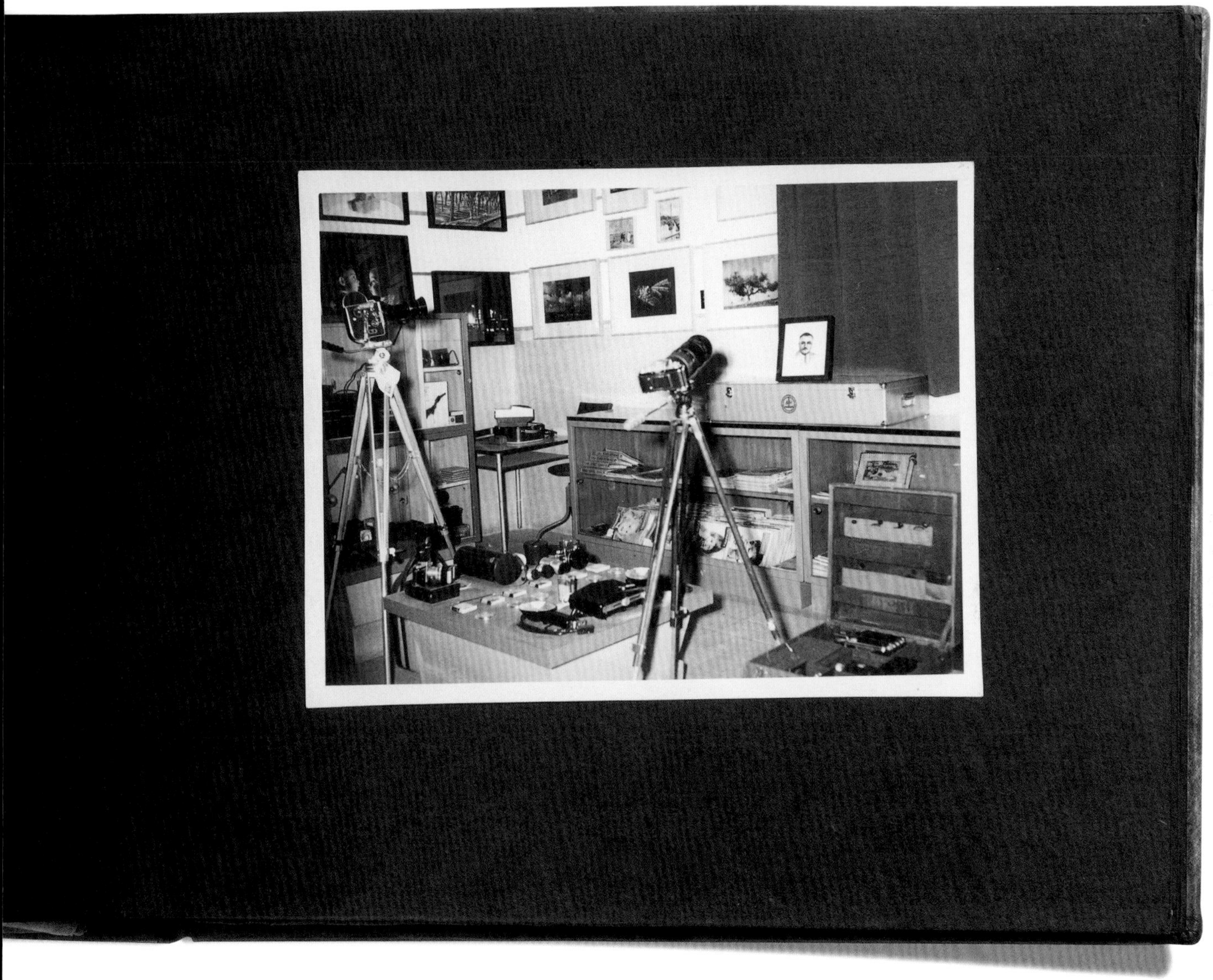

Heba Farid / هبة فريد, *Making Heroes – Photograph Albums from Egyptian Military and Police Officers*, early 1920s to late 1970s / *Fotoalben von ägyptischen Militär- und Polizeioffizieren*, frühe 1920er bis späte 1970er Jahre / ألبومات لأفراد من الجيش و الشرطة المصرية، أوائل العشرينات حتى أواخر السبعينات من القرن العشرين → pp. / S. 135 - 136 / ص. ٥٤, Collection / Sammlung: Amgad Naguib / مقتنيات أمجد نجيب

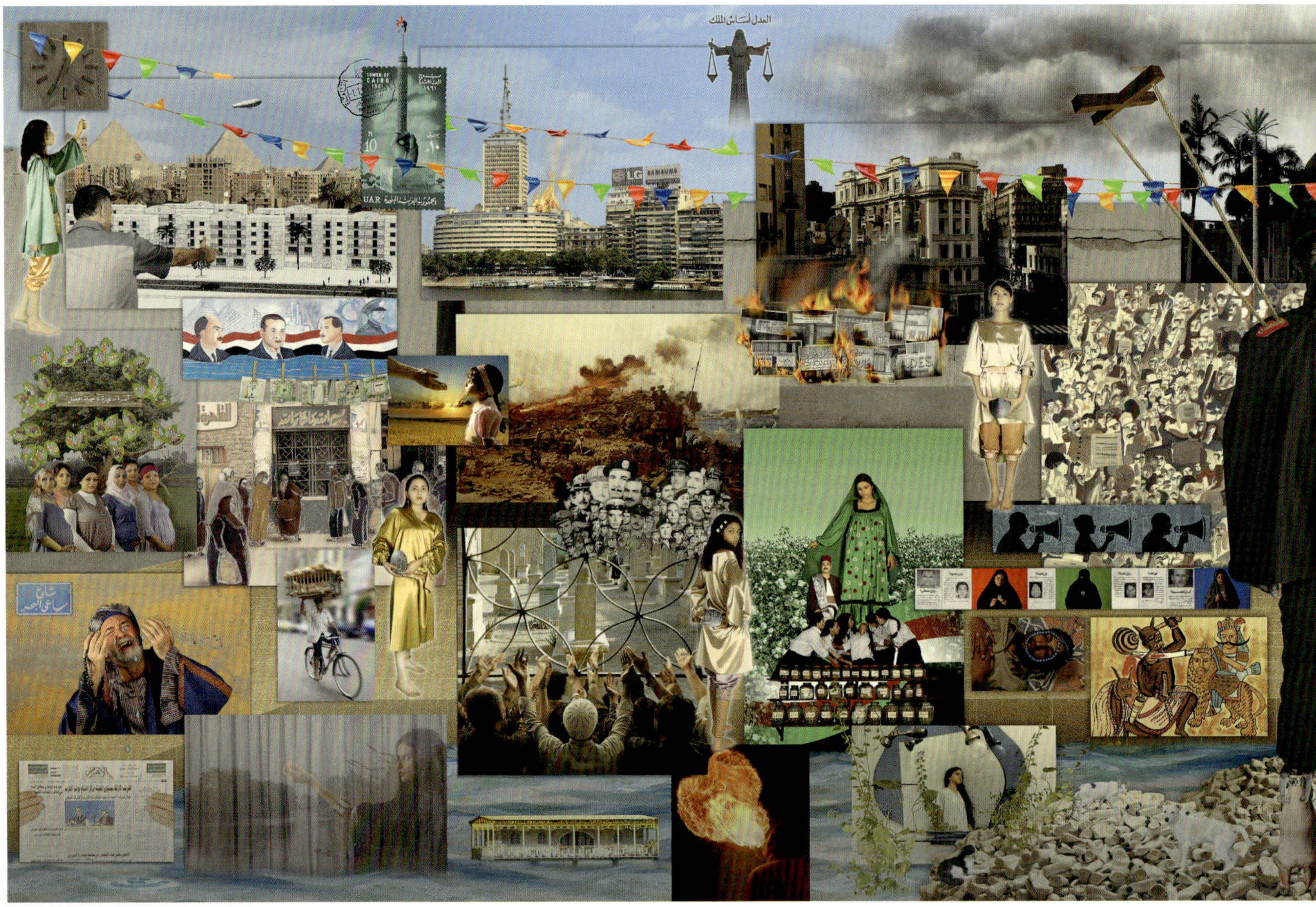
العدل أساس الملك
UAR
LG
SAMSUNG

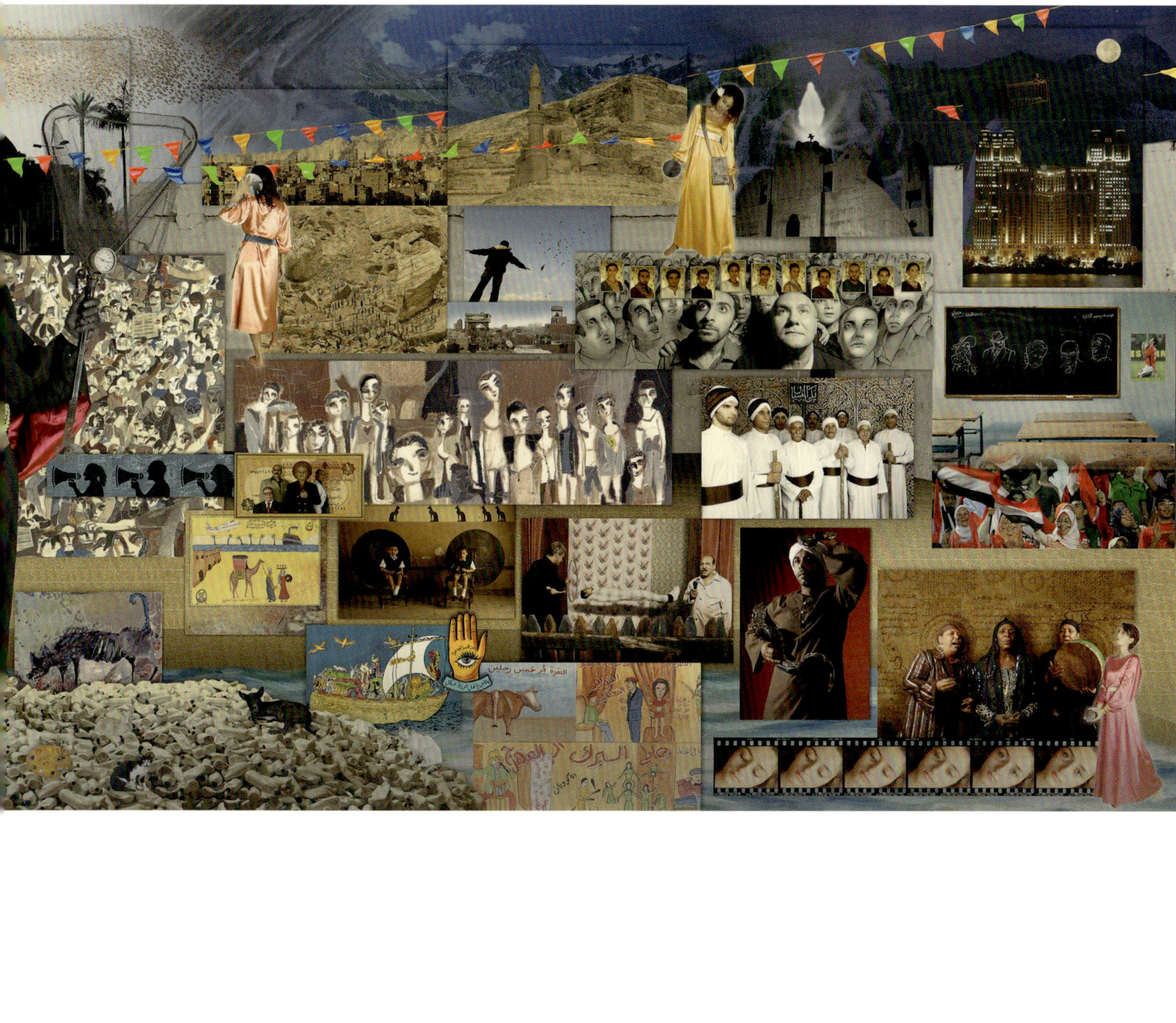

Hala Elkoussy / هالة القوصي, *The Myths & Legends Room – The Mural*, 2010
48 C-prints, 900 × 300 cm / 48 مطبوعة- صور ملونة ⟶ pp. / S. 133–134 / ص. ٥٢

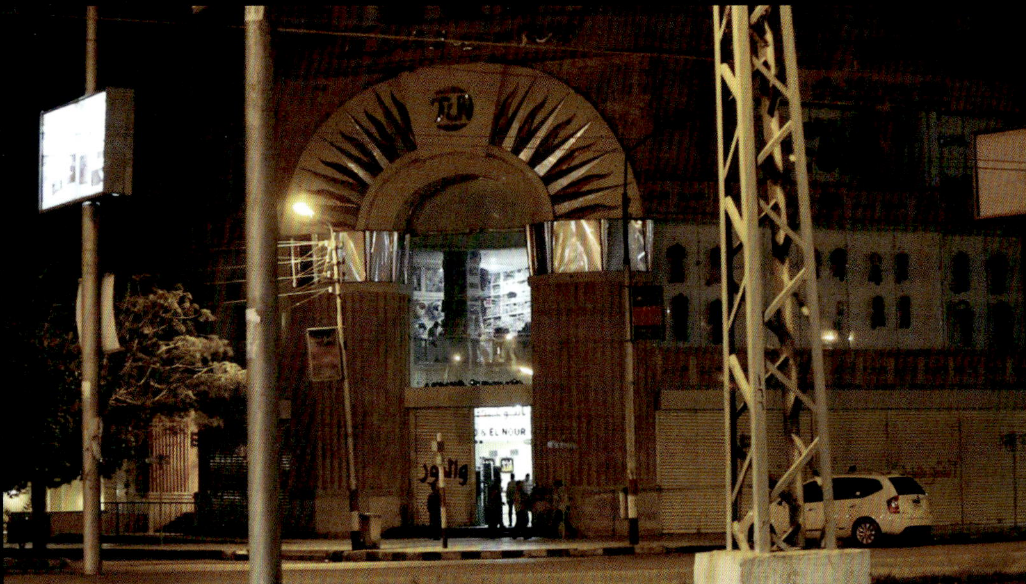

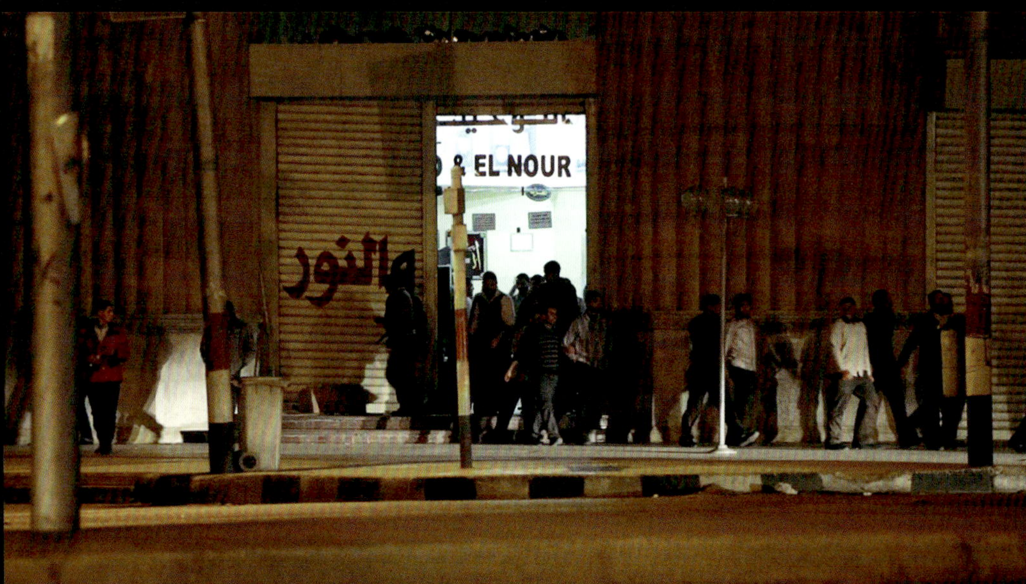
& EL NOUR
النور

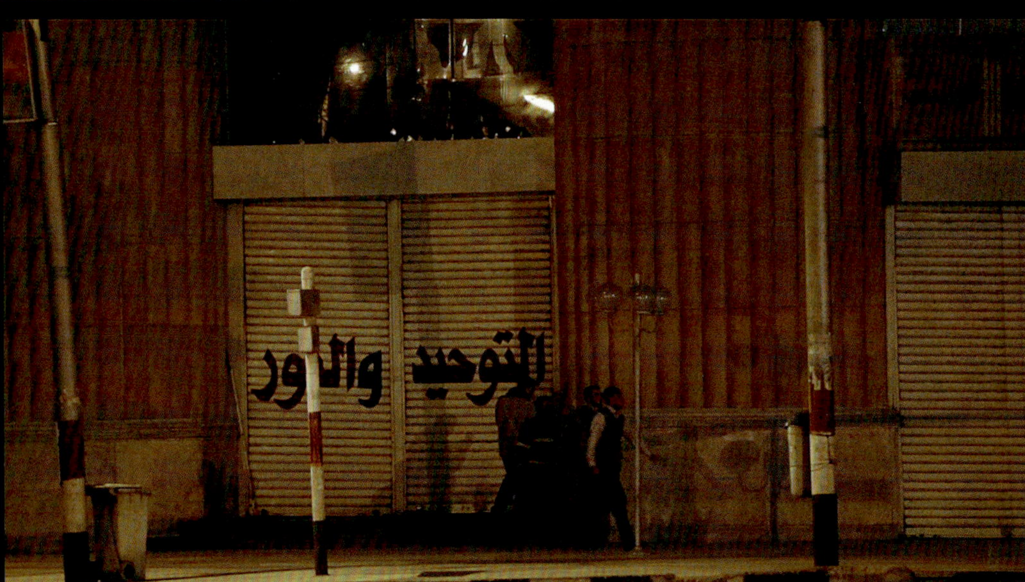
التوحيد والنور

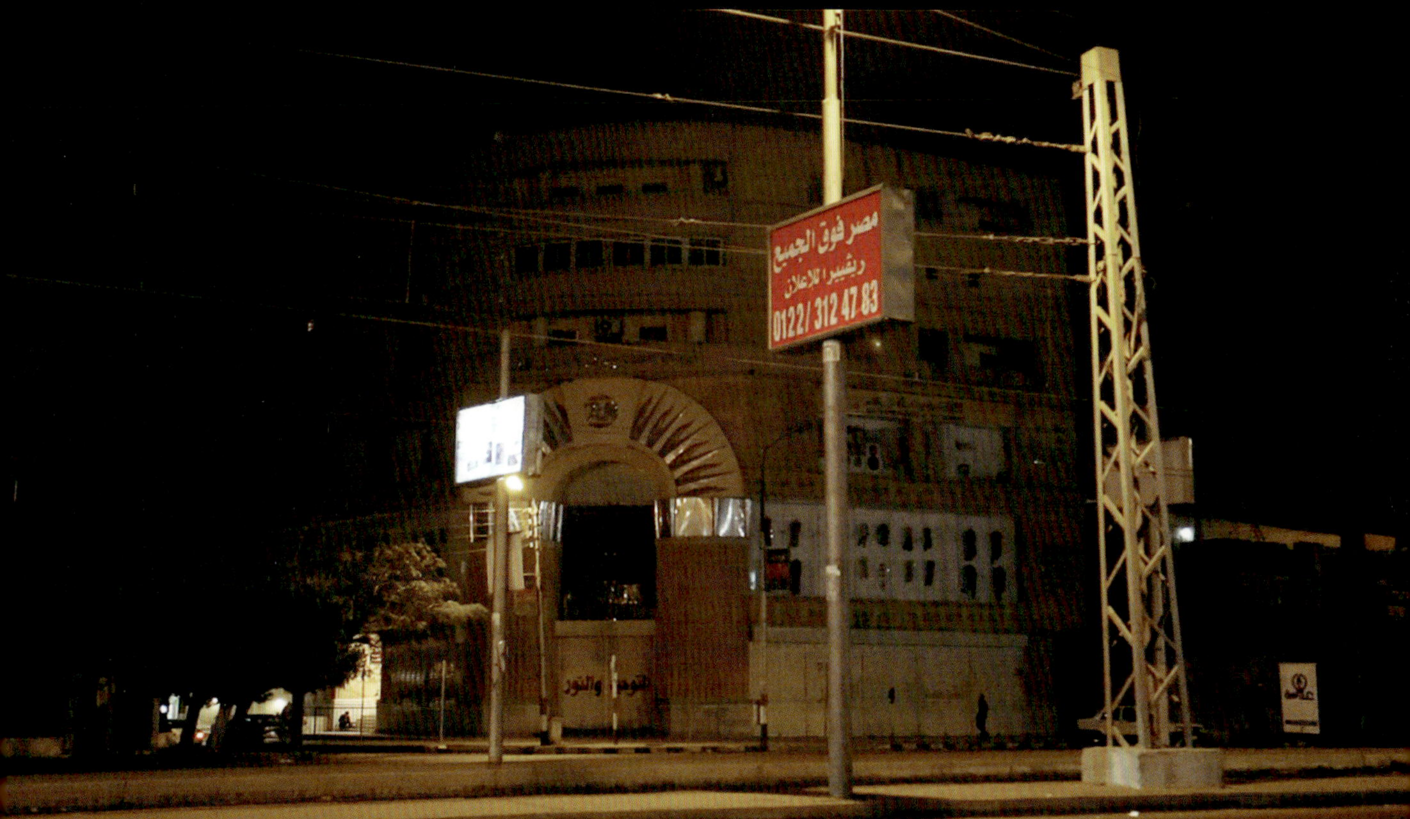

Osama Dawod / أسامة داوود, *El Tawheed & El Nour*, 2013
HD video, 2:30 min. / فيديو عالي الدقة، 2:30 دقيقة → p. / S. 132 / ص.٥٣

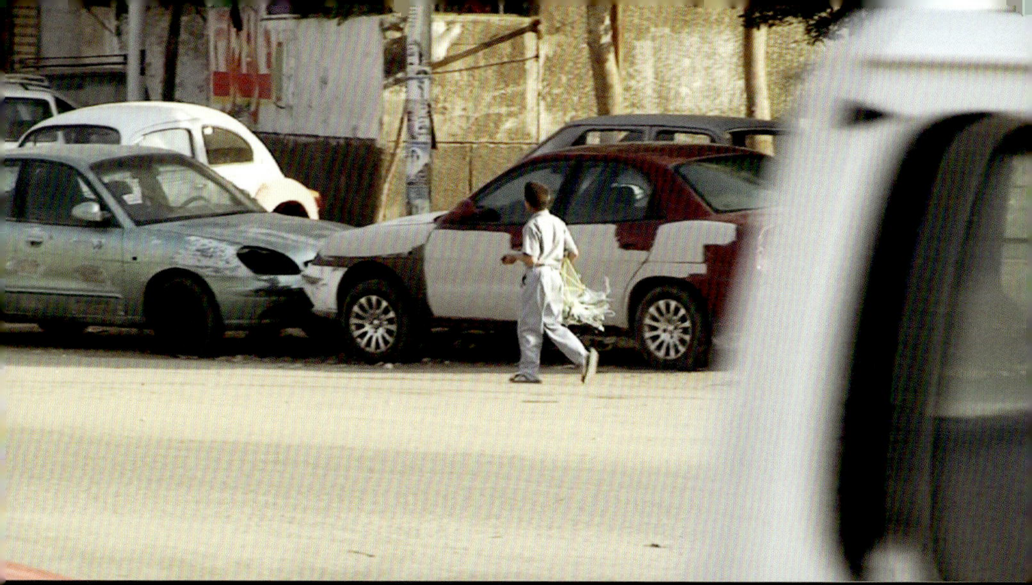

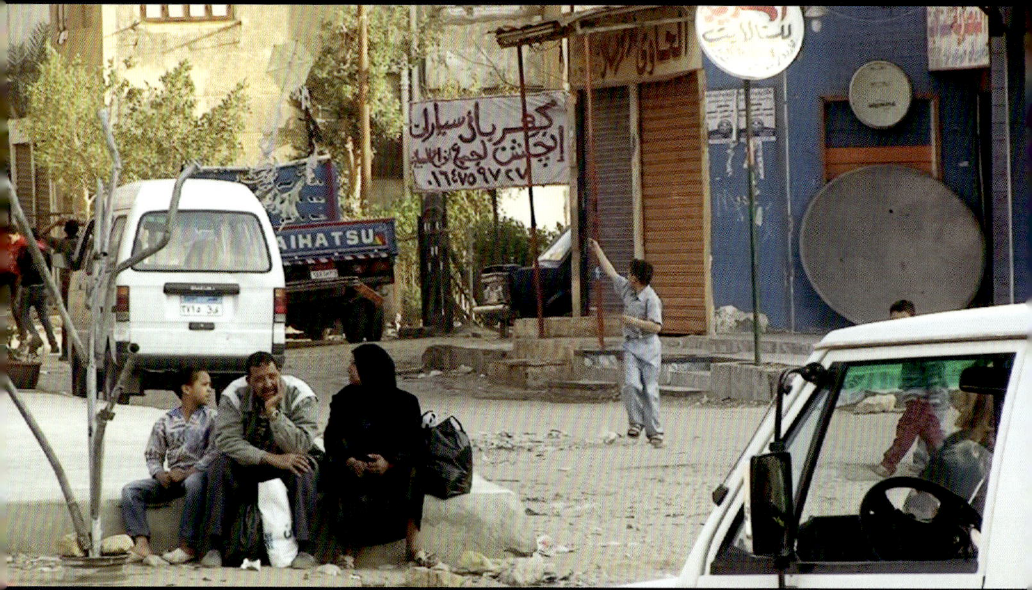
AIHATSU

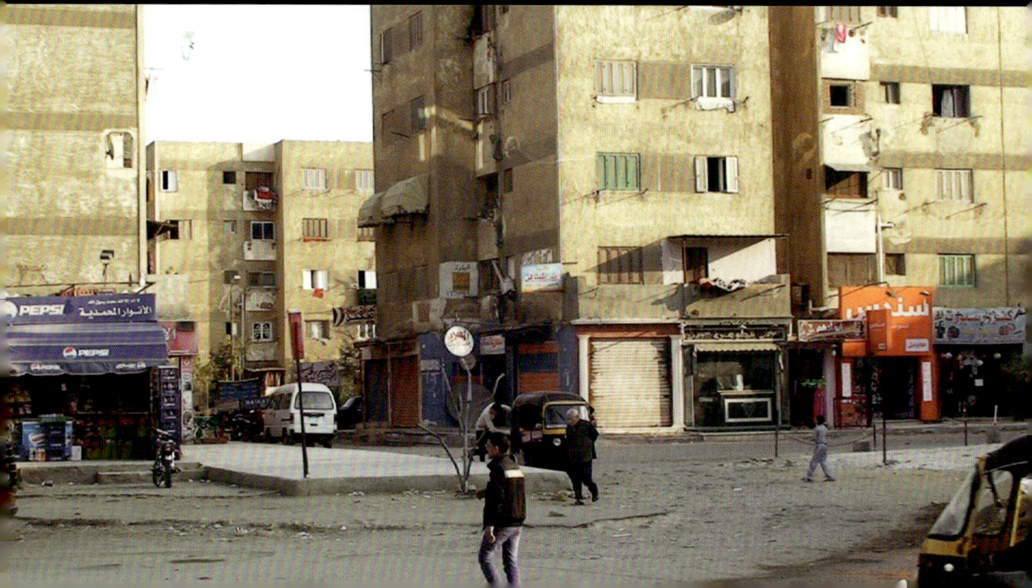
PEPSI
PEPSI

Conversations with children recorded on March 30–31, 2012, in the Mokattam district of Cairo. This video sequence was produced at the same time. / Aus Gesprächen mit Kindern, die am 30. und 31. März 2012 im Kairoer Stadtteil Mokattam aufgenommen wurden. Zeitgleich entstand diese Videosequenz. / من محادثات مع أطفال، سجلت في 30 و 31 مارس 2012 في المقطم. عندما سجلت مقاطع الفيديو

أول مرة كنت بلعب في الشارع لقيتهم بيقولوا

The first time I heard about it I was playing on the street.

بس أنا عارف إنه هو كان في ثورات قبل كده بس كانوا بيضربوهم ويمشوا تاني

I knew that some people had tried it before, but the protests were always crushed.

هو اللي أنا عرفته إن ساعة بيقولوا إن الناس دخلت خربت في القسم بقيت تضرب في الأقسام علشان يخرجوا المساجين وفي ناس تانية بتقول إن الظباط هم أساساً اللي خرجوهم

I heard that a lot of people had attacked the police station to free the prisoners, though some said that it was the police who freed the prisoners.

فأنا يعني معرفش لكن معدش أقول إن دوت حصل وده حصل ومفيش حاجة حصلت وأنا بقول كدب

But I don't know anything. I don't think either is true.

الرئيس اللي هيمسك مصر مش هيقدر يعمل زي مبارك خالص لأنه هو عارف إحنا عملنا إيه في حسني مبارك، فهو طبعاً مش حيعمل زيه، و مش هيبقى عايز إنه الناس تنزل الشارع تاني و تتظاهر ضده زي المظاهرات دي

The next president won't do what Mubarak did because he won't want the people to take to the streets again and protest against him.

إنت بتعمل في البلد ديه للآخرة مش للدنيا يعني إنت كل حاجة مبتعملهاش ليك هنا

Everything that the people are doing is not for the present but for the years ahead.

Chris Michalski / كريس ميشالسكي & Sebastian Stumpf / سيباستيان شتومف,
We didn't see it, but we heard about it, 2012
Video and sound installation / Video- und Toninstallation, 11:50 min. / عمل تركيبي فيديو وصوت، 11:50 دقيقة
→ p. / S. 138 / ص.٥٥

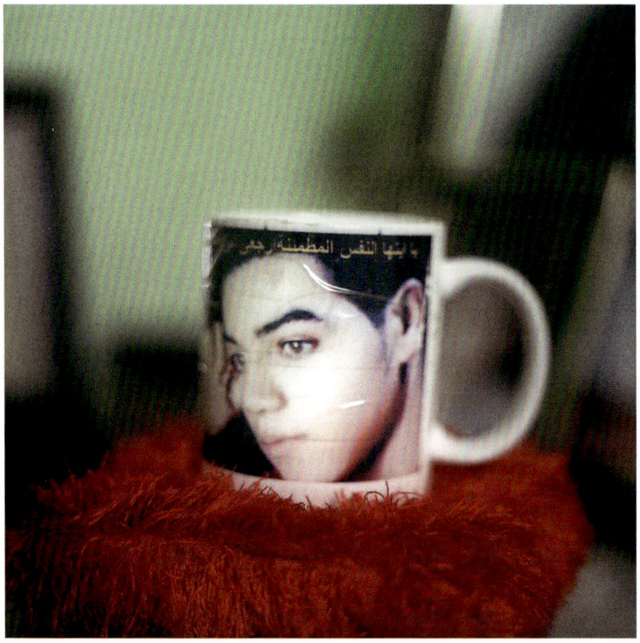
يا ايتها النفس المطمئنة ارجعي

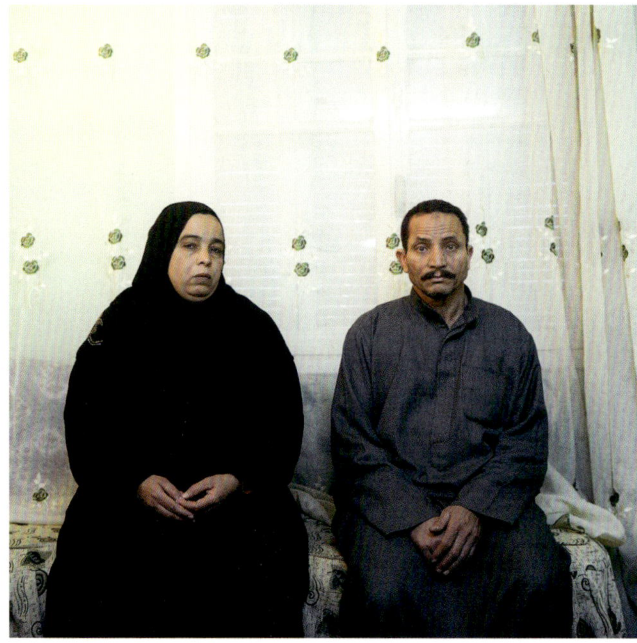

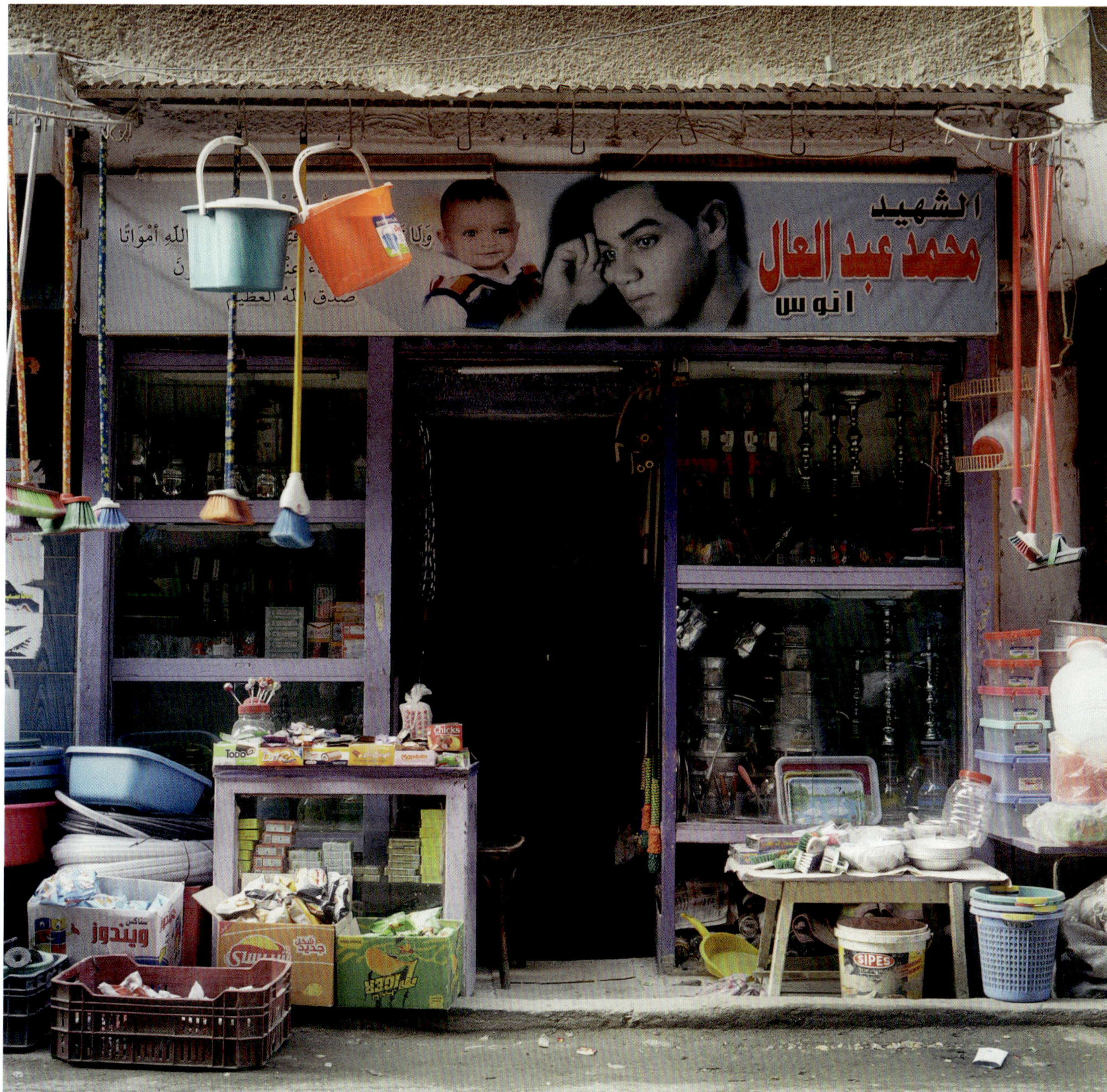
الشهيد
محمد عبد العال
انوس
صدق الله العظيم
ويندوز
Chicks
SIPES

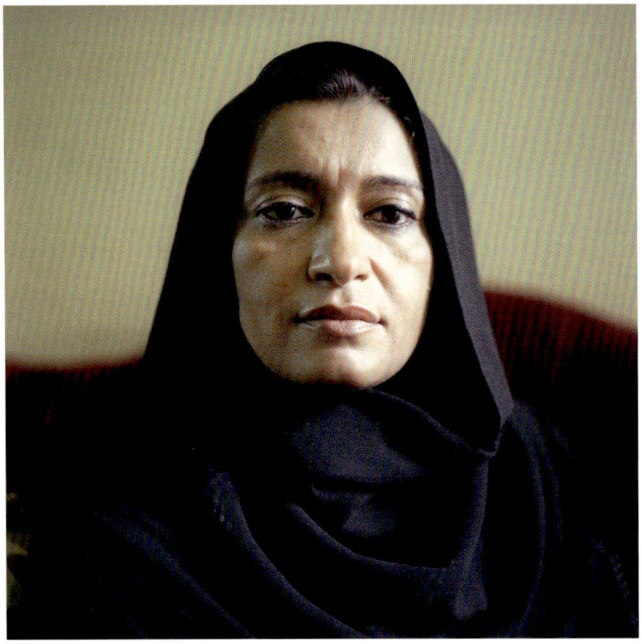

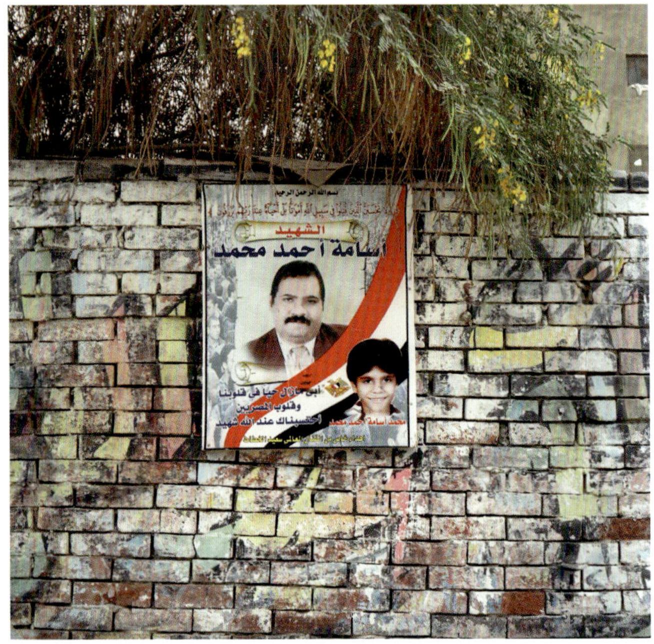
بسم الله الرحمن الرحيم
الشهيد
أسامة أحمد محمد
وقلوب المصريين
احتسبناك عند الله شهيد

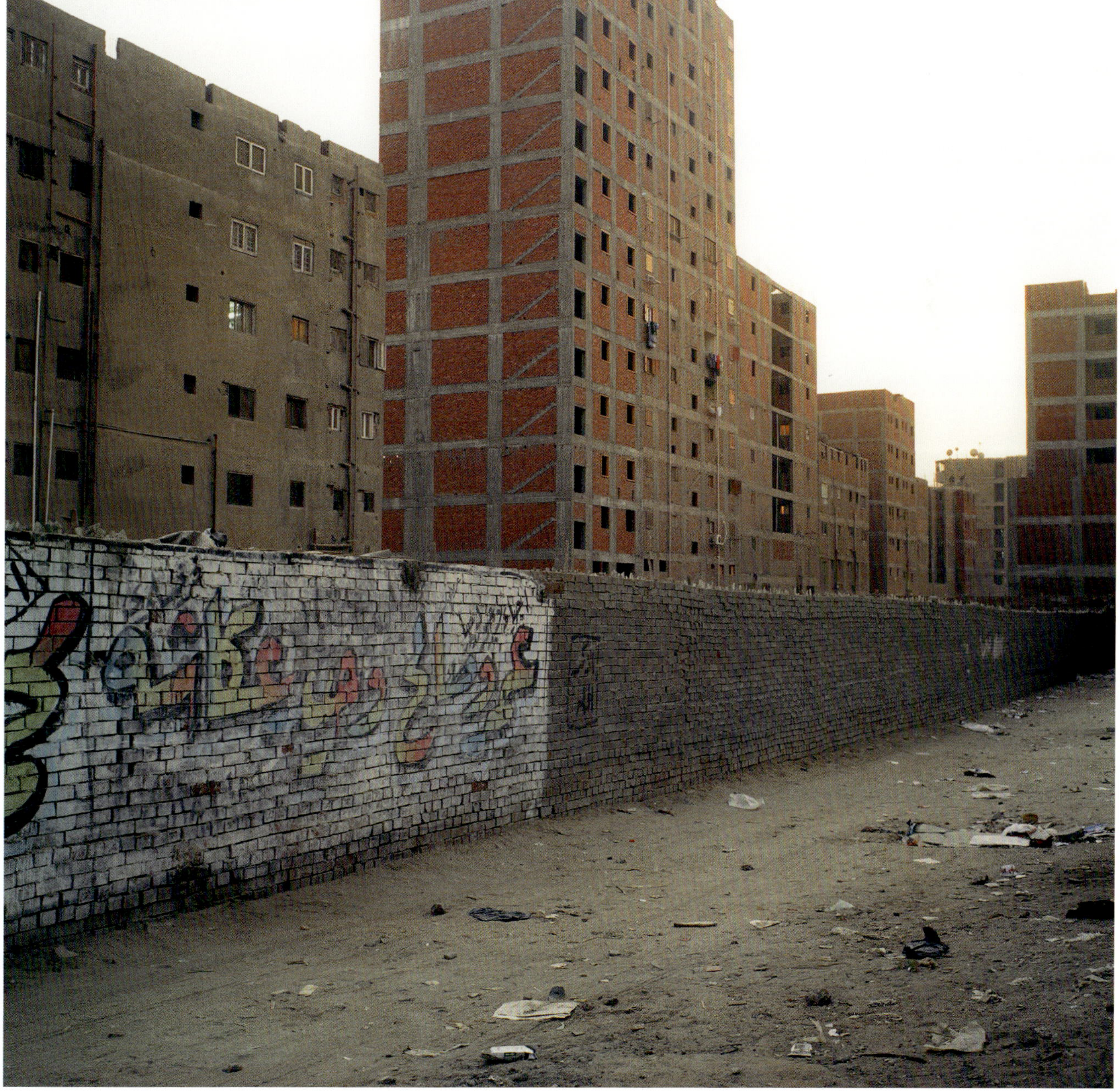

Denis Dailleux / دينيس دايو, *Memories of a Revolution*, 2012
Inkjet prints, 30 × 30 cm, 60 × 60 cm / طباعات حبر سائل → p. / S. 132 / ص. ٥٣

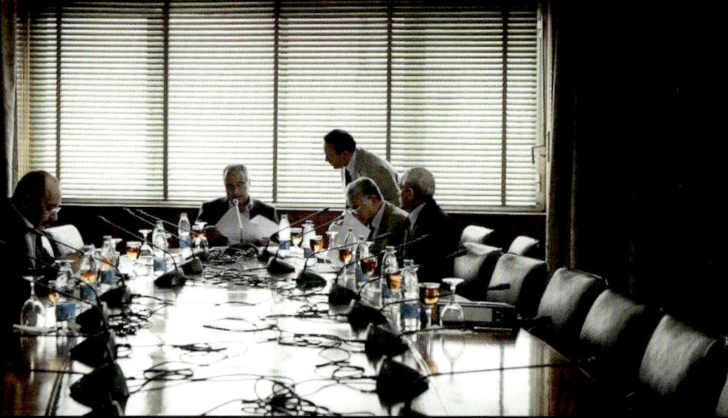

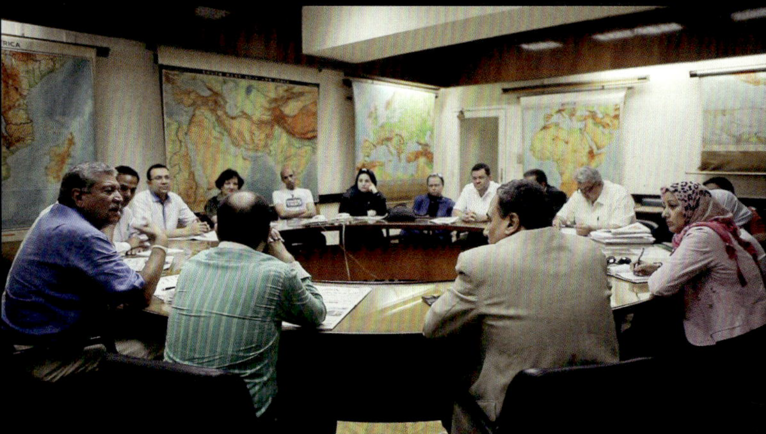

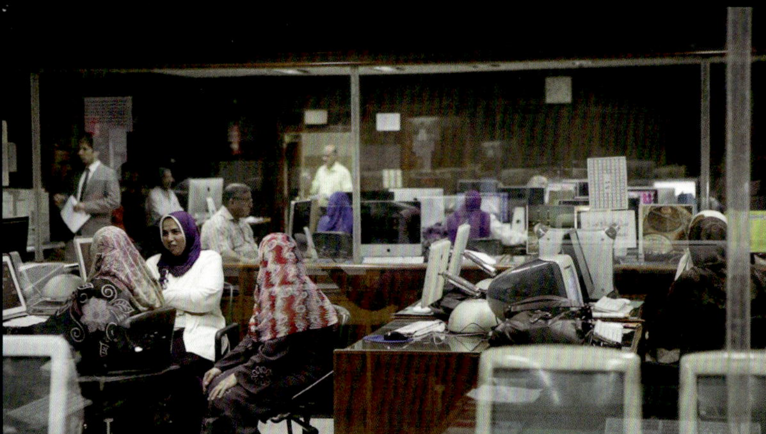

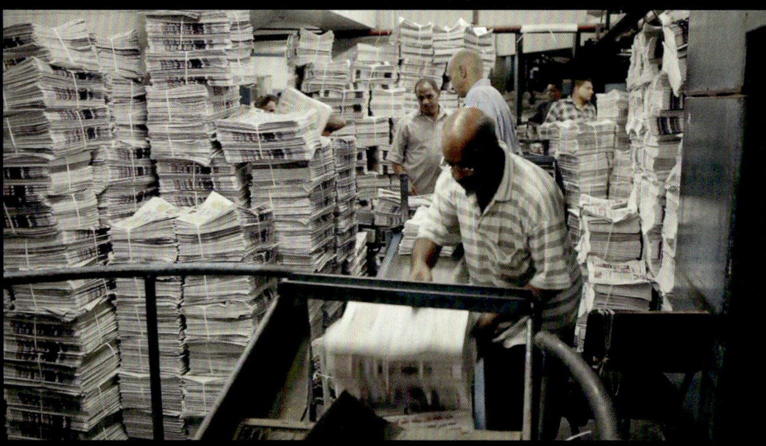

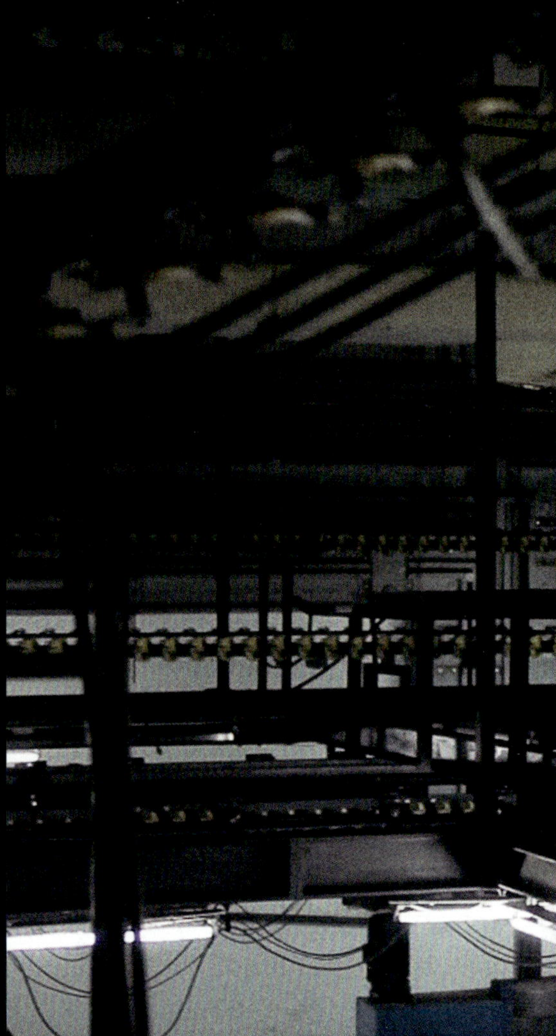

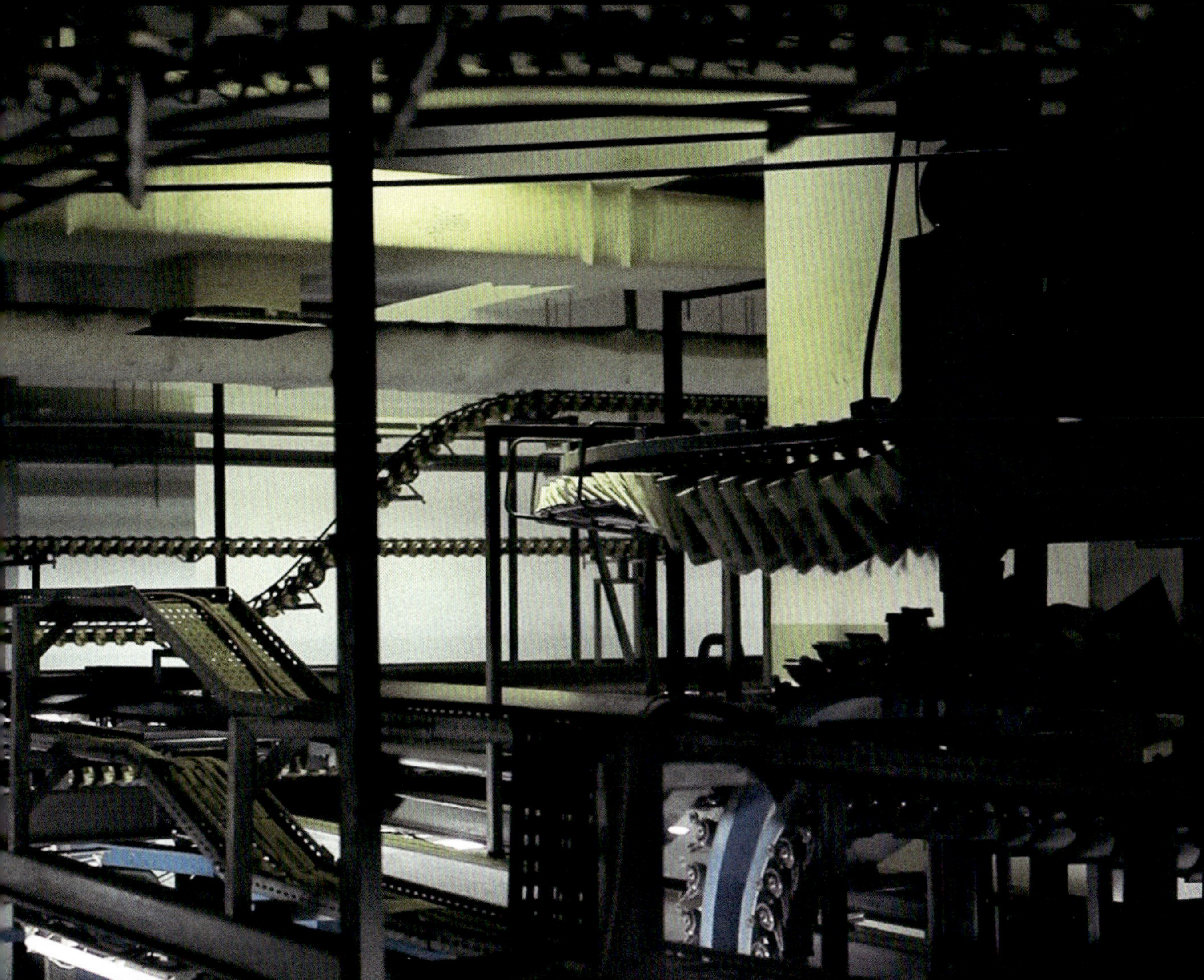

“My name is Ahmed but it could also be Amr—what I remember is that I am a photographer. They told me that I am in hospital, recovering from a heart attack ….
I had spent the entire eighteen days of the revolution in hospital. Everybody said I missed a great moment in my country’s history … I was only glad, I did not have to be out there. During all my career as a photo journalist I had tried to avoid political events. I always felt my pictures were used to show something unreal.”

Johanna Domke / يوهانا دومكة & Marouan Omara / مروان عمارة, *CROP*, 2013
HD video, 45:09 min. / فيديو عالي الدقة، 45:09 دقيقة → pp. / S. 132–133 / ص. ٥٤

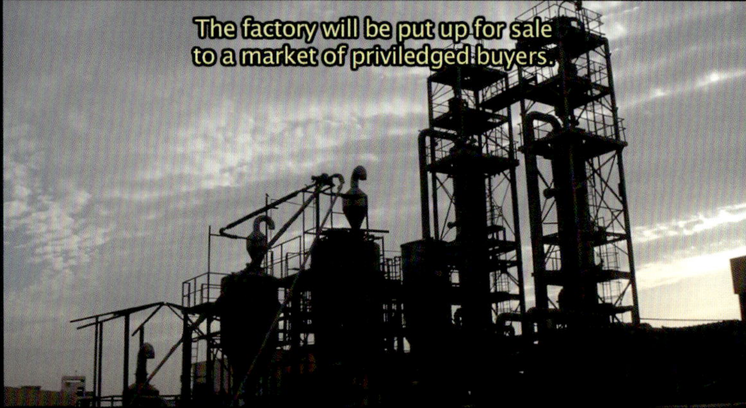

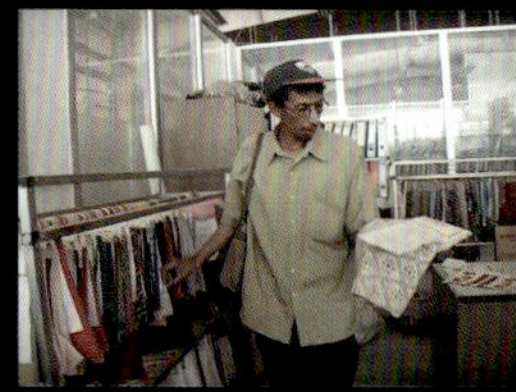

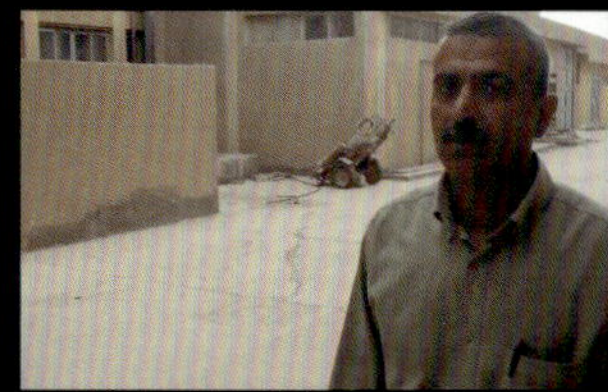

Isn't this our country?

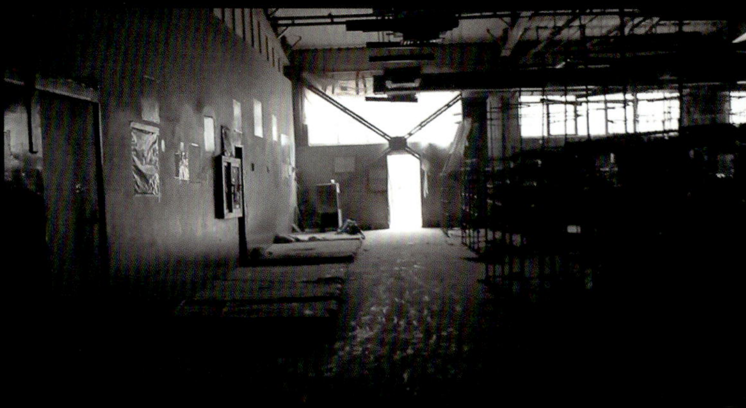

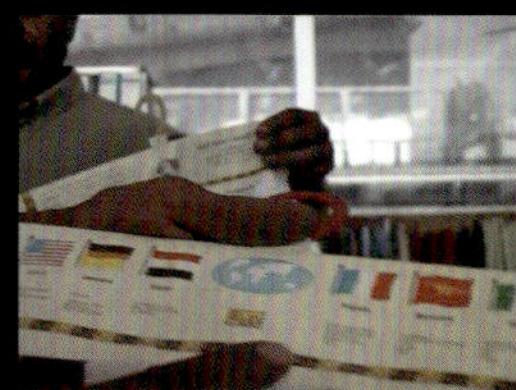

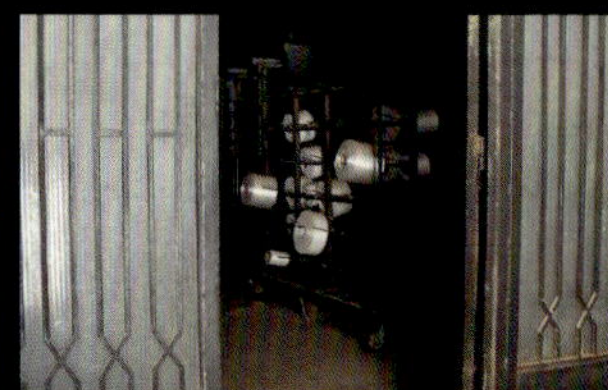

And this is the company's logo.

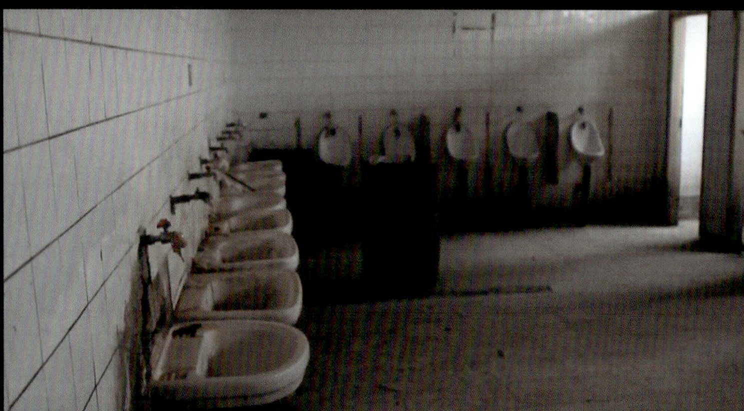

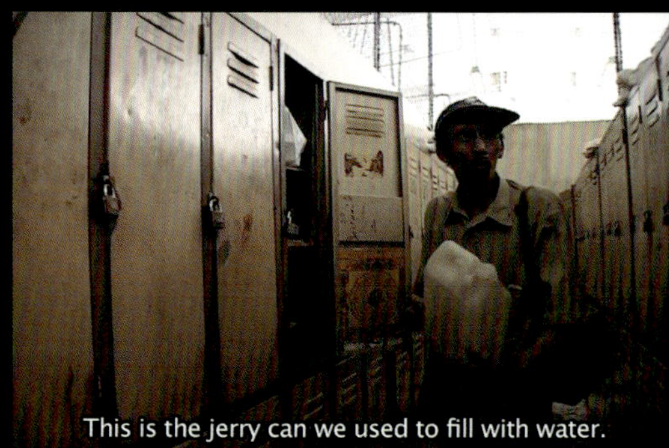

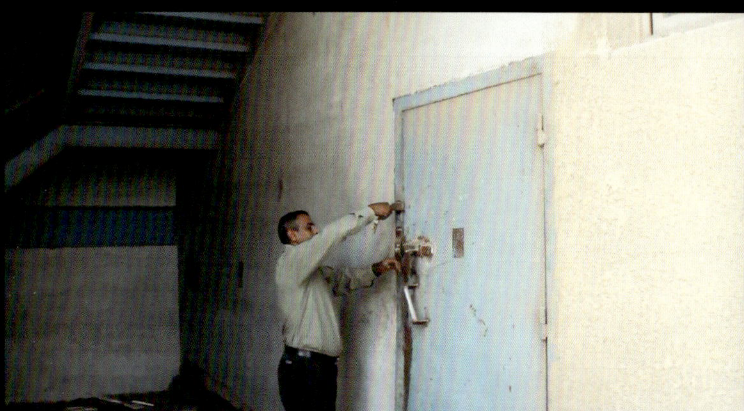

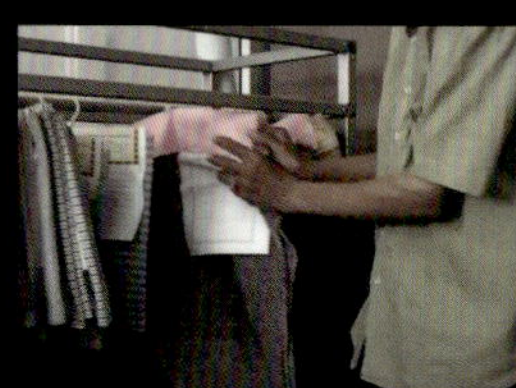

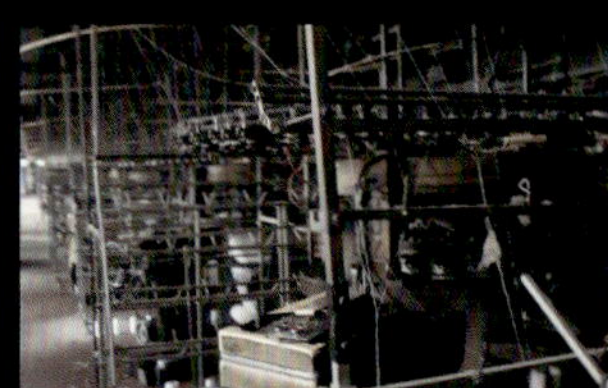

left idle.

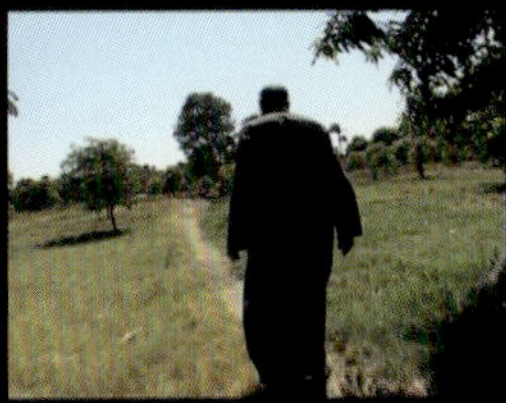
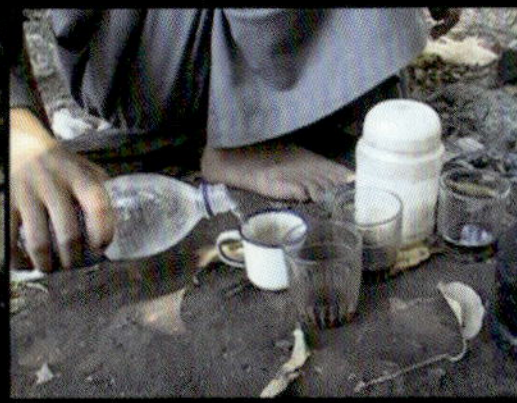

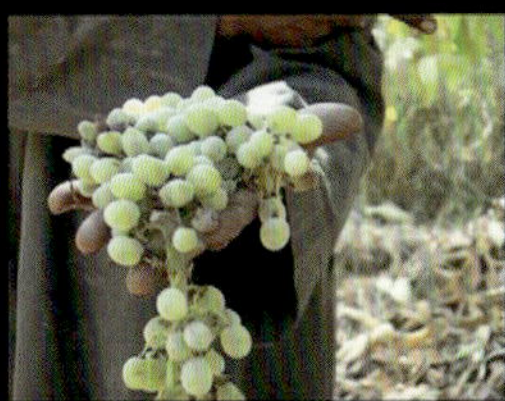
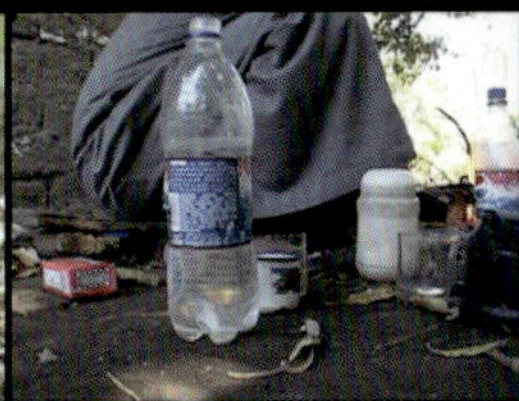

See how the leaves have gone dry of thirst.

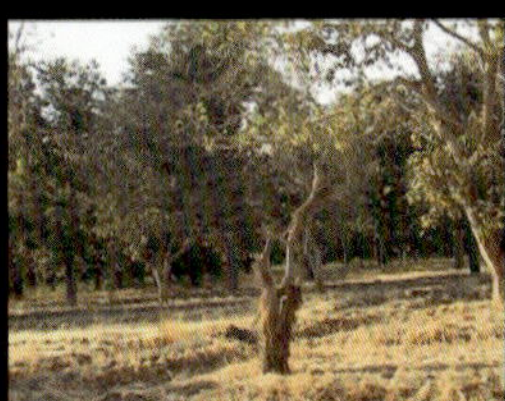
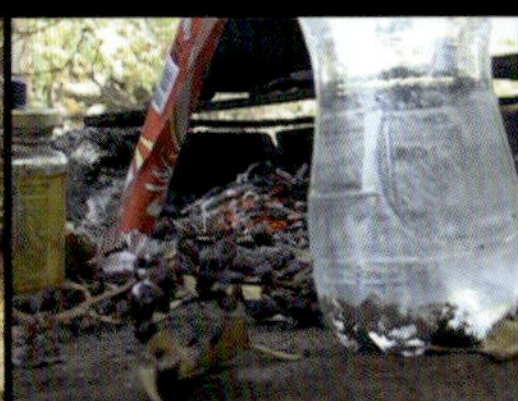

I swear I get annoyed,
I don't want to uproot her.

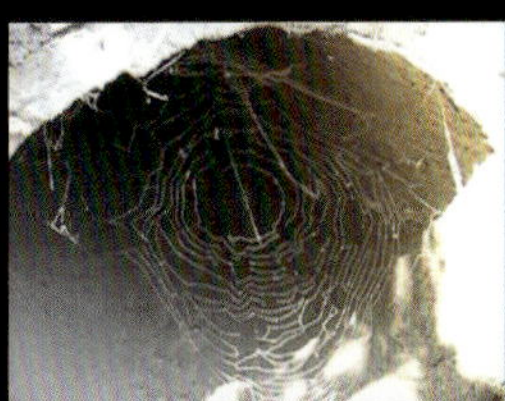
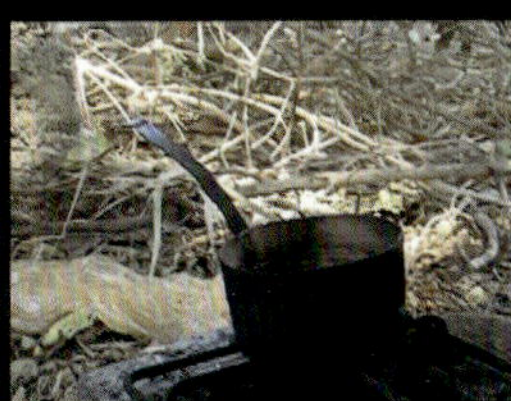

And where is the water?

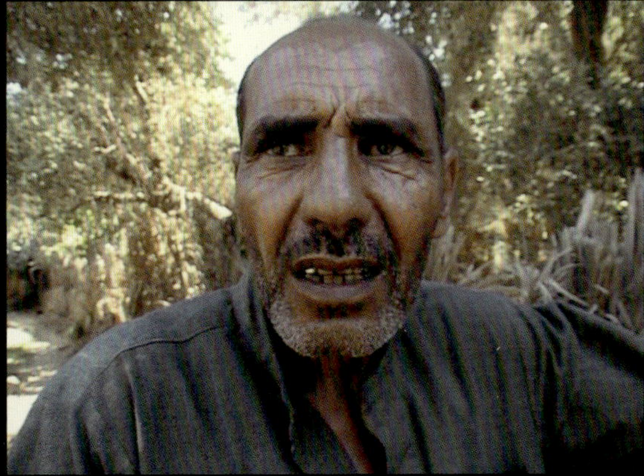

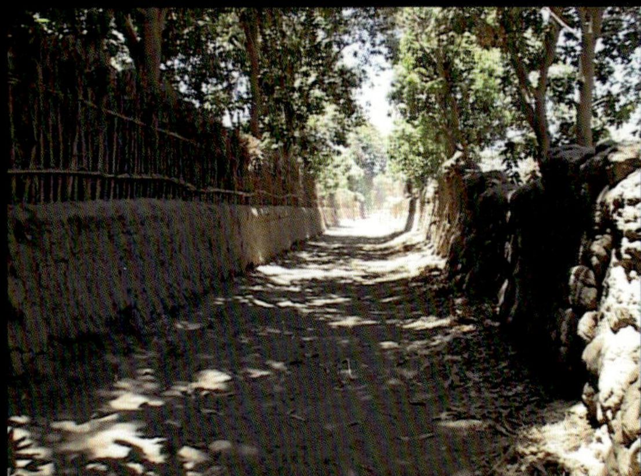

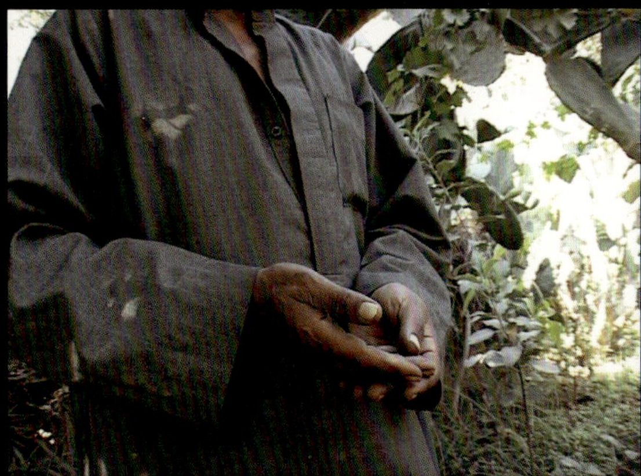

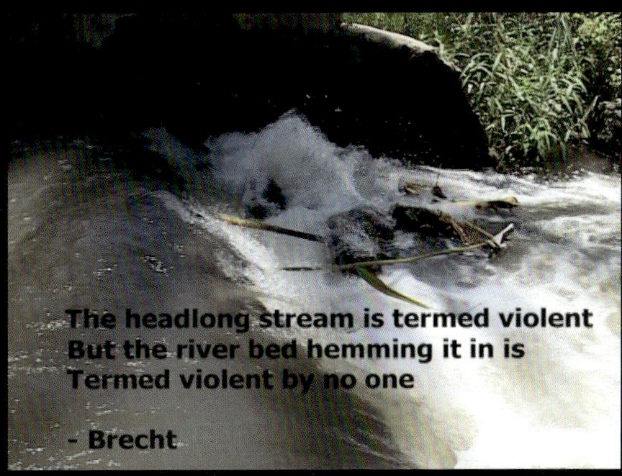

Philip Rizk / فيليب رزق, *Sturm: Fayoum*, 2010
HD video, 4:53 min. / فيديو عالي الدقة، 4:53 دقيقة ⟶ p. / S. 139 / ص.٥٤

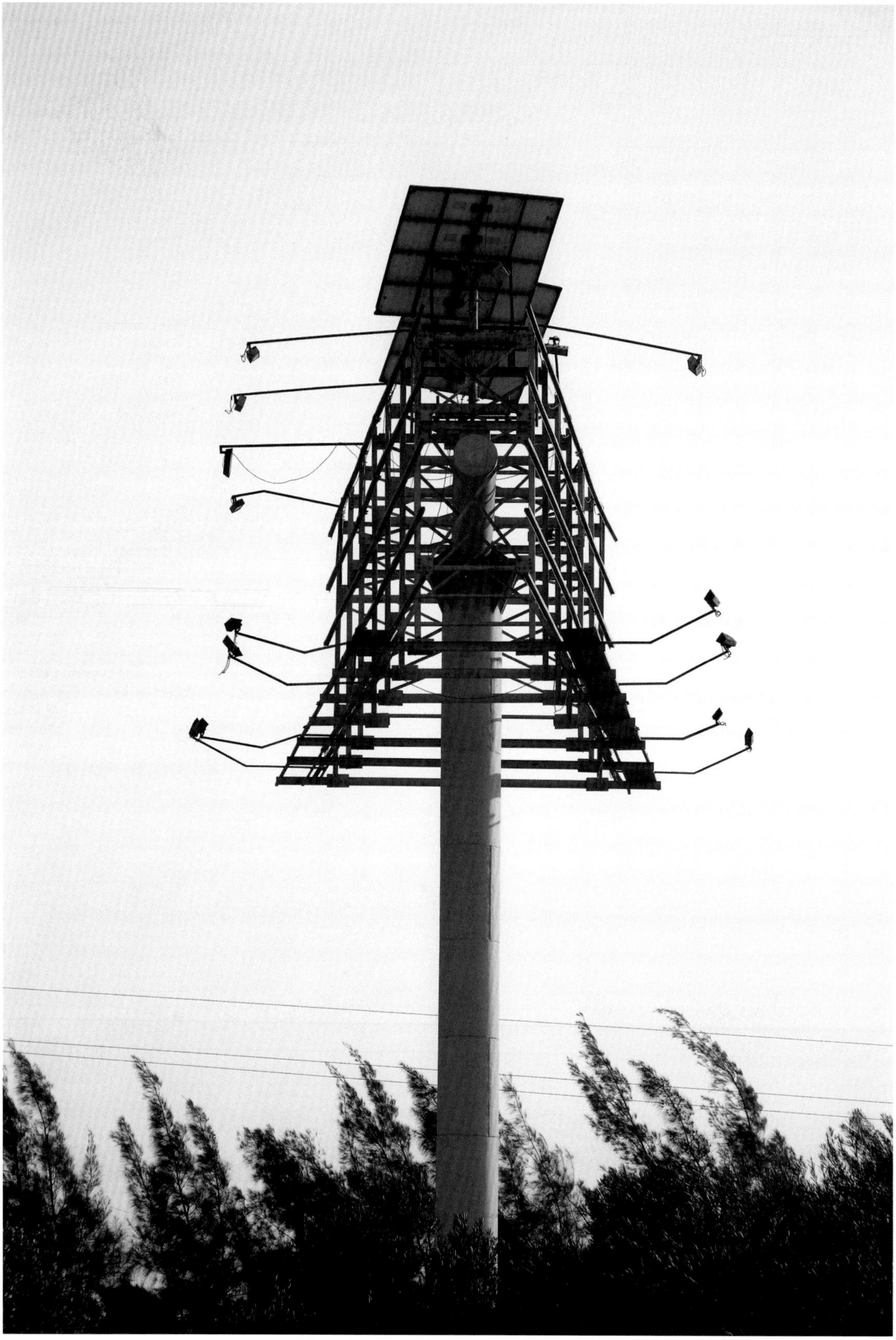

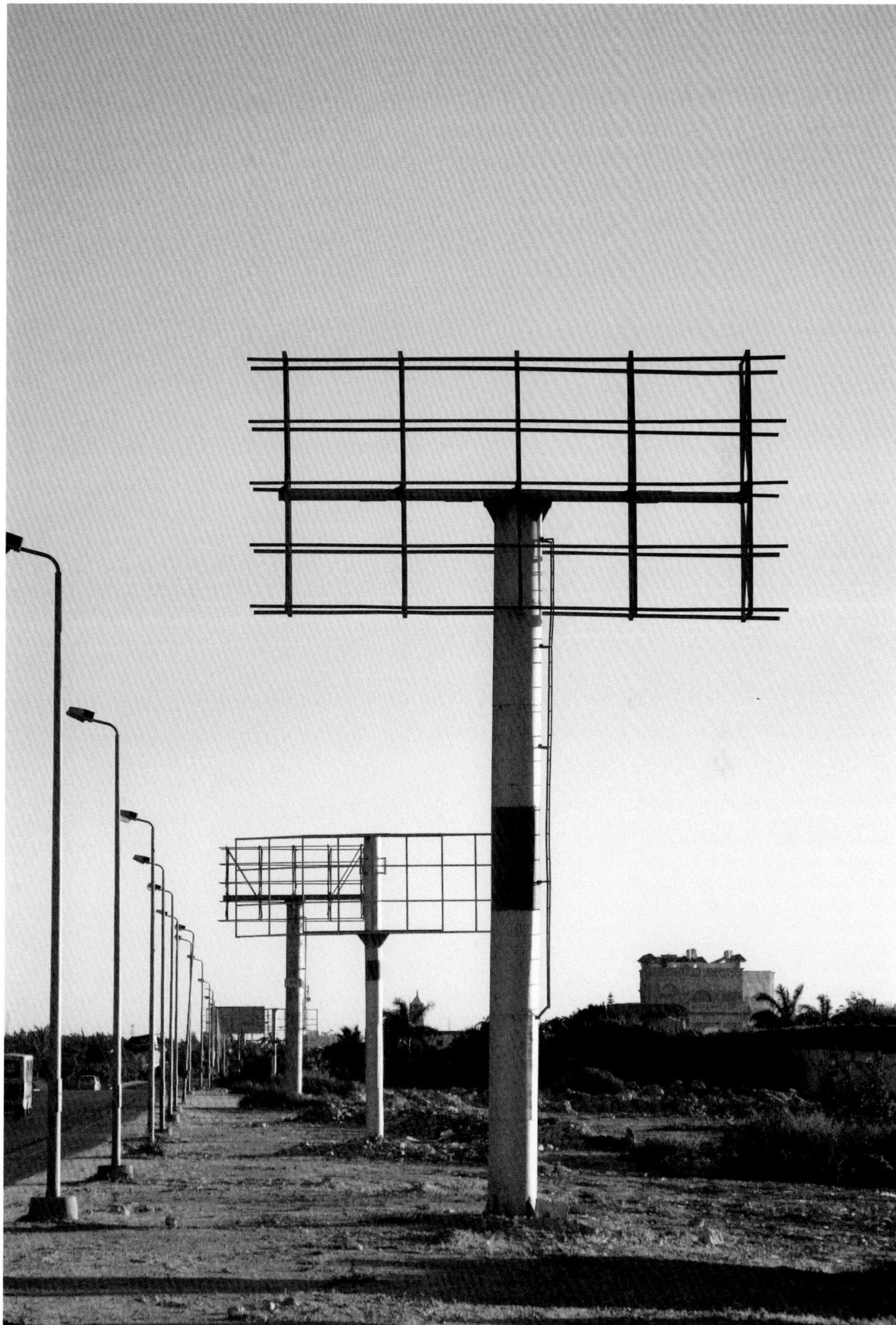

Tarek Hefny / طارق حفني, from the series / aus der Serie / من سلسلة *you two faced whore!*, 2008
Monochrome print on newspaper / Schwarzweißdruck auf Zeitungspapier / طباعة أبيض وأسود على ورق جرائد → p. / S. 136 / ص.٥٣

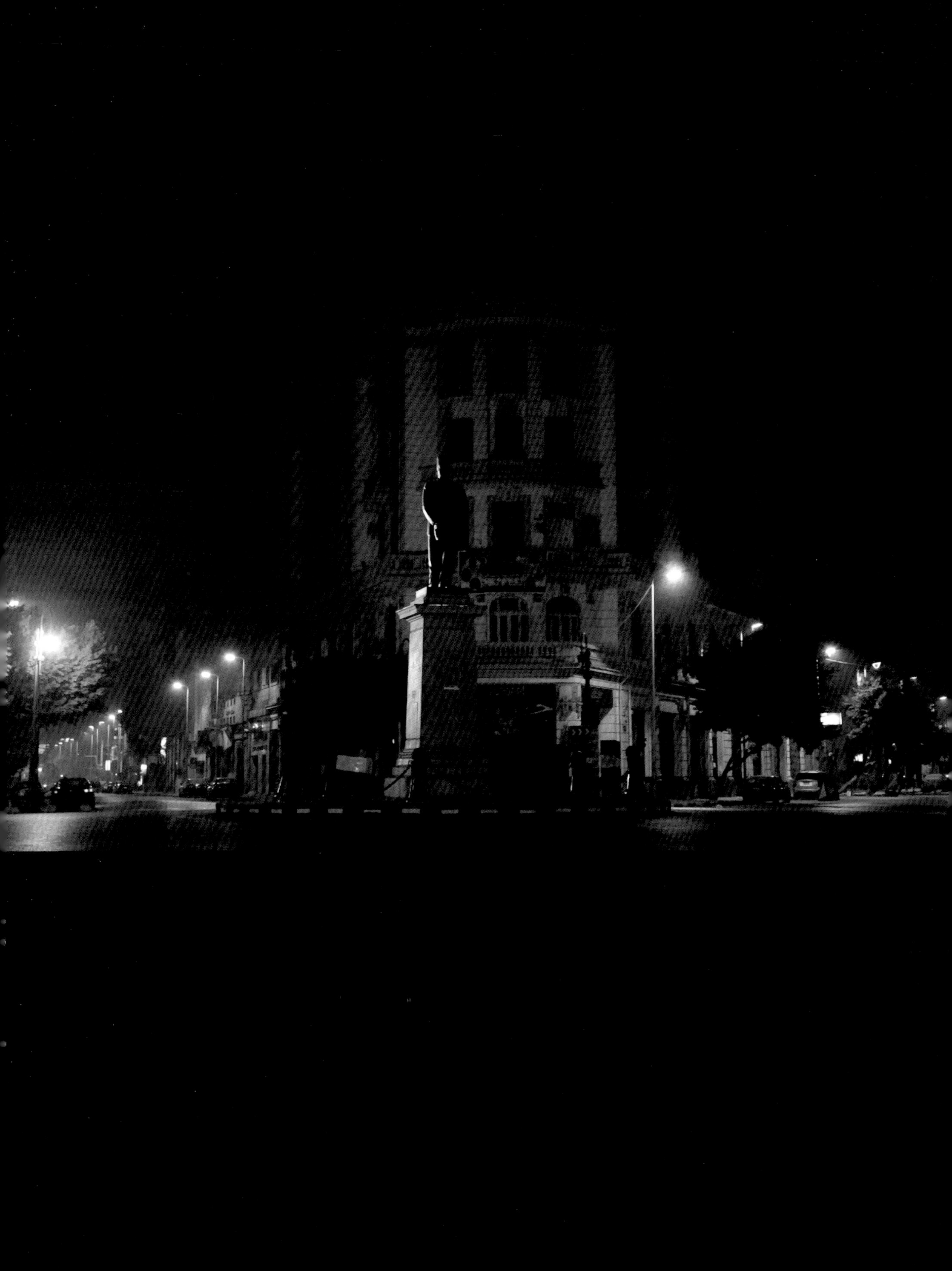

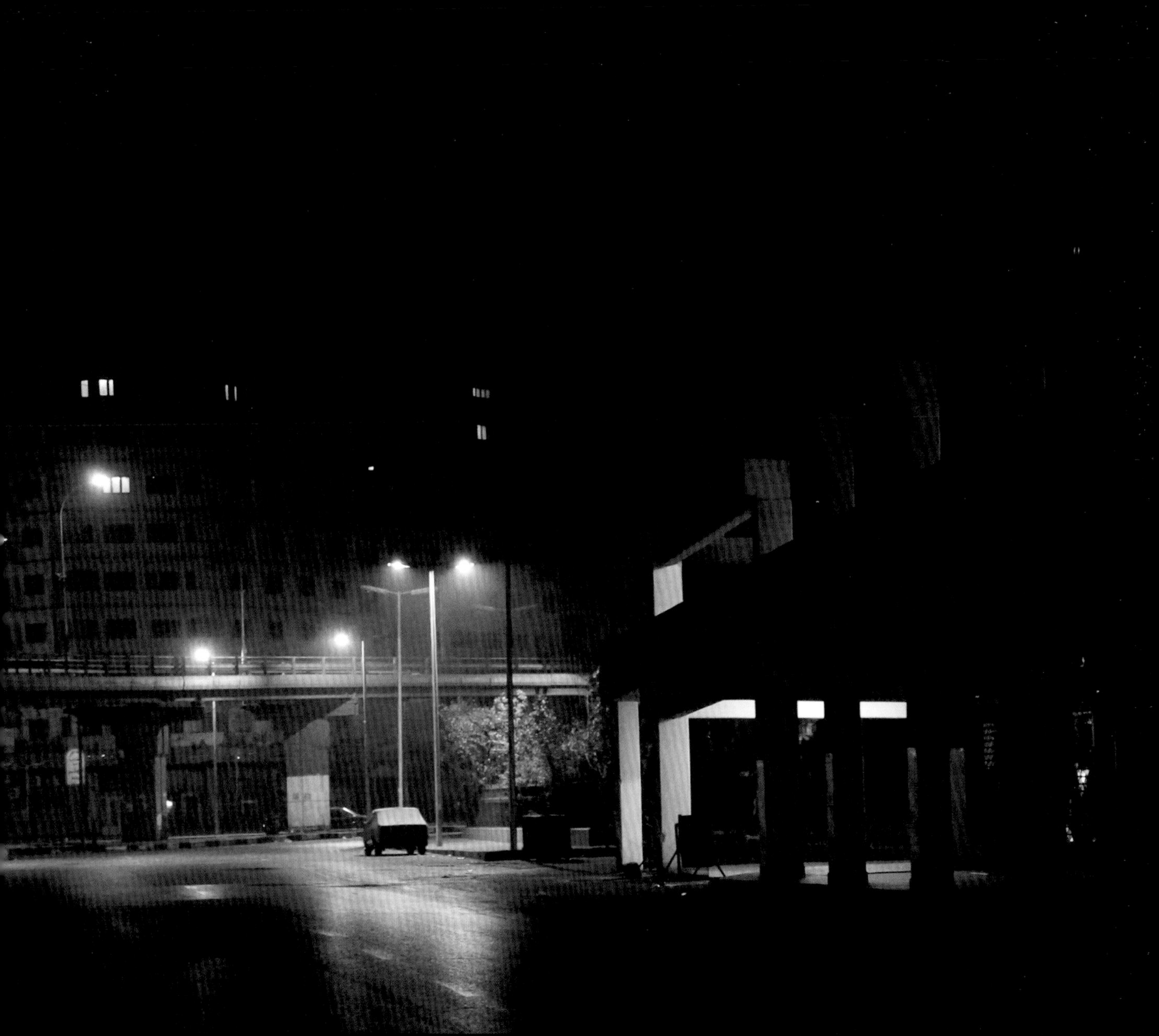

Voice-over: Dream accounts, collected between Feb. 18 and Mar. 10, 2011, in downtown Cairo / Stimme aus dem Off: Erzählte Träume, gesammelt in der Kairoer Innenstadt zwischen dem 18. Februar und 10. März 2011 / صوت في الخلفية: أحلام محكيّة، مجمّعة بين 18 فبراير و 10 مارس، 2011 في مركز المدينة في القاهرة

I was surrounded by snakes. They were very ugly, really big and fat. It wasn't real, I had never seen such snakes before. I knew I was imagining them. There were lots of snakes and more of them kept coming. My family was with me, and I feared that the snakes would kill them. (Ragma, school student, 14 years old)
I am sleeping. The telephone rings and wakes me up. Somebody is asking me: What are your plans? I have no plan, I wonder. Yes you do, the voice insists. What is it, I am asking, but there is only silence. I am begging for an answer. Finally the voice says: "Your plan is to grow." (Dowa, student)

Kaya Behkalam / كايا بهكالام, *Excursions in the Dark*, 2011
HD video, 19:40 min. / فيديو عالي الدقة، 19:40 دقيقة → p. / S. 131 / ص.٥٣

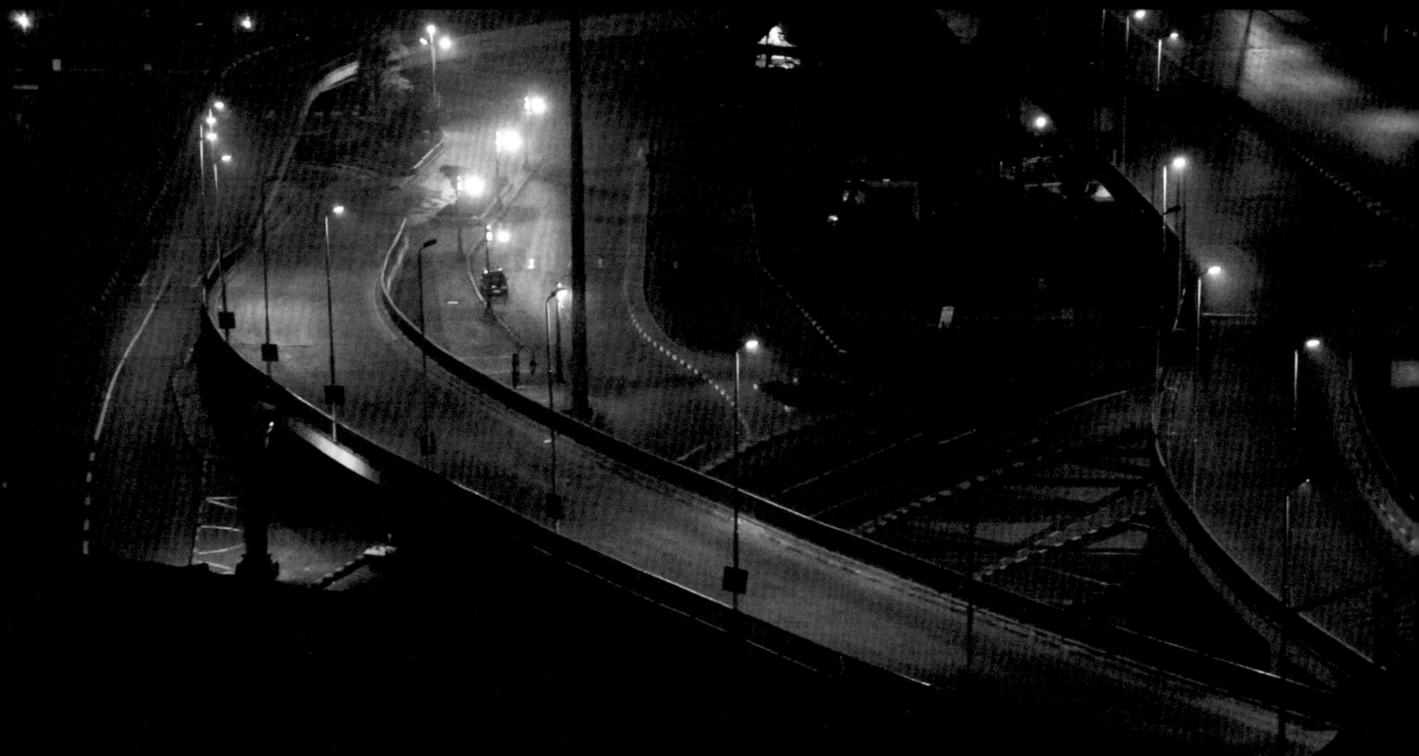

Myriam Abdelaziz

from the series/aus der Serie
Egyptian Revolt, 2011
⟶ fig./Abb. 46+47
from the series/aus der Serie
Cell Phone Stories, 2012
⟵ fig./Abb. 16, ⟶ fig./Abb. 14

Crowds are a prevalent motif in public images produced during the eighteen days. Portrait photographer Myriam Abdelaziz, who was born in Cairo and lives in New York and Cairo, has a dual perspective, both from inside her native country and from abroad. She focuses on the individual, on details and gestures, which are more significant than the broad perspective and reflect the moment of image making itself.

Myriam Abdelaziz is a French photographer of Egyptian origin. Her career started in the marketing field, where she worked for seven years after studying political science, journalism and marketing. She then decided to pursue a career in photography and graduated from the International Center of Photography in New York in 2006. Since then her work has been published in prestigious magazines such as Le Monde, Newsweek, Time Magazine, Courrier International, and Eyemazing, and has been exhibited worldwide. She is a member of the Middle Eastern women's photography collective: RAWIYA. She mainly works on stories in the Middle East and Africa.

Menschenmassen sind das vorherrschende Motiv der öffentlichen Bilderflut während der ersten achtzehn Tage der Revolution. Die Porträtfotografin Myriam Abdelaziz, in Kairo geboren und in New York und Kairo lebend, hat beide Perspektiven, von innen und von außen. Sie fokussiert auf das Individuum, auf die einzelne Person, auf Details und Gesten, die signifikanter sind als der weite Blick, und reflektiert dabei nicht zuletzt das Bildermachen selbst.

Myriam Abdelaziz ist eine französische Fotografin ägyptischer Herkunft. Ihre berufliche Laufbahn begann im Marketingbereich, wo sie sieben Jahre arbeitete, nachdem sie Politikwissenschaften, Journalismus und Marketing studiert hatte. Anschließend entschied sie sich, verstärkt fotografisch zu arbeiten, sie machte 2006 einen Abschluss am International Center of Photography in New York. Seitdem werden ihre Arbeiten in renommierten Magazinen wie Le Monde, Newsweek, Time Magazine, Courrier International und Eyemazing publiziert und sind weltweit in Ausstellungen zu sehen. Abdelaziz ist Mitglied des Künstlerkollektivs Middle Eastern Woman Photographer: RAWIYA. Hauptsächlich arbeitet sie an Reportagen in Nahost und Afrika.

Peter van Agtmael

Egypt. Cairo. Feb. 3, 2011.
Mubarak supporters flee across the 6th of October Bridge, which crosses the Nile, after being routed from Tahrir Square by anti-Mubarak fighters following a 24-hour street battle./Mubarak-Anhänger fliehen über die Brücke des 6. Oktober, die den Nil überspannt, nachdem sie von Mubarak-Gegnern am Tahrir-Platz nach einer 24-stündigen Straßenschlacht besiegt wurden.
⟵ fig./Abb. 55
Egypt. Cairo. Feb. 3, 2011.
The street battle between pro-and anti-Mubarak protesters continues. The battle is fought with primitive weapons, rocks, sticks, and Molotov cocktails./Das Straßengefecht zwischen Mubarak-Anhängern und -Gegnern wird fortgesetzt. Der Kampf wird mit primitiven Waffen ausgetragen, Steinen, Stöcken und Brandflaschen.
⟵ fig./Abb. 56

"These photographs were taken from the balcony of the Ramses Hilton Hotel on February 2–3, 2011. I had been covering the revolution for about a week, struggling to take pictures that conveyed the enormity and power of the event. On February 2, a careless miscalculation resulted in my being beaten by a mob of Mubarak supporters. I made it back to the Hilton with the help of some sympathetic Egyptians who had intervened. However, my injuries—and strained nerves—made it impossible for me to go back on the streets. I had an extra camera in my room with a cheap long lens and began photographing the rhythms of the violence throughout the night and into the next day, when the Mubarak supporters finally broke and sprinted in fear across the 6th of October Bridge."

Peter van Agtmael was born in Washington D.C. in 1981. He studied history at Yale University and graduated with honors in 2003. In 2008, he helped to organize the book and exhibition *Battlespace*, a retrospective of the events that took place in Iraq and Afghanistan. He won the ICP Infinity Award for Young Photographer in 2011, the Lumix FreeLens Award in 2012, as well as awards from World Press Photo, the American Photography Annual, and Photo District News. Van Agtmael became a nominee member of Magnum in 2008 and an associate member in 2011. Most of the time he works in Iraq, Afghanistan, and the USA.

„Die Bilder wurden am 2. und 3. Februar 2011 vom Balkon des Ramses Hilton Hotels aufgenommen. Ich hatte zuvor ungefähr eine Woche lang die Ereignisse der Revolution fotografiert und vergeblich versucht, die Größe und Kraft des Geschehens in meinen Bildern zu transportieren. Am 2. Februar hatte eine leichtsinnige Fehleinschätzung von mir dazu geführt, dass ich von einem Mob von Mubarak-Anhängern zusammengeschlagen wurde. Mit der Hilfe einiger Ägypter, die dazwischen gegangen waren, schaffte ich es zurück ins Hotel, doch meine Verletzungen – und strapazierten Nerven – erlaubten es mir nicht, auf die Straße zurückzukehren. Ich hatte noch eine Ersatzkamera mit einem billigen Zoomobjektiv in meinem Zimmer und fing an, den Rhythmus der Gewalt im Verlauf der Nacht und des darauffolgenden Tages zu fotografieren, als die Anhänger Mubaraks endlich aufgaben und voller Angst über die Brücke des 6. Oktober flüchteten."

Peter van Agtmael wurde 1981 in Washington D.C. geboren. Er studierte Geschichte an der Yale University und beendete sein Studium 2003 mit Auszeichnung. 2008 war er an der Organisation der Ausstellung *Battlespace*, einer Retrospektive zu den Ereignissen aus dem Irak und Afghanistan, beteiligt. Er gewann 2011 den ICP Infinity Award for Young Photographer, 2012 den Lumix Freelens Award sowie Preise von World Press Photo, dem American Photography Annual und der Photo District News. Van Agtmael wurde 2008 für Magnum nominiert und ist seit 2011 Vollmitglied. Er arbeitet überwiegend im Irak, in Afghanistan und den USA.

Kim Badawi

People watching Facebook projections in Tahrir Square, Cairo/ Zuschauer bei Projektionen von Facebook auf dem Tahrir-Platz, Kairo, Feb. 6, 2011
⟵ fig./Abb. 59

"Nightly projections of videos uploaded on Facebook and other social networking sites caught the attention of a myriad of Egyptians from extremely different social and economic classes and beliefs. Indeed, Egypt was a society used to living with a coded language. Evaluations of your appearance, stature, demeanor, conversation, and even sex all fed into your reputation. Somehow for the first eighteen days of the uprising, in Tahrir itself this was not the case. Egyptians all stood side by side. That in itself was extraordinary and an eye-opener, even to Egyptians themselves. This made them grow together somehow, giving the crowd the drive to carry on. Having very little light available, I chose to frame this image around the projection of light itself, in an attempt to show the wide variety of personalities present."

Born in Paris in 1980, Kim Badawi is an American documentarian of French, Egyptian, and Slovenian background. Badawi has been in Cairo as of the first days of the Egyptian Revolution and has documented its progression, and now its aftermath, from a unique vantage point. Kim Badawi's very first solo retrospective opened at the Galerie Rauchfeld in Paris in November 2012, in conjunction with Paris Photo.

„Nächtliche Vorführungen von Videos, die bei Facebook und anderen sozialen Netzwerken hochgeladen wurden, zogen unzählige Ägypter aus den unterschiedlichsten sozialen und wirtschaftlichen Verhältnissen und mit den verschiedensten Überzeugungen an. Normalerweise ist das gesellschaftliche Leben in Ägypten stark von Sprachcodes geprägt. Erscheinung, Statur, Benehmen, die Art der Konversation und sogar Sexualität schlagen sich im Ansehen einer Person nieder. Doch irgendwie traf dies während der ersten achtzehn Tage des Aufruhrs auf dem Tahrir nicht zu. Die Ägypter standen Seite an Seite. Das alleine war für sie schon alarmierend und bemerkenswert. Es ließ sie zusammenwachsen und verlieh der Menge irgendwie die Kraft, weiterzumachen. Da mir sehr wenig Licht zur Verfügung stand, entschloss ich mich dazu, das Bild um die Projektion des Lichts an sich zu arrangieren, um so die Vielfalt, die Unterschiedlichkeit der anwesenden Personen zur Geltung zu bringen."

Kim Badawi, geboren 1980 in Paris, ist ein amerikanischer Dokumentarfotograf mit französischem, ägyptischem und slowenischem Hintergrund. Seit den ersten Tagen der ägyptischen Revolution hält sich Badawi in Kairo auf und hat dort sowohl die Entwicklung der Revolution als auch ihre Nachwirkungen von einem einzigartigen Blickwinkel aus festgehalten. Badawis erste Retrospektive in der Galerie Rauchfeld eröffnete im November 2012 in Paris im Rahmen der Paris Photo.

Mostafa Bahgat

Videos about the confrontations and street fighting that took place between November 2011 and February 2012 / Videos über Auseinandersetzungen und Straßenschlachten im Zeitraum von November 2011 bis Februar 2012
⟶ pp. 163–167 / S. 167–172

The video journalist Mostafa Bahgat has been a long-standing legend amongst young activists. He is always in the frontline. According to reports, he has managed to find the perfect balance between the length of his zoom and the length of his legs. As a reporter he leads a double life. His main job is working as a cameraman for ONtv but a lot of his takes, which are too radical or which he shoots for his own purposes, find their way into his personal montages.

Der Videojournalist Mostafa Bahgat ist unter den jungen Aktivisten längst legendär. Er steht stets an vorderster Front. Man sagt, er sei in der Lage, die Schnelligkeit seiner Beine und die Brennweite seines Zoomobjekts perfekt aufeinander abzustimmen. Als Berichterstatter führt er ein „Doppelleben". Hauptberuflich arbeitet er als Kameramann für den Sender ONtv, viele seiner Aufnahmen jedoch, die zu drastisch sind oder die er gleich für seine Zwecke macht, verwendet er in seinen eigenen Bildmontagen.

Lara Baladi

Alone, Together... In Media Res, 2012
Three-channel video installation / Drei-Kanal-Videoinstallation, 42:00 min.
Research / Recherche: Lara Baladi Archive (videos, articles, photos) / Archiv (Videos, Artikel, Fotos): Lara Baladi & Amina Diab
MAX/MSP/Jitter Programming / Programmierung: Michael Carter
⟵ pp. / S. 83–85

"In January 2011, just as the YouTube video 'Tiananmen-Like Courage in Cairo' went viral, a friend posted on Facebook a speech Jean Paul Sartre had delivered to striking French autoworkers forty years earlier. As the political tension grew, more images and videos of a packed Tahrir Square were uploaded to the Internet. They echoed footage from other uprisings across the Middle East and North Africa, as well as the sights and sounds of a vast array of past social movements. It was as though Sartre was protesting with us in Tahrir.

I initiated an ongoing archival project called Vox Populi, *gathering videos, articles and photographs related to the events on the ground, while also collecting material on major events that had taken place around the world since January 25, 2011. I researched and brought together footage that resonated with Tahrir Square and everything that followed—from historical films to philosophical speeches to banned cartoons, and more.* Alone, Together... In Media Res *is the first work taken from this archive—a narrative that weaves together video sequences and reflects on many of the questions raised during the Arab uprisings. These revolutions signal the beginning of the unraveling of a major historical period. In the middle of this I fell—like Alice in Wonderland—into a hole: YouTube."*

Egyptian-Lebanese artist Lara Baladi was born in Beirut, raised in Cairo and Paris, and educated in London. She has lived in Egypt since 1997. Baladi publishes and exhibits worldwide. Her body of work encompasses photography, video, visual montages/collages, installations, architectural constructions, tapestries, and even perfume. During the 2011 Egyptian uprising, Baladi cofounded two media initiatives: Radio Tahrir and Tahrir Cinema. Both projects served as a public platform to build and share an archive on, and for, the revolution. Baladi has been a member of the Arab Image Foundation since its creation in 1997. She is represented by the Townhouse Gallery in Cairo and Gallery ISVDE in Dubai.

„Januar 2011, gerade als das YouTube-Video ‚Tiananmen-Like Courage in Cairo' sich rasend schnell verbreitete, stellte ein Freund von mir eine Rede von Jean-Paul Sartre auf Facebook, die dieser vierzig Jahre zuvor an streikende Arbeiter der französischen Automobilindustrie gerichtet hatte. Als die politischen Spannungen zunahmen, wurden immer mehr Fotos und Videos vom übervollen Tahrir-Platz im Internet hochgeladen. Sie waren vergleichbar mit Bildern von anderen Aufständen in Nahost und Nordafrika und – in dem Anblick und mit der Geräuschkulisse, die sie boten – mit Bildern, die man von früheren sozialen Bewegungen kannte. Es war, als ob Sartre mit uns auf dem Tahrir-Platz protestierte.

Ich begann ein fortlaufendes Archiv mit dem Namen Vox Populi *anzulegen. Dafür suchte ich Videos, Artikel und Fotografien zusammen, die mit dem Geschehen vor Ort zu tun hatten, sowie Material zu wichtigen Ereignissen weltweit nach dem 25. Januar 2011. Ich recherchierte und sammelte Filmmaterial, das den Tahrir-Platz und alles, was damit zusammenhing, zum Thema hat, von historischen Filmen über philosophische Reden bis hin zu verbotenen Karikaturen und vieles mehr.* Alone, Together... In Media Res *ist die erste Arbeit, die ich aus den Materialien dieses Archivs entwickelt habe. Es ist eine Erzählung, die aus der Verflechtung von Video-Ausschnitten entsteht und über die vielen Fragen nachdenkt, die sich während der arabischen Aufstände stellten. Die Revolution markiert den Beginn des Zusammenbruchs einer historischen Epoche, und mittendrin fiel ich, wie Alice im Wunderland, in ein Loch: YouTube."*

Die ägyptisch-libanesische Künstlerin Lara Baladi wurde in Beirut geboren, wuchs in Kairo und Paris auf und erhielt ihre Ausbildung in London. Seit 1997 lebt sie in Ägypten. Baladis Arbeiten werden international veröffentlicht und ausgestellt. Ihr künstlerisches Werk umfasst Fotografie, Video, visuelle Collagen/Montagen, Installationen, architektonische Konstruktionen, Teppiche und sogar Parfum. Während der Aufstände 2011 hat Baladi zwei Medieninitiativen mitbegründet: Radio Tahrir und Tahrir Cinema. Beide Projekte dienen dazu, ein Archiv von und über die Revolution aufzubauen und mit anderen zu teilen. Baladi ist seit der Gründung 1997 Mitglied der Arab Image Foundation. Sie wird von der Townhouse Galerie in Kairo und von der Gallery ISVDE in Dubai vertreten.

Ahmed Basiony

January 26, 2011
HD video, 2:30 min.
⟶ fig. / Abb. 33

Ahmed Basiony was one of the most important young contemporary sound and visual artists in Egypt. He was born in Cairo in 1978 and studied art in the Faculty of Art Education at Helwan University in Cairo, where he went on to work as an assistant professor in the Department of Painting and Drawing. He also attained an MA in philosophy of art, completing his graduate studies in sound art and electronics. He was interested in researching the structural and physical relations between sound and visuals, as manifested in structural systems or in the environmental fabric, and how to develop these relations in ideological terms. These relations are examined in contemporary frameworks and include creative projects such as *Copia, Symmetrical System, The Verbal is Kohli, Madina, 30 Days of Running in Place,* and *ASCII Does Not Speak Arabic.* The projects relate to various experiences in fields such as video, performance, interactive sound installation, and live sound.

On January 28, 2011, artist and musician Ahmed Basiony was killed by snipers on the Friday of Anger in Tahrir Square in Cairo. He died at the age of thirty-two but immediately became an emblem of hope to millions of Egyptians who were determined to devote their lives to helping the nation emerge from a state of repression to a state of freedom. A man who died for his country, an artist honored for his courage and his love, Basiony had already achieved a certain mystique amongst his friends, colleagues, and students, who were proud to learn from his life, and even more from the cause he stood for that fateful day. Basiony's words posted on his Facebook status on his last Wednesday and Thursday evenings showed his absolute determination to continue the revolution in peace, despite having been beaten by police batons.

"Please, O Father, O Mother, O Youth, O Student, O Citizen, O Senior, and O more. You know this is our last chance for our dignity, the last chance to change the regime that has lasted the past thirty years. Go down to the streets, and revolt, bring your food, your clothes, your water, masks and tissues, and a vinegar bottle, and believe me, there is but one very small step left... If they want war, we want peace, and I will practice proper restraint until the end, to regain my nation's dignity." (This biography was written by Basiony's friend Shady El Noshokaty.)

Ahmed Basiony gehörte zu den wichtigsten Vertretern der jungen ägyptischen zeitgenössischen Klangkunst und bildenden Kunst. Er wurde 1978 in Kairo geboren und studierte an der Helwan Universität an der Fakultät für Kunsterziehung, wo er später als wissenschaftlicher Mitarbeiter am Institut für Malerei und Grafik tätig war. Er schloss sein Studium mit einem MA in Kunstphilosophie ab und hat darüber hinaus Studien in Klangkunst und Elektronik absolviert. Sein Interesse galt der Suche nach Strukturen und physikalischen Beziehungen zwischen Klang und Optik, sowohl in strukturellen Systemen als auch in der Zusammensetzung der Umwelt, und der Frage, wie diese Verknüpfungen ideologisch umgesetzt werden. Diese Beziehungen untersuchte er beispielsweise in Kreativprojekten wie *Copia, Symmetric System, The Verbal is Kohli, Medina, 30 Days Running in the Place* und *ASCII Doesn't Speak Arabic*, die Video, Performance, interaktive Soundinstallationen und Livesound umfassen.

Am 28. Januar 2011, dem Tag des Zorns, wurde Ahmed Basiony durch Heckenschützen auf dem Tahrir-Platz in Kairo getötet. Er starb im Alter von nur 32 Jahren. Basiony entwickelte sich über Nacht zu einem Symbol der Hoffnung für Millionen Ägypter, die entschlossen sind, ihr Leben dem Umbruch Ägyptens von einer unterdrückten zu einer freien Nation zu widmen. Als ein Mann, der für sein Land gestorben ist, und ein Künstler, der für seinen Mut und seine Liebe verehrt wurde, hatte sich Basiony bereits zu einem Mythos unter seinen Freunden, Kollegen und Studenten entwickelt, die alle stolz darauf waren, von seinem Leben und mehr noch von der Sache zu lernen, für die er an diesem schicksalsreichen Tag stand. Obwohl er von der Polizei niedergeknüppelt wurde, drücken Basionys an den letzten beiden Abenden vor seinem Tod veröffentlichten Facebook-Beiträge seine Entschlossenheit aus, die Revolution friedlich voranzutreiben.

„Bitte, oh Vater, oh Mutter, oh Jugend, oh Student, oh Bürger, oh Greis und oh viele mehr. Ihr wisst, dass dies Eure letzte Chance auf Würde ist, Eure letzte Chance, die Regierung zu wechseln, die die letzten dreißig Jahre überdauert hat. Geht auf die Straße und lehnt Euch auf, bringt Euch Essen mit, Kleidung, Wasser, Maskierungen und Verbandszeug und eine Flasche Essig und glaubt mir, es ist nur noch ein kleiner Schritt. Wenn sie Krieg wollen, wollen wir Frieden, und ich werde mich bis zuletzt beherrschen, um die Würde meiner Nation wiederzugewinnen." (Die Biografie verfasste Basionys Freund Shady El Noshokaty.)

Kaya Behkalam

Excursions in the Dark, 2011
HD video, 19:40 min.
⟵ pp./S. 126–128

"Cairo, February 2011. Mubarak has been deposed, and calm has returned to the streets. Yet the dark alleyways and city squares seem strangely empty. The night curfews have turned the site of the revolution into a place outside of chronological time, a stage waiting to be filled after one curtain has fallen and before the next is raised. Who or what will occupy this stage?

Fragments of conversations with women and men who speak of dreams, unconscious fears, and formless images are contrasted by a motionless camera that views the city as a manifestation of the desires and projections of previous ages. Excursions in the Dark *traces—in the words of Walter Benjamin—the 'moment that the historian takes upon himself the task of dream interpretation,' the vanishing point connecting the city's architecture, collective dreamscapes, and political agency."*

Kaya Behkalam was born in Berlin in 1978. He is an artist and the author of various books, including *A Spectre Haunting Europe: The Middle Eastern Migrant and the German Angst*. Behkalam owns a factory in Adana, Turkey, that produces art installations on demand. Since 2006, he has been a codirector of the Reloading Images Immaterial Museum. Behkalam currently lives in Cairo and teaches in the Arts Department at the American University in Cairo.

„Kairo, Februar 2011. Der Diktator Husni Mubarak war abgesetzt worden, und Ruhe kehrte auf die Straßen zurück. Aber die dunklen Gassen und Plätze der Stadt erscheinen auf eine eigenartige Weise leer. Die nächtliche Ausgangssperre hat die Orte der revolutionären Handlungen in einen Raum außerhalb der Zeit verwandelt, in eine Bühne, die darauf wartet, benutzt zu werden, nachdem der Vorhang gefallen und noch nicht wieder geöffnet ist. Womit soll die Bühne bespielt werden?

Fragmentierte Gespräche mit Frauen und Männern, die sich an Träume erinnern, von unbewussten Ängsten und gestaltlosen Bildern sprechen, kontrastieren mit der bewegungslosen Kamera, die auf die Stadt als Manifestation der Wünsche und Projektionen vergangener Epochen gerichtet ist. Excursions in the Dark *spürt – mit Walter Benjamins Worten – dem ‚Augenblick' nach, ‚wo der Historiker selbst die Aufgabe der Traumdeutung übernimmt', und geht auf den Fluchtpunkt zu, an dem sich die Architektur der Stadt, kollektive Traumlandschaften und politische Instanzen treffen."*

Kaya Behkalam wurde 1978 in Berlin geboren. Er ist Künstler und Autor zahlreicher Bücher, darunter *A Spectre Haunting Europe: The Middle Eastern Migrant and the German Angst*. Behkalam besitzt eine Fabrik in Adana, Türkei, die auf Bestellung Kunstinstallationen produziert. Seit 2006 ist er der Kodirektor des Museums Reloading Images Immaterial. Zurzeit lebt er in Kairo und lehrt dort an der Kunstfakultät der American University.

Taha Belal

The Death of Pope Shenouda, 2012
Newspaper transfer on paper / Tageszeitung auf Papier übertragen, 29.7 cm × 42 cm
⟵ pp./S. 98–99

"Egyptian Coptic Christian Pope Shenouda III, the patriarch of most of Egypt's estimated 12 million Christians, died of old age on Saturday, March 17, 2012. Bells tolled in Cairo's Abbasiya district, site of Egypt's main Coptic cathedral, as the news spread. Shenouda, 88, became the 117th Pope of Alexandria in November 1971 and was popular among Egypt's Christians and Muslims alike during his four decades in power."

Taha Belal was born in Cairo in 1984. In 2001, he went to the United States to earn his BA, and then took a year off before returning to the United States to get his MA from the California College of the Arts in San Francisco in 2008. Belal was awarded a residency at the Headlands Center for the Arts and was nominated for the San Francisco Museum of Modern Art SECA Award. His works have been shown in numerous exhibitions. He currently lives and works in Cairo.

„Der koptische Papst Shenouda III., Patriarch des Großteils der geschätzten zwölf Millionen ägyptischen Christen, starb am Samstag, den 17. März 2012 im hohen Alter. Glockengeläut ertönte im Kairoer Stadtteil Abbasiya (Sitz der wichtigsten ägyptischen koptischen Kathedrale), wie es die Nachrichten verbreiteten. Shenouda, 88, wurde im November 1971 in Alexandria zum hundertsiebzehnten Papst ernannt. Unter ägyptischen Christen und Muslimen war er während seiner vier Amtsdekaden sehr beliebt."

Taha Belal wurde 1984 in Kairo geboren. Im Jahr 2001 ging er zum Studium in die USA, 2008 schloss er mit dem MA am California College of the Arts in San Francisco ab. Belal erhielt eine Residenz am Headlands Center for the Arts und wurde für den San Francisco Museum of Modern Art SECA Preis nominiert. Seine Arbeiten wurden in verschiedenen Ausstellungen gezeigt. Zurzeit lebt und arbeitet er in Kairo.

Eva Bertram

High Seats, 2008–2012
C-prints, 20×30 cm
⟵ pp./S. 94–97

"High Seats *shows both 'manned' and 'unmanned' security checkpoints in and around Cairo, set up outside military, government, and other buildings of strategic and operational importance. Taken secretly or from a great distance, the photographs provide an everyday view from the perspective of an observer who is perhaps also being observed. The area being monitored does not seem to fulfill the strategic criteria according to which it was created, which results in absurd coincidences. The exposed security checkpoints become the misplaced relicts of a weakening power."*

Eva Bertram was born in 1964. She studied communication design at the Folkwang University in Essen with a focus on artistic photography under Jürgen Klauke. Since 1993 Bertram has exhibited nationally and internationally, and her works are also part of several collections, including that of the Museum Folkwang in Essen and the Centre National de l'Audiovisuel in Luxembourg. Bertram has been teaching at the New School of Photography in Berlin since 2007 and at the Berlin University of the Arts since 2012. She lives and works in Berlin.

„High Seats *zeigt ‚bemannte' und ‚unbemannte' Kontrolltürme in Kairo und Umgebung, wie man sie rund um militärische Einrichtungen, Behörden oder Anlagen von strategischer, operativer Bedeutung findet. Es sind schnell, teils verstohlen oder aus großer Entfernung gemachte Aufnahmen aus der Perspektive eines alltäglichen Beobachters – der möglicherweise selbst beobachtet wird. Das zu überwachende Gelände scheint die strategischen Kriterien seiner Planung größtenteils nicht zu erfüllen. Die exponierten Kontrolltürme mutieren so zu deplatzierten Relikten der Machtdemonstration."*

Eva Bertram, geboren 1964, studierte Kommunikationsdesign an der Universität GHS/Folkwang in Essen mit Schwerpunkt künstlerische Fotografie bei Jürgen Klauke. Seit 1993 war sie national und international an Ausstellungen beteiligt. Ihre Arbeiten sind in verschiedenen Sammlungen vertreten, u.a. im Museum Folkwang, Essen, und im Centre National de l'Audiovisuel in Luxembourg. Bertram lehrt seit 2007 an der Neuen Schule für Fotografie Berlin sowie seit 2012 an der Universität der Künste Berlin. Sie lebt und arbeitet in Berlin.

Sarah Carr

from the Flickr albums / aus den Flickr-Alben
Tahrir, Day 17 / Tahrir, Tag 17, Feb. 10, 2011
⟵ fig. / Abb. 11
Khaled Said, One Year Later / Khaled Said, Ein Jahr später, June 6, 2011
⟵ fig. / Abb. 6
November 23, Nov. 23, 2011
⟵ fig. / Abb. 46
Cabinet Sit-In Attack Protests / Proteste gegen den Angriff auf die Kabinettsbesetzung, Dec. 18, 2011
⟵ fig. / Abb. 43
1st Anniversary / Erster Jahrestag, Jan. 25, 2012
⟵ fig. / Abb. 9
Port Said Clashes, Day 2 / Auseinandersetzung in Port Said, zweiter

Tag, Feb. 3, 2012
⟵ fig./Abb. 44+45
SCC, June 14, 2012
⟵ fig./Abb. 13, 42
Womens's March/Demonstration der Frauen, Dec. 20, 2011
⟶ p./S. 183
Maspero March/Demonstration bei Maspero, Oct. 9, 2012
⟶ p./S. 197

"1/2 Egyptian. It's my country too you bastards."

This provocative slogan stands at the top of the blog produced by Anglo-Egyptian journalist Sarah Carr. In parallel to her articles for Egypt Independent, she uses her blog to comment on the political and social situation in today's Egypt. In her texts, she blends everyday-life observations with political analysis, often accompanied by sarcastic remarks. Her laconic photographs are in the same vein.

Sarah Carr is an Anglo-Egyptian photographer based in Cairo. She works as a journalist for the newspaper Egypt Independent. Carr blogs at www.inanities.org.

„1/2 Egyptian. It's my country too you bastards"

Dieser provokante Slogan steht über dem Blog der britisch-ägyptischen Journalistin Sarah Carr. Neben ihren Artikeln für Egypt Independent kommentiert sie in ihrem Blog die politische und soziale Lage des heutigen Ägyptens. Ihre Texte verbinden Alltagsbeobachtungen mit politischen Analysen, oftmals begleitet von sarkastischen Kommentaren. Von ähnlicher Art sind ihre lakonischen Fotografien.

Sarah Carr ist eine britisch-ägyptische Fotografin aus Kairo. Sie arbeitet als Journalistin u.a. für Egypt Independent und schreibt für die Internetseite www.inanities.org.

Denis Dailleux

Memories of a Revolution, 2012
Inkjet prints, 30×30cm, 60×60cm
⟵ pp./S. 116–119

"April 5, 2008, Cairo. One of my French friends phoned me up and said: 'Don't go out tomorrow. They're calling for a strike on the social networks.' And yet I did go out on April 6, making my way to Tahrir Square. There wasn't a single demonstrator there, but there were hundreds of police, arbitrarily stopping Egyptians as they came out of the metro exits, thus creating panic. The police were prepared for the possibility of a civil disturbance that day, although this never materialized. I told myself that Egyptians would have to have the courage to die for the revolution.

On January 28, 2011, at around 4 pm, I went with a friend to Tahrir Square. On the way we saw signs that a struggle had taken place: barriers were torn down, the ground was strewn with debris, and the smell of teargas lingered in the air. As we came to Kasr El Nil Bridge, young people were running in all directions, some of them carrying the injured with them. I saw young men in the prime of their lives, yelling to build up the courage to fight with heavily armed policemen. Some just had stones in their hands, others only had their courage. We didn't know it, but at that very moment the uprising was going on throughout Cairo. From all sides young people were coming together to express their anger toward the police. They weren't activists, just ordinary citizens. Many of them were shot down by the police, who were firing from the rooftops.

Two days later photos of the martyrs were all over Tahrir Square, distributed by their friends. I resolved then and there to pay my respects to them one day by taking pictures of their parents and the world they lived in. In this way those who had died would not be forgotten."

Denis Dailleux was born in Angers, France, in 1958. He lives and works in Paris and Cairo and has been a practicing photographer for more than twenty years. Dailleux is a member of l'Agence Vu, an agency for photographers.

„5. April 2008, Kairo. Einer meiner französischen Freunde rief mich an und teilte mir mit: ‚Geh morgen nicht raus, über die sozialen Netzwerke gibt es einen Aufruf zum Streik'. Dennoch bin ich am 6. April rausgegangen, um mich auf den Tahrir-Platz zu begeben. Dort war kein einziger Demonstrant, jedoch Hundertschaften von Polizisten, die willkürlich die Ägypter aufhielten, die aus den Ausgängen der Metro kamen, und so Panik verbreiteten. An diesem Tag waren die Polizisten auf einen möglichen Aufstand vorbereitet, der jedoch nicht stattfand. Ich sagte mir, dass die Ägypter den Mut haben müssten, für die Revolution zu sterben.

Am 28. Januar 2011, gegen 16 Uhr, lief ich mit einem Freund zum Tahrir-Platz. Unterwegs fielen uns die Spuren des Kampfes auf: herausgerissene Absperrungen, der Boden übersät mit Schutt, der Geruch von Tränengas in der Luft. Als wir an der Kasr-El-Nil Brücke ankamen, liefen junge Leute in alle Richtungen, einige von ihnen trugen Verletzte. Ich sah diese jungen Burschen in der Blüte ihrer Jahre, sie schrien, um sich Mut zu machen für den Kampf mit den bis an die Zähne bewaffneten Polizisten. Einige trugen nur Steine, andere hatten als einzige Waffe ihre Wut. Zu diesem Zeitpunkt wussten wir es noch nicht, aber im selben Moment fand der Aufstand in ganz Kairo statt. Von überall liefen Jugendliche herbei, um ihre Wut auf die Polizei zum Ausdruck zu bringen. Es waren keine Aktivisten, sondern einfache Bürger. Viele von ihnen wurden von Polizisten niedergestreckt, die von den Dächern herunterschossen.

Zwei Tage später waren die Fotos der Märtyrer überall auf dem Platz zu sehen, ihre Freunde verteilten sie. Genau in diesem Moment beschloss ich, dass ich ihnen eines Tages meine Ehre erweisen würde, indem ich ihre Eltern und ihr Lebensumfeld fotografieren würde, damit die Verstorbenen nicht in Vergessenheit geraten."

Denis Dailleux wurde 1958 in Angers, Frankreich, geboren. Er lebt und arbeitet in Paris und Kairo und beschäftigt sich hauptberuflich seit über zwanzig Jahren mit Fotografie. Dailleux ist Mitglied der Agence Vu, einer Agentur für Fotografen.

Osama Dawod

Maspero, 2012
⟶ pp./S. 148–149
El Tawheed & El Nour, 2013
HD video, 2:30 min.
⟵ pp./S. 112–113

El Tawheed & El Nour

Osama Dawod's video project shows workers leaving companies that belong to members of the Muslim Brotherhood. On the one hand, the short video sequences make reference to one of the earliest films in history (the Lumière brothers' Workers Leaving the Lumière Factory, *1895), on the other, they show the rigid organization of these companies.*

Osama Dawod was born in Ismaïlia, Egypt, in 1980. He earned a bachelor's degree in design and printmaking from the Faculty of Fine Arts at Helwan University in Cairo in 2003, and afterward he received his master's degree from the San Francisco Art Institute in California. Dawod has participated in various exhibitions in Egypt, Europe, and Asia, including solo shows at the Townhouse Gallery and at the Artellewa Art Space, both in Cairo. He currently teaches photography at the American University in Cairo and lives in Cairo and Ismaïlia.

El Tawheed & El Nour

Im Video von Osama Dawod sieht man, wie Arbeiter oder Angestellte Gebäude von Firmen verlassen, die sich im Besitz der Muslimbruderschaft befinden. Neben der Referenz auf eines der frühesten Stücke der Filmgeschichte – Louis und Auguste Lumière, Arbeiter verlassen die Lumière-Werke, *1895 – geben die kurzen Videosequenzen einen Eindruck von der straffen Organisation der Unternehmen.*

Osama Dawod wurde 1980 in Ismaïlia, Ägypten, geboren. Bis 2003 studierte er Design und Druckgrafik an der Kunstfakultät der Helwan Universität in Kairo und machte anschließend seinen MA am San Francisco Art Institute in Kalifornien. Dawod nahm an zahlreichen Ausstellungen in Ägypten, Europa und Asien teil, darunter Einzelausstellungen in der Townhouse Galerie und im Artellewa Art Space, beide in Kairo. Zurzeit lehrt er Fotografie an der American University in Kairo und lebt sowohl in Kairo als auch in Ismaïlia.

Johanna Domke & Marouan Omara

CROP, 2013
HD video, 45:09 min.
⟵ pp./S. 120–121

"CROP is a documentary film that reflects the impact of images on the Egyptian revolution. The film does not show any images from the uprisings but reveals the inner life of Egypt's oldest and most influential state newspaper, Al-Ahram. In a row of carefully created tableaux we become witness to the proceedings inside the institution—from the highest executive offices to individual workers. A voice-over tells the story of a photojournalist who missed the revolution because he was in hospital. His voice offers a personal reflection on the media ploys of the old regime."

Johanna Domke is a visual artist who works with film, video, and photography. She was born in Kiel, Germany, in 1978, and grew up in both Germany and Argentina. Domke studied fine arts at the Royal Danish Academy of Fine Arts in Copenhagen, Denmark, and at the Malmö Art Academy in Sweden. Her work has been shown in international group exhibitions and in solo shows, and recently at the Shedhalle Zurich, the Berlinische Galerie in Germany, the Kunsthallen Nikolaj in Copenhagen, and the Casino Luxembourg. She currently lives in Berlin, Istanbul, and Copenhagen, creating pieces in the crossover field of art and cinema.

Marouan Omara is a filmmaker from Cairo, born in 1987. He studied photography at the Faculty of Applied Arts in Cairo and joined the Academy of Cinema Arts and Technology in

2006 to follow his passion for filmmaking. Starting his career as a freelance photographer, he showed his work in photography exhibitions at both national and international level. He has produced a series of documentaries and worked in a number of productions in different capacities. He took part in the Arabia Offscreen cultural expedition and participated in the Durban Talent Campus for young filmmakers. Omara is currently preparing his first feature film *Repeated Stopping*, which will be produced at the beginning of 2013.

"CROP *ist ein Dokumentarfilm, der die Bedeutung der Bilder in der ägyptischen Revolution reflektiert. Der Film zeigt nicht etwa Aufnahmen von den Aufständen, er macht das Innenleben der ältesten und einflussreichsten staatlichen Zeitung Ägyptens, Al-Ahram, sichtbar. In einer Sequenz sorgfältig komponierter Standbilder werden wir Zeugen der Vorgänge im Inneren dieser Institution – vom Büro der Geschäftsführung bis zur Tätigkeit des einzelnen Arbeiters. Als Voice-over hören wir die fiktive Geschichte eines Fotojournalisten, der die Revolution eines Krankenhausaufenthalts wegen verpasst hat. Seine Erzählung liefert eine persönliche Einschätzung der Medienstrategien des alten Regimes.*"

Johanna Domke wurde 1978 in Kiel geboren und wuchs in Deutschland und Argentinien auf. Sie studierte an der Königlichen Dänischen Kunstakademie in Kopenhagen und an der Malmö Art Academy in Schweden. Domke arbeitet mit den Medien Film, Video und Fotografie. Ihre Werke wurden in internationalen Gruppen- und Einzelausstellungen gezeigt, jüngst in der Shedhalle in Zürich, der Berlinischen Galerie, der Kunsthalle Nikolaj in Kopenhagen und im Casino Luxemburg. Heute lebt sie in Berlin, Istanbul und Kopenhagen und produziert Arbeiten, die an der Schnittstelle zwischen Kunst und Kino angesiedelt sind.

Marouan Omara, geboren 1987, ist ein Filmemacher aus Kairo. Er studierte Fotografie an der Hochschule für Angewandte Künste in Kairo und ab 2006 an der Academy of Cinema Arts And Technology. Er arbeitete als freischaffender Fotograf, seine Arbeiten wurden im In- und Ausland gezeigt. Er hat mehrere Dokumentarfilme gedreht und wirkte an verschiedenen Produktionen mit. Er war Teilnehmer des Programms Arabia Off Screen und Durban Talent Campus für junge Filmemacher. Sein erster Spielfilm *Repeated Stopping* wird 2013 produziert.

Amira El Ahl

Interview with video journalist Mostafa Bahgat/Interview mit dem Videojournalisten Mostafa Bahgat, 2012

⟶ pp. 163–167/S. 167–172

Amira El Ahl's Egyptian and German heritage has provided her with a rich insight into the Middle East. After finishing her training at a local newspaper in Germany, she worked for two years as the Middle East correspondent for Der Spiegel in Cairo. Today she works as a freelance correspondent and expert in the region. Her travels have taken her all over the world, to Lebanon, Algeria, Jordan, Syria, and the United Arab Emirates, as well as to the USA, Canada, South Africa, and most of the countries in western Europe. Her language skills and her cultural heritage allow her a deep access and insight into the Arab world. Her aim is to report fairly and truthfully about the people, their traditions, and their way of life, free from stereotypes and prejudices.

Als Tochter eines Ägypters und einer Deutschen ist Amira El Ahl von Kindesbeinen an mit der arabischen Kultur vertraut. Nach ihrer Ausbildung zur Journalistin hat sie zwei Jahre lang als Auslandskorrespondentin für den Spiegel aus Kairo berichtet und arbeitet heute als freie Korrespondentin und Expertin im Nahen Osten. Ihre Reisen führten sie u.a. in den Libanon, nach Algerien, Jordanien, Syrien und die Vereinigten Arabischen Emirate sowie in die USA, Kanada, Südafrika und fast alle Länder Westeuropas. Ihre Sprachkenntnisse und ihre Herkunft erlauben ihr Zugang und Einblick in die arabische Welt, wie er nur wenigen ausländischen Journalisten möglich ist. Ihr Ziel ist es, gerecht und wahrheitsgemäß über die Menschen, ihre Traditionen und Lebensarten zu berichten, jenseits gängiger Klischees und Stereotype.

Hossam el-Hamalawy

The Revolution Will Be Flickrized/ Die Revolution wird flickrisiert werden, May 8, 2008

⟶ p. 190/S. 191

from the Flickr album/aus dem Flickr-Album *Egyptian Street Art*

⟶ p./S. 193, 196–197

In May 2008, the blogger and journalist Hossam el-Hamalawy wrote in a number of texts about the revolutionary power of images. This was prompted by pictures taken by the Egyptian photojournalist Nasser Nouri covering the workers' insurrection in El-Mahalla El-Kubra. Of course, it was not just the "distribution of pictures" that led to the January 2011 uprisings in Tunisia, Egypt, and the Arab world, although the new digital information channels had their part to play.

Hossam el-Hamalawy, an Egyptian journalist, photographer, and blogger, was born in 1977. He received his BA in economics from the American University in Cairo and his MA in political science from the same university. During his time at university, he joined the Revolutionary Socialists, a Trotskyite organization in Egypt that is currently involved in establishing the Workers Democratic Party. El-Hamalawy was one of the first participants and organizers of the Egyptian Revolution, and since that day he has blogged for the website 3arabawy.

Bereits im Mai 2008 schrieb der Blogger und Journalist Hossam el-Hamalawy über die revolutionäre Macht der Bilder. Anlass waren Aufnahmen des ägyptischen Fotojournalisten Nasser Nouri vom Arbeiteraufstand in El-Mahalla El-Kubra. Gewiss lag es nicht nur an der Verbreitung der Bilder, dass es im Januar 2011 zu den Aufständen in Tunesien, Ägypten und anderen Teilen der arabischen Welt kam, auch wenn die neuen digitalen Informationskanäle sicher ihren Anteil daran hatten.

Hossam el-Hamalawy, ein ägyptischer Journalist, Fotograf und Blogger, wurde 1977 geboren. Er erhielt seinen BA von der American University in Kairo in Wirtschaft und seinen MA von derselben Universität in Politikwissenschaft. Bereits während seiner Zeit an der Universität wurde er Mitglied der Revolutionary Socialists, einer trotzkistischen Organisation in Ägypten, die sich zurzeit mit dem Aufbau einer demokratischen Arbeiterpartei beschäftigt. El-Hamalawy war einer der ersten Teilnehmer und Organisatoren der ägyptischen Revolution und berichtet darüber für die Internetseite 3arabawy.

Hala Elkoussy

The Myths & Legends Room – The Mural, 2010

48 C-prints, 900×300 cm

⟵ pp./S. 110–111

"Hala Elkoussy's The Myths & Legends Room – The Mural *is a series of photographic tales based on historical facts, rumors, religious beliefs, traditions, myths, and legends. Narratives are conjured up that allow reality to shimmer through: life in Cairo, the city that lies at the root of almost all of Elkoussy's works. The large mural explores the genre of the photomontage that has become ubiquitous in the advertising industry. Elkoussy uses the montage principle on a massive and colorful scale, bringing together staged images and street photography, old photographs, original drawings, illustrations and computer-generated graphics and design. Reference is made to commemorative wall paintings such as those in the National Military Museum in Cairo depicting war scenes from Egyptian history, and military heroism and its popular celebration."*

Hala Elkoussy was born in Cairo in 1974. She studied at the American University before completing an MA in image and communication at Goldsmiths College, University of London. She lectured on photography in 2002 and 2003. In 2004, she cofounded the Contemporary Image Collective (CIC) in Cairo. In 2006, she completed a two-year residency at the Rijksakademie van Beeldende Kunsten in Amsterdam. In 2010, Elkoussy was a recipient of the Abraaj Capital Art Prize. Most recently, her feature film treatment entitled *Cactus Flower* received a development grant from the Rotterdam International Film Festival's Hubert Bals Fund.

„Hala Elkoussys The Myths & Legends Room – The Mural *besteht aus fotografischen Geschichten, die auf historischen Fakten, Gerüchten, religiösen Vorstellungen, Traditionen, Mythen und Legenden basieren. Es sind beschwörende Erzählungen, durch die die Wirklichkeit hindurchschimmert: die Realität des Lebens in Kairo, der Stadt, die Ausgangspunkt fast aller Arbeiten von Elkoussy ist. Künstlerisch untersucht dieses Wandbild das Prinzip der Fotomontage. Elkoussy nutzt es im großen und farbenprächtigen Stil, indem sie kommerzielle Studiofotografien, Aufnahmen aus dem Alltag, gefundene alte Fotos, Zeichnungen, Illustrationen und am Computer erstellte Grafiken und Designelemente kombiniert. Die Arbeit verweist auf Wandmalereien, die Kriegsszenen aus der ägyptischen Geschichte oder Heldentaten des Militärs und dessen Unterstützung durch das Volk darstellen, wie sie zum Beispiel im National Military Museum in Kairo ausgestellt sind."*

Hala Elkoussy wurde 1974 in Kairo geboren. Bevor sie ihr Studium der Bild- und Kommunikationswissenschaften am Goldsmiths College in London abschloss, hatte sie bereits an der American University in Kairo studiert. Zwischen 2002 und 2003 hielt sie Vorlesungen zum Thema Fotografie. Im Jahr 2004 war sie eine der Mitbegründer des Contemporary Image Collective (CIC) in Kairo. 2006 beendete sie eine zweijährige Künstlerresidenz an der Rijksakademie Van Beeldende Kunsten in Amsterdam. 2010 wurde Elkoussy der Abraaj Capital Art Prize verliehen. Zuletzt erhielt sie für ihren Spielfilm *Cactus Flower* Fördermittel vom Hubert Bald Fund des Internationalen Filmfestivals Rotterdam.

Mosa'ab Elshamy

from the Flickr albums / aus den Flickr-Alben
Protesters during a speech, Tahrir Square / Demonstranten während einer Rede, Tahrir-Platz, Apr. 8, 2011
⟶ fig. / Abb. 50
Revolution Graffiti / Graffiti der Revolution, July 15, 2011
⟶ p. / S. 193
El-Fan Midan / Veranstaltung „Kunst ist ein Platz", Jan. 7, 2012
⟶ p. / S. 183
Jan. 25 Anniversary / Jahrestag, Jan. 27, 2012
⟶ p. / S. 196
Downtown Walls / Mauern in der Kairoer Innenstadt, Mar. 12, 2012
⟶ pp. / S. 184–185
Revolution's 2nd Anniversary / Zweiter Jahrestag der Revolution, Jan. 25, 2013
⟵ fig. / Abb. 14
Most Popular / Am beliebtesten, July 4, 2013
⟶ p. / S. 194–195
Masks of Tahrir / Masken auf dem Tahrir, 2011–13
⟶ pp. / S. 186–187

Masks of Tahrir
"Tahrir sometimes feels like an unintended costume party. The diversity of the people who have been attending the demonstrations since day one can be seen in the clothing they wear. In the project, I have focused on their faces."

Mosa'ab Elshamy, born in 1990, is an independent young photographer based in Cairo. His images and photo stories of the Egyptian Revolution have appeared in Time Magazine, The Economist, Foreign Policy Magazine, Al Jazeera, and Al Akhbar English, as well as in other print and online media.

Masken auf dem Tahrir
„Der Tahrir-Platz wirkt manchmal wie der Veranstaltungsort eines unbeabsichtigten Kostümfests. Die Unterschiedlichkeit der Menschen, die seit Tag eins der Revolution bei den Demonstrationen dabei sind, spiegelt sich in der Kleidung wider. In diesem Projekt habe ich mich auf ihre Gesichter konzentriert."

Mosa'ab Elshamy, geboren 1990, ist ein freiberuflicher Fotograf, der in Kairo lebt und arbeitet. Seine Bilder und Fotostrecken über die ägyptische Revolution waren im TIME Magazin, in The Economist, im Foreign Policy Magazin, bei Al Jazeera und Al Akhbar English sowie in weiteren Print- und Online-Medien vertreten.

Rowan El Shimi

Graffiti against the Power of the State Media / Graffiti gegen die Macht der Staatsmedien
⟶ pp. / S. 150–151
The Woman in the Blue Bra / Die Frau mit dem blauen BH
⟶ pp. / S. 182–183
from the Flickr album / aus dem Flickr-Album *Kasr El Aini Street Battle / Kasr-El-Aini Straßengefechte*, Dec. 18, 2011
⟶ p. / S. 183
Walls in Downtown Cairo / Barrikaden in der Kairoer Innenstadt
⟶ pp. / S. 184–185

Rowan El Shimi is a journalist who writes on culture and sustainable development. She is also actively involved on a grassroots level, in addition to her job as a reporter. She has a keen interest in photography and has participated in collaborative initiatives including the 2012 Alternative News Agency II workshop at the Contemporary Image Collective, a Cairo-based visual arts center. Her snapshots of the ongoing Egyptian Revolution have featured in several venues and magazines both locally and internationally. Alongside her interest in photography, El Shimi has found a niche in volunteerism, a movement that inspires her myriad interests.

Rowan El Shimi ist Journalistin, sie schreibt über kulturelle Ereignisse und nachhaltige Entwicklung. Daneben ist sie auch in Bürgerbewegungen aktiv. Sie hat ein starkes Interesse an Fotografie und nahm an verschiedenen Gemeinschaftsinitiativen teil, u.a. 2012 am Alternative News Agency II Workshop am Contemporary Image Collective, einem Zentrum für bildende Kunst in Kairo. Ihre Schnappschüsse von der andauernden ägyptischen Revolution waren sowohl national als auch international zu sehen. Sie engagiert sich ehrenamtlich und findet in dieser Arbeit Inspiration.

Mohamed Ezz

Vinegar.. Soldier.. Coke, 2011
Cyanotype prints on cotton paper / Cyanotypie-Drucke auf Baumwollpapier, 120 × 60 cm
⟵ pp. / S. 102–103

"'We tried that in Tunis until their bombs became useless... God be with you, Egyptians.'

These kinds of messages spread quickly after the first night of the Egyptian Revolution, when police forces successfully put an end to the demonstrations. The teargas and the lack of experience on the part of the protesters were what ended the demonstrations. The next day messages arrived from Tunisian protesters explaining how to protect oneself from the gas. On the Friday of Anger, Egyptians carried bottles of vinegar and coke. They could finally stand up to the soldiers, restarting the protests that would ultimately lead to the downfall of the thirty-year regime."

Mohamed Ezz, an Egyptian photographer and engineer, was born in 1985 in Cairo, where he currently lives. In his work, he captures different kinds of scenes taking place in his surrounding community. Ezz draws attention to the people and situations that are a part of his daily life in Egypt, and to various aspects of Egyptian society. In 2005, he began participating in artistic events and exhibitions. Most recently, he won the Jury Award at the EU Delegation's first photography competition in 2008 and the Gold Medal at the Sharjah Award for Arab Photography in 2011.

„,Das haben wir in Tunis ausprobiert, bis ihre Bomben unbrauchbar wurden ... Gott sei mit Euch, ägyptisches Volk.'

Solche Nachrichten verbreiteten sich nach der ersten Nacht der ägyptischen Revolution, als Polizeikräfte erfolgreich die Demonstrationen aufgelöst hatten. Es lag an den Tränengasbomben und der Unwissenheit der Demonstranten, die sich nicht dagegen zu schützen wussten. Am nächsten Tag trafen die Mitteilungen von tunesischen Aktivisten ein, die den Umgang mit dem Gas erklärten. Am Tag des Zorns, einem Freitag, hatten die Ägypter Flaschen mit Essig und Cola dabei. Endlich konnten sie den Soldaten standhalten, und die Proteste, die zum Sturz des seit dreißig Jahren bestehenden Regimes führen sollten, begannen von Neuem."

Mohammed Ezz, Fotograf und Ingenieur, wurde 1985 in Kairo geboren, wo er zurzeit auch lebt und arbeitet. Er fotografiert Szenen und Geschehnisse in seiner unmittelbaren Umgebung und lenkt die Aufmerksamkeit damit auf die Menschen und die Alltagsrealität und gleichzeitig auf die verschiedensten Aspekte der ägyptischen Gesellschaft. Seit 2005 nimmt er an Ausstellungen und Kunstaktionen teil. Zu seinen jüngsten Preisen zählen der Jury-Preis des ersten Fotografie-Wettbewerbs der Delegation der Europäischen Union, 2008, und der Golden Award beim Sharjah Award for Arab Photo, 2011.

Al Shorouk Photojournalists / -Fotojournalisten

Roger Anis (studied fine arts; with Al Shorouk since 2010 / studierte bildende Kunst, seit 2010 bei Al Shorouk)
⟵ fig. / Abb. 15,
⟶ fig. / Abb. 34, 35, 42
Ahmed Abdellatif (studied mass communication; with Al Shorouk since it started in 2008 / studierte Kommunikationsdesign, seit der Gründung 2008 bei Al Shorouk)
⟵ fig. / Abb. 50
Fadi Ezzat
⟵ fig. / Abb. 12, 48
Thomas Hartwell
⟵ fig. / Abb. 52, ⟶ p. / S. 151, 197
Aly Hazza'a (studied engineering; with Al Shorouk since 2011 / studierte an der Fakultät für Ingenieurwesen, seit 2011 bei Al Shorouk)
⟵ fig. / Abb. 54, ⟶ p. / S. 183 + cover,
⟶ fig. / Abb. 11, 36
Eman Helal
⟶ fig. / Abb. 39
Magdy Ibrahim (studied mass communication; with Al Shorouk since it started in 2008 / studierte Kommunikationsdesign, seit der Gründung 2008 bei Al Shorouk)
⟶ fig. / Abb. 40
Sabry Khaled (studied dentistry; with Al Shorouk since end of 2012 / studierte an der Zahnärztlichen Fakultät, seit Ende 2012 bei Al Shorouk)
⟶ fig. / Abb. 45
Heba Khalifa (studied fine arts; with Al Shorouk since 2009 / studierte bildende Kunst, seit 2009 bei Al Shorouk)
⟵ fig. / Abb. 47
Heba el Kholy (studied fine arts; with Al Shorouk since 2012 / studierte bildende Kunst, seit 2012 bei Al Shorouk)
⟶ fig. / Abb. 13
Mohamed el Maymony (studied commerce; with Al Shorouk since it started in 2008 / studierte Wirtschaft, seit der Gründung 2008 bei Al Shorouk)
⟶ fig. / Abb. 44
George Mohsen (studied commerce; with Al Shorouk since 2012 / studierte

Wirtschaft, seit 2012 bei Al Shorouk)
⟶ fig. / Abb. 41
Samuel Mohsen (studied commerce; with Al Shorouk since 2012/ studierte Wirtschaft, seit 2012 bei Al Shorouk)
⟶ fig. / Abb. 37
Amira Mortada (studied mass communication; with Al Shorouk since 2010/studierte Kommunikationsdesign, seit 2010 bei Al Shorouk)
⟵ fig. / Abb. 53
Jihan Nasr (studied sociology; with Al Shorouk since 2009/ studierte Soziologie, seit 2009 bei Al Shorouk)
⟵ fig. / Abb. 49
Randa Shaath (studied mass communication and Middle Eastern studies, with Al Shorouk since it started in 2008/studierte Nahoststudien und Kommunikationsdesign, seit der Gründung 2008 bei Al Shorouk)
⟶ fig. / Abb. 43
Rafi Shaker (studied law; with Al Shorouk since 2010/studierte Rechtswissenschaften, seit 2010 bei Al Shorouk)
⟶ fig. / Abb. 38
Lobna Tarek (studied mass communication; with Al Shorouk since 2010/studierte Kommunikationsdesign, seit 2010 bei Al Shorouk)
⟵ fig. / Abb. 51

"The 'red line' refers to the unwritten rules that stifled Egypt for over thirty years. Under the Mubarak regime, the 'red lines' not to be crossed limited what was said and done, and more importantly what was publicly disseminated. One either imposed self-censorship or was punished. Decades of a state of emergency and the selective application of laws helped to control dissent. The January 25 Revolution took place because public resentment had reached boiling point.

The young photographers from Al Shorouk newspaper were among the vanguard of those who found an audience for their voices and a venue for images that previously would have been unpublished. The fear of confronting authoritarian rule evaporated almost overnight. Egyptians raised their voices and began to define their own 'red lines' for society and those who govern the country. Working closely as a team, the photographers from Al Shorouk continue to document the revolution, as Egypt continues to protest, debate, speak out, and search for a new order."
(Thomas Hartwell)

Thomas Hartwell was born in Texas in 1955. He received a degree in Middle Eastern studies and photojournalism from the University of Texas. Hartwell has spent over thirty years in the Middle East, living in Iran, Egypt, and Algeria, photographing news, features, and documentary projects on assignment for a variety of international publications and organizations. He has participated in exhibitions in Egypt, Algeria, Bahrain, Switzerland, and the USA. Currently he is a photo editor on the Middle East regional photo desk at the Associated Press in Cairo.

„Die ‚rote Linie' bezieht sich auf die ungeschriebenen Gesetze, die Ägypten mehr als dreißig Jahre gelähmt haben. Unter dem Mubarak-Regime markierte die nicht zu übertretende ‚rote Linie', was gesagt oder getan werden durfte und – vielleicht fast wichtiger – was öffentlich verbreitet werden durfte. Man hatte die Wahl zwischen Selbstzensur oder Strafe. Jahrzehnte des Ausnahmezustands und die selektive Anwendung von Gesetzen halfen dabei, abweichende Meinungen zu kontrollieren. Der über die Jahre aufgebaute Druck entlud sich in der Revolution vom 25. Januar.

Die jungen Fotografen der Tageszeitung Al Shorouk waren unter den ersten, die ein Publikum für ihre Stimmen und Bilder fanden, die anderenfalls unveröffentlicht geblieben wären. Die Angst vor einer Konfrontation mit der Obrigkeit verschwand beinahe über Nacht. Die Ägypter erhoben ihre Stimmen und begannen, ihre eigene ‚rote Linie' für die Gesellschaft und die Regierenden zu definieren. In Teamarbeit setzen die Fotografen von Al Shorouk die Berichterstattung über den Wandel fort, während Ägypten weiterhin protestiert, debattiert, sich artikuliert und nach einer neuen Ordnung sucht."
(Thomas Hartwell)

Thomas Hartwell wurde 1955 in Texas geboren. Er studierte an der University of Texas Nahoststudien und Fotojournalismus. Hartwell hat über dreißig Jahre im Nahen Osten gelebt und fotografierte im Auftrag verschiedener internationaler Medien und Organisationen. Seine Bilder wurden in Ausstellungen in Ägypten, Algerien, Bahrain, der Schweiz und den USA gezeigt. Im Moment ist er Bildredakteur für den Bereich Nahost bei der Associated Press in Kairo.

Heba Farid

Making Heroes–Photograph Albums from Egyptian Military and Police Officers / Konstruktion von Helden – Fotoalben von ägyptischen Militär- und Polizeioffizieren
⟵ fig. / Abb. 1, ⟵ pp. / S. 106–109
Testimonies, Protests, and Photojournalism / Zeugnisse, Proteste und Fotojournalismus
Interpretation of the photographs / Interpretation der Bilder: Heba Farid, Amgad Naguib, Menna Khalil
from the collection of / aus der Sammlung von Amgad Naguib
⟵ fig. / Abb. 2, 3, ⟶ fig. / Abb. 2–4

Making Heroes – Photograph Albums from Egyptian Military and Police Officers
Facsimiles (bound photographic prints) of eight vintage photograph albums (paper and plastic albums, silver gelatin and c-prints, some handcolored / retouched).

Albums and individual photographs originate from the early 1920s to the late 1970s. Photo albums compiled by members of the army or security forces or by police officers have now become artifacts documenting the construction of a self-image.

"General" Louis Ibrahim Album
from the collection of Amgad Naguib
⟵ fig. 1, ⟵ pp. 106–107
Photograph wallet album (14×10×1 cm) showing ID cards for and portraits of Louis Ibrahim and his wife, 1960s: plastic, commercially available photograph album, 4 interior plastic sleeve pages (1 fold-out, 3 panels), 4 silver gelatin prints, 8×11 cm, 3 ID cards with photographs, 1 relic (human remains), souvenir (Jerusalem) on card, 1 religious icon color reproduction 7×10.5 cm

The *"General" Louis Ibrahim Album* shows the well decorated maestro, director of the Egyptian military band from the mid-1960s to early 1970s. It reveals his propensity for the theatrical, his penchant for self-portraiture, and his love for his wife.

Police Academy Album
from the collection of Amgad Naguib
⟵ pp. 108–109
Photograph album depicting the Egyptian Police Academy, souvenir photographs, 1960s: leather, commercially available photograph album, gold embossed title "Album", string binding, cloth inside cover, paper interior, 16 pages, 15 silver gelatin photographs: 13.5×18.5cm, 24 photographs: 9×14cm, adhesive, calc page separators, cover left-opening. 24.5×30.5×2cm

The *Police Academy Album*, perhaps a maquette for a final version, documents an official visit, highlights the contemporary identity of the security forces in post-1952 revolutionary Egypt and its own self-promotional institutional spirit.

Heba Farid, born in Cairo in 1966, is a multidisciplinary artist with a background in landscape architecture and fine arts. Aside from her artistic practice, she is also a founding board member of the Contemporary Image Collective, an independent nonprofit art initiative founded in Cairo in 2004. Since 2008, Farid has been coordinating the Photographic Memory of Egypt program for the Center for Documentation of Cultural and Natural Heritage, a research-based initiative focused on the historiography of photographic practice in Egypt. Farid currently lives and works in Cairo.

Konstruktion von Helden – Fotoalben von ägyptischen Militär- und Polizeioffizieren
Faksimiles (gebundene fotografische Abzüge) von acht Vintage-Fotoalben (Papier- und Plastikalben, Silbergelatineabzüge und C-Prints, einige handkoloriert / retuschiert).

Die Alben und einzelnen Fotografien datieren aus den frühen 1920er bis späten 1970er Jahren. Die von Militärangehörigen, Polizeibeamten oder Sicherheitspersonal zusammengestellten Fotoalben sind Artefakte, die dem Betrachter die Konstruktion eines Selbstbildes vor Augen führen.

„General" Louis Ibrahim Album
aus der Sammlung von Amgad Naguib
⟵ Abb. 1, S. 106–107
Taschenfotoalbum (14×10×1 cm) mit Ausweisen und Porträts von Louis Ibrahim und seiner Frau, 1960er: Plastik, im Handel erhältliches Fotoalbum, 4 Einsteckseiten aus Plastik (1 ausfaltbar, 3 Tafeln), 4 Silbergelatineabzüge, 8×11 cm, 3 Ausweise mit Foto, 1 Relikt (menschlichen Ursprungs), Souvenir (Jerusalem) auf Pappe 1 farbige Reproduktion einer religiösen Ikone, 1 farbige Reproduktion einer religiösen Ikone 7×10,5 cm

Das *„General" Louis Ibrahim Album* zeigt den exzentrischen und hoch dekorierten Maestro, Mitte der 1960er bis in die frühen 1970er Jahre Dirigent der ägyptischen Militärkapelle. Es offenbart seinen Hang zu Theatralik und Selbstdarstellung und die Liebe zu seiner Frau.

Polizeiakademie-Album
aus der Sammlung von Amgad Naguib
⟵ S. 108–109
Fotoalbum, welches die ägyptische Polizeiakademie zeigt, Souvenir-Fotografien, 1960er: Leder, im Handel erhältliches Fotoalbum, auf dem Titel das Wort „Album" in Goldprägung, Fadenbindung, Innendeckel Stoff, Innenseiten Papier, 16 Seiten, 15 Silbergelatineabzüge: 13,5×18,5cm, 24 Fotografien: 9×14 cm, Klebstoff, Trennseiten aus Pergamin, Album öffnet links. 24,5×30,5×2 cm

Das *Polizeiakademie-Album*, eventuell ein Probeexemplar der endgültigen Version, dokumentiert einen offiziellen Besuch und betont die zeitgenössische Identität der Sicherheitskräfte im Ägypten nach der Revolution von 1952 sowie ihren Wunsch nach Selbstdarstellung.

Heba Farid, geboren 1966 in Kairo, ist eine interdisziplinär arbeitende Künstlerin, die Landschaftsarchitektur und bildende Kunst studiert hat. Abgesehen von ihren eigenen künstlerischen Aktivitäten, ist sie Gründungsmitglied des Contemporary Image Collective (CIC), einer unabhängigen gemeinnützigen Künstlerinitiative, die 2004 in Ägypten ins Leben gerufen wurde. Seit 2008 koordiniert Farid das Programm für Photographic Memory of Egypt des Center for Documentation of Cultural and Natural Heritage, einer auf Forschung basierten Initiative, die sich auf die Geschichte fotografischer Praxis in Ägypten konzentriert. Zurzeit lebt und arbeitet Farid in Kairo.

Nermine Hammam

from the series / aus der Serie
Upekkha, 2011
Inkjet prints, 60×90 cm, 50×90 cm
⟵ pp. / S. 104–105

"In the course of the January Revolution we were frightened to hear that the army was on its way. This legendary force was leaving its barracks in the desert to take on the citizens in Tahrir Square. Heavy tanks rushed through Cairo's deserted streets, but when the hatches opened, what emerged was not the angry stereotypes of power and masculinity that we expected, but wide-eyed youths with tiny frames and ill-fitting army fatigues. The soldiers' vulnerability and youth baffled me. I realized then and there: power is a myth, a construct. It is found only in images, not in an inherent reality. The power of the military was a projection of the soldiers and citizens alike. Power is an elaborately choreographed performance, complete with props, which transforms young men into military symbols.

During the eighteen days of the revolution, faced with thousands of peaceful protesters the army seemed passive, mere observers of the scene. I felt an urge to parody propaganda posters from the 1940s and 1950s with their idealized images of strong men and women. The background motifs in my pictures emphasize how disparate the presence of the armed men among the civilians in Tahrir was: men of war in Paradise."

Nermine Hammam, born in Cairo in 1967, is a visual artist. She obtained her BA in filmmaking from New York University's Tisch School of Arts. She makes densely composed figurative prints that exist somewhere between painting and photography. Hammam's work has been widely exhibited and is part of public and private collections around the world.

„Während der ägyptischen Revolution im Januar haben wir mit Besorgnis vernommen, dass die Armee im Anmarsch war. Diese legendäre Kraft verließ ihr Lager in der Wüste, um zu den Bürgern auf dem Tahrir zu stoßen. Schwerfällige Panzer ächzten durch die verlassenen Straßen Kairos. Und als die Luken sich öffneten, kamen nicht, wie von uns erwartet, wütende Stereotypen der Macht und Männlichkeit heraus, sondern Jugendliche mit großen Augen, schmalem Kreuz und schlecht sitzenden Tarnanzügen. Die Verletzlichkeit der Soldaten und ihre Jugend verblüfften mich. In diesem Moment wurde mir bewusst, dass Macht ein Mythos ist, eine Konstruktion – sie existiert nur auf Bildern, nicht in der Realität. Die Macht des Militärs war eine wechselseitige Projektion, Soldaten und Bürger waren gleichermaßen daran beteiligt. Macht ist zugleich eine sorgfältig choreografierte Performance, inklusive Requisiten, welche diese Jugendlichen in militärische Symbole verwandelten.

Während der achtzehn Tage der Revolution schien die Armee angesichts Tausender friedlicher Demonstranten inaktiv, ausschließlich Beobachter der Ereignisse zu sein. Ich hatte das Bedürfnis, Propagandaposter aus den Vierziger- und Fünfzigerjahren mit starken, idealisierten Männern und Frauen zu parodieren. Die Hintergrundmotive in meiner Arbeit betonen, wie unstimmig die Anwesenheit der bewaffneten Männer unter den Zivilisten auf dem Tahrir wirkte: Männer des Krieges im Paradies."

Nermine Hammam wurde 1967 in Kairo geboren. Sie studierte am Institut für Film der Tisch School of Arts in New York. Die Künstlerin komponiert dichte figurative Bilder zwischen Malerei und Fotografie. Ihre Arbeiten wurden bereits vielfach ausgestellt und sind Teil öffentlicher und privater Sammlungen weltweit.

Tarek Hefny

from the series / aus der Serie
you two faced whore!, 2008
Monochrome print on newspaper / Schwarzweißdruck auf Zeitungspapier
⟵ pp. / S. 124–125

Since the financial crisis of 2008, the billboards along Egypt's highways have been empty. The desolate landscape of the Cairo–Alexandria road is framed and emphasized by these monstrous yet powerless structures. Hefny's images recall a topographical photographic tradition documenting the "man-altered landscapes" that result from the excesses of modernity.

Tarek Hefny is a photographer based in Cairo. He received his bachelor's degree with honors in painting from the Helwan University Faculty of Fine Arts in Cairo in 2005. Hefny has participated in several group exhibitions, showing his work in both painting and photography shows. He focuses mainly on modern urban life and its effects. Hefny has spent his whole life immersed in the intense atmosphere of Cairo, and most of his work revolves around the relation between a person and the place where he or she lives.

Seit der Finanzkrise 2008 bleiben die vielen Billboards an den ägyptischen Überlandstraßen leer. Die desolate Landschaft an der Verbindungsstraße zwischen Kairo und Alexandria wird von den monströsen, aber machtlosen Strukturen neu gerahmt und akzentuiert. Hefnys Bilder knüpfen an die Tradition der topografischen Fotografie an, die eine vom Menschen veränderte Landschaft dokumentiert, in der sich die Exzesse der Moderne niederschlagen.

Tarek Hefny ist Fotograf. Er erhielt 2005 seinen BA mit Auszeichnung in Malerei von der Fakultät der bildenden Künste der Helwan Universität in Kairo. Hefny nahm sowohl mit fotografischen wie auch malerischen Werken an zahlreichen Gruppenausstellungen teil. Sein Interesse gilt dem modernen urbanen Leben und dessen Auswirkungen. Geprägt durch das Leben in Kairo, beschäftigt Hefny sich in seinen Arbeiten hauptsächlich mit der Beziehung zwischen Personen und den Orten, in denen diese leben.

Ahmed Kamel

Hypothetical Society, 2009
Drawings on paper / Zeichnungen auf Papier, 49.5×56 cm, 32×50 cm
⟵ pp. / S. 100–101

"What I call 'hypothetical society' is an internet-based community that allows 'friends' who might or might not know each other in 'real life' to view one another's profiles. Participants are aware of their appearance and pose for the pictures in a certain manner. Through the upload and display of such photos, the private becomes public and is given short-term attention as a projection, which one can comment on: 'Like' or 'Dislike.' In this way the hypothetical society allows Internet users to view a wide range of groups and communities and their behaviors in their environments.

These photographic images are converted into drawings with non-expressive lines by means of a projector-machine and the 'real' background is turned into a neutral gray. In this way a new focus of attention is created, individual features and concrete surroundings disappear, and details in clothing and accessories are reduced. The uploaded screenshot becomes a drawing on the wall, assuming the function of an iconographical locum in a non-objective space."

Ahmed Kamel was born in Cairo in 1981. He studied painting at Helwan University in Cairo and received his BA in 2003. Kamel has had various solo shows and participated in group exhibitions in the Middle East and Europe, including the Contemporary Image Collective in Cairo, the Townhouse Gallery in Cairo, the Brandts Museet for Fotokunst in Denmark, and the Kunstraum Düsseldorf. The artist lives and works in Cairo and Berlin, and has been a student with Tina Bara's master class at the Academy of Visual Arts, Leipzig, since 2012.

„Was ich als ‚hypothetische Gesellschaft' bezeichne, ist eine Gemeinschaft im Internet, die ‚Freunden' – unabhängig davon, ob sie sich tatsächlich kennen oder nicht – den gegenseitigen Zugang zu ihren Bildprofilen erlaubt. Die Beteiligten sind sich ihrer Erscheinung bewusst, sie posieren und kleiden sich für die Aufnahmen in einer bestimmten Art. Durch den Upload und die Veröffentlichung im Internet wird das Private vorübergehend öffentlich und erhält Aufmerksamkeit als eine Projektion, die man kommentieren kann, indem man den Like- oder Dislike-Button klickt.

Bei der Übersetzung der Fotografien mittels eines Projektors in nichtexpressive Zeichnungen wird der ‚reale' Hintergrund in ein neutrales Grau gewandelt. Auf diese Weise verschiebt sich der Fokus. Die individuellen Gesichtszüge, das konkrete Umfeld verschwinden, die Details der Kleidung und Accessoires sind reduziert. Das hochgeladene Bildschirmbild wird so zu einer Zeichnung an der Wand, und die dargestellten Personen nehmen die Funktion ikonografischer Stellvertreter an einem ungegenständlichen Ort an."

Ahmed Kamel wurde 1981 in Kairo geboren. Er studierte Malerei an der Helwan Universität in Kairo und erhielt seinen BA im Jahr 2003. Kamel hatte bereits Einzel- und Gruppenausstellungen im Nahen Osten und Europa, u.a. am Contemporary Image Collective in Kairo, in der Townhouse Galerie in Kairo, am Brandts Museet for Fotokunst in Dänemark und im Kunstraum Düsseldorf. Der Künstler lebt und arbeitet in Kairo und Berlin und ist seit 2012 Student in der Meisterklasse von Tina Bara an der Hochschule für Grafik und Buchkunst, Leipzig.

Nadine Khan & Mariam Mekiwi

I Will Speak of the Revolution, 2011
HD video, 1:07 min.
← pp./S. 88–89

"I will speak of the revolution. Consider this moment. Many victories, yes, yet there remains much more before its completion. A great moment for new, different works not possible before. Yet the power of Tahrir is that it cannot be owned or framed. So why should I frame it? In a personal or group victory, a point of view, a soldier's story, a slogan, a martyr, a tear, etc. All beautiful inspiring stories, one day they will be told, but at the right moment. The day we feel that the Square has really won. When the opportunity of change has become a reality. When achievements are not just commodities. I think now I would rather not speak of the revolution." (Voice-over from I Will Speak of the Revolution*)*

Egyptian filmmaker Nadine Khan holds a BA in film directing from the Higher Institute of Cinema in Cairo. Khan has worked as assistant director and producer with many Egyptian directors, including her father, Mohamed Khan, as well as Yousry Nasrallah and Nabil Ayouch.

Mariam Mekiwi is also a director from Egypt. She received her BA from the American University in Cairo and is currently doing her MFA in film, video, and photographic arts at the University of Fine Arts of Hamburg. Since 2008 Mekiwi has been working as a freelance film director and film editor.

„Ich werde über die Revolution sprechen. Man sollte über diesen Augenblick nachdenken. Es gab viele Siege, ja, dennoch bleibt bis zu ihrer Vollendung noch weitaus mehr zu tun. Ein großartiger Moment für neue, bisher nicht möglich gewesene Arbeiten. Doch die Kraft des Tahrir liegt genau darin, dass sie nicht in Beschlag genommen oder ins Bild gesetzt werden kann. Warum sollte ich sie also abbilden? Einen persönlichen oder kollektiven Sieg, eine Haltung und Sichtweise, die Geschichte eines Soldaten, einen Slogan, einen Märtyrer, eine Träne etc. Alles wunderbar ermutigende Geschichten, eines Tages werden sie erzählt, aber dann im richtigen Moment – an dem Tag, an dem wir spüren, dass die Bewegung vom Tahrir wirklich gewonnen hat. Wenn die Chance auf den Wandel Wirklichkeit geworden ist. Wenn die Errungenschaften mehr ausmachen als ein paar Annehmlichkeiten. Ich denke, dass ich jetzt lieber nicht von der Revolution sprechen möchte." (Voice-over aus I Will Speak of the Revolution*)*

Die ägyptische Filmemacherin Nadine Khan hat am High Institute of Cinema in Kairo mit einem BA in Filmregie abgeschlossen. Als Regieassistentin und Produzentin hat sie mit verschiedenen ägyptischen Regisseuren zusammengearbeitet, darunter ihr Vater, Mohammed Khan, Yousry Nasrallah und Nabil Ayouch.

Mariam Mekiwi ist ebenfalls eine ägyptische Filmregisseurin. Sie studierte an der American University in Kairo und macht gerade ihren MA in Film/Video und künstlerischer Fotografie an der Hochschule für bildende Künste in Hamburg. Seit 2008 arbeitet Mekiwi freiberuflich als Regisseurin und Cutterin.

Maha Maamoun

Night Visitor: The Night of Counting the Years, 2011
HD video, 8:00 min.
← pp./S. 86–87

"A look at YouTube videos made by the many men and women who broke into Egyptian state security buildings on March 5, 2011, reveals different narratives of this highly charged political space. Videos recorded by means of cell-phone cameras offer not only glimpses into the actions and desires of previous tenants of this space but open up psychological spaces in both the visitor and visited."

Maha Maamoun is an artist living and working in Cairo. Her work has been shown in several exhibitions worldwide, including the Witte de With Center for Contemporary Art in Rotterdam, the Museum of Modern Art in New York, and the Philadelphia Museum of Art. Maamoun has cocurated several exhibitions and art projects including *PhotoCairo3*, a visual arts exhibition in Cairo, *Meeting Points 5*, an itinerant contemporary arts festival in the Middle East, and *The Middle Ear*, a book project. The artist is a founding board member of the Contemporary Image Collective, an independent nonprofit space for contemporary art, founded in Cairo in 2004.

„Wenn man sich Filmmaterial auf YouTube anschaut, welches von den unzähligen Männern und Frauen aufgenommen wurde, die am 5. März 2011 in das Gebäude der ägyptischen Staatssicherheit einbrachen, stößt man auf unterschiedliche Erzählungen über diesen politisch höchst aufgeladenen Ort und Moment. Die Aufnahmen der Handykameras bieten nicht nur einen oberflächlichen Blick auf die Taten und Motive der ehemaligen Herren dieses Gebäudes, sie offenbaren auch eine psychologische Dimension, sowohl der Aktivisten als auch der dort Herrschenden."

Maha Maamoun lebt und arbeitet als Künstlerin in Kairo. Ihre Arbeiten wurden in zahlreichen Ausstellungen weltweit gezeigt, u.a. im Witte de With Center for Contemporary Art in Rotterdam, im Museum of Modern Art in New York und im Philadelphia Museum of Art. Maamoun ko-kuratierte diverse Ausstellungen und Kunstprojekte, darunter *PhotoCairo3* in Kairo, *Meeting Points 5*, eine Ausstellung zeitgenössischer Kunst, die im Nahen Osten tourt, sowie das Buchprojekt *The Middle Ear*. Die Künstlerin ist Gründungsmitglied des Contemporary Image Collective, einer unabhängigen gemeinnützigen Initiative für zeitgenössische Kunst, gegründet 2004 in Kairo.

Alex Majoli

Egypt. Cairo. Feb. 5, 2011.
Almost two weeks after the uprising began, protesters are back in Tahrir Square. / Knapp zwei Wochen nach dem Beginn des Aufstands sind die Demonstranten zurück auf dem Tahrir-Platz.
→ fig./Abb. 48+49

Alex Majoli, born in 1971, is an Italian photographer. At the age of fifteen, Majoli joined the F45 Studio in Ravenna and graduated from art school in 1991. After becoming a full member of Magnum Photos in 2001, Majoli covered the fall of the Taliban regime in Afghanistan and, two years later, the invasion of Iraq. He continues to document various conflicts worldwide for Newsweek, The New York Times Magazine, Granta, and National Geographic. In 2003, he won the Infinity Award in Photojournalism at the International Center of Photography in New York. Currently Majoli lives and works in New York and Milan.

Alex Majoli, geboren 1971, ist ein italienischer Fotograf. Im Alter von fünfzehn Jahren trat er dem F45 Studio in Ravenna bei und machte seinen Abschluss an der dortigen Kunstakademie 1991. Nachdem er 2001 ein Vollmitglied von Magnum Photos geworden war, widmete er sich thematisch dem Sturz des Taliban-Regimes in Afghanistan und zwei Jahre später dem militärischen Einmarsch der USA in den Irak. Er hat zahlreiche Konflikte weltweit für Newsweek, das New York Times-Magazin, Granta und National Geographic dokumentiert. Im Jahr 2003 erhielt der den Infinity Award of Photojournalism vom International Center of Photography in New York. Zurzeit lebt und arbeitet Majoli in New York und Mailand.

Jasmina Metwaly

Play Time, 2012
Installation based on a video projection (5:00 min.) and a slide projection (20 video stills transferred on to slide transparencies) / Installation aus Videoprojektion (5:00 min.) und Diaprojektion (20 Videostills, transferiert auf Diafilm)
← pp./S. 90–91

"Metwaly uses footage taken from activist documentaries that she produced parallel to her own artistic work in 2011 and 2012. One implication of the events of the last year is that narrative is no longer able to withstand nuance: images must quickly be put to use before another interest group gains control of the narrative. Uncertain or uninformative images are not only unnecessary but dangerous." (Mia Jankowicz)

Jasmina Metwaly, born in Warsaw in 1982, is a visual artist who grew up in Warsaw and Cairo. In 2006 she completed her master's degree at the Academy of Fine Arts in Poznan, Poland, followed by a postgraduate diploma at the Byam Shaw School of Art at Central Saint Martins, London. In 2009, Metwaly moved to Cairo and held an exhibition at the Townhouse Gallery. In 2011, Philip Rizk and Jasmina Metwaly together established a video collective and codirected a series of short videos on and around the January 25 Revolution called *Remarking January 25: A Series of Six.*

„Metwaly arbeitet mit Material, das sie aus ihren eigenen dokumentarischen Filmen schneidet, die 2010 und 2011 entstanden, als sie neben ihrer künstlerischen Praxis politische Aktionen aufnahm. Raum für Nuancierung gab es bei dieser Arbeit nicht. Die Bilder mussten schnell verarbeitet werden, um zu verhindern, dass andere Interessengruppen die Nachrichten kontrollierten. Zufällig entstandene oder

uninformative Bilder waren nicht nur unnötig, sondern gefährlich." (Mia Jankowicz)

Jasmina Metwaly, geboren 1982 in Warschau, wuchs in Warschau und Kairo auf. 2006 erhielt sie ihren MA von der Akademie der bildenden Künste in Poznan, Polen, gefolgt von einem Diplom an der Byam Shaw Kunsthochschule am Central Saint Martins, London. 2009 zog Metwaly nach Kairo und zeigte ihre Werke dort in einer Ausstellung in der Townhouse Galerie. Im Jahr 2011 haben Philip Rizk und Jasmina Metwaly gemeinsam ein Videokollektiv gegründet und eine Serie von Kurzfilmen über die Ereignisse während und um die Revolution vom 25. Januar 2011 gedreht, mit dem Titel *Remarking January 25: A series of Six.*

Chris Michalski & Sebastian Stumpf

We didn't see it, but we heard about it, 2012
Video and sound installation/ Video- und Toninstallation, 11:50 min.
⟵ pp./S. 114–115

"The video and sound installation features the opinions and perceptions of children and teenagers living in Mokattam, a neighborhood on the southeastern edge of Cairo. These young people did not participate in the revolution, nor were they eyewitnesses to it. They saw the events on television and heard about it from their families, friends, and neighbors. They do not live very far from where the conflicts took place, and some of them even have family members or friends who were involved in the protests. As a result they are faced with an overabundance of information, some of which is contradictory. Their statements make clear that they are trying to make sense of the complex chain of events and the effects that they will have. The children's statements are juxtaposed with a short video sequence showing a young boy completely absorbed in flying a kite amid daily life on the streets of Mokattam."

Chris Michalski, born in New York in 1976, currently lives in Leipzig, Germany, and Novosibirsk, Russia. He is a writer, artist, and translator.

Sebastian Stumpf, born in Würzburg in 1980, works with photography and video installations. After completing his master's degree at the Academy of Visual Arts Leipzig, studying under Timm Rautert, he received the Marion Ermer Award in 2010 and a grant from the Kulturstiftung der Länder in 2010/11. His work has been part of various exhibitions, for example at the ZKM Karlsruhe, the Fotomuseum Winterthur, and the Museum der bildenden Künste Leipzig.

„*Die Ton- und Videoarbeit* Wir haben es nicht gesehen, aber wir haben davon gehört *gibt die Meinungen und Wahrnehmungen von Kindern und Jugendlichen wieder, die im Stadtteil Mokattam am südöstlichen Rand von Kairo leben. Diese jungen Menschen sind keine Teilnehmer oder Augenzeugen der Revolution. Sie haben von den Ereignissen durch das Fernsehen, durch die Äußerungen ihrer Familien, Freunde und Nachbarn erfahren. Sie leben nicht weit vom Zentrum der Auseinandersetzungen entfernt, manche haben Familienangehörige oder Freunde, die an den Protesten beteiligt waren. Doch sind sie mit einer Fülle an vermittelten, teilweise widersprüchlichen Informationen konfrontiert. Ihre Äußerungen zeigen ihr Bemühen, die dramatischen Veränderungen zu begreifen und sinnvolle Zusammenhänge herzustellen. Es sind individuelle Versuche, ein Verständnis der komplexen Ereignisse und möglichen Auswirkungen zu entwickeln. Die Äußerungen der Kinder werden von einer Videosequenz begleitet, die einen Jungen zeigt, der inmitten des alltäglichen Treibens auf den Straßen von Mokattam in sein Spiel vertieft ist."*

Chris Michalski, geboren 1976 in New York, lebt zurzeit in Leipzig und Nowosibirsk, Russland. Er ist Autor, Künstler und Übersetzer.

Sebastian Stumpf, 1980 in Würzburg geboren, arbeitet mit Fotografie und Videoinstallationen. Nach seinem Studium an der Hochschule für Grafik und Buchkunst in Leipzig, als Meisterschüler von Timm Rautert, erhielt er 2010 den Marion-Ermer-Preis und 2010/11 das Stipendium der Kulturstiftung der Länder. Seine Arbeiten wurden u.a. in Ausstellungen im Zentrum für Kunst und Medientechnologie in Karlsruhe, im Fotomuseum Winterthur und im Museum der bildenden Künste Leipzig gezeigt.

Alex Nunns

A Revolution in Tweets/ Die Revolution erzählt in Twitternachrichten, 2011–13
⟶ pp./S. 146–147, 202–203

"When the Egyptian uprising began, some commentators in the West called it a 'Twitter revolution.' It was not. Revolutions do not come out of thin air, or even cyberspace. But Twitter did provide a real-time account of the revolution that has no parallel in history. This was recorded in the book Tweets from Tahrir, *made up of Twitter posts from the eighteen-day uprising that overthrew Hosni Mubarak. Of course, the revolution did not stop there, and for* Cairo. Open City. New Testimonies from an Ongoing Revolution *the approach and method of* Tweets from Tahrir *has been extended right up to the present to provide a framework narrative of events. The same group of tweeters has been used throughout, but as the political situation has become more complicated, their views have inevitably diverged. This fragmentation of the narrative reflects the reality that the post-Mubarak period has been far more difficult to navigate than the initial eighteen days. The selected group of tweeters is in no way representative of the whole Egyptian Twittersphere, the revolutionaries, or the wider polity. But their accounts continue to provide a compelling insight into the ongoing Egyptian revolution."*

Alex Nunns is a writer, political activist, and musician from London. He coedited *Tweets from Tahrir: Egypt's Revolution As It Unfolded, in the Words of the People Who Made It*, the first book to tell the story of a historical event using tweets. It was later made into a documentary film of the same title by Al Jazeera English. Alex Nunns studied history at Cambridge University.

„Als der Aufstand in Ägypten begann, wurde er von manchen westlichen Kommentatoren ‚Twitter-Revolution' genannt. Doch sie täuschten sich. Revolutionen kommen nicht aus dem Nichts oder gar aus dem Cyberspace. Twitter jedoch lieferte einen Echtzeitbericht der Revolution, wie er in der Geschichte einzigartig ist. Im Buch Tweets from Tahrir *sind Twitter-Mitteilungen aufgezeichnet, die in der Zeit des achtzehntägigen Aufstandes, welcher Husni Mubarak zum Sturz brachte, entstanden. Natürlich hörte die Revolution dort nicht auf. Für* Kairo. Offene Stadt. Neue Bilder einer andauernden Revolution *wurde die Methode von* Tweets from Tahrir *in die Gegenwart hinein erweitert, um aus den Ereignissen einen berichtenden Rahmen zu machen. In beiden Publikationen taucht dieselbe Gruppe von Twitter-Autoren auf, aber da die politische Situation komplizierter geworden ist, gehen die Meinungen nun unvermeidlich auseinander. Diese Fragmentarisierung des Berichtens spiegelt die Realität der Post-Mubarak-Periode wider, die weit schwieriger zu steuern war, als die anfänglichen achtzehn Tage. Die ausgewählte Gruppe von Twitterern ist in keiner Weise repräsentativ für die gesamte ägyptische Twittersphäre, die Revolutionäre oder das weitere politische System. Aber ihre Berichte übermitteln noch immer fesselnde Einblicke in die anhaltende ägyptische Revolution."*

Alex Nunns ist Schriftsteller, politischer Aktivist und Musiker aus London. Er war Mitherausgeber des ersten Buches, das die Geschichte eines historischen Ereignisses mittels Tweets erzählt: *Tweets from Tahrir: Egypts revolution as it unfolded, in the words of the people who made it.* Aus dem Buch ging später ein Dokumentarfilm gleichen Titels von El Jazeera English hervor. Alex Nunns hat Geschichte an der Cambridge University studiert.

Ivor Prickett

from the series/aus der Serie *Days of Anger*, 2011
These images, taken between Jan. 28 and Feb. 12, 2011, document the scenes that I witnessed in and around the streets of downtown Cairo./Diese Bilder, aufgenommen zwischen dem 28. Januar und 12. Februar 2011, dokumentieren die Szenen, deren Zeuge ich auf den Straßen der Kairoer Innenstadt wurde.
⟵ fig./Abb. 57+58

Ivor Prickett was born in Ireland in 1983. He is a documentary photographer with a particular interest in postwar situations. For two years he lived and worked in the Middle East, where he documented the uprisings in Egypt and Libya in 2011. Prickett's clients range from magazines such as The Sunday Times Magazine to Newsweek, and his work has been exhibited widely, including at the Foam Fotografiemuseum Amsterdam, Foto8 in London, and the Gallery of Photography in Dublin. He is now based between Istanbul and London.

Ivor Prickett wurde 1983 in Irland geboren. Er ist Dokumentarfotograf mit einem besonderen Interesse für Nachkriegssituationen. Zwei Jahre hat er im Nahen Osten verbracht, wo er 2011 die Aufstände in Ägypten und Libyen dokumentierte. Zu seinen Auftraggebern gehören verschiedene Magazine wie The Sunday Times Magazine und die Newsweek. Seine Bilder wurden vielfach ausgestellt, u.a. im Foam Fotografie-Museum Amsterdam, in Foto8 in London und in der Gallery of Photography in Dublin. Zurzeit lebt Prickett in Istanbul und London.

Jonathan Rashad

from the Flickr albums/ aus den Flickr-Alben
Egypt Clashes / Die ägyptischen Zusammenstöße, May 2012
← fig./Abb. 36–38
Brotherhood's Headquarters Stormed / Zentrale der Muslimbruderschaft gestürmt, Dec. 6, 2012
← fig./Abb. 39–41
Presidental Palace Sit-In / Sitzstreik vor dem Präsidentenpalast, Dec. 2012
→ p./S. 192
Egypt Clashes / Die ägyptischen Zusammenstöße, Jan. 2013
← Cover illustration / Umschlagmotiv

Jonathan Rashad is a young, Cairo-based freelance photojournalist. In 2008, he started his career as a photographer and drifted into journalism in 2010. Rashad's photographs have been used as cover designs for *Tweets from Tahrir* and *Im Land Ägypten*, and have also featured in hundreds of articles on the web, and in various magazines. His works have been featured in public exhibitions across many countries, including Egypt, the USA, England, Tunisia, and France. In March 2011, Rashad won the IFES photography contest.

Jonathan Rashad ist ein junger Fotojournalist aus Kairo. Im Jahr 2008 begann er seine berufliche Laufbahn als Fotograf und verlagerte seinen Schwerpunkt ab 2010 auf den Journalismus. Rashads Fotografien wurden als Titelmotive für die Bücher *Tweets from Tahrir*, *Im Land Ägypten* sowie für Hunderte von Artikeln im Internet und unterschiedlichen Magazinen verwendet. Seine Werke waren in Ausstellungen in vielen verschiedenen Ländern, u.a. Ägypten, USA, England, Tunesien und Frankreich zu sehen. Im März 2011 gewann Rashad den IFES Fotografie Wettbewerb.

Philip Rizk

Sturm: Ahmonseto, 2010, HD video, 6:09 min.
← p./S. 122
Sturm: Fayoum, 2010, HD video, 4:53 min.
← p./S. 123

Sturm: Ahmonseto
"In 2002 Mohammed Khamis, a business tycoon closely associated with the Mubarak regime, tried to become a partner in the Ahmonseto textile factory. Shortly after owner Adel Agha rejected Khamis's offer, Agha was accused of fraud and imprisoned. After his release three years later, Agha filed a loan dispute against Banque Misr and was again sentenced, to three years in prison. After being sentenced, Agha fled the country. Caught in the middle of this dispute were the two thousand workers employed at the Ahmonseto textile factory. They went to court and demanded that they be allowed to manage the factory themselves in Agha's absence to avoid losing their jobs. After years of inactivity, a government committee finally deemed the factory nonfunctional. Overseeing the factory assessment process was Mohamed Khamis. Since the shutdown ruling, the workers have been fighting to receive even a small amount of the severance pay owed to them by Banque Misr, now the owners of Agha's assets."

Sturm: Fayoum
"In the village of Abu Ksa, in the governorate of Fayoum, the Nile's water doesn't flow as it once did. Though Fayoum is considered part of the 'food basket' of Egypt, today many fields are drying up. One reason why the water does not flow where it used to is that those responsible for overseeing water distribution attempt to obtain personal benefits, accepting bribes, taking more than their fair share, and giving priority to friends and relatives. In some places this small-scale theft becomes full-fledged corruption. The agricultural operations that have sprung up around the city of Fayoum in recent years require massive amounts of water. The owners export most of the produce to maximize profits. Many of these operations are owned by former members of parliament and employees of the government's security apparatus. Furthermore, government policy actually encourages food export, as higher exports are said to benefit the economy. Meanwhile food prices in Egypt increased by eighteen percent in 2011."

Philip Rizk, born in Limassol, Cyprus, in 1982, is a video-maker and writer based in Cairo. Rizk studied philosophy and anthropology and received his MA from the American University in Cairo. In the summer of 2008, he directed his first documentary, entitled *This Palestinian Life*, which premiered at the London International Documentary Festival. In 2011, Philip Rizk and Jasmina Metwaly together established a video collective and co-directed a series of short videos on and around the January 25 Revolution called *Remarking January 25: A Series of Six*. Rizk is also part of Mosireen, a media collective that covers the ongoing revolution in Egypt.

Sturm: Ahmonseto
„Im Jahr 2002 versuchte Mohammed Khamis, ein dem Mubarak-Regime nahestehender Großindustrieller, Teilhaber der Textilfabrik Ahmonseto zu werden. Kurz nachdem der Besitzer, Adel Agha, Khamis' Angebot abgelehnt hatte, wurde er der Unterschlagung bezichtigt und ins Gefängnis geworfen. Nach seiner Freilassung drei Jahre später war Agha in einen Streit um einen Kredit mit der staatlichen Banque Misr verwickelt und wurde erneut zu drei Jahren Gefängnis verurteilt. Er floh aus dem Land. Die zweitausend Arbeiter der Textilfabrik zogen vor Gericht und forderten zur Sicherung ihrer Arbeitsplätze, dass ihnen während Aghas Abwesenheit die Leitung der Fabrik überlassen werde. Nach jahrelangem Stillstand befand eine Regierungskommission die Fabrik schließlich für funktionsuntüchtig. Mohammed Khamis hatte die Kontrolle über die Wertfeststellung und das Gutachten. Seit der Stilllegung der Fabrik kämpfen die Arbeiter dafür, wenigstens eine geringfügige Abfindung für den Verlust ihrer Arbeitsplätze von der Banque Misr zu erhalten, in deren Besitz Aghas Vermögen übergegangen ist."

Sturm: Fayoum
„In dem Dorf Abu Ksa im Regierungsbezirk Fayoum führt der Nil weniger Wasser als früher. Fayoum ist bekannt für seine Obst- und Gemüseproduktion, doch sind viele Felder heute ausgetrocknet. Eine Ursache dafür, dass das Wasser nicht mehr so weit ins Land reicht wie früher, ist darin zu suchen, dass die für die Verteilung des Wassers Verantwortlichen oft zu ihrem persönlichen Vorteil handeln: Sie sind bestechlich, nehmen sich mehr, als ihnen zusteht, und begünstigen Freunde und Bekannte. In manchen Gegenden sind diese kleinen Delikte zur Korruption im großen Stil mutiert. Die Agrarindustrie, die in den letzten Jahren um die Stadt Fayoum gewachsen ist, benötigt Unmengen von Wasser. Ein Großteil der landwirtschaftlichen Produkte wird exportiert, damit die Besitzer der Agrarbetriebe ihre Profite maximieren können. Viele der Betriebe sind Eigentum ehemaliger Parlamentsmitglieder oder von Angehörigen des Sicherheitsapparates der Regierung. Dazu kommt: die Regierungspolitik fördert den Export von Lebensmitteln; steigende Exporte würden ‚die Wirtschaft des Landes stärken'. Für die Ägypter jedoch sind die Lebensmittelpreise 2011 um achtzehn Prozent gestiegen."

Philip Rizk, geboren 1982 in Limassol, Zypern, lebt als Videofilmer und Autor in Kairo. Er studierte Philosophie und Anthropologie an der American University in Kairo. Im Sommer 2008 lieferte er mit dem Dokumentarfilm *This Palestinian Life* seine erste Regiearbeit, die auf dem Internationalen Londoner Dokumentarfilmfestival seine Premiere feierte. Im Jahr 2011 gründete er mit Jasmina Metwaly ein Videokollektiv, zusammen realisierten sie eine Serie von Kurzfilmen über die Ereignisse während der Revolution vom 25. Januar 2011 mit dem Titel *Remarking January 25: A series of Six*. Rizk ist außerdem Mitglied des Medienkollektivs Mosireen, welches die fortlaufende Revolution in Ägypten dokumentiert.

Ibrahim Saad

The House of the Republic, 2012
Installation with large-scale photomontage and two-channel video presentation / Installation aus großflächiger Fotomontage und Zwei-Kanal-Videopräsentation, 10:06 min.
← pp./S. 92–93

"The House of the Republic *is an artistic project that seeks to compare the Egyptian Revolution with the Romanian Revolution, identifying similarities and exploring why the movements began and how they ended."*

Ibrahim Saad is a visual artist who lives and works in Cairo, Egypt. He received his BA at the Faculty of Fine Arts at Helwan University in Cairo. His artistic projects have been displayed in various exhibitions in Egypt, Europe, and Asia, and Saad has also been awarded numerous residencies and participated in many workshops in Egypt, China, the Netherlands, and Switzerland. His work can be seen as an investigation into the depths of the human soul. He tries to find new ways of communicating human emotions. He uses himself as a model in his performances, photographs, and videos.

„The House of the Republic *ist ein Projekt, das die ägyptische Revolution mit der rumänischen Revolution vergleicht und Ähnlichkeiten herausarbeitet. Zum Beispiel stellt es die Frage, warum diese Revolutionen stattfanden, wie sie begannen und endeten."*

Ibrahim Saad ist bildender Künstler, er lebt und arbeitet in Kairo und studierte an der Fakultät der bildenden Künste der Helwan University. Seine künstlerischen Projekte wurden in verschiedenen Ausstellungen in Ägypten, Europa und Asien gezeigt. Saad hat an zahlreichen Residenzprogrammen und Workshops in Ägypten, China, den Niederlanden und der Schweiz teilgenommen. Seine Arbeiten untersuchen die Tiefen der menschlichen Seele; er sucht nach neuen Wegen, menschliche Empfindungen zu kommunizieren. In seinen Performances, Fotografien und Videos benutzt er sich selbst als Model.

Randa Shaath

Tahrir Square, the First Day of the American Invasion of Iraq / Tahrir-Platz am ersten Tag der amerikanischen Invasion in den Irak, Mar. 21, 2003, from the series / aus der Serie *Under the Same Sky: Cairo*, 2003, silver gelatin prints / Silbergelatineabzüge, 25×20 cm
⟵ fig. / Abb. 4+5

"March 21, 2003—the first day of the American invasion of Iraq—saw the biggest demonstration in Egypt in decades. Up until then the police had always known when a demonstration was going to take place and would amass security at the location to limit the number of protesters. A few dozen demonstrators would be surrounded by hundreds of police, often using violence and making arrests to dissuade others from joining in. But anger against the war in Iraq was intense and the call for protests that came from a variety of groups was heeded by Egyptians across the political spectrum.

I marched in the demonstration and took pictures along the way. After losing my voice and growing tired, I looked for an elevated location to shoot pictures from. What I saw was quite graphic—different shapes and masses of people. After this demonstration the authorities set up barriers, blocking sidewalks and restricting movement in the square. It was not until January 25, 2011, that Tahrir Square once again became a place for mass dissent."

Randa Shaath was born in Philadelphia in 1963 to a Palestinian father and an Egyptian mother. She received her BA in Middle Eastern studies from the American University in Cairo and her MA in mass communication from the University of Minnesota. Shaath has worked as a photographer for newspapers, magazines, and photo agencies. Her work has been exhibited worldwide, for example in Egypt, Lebanon, Brazil, Spain, Germany, and the USA. Shaath is currently the photo editor of the daily newspaper Al Shorouk in Cairo.

„Am 21. März 2003, dem ersten Tag der amerikanischen Invasion in den Irak, fand die seit Jahrzehnten größte Demonstration in Ägypten statt. Bis zu diesem Tag wusste die Polizei immer, wann eine Demonstration stattfinden würde, und zog ihre Sicherheitskräfte vor Ort zusammen, um die Zahl der Protestierenden zu begrenzen. Gruppen von bis zu hundert Demonstranten wurden von Hunderten Polizisten umringt, Gewalt und Verhaftungen sollten andere von der Teilnahme abschrecken. Aber die Wut wegen des Krieges im Irak war mächtig, und der Aufruf zum Protest kam von ganz verschiedenen Gruppen. Ägypter aus allen Teilen der Gesellschaft folgten ihm.

Ich lief mit der Demonstration mit und fotografierte dabei. Als ich heiser und müde war, habe ich mir einen erhöhten Standpunkt zum Fotografieren gesucht. Der Blick von oben bot ein grafisches Bild – Formen von Menschenmassen. Nach dieser Demonstration wurden Barrieren errichtet, die die Gehsteige blockierten und die Bewegung auf dem Platz einschränkten. Erst am 25. Januar 2011 wurde der Tahrir wieder zu einem Ort der Massenproteste."

Randa Shaath wurde 1963 in Philadelphia als Tochter eines palästinensischen Vaters und einer ägyptischen Mutter geboren. Sie studierte an der American University in Kairo und machte ihren MA in Kommunikationsdesign an der University of Minnesota. Shaath hat als Fotografin für Zeitungen, Magazine und Fotoagenturen gearbeitet. Ihre Bilder wurden weltweit ausgestellt, u.a. in Ägypten, dem Libanon, Brasilien, Spanien, Deutschland und den USA. Im Moment ist sie Bildredakteurin bei der Tageszeitung El Shorouk in Kairo.

Lilian Wagdy

Friday of Anger... Streets and Memories, 2011
Photographs collected on Facebook / Fotografien auf Facebook gesammelt
⟶ pp. / S. 188–189

Lilian Wagdy is a citizen journalist and photographer who worked in mainstream media for nine years before turning to citizen journalism. She documented the Egyptian Revolution by taking thousands of pictures and by showing numerous citizens in and around Cairo how to use citizen journalism as a means to keep the authority of the state in check.

Lilian Wagdy ist eine Bürgerjournalistin. Als Fotografin hat sie neun Jahre lang für die Massenmedien gearbeitet, bevor sie sich dem partizipativen Journalismus zugewendet hat. An der Berichterstattung der ägyptischen Revolution war sie mit tausenden von Bildern beteiligt und hat zahlreiche Bürger in und außerhalb Kairos angeleitet, wie man sich durch partizipativen Journalismus gegen die Autorität des Staates wehren kann.

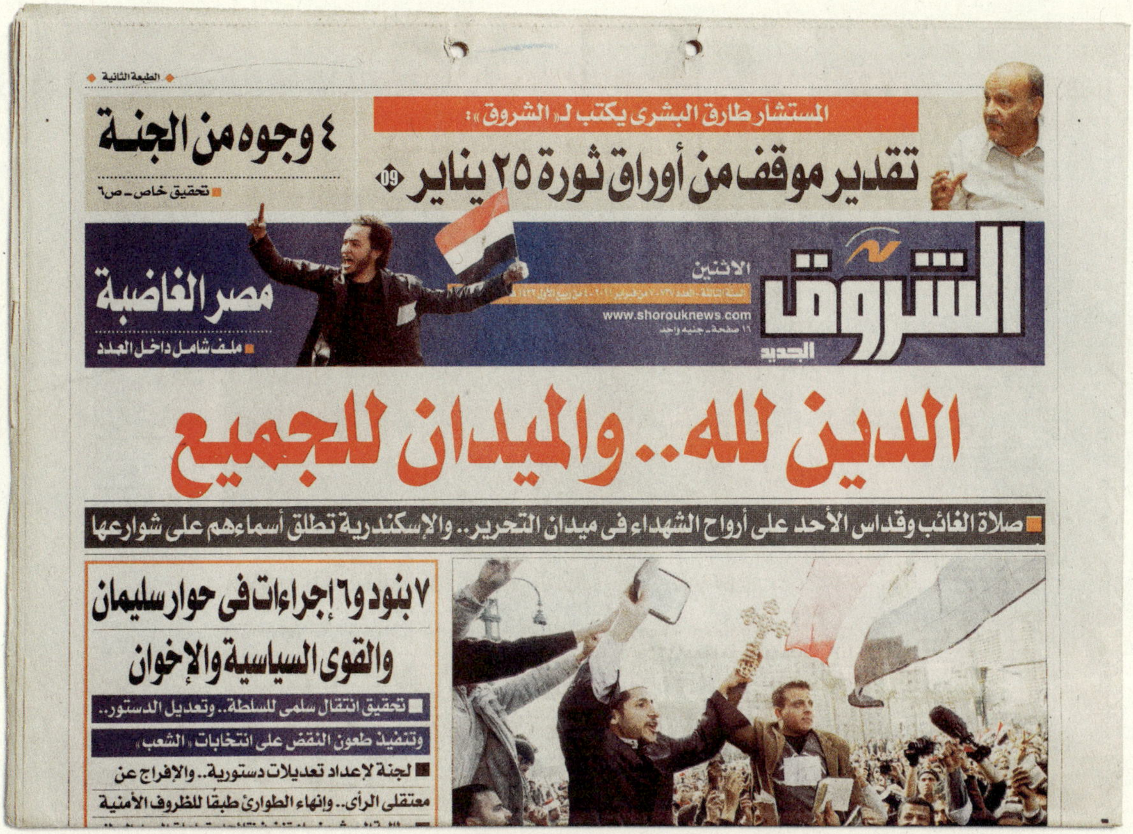

الطبعة الثانية

المستشار طارق البشرى يكتب لـ«الشروق»:

تقدير موقف من أوراق ثورة ٢٥ يناير 09

٤ وجوه من الجنة

تحقيق خاص – ص٦

الشروق الجديد

الاثنين

www.shorouknews.com

١٦ صفحة – جنيه واحد

مصر الغاضبة

ملف شامل داخل العدد

الدين لله.. والميدان للجميع

صلاة الغائب وقداس الأحد على أرواح الشهداء فى ميدان التحرير.. والإسكندرية تطلق أسماءهم على شوارعها

٧ بنود و٦ إجراءات فى حوار سليمان والقوى السياسية والإخوان

- تحقيق انتقال سلمى للسلطة.. وتعديل الدستور.. وتنفيذ طعون النقض على انتخابات «الشعب»
- لجنة لإعداد تعديلات دستورية.. والإفراج عن معتقلى الرأى.. وإنهاء الطوارئ طبقًا للظروف الأمنية

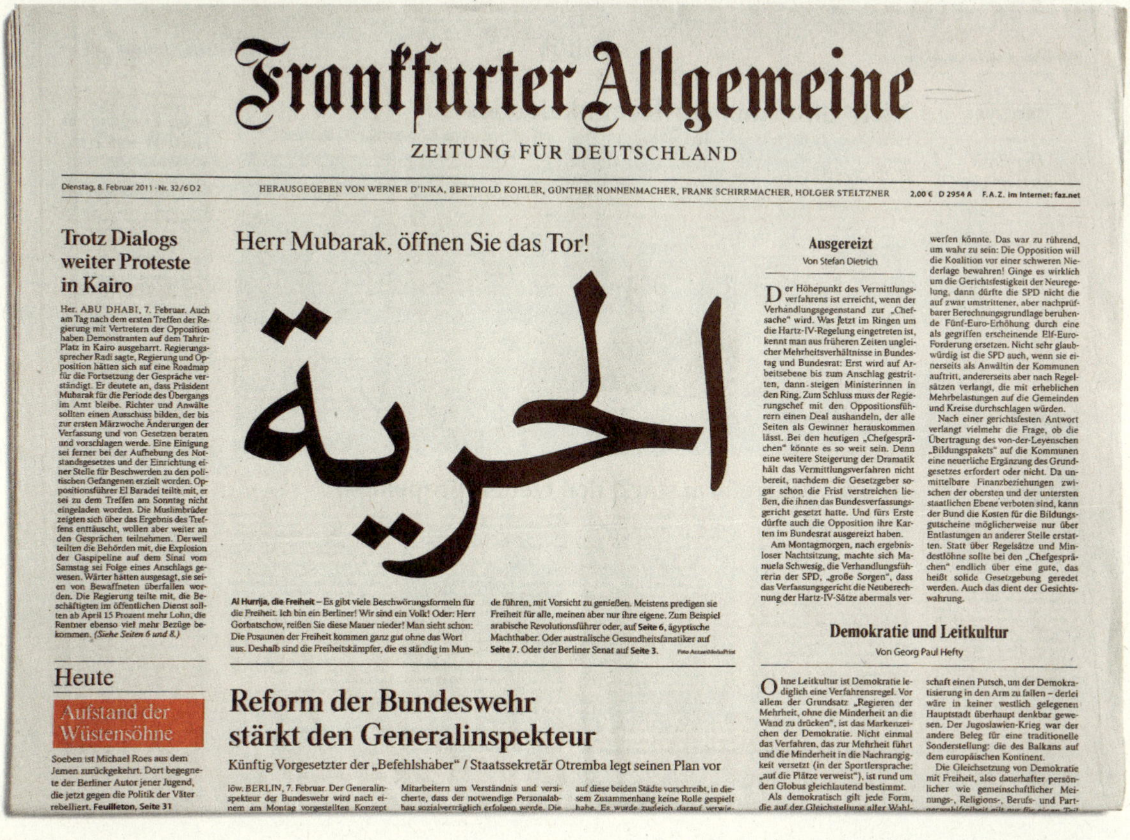

Frankfurter Allgemeine

ZEITUNG FÜR DEUTSCHLAND

Dienstag, 8. Februar 2011 · Nr. 32/6 D2 — HERAUSGEGEBEN VON WERNER D'INKA, BERTHOLD KOHLER, GÜNTHER NONNENMACHER, FRANK SCHIRRMACHER, HOLGER STELTZNER — 2,00 € D 2954 A F.A.Z. im Internet: faz.net

Trotz Dialogs weiter Proteste in Kairo

Her. ABU DHABI, 7. Februar. Auch am Tag nach dem ersten Treffen der Regierung mit Vertretern der Opposition haben Demonstranten auf dem Tahrir-Platz in Kairo ausgeharrt. Regierungssprecher Radi sagte, Regierung und Opposition hätten sich auf eine Roadmap für die Fortsetzung der Gespräche verständigt. Er deutete an, dass Präsident Mubarak für die Periode des Übergangs im Amt bleibe. Richter und Anwälte sollten einen Ausschuss bilden, der bis zur ersten Märzwoche Änderungen der Verfassung und von Gesetzen beraten und vorschlagen werde. Eine Einigung sei ferner bei der Aufhebung des Notstandsgesetzes und der Einrichtung einer Stelle für Beschwerden zu den politischen Gefangenen erzielt worden. Oppositionsführer El Baradei teilte mit, er sei zu dem Treffen am Sonntag nicht eingeladen worden. Die Muslimbrüder zeigten sich über das Ergebnis des Treffens enttäuscht, wollen aber weiter an den Gesprächen teilnehmen. Derweil teilten die Behörden mit, die Explosion der Gaspipeline auf dem Sinai vom Samstag sei Folge eines Anschlags gewesen. Wärter hätten ausgesagt, sie seien von Bewaffneten überfallen worden. Die Regierung teilte mit, die Beschäftigten im öffentlichen Dienst sollten ab April 15 Prozent mehr Lohn, die Rentner ebenso viel mehr Bezüge bekommen. *(Siehe Seiten 6 und 8.)*

Heute

Aufstand der Wüstensöhne

Soeben ist Michael Roes aus dem Jemen zurückgekehrt. Dort begegnete der Berliner Autor jener Jugend, die jetzt gegen die Politik der Väter rebelliert. **Feuilleton, Seite 31**

Herr Mubarak, öffnen Sie das Tor!

الحرية

Al Hurrija, die Freiheit – Es gibt viele Beschwörungsformeln für die Freiheit. Ich bin ein Berliner! Wir sind ein Volk! Oder: Herr Gorbatschow, reißen Sie diese Mauer nieder! Man sieht schon: Die Posaunen der Freiheit kommen ganz gut ohne das Wort aus. Deshalb sind die Freiheitskämpfer, die es ständig im Munde führen, mit Vorsicht zu genießen. Meistens predigen sie Freiheit für alle, meinen aber nur ihre eigene. Zum Beispiel arabische Revolutionsführer oder, auf **Seite 6**, ägyptische Machthaber. Oder australische Gesundheitsfanatiker auf **Seite 7**. Oder der Berliner Senat auf **Seite 3**.

Reform der Bundeswehr stärkt den Generalinspekteur

Künftig Vorgesetzter der „Befehlshaber" / Staatssekretär Otremba legt seinen Plan vor

löw. BERLIN, 7. Februar. Der Generalinspekteur der Bundeswehr wird nach einem am Montag vorgestellten Konzept [...] Mitarbeitern um Verständnis und versicherte, dass der notwendige Personalabbau sozialverträglich erfolgen werde. Die [...] auf diese beiden Städte vorschreibt, in diesem Zusammenhang keine Rolle gespielt habe. Es wurde zugleich darauf verwie-

Ausgereizt

Von Stefan Dietrich

Der Höhepunkt des Vermittlungsverfahrens ist erreicht, wenn der Verhandlungsgegenstand zur „Chefsache" wird. Was jetzt im Ringen um die Hartz-IV-Regelung eingetreten ist, kennt man aus früheren Zeiten ungleicher Mehrheitsverhältnisse in Bundestag und Bundesrat: Erst wird auf Arbeitsebene bis zum Anschlag gestritten, dann steigen Ministerinnen in den Ring. Zum Schluss muss der Regierungschef mit den Oppositionsführern einen Deal aushandeln, der alle Seiten als Gewinner herauskommen lässt. Bei den heutigen „Chefgesprächen" könnte es so weit sein. Denn eine weitere Steigerung der Dramatik hält das Vermittlungsverfahren nicht bereit, nachdem die Gesetzgeber sogar schon die Frist verstreichen ließen, die ihnen das Bundesverfassungsgericht gesetzt hatte. Und fürs Erste dürfte auch die Opposition ihre Karten im Bundesrat ausgereizt haben.

Am Montagmorgen, nach ergebnisloser Nachtsitzung, machte sich Manuela Schwesig, die Verhandlungsführerin der SPD, „große Sorgen", dass das Verfassungsgericht die Neuberechnung der Hartz-IV-Sätze abermals verwerfen könnte. Das war zu rührend, um wahr zu sein: Die Opposition will die Koalition vor einer schweren Niederlage bewahren! Ginge es wirklich um die Gerichtsfestigkeit der Neuregelung, dann dürfte die SPD nicht die auf zwar umstrittener, aber nachprüfbarer Berechnungsgrundlage beruhende Fünf-Euro-Erhöhung durch eine als gegriffen erscheinende Elf-Euro-Forderung ersetzen. Nicht sehr glaubwürdig ist die SPD auch, wenn sie einerseits als Anwältin der Kommunen auftritt, andererseits aber nach Regelsätzen verlangt, die mit erheblichen Mehrbelastungen auf die Gemeinden und Kreise durchschlagen würden.

Nach einer gerichtsfesten Antwort verlangt vielmehr die Frage, ob die Übertragung des von-der-Leyenschen „Bildungspakets" auf die Kommunen eine neuerliche Ergänzung des Grundgesetzes erfordert oder nicht. Da unmittelbare Finanzbeziehungen zwischen der obersten und der untersten staatlichen Ebene verboten sind, kann der Bund die Kosten für die Bildungsgutscheine möglicherweise nur über Entlastungen an anderer Stelle erstatten. Statt über Regelsätze und Mindestlöhne sollte bei den „Chefgesprächen" endlich über eine gute, das heißt solide Gesetzgebung geredet werden. Auch das dient der Gesichtswahrung.

Demokratie und Leitkultur

Von Georg Paul Hefty

Ohne Leitkultur ist Demokratie lediglich eine Verfahrensregel. Vor allem der Grundsatz „Regieren der Mehrheit, ohne die Minderheit an die Wand zu drücken", ist das Markenzeichen der Demokratie. Nicht einmal das Verfahren, das zur Mehrheit führt und die Minderheit in die Nachrangigkeit versetzt (in der Sportlersprache: „auf die Plätze verweist"), ist rund um den Globus gleichlautend bestimmt.

Als demokratisch gilt jede Form, die auf der Gleichstellung aller Wahl- [...] schaft einen Putsch, um der Demokratisierung in den Arm zu fallen – derlei wäre in keiner westlich gelegenen Hauptstadt überhaupt denkbar gewesen. Der Jugoslawien-Krieg war der andere Beleg für eine traditionelle Sonderstellung: die des Balkans auf dem europäischen Kontinent.

Die Gleichsetzung von Demokratie mit Freiheit, also dauerhafter persönlicher wie gemeinschaftlicher Meinungs-, Religions-, Berufs- und Part-

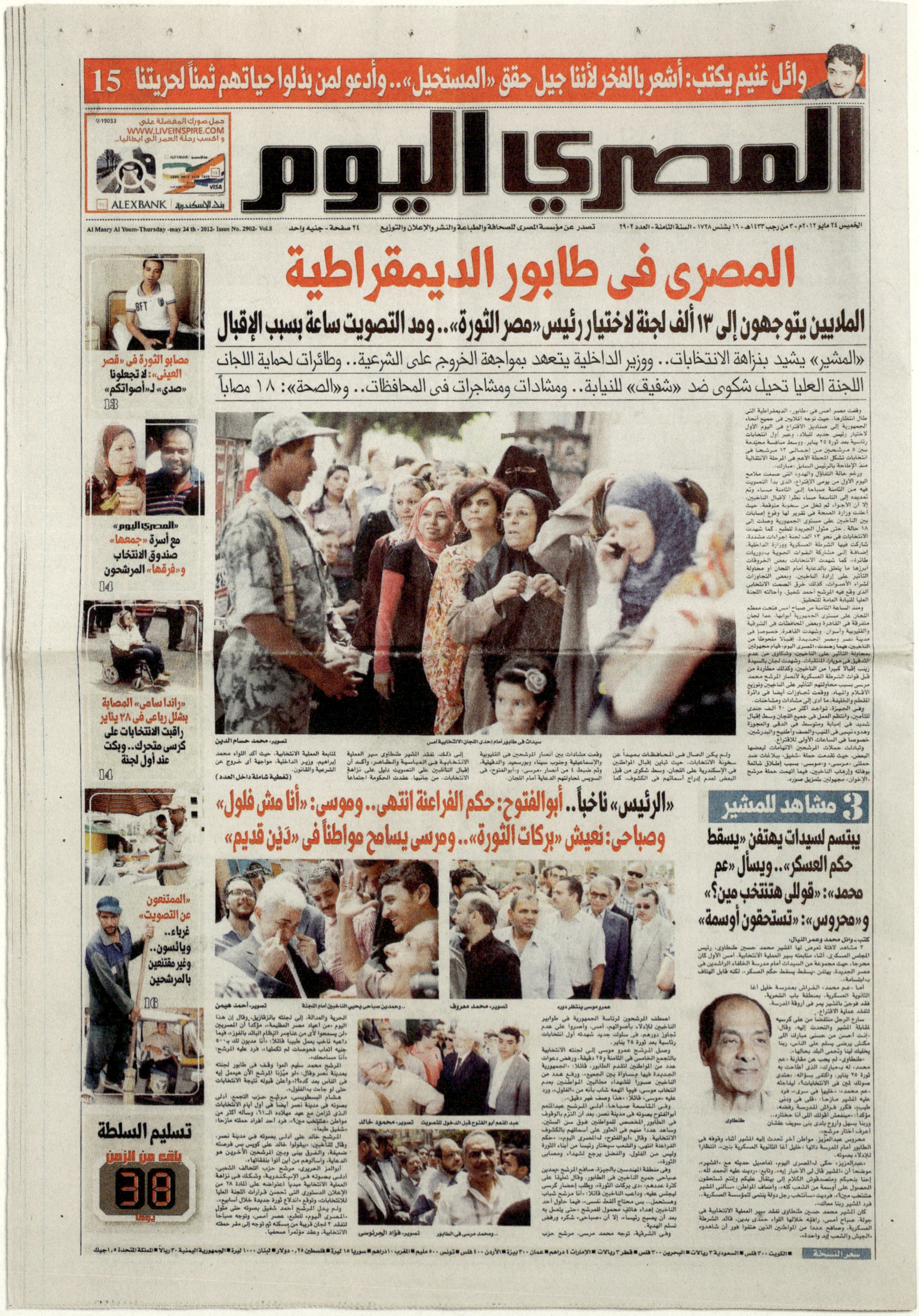

وائل غنيم يكتب: أشعر بالفخر لأننا جيل حقق «المستحيل».. وأدعو لمن بذلوا حياتهم ثمناً لحريتنا 15

المصري اليوم

الخميس ٢٤ مايو ٢٠١٢م - ٣ من رجب ١٤٣٣هـ - ١٦ بشنس ١٧٢٨ - السنة الثامنة - العدد ٢٩٠٢ — تصدر عن مؤسسة المصرى للصحافة والطباعة والنشر والإعلان والتوزيع — ٢٤ صفحة - جنيه واحد — Al Masry Al Youm-Thursday -may 24 th - 2012- Issue No. 2902- Vol.8

المصرى فى طابور الديمقراطية

الملايين يتوجهون إلى ١٣ ألف لجنة لاختيار رئيس «مصر الثورة».. ومد التصويت ساعة بسبب الإقبال

«المشير» يشيد بنزاهة الانتخابات.. ووزير الداخلية يتعهد بمواجهة الخروج على الشرعية.. وطائرات لحماية اللجان

اللجنة العليا تحيل شكوى ضد «شفيق» للنيابة.. ومشادات ومشاجرات فى المحافظات.. و«الصحة»: ١٨ مصاباً

وقفت مصر امس فى «طابور» الديمقراطية التى طال انتظارها، حيث توجه الملايين فى جميع أنحاء الجمهورية إلى صناديق الاقتراع فى اليوم الأول لاختيار رئيس جديد للبلاد، وعبر أول انتخابات رئاسية بعد ثورة ٢٥ يناير، ووسط منافسة محتدمة بين ٥ مرشحين من إجمالى ١٣ مرشحاً فى انتخابات تشكل المحطة الأهم فى المرحلة الانتقالية منذ الإطاحة بالرئيس السابق «مبارك».

تصوير - محمد حسام الدين

سيدات فى طابور أمام إحدى اللجان الانتخابية أمس

(تغطية شاملة داخل العدد)

مصابو الثورة فى «قصر العينى»: لا تجعلونا «صدى» لـ«أصواتكم» 13

«المصري اليوم» مع أسرة «جمعها» صندوق الانتخاب و«فرقها» المرشحون 14

«راندا سامى» المصابة بشلل رباعى فى ٢٨ يناير راقبت الانتخابات على كرسى متحرك.. وبكت عند أول لجنة 14

«الممتنعون عن التصويت» غرباء.. ويائسون.. وغير مقتنعين بالمرشحين 16

تسليم السلطة باقٍ من الزمن 38 يوماً

«الرئيس» ناخباً.. أبوالفتوح: حكم الفراعنة انتهى.. وموسى: «أنا مش فلول» وصباحى: نعيش «بركات الثورة».. ومرسى يسامح مواطناً فى «دَيْن قديم»

..وحمدين صباحى يحيى الناخبين أمام اللجنة — تصوير - أحمد هيمن

عمرو موسى ينتظر دوره — تصوير - محمد معروف

عبد المنعم أبو الفتوح قبل الدخول للتصويت — تصوير - محمود خالد

..ومحمد مرسى فى الطابور — تصوير - فؤاد الجرنوسى

اصطف المرشحون لرئاسة الجمهورية فى طوابير الناخبين للإدلاء بأصواتهم، أمس، وأصروا على عدم تجاوز دورهم، فى سلوك جديد شهدته أول انتخابات رئاسية بعد ثورة ٢٥ يناير.

3 مشاهد للمشير

يبتسم لسيدات يهتفن «يسقط حكم العسكر».. ويسأل «عم محمد»: «قوللى هتنتخب مين؟» و«محروس»: «تستحقون أوسمة»

كتب - وائل محمد وعمر النيال

٣ مشاهد لافتة تعرض لها المشير محمد حسين طنطاوى، رئيس المجلس العسكرى، أثناء متابعته سير العملية الانتخابية، أمس الأول كان محرجاً، حيث مجموعة من السيدات أمام مدرسة الخلفاء الراشدين فى مصر الجديدة، يهتفن «يسقط يسقط حكم العسكر»، لكنه قابل الهتاف بابتسامة.

طنطاوى

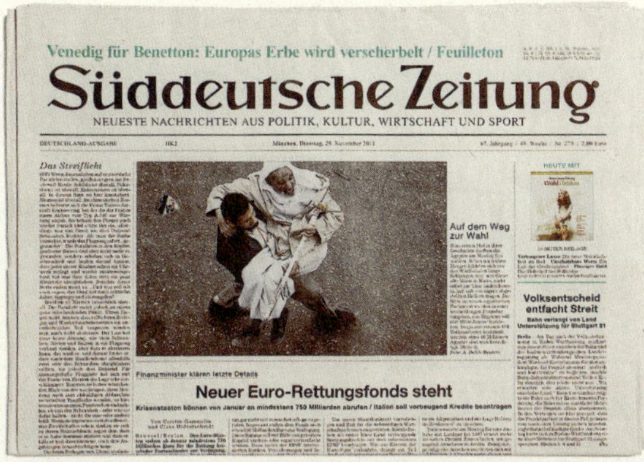

Venedig für Benetton: Europas Erbe wird versccherbelt / Feuilleton

Süddeutsche Zeitung

NEUESTE NACHRICHTEN AUS POLITIK, KULTUR, WIRTSCHAFT UND SPORT

Das Streiflicht

Auf dem Weg zur Wahl

Volksentscheid entfacht Streit

Finanzminister klären letzte Details

Neuer Euro-Rettungsfonds steht

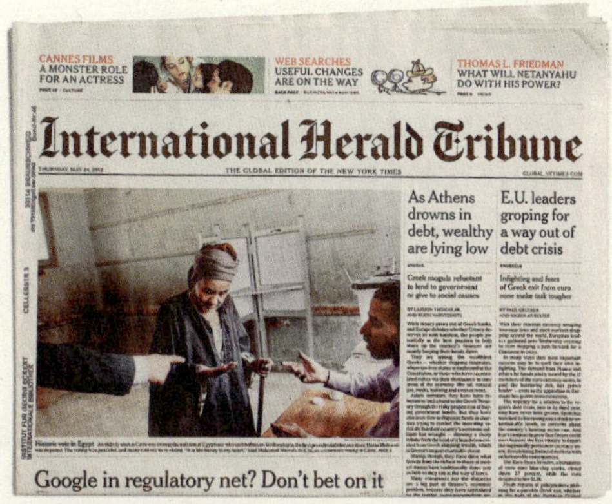

CANNES FILMS A MONSTER ROLE FOR AN ACTRESS

WEB SEARCHES USEFUL CHANGES ARE ON THE WAY

THOMAS L. FRIEDMAN WHAT WILL NETANYAHU DO WITH HIS POWER?

International Herald Tribune

THE GLOBAL EDITION OF THE NEW YORK TIMES

As Athens drowns in debt, wealthy are lying low

E.U. leaders groping for a way out of debt crisis

Google in regulatory net? Don't bet on it

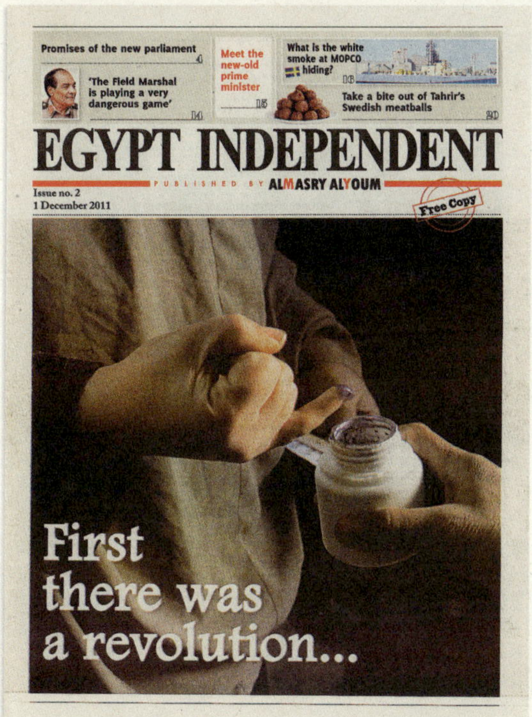

Promises of the new parliament

'The Field Marshal is playing a very dangerous game'

Meet the new-old prime minister

What is the white smoke at MOPCO hiding?

Take a bite out of Tahrir's Swedish meatballs

EGYPT INDEPENDENT

PUBLISHED BY ALMASRY ALYOUM

Issue no. 2

1 December 2011

Free Copy

First there was a revolution...

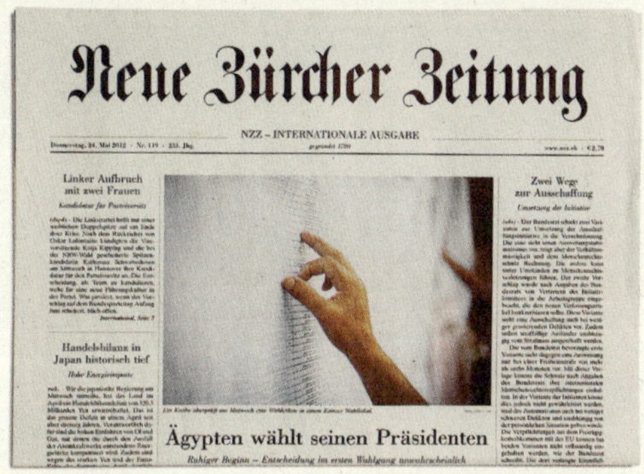

Neue Zürcher Zeitung

NZZ – INTERNATIONALE AUSGABE

Linker Aufbruch mit zwei Frauen

Handelsbilanz in Japan historisch tief

Zwei Wege zur Ausschaffung

Ägypten wählt seinen Präsidenten

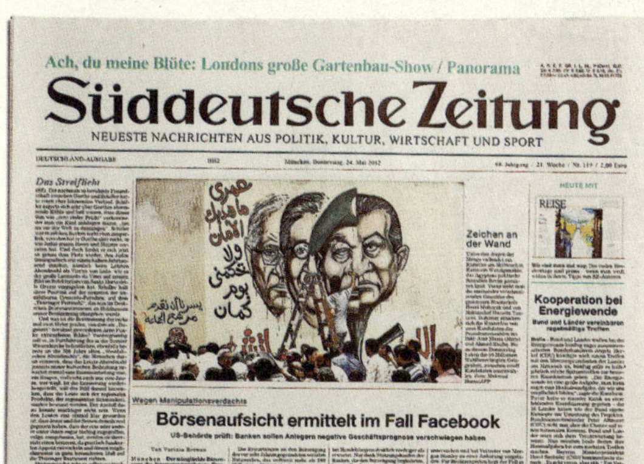

Ach, du meine Blüte: Londons große Gartenbau-Show / Panorama

Süddeutsche Zeitung

NEUESTE NACHRICHTEN AUS POLITIK, KULTUR, WIRTSCHAFT UND SPORT

Das Streiflicht

Zeichen an der Wand

Kooperation bei Energiewende

Wegen Manipulationsverdachts

Börsenaufsicht ermittelt im Fall Facebook

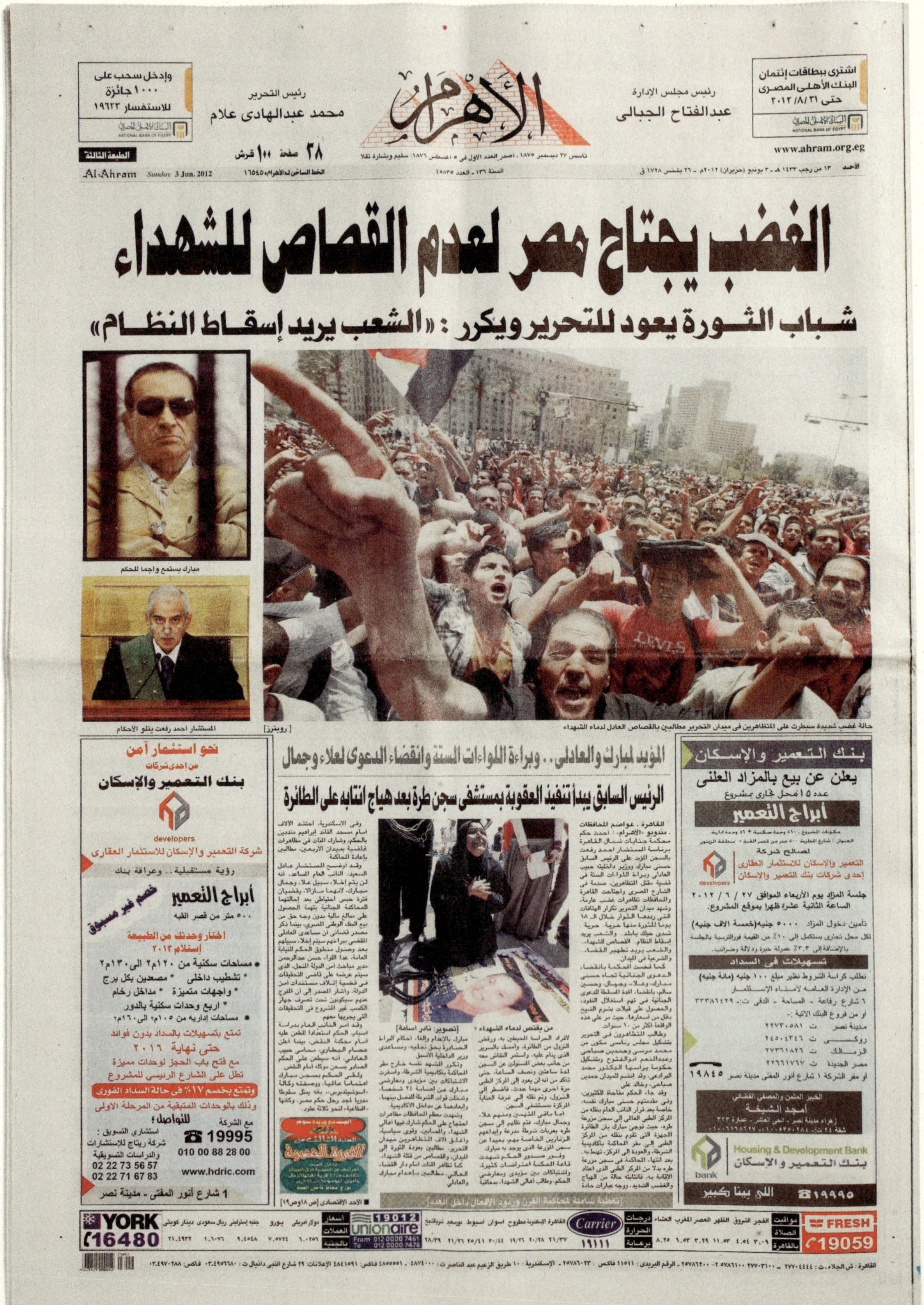
الأهرام
رئيس مجلس الإدارة
عبدالفتاح الجبالى
رئيس التحرير
محمد عبدالهادى علام
www.ahram.org.eg
٣٨ صفحة ١٠٠ قرش
الطبعة الثالثة
Al-Ahram Sunday 3 Jun. 2012
الأحد ١٣ من رجب ١٤٣٣ هـ - ٣ يونيو (حزيران) ٢٠١٢م - ٢٦ بشنس ١٧٢٨ ق
السنة ١٣٦ - العدد ٤٥٨٣٥
الغضب يجتاح مصر لعدم القصاص للشهداء
شباب الثورة يعود للتحرير ويكرر: «الشعب يريد إسقاط النظام»
مبارك يستمع واجما للحكم
المستشار احمد رفعت يتلو الأحكام
حالة غضب شديدة سيطرت على المتظاهرين في ميدان التحرير مطالبين بالقصاص العادل لدماء الشهداء
[رويترز]
المؤبد لمبارك والعادلى.. وبراءة اللواءات الستة وانقضاء الدعوى لعلاء وجمال
الرئيس السابق يبدأ تنفيذ العقوبة بمستشفى سجن طرة بعد هياج انتابه على الطائرة
بنك التعمير والإسكان
أبراج التعمير

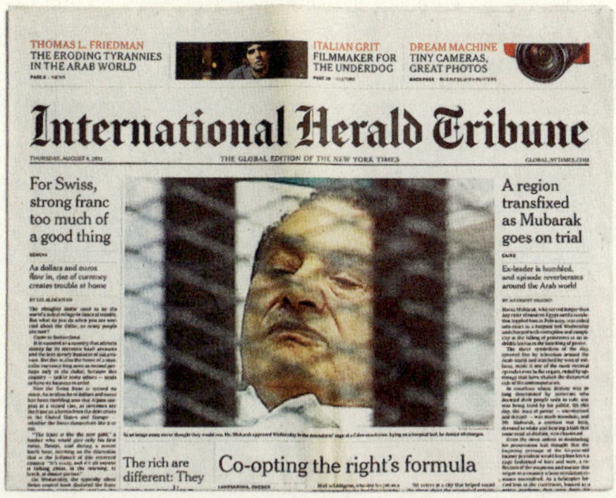

THOMAS L. FRIEDMAN
THE ERODING TYRANNIES IN THE ARAB WORLD

ITALIAN GRIT
FILMMAKER FOR THE UNDERDOG

DREAM MACHINE
TINY CAMERAS, GREAT PHOTOS

International Herald Tribune

THE GLOBAL EDITION OF THE NEW YORK TIMES

For Swiss, strong franc too much of a good thing

A region transfixed as Mubarak goes on trial

The rich are different: They

Co-opting the right's formula

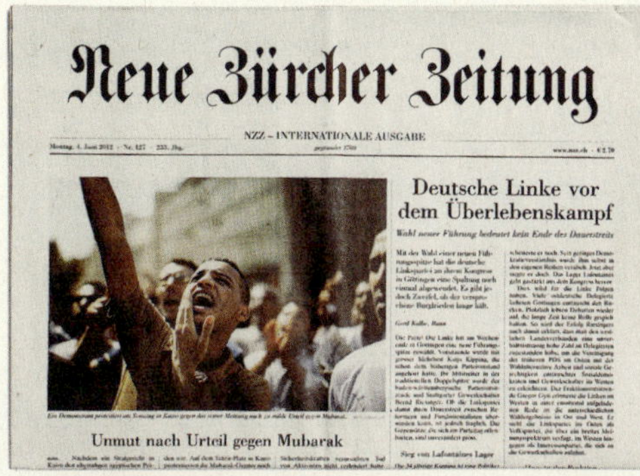

Neue Zürcher Zeitung

NZZ – INTERNATIONALE AUSGABE

Deutsche Linke vor dem Überlebenskampf

Unmut nach Urteil gegen Mubarak

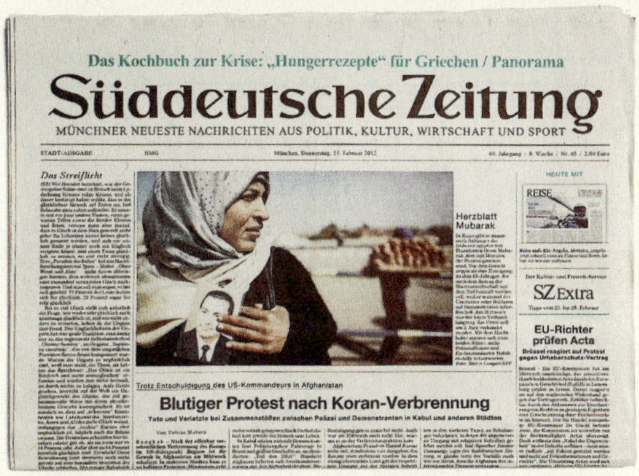

Das Kochbuch zur Krise: „Hungerrezepte" für Griechen / Panorama

Süddeutsche Zeitung

MÜNCHNER NEUESTE NACHRICHTEN AUS POLITIK, KULTUR, WIRTSCHAFT UND SPORT

Das Streiflicht

Herzblatt Mubarak

SZ Extra

EU-Richter prüfen Acta

Trotz Entschuldigung des US-Kommandeurs in Afghanistan

Blutiger Protest nach Koran-Verbrennung

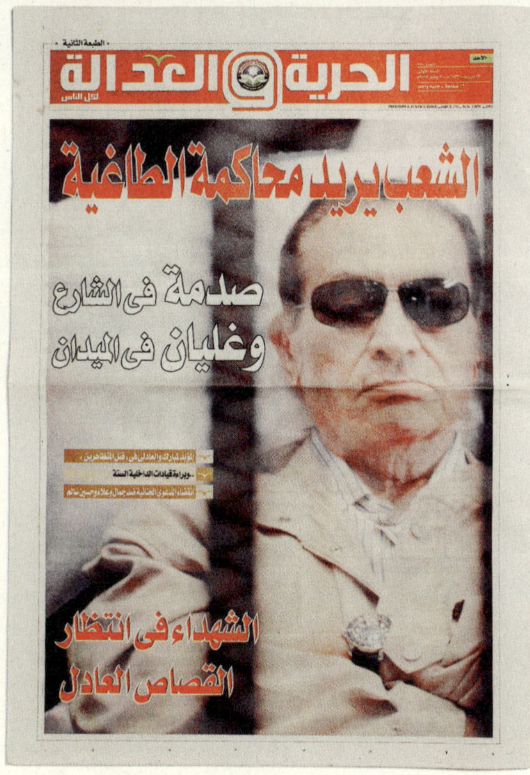

الحرية والعدالة

الشعب يريد محاكمة الطاغية

صدمة فى الشارع
وغليان فى الميدان

الشهداء فى انتظار
القصاص العادل

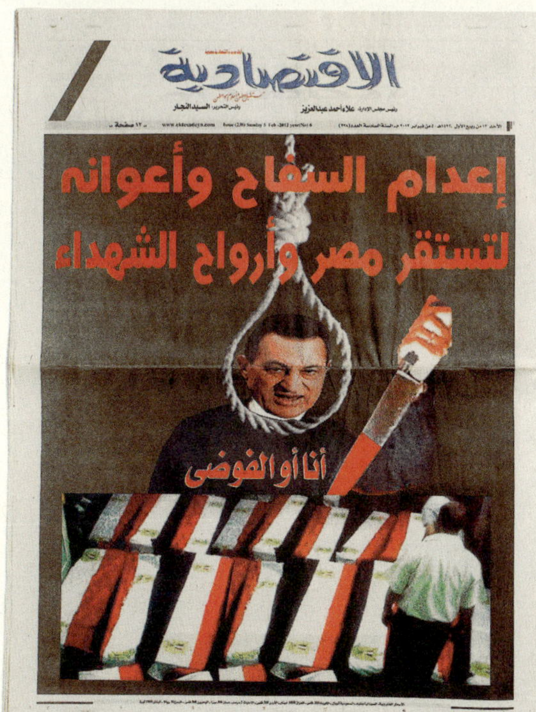

الاقتصادية

إعدام السفاح وأعوانه
لتستقر مصر وأرواح الشهداء

أنا أو الفوضى

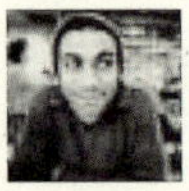

3arabawy Hossam عمو حسام
@shadihamid I'm not expecting a revolution today. I'm expecting protests. So let's not shoot high so as not to disappoint people later.
11:02 Jan 25, 2011

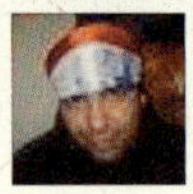

Sandmonkey Mahmoud Salem
Huge demo going to tahrir #jan25 shit just got real
13:21 Jan 25, 2011

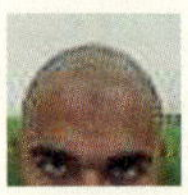

TravellerW Mo-ha-med
Police throws rocks @ demonstrtrs while we raised our arms. We're unarmed, they're in full gear. We are strong, they're weak. #25jan #Egypt
16:27 Jan 25, 2011

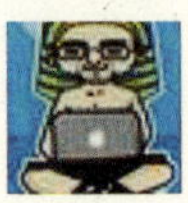

Ghonim Wael Ghonim
Egypt after #Jan25 is no way going to be the same as Egypt before it. Today we proved so many points.
00:45 Jan 26, 2011

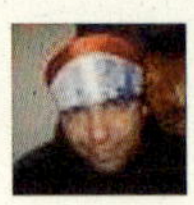

Sandmonkey Mahmoud Salem
NDP building burnt, police trucks burnt, graffiti against regime in Ramsis and everywhere #Jan25 #Egypt
13:42 Jan 29, 2011

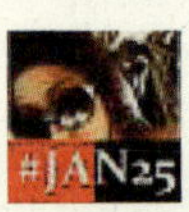

Gsquare86 Gigi Ibrahim جيييج
Fear is over in EGYPT!!!
Fear has left the people and now with Muabark
16:14 Jan 30, 2011

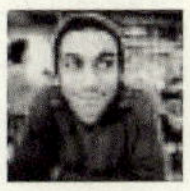

3arabawy Hossam عمو حسام
Plainclothes thugs (police) are on horses now, trying to storm Tahrir Square, with whips! #Jan25
15:01 Feb 2, 2011

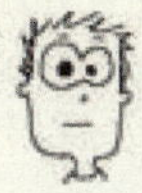

beleidy Amr El Beleidy
The hope of the whole region is now in one public square!
16:43 Feb 2, 2011

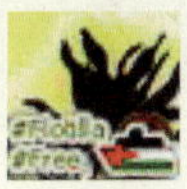

monasosh monasosh
Ppl r using the car ruins & rubbish around them 2 create shields to advance to the frontline.
I feel as if reporting on a battlefield #Jan25
03:52 Feb 3, 2011

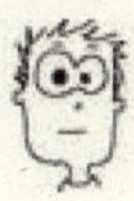

beleidy Amr El Beleidy
I cannot believe what just happened!
Hosny Mubarak resigned! The army now controls the country!
18:03 Feb 11, 2011

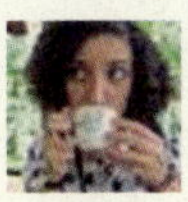

ManarMohsen Manar Mohsen
The streets in Cairo are going wild with patriotism & happiness! Flags waving out of every car, strangers congratulating each other! "MASR!"
19:29 Feb 11, 2011

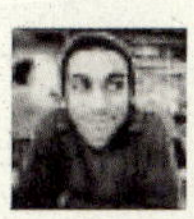

3arabawy Hossam عمو حسام
i am 33 years old and today i voted for the first time in my life :) #egypt
10:23 Mar 19, 2011

"Maspero is the 'media tank', the building that houses the Egyptian Radio and Television Union. It is owned and run by the Egyptian army generals who have ruled and—with their successors—inherited the country for decades. Ever since the late fifties and early sixties, Maspero has had a penchant for censorship. This may not be immediately destructive, but it always poisons the mind. Beware of the 'media tank.' Beware of the beast."

(Osama Dawod)

„Das ‚Maspero' ist das Schlachtschiff der Medien. Das Gebäude befindet sich nicht nur im Besitz der ägyptischen Militärgeneräle, die das Land seit mehreren Jahrzehnten regieren (und auch weiterregieren werden). Die staatliche Rundfunk- und Fernsehanstalt, die es beherbergt, steht auch unter ihrer Kontrolle. Seit den späten fünfziger und frühen sechziger Jahren steht ‚Maspero' für Zensur. Sie hat nicht unbedingt sofort verheerende Auswirkungen, durchdringt und vergiftet aber die gesellschaftliche Atmosphäre. Hütet euch vor dem ‚Medienschlachtschiff' – hütet euch vor der Bestie."

(Osama Dawod)

"يعتبر مبنى 'ماسبيرو' القوة الإعلامية الرئيسية في مصر. لا يقع المبنى تحت سيطرة جنرالات الجيش المصري، الذين يحكمون مصر منذ عقود (وسيظلون حاكمين لها) وحسب، بـل وحتى إتحاد الإذاعـة والتلفزيون المتواجد به يقع تحت سيطرتهم أيضـاً. يعتبر مبنى 'ماسبيرو' منذ نهايـات الخمسينات وبداية الستينات رمزاً للرقابة الإعلامية. قد لا يظهر التأثير الوخيم للرقابة الإعلامية مبـاشرةً ولكنـه يخترق الوسط المجتمعـي ويسممه. إحذروا 'ماسبيرو' وحش الإعلام المصري."

(أسامة داوود)

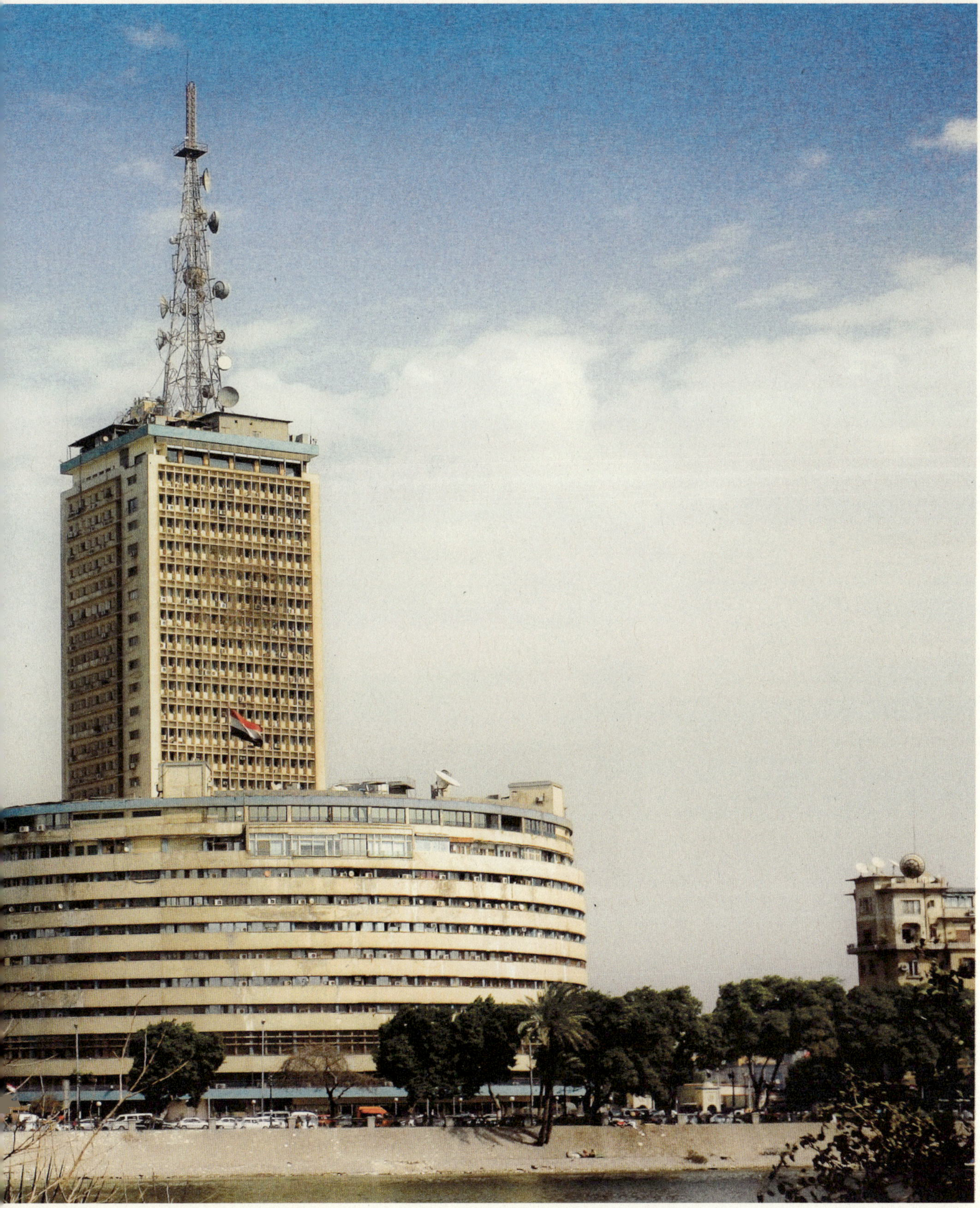

The state media has proven on more than one occasion that they are more committed to serving the rulers than they are to conveying the truth. The state propaganda machine uses images as a weapon just as much as the protesters do, but the difference is that it conveys a very different reality from the one out on the streets. And people reacted strongly to this: they broadcast their feelings on computer screens or painted them across walls. The most potent symbol for this criticism of the media is the Maspero, the state television building.

(Documents collected by Rowan El Shimi)

Bei mehr als einer Gelegenheit haben die staatlichen Medien bewiesen, dass sie eher daran interessiert sind, den Machthabern von Nutzen zu sein, als die Wahrheit ans Licht zu bringen. Die Propagandamaschinerie des Staates setzt ebenso wie die Protestbewegung Bilder als Waffe ein – nur zeigen ihre Bilder eine Realität, die sich grundlegend von jener der Straße unterscheidet, was die Bevölkerung stark provoziert hat. Während die einen ihre Reaktionen über die Computerbildschirme verbreiteten, sprühten die anderen sie auf die Mauern. Zentrales Motiv der Medienkritik ist das „Maspero“, das Gebäude des staatlichen Fernsehens.

(Dokumente gesammelt von Rowan El Shimi)

أثبتت أجهزة الإعلام التابعة للدولة في أكثر من واقعة بأنها تفضل خدمة الفئة الحاكمة على إظهار الحقيقة. تستخدم آلة البروباجاندا السياسية التابعة للدولة الصور كسلاح كما يستخدمها المحتجون أيضاً، مع الفارق، بأنها تعكس حقيقة تختلف كلياً عن الواقع الملموس، الأمر الذي يؤدي إلى زيادة الإثارة لدى الجماهير. وبينما ينشر البعض منهم ردة فعله على شاشات الكمبيوتر يقوم البعض الآخر برشها على الجدران. الموضوع الرئيسي لهذا النقد الإعلامي هو مبنى "ماسبيرو"، مبنى إتحاد الإذاعة والتلفزيون التابع للدولة.

(تجميع الوثائق روان الشيمي)

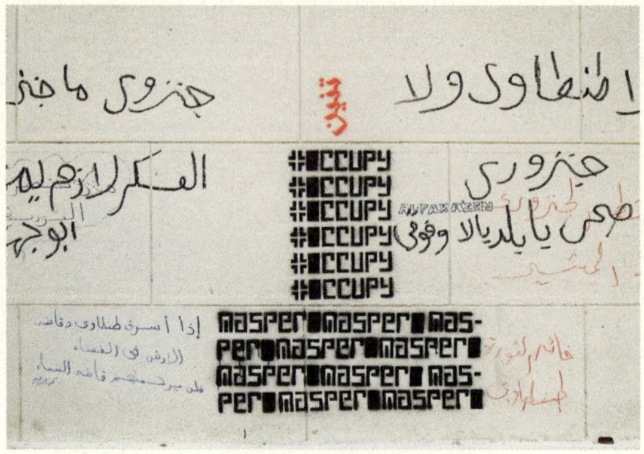

1

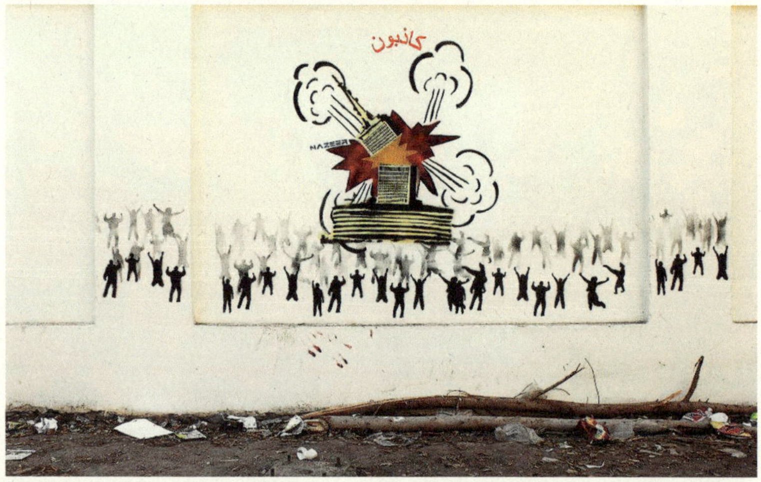
2

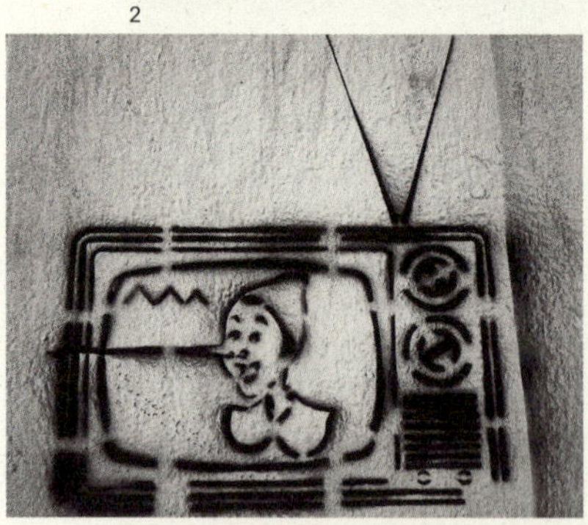
3

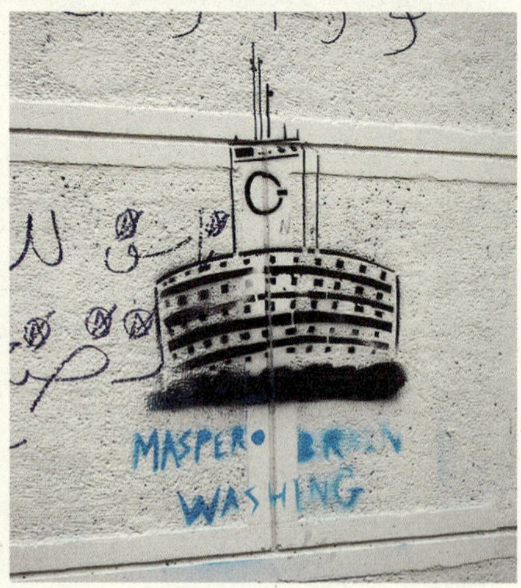

4

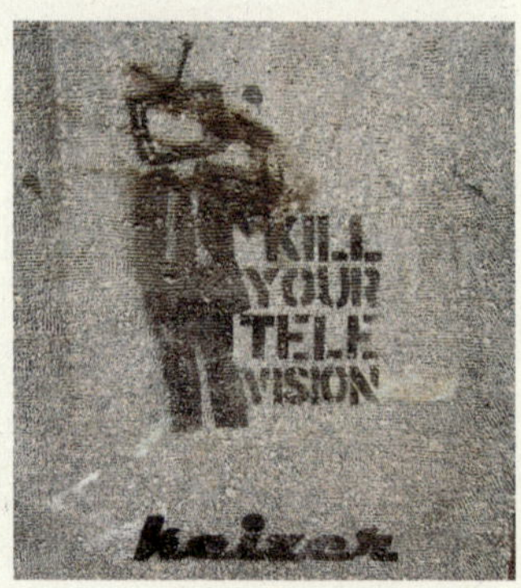

5

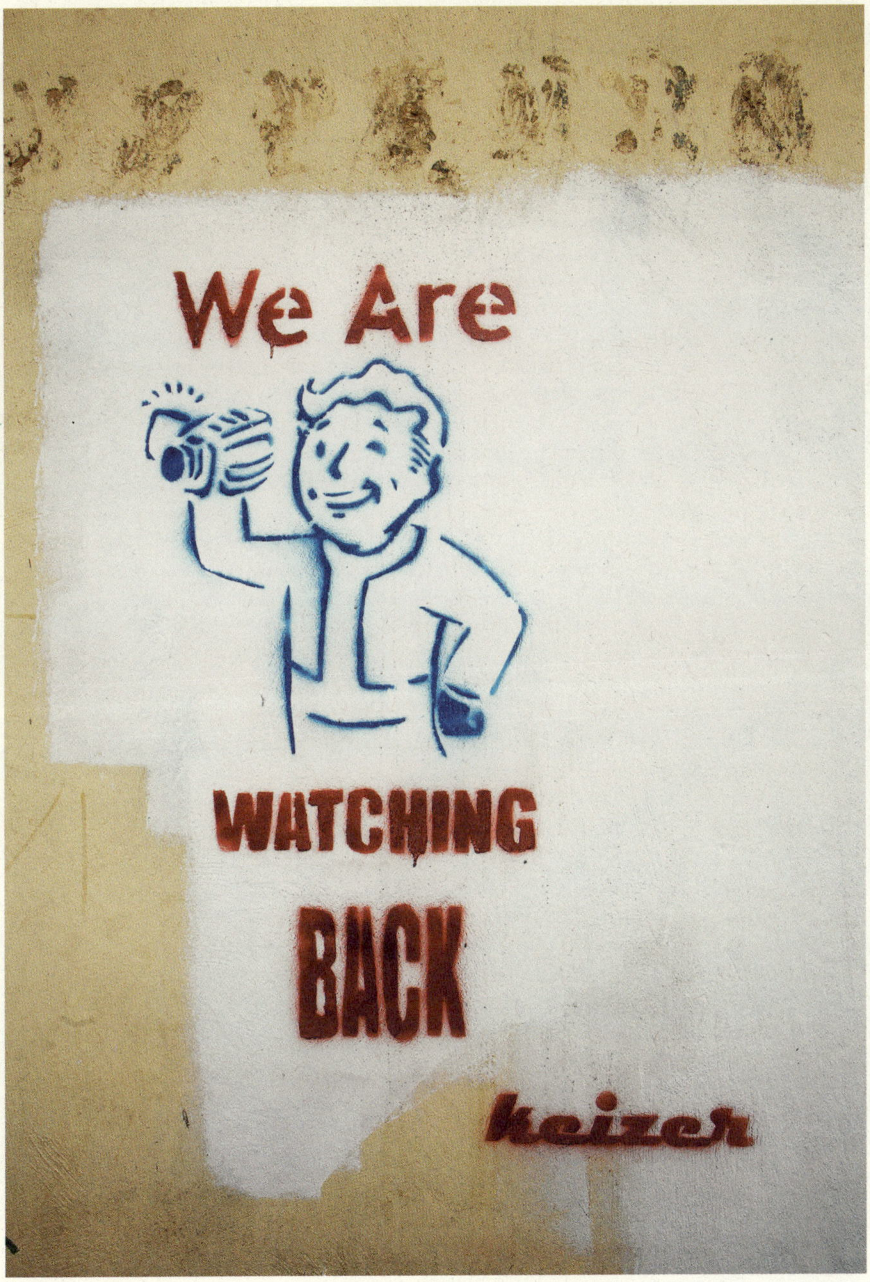

6

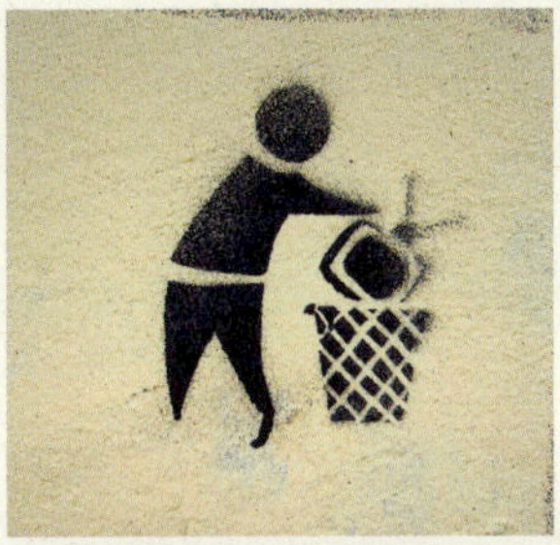
7

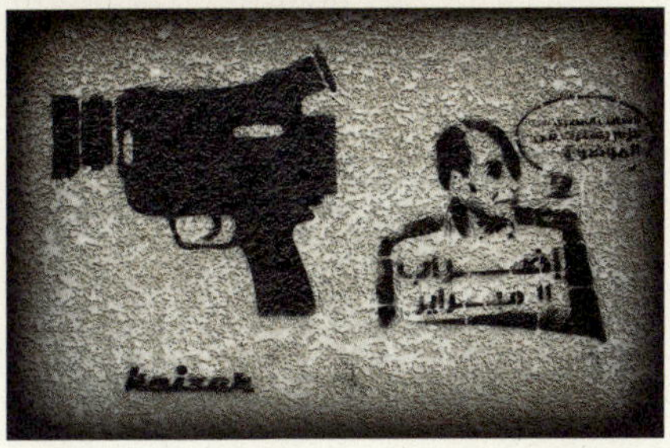

8

1 *Occupy Maspero*
(Photo / Foto / صورة: Gigi Ibrahim / جيجي إبراهيم
from the Flickr album / aus dem Flickr-Album /
من ألبوم على موقع فليكر تحت عنوان *Egypt Graffiti: Street Art*, Nov. 28, 2011)

2 "*Lying Media*"
(Graffiti by / von Amr Nazeer / جرافيتي عمرو نظير)

3 *Pinocchio TV*
(Photo / Foto / صورة: Gigi Ibrahim / جيجي إبراهيم
cf. / vgl. / #1 انظر, Nov. 2, 2011)

4 *Maspero – Occupy Cabinet*
(Photo / Foto / صورة: Sally Zohney / سالي زهني
from the Flickr album / aus dem Flickr-Album /
من ألبوم على موقع فليكر تحت عنوان *Cairene Street Art*, Dec. 2, 2011)

5 *Kill your TV*
(Photo / Foto / صورة: Gigi Ibrahim / جيجي إبراهيم
cf. / vgl. / #1 انظر, Jan. 22, 2012)

6 *We Are Watching Back*
(Photo / Foto / صورة: Thomas Hartwell /
توماس هارتويل, from the exhibition / aus der Ausstellung / من معرض *The Red Line*, 2011)

7 *Trash your TV*
(Photo / Foto / صورة: Gigi Ibrahim / جيجي إبراهيم
cf. / vgl. / #1 انظر, Jan. 20, 2012)

8 *Fear us . . .*
(Photo / Foto / صورة: Gigi Ibrahim / جيجي إبراهيم
cf. / vgl. / #1 انظر, Apr. 20, 2012)

Initiatives like Mosireen and ThawraMedia were started in 2011, when citizen journalism and cultural activism virtually exploded on the scene. Both initiatives offer platforms for the kind of reporting that makes space for new perspectives and approaches—beyond the state-controlled media. The actor, activist, and cofounder of Mosireen, Khalid Abdalla, puts it like this:

"During periods of fundamental social upheaval, it is vitally important to ask who has ownership of history and the truth. This is one of the first revolutions in history that is being documented by the people involved in it rather than by news agencies. Mosireen is, to some extent, a response to this."

The two initiatives are also associated with the idea of the archive, which is the subject of intense discussion among creative artists in the Arab world following the work of the Beirut art collective *Arab Image Foundation*.

ThawraMedia came into being in the wake of the eighteen days and Mubarak's resignation, when digital recordings of the events were collected using memory cards and USB sticks in a "media tent" on Tahrir Square. Mosireen was established during the constant wave of protests that took place in summer 2011. The videos about the Coptic demonstrators who were killed in October 2011 gave them a strong Internet presence and towards the end of the year they reached a worldwide audience. At the local level, in tandem with initiatives like Tahrir Cinema and Kazeboon, they seek to carry on a public debate within the physical space of the city. Tahrir Cinema began in July 2011 with videos being projected at night in Tahrir Square. The activists from the Kazeboon group (Kazeboon means "Liar") showed their own recordings of their protests on the walls of buildings, and even on the Maspero itself. In districts where inhabitants had no Internet, the activities of Kazeboon also helped to counter the official media reports that were coming out.

Initiativen wie Mosireen und ThawraMedia entstanden 2011, als Bürgerjournalismus und kultureller Aktivismus geradezu „explodierten". Beide Initiativen bieten Plattformen für diese Art von Berichterstattung, die neue Blickwinkel und Betrachtungsweisen möglich macht – jenseits der staatlich kontrollierten Medien. Der Schauspieler, Aktivist und Mitbegründer von Mosireen Khalid Abdalla äußert sich so: „In Zeiten eines grundlegenden sozialen Umbruchs wird es dringend notwendig, die Frage zu stellen, wem die Geschichte und die Wahrheit gehören. Dies ist eine der ersten Revolutionen in der Geschichte, die viel mehr von den Beteiligten selbst dokumentiert wird als von Nachrichtenagenturen. Mosireen ist zum Teil eine Reaktion darauf." Mit den beiden Initiativen verbindet sich zudem die Idee des Archivs, die unter den Kulturschaffenden im arabischen Raum in Anlehnung an das Beiruter Künstlerkollektiv *Arab Image Foundation* intensiv diskutiert wird.

ThawraMedia entstand im Anschluss an die achtzehn Tage und den Rücktritt Mubaraks, als in einem „Medienzelt" auf dem Tahrir-Platz die digitalen Aufnahmen von den Ereignissen per Speicherkarte und USB-Stick gesammelt wurden. Mosireen gründete sich während der anhaltenden Proteste im Sommer 2011. Mit den Videos über die getöteten koptischen Demonstranten im Oktober 2011 wurden sie sehr stark im Internet wahrgenommen und fanden gegen Ende des Jahres eine weltweite Öffentlichkeit. Auf lokaler Ebene versuchen sie gemeinsam mit Initiativen wie Tahrir Cinema und Kazeboon, eine öffentliche Debatte im physischen Raum der Stadt zu führen. Das Tahrir Cinema begann im Juli 2011 auf dem nächtlichen Tahrir-Platz mit der Projektion von Videos. Die Aktivisten der Gruppe Kazeboon (zu deutsch „Lügner") zeigten ihre Videos der Proteste, die sie auf Wände von Gebäuden, auch des „Maspero", projizierten. Auch in Stadtvierteln, in denen die Bewohner nicht über Internet verfügen, versuchten die Aktionen von Kazeboon, der offiziellen Berichterstattung etwas entgegenzusetzen.

نشأت مبادرتا "مُصرّين" و"ثورة ميديا" في العام 2011، عندما عمت وإنتشرت أنشطة الصحافة المدنيّة لغير المحترفين والنشاطات الثقافية إلى حد بعيد. تقدم كلتا المبادرتان مواقع لهذا النوع من التغطية الصحافيّة، حيث تقدم وجهات نظر وطرق جديدة خارجة عن سيطرة إعلام الدولة. يُعبرِّ الممثل والناشط وأحد المؤسسين لمبادرة "مُصرّين" خالد عبدالله عن ذلك بقوله: "في أزمنة التغيرات الإجتماعيّة الجذريّة يصبح من الضروري أن نطرح السؤال التالي، من يملك الحقيقة والتاريخ. هذه هي أول ثورة يتم توثيقها من قبل المشاركين بها عوضاً عن وكالات الأخبار. و"مُصرّين" هي لحد ما رد فعل لها." تتقاسم المبادرتان فكرة الأرشفة على غرار المؤسسة العربيَّة للصورة ومركزها بيروت، وتتم مناقشة هذا الأمر في الوقت الحالي بكثافة في أوساط الفنانين العرب.

أُنشئت "ثورة ميديا" في "خيمة الإعلام" في ميدان التحرير بعد مضي الـ"18 يوم" وتنحي مبارك، حيث تم جمع الصور الرقمية للأحداث على بطاقات الذاكرة والفلاشات. أمّا "مُصرّين" فقد أُنشئت أثناء المظاهرات المستمرة في صيف 2011 وجذبت الإنتباه لها بشكل أكبر بالإنترنت عندما قامت بنشر مقاطع فيديو عن مقتل المتظاهرين الأقباط في أكتوبر 2011، وفي نهاية العام أصبحت "مُصرّين" معروفة عالمياً. أما على الصعيد المحلي فإن مجموعة "مُصرّين" تحاول التعاون مع مبادرات أخرى كـ "سينما التحرير" و"كاذبون" لإثارة جدل ضمن المدينة ذاتها. بدأت "سينما التحرير" في يوليو 2011 بعرض مقاطع فيديو ليلاً. أما مجموعة "كاذبون" فقد كانت تعرض مقاطع فيديو على واجهات جدران المباني ومن ضمنها واجهات "ماسبيرو" للمظاهرات التي كانوا يقومون بها بأنفسهم وتصويرها بأنفسهم. واظبت مجموعة "سينما التحرير" على تقديم عروضها أيضاً في الأحياء التي لا يصلها الإنترنت لمواجهة تأثير الإعلام الرسمي.

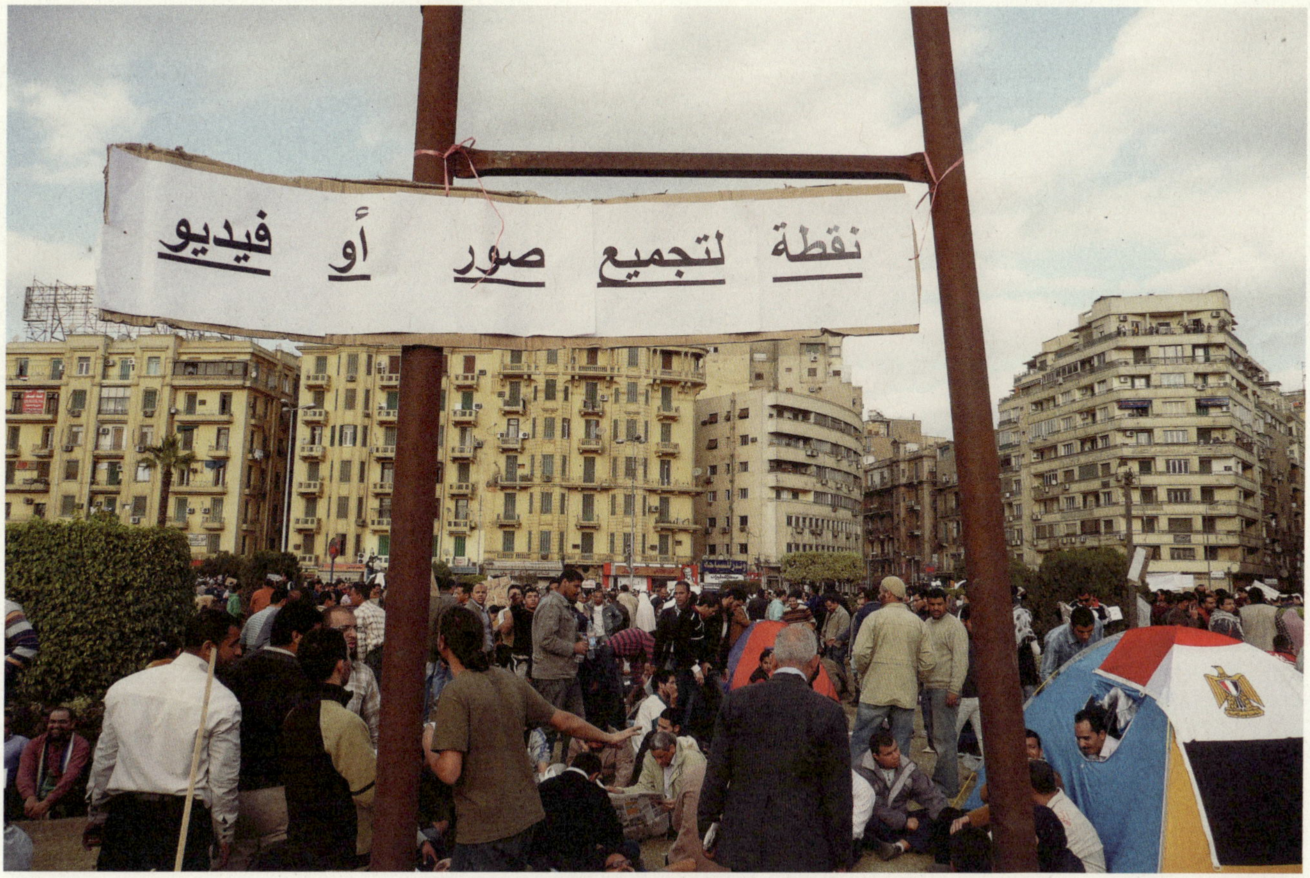

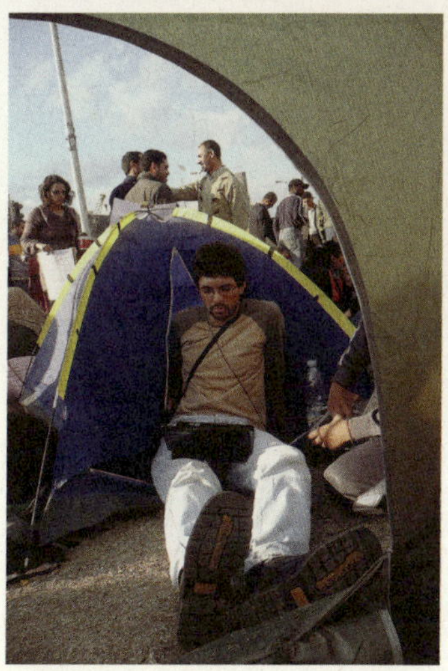

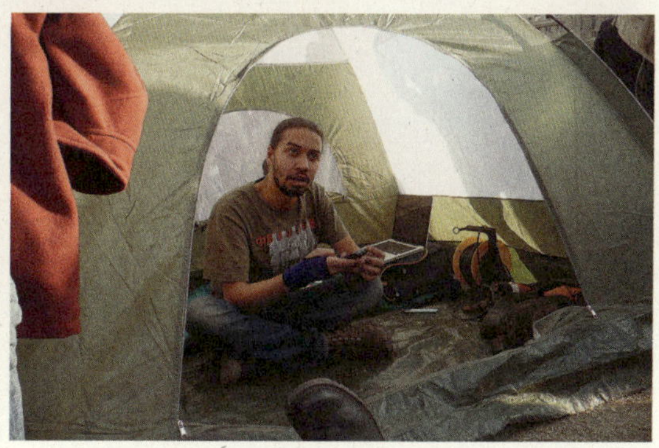

The ThawraMedia tent on Tahrir Square, collecting point for image files, February 2011 /
Das Zelt von ThawraMedia auf dem Tahrir-Platz, Sammelstelle für Bilddaten, Februar 2011 /
خيمة ثـورة ميديـا في ميدان التحرير، مكان تجميع الصور، فبراير 2011

Mosireen is a non-profit media collective in downtown Cairo born out of the explosion of citizen media and cultural activism in Egypt during the revolution. Armed with mobile phones and cameras, thousands upon thousands of citizens kept the balance of truth in their country by recording events as they happened in front of them, wrong-footing censorship and empowering the voice of a street-level perspective. Egypt's march towards the future its millions demanded did not end with Mubarak leaving power, it began.

Mosireen, which is a play on the Arabic words for "Egypt" and "determined" was founded in the wake of Mubarak's fall by a group of film makers and activists who got together to found a collective space dedicated to supporting citizen media of all kinds.

(www.mosireen.org)

Mosireen ist ein nicht profitorientiertes Medienkollektiv im Zentrum Kairos, das aus der sprunghaften Vermehrung der Bürgermedien und des kulturellen Aktivismus in Ägypten während der Revolution hervorging. Bewaffnet mit Mobiltelefonen und Kameras gelang es Abertausenden von Bürgern, ihrer Wahrheit eine Stimme zu geben, indem sie die Ereignisse so festhielten, wie sie sich vor ihnen vollzogen. Damit schlugen sie der Zensur ein Schnippchen und stärkten zugleich den Einfluss jener Perspektive der Straße. Der von Millionen Einwohnern Ägyptens geforderte Aufbruch in die Zukunft endete nicht in dem Moment, da Mubarak von seinem Amt zurücktrat, dort begann er.

Mosireen, was ein Wortspiel mit den arabischen Wörtern für „Ägypten" und „entschieden" ist, wurde in der Folge von Mubaraks Sturz von einer Gruppe von Filmemachern und Aktivisten gegründet, die zusammenkamen, um einen gemeinschaftlichen Raum zu gründen und so die verschiedenartigen Bürgermedien zu unterstützen.

(www.mosireen.org)

منذ بداية الثورة في 25 يناير و حتى الآن، لعب الإعلام الشعبي دوراً محورياً في نقل الأحداث، فكان للأخبار و الصور و مقاطع الفيديو التي تناقلها المصريون دوراً مركزياً في خلق خطاب إعلامي شعبي أكثر صدقاً وشمولاً و في الضغط على الإعلام المؤسسي لتبني هذا الخطاب.

من وسط أحداث الثورة خلقت مُصرّين، كتعاونية إعلامية تهدف لدعم جهود الإعلام الشَعبي و النشاط الثقافي في مصر. كما تهدف لدعم جهود كل من يريد تقديم دور في دعم الثورة إعلامياً أو ثقافياً.

لذا فنحنُ مُصرّون

- أن تكون مُصرّين مكاناً مفتوحاً لكلٍّ من يُؤمن بمطالب الثورةَ و يعتقد أن الثورة مازالت مستمرة و يَوَدُ أن يدعمها بإنتاج مواد إعلامية، و لكل من يؤمن
- أننا قادرون على خلق إعلام بديل يعبر عن وجهات نظرنا على اختلافها وينقل الحقيقة بلا زيف.
- أن نكون مكاناً يقدم كل الدعم المستطاع لكل صانع أفلام داعمة للثورة، محترفاً كان أم هاوياً يصورها علي تليفون محمول أو كاميرا بسيطة.
- أن تكون مساحة لتبادل المهارات والتدريب بين الأفراد المختلفين، كانوا صنّاع أفلام أو ناشطين سياسياً أو مهتمين بتنمية مهاراتهم في صناعة الأفلام و الصحافة الشعبية.
- أن تخلق مساحة لعرض الأفلام و المناقشة حولها في المساحات المفتوحة كما في المواقع المغلقة.
- أن تخلق أرشيفاً بصرياً و صوتياً للثورة والأحداث السياسية التي تمر بنا.
- أن تعمل كنقطة تلاقٍ للتنسيق بين المجموعات المختلفة و المبادرات المختلفة.
- أن تنتج أفلاماً تدعم الثورة و مطالبها وتعبر عن تجربة الذين شاركوا فيها.

مُصرّين هي مبادرة من مجموعة من النشطاء و صنّاع السينما المستقلين.

أبواب مُصرّين مفتوحة لجميع صنّاع الأفلام المساندين للثورة، بلا تمييز. وهي مجموعة لا تهدف للربح. وحتى نستطيع الاستمرار في تقديم خدماتنا فسيكون لبعض الخدمات قيمة رمزية مقترحة، وقد يختار الأفراد أن يساهموا بأكثر من القيمة المقترحة أو أقل منها أو يستخدموا الخدمة بصورة مجانية حسب إمكانياتهم

نحن نرحب بكل مساهماتكم حتى تصبح مُصرّين قادرة على تقديم خدماتها بشكل أفضل، نرحب بكاميرات مستخدمة أو أجهزة كمبيوتر محمولة مستخدمة في حالة جيدة. من الممكن أيضاً أن تساهموا بكتب أو دوريات مستقلة. ونرحب بإقتراحاتكم.

مواعيد العمل الأحد: 2 – 8

الإثنين إلى الخميس: 12 – 8

العنوان: 34 شارع طلعت حرب، عمارة يعقوبيان، الدور السادس، شقة 26. وسط البلد.

(www.mosireen.org)

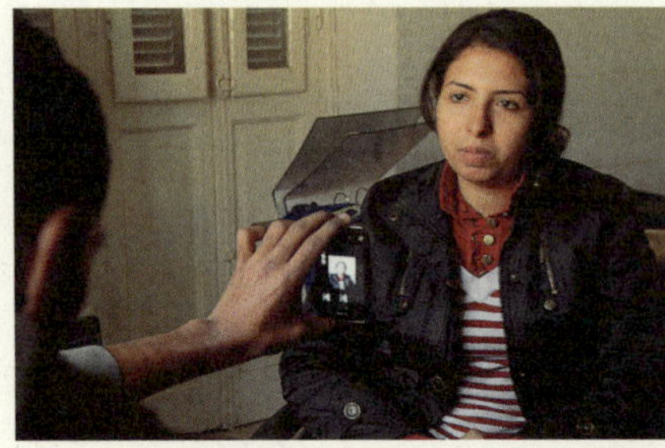

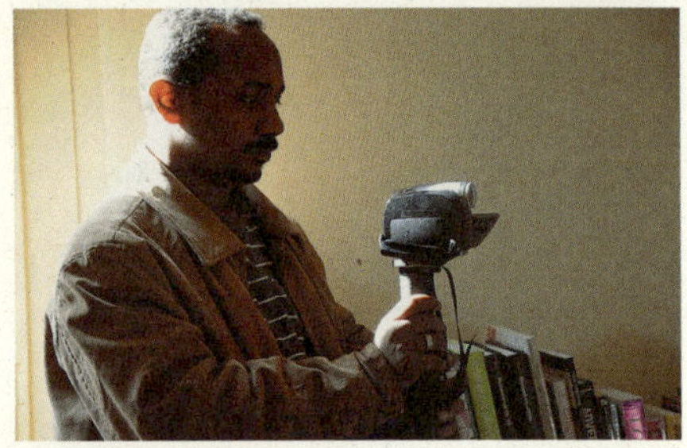

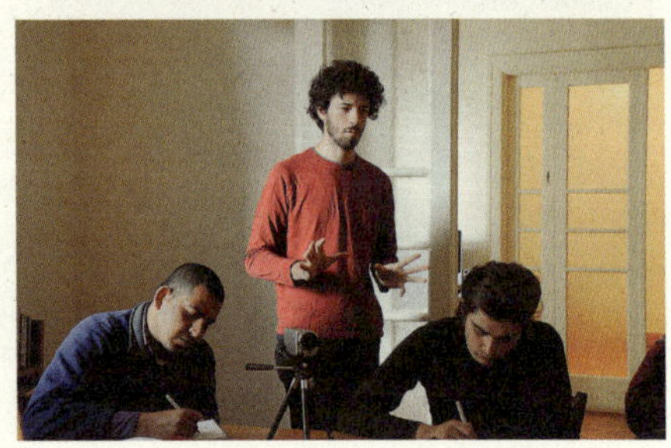

Members of the Mosireen collective conduct workshops on filming, editing, animation, or the intricacies of interviewing victims of torture. In early 2012 Mosireen launched the Ra7al workshops, which take place in governorates outside of Cairo. Ra7al is a crash course in revolutionary filmmaking, training participants about issues such as copyleft footage, social media, editing, filmmaking with a mobile phone, and setting up street screenings./
Mitglieder des Kollektivs bieten Schulungen zu Film, Schnitt und Animation an oder sensibilisieren in Seminaren für die Schwierigkeiten, ein Folteropfer zu interviewen. Zu Beginn des Jahres 2012 initiierte Mosireen die Ra7al-Workshops in Gouvernements außerhalb Kairos. Dabei handelt es sich um Crashkurse über das Filmen für die Revolution, wobei die Teilnehmer zu Fragen des „Copyleft"-Materials, über soziale Medien, Filmschnitt, Filmen mit dem Mobiltelefon und für die Einrichtung von Filmvorführungen im Freien geschult werden./
يقوم أعضاء مجموعة مُصرّين بتدريس ورش عمل عن الأفلام، المونتاج والأنيميشن و يقيمون ندوات عن كيفية ومدى صعوبة إجراء حوار مع ضحية تعذيب على سبيل المثال. أسسوا في عام 2012 مبادرة أسموها ورش عمل "رحّال" في محافظات مصر خارج القاهرة. تتكون من كورسات مكثفة عن تصوير الثورة، يتلقى فيه المشتركون المعلومات عن كيفية التعامل مع مواد الكوبي لفت أو الحقوق المتروكة الموجودة على مواقع التواصل الاجتماعي، المونتاج، التصوير بالتليفون المحمول وتنظيم عروض للأفلام في الأماكن المفتوحة.

Khalid Abdalla

Actor, activist and cofounder of Mosireen Media Collective

Testimony

A revolution is an act of sight. Like a miracle, it makes visible what seemed beyond the horizon, bringing power structures into focus, reshaping what once appeared indestructible. As such, a revolution is also a battle with time. How long does it take to react to what you've seen? Meanwhile, miracles develop into stories, and stories are easily manipulated. The more time passes, the more stories are told, the more the miracle is called a delusion, and the more the sight is turned into darkness. At each step of this miraculous journey, violence is inescapable. As people face authority, two visions of truth lock in a struggle for existence. Claims on the past and the future collide with purpose, and, at each turn of the wheel, blood marks the trail.

Those of us who witness the miraculous have a duty to others. The story of what we see no longer belongs to us because it changes everything. In a revolution, this change is a whole political reality worth dying for, not because death is an ideal but because the economy of life has become such that risking death is the only way of securing life for others. Such is the culture of lies pervading the old order that it will kill you and claim that no one died. Another darker miracle.

The bodies caught in this battleground, and the families from which their blood came, are the real storytellers of this history. The heart that moves mountains has something to tell us all. And yet so many of those hearts are silenced. The act of testimony becomes our closest witness.

Something of this world is present when you walk into a room and switch on a camera to be faced with someone who wants to speak through you. Inasmuch as they tell you their experience of what happened, they engage in an act of the kindest faith in their audience. Their words say that if you truly hear me, you will see a world that you are blind to. Meanwhile, their method of speech is twofold: to provide proof of their story and to move. Sometimes, it is only to move, because that is the truest statement, even if it falls on deaf ears.

Rotten ideologies create societies dependent on a culture of lies. Sometimes those lies are comforting. More often than not they serve authority. When authority lies, it must be overthrown. For this to happen, you must disprove the lies. But doing so takes time. The burden of providing proof is a longer process than the ability to lie, especially when the lie is as comforting and invisible as sleep.

But when someone says what you're thinking without you saying it, that person has a hold on you. When their story confirms your hidden fears, a process of trust around a discourse begins. A revolution is a period of time in which massive social change is possible within a very short period of time. The moment at which people believe something collectively without another word being spoken is the moment a whole power structure begins to shift. They need to believe at the same time, especially when they are leaderless. And so timing is essential if you wish to catch a fleeting moment. The rhythm of our story is the rhythm of our testimonies and acts of witness. Just as they protect us, they protect our narratives—the story of where we have come from, and also where we are going.

Our words, our eyes, our cameras, our ink are all witnesses to the deeper truths in this power shift. Which is not to say that we are always right, but that we are always reaching out for something truer than just mere evidence. We are searching for evidence of the future, just as we saw it when one horizon collapsed into another. You can only find it if you keep looking.

So beware those of you who would silence a revolution and its demands. When something with the resonance of such humanity happens, everyone looks and everyone listens, eventually.

Turbulence

Stability is a lie. The idea that stability protects us is another lullaby. What protects us is our ability to adapt, endlessly. Change is more valuable than nostalgia. While beautiful moments repeat themselves, just like darker ones, each repeat is never the same. Renewal is better than repetition, and more daring.

In a revolution, you have to dare and risk failure because you have already accepted that what you knew as stability is certain disaster. But daring is exhausting, and laziness is a human right. Where do you strike the balance? For a good while, you don't.

Being driven to exhaustion and lapsing into laziness is a necessary rhythm. Rhythms are essential to collective action, and it is better to acknowledge a rhythm than behave as if it doesn't exist. Never sail the high seas as you would Lake Geneva. Better to follow the wave than sail against it, unless you are forced to, at which point know your limits. The sea is more powerful than any vessel.

Change comes in waves, and never in straight lines. You can't predict when the next wave will come, but you always know when a storm is brewing.

Turbulence protects us against authority. As things stand, we know that authority does not have our interests at heart. So, by default, we know that as long as we continue moving in a threatening rhythm, authority cannot control us. Time and again we have learnt that they will never voluntarily accept our demands, so we have to make it necessary to them. Only when they listen, or we guarantee our advantage, will the calm begin to come.

But calm is not stability. It is a sign of having found a common ground where each individual is able to get on with their life, in which our stories have become our history. We cannot live for each other forever, except in mythology.

Martyrs

We have had over a thousand martyrs since this revolution began, and at no point on our journey have we not known that there will be more. Despite having filmed hundreds of videos with martyrs' families, no one has ever filmed a martyr speak. Even when they seemed to have foreknowledge of their death, their words only ever exist in retrospect, and the images of their dead bodies are often something like a final statement. Still their words and images live on like imperfect reminders of their families' pain, as they become symbols of a wider struggle they had each consciously chosen.

The names of every martyr are not known one by one. Indeed some have never been identified. It is deeply unfair that some martyrs' names ring out louder than others, but that is the fault of the living, not theirs. While some martyrs have become icons of particular moments and particular identities, each marks a chapter on our onward journey.

More testimonies belong to the martyrs' families than any other. Images of violence in Egypt have expressed many extraordinary truths, but they have become standardized as a mode of expression over time. Almost everything they can say has now been said. But while these images have exhausted themselves into repetition, there are still truths burning to be spoken. Principles are not easily embodied. From the very beginning, the fact that this revolution has been fought for a series of common ideals has meant they lack representation in a single identity or ideological organization. In turn, the right to speak is the rarest privilege.

Experts and politicians have a right to convince. All of us have a right to participate. It is only the martyrs' families who have an indisputable right to speak. Every one of us has moments in which what we say or write might be of value. But the right to speak is a very particular mantle, which is perhaps why images have been such a crucial part of how the living in our revolution have made the dead speak. Those of you who have only seen our revolution through the lens of international media, make note that you have probably not heard from a martyr's mother or father, their brother or sister, their wife or fiancé.

At a martyr's funeral, the family is meant to ululate. It is a sound like no other at a funeral, traditionally kept for a wedding. If you understand that sound, you will understand our revolution.

Celebration

The world witnessed a celebration on February 11, 2011. It has since decided to disregard that vision and written into the story a failed process of transition to democracy, hijacked quite simply by the Muslim Brotherhood. Which is to say, it wrote its own ending onto the story of what is happening, taking with it the days when people approached an Egyptian with a sense of complicit happiness, and replacing them with a moment when the subject is approached with awkwardly apologetic curiosity.

But your eyes did not lie to you that day. Like every other Egyptian who was happy to see the fall of Mubarak, you wrote another ending far too soon. We have seen that moment come time and again, when a false sense of ending is given the authority of augury.

The truth is that it's too early to tell where we'll be even a year from now. In under two years the revolution has dealt massive blows to the three major organized powers in Egypt: the Police State, the Army, and the Muslim Brotherhood. The fact that each of them has tried to enforce its authority outright, and not one of them has succeeded, means the story of Mubarak's state unraveling continues, by the will of the people.

It is easy to forget that the most important attribute of democracy is participation beyond the ballot box. Such is the state of complacent democracy in places where it seems to work for the nation-state, that we forget that the guarantors of a state worth protecting are not the voting system, but everything that sits around it. A vote between two fascist authoritarians is worthless in a state apparatus unable to guarantee any form of justice for its most vulnerable.

On the second anniversary of Mubarak's fall, we continue to celebrate the fact that the revolution has continued despite the various attempts to thwart it. It is an extraordinary thing to learn that two years later we still have the energy to fight a battle we thought might last a number of days.

The act of testimony is a choice as to what you confess to yourself and others to having seen. It's a peculiarity of our complacent vision in normal times that we believe we can see, when we are blind to most of what happens in the world. And yet the whole world saw something to celebrate, the day Mubarak stepped down. There have been few more numerous acts of collective witness in history, if any. Those of us who can still see it know there is a certain history following from its arc. What we witnessed was not just the toppling of a dictator, it was a human vision we all have a duty to make manifest.

Systems

What is happening in Egypt is not happening out there, it is happening to all of us, just as intensely as it did to Mohamed Bouazizi's body, when he set himself on fire. Just as Egypt's democracy brought us another dictator, so Western democracies secured the dictator we toppled. When the tools of democracy are used to create dictatorships with a taste for blood, it is only a matter of time before the deep hypocrisy releases an earthquake.

So when you listen to the testimony of a poor Egyptian family, do not pity them, pity yourself, at least until you know deep inside you that you are doing something about it.

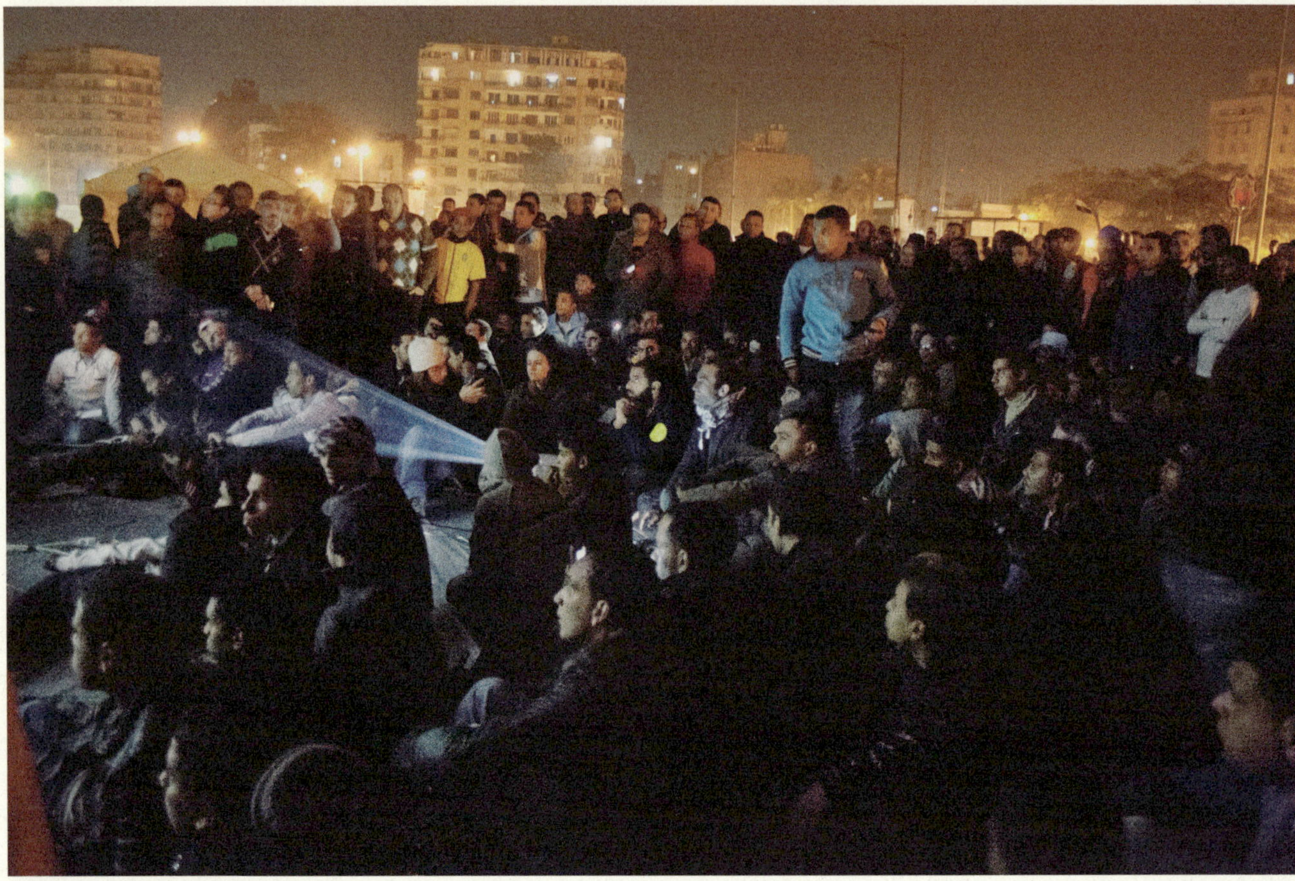

Tahrir Cinema, Dec. 2, 2011, Cairo
The actor and activist Khalid Abdalla presents photographs and videos taken by citizen journalists/
Der Schauspieler und Aktivist Khalid Abdalla präsentiert Fotos und Videos von Bürgerjournalisten/
سينما التحرير، 2 ديسمبر 2011، القاهرة، الممثل والناشط خالد عبد الله يعرض صور ومقاطع فيديو لصحفيين هواة (صحافة شعبية)

Khalid Abdalla

Schauspieler, Aktivist und Mitbegründer von Mosireen Medienkollektiv

Zeugenbericht

Eine Revolution ist eine Handlung, die gesehen wird. Sie gleicht einem Wunder, sie macht sichtbar, was sich hinter dem Horizont verborgen zu haben schien, rückt Machtstrukturen in den Blick und formt neu, was unveränderlich und unzerstörbar wirkte. Die Revolution als solche ist ein Kampf mit der Zeit. Wie lange dauert es, um [dauerhaft das] zu erreichen, was man [als Möglichkeit] vor Augen geführt bekam? Im Laufe der Zeit werden aus Wundern Geschichten, die leicht manipuliert werden können. Je mehr Zeit vergeht, umso mehr Geschichten werden erzählt, und umso häufiger wird das Wunder als Täuschung bezeichnet, und umso stärker trübt sich der Blick und es rückt auch das, was zuvor gesehen werden konnte, in die sich ausbreitende Dunkelheit. Jeder Schritt dieser Wunderreise ist unvermeidlich von Gewalt begleitet. Wenn die Menschen den Autoritäten gegenüberstehen, geraten zwei Visionen von Wahrheit in einen Daseinskampf. Forderungen an die Vergangenheit und die Zukunft kollidieren mit kalkuliertem Bedacht, und jede Bewegung hinterlässt blutige Spuren auf ihrem Weg.

Jene unter uns, die Zeugen des Wunders wurden, stehen den anderen gegenüber in der Pflicht. Die Erzählung dessen, was wir sehen, gehört uns nicht länger [allein], denn sie verändert alles. In einer Revolution ist diese Veränderung eine politische Realität, die es wert wäre, für sie zu sterben; nicht, weil der Tod ein Ideal darstellt, sondern weil die Ökonomie des Lebens sich mittlerweile so darstellt, dass den Tod zu riskieren die einzige Möglichkeit geworden ist, das Leben anderer zu sichern. Die Kultur der Lügen durchdringt die alte Ordnung und befähigt sie, dich zu töten und am Ende zu behaupten, niemand wäre gestorben. Ein weiteres, [jedoch bedeutend] dunkleres Wunder.

Die Toten, die diese Schlacht forderte, und das Blut der Familien, das in den Adern der Toten floss, sind die wahren Erzähler dieser Geschichte. Ein Herz, das Berge versetzt, kann uns alle etwas lehren. Und dennoch werden so viele dieser Herzen zum Verstummen gebracht. Der Zeugenbericht wird unser wichtigster Zeuge.

Etwas von dieser Welt ist anwesend, wenn du einen Raum betrittst, eine Kamera anschaltest und jemandem gegenüberstehst, der durch dich sprechen möchte. Indem sie dir ihre Erfahrungen erzählen, zeigen sie eine Handlung des wohlwollendsten Glaubens an ihr Publikum. Ihre Worte sagen: Wenn du mich wirklich hörst, dann wirst du eine dir verschlossene Welt sehen, eine Welt, für die du blind bist. Dabei ist ihre Sprechweise eine zweigleisige: Sie will Beweise ihrer Geschichte liefern und [zugleich] bewegen. Manchmal geht es nur darum zu bewegen, denn ein solches Statement ist das aufrichtigste, selbst dann, wenn es auf taube Ohren stößt.

Verdorbene Ideologien erschaffen Gesellschaften, die auf einer Kultur der Lügen basieren. Manchmal sind diese Lügen angenehm. Zumeist dienen sie der Autorität. Wenn die Autorität eine verlogene ist, muss sie gestürzt werden. Dafür müssen die Lügen widerlegt werden. Aber das beansprucht viel Zeit. Man muss länger die Bürde des Beweiselieferns tragen, als es dauert, die Fähigkeit des Lügens zu erlernen und anzuwenden, vor allem, wenn die Lügen so angenehm und unsichtbar sind wie der Schlaf.

Wenn jedoch jemand sagt, was du denkst und nicht du hast es gesagt, dann liegst du in den Händen dieser Person. Wenn deren Geschichte deine verborgenen Ängste bestätigt, bildet sich aus dem Bericht Vertrauen. Eine Revolution ist eine Phase, in der massive soziale Veränderungen innerhalb einer sehr kurzen Zeit möglich sind. Der Moment, in welchem Menschen wortlos kollektiv an etwas glauben, ist der Moment, in dem eine Machtstruktur ins Rutschen kommt. Die Menschen müssen den Glauben zur selben

Zeit teilen, vor allem dann, wenn sie führerlos sind. Und folglich ist das Timing von essenzieller Wichtigkeit, wenn es darum geht, einen flüchtigen Moment einzufangen. Der Rhythmus unserer Geschichte ist der Rhythmus unserer Zeugenschaft und Berichte. Genau so, wie diese uns beschützen, beschützen sie unsere Erzählungen: die Geschichten unserer Herkunft und unseres künftigen Weges.

Unsere Worte, unsere Augen, unsere Kameras, unsere Tinte – sie alle sind Zeugen unserer tieferen Wahrheiten in diesem Machtwechsel. Was nicht heißen soll, dass wir immer im Recht sind, aber dass wir immer etwas zu erreichen suchen, das wahrer ist, als der schiere Beweis. Wir suchen nach deutlichen Anzeichen der Zukunft, so wie wir sie sahen, als ein Horizont in einen anderen stürzte [, als sich uns eine andere Welt offenbarte]. Man kann diese Anzeichen nur finden, wenn man unablässig nach ihnen sucht.

Also hütet euch, ihr, die ihr eine Revolution und ihre Forderungen zum Verstummen bringen würdet. Wenn sich etwas mit der Resonanz solcher Menschenmassen und in Menschlichkeit vollzieht, sieht letztendlich jeder hin und hört jeder zu.

Turbulenz

Stabilität ist eine Lüge. Die Behauptung, dass Stabilität uns schütze, ist nur ein weiteres Schlaflied. Was uns schützt, ist unsere endlose Fähigkeit zur Anpassung. Veränderung ist wertvoller als Nostalgie. Wenngleich schöne Momente und auch unschöne, dunklere, sich selbst wiederholen, ist jede Wiederholung anders. Erneuerung ist wichtiger als Wiederholung, und sie ist auch wagemutiger.

In einer Revolution muss man das Risiko des Versagens eingehen, denn man hat dann schon akzeptiert, dass das, was du als Stabilität kanntest, nichts als ein garantiertes Desaster war. Jedoch ist es erschöpfend, wagemutig zu sein, und der Mensch hat ein Recht auf Faulheit. Wie findet man ein Gleichgewicht? Für eine ganze Weile findet man schlichtweg keines.

In die Erschöpfung getrieben zu werden und [anschließend] in die Faulheit zu fließen, das ist ein notwendiger Rhythmus. Rhythmen sind für kollektive Handlungen wesentlich, und es ist besser, einen Rhythmus anzuerkennen, als ihn zu negieren. Befahre die Meere nie wie den Genfer See. Es ist besser, mit der Welle zu gehen, als gegen sie zu segeln, es sei denn, du hast keine Wahl, und dann wisse um deine Grenzen. Das Meer ist stärker als jedes Schiff.

Veränderung kommt in Wellen, nie kommt sie geradlinig. Man kann nicht voraussagen, wann die nächste Welle kommen wird, aber man weiß immer, wann sich ein Unwetter zusammenbraut.

Turbulenzen beschützen uns vor Autoritäten. So wie es aussieht, wissen wir, dass unsere Interessen den Autoritäten kein Anliegen sind. Solange wir in einem [nicht vorhersagbaren] Rhythmus in Bewegung bleiben, sind wir für die Autoritäten unkontrollierbar und bedrohlich. Wieder und wieder mussten wir begreifen, dass sie unsere Forderungen niemals freiwillig akzeptieren werden, also müssen wir ihnen das zu einem dringenden Anliegen machen. Nur wenn sie zuhören oder wenn die Macht auch garantiert zu unseren Gunsten verteilt ist, wird die Ruhe beginnen sich auszubreiten.

Aber Ruhe ist nicht Stabilität. Sie ist ein Zeichen dafür, eine gemeinsame Basis gefunden zu haben, auf welcher jedes Individuum befähigt wird, mit seinem Leben fortzufahren, mit jenem Leben, in dem unser aller Erzählungen zu unser aller Geschichte geworden ist. Nur in der Mythologie können wir alle für immer miteinander leben.

Märtyrer

Seit die Revolution begann, gab es über tausend Märtyrer. Wir wussten an jedem Punkt unserer Reise, dass es noch mehr werden würden. Obwohl mit den Familien der Märtyrer viele Videos gefilmt wurden, hat niemand je eine Filmaufnahme eines sich äußernden Märtyrers angefertigt. Selbst wenn sie um ihren anstehenden Tod wussten, existieren ihre Worte immer nur in der [erinnernden] Rückschau, und die Bilder ihrer toten Körper sind oft eine Art abschließendes Statement. Ihre Worte und Bilder leben wie unvollkommene Mahnungen an den Schmerz ihrer Familien, während sie zu Symbolen eines größeren Kampfes werden, für den sie sich alle bewusst entschieden haben.

Die Namen aller einzelnen Märtyrers sind nicht bekannt. Manche wurden auch niemals identifiziert. Es ist zutiefst ungerecht, dass die Namen mancher Märtyrer lauter tönen als andere, aber das ist der Fehler jener, die leben. Wenngleich manche Märtyrer zu Ikonen eines speziellen Moments und zu besonderen Persönlichkeiten geworden sind [und andere nicht], markiert jeder ein Kapitel unserer andauernden Reise.

Von den Familien der Märtyrer stammen mehr Zeugenberichte als von irgendeiner anderen Quelle. Die Bilder der Gewalt in Ägypten haben viele außergewöhnliche Wahrheiten ausgedrückt, aber sie sind im Laufe der Zeit zu einer standardisierten Ausdrucksform geworden. Alles, was sie sagen können, ist mittlerweile gesagt worden. Aber wenngleich sich diese Bilder bis zur Verausgabung wiederholt haben, gibt es doch noch Wahrheiten, die darauf brennen, ausgesprochen zu werden. Prinzipien können nicht leicht in Form gegossen werden. Von Anfang an bedeutete der Umstand, dass diese Revolution für eine ganze Reihe allgemeiner Ideale und Ziele ausgetragen wurde, dass es ihr an repräsentativen Einzelpersonen und repräsentativen ideologischen Organisationen mangelte. Im Gegenzug ist das Recht auf freie Rede das kostbarste Privileg.

Experten und Politiker haben das Recht zum Überzeugen. Alle von uns haben ein Recht zur Teilnahme. Allein die Märtyrerfamilien haben ein unumstößliches Recht zum Sprechen. Wir anderen haben alle Momente, in denen das, was wir sagen oder schreiben von Wert sein könnte. Aber das Rederecht ist eine sehr besondere Verpackung [der unterschiedlichsten Inhalte und Interessen], was vielleicht der Grund dafür ist, dass die Bilder eine so entscheidende Rolle darin spielten, wie die Lebenden unserer Revolution die Toten sprechen ließen. Die unter euch, die die Revolution nur mit den Augen der internationalen Medien gesehen habt, merkt euch, dass ihr nichts von Vater oder Mutter, von Bruder oder Schwester, von Ehefrau oder Verlobter des Märtyrers gehört habt.

Auf der Beerdigung eines Märtyrers soll die Familie heulend wehklagen. Das Klagen, das traditionellerweise für Hochzeiten reserviert ist, ist auf der Beerdigung ein Geräusch wie kein anderes. Wenn ihr dieses Geräusch versteht, versteht ihr die Revolution.

Feier

Am 11. Februar 2011 wurde die Welt Zeugin einer Feier. Seitdem hat sie sich entschieden, die Vision [die an diesem Tag sichtbar wurde] zu ignorieren und hat der Geschichte einen gescheiterten Prozess des Übergangs zur Demokratie eingeschrieben. Die Demokratie wäre ziemlich simpel von den Muslimbrüdern entführt worden. Was heißen soll: die Welt hat ihre eigene Version vom Ende der Erzählung dessen, was sich da vollzieht, gesetzt. Sie reißt die Tage an sich, in denen man den Ägyptern in einer Art eingeschworenem Glücklichsein begegnete und setzte an die Stelle dieser Tage den Moment, in dem dem [ägyptischen] Gegenüber mit unbeholfen entschuldigender Neugierde begegnet wird.

Aber an diesem Tag [, am 11. Februar 2011] haben eure Augen euch nicht belogen. Wie jeder andere Ägypter, der glücklich war, den Sturz von Mubarak zu sehen, hast du viel zu früh ein anderes Ende geschrieben. Wir haben diesen Moment ein ums andere Mal kommen sehen: Die Allmacht über die Zukunftsvoraussage wird einem falschen Gespür für das Ende überlassen.

Die Wahrheit ist [jedoch], dass es sogar zu früh ist, um sagen zu können, wo wir uns in einem Jahr befinden werden. In weniger als zwei Jahren hat die Revolution den drei größten organisierten Kräften Ägyptens massive Schläge versetzt: dem Polizeistaat, der Armee und den Muslimbrüdern. Der Umstand, dass jeder von ihnen versuchte, seine eigene Autorität vollständig durchzusetzen, aber keiner von ihnen dabei erfolgreich war, bedeutet, dass die Geschichte von der Entwirrung von Mubaraks Staat sich fortsetzt – durch den Willen des Volkes.

Es ist leicht zu vergessen, dass das wichtigste Attribut der Demokratie eine Teilnahme ist, die darüber hinausgeht, am Wahltag Häkchen zu setzen. Denn in einem selbstgefälligen Staat, wo alles für diesen Nationalstaat zu arbeiten scheint, verhält es sich so, dass wir vergessen, dass der Garant eines schützenswerten Staates nicht das Wahlsystem ist, sondern alles, was sich darum herum befindet. Eine Wahl zwischen zwei faschistischen Autoritäten in einem Staatsapparat, der nicht in der Lage ist, seinen verwundbarsten Mitgliedern irgendeine Form der Gerechtigkeit zu garantieren, ist wertlos.

Am zweiten Jahrestag von Mubaraks Sturz feiern wir noch immer, dass die Revolution, trotz der verschiedenen Versuche, sie zu unterbinden, anhält. Es ist außergewöhnlich zu sehen, dass wir zwei Jahre später noch immer die Kraft haben, eine Schlacht zu schlagen, von der wir annahmen, dass sie nur wenige Tage dauern würde.

Der Zeugenbericht ist eine Entscheidung hinsichtlich dessen, was man sich selbst und anderen einräumt, gesehen zu haben. Es ist eine Besonderheit unseres selbstzufriedenen Sehvermögens in normalen Zeiten, dass wir annehmen, sehen zu können, dabei aber doch für die meisten Vorgänge in der Welt blind sind. Aber dennoch sah die ganze Welt an dem Tag, da Mubarak zurücktrat, etwas Feierliches. Es gab nur wenige Ereignisse kollektiver Zeugenschaft in der Geschichte, falls es überhaupt welche gab. Jene unter uns, die es noch sehen können, wissen, dass es eine bestimmte Geschichte gibt, die sich aus ihrem bisherigen Verlauf ergibt. Wessen Zeugen wir wurden, war nicht nur der Sturz eines Diktators, es war eine menschliche Vision, die zu manifestieren wir alle verpflichtet sind.

Systeme

Was in Ägypten passiert, passiert nicht da draußen. Es widerfährt uns allen. Genauso intensiv, wie es Mohammed Bouazizis Körper widerfuhr, als er sich selbst anzündete. So, wie uns die ägyptische Demokratie einen weiteren Diktator bescherte, stützten die westlichen Demokratien den Diktator, den wir stürzten. Wenn die Werkzeuge der Demokratie genutzt werden, um Diktatoren mit einem Faible für Blut zu erschaffen, ist es nur eine Frage der Zeit, bis die tiefe Scheinheiligkeit ein Erdbeben auslöst.

Wenn du dir also die Berichte einer armen ägyptischen Familie anhörst, dann habe kein Mitleid mit ihnen, habe Mitleid mit dir, zumindest bis du tief in dir weißt, dass du etwas unternehmen wirst.

Interview with Mostafa Bahgat

By Amira El Ahl

The interview focuses on the political situation during summer 2012.

Amira El Ahl (AEA): How would you define yourself?

Mostafa Bahgat (MB): I'm a video journalist who would like to be a war videographer.

AEA: Do you have a role model?

MB: No. I've been participating in demonstrations for a long time, before I started working in journalism. And I always had this crisis that what I saw on these demonstrations I would not see afterwards on TV or on the Internet. That is what drives me. I want the people to see what I see from close up. Of course there are people that I admire, but I don't have an idol.

AEA: Did you study filmmaking?

MB: I became a filmmaker by chance. I started working at Masry al-Youm as an Internet moderator, filtering comments on their Internet platform. And it was a lucky coincidence that my office was in the same office as that of the multimedia department.

AEA: When was that?

MB: In October 2009. The multimedia department was meant to have the journalists themselves filming events. But then there were administrative problems and the journalists decided that they wouldn't film. Then came the first labor sit-in at the parliament in 2010. There was a discussion in the office about whether somebody should go film and if one of the journalists would do it. Nobody wanted to go, so I told them, "I want to go down and film." So I took a ten-minute crash course.

AEA: And you knew how the camera worked after that crash course?

MB: It was a small camera, just like a Flip cam or a mobile camera, nothing too difficult. They told me about the sizes of the frames, which frame to choose when I do an interview or a long shot. And ever since then I haven't stopped filming. Every time something was going on I had to go down and film.

AEA: As a video journalist, you do the job of four people. It's quite stressful.

MB: Yes, I have to concentrate on what I am filming, I have to concentrate on the sound, I have to focus on the questions and the answers, and I also have to concentrate on what's happening around me—and all that is just one part. I also sit and do the montage and direct the piece later on. And all that started with the ten-minute crash course. (laughs)

AEA: You are a journalist who works for an official media outlet. At the same time you have a YouTube channel, and the videos you post there would definitely never be broadcast on TV. The language and images they use are too strong. So you're both, a journalist but also a social media activist. How difficult is this balance?

MB: For me the official media is my bread and butter. I work in order to make money. And I get very clear orders from my employers: "Go down and cover this or that topic for us." When I sit and cut the piece and put it together, and I have filmed somebody who is cursing the military council, I will not use these images. Of course that bothers me, and I am not happy that I have to do this. But I can take exactly the same material that I gave the channel and make another video with it. I understand that they are enchained by the rules. The TV bosses are not bad. That's not the reason they don't want to broadcast this material. They are enchained, just like I'm enchained.

AEA: But the second video you will make with the same material, plus extra material you cannot show on TV, is the one that is the more accurate, the more truthful one?

MB: Yes, of course. The thing is, I don't interfere. My role is to tape everything that is happening and try to broadcast it without me reformulating the information. The important thing is that you do not take sides, that you are objective. I have to be in the middle and show both sides, even if my political or personal affiliations are leaning towards a certain group.

AEA: Do you do your YouTube channel out of a journalistic drive or because you have a political goal as an activist?

MB: Maybe it's a mix of the two. One part has to do with something I know how to do, the tool that I can master. And another part is where I say what happened in an incident. I see it like this: I do something that has both sides, and at the same time I explain the violence, because violence breeds violence. The security forces fire at the protesters, so of course the people will defend themselves. What are the tools in their hands? Stones or Molotov cocktails. I see these as legitimate means. It is not something that makes us ashamed as protesters. It is just something that happens and that's how it is.

AEA: Are you also a protester?

MB: Yes, I'm also a protester.

AEA: So you are both at the same time, journalist and protester. That isn't a problem for you, a contradiction?

MB: As long as I maintain my objectivity, I don't have a problem. It becomes a problem when all the footage you see has no protesters throwing Molotov cocktails, for example, and I concentrate the whole time on the fact that all the violence comes from the police. And the truth of the matter is that this is not the reality.

AEA: Do you feel different from the people who stand next to you as protesters? Do you feel that there is a distance between you and them because you are there as a journalist?

MB: No, not at all. The protester beside me has got the tool that he knows how to use and I've got the tool I know how to use. I have my camera and he has a stone or something else. But in the end the two of us are standing in the same line. At the beginning of the revolution I had the problem that I kept thinking: I want to participate myself in throwing stones. But then I felt that a lot of people are doing this. And nobody is doing what I am doing. So I have to concentrate on what I am doing. But the whole time I feel that we are together. When a teargas bomb falls, I throw it back, for example. I always say: "Respect the thing you're holding." So if you decided to turn on a camera and film, respect the role that you chose. And if you've turned off the camera and decided enough filming now, you are free.

AEA: So the camera and your videos are your weapons?

MB: Yes. Only once I went down and did not film, although I had my camera with me. I had decided beforehand that I would not film, but I took it with me in case something happened.

AEA: Maybe videos like the ones you take are a better tool to fight the battle that you are fighting. They might even be a stronger weapon because you get the message out into the world.

MB: Not just that. The footage is not just strong, it is one of the things that will remain in the future. I think that after ten years, when, the people are talking about the revolution, or if they want to do a film on the revolution, this footage will be one of the things that they use from me or from Mosireen [media collective] and all the other people that took footage of the events. Stones are gone as soon as you have thrown them.

AEA: You are always on the frontline. As you said, you want to be a war videographer. Are you never afraid for your life, that you could be killed because of what you're doing?

MB: If I thought like this, I would not stand on the frontline. I think in a different way. I use protection tools and rules that I lay down for myself.

AEA: Which are?

MB: I don't always use these precautions but most of the time. I wear a gas mask, whose plastic also protects the eyes from shotgun bullets, and gloves, because of the gas bombs and because lately I was being hit on my hands a lot. And I always use the things around me, like a tree or an electricity box. And I take care that I keep my face down, so nothing gets into my eyes. I hold my camera down [he demonstrates looking into it from the viewfinder on top] or I crouch behind a lamppost and hold the camera to the side of it with one hand, so my body is protected. So I am always sure that the sensitive parts of my body are hidden.

AEA: What is your drive, what do you want to achieve?

MB: Before I started filming, whenever there were casualties among the protesters, the general opinion of the people was one of two things: either the protesters are wrong because they started the violence, or the officer definitely did not want to do something like this. These were the two arguments that I was hearing all the time. I wanted to show that the violence is on purpose. And the targeting is real. It is not only bad luck that the shot hit a protester. It was on purpose. And from the back I cannot do that. I cannot capture the determination of the officer who is running from one place to another and is aiming and shooting at people. I saw that it's important that people see this. There are other people standing next to me who are dying, people who have their eyes shot and I think that it is necessary that somebody films that. I am content with my role and I have to be in this area. If I thought about it differently I guess I wouldn't go.

AEA: So you also feel a kind of responsibility to be there for these people in order to show what is really happening.

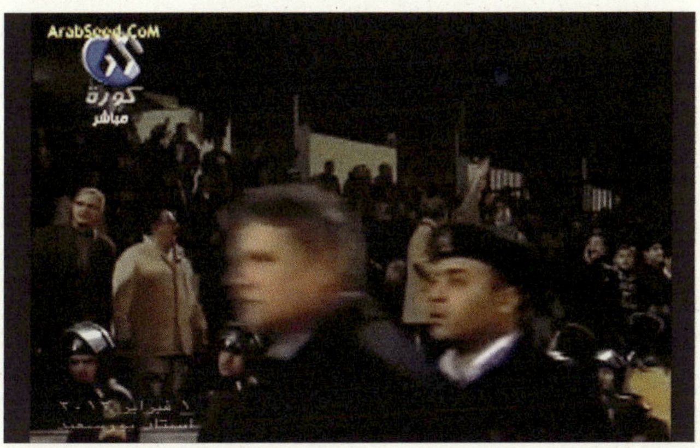

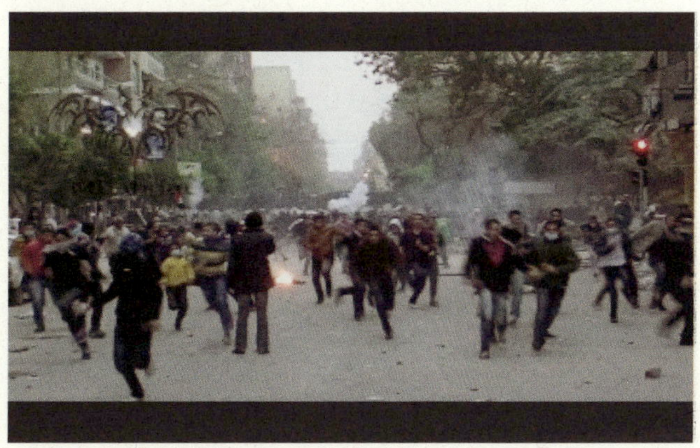

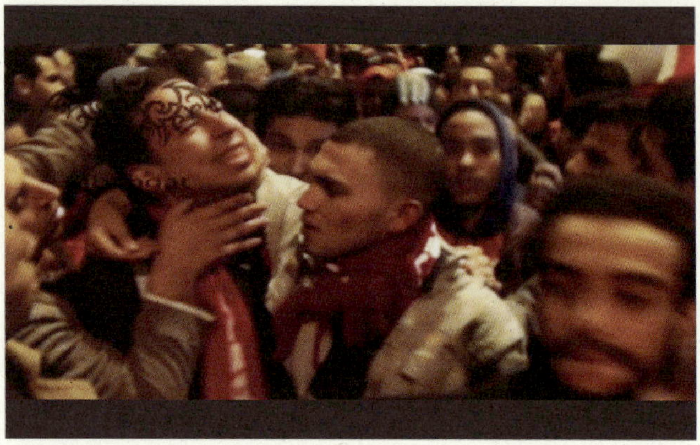

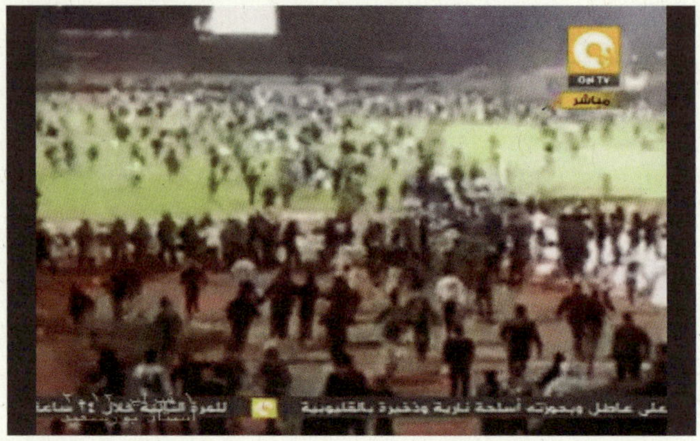

MB: I guess that's the motive that makes me work three, four days without sleep, without eating, and also being shot at.

AEA: What you do is very intense. It takes a lot of energy, mentally and physically.

MB: I feel I have a responsibility for these people. I feel that I take good images and that I have to stay there. Often the battery of my camera runs out and I can't leave. I would like to go somewhere to charge the battery and rest for a little while, but I can't. I stay and give my camera to somebody to charge it and bring it back to me. But I cannot leave.

AEA: Do you feel there is hope, or do you ever despair. Do you ever feel or think that what you are doing makes no difference?

MB: Some months ago I had a phase like this. I thought that everything I'm doing makes no sense. I thought that when people see what is happening, there will be a change in the situation. But after I calmed down a bit, I realized that I had over-exaggerated more than was necessary. People choose to watch these videos or not. It is not my job to correct their understanding.

AEA: Do you think you have two lives—as a journalist and a social activist—or is it one life that is easy to combine?

MB: It's not easy. Sometimes it obliges me to do things that I'm not able to do. And I don't like doing. But it is just like any work. Sometimes you do things you like and sometimes you have to do things you're not happy with. And from another side I see that I am performing my role with a clear conscience. And I do the things that I see need to get out.

AEA: But it's like two parallel lives.

MB: Well, I would say that work takes up 30 percent of my time and the rest of the things I do takes up 70 percent. It's not the same thing and they're also not completely exclusive from one other. I can't say they're the same life or that they're totally separate. It is somewhere in between the two.

AEA: If people like you were not there standing in the frontline and risking their lives to show what's happening, then the people who are throwing the stones would never really get a voice. They would not be known to the world.

MB: But I don't give them a voice. That would mean I speak for them. I don't do that. I could say that I see myself as one of them. I could say that my role is as important as theirs. But I cannot carry the responsibility that I am speaking in their name. They speak for themselves. And that is precisely why I have to film with the people. They tell the story.

AEA: Are you optimistic or pessimistic?

MB: For the future I am optimistic, but for now I am not. The scenario is going exactly as the military wants it. The difference from my point of view is that there is a whole generation of youngsters that for the first time is breathing freedom. And it is difficult to take that away from them again. Before the revolution we were used to the fact that we would always just be a small group of people that would demonstrate. In front of the journalist syndicate we would be two hunderd people on a demonstration. Now there are lots of people and Tahrir Square is for them the place where they can talk and discuss things. It is really the first time in our lives that we are doing such a thing. We never used to discuss politics. So in the long run I am optimistic. But at the moment and for now, no.

AEA: Besides all the political difficulties, I think people have changed and Egypt has changed too.

MB: On the political level we have not changed, but the people have changed. It is not a lot, but it is a start.

AEA: Did you change as well?

MB: For sure. I have more trust in people now.

Interview mit Mostafa Bahgat

Von Amira El Ahl

Das Gespräch bezieht sich auf die politische Situation im Sommer 2012, als das Gespräch in Kairo stattfand.

Amira El Ahl (AEA): Wie würdest du dich selbst beschreiben?

Mostafa Bahgat (MB): Ich bin ein Videojournalist, aber ich würde gern verstärkt aus Kriegsgebieten berichten.

AEA: Hast du ein Vorbild?

MB: Nein. Schon lange, bevor ich anfing im Journalismus zu arbeiten, nahm ich an Demonstrationen teil. Und immer wieder hatte ich ein Problem damit, dass das, was ich auf diesen Demonstrationen beobachtet hatte, anschließend nicht im Fernsehen oder im Internet zu sehen war. Das ist es, was mich antreibt. Ich will, dass die Menschen sehen, was ich aus der Nähe sehe. Natürlich gibt es Menschen, die ich bewundere, aber ich habe kein Idol.

AEA: Hast du Film studiert?

MB: Eigentlich wurde ich durch Zufall Filmemacher. Ich begann bei Al-Masry al-Youm (eine private ägyptische Tageszeitung, d.ÜS) als Internetmoderator zu arbeiten und filterte Kommentare auf deren Internetplattform. Es war ein glücklicher Zufall, dass sich mein Büro in demselben Bürokomplex befand wie das der Multimedia-Abteilung.

AEA: Wann war das?

MB: Im Oktober 2009. Die Multimedia-Abteilung von Masry al-Youm hat ihre eigenen Journalisten, die normalerweise die Ereignisse filmen.

Aber es gab dann administrative Probleme und die Journalisten entschieden, dass sie nicht filmen würden. 2010 geschah die erste Sitzblockade der Arbeiter im Parlament. Im Büro gab es eine Diskussion darüber, ob jemand dort filmen sollte und ob das einer der Journalisten machen würde. Niemand fand sich bereit, deshalb habe ich zu ihnen gesagt „Ich will hingehen und filmen“. Daraufhin bekam ich einen zehnminütigen Crashkurs.

AEA:. Und nach dem Crashkurs wusstest du, wie die Kamera funktioniert?

MB: Es war eine kleine Kamera, ähnlich einer Flip-Cam oder einer Handykamera, nichts zu Schwieriges. Mir wurde erklärt, wie groß die Bildausschnitte zu sein hätten und welchen ich bei einem Interview und welchen bei einer Totalaufnahme auswählen sollte. Seitdem habe ich nicht mehr aufgehört. Immer wenn etwas im Gange war, musste ich hingehen und filmen.

AEA: Als Videojournalist erledigst du den Job von vier Menschen gleichzeitig. Das ist ziemlich anstrengend.

MB: Ja, ich muss mich darauf konzentrieren, was ich filme, ich muss auf den Ton achten, muss meine Aufmerksamkeit auf die Fragen und Antworten richten und gleichzeitig noch darauf, was um mich herum passiert – und das ist nur ein Teil der ganzen Arbeit. Hinzu kommt, dass ich mich später hinsetze und mich um Regie und Montage kümmere. Und all das begann mit diesem zehnminütigen Crashkurs. (lacht)

AEA: Du bist ein Journalist, der für eine Sendeanstalt der offiziellen Medien arbeitet. Zugleich hast du aber auch einen YouTube-Kanal und die Videos, die du dort zeigst, werden bestimmt nie im Fernsehen ausgestrahlt. Sie sind zu stark in ihrer Sprache und ihren Bildern. Also bist du beides, ein Journalist, aber gleichzeitig auch ein Aktivist in den sozialen Netzwerken. Wie schwierig ist dieser Spagat?

MB: Die offiziellen Medien sichern mir meinen Lebensunterhalt. Ich arbeite dort, um Geld zu verdienen. Und ich bekomme ziemlich deutliche Anweisungen von meinen Vorgesetzten: „Geh und bearbeite dieses oder jenes Thema für uns“. Wenn ich das Material anschließend zusammenschneide und jemanden gefilmt habe, der den Militärrat verflucht, dann werde ich diese Bilder nicht in den Film nehmen. Natürlich macht mir das etwas aus, und ich bin nicht glücklich darüber, dass es so ist. Aber ich kann aus genau dem Material, das ich dem Fernsehsender gegeben habe, ein anderes Video machen. Ich verstehe, dass die Regeln den Sendern Fesseln anlegen. Die Leiter der Fernsehsender sind keine schlechten Menschen, aber sie können eben dieses Material nicht ausstrahlen. Sie sind gefesselt, so wie auch ich gefesselt bin.

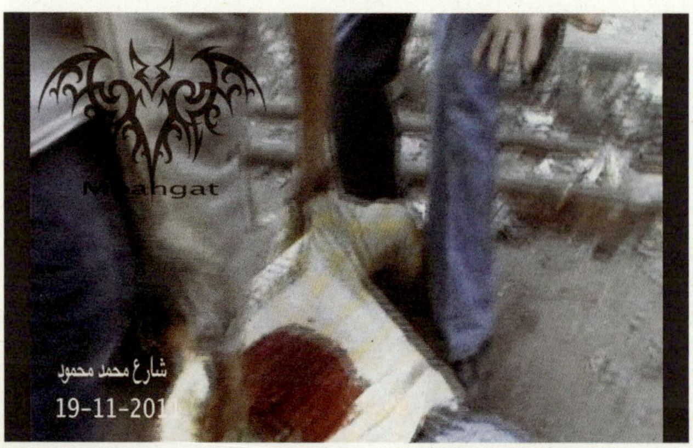

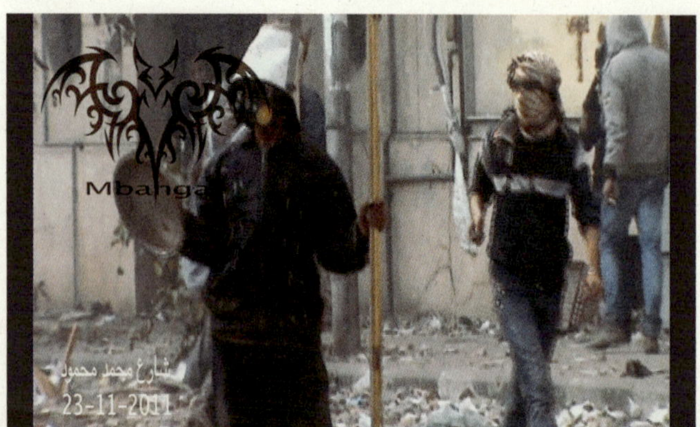

AEA: Aber ist das zweite Video, dass du aus demselben und aus zusätzlichem Material machst und dass du nicht im Fernsehen zeigen kannst, das genauere, das wahrhaftigere?

MB: Ja, natürlich. Die Sache ist die, dass ich nicht eingreife. Meine Aufgabe ist es, alles was passiert aufzunehmen, ohne die Informationen und Aussagen umzuformulieren. Das Wichtigste ist eigentlich, dass man sich auf keine Seite stellt, dass man objektiv bleibt. Ich muss in der Mitte stehen und beide Seiten zeigen, auch dann, wenn ich mich mit meiner politischen oder persönlichen Haltung einer bestimmten Gruppe zugehörig fühle.

AEA: Betreibst du deinen YouTube-Kanal aus einem journalistischen Antrieb heraus oder weil du damit ein politisches Ziel als Aktivist verfolgst?

MB: Wahrscheinlich ist es eine Mischung aus beidem. Der eine Teil hat mit den Dingen zu tun, die ich kenne und beherrsche. Und der andere Teil besteht daraus, dass ich darüber berichte, was bei einem Ereignis passiert ist. Ich sehe es so: Ich mache etwas, das beide Seiten beinhaltet und zur gleichen Zeit erkläre ich die Gewalt, weil aus Gewalt immer neue Gewalt entsteht. Die Sicherheitskräfte schießen auf die Demonstranten, selbstverständlich verteidigen sich die Menschen dann. Und welche Mittel stehen ihnen dafür zur Verfügung? Steine oder Molotowcocktails. Für mich ist das ein legitimer Weg, der uns als Demonstranten nicht beschämt. Es ist nun einmal etwas, das passiert, und so ist es.

AEA: Du bist also auch ein Demonstrant?

MB: Ja, ich bin auch ein Demonstrant.

AEA: Also bist du beides zur gleichen Zeit, Journalist und Demonstrant. Ist das nicht ein Problem oder ein Widerspruch für dich?

MB: Solange ich meine Objektivität aufrechterhalte, habe ich kein Problem damit. Es kann zu einem Problem werden, wenn zum Beispiel das Filmmaterial keine Demonstranten zeigt, die Molotowcocktails werfen und ich mich nur darauf konzentrieren würde, zu zeigen, dass die Gewalt ausschließlich von der Polizei ausgeht. Die Wahrheit ist, dass dies nicht der Realität entspricht.

AEA: Fühlst du dich anders als die Demonstranten direkt neben dir? Gibt es Distanz zwischen dir und ihnen, weil du als Journalist vor Ort bist?

MB: Nein, überhaupt nicht. Der Demonstrant neben mir hat sein Mittel und weiß dieses anzuwenden, und ich habe mein Mittel und weiß ebenso, wie ich es einsetzen kann. Ich habe meine Kamera und der Demonstrant hat einen Stein oder etwas anderes. Aber letztendlich befinden wir uns in derselben Situation. Am Anfang der Revolution dachte ich immerzu: Ich will mich auch am Steinewerfen beteiligen. Aber dann bemerkte ich, dass das ja viele Menschen machen. Und niemand macht das, was ich mache. Also muss ich mich auf das konzentrieren, was ich tue. Aber die ganze Zeit fühle ich Verbundenheit. Wenn zum Beispiel eine Tränengasbombe bei mir landet, dann werfe ich sie auch zurück. Ich sage immer: „Behandele mit Respekt, woran du beteiligt bist“. Wenn du dich dazu entschlossen hast, deine Kamera anzuschalten und zu filmen, dann respektiere auch diese Aufgabe. Und wenn du die Kamera ausmachst und beschlossen hast, dass du für den Moment genug gefilmt hast, dann bist du frei.

AEA: Sind die Kamera und deine Filme folglich deine Waffen?

MB: Ja. Ich bin nur einmal ohne zu filmen bei den Protesten gewesen, obwohl ich meine Kamera dabei gehabt hatte. Ich hatte mich im

Vorfeld dazu entschlossen, nicht zu filmen, aber ich nahm die Kamera mit für den Fall, das etwas Wichtiges passieren würde.

AEA: Vielleicht sind Videos wie deine das bessere Werkzeug in diesem Kampf, den du austrägst. Sie könnten sogar eine stärkere Waffe sein, weil du es schaffst, die Botschaften in die Welt zu transportieren.

MB: Nicht nur das. Das Filmmaterial ist nicht einfach nur kraftvoll, sondern es ist auch ein Teil dessen, was in der Zukunft noch erhalten sein wird. Ich glaube, dass in zehn Jahren, wenn die Menschen über die Revolution reden oder wenn sie einen Film über die Revolution machen wollen, dann werden sie dieses Filmmaterial oder das von Mosireen und das von all den anderen Menschen, die bei den verschiedenen Anlässen Aufzeichnungen anfertigten, verwenden. Steine sind weg, sobald man sie geworfen hat.

AEA: Du bist immer ganz vorne mit dabei. Wie du bereits erwähnt hast, würdest du gerne aus Kriegsgebieten berichten. Hast du niemals Angst um dein Leben, dass du bei dem, was du tust, getötet werden könntest?

MB: Wenn ich so denken würde, würde ich nicht an vorderster Front stehen. Ich denke anders. Ich verwende Mittel, um mich zu schützen und halte mich an Regeln, die ich für mich selber aufgestellt habe.

AEA: Als da wären?

MB: Ich halte mich nicht immer an diese Vorsichtsmaßnahmen, aber meistens: Ich trage eine Gasmaske, deren Plastikschale auch meine Augen vor den Schrotflintenkugeln schützt, Handschuhe wegen den Gasbomben und weil ich in letzter Zeit oft an meiner Hand getroffen worden bin. Ich benutze auch immer die Gegenstände um mich herum, wie zum Beispiel einen Baum oder einen Stromkasten. Und ich passe auf, dass ich mein Gesicht nach unten halte, damit nichts in meine Augen kommt. Ich halte meine Kamera nach unten (er zeigt, wie er von oben in den Kamerasucher hineinsieht) oder ich hocke hinter einem Laternenmast und halte die Kamera mit nur einer Hand, strecke sie nur seitlich raus, damit mein Körper in Deckung bleibt. Darum gehe ich immer davon aus, dass die empfindlichen Teile meines Körpers geschützt sind.

AEA: Was ist dein Antrieb, was willst du erreichen?

MB: Bevor ich mit dem Filmen begonnen hatte, war die vorherrschende Meinung der Menschen, sobald es Verletzte in den Reihen der Demonstranten gab, von zwei Aspekten geprägt: Entweder die Demonstranten haben sich falsch verhalten, weil sie mit der Gewalt begonnen haben, oder der Polizist hat das eben nicht mit Absicht gemacht. Das waren die zwei Meinungen, die ich die ganze Zeit gehört habe. Ich wollte zeigen, dass die Gewalt eine vorsätzliche ist. Und dass wirklich auf Menschen gezielt wird. Es ist ja nicht so, dass ein Demonstrant nur durch ein Missgeschick getroffen wird. Es geschieht mit Absicht. Und irgendwo weit hinten stehend kann ich nicht zeigen, was ich zeigen will. Ich kann die Entschlossenheit des Polizisten, der von einem Ort zum anderen rennt und auf die Menschen zielt und schießt, nicht einfangen. Ich habe erkannt, dass es wichtig ist, dass die Menschen dies sehen. Es gibt Menschen, die neben mir stehen und sterben, Menschen, in deren Augen geschossen wurde, und ich glaube, dass es wichtig ist, dass jemand das alles filmt. Ich bin mit meiner Rolle zufrieden und ich muss einfach mit dabei sein. Wenn ich anders darüber denken würde, würde ich wahrscheinlich nicht dorthin gehen.

AEA: Du fühlst also eine Art Verantwortung dafür, vor Ort für die Menschen da zu sein, um zu zeigen, was wirklich passiert.

MB: Ich glaube, dass ist der Beweggrund, der mich drei oder vier Tage ohne Schlaf, ohne Essen und trotz Schussverletzung arbeiten lässt.

AEA: Was du machst, ist wirklich anstrengend und intensiv. Es braucht sehr viel Kraft, geistig und körperlich.

WB: Ich empfinde eine Verantwortung für diese Menschen. Ich glaube, dass ich gute Bilder mache und dass ich vor Ort sein muss. Wenn der Akku meiner Kamera leer wird, kann ich nicht gehen. Ich würde gerne irgendwo meine Kamera aufladen und eine kleine Pause machen, aber ich kann nicht gehen. Ich bleibe und gebe meine Kamera jemandem, damit er sie auflädt und er bringt sie mir anschließend zurück. Aber ich kann nicht gehen.

AEA: Hast du das Gefühl, dass es Hoffnung gibt oder zweifelst du je daran? Glaubst du oder fühlst du, dass das, was du machst, etwas verändern kann?

MB: Vor einigen Monaten gab es so eine Phase. Ich dachte, alles was ich tue, hat keinen Sinn. Ich hatte geglaubt, dass sich an der Situation etwas verändern würde, wenn die Menschen sehen, was wirklich passiert. Nach einiger Zeit habe ich mich etwas beruhigt und festgestellt, dass ich ziemlich übertrieben habe, mehr als nötig erwartet hatte. Die Menschen entscheiden selbst, ob sie diese Videos sehen wollen oder nicht. Es ist nicht meine Aufgabe, zu korrigieren, was und wie die Menschen etwas verstehen.

AEA: Glaubst du, dass du zwei verschiedene Leben hast – als Journalist und als sozialer Aktivist – oder ist es ein einziges Leben, das sich leicht kombinieren lässt?

MB: Leicht ist es nicht. Manchmal verlangt es von mir Dinge, die zu tun ich gar nicht in der Lage bin. Und die ich auch nicht gerne mache. Aber das ist bei jedem Beruf so. Manchmal machst du Dinge, die du magst, und manchmal musst du etwas tun, womit du nicht einverstanden bist. Andererseits glaube ich, dass ich meine Rolle mit einem reinen Gewissen ausübe. Und ich kümmere mich um die Dinge, von denen ich meine, dass sie öffentlich sein müssen.

AEA: Aber es hört sich nach zwei parallelen Leben an.

MB: Gut, ich würde sagen, dass meine Arbeit 30 Prozent und der Rest der Dinge, die ich mache, 70 Prozent meines Lebens einnimmt. Es ist nicht die gleiche Sache, aber andererseits lassen sie sich auch nicht komplett voneinander trennen. Ich kann weder behaupten, dass sie das gleiche Leben formen, noch dass sie komplett voneinander getrennt sind. Es ist etwas dazwischen.

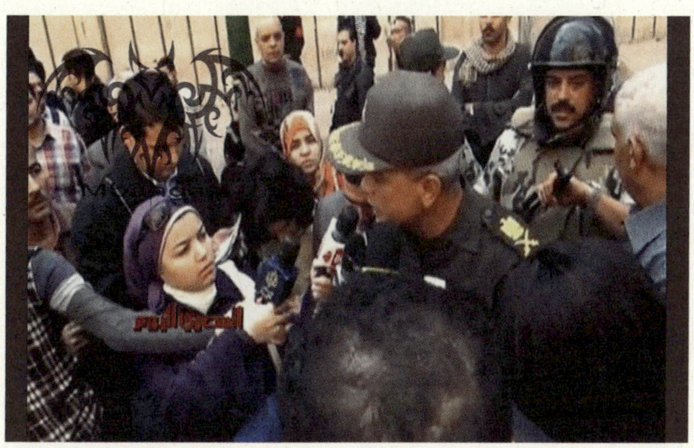

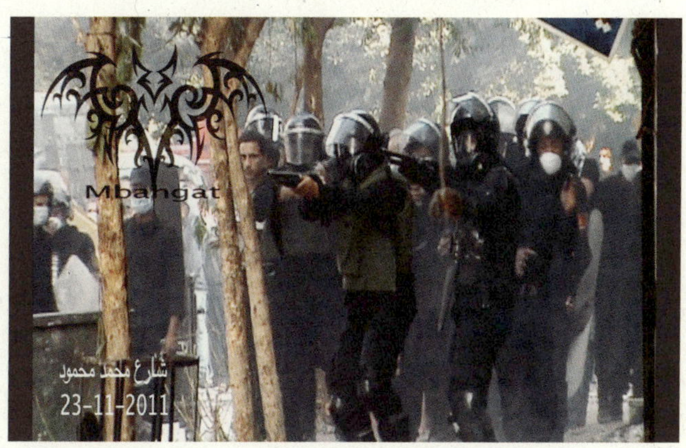

AEA: Wenn es keine Menschen wie dich geben würde, die sich in die Frontlinie stellen und ihr Leben riskieren, um zu zeigen, was vor sich geht, dann würden die Menschen, die Steine schmeißen, auch keine Stimme bekommen. Die Welt wüsste gar nicht von ihrer Existenz.

MB: Aber ich gebe ihnen keine Stimme. Das würde bedeuten, dass ich für sie spreche. Das tue ich nicht. Ich könnte sagen, dass ich mich als ein Teil von ihnen betrachte. Ich könnte sagen, dass meine Aufgabe genauso wichtig wie ihre ist. Aber ich könnte nicht die Verantwortung dafür tragen, in ihrem Namen zu sprechen. Sie sprechen für sich selbst. Und genau deshalb muss ich diese Menschen filmen. Sie erzählen die Geschichte.

AEA: Bist du ein Optimist oder ein Pessimist?

MB: Für die Zukunft bin ich optimistisch, aber im Moment bin ich es nicht, denn die Ereignisse entwickeln sich genau so, wie das Militär es möchte. Von meinem Standpunkt aus gibt es jedoch einen Unterschied: es gibt eine neue Generation Jugendlicher, die zum ersten Mal das Gefühl von Freiheit verspüren. Und es wird schwer sein, ihnen das wieder wegzunehmen. Vor der Revolution waren wir daran gewöhnt, immer nur eine kleine Gruppe von Demonstranten zu sein. Wir standen als eine Gruppe von 200 Menschen einem Syndikat von Journalisten gegenüber. Jetzt sind es sehr viele Menschen und der Tahrir-Platz ist für sie der Ort, an dem sie sprechen und diskutieren können. Es ist wirklich das erste Mal in unserem Leben, das wir dergleichen erleben. Wir waren es nicht gewöhnt, über politische Themen zu diskutieren. Deshalb bin ich auf lange Sicht optimistisch. Aber im Moment nicht, nein.

AEA: Abgesehen von den politischen Problemen habe ich das Gefühl, dass sich die Menschen und Ägypten verändert haben.

MB: Auf der politischen Ebene haben wir uns nicht verändert, aber die Menschen haben sich verändert. Das ist nicht viel, aber immerhin ein Anfang.

AEA: Hast du dich auch verändert?

MB: Ganz bestimmt. Ich habe jetzt mehr Vertrauen in die Menschen.

س: هل تعتقد أن لديك حياتان – صحفي وناشط إجتماعي – أم أنها حياة واحدة سهلة الدمج؟

ج: إنها ليست مسألة سهلة. أحياناً يتطلب الأمر أن أفعل أشياءً لا أستطيع فعلها ولا أحب عملها. مثل أي عمل آخر، أحياناً تفعل أشياءً تحبها وأحياناً أخرى تكون مجبراً على عمل ما لا تحبه. ومن ناحية أُخرى فأنا أشعر أني أؤدي عملي بضمير مرتاح. كما أني أفعل الأشياء التي أرى أنها يجب أن تظهر.

س: ولكن هي تبدو فعلاً كحياتين متوازيتين.

ج: حسناً، أستطيع أن أقول أن عملي يأخذ 30% وباقي الأشياء التي أفعلها 70%. هما ليسا بالشيء الواحد ولكن أيضاً لا يمكن فصلهما تماماً. لا أستطيع القول بأنهما شيء واحد ولا شيئان منفصلان تماماً. إنه شيء بين الاثنين.

س: لو لم يكن أمثالك من الناس موجوداً في الصفوف الأمامية يخاطرون بحياتهم لنقل الحدث، فلن يكون للناس الأخرى الذين يقذفون بالحجارة صوتاً. ولم يكن للعالم أن يعرفهم.

ج: ولكني لا أعطيهم صوتاً. هذا يعني أني أتكلم عنهم، الشيء الذي لا أفعله. أستطيع أن أقول أني جزء منهم. وأن دوري مهم كدورهم. ولكني لا أستطيع تحمل مسؤولية الكلام نيابة عنهم. هم يُعَبِرون عن أنفسهم. وذلك بالتحديد السبب الذي يجب من أجله التصوير مع الناس. إنهم يقصون الحكايات.

س: هل أنت متفائل أم متشائم؟

ج: إني متفائل بالمستقبل ولكني غير متفائل في الوقت الحالي، فالسيناريو يسير بالضبط كما يريده الجيش. الفارق من وجهة نظري هو أن هناك جيل كامل من الشباب الذين تنفسوا الحرية للمرة الأولى. ومن الصعب أخذها منهم مرة أخرى. قبل الثورة كنّا معتادين حقيقة أن هناك دائماً مجموعة صغيرة هي التي تتظاهر. أمام نقابة الصحفيين كنا 200 متظاهر. الآن هناك الكثير من الناس وميدان التحرير بالنسبة لهم هو مكان الكلام والنقاش. إنها فعلاً المرة الأولى في حياتنا التي نفعل فيها شيئاً كهذا. لم نكن نتناقش في السياسة أبداً، ولذلك أنا متفائل على المدى البعيد. ولكن في الوقت الحالي لا.

س: بجانب كل الصعوبات السياسية، أعتقد أن المصريين قد تغيروا وأن مصر أيضاً تغيرت.

ج: نحن لم نتغير على الصعيد السياسي ولكن الشعب قد تغير. إنه ليس تغيراً كبيراً ولكنه بداية.

س: هل تغيرت أنت أيضاً؟

ج: بالطبع. أصبحت لدي ثقة بالناس.

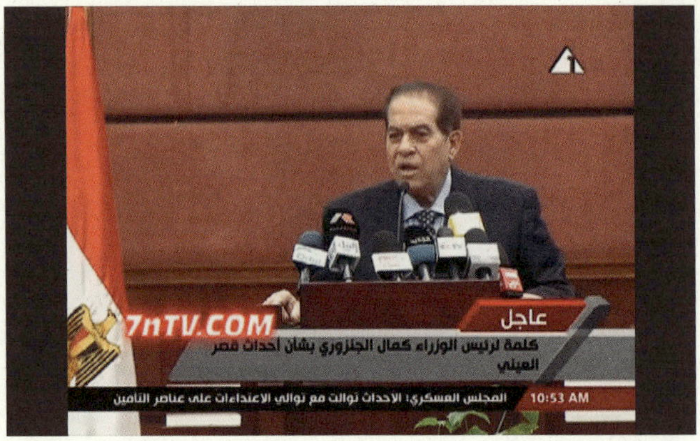

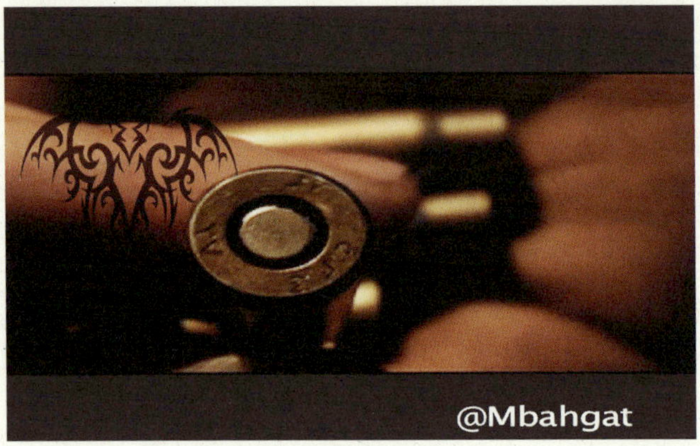

ج: إذا فكرت بهذه الطريقة فلن أقف في الصفوف الأمامية. أنا أفكر بطريقة مختلفة. فأنا أستخدم أدوات حماية وأضع لنفسي قواعد

س: ألا وهي؟

ج: أنا لا أستخدم هذه الأدوات بشكل دائم ولكنها غالباً تكون كلآتي: أرتدي القناع الواقي من الغازات، يحمي البلاستيك الموجود في القناع عيناي من الرصاص، وأرتدي قفازات أتعامل بها مع قنابل الغاز ولأنني مؤخراً تعرضت للضرب على يداي بشكل متكرر. غير ذلك أستخدم كل ما هو حولي مثل الأشجار أو منفذ الكهرباء. أحاول أيضاً أن أبقي رأسي منخفضاً لكي لا يدخل شيئاً في عيني. أخفض كاميرتي (يستعرض كيف ينظر في عدسة الكاميرا من أعلى) أو أختبىء خلف أحد أعمدة الإنارة وأمسك الكاميرا بجانبي بيد واحدة، بذلك يكون جسدي محمياً. أتأكد دائماً من أن جميع المناطق الحساسة في جسدي محمية.

س: ما الذي يحفزك، ماذا الذي تريد إنجازه؟

ج: قبل أن أبدأ في مجال صناعة الأفلام، كان النقاش في المظاهرات دائماً -عند وقوع ضحايا- عما إذا كان ذلك خطأ المتظاهرين لأنهم هم من بدأ العنف أو أن الشرطة لم تقصد قتل كل هؤلاء. هذه هي الآراء التي كنت أسمعها. كنت أريد أن أكشف حقيقة أن العنف في الواقع مقصود. وأن الاستهداف موجود. وأن الطلقات التي تصيب المتظاهرين ليست مجرد سوء حظ. ولكنها مقصودة. ولن أستطيع أن أنقل الصورة من الصفوف الخلفية. لن أتمكن من تصوير إصرار الضابط الذي يجري من مكان لآخر يستهدف الناس. وفي رأي أنه من المهم أن يرى الناس هذا. يموت الناس بجانبي وآخرين يفقدون أعينهم وأرى أنه من المهم أن يصور أحد هذه المشاهد. أنا راضٍ عن دوري ومن واجبي أن أظل في هذه المنطقة. إذا فكرت في الأمر بشكل مختلف، أظن أنني لم أكن لأشارك.

س: إذاً أنت تشعر بالمسؤولية اتجاه هؤلاء، أن تكون موجوداً لهم، لكي تعرض ما يحدث حقاً.

ج: أظن أن هذا هو السبب الذي يجعلني أعمل ثلاثة أو أربعة أو خمسة أيام بدون نوم، أو طعام مع التعرض لضرب النار.

س: ما تفعله مكثف جداً ويستلزم الكثير من الجهد الفكري والعضلي.

ج: أشعر بالمسؤولية اتجاه هؤلاء الناس. أشعر أني قد ألتقط صوراً جيدة وأن علي البقاء هناك. يحدث كثيراً أن تفرغ بطارية الكاميرا ولا أستطيع مغادرة المكان. أتمنى أن أذهب إلى أي مكان حيث يمكنني شحن البطارية و الإستراحة لبعض الوقت ولكن لا أستطيع. دائماً أبقى وأطلب من أي شخص الذهاب بدلاً مني لشحن الكاميرا وإعادتها لي. ولكن أنا لا أستطيع المغادرة.

س: هل تشعر أن هناك أمل أم تشعر باليأس أحياناً؟
هل تشعر أو تفكر أن ما تفعله لا يُحدث فرقاً حقاً؟

ج: مرّت علي أشهر شَعَرتُ فيها بذلك. وأن ما أفعله لا يغير أي شيء. اعتقدت أنه لو رأى الناس ما يحدث يمكن أن يغيروا موقفهم. ولكن بعد ما هدأت بعض الشيء اكتشفت أني بالغت في الأمر أكثر من اللزوم. الناس هي التي تختار أن تشاهد هذه الفيديوهات أو لا. ليس من شأني تصحيح تفكير الناس.

ج: هو خليط من الإثنين. جزء منها هو شيء أنا أعرف كيفية استخدامه وتوظيفه وأنا متحكم فيه. والجزء الآخر هو جزء يقول أن ما حدث هو واقعة. هكذا أرى الموضوع: أنا أفعل شيئاً يضم الناحيتين وفي نفس الوقت أشرح العنف، لأن العنف يولد عنف. تطلق قوات الأمن الرصاص على المتظاهرين، فيقوم المتظاهرون بالطبع بالدفاع عن أنفسهم. والشيء الذي يحملونه في أيديهم؟ أحجار ومولوتوف. في رأيي هذه طرق مشروعة، هذا شيء لا نخجل منه كمتظاهرين. هذا شيء يحدث وهذا هو الحال.

س: هل أنت أيضاً متظاهر؟

ج: أجل أنا متظاهر أيضاً.

س: إذا أنت الإثنين في نفس الوقت، صحفي ومتظاهر. ألا يمثل هذا مشكلة لك؟ تناقض؟

ج: طالما أنجح في الحفاظ على الحيادية فلا توجد أي مشكلة. تكون المشكلة عندما تكون لدي مادة تعرض متظاهرين وهم يلقون المولوتوف، وأنا أركز على أن العنف كله قادم من جهة الشرطة. والحقيقة هي أن ليس هذا هو الواقع.

س: هل تشعر بفرق بينك وبين المتظاهر الواقف بجانبك؟ هل تشعر أن بينك وبينه مسافة لأنك موجود بصفتك صحفي؟

ج: لا أبداً. فالمتظاهر الذي يقف بجانبي معه الأداة التي يجيد استخدامهما، ومعي أنا الأداة التي أجيد استخدامها. معي الكاميرا وهو معه حجر أو شيء آخر. ولكن في آخر الأمر نقف نحن الإثنين في نفس الصف. كنت أواجه مشكلة في أول الثورة لأنني كنت أفكر دائماً: أريد أن ألقي بالحجارة أنا أيضاً. ثم أحسست أن هناك الكثير يفعل هذا بالفعل. ولا يوجد أحد يفعل ما أفعله. ولهذا يجب علي التركيز في ما أفعله. ولكني أشعر كل الوقت أننا سوياً. عندما تسقط علينا قنبلة غاز أقوم بالتقاطها ورميها، على سبيل المثال. أقول دائماً: احترم ما في يدك. إذا قررت أن تمسك كاميرا لتصنع فيلم، احترم الدور الذي اخترته. وإذا قررت إغلاق الكاميرا وأنك صورت ما يكفي، فأنت حر.

س: إذا فالكاميرا والفيديوهات هي أسلحتك؟

ج: أجل. مرة واحدة فقط هي التي نزلت فيها ولم أصور بالرغم من أنني كنت أحمل الكاميرا معي. ولكنني كنت قررت قبل النزول بألا أصور ولكنني أخذت الكاميرا معي في حالة حدوث أي شيء.

س: قد تكون الفيديوهات التي تصورها هي أداة أفضل للمحاربة في المعركة. قد تكون سلاح أقوى من السلاح الحقيقي لأنها تحتوي على رسالة ترسلها للعالم.

ج: ليس هذا فقط. إن المادة ليست قوية فقط ولكن هي جزء من شيء سيبقى في المستقبل. أعتقد أنه بعد عشر سنوات، عندما يتحدث الناس عن الثورة أو إذا أرادوا صنع فيلم عن الثورة، سوف تكون هذه المادة جزء من المواد التي سوف يستخدمونها من عملي أو عمل مُصرِّين وكل من جمع مادة من الأحداث. فالأحجار تختفي بعد إلقائها.

س: أنت دائماً تقف في الصفوف الأمامية. فأنت قلت أنك تريد أن تصبح مصور حرب. ألا تخشى أن تقتل بسبب ما تفعله؟

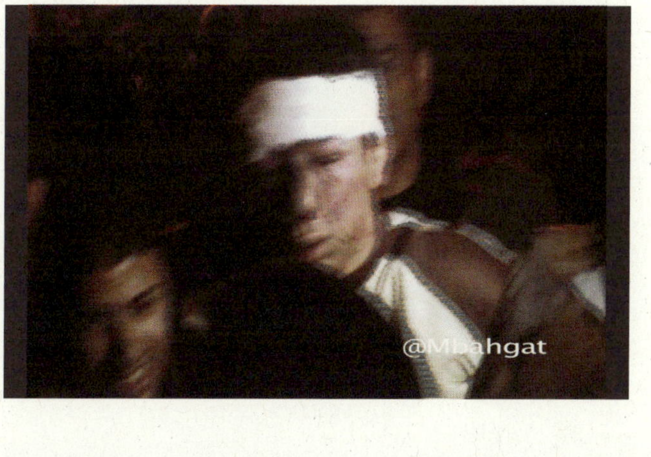

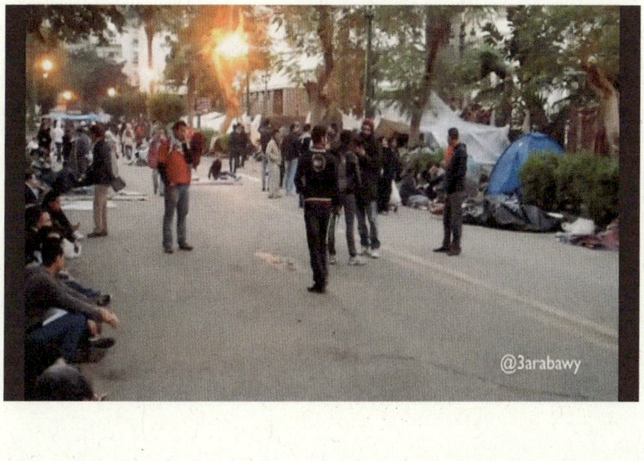

حوار مع مصطفى بهجت

أجرت الحوار أميرة الأهل

اللقاء يعود إلى الحالة السياسية في صيف 2012

س: كيف تقدم نفسك؟

ج: أنا صحفي فيديو يريد أن يكون مصور فيديو حربي.

س: هل لديك قدوة؟

ج: لا. كنت دائماً أشارك في المظاهرات، حتى قبل أن أعمل بالصحافة. وكان ما يثير غضبي هو أن ما كنت أراه في المظاهرات لا أراه بعد ذلك في التلفاز أو الإنترنت. هذا ما يحركني. أريد أن يرى الناس ما أراه عن قرب. هناك بالطبع شخصيات أنا معجب بها، ولكن ليس لدي قدوة.

س: هل درست صناعة الأفلام؟

ج: لقد أصبحت صانع أفلام بالصدفة. بدأت بالعمل في صحيفة المصري اليوم كمدير للمنتدى، أراقب التعليقات. وكان من حسن حظي أن يكون مكتبي في نفس مكان قسم الوسائط المتعددة.

س: متى حدث هذا؟

ج: في أكتوبر 2009. كان قسم الوسائط المتعددة في المصري اليوم يكلف الصحفيين بتصوير الأحداث بنفسهم. ثم حدثت بعض المشاكل الإدارية فقرر الصحفيون عدم التصوير بأنفسهم. ثم جاءت أحداث أول اعتصام عمّالي عند مجلس الشعب في عام 2010. بدأ النقاش في المكتب حول إرسال أحدٍ ما لتصوير الأحداث وحول ما إذا كان أحد من الصحفيين سوف يصوره. لم يكن هناك أحد على استعداد للذهاب، لذا قلت أنا: " أريد الذهاب للتصوير". بعدها حصلت على دورة مكثفة لمدة عشر دقائق.

س: وتعلمت كيفية تشغيل الكاميرا بعد تلك الدورة المكثفة؟

ج: كانت كاميرا صغيرة، مثل كاميرات اليد أو الموبايل، وتقنيتها ليست متطورة. شرحوا لي مقاسات الكوادر، أيها للقاءات أو للصور الكبيرة. لم أتوقف عن التصوير منذ ذلك الوقت. كنت أنزل للتصوير في كل الأحداث.

س: يقوم صحفي الفيديو بعمل أربعة أشخاص وهذا شيء صعب وعمل مرهق للأعصاب.

ج: أجل، فأنا أركز على ما أصوره وعلى الصوت وعلى الأسئلة والأجوبة وعلى ما يدور حولي- وكل هذا جزء واحد فقط. بعد ذلك أجلس وأقوم بالمونتاج وأخرج المقطع بعد ذلك. بدأ كل هذا بعشر دقائق. (يضحك)

س: أنت تعمل لدى وسيلة إعلام رسمية. وفي نفس الوقت عندك قناة على اليوتيوب تحتوي على فيديوهات لن يتم عرضها على التلفاز بدون أدنى شك. فاللغة السائدة والصور المعروضة قوية أكثر من اللازم. إذاً أنت الإثنين: صحفي ولكن أيضاً ناشط على مواقع التواصل الاجتماعي. ما مدى صعوبة حفظ الإتزان؟

ج: إن وسائل الإعلام الرسمية هي أكل عيشي. أعمل فيها من أجل المال. أحصل في هذا العمل على أوامر من رؤسائي: "إذهب لكي تغطي هذا الموضوع لنا!" عند جلوسي لتحرير الفيديو أضطر لحذف المشهد الذي يهين هذا الشخص أو ذاك المجلس العسكري. هذا يحزنني ولا أحب كوني مضطرٌ لعمل هذا. ولكنني أتمكن من أخذ المادة التي جمعتها للقناة وأصنع منها فيديو آخر. أعرف أن الجريدة مجبرة على اتباع قواعد معينة. إن المدراء بالتلفاز ليسوا أشخاصاً سيئين يعارضون عرض هذه المادة. ولكنهم مقيدين، تماماً مثلي.

س: وهذا الفيديو الثاني الذي تخرجه من نفس المادة مع المادة الإضافية التي لا يمكن عرضها على التلفاز، هل هذا الفيديو أدق وأصدق؟

ج: بالطبع. الموضوع هو أنني لا أتدخل. دوري هو تسجيل كل شيء وإذاعته دون أي تغيير في المعلومة. الشيء المهم هو عدم الانحياز لأي جانب، أن أكون موضوعياً. يجب أن أكون في المنتصف وأعرض الناحيتين، حتى وإن كانت قناعاتي وانتمائاتي الشخصية تميل إلى فريق بعينه.

س: هل لقناة اليوتيوب الخاصة بك أهداف مهنية بصفتك صحفي أم هي موجودة لأهداف سياسية بصفتك ناشط؟

Al Shorouk – Photojournalists from an Independent Newspaper / Fotojournalisten einer unabhängigen Zeitung / الصحفيون المصورون من الصحيفة المصرية المستقلة الشروق

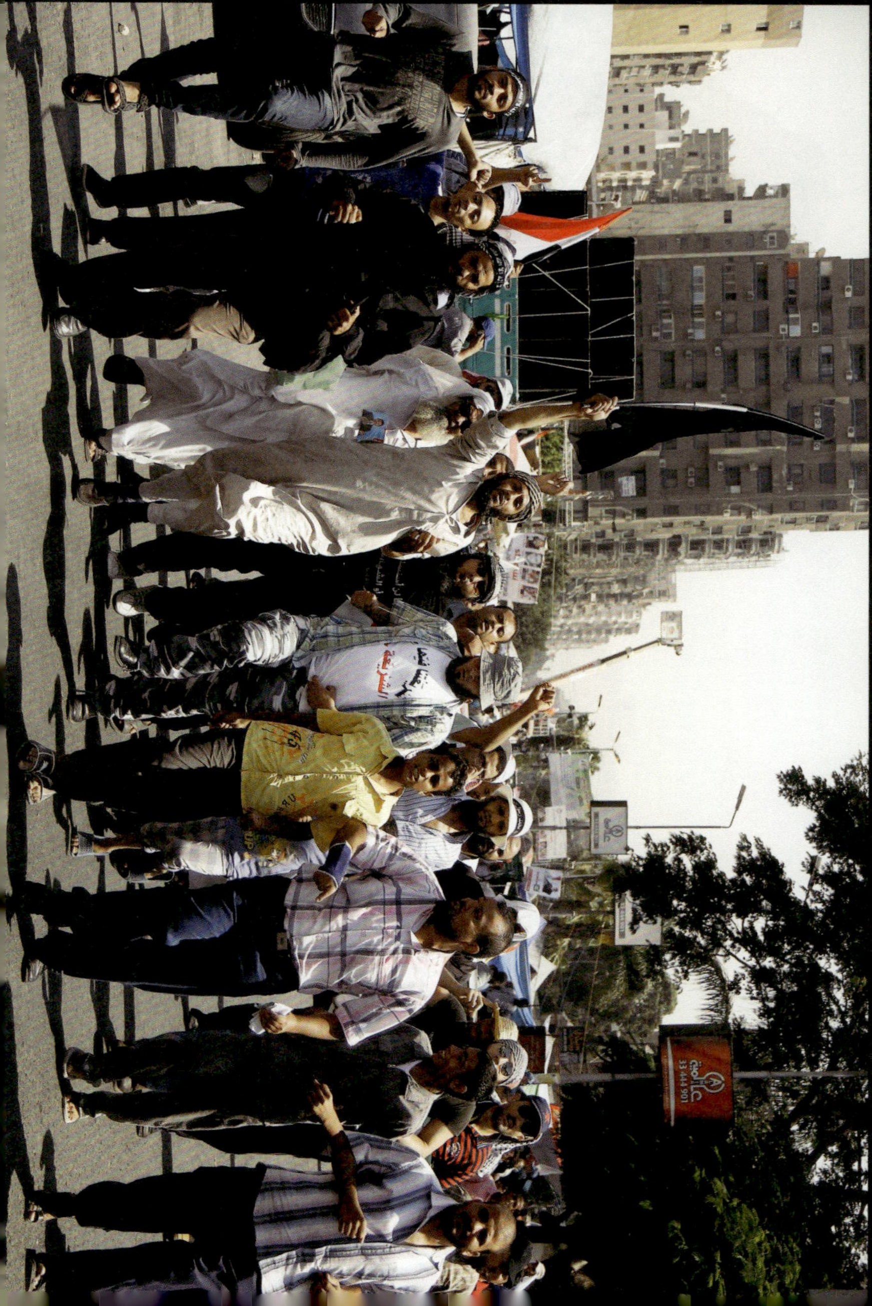

Sabry Khaled, Nasr City, July 27, 2013. Pro-Morsi protesters place barriers on Nasr road / Mursi-Anhänger bauen Straßensperren auf der Nasr Road auf / صبري خالد، مدينة نصر، 27 يوليو 2013. متظاهرون مؤيدون لمرسي يضعون الحواجز على طريق نصر

Aly Hazza'a, *Rabaa Al-Adaweya, Cairo, June 29, 2013.* Morning prayers conducted by members of the Muslim Brotherhood inside the protest zone / Morgengebete von Mitgliedern der Mulsimbrüder in der Protestzone / علي هزاع، رابعة العدوية، القاهرة 29 يونيو 2013. أفراد جماعة الإخوان المسلمين يؤدون صلاة الفجر داخل منطقة المظاهرة

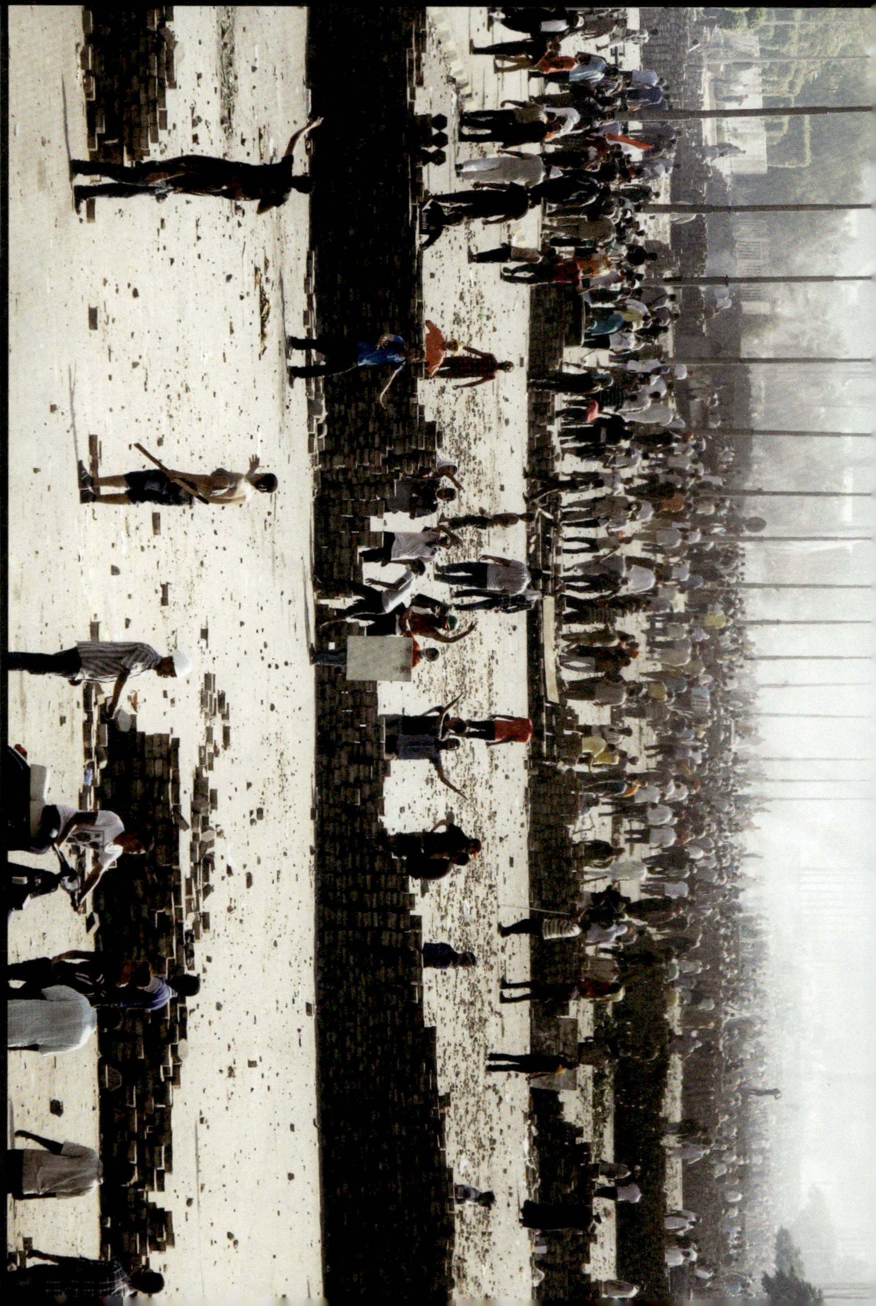

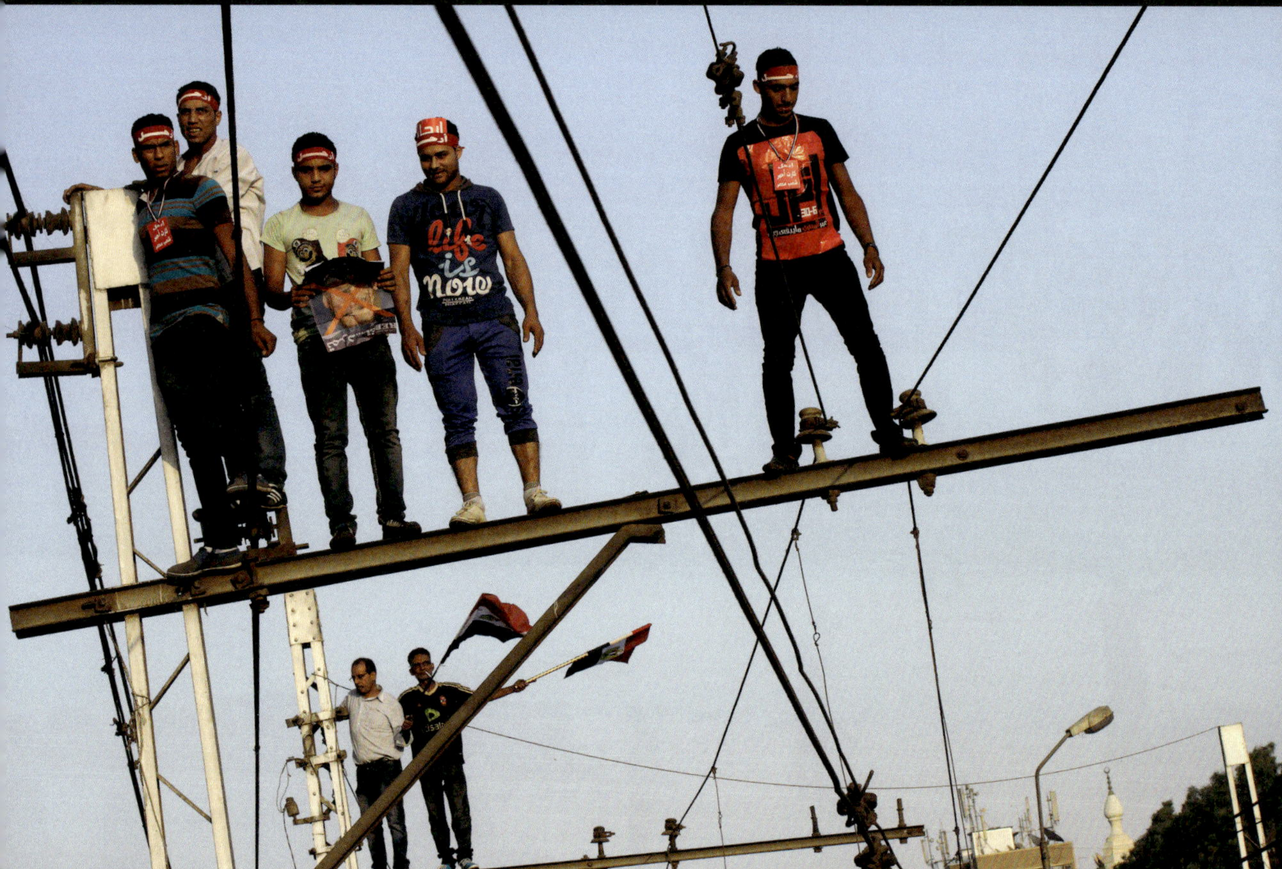

Sabry Khaled, *Itihadya*, *Cairo*, *June 30, 2013*. Anti-Morsi protesters on top of electricity poles outside the presidential palace / Mursi-Gegner auf Strommasten vor dem Präsidentenpalast / صبري خالد، الإتحادية، القاهرة، 30 يونيو 2013. متظاهرون ضد مرسي يتسلقون عامود كهرباء خارج القصر الرئاسي

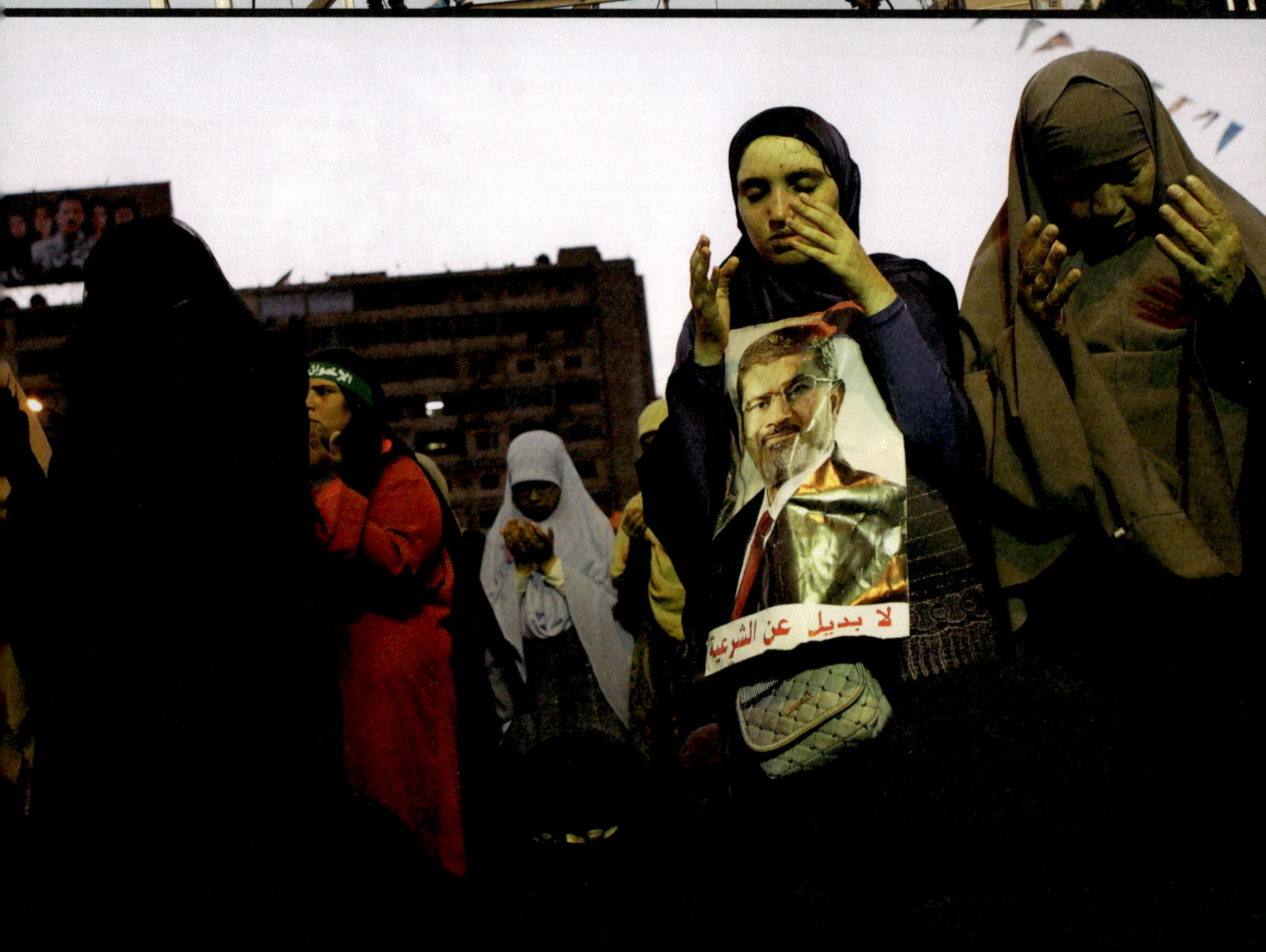

Sabry Khaled, *Rabaa Al-Adaweya*, *Cairo*, *July 10, 2013*. Supporters of ousted president Mohamed Morsi praying in Nasr City on the first day of Ramadan / Anhänger des gestürzten Präsidenten Mohammed Mursi beten am ersten Tag des Ramadan in Nasr City / صبري خالد، رابعة العدوية، القاهرة، 10 يوليو 2013. أنصار الرئيس محمد مرسي المعزول وهم يصلون في مدينة نصر أول أيام شهر رمضان

Cairo. Open City / Kairo. Offene Stadt

New Testimonies from an Ongoing Revolution /

Neue Bilder einer andauernden Revolution

The documents, texts, and photographs set out in the book *Cairo. Open City* go up until July 2013 and Morsi's overthrow. The bloody events that followed now make clear the degree to which the images we had previously selected seem to have changed, both in terms of their significance and in our way of reading them, shifting in line with the political situation and thus providing a new vantage point from which to view the pictures afresh.

The pages in this annex highlight the growing polarization within Egyptian society, presenting new visuals captured by the authors of the images already represented in the main book. /

Die in *Kairo. Offene Stadt* präsentierten Dokumente, Texte und Fotografien berücksichtigen die Ereignisse und Entwicklungen bis zum Juli 2013, bis zu Mursis Sturz. Die darauf folgenden blutigen Ereignisse machen nun deutlich, wie sich Bedeutung und Lesart der vor diesem Zeitpunkt ausgewählten Bilder zu verändern scheinen – vor dem Hintergrund der jeweiligen politischen Situation, aus der man sie betrachtet.

Die vorliegenden Seiten legen den Schwerpunkt auf die zunehmende Polarisierung innerhalb der ägyptischen Gesellschaft, indem sie neue Aufnahmen von den bereits im Buch vertretenen Bildautoren zeigen.

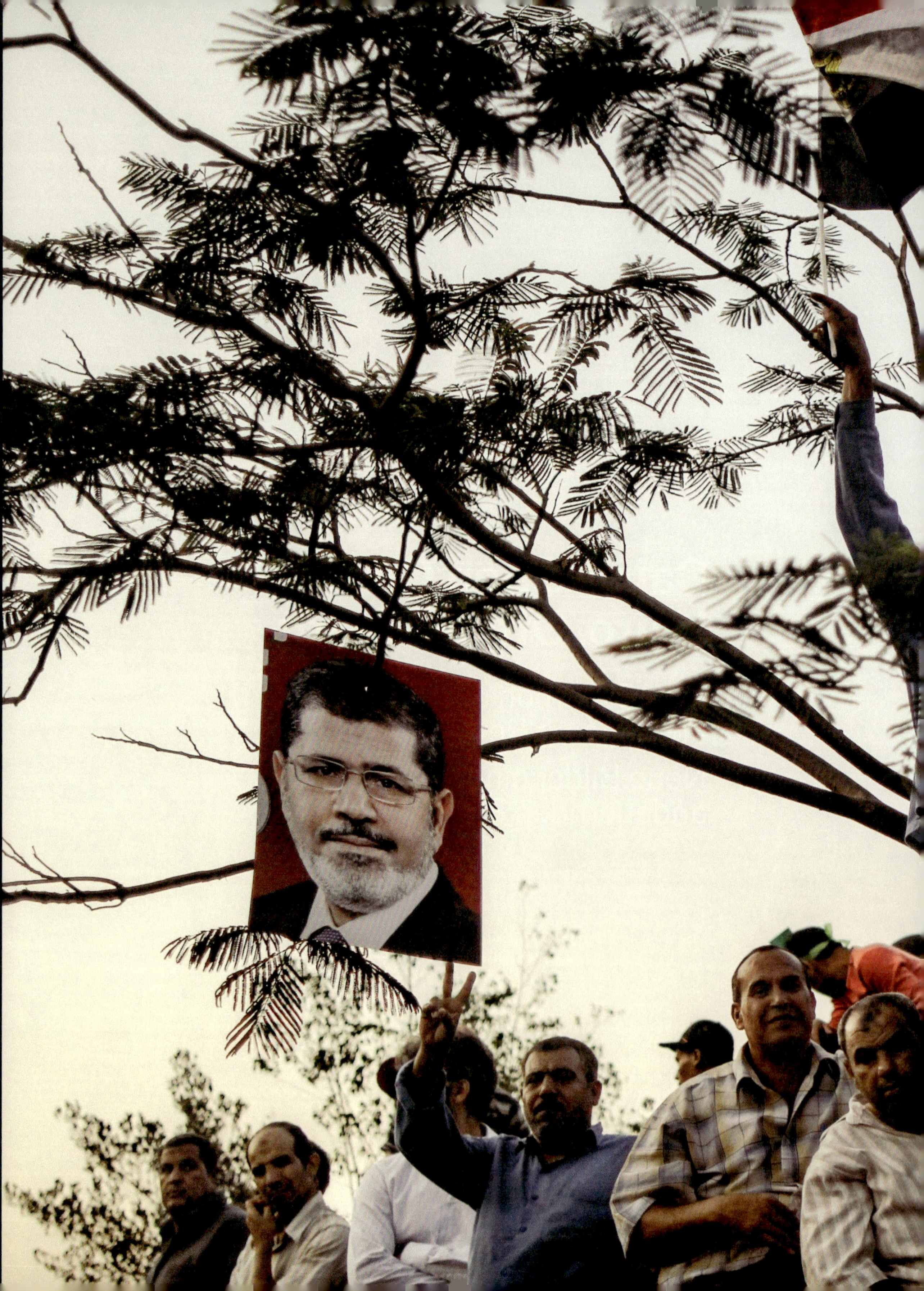

–from the Flickr album / aus dem Flickr-Album *June 30 protests* / من البوم فليكر
– مظاهرات *30* يونيو

of his taking office. / Anhänger von Mohammed Mursi demonstrieren am Jahrestag seiner Amtseinführung für ihren Präsidenten, July 3, 2013. / أنصار محمد مرسي يتظاهرون لدعم رئيسهم في أول ذكرى لتوليه الحكم

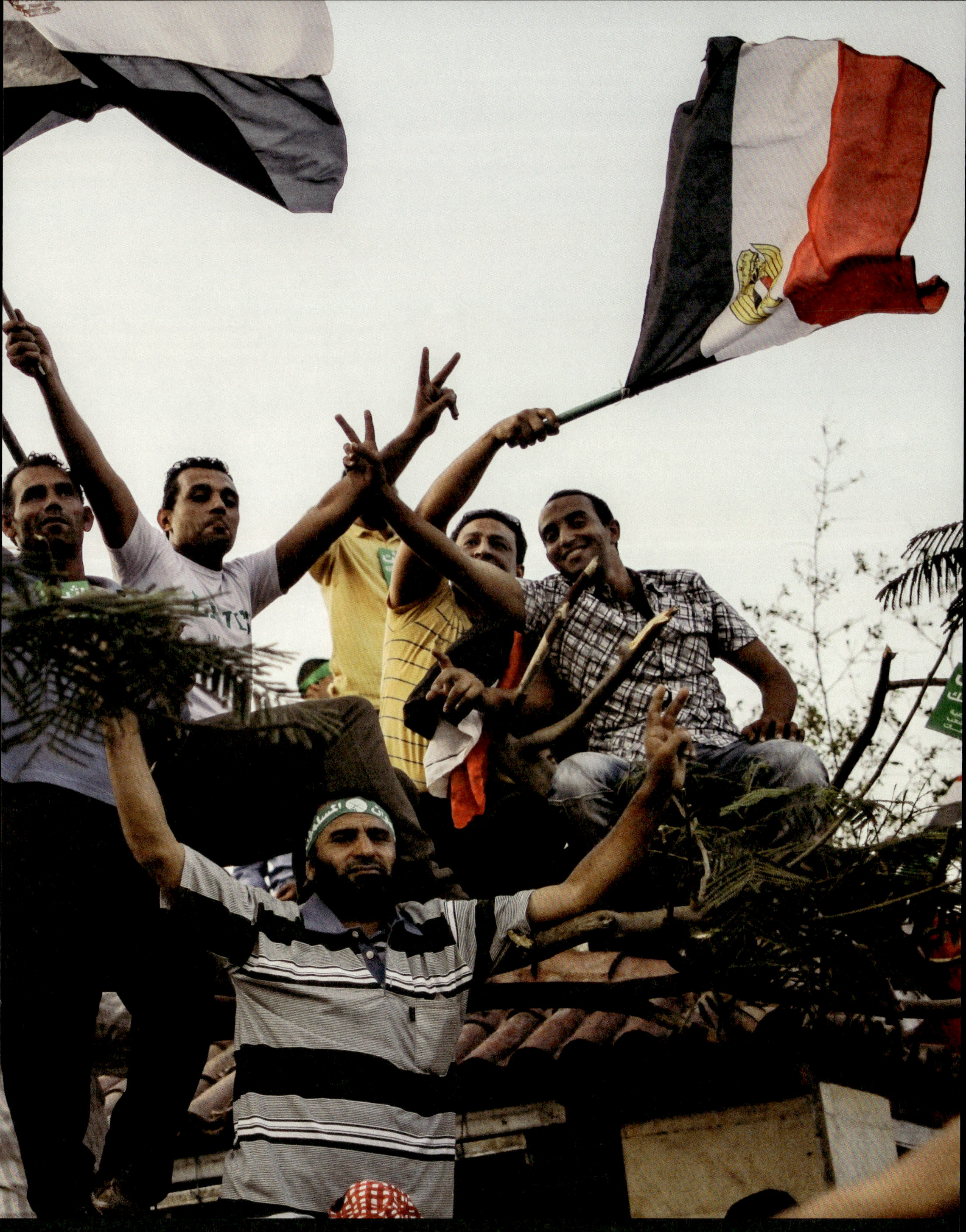

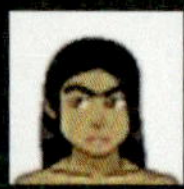

gharbeia Amr Gharbeia
Today is possibly Egypt's largest, most spread protests I saw, dozens of towns, seas of people. I'd be scared if I were Muslim Brotherhood.
18:26 Jun 30, 2013

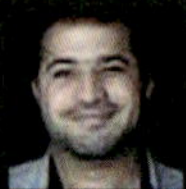

ashrafkhalil ashraf khalil
The 20 min walk from edge of palace protest area to nearest metro is one continuous anti-Morsi rally. It never actually stops #june30
21:21 Jun 30, 2013

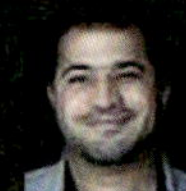

ashrafkhalil ashraf khalil
So people are trying to burn down FJP HQ&police refuse to protect. Doesn't this confirm MB claims that they're being conspired against??
03:06 Jul 1, 2013

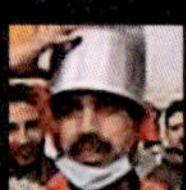

moftasa Mostafa Hussein
EGYPTIAN ARMY: NATIONAL SECURITY IN GREAT DANGER, GIVES 'EVERYONE' 48 HOURS TO RESPOND TO THE DEMANDS OF THE PEOPLE.
16:34 Jul 1, 2013

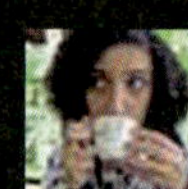

ManarMohsen Manar Mohsen
Morsi now cornered. People will not leave, and armed forces will carry out a coup on 48 hours if he doesn't. #June30
16:46 Jul 1, 2013

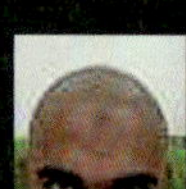

eldahshan Mohamed El Dahshan
Egyptians are a nation with the memory of a goldfish. #Maspero #Abbasseya #VirginityTests … This is what you're welcoming back? #June30
18:09 Jul 1, 2013

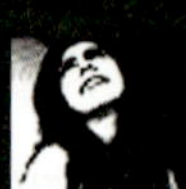

Egyptocracy Egyptocracy
We, the Egyptian people, are deciding our fate. Allowing the army to aid us is our choice. If anything goes wrong, we will correct it. #Egypt
16:01 Jul 3, 2013

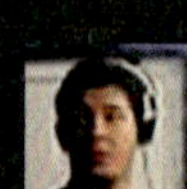

sharifkouddous Sharif Kouddous
Military love is widespread. Cheering choppers and carrying pics of Sissi and Abdel Nasser #nationalamnesia #Tahrir http://t.co/h3DvDy2woO
19:59 Jul 3, 2013

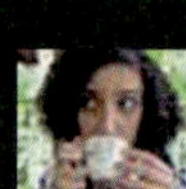

ManarMohsen Manar Mohsen
Constitution suspended, head of constitutional court now president, early presidential elections.
21:07 Jul 3, 2013

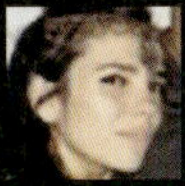

NevineZaki Nevine
It's like the army wrote everyone's dream impeachment statement! They checked all the boxes! #egypt
21:22 Jul 3, 2013

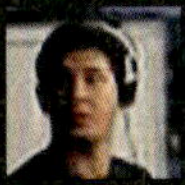

sharifkouddous Sharif Kouddous
After two and a half years, Egypt just went back to square one in its post-Mubarak transition
21:22 Jul 3, 2013

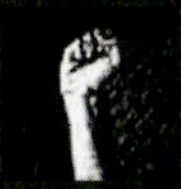

JanoCharbel Jano Charbel
Several 1,000 troops now deployed across Cairo. Police trucks, army APCs & military police jeeps on all major streets. Not liking this vibe!
23:13 Jul 3, 2013

ORHamilton Omar Robert Hamilton
We've swapped one hierarchical, secretive, armed, patriarchal, capitalist, violent organisation for another. Again. The revolution continues
23:18 Jul 3, 2013

ManarMohsen Manar Mohsen
In another exercise of swapping allies and chants in Egypt's 3-year political fiasco, MB are now the ones standing against the armed forces.
17:58 Jul 4, 2013

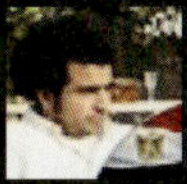

tarekshalaby Tarek Shalaby
It's important to acknowledge that #June30 is not a continuation of #Jan25. It's an attempt by SCAF to end it. We must fight both SCAF & MB.
02:05 Jul 8, 2013

sharifkouddous Sharif Kouddous
Bloodbath at Republican Guard HQ. Dozens of Morsi supports killed. 1 soldier dead. Army claims group tried to storm building.
09:05 Jul 8, 2013

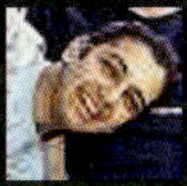

MohammedY Mohammed Yahia
It sickens me how far people are going to justify the killing of protesters this morning just because they are pro-#Morsi
12:44 Jul 8, 2013

Alex Nunns, *A Revolution in Tweets / Die Revolution erzählt in Twitternachrichten*, 2013 / 2013, ألكس نانس، ثورة في تغريدات،

Video circulated on the Internet, apparently showing two young Morsi opponents being thrown from a roof in Alexandria by supporters of the Muslim Brotherhood, July 6, 2013 / Im Internet zirkulierendes Video zeigt, wie vermutlich zwei jugendliche Mursi-Gegner von Anhängern der Muslimbruderschaft von einem Dach in Alexandria geworfen werden, 6. Juli 2013 / فيديـو انتشر في الإنترنـت يظهر كما يبدو إلقاء اثنين من الشباب المعارضين لمرسي من فوق سطح في الإسكندرية من قبل أنصار الإخوان المسلمين 6 يوليو 2013
(english.alarabiya.net/en/News/middle-east/2013/07/06/Video-shows-anti-Mursi-protesters-thrown-off-building-in-Alexandria)

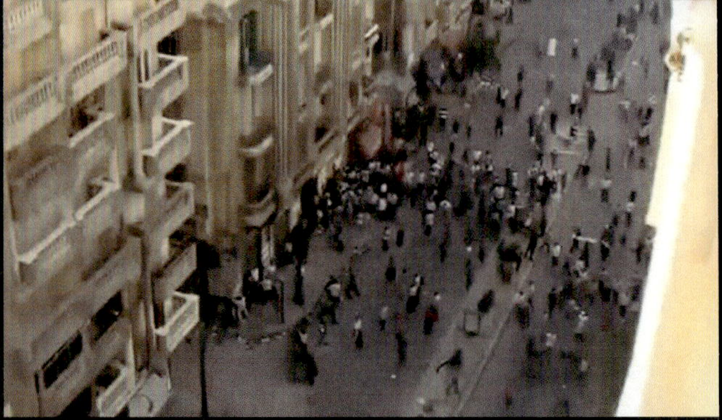

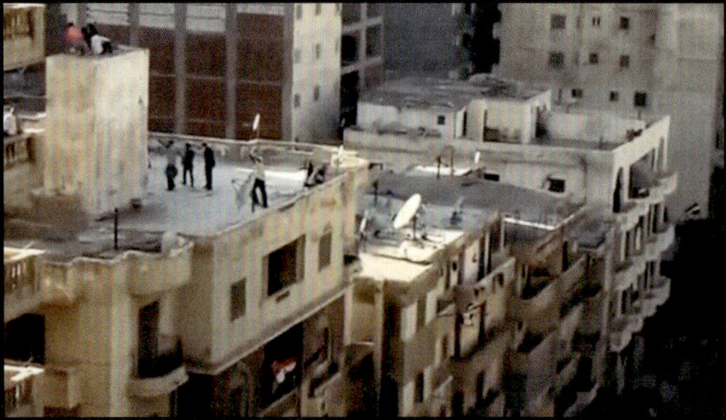

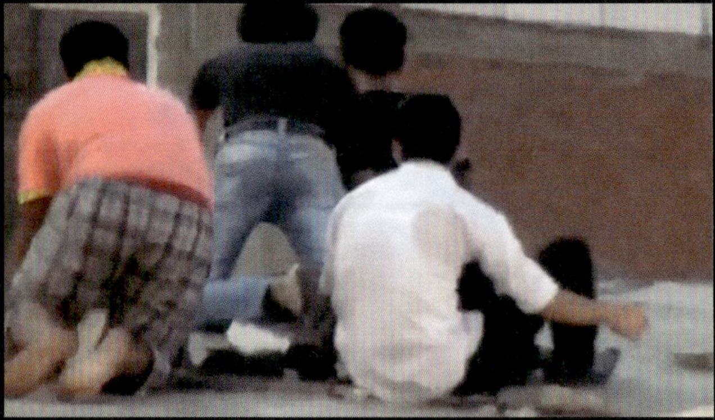

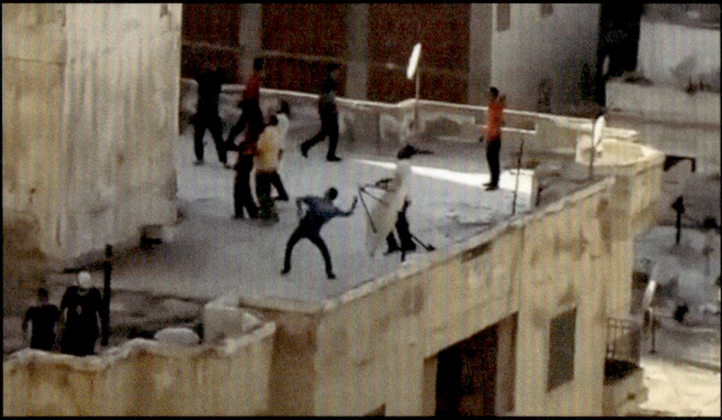

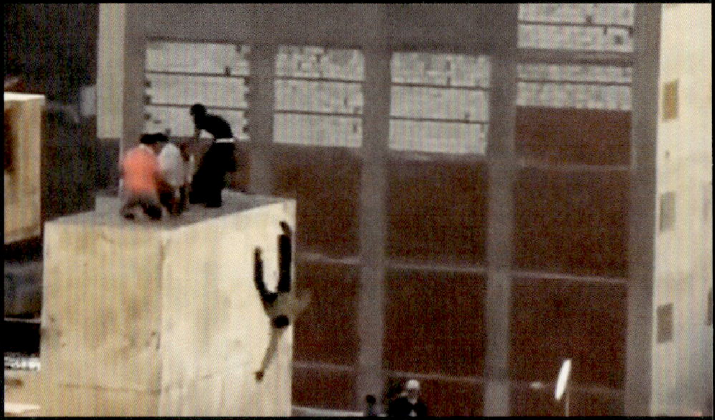

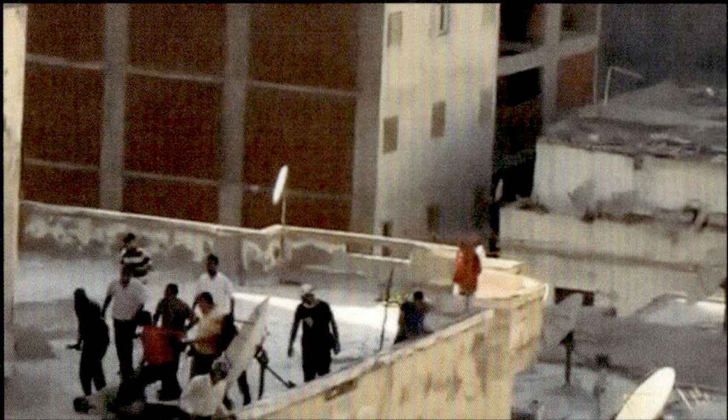

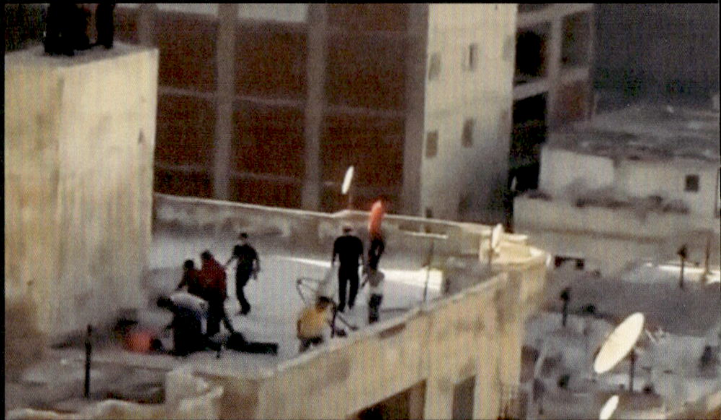

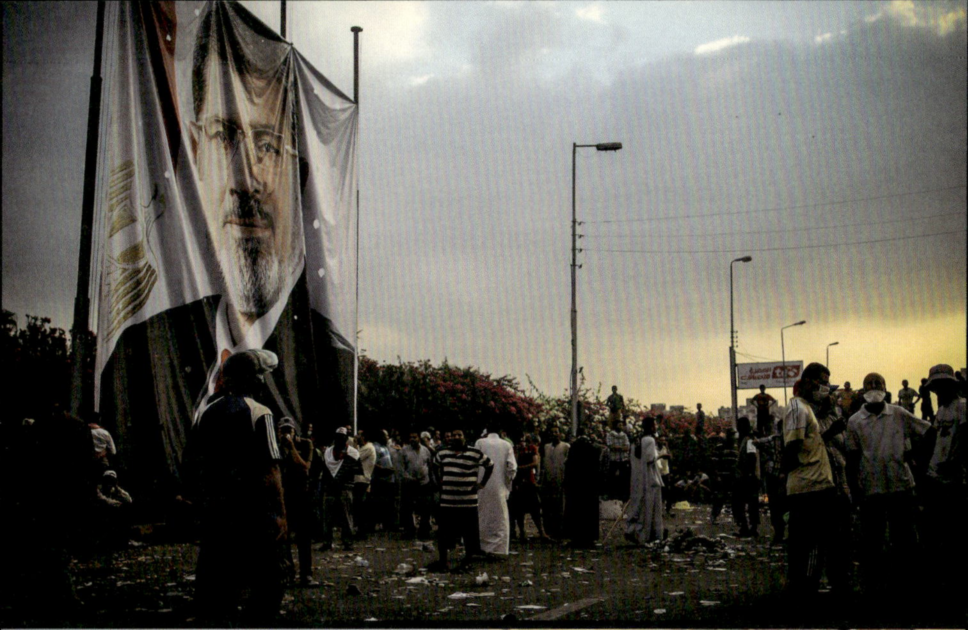

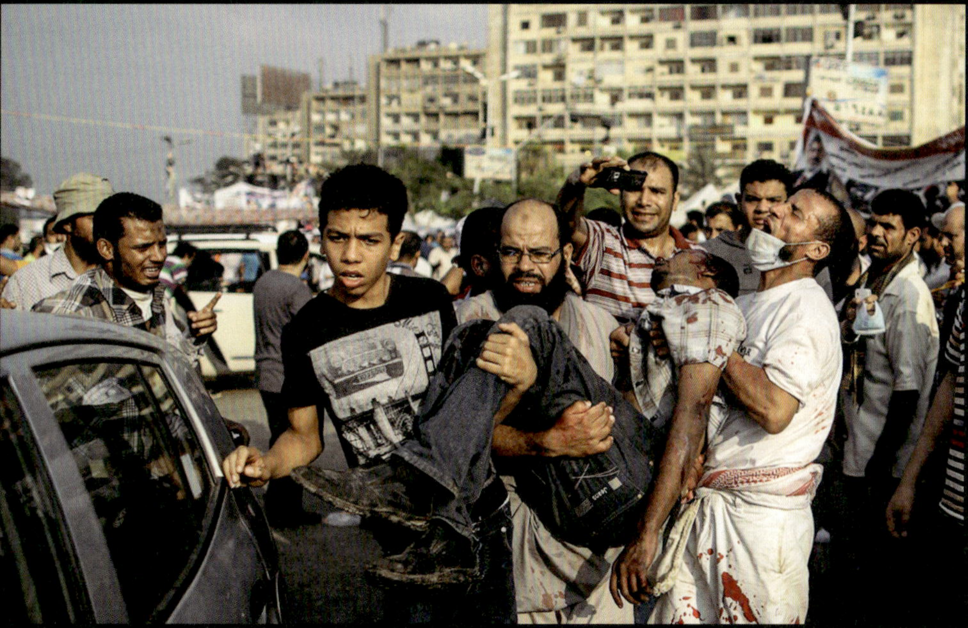

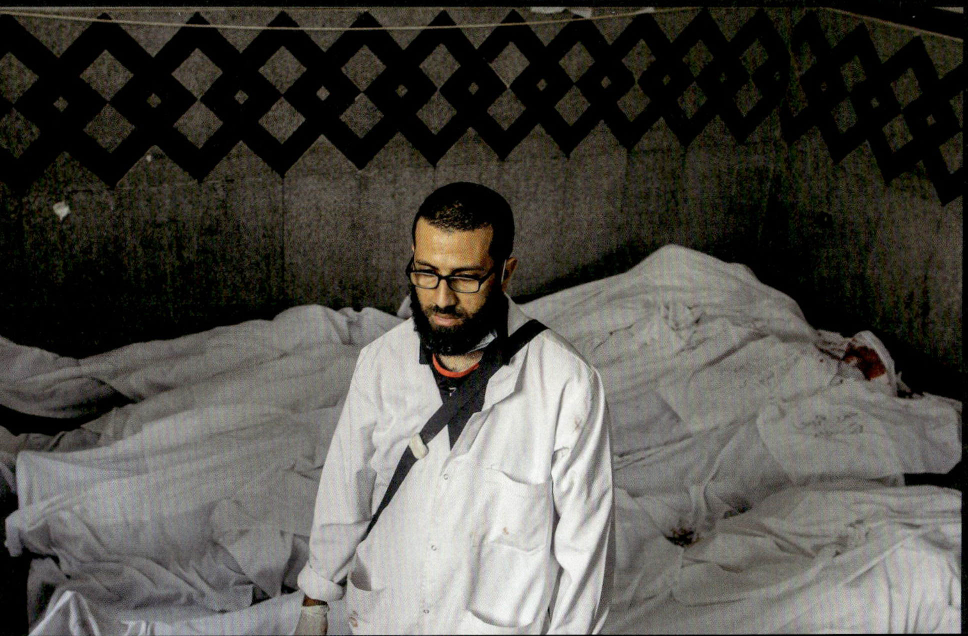

Mosa'ab Elshamy, *Rabaa Adaweya Clashes*, July 27, 2013 / 2013 اشتباكات رابعة العدوية، 27 يوليو

From the Flickr album / aus dem Flickr-Album *Rabaa Adaweya Clashes* / من ألبوم موقع فليكر، اشتباكات رابعة العدوية

The many failures of the Muslim Brotherhood's (MB) regime to manage the state's affairs and the accelerating downward spiral of the national economy meant that a significant number of the protesters came from the poorer segments of the country. They were expecting the Egyptian Revolution to bring social changes and punishment for those who had been in power, and accordingly some youth groups took the initiative of collecting signatures from across the country demanding early presidential elections. The campaign was given the name "Tamarrod," which means "rebel."

More than thirty million signatures were collected in a very short period of time. But the reaction of the MB was to ignore this popular demand, which resulted in the call for a large-scale demonstration on June 30, 2013, the anniversary of Mohamed Morsi's presidential inauguration. Despite the massive protests, the MB's response was once again negative as it turned a blind eye to what was happening.

The Egyptian military, however, seemed more sympathetic to the people's demands and gave the president an ultimatum of seven days (plus two extra days) to acknowledge the de facto call for early presidential elections. Morsi did not respond, so the army took action and removed him.

After Morsi's ouster a temporary president was appointed, and a road map for the future was drawn up, starting with the drafting of a new constitution, followed by parliamentary elections, and culminating in the voting in of a new president.

On August 14, 2013, security forces stormed two protest camps in Rabaa and Nahda squares, set up and occupied up to that point by supporters of deposed president Mohamed Morsi. Extreme force was used, with the violence continuing for days, during which hundreds of people lost their lives. Despite the brutality, many people hailed this new role for the military. It seemed as though Egypt had reverted to the political situation that had existed prior to the outbreak of the revolution on January 25, 2011. /

Mirette Bakir

Enttäuscht von den zahlreichen Versäumnissen der regierenden Muslimbruderschaft bei der Führung der Staatsgeschäfte und von der sich rapide verschlechternden wirtschaftlichen Situation beteiligten sich viele Menschen aus den armen Schichten des Landes an den Protesten. Sie erwarteten, dass die Revolution soziale Veränderungen bringen würde und endlich auch die ehemaligen Machthaber bestraft würden, die für die vielen Toten der vergangenen Jahre verantwortlich sind. Folglich ergriffen einige junge Leute die Initiative und sammelten landesweit Unterschriften für eine vorgezogene Präsidentschaftswahl. Der Titel der Kampagne lautete „Tamarod", was so viel bedeutet wie „Rebell".

In sehr kurzer Zeit kamen mehr als dreißig Millionen Unterschriften zusammen. Die Muslimbrüder aber reagierten nicht, sie ignorierten ganz einfach die Forderung des ägyptischen Volkes. Daher rief man für den 30. Juni 2013, den Jahrestag von Mursis Amtsantritt, zu einer Massendemonstration auf. Trotz der massiven Proteste an diesem Tag missachteten die Muslimbrüder den Willen des Volkes aufs Neue.

Das ägyptische Militär jedoch schien mit den Forderungen der Masse zu sympathisieren und stellte dem Präsidenten ein Ultimatum von sieben (plus zwei weiteren) Tagen, in denen er der bestehenden Forderung nach vorgezogener Präsidentschaftswahl nachkommen sollte. Als Mursi nicht reagierte, handelte das Militär und setzte den Präsidenten ab.

Nach Mursis Sturz wurde ein Übergangspräsident berufen und eine „Roadmap" festgelegt, nach der als Erstes eine neue Verfassung ausgearbeitet werden sollte, gefolgt von Parlamentswahlen und schließlich der Wahl eines neuen Präsidenten.

Am 14. August 2013 stürmten Sicherheitskräfte die beiden Protestlager, die Anhänger Mohammed Mursis auf dem Kairoer Nahda-Platz und dem Platz vor der Rabaa-Moschee errichtet und bis zu diesem Zeitpunkt besetzt hatten. Es folgten Tage exzessiver Gewalt, Hunderte von Menschen starben. Dennoch begrüßten viele die neue Haltung des Militärs. Es schien, als wäre Ägypten in die politische Situation vor dem Ausbruch der Revolution am 25. Januar 2011 zurückgefallen. /

فشل نظام الإخوان في إدارة شؤون الدولة، فجاءت النوبات الإحتجاجية من جانب الفئات الأكثر فقراً والتي كانت تتوقع الكثير من نتائج الثورة المصرية، فتصدت مجموعة من الشباب لحملة جمع توقيعات لإجراء انتخابات رئاسية مبكرة تحت اسم "تمرد" وقد وصل عدد التوقيعات إلى أكثر من ثلاثين مليون توقيع فى خلال فترة زمنية قصيرة، ولكن كان رد فعل نظام الإخوان هو تجاهل مطلب الشعب والإستهانة به. فكانت الدعوة إلى التظاهر يوم 30 يونيو 2013 وهو الموافق ذكرى مرور سنة كاملة على تولي محمد مرسي رئاسة الجمهورية.

ورغم ضخامة الحشد الذي تجمع في هذا اليوم إلّا أن رد فعل الإخوان كان سلبياً، متجاهلاً مرة أخرى مطالب الشعب.

فاستشعرت قيادة القوات المسلحة المصرية أن عليها التلبية فتم إمهال رئيس الجمهورية مدة أسبوع زاد إلى تسعة أيام للإقرار بالأمر الواقع والإعلان عن انتخابات رئاسية مبكرة ولكنه لم يستجب فقامت القوات المسلحة بالإطاحة به.

وتم إعلان عزل الرئيس وتعيين رئيس مؤقت للبلاد وإعلان خارطة للطريق تبدأ بإعداد دستور جديد للبلاد يليه انتخابات نيابية للوصول إلى مجلس تشريعي ثم يلي ذلك إنتخاب رئيس جديد للبلاد.

في 14 أغسطس عام 2013، داهمت قوات الأمن المصرية إعتصامين لمؤيدي الرئيس المعزول محمد مرسي في القاهرة، واستخدمت القوة، واستمر العنف لعدة أيام ، فقد مئات الاشخاص حياتهم . وعلى الرغم من العنف ، فقد أشاد كثير من الناس بهذا الدور الجديد للجيش. وإن بدا الأمر وكأن مصر قد عادت إلى الوضع السياسي الذي كان قائماً قبل اندلاع الثورة في 25 يناير 2011.

تمتد الوثائق والنصوص ، و الصور الواردة في كتاب "القاهرة. مدينة مفتوحة" إلى يوليو 2013، والإطاحة بمرسي. الأحداث الدامية التي حدثت مؤخراً جعلت الصور التي اخترناها مسبقاً تبدو وكأنها تغيرت، سواء من حيث أهميتها أوطريقتنا في قراءتها وتحولها تماشياً مع الوضع السياسي، وبالتالي توفير رؤية جديدة لمنظور حديث.

تسلط بعض الصفحات في هذا الملحق الضوء على الاستقطاب المتزايد داخل المجتمع المصري، وتقدم صوراً جديدة بعدسة المصورين أنفسهم الممثلين في الكتاب الرئيسي.

ميريت بكير

Ongoing, some websites /
Fortlaufend, einige Webseiten /
استمرار، بعض المواقع

www.mosireen.org
tweetsfromtahrirlive.com
www.jadaliyya.com
www.arabawy.org
tabulagaza.blogspot.com
www.inanities.org
www.flickr.com/photos/mosaaberising
www.flickr.com/photos/drumzo

case yelling at media: "Does my son look like a thug?" / Eine Mutter der 21 Fußballanhänger, die im Verfahren zu den Ausschreitungen im Stadion von Port Said zum Tode verurteilt wurden, schreit zu den Medien: „Sieht mein Sohn wie ein Verbrecher aus?"

round Kasr el Nil Bridge near Tahrir Square / Anti-Mursi-Demonstrant bei Auseinandersetzungen mit Sicherheitskräften bei der Kasr el Nil Bridge nahe des Tahrir-Platzes /

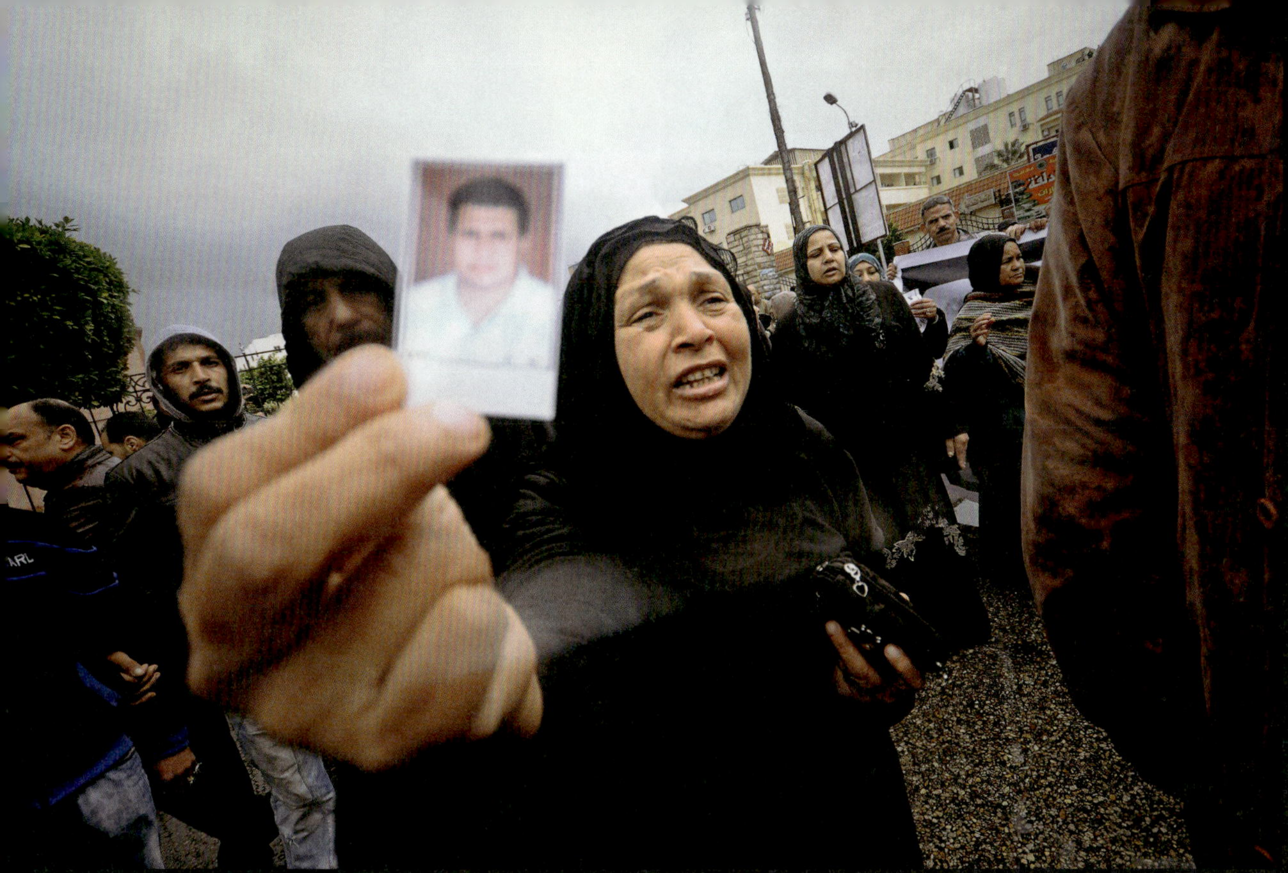

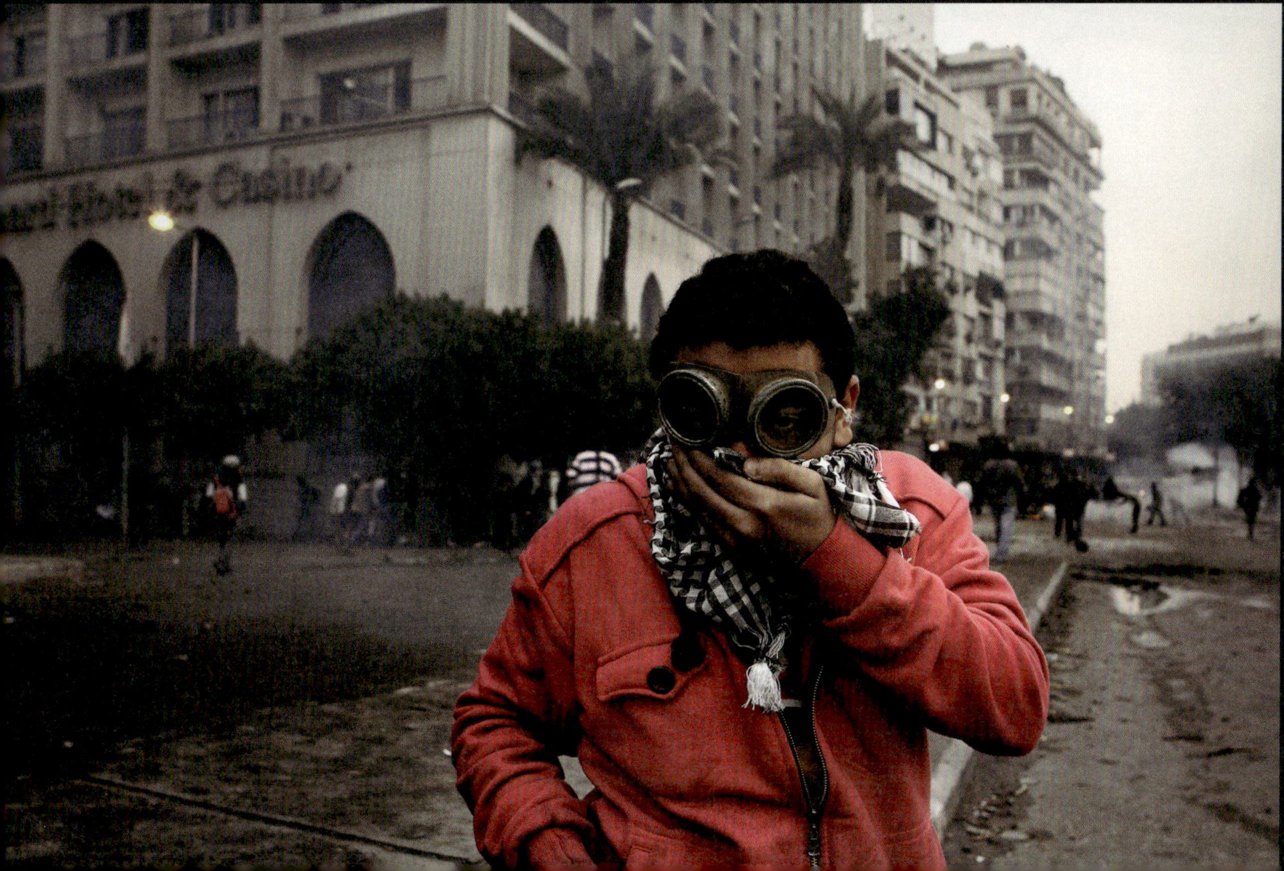

From the Flickr album / aus dem Flickr Album Port Said – February 2013
and / und *Egypt Clashes* – January 2013 / 2013

لبومان من فليكر، بورسعيد - فبراير 2013
اشتباكات مصرية - يناير 2013

A Coup or a Continuation of the Revolution? / Ein Staatsstreich oder die Fortsetzung der Revolution? / استمرار للثورة أم انقلاب؟
Video, 6:59 min., uploaded on July 14, 2013 / 2013 فيديو، 6:59 د، 14 يوليو
(www.youtube.com/watch?v=xrmhe5JuuNc)

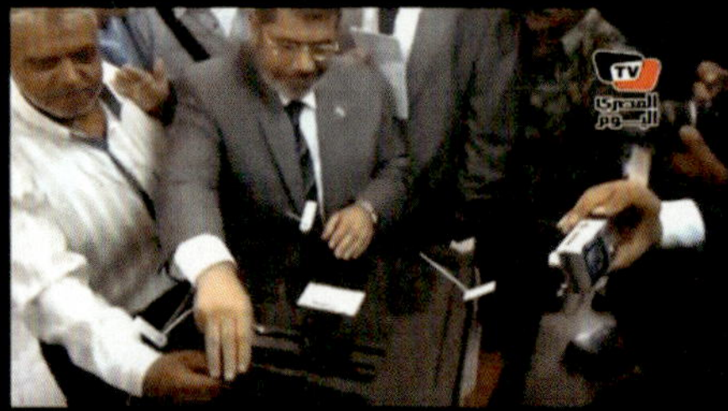

It is obvious people now understand that ballot boxes are just a means for the elite to monopolize power.

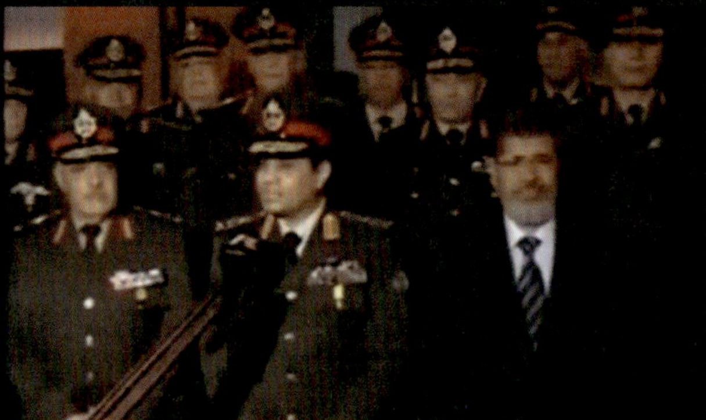

which was a large part of the bargain between them.

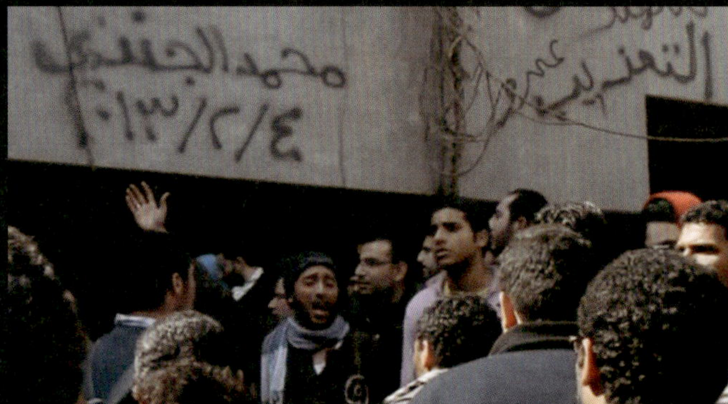

– Mohammad Gindy, your blood is freeing this nation!

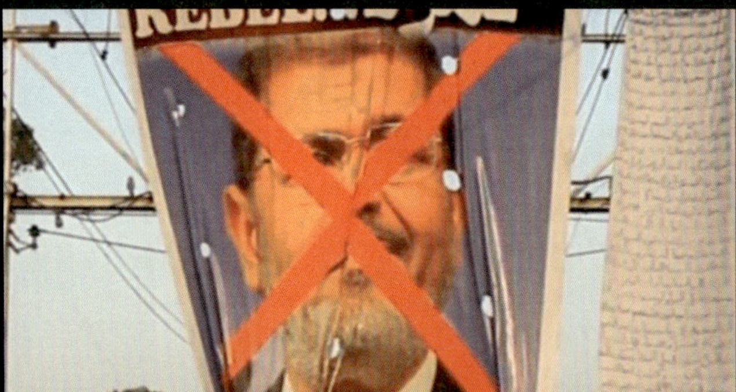

just because of their total failure in government, and their having lost the support of the public.

We got rid of Morsi and his clan. But we are facing new dangers.

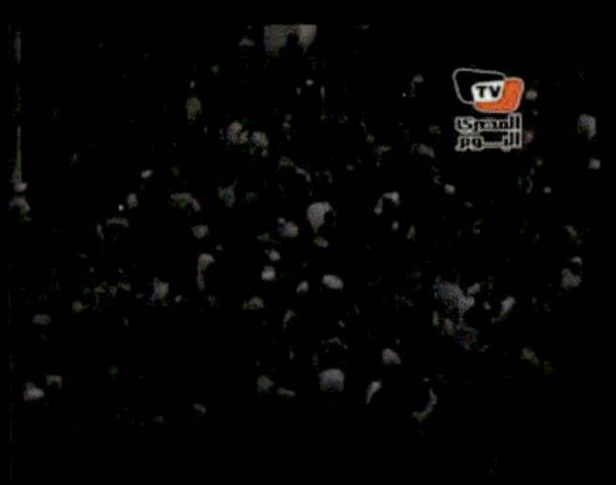

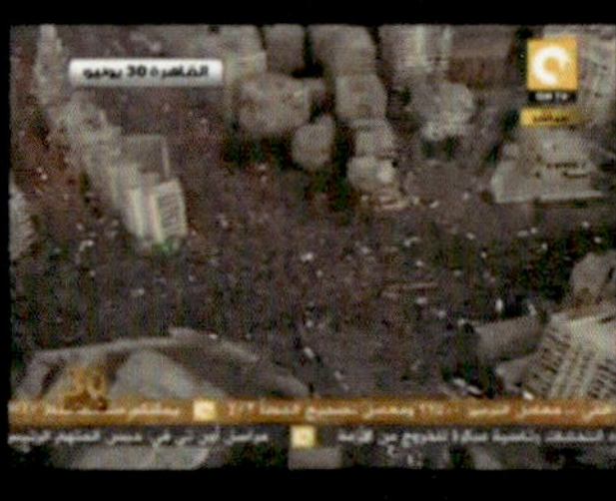

Glory to the people! The revolution continues!

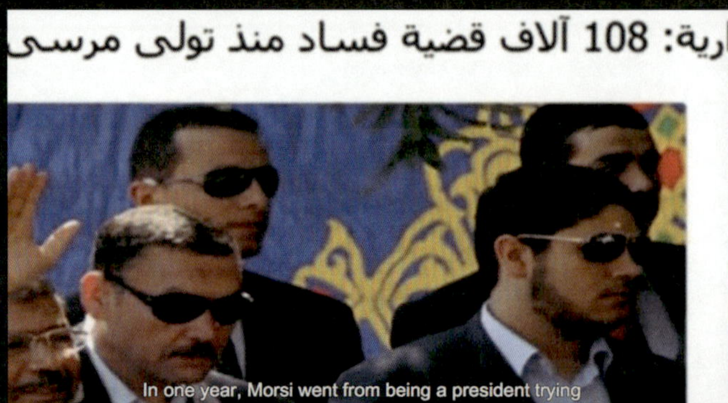

In one year, Morsi went from being a president trying to monopolize power, to a completely powerless one.

Mosireen – Media Collective / Medienkollek

القاهرة. مدينة مفتوحة

صور جديدة
من ثورة مستمرة

تمتد الوثـائق والنصوص ، و الصور الواردة في كتاب ”القاهرة. مدينة مفتوحة“ إلى يوليو 2013، والإطاحة بمحمد مرسي. الأحداث الدامية التي حدثت مؤخراً جعلت الصور التى اخترناها مسبقاً تبدو وكأنها تغيرت، سواء من حيث أهميتها أوطريقتنا في قراءتها ، وتحولها تماشياً مع الوضع السياسي ، وبالتالي توفير رؤية جديدة لمنظور حديث.
تسلط بعض الصفحات في هذا الملحق الضوء على الاستقطاب المتزايد داخل المجتمع المصري، وتقدم صوراً جديدة بعدسة المصورين أنفسهم الممثلين في الكتاب الرئيسي.

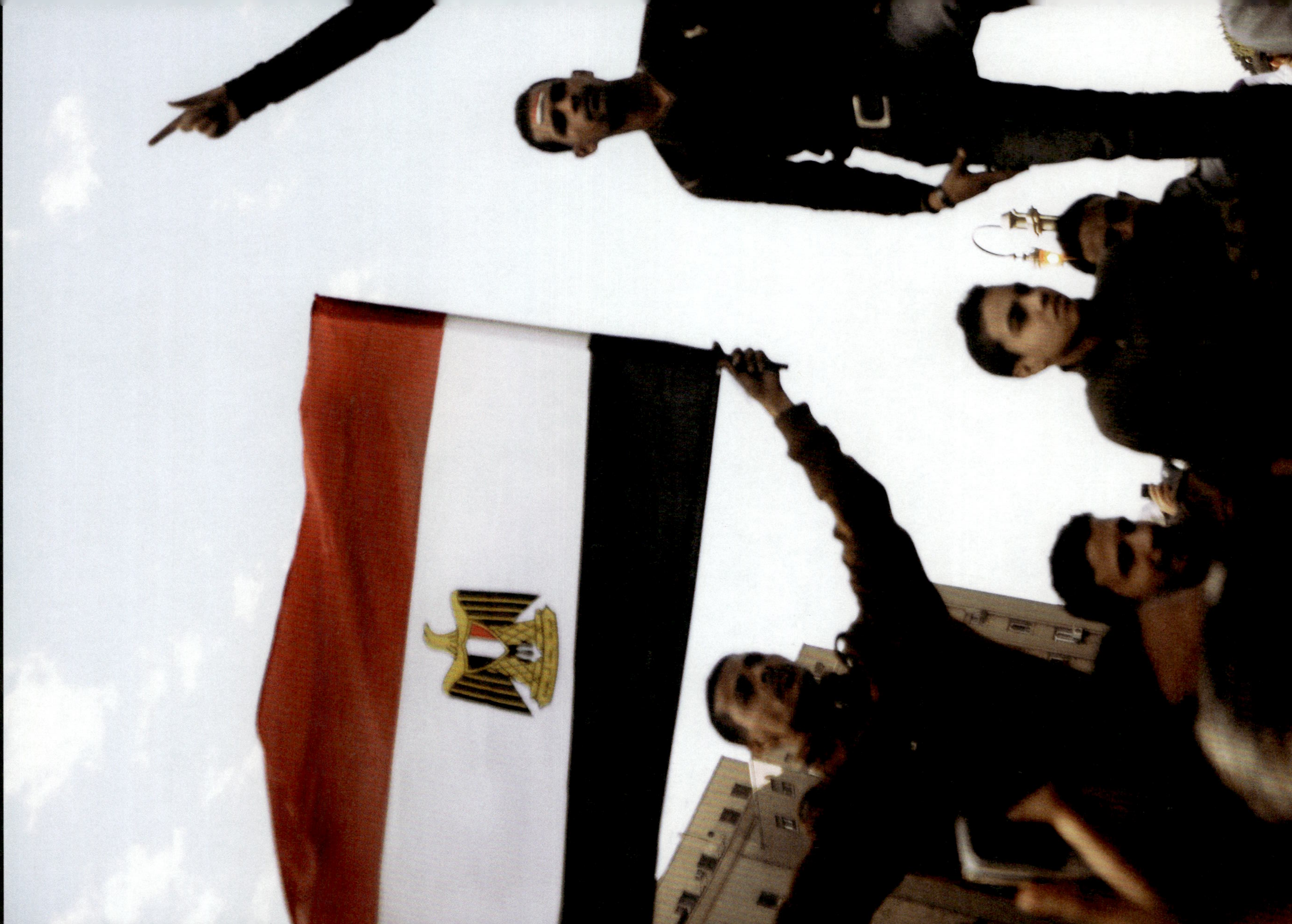

From the Flickr album / aus dem Flickr-Album *Egypt Clashes* –
January 2013 / *2013* من ألبوم فليكر – اشتباكات مصر – يناير

Jonathan Rashad, A protester leads chants amidst clashes with police on the second anniversary of the Egyptian Revolution. / Eine Demonstrantin stimmt am zweiten Jahrestag der Revolution inmitten der Auseinandersetzungen mit der Polizei den Protestgesang an, Jan. 25, 2013. / جوناثان رشاد، القاهرة. متظاهر يقود الهتاف وسط اشتباكات مع الشرطة في ثاني ذكرى للثورة المصرية

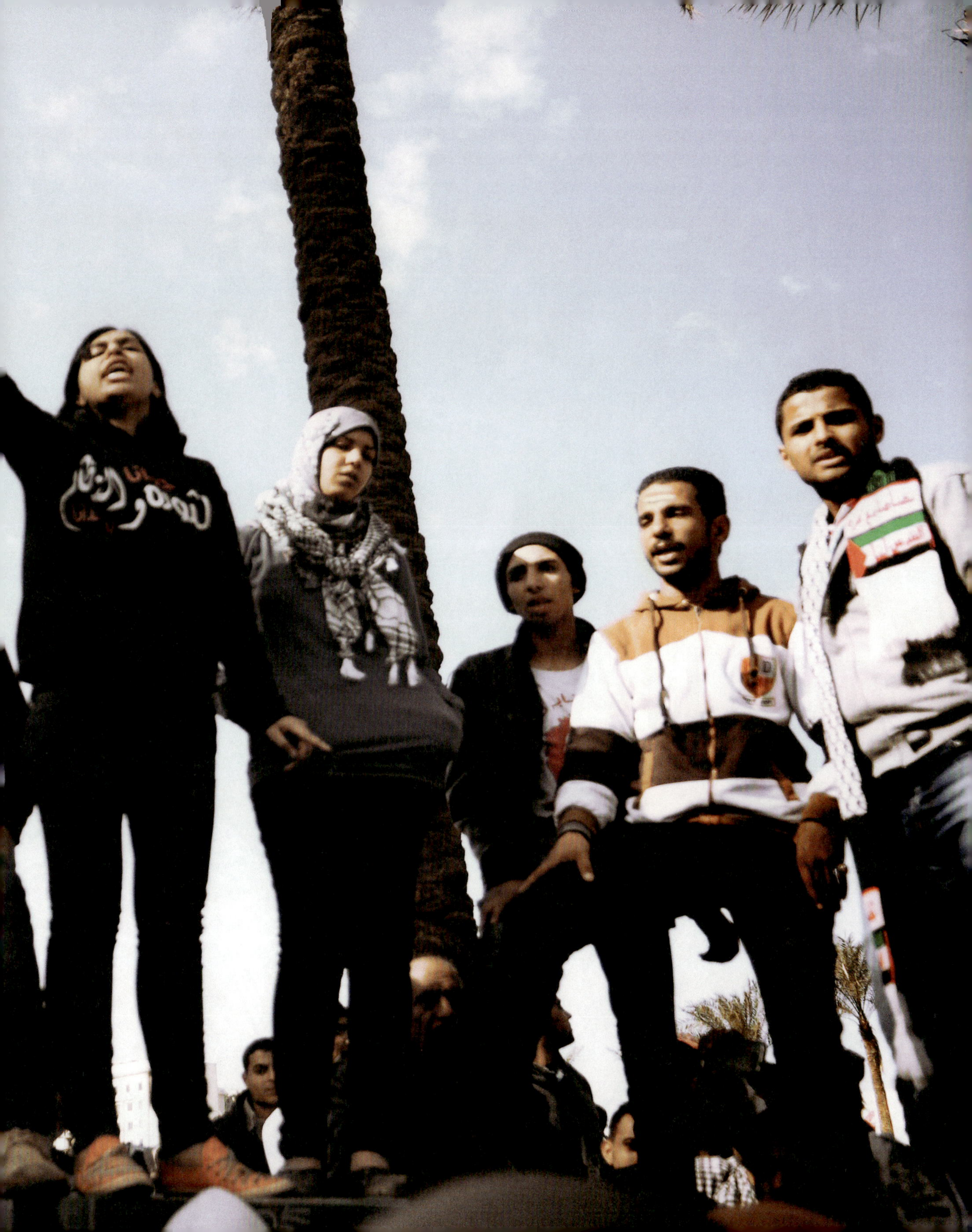

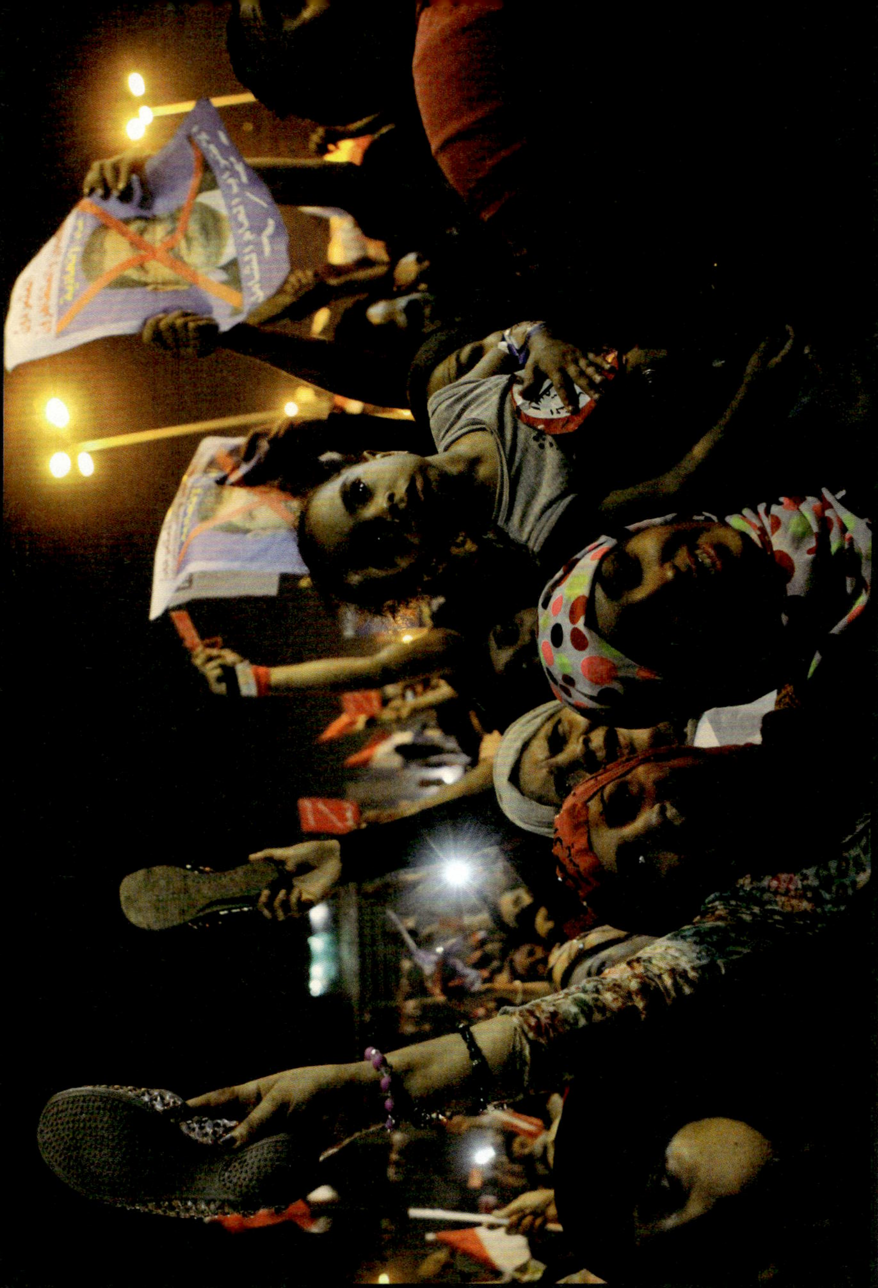

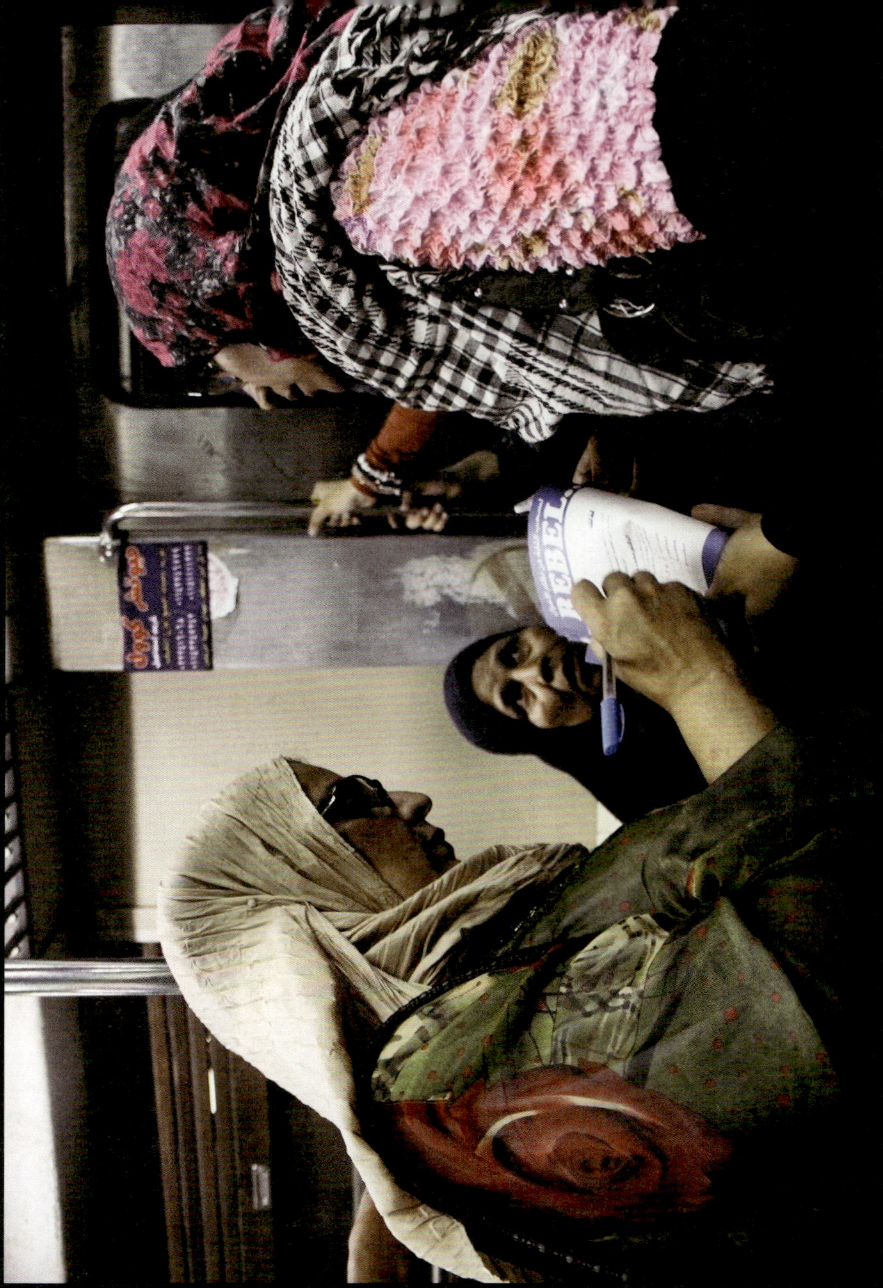

Sabry Khaled, *Tahrir, Cairo, June 6, 2013*. Anti-Morsi protesters listening to a speech by Morsi / Mursi-Gegner während einer Rede von Mursi / صبرى خالد، *6 يونيو 2013*. التحرير، القاهرة، محتجون مناهضون للإخوان المسلمين أثناء الاستماع إلى خطاب مرسي في ميدان التحرير

Heba el Kohly, *Subway, Cairo, May 30, 2013*. Women signing petition in the Cairo subway in support of the Tamarod ("rebel") movement / Frauen unterzeichnen den Aufruf der Tamarod-Bewegung in der Kairoer U-Bahn / هبة الخولي، مترو الأنفاق، القاهرة، *30 مايو 2013*. سيدات توقعن وثائق حملة "تمرد".

Al Shorouk – Photojournalists from an Independent Newspaper / Fotojournalisten einer unabhängigen Zeitung / الصحفيون المصورون من الصحيفة المصرية المستقلة الشروق

الإنتخابي ولكن كل شئ آخر حوله. إن الاختيار في التصويت بين نظامين فاشيين لا قيمة له في دولة لا تستطيع مؤسساتها ضمان أي نوع من أنواع العدل للمستِضعفين.

في الذكرى الثـانية لسقوط مبـارك، نحتفل بأن الثـورة لازالت مستمرة بالرغم من المحاولات العديـدة لإحباطها. إنه في الواقع شيء مدهش أنه لازالت لدينـا القوة للمحاربـة في معركة ظننا أنــها لن تستمر سوى عدة أيـام.

إن عملية الإدلاء بالشهادة هي اختيـار لما سوف تعترف به أمام نفسك وأمام الآخريـن بأنك رأيتـه. من خصائص نظرنا الراضي في الأوقات العاديـة أن نعتقد بأننا نرى، في حين أننا لا ندري شيئاً عن معظم ما يجري في العالم. ومع ذلك رأى العالم كله سبباً للإحتفال يوم تنحي مبـارك. قلما وجد في التاريخ أحداث رصد مشابهة في جمعيتها. كل من لا يزال قادراً على المتابعة، يعرف أن هناك تاريـخاً معيناً يتتابع من بداية هذا الحدث. ما شهدناه لم يكن مجرد سقوط ديكتاتور، ولكنه كان حلمٌ آدمي يتوجب علينا جميعاً أن نثبته ونظهره.

النظم

ما يحدث في مصر، لا يحدث هنـاك فقط ولكنـه يحدث لنا جميعاً، بنفس الحدة التي حدثت لجسد بوعزيزي. وكما أتت لنا الديموقراطية في مصر بديكتاتور آخر، قامت الديموقراطيات الغربية بتأمين الديكتاتور الذي أسقطناه. عندما تُستغل الأدوات الديموقراطيـة لخلق ديكتاتوريـات ذات مزاج دموي، تكون المسألة فقط مسألة وقت حتى يتسبب هذا النفاق في زلزال.

عندما تستمع إذاً إلى شهادة عائلة مصرية فقيرة، لا تشعر بالشفقة تجاهها ولكن حاول أن تشعر بالشفقة تجاه نفسك، على الأقل حتى تتأكد من أنك تفعل شيئاً مفيداً.

إنك لا تبحر في المحيط بنفس الطريقة التي تبحر بها في بحيرة جنيف. فمن الأفضل أن تتبع الموجة لا أن تبحر ضدها، إلا إذا أجبرت على ذلك وفي هذه الحالة من الأفضل أن تعرف حدودك. فالبحر أعتى من أي سفينة.

يأتي التغيير دائماً في موجات ولا يأتي أبداً في خطوط مستقيمة. ولن تستطيع التنبؤ بميعاد قدوم الموجة التالية، ولكنك تعرف دائماً عندما تكون العاصفة على وشك أن تهب.

يحمينا الاضطراب من السُلطة. طالما استمر الحال كما هو عليه، نعلم نحن أن السلطة لا تهتم بمصالحنا. ولهذا فنحن نعلم أنه طالما تحركنا في إيقاع تهديدي، لن تستطيع السلطة التحكم فينا. تعلمنا مرة تلو الأخرى أنهم لن يقبلوا طلباتنا طواعية ولهذا فعلينا جعلها ضرورة لهم. ولن يسود الهدوء مرة أخرى قبل أن يستمعوا لنا أو أن نضمن حقوقنا.

ولكن الهدوء ليس استقراراً. هو ليس إلا دليل على النجاح في العثور على أساس مشترك، يستطيع عليه كل فرد المضي بحياته، وفيه تصبح حكاياتنا تاريخاً. لن نستطيع أن نعيش عمرنا كله للآخرين، إلا في الأساطير.

الشهداء

منذ بدء الثورة سقط أكثر من ألف شهيد وفي كل لحظة من هذه الرحلة كنا على يقين أن المزيد من الشهداء سوف يسقطون. وبالرغم من وجود المئات من التسجيلات لعائلات الشهداء، لم ينجح أحدٌ في التسجيل مع شهيد يتحدث. حتى الذين أحسوا بقدوم الموت، تعيش كلماتهم فقط في الماضي وصور جثامينهم تشبه التصريح الأخير. تعيش كلماتهم وصورهم تذكاراً مُراً لوجع عائلاتهم، وقد تحولوا إلى رمز لنضال أكبر اختاروه بإرادتهم.

أسماء الشهداء ليست معروفة كلها. وهناك العديد من الجثامين لم يتعرف عليها أحد. وهو ليس من العدل أن يكون لأسماء بعض الشهداء صدىً أعلى من آخرين، ولكن هذه غلطة من هم على قيد الحياة وليست غلطة الشهداء. وفي حين تحولت بعض الأسماء إلى أيقونات للحظات وهويات معينة، فإن كل منهم يشكل فصلاً في رحلتنا.

أغلب الشهادات الموجودة هي لأهالي الشهداء. عبّرت صور مشاهد العنف عن حقائق كثيرة مدهشة ولكنها تحولت إلى طريقة تعبير طبيعية مع مرور الوقت. ولقد قالت الصور كل ما يمكن أن تقوله. وفي حين استنفد التكرار معنى هذه الصور، لا تزال هناك حقائق يجب أن تُكشف. إنه من الصعب تجسيد

المبادئ. فمنذ بدء الثورة كان جلياً أنها ثورة تحارب من أجل مجموعة من أفكار عامة وهذا يعني أنه لم يكن هناك من يمثل هذه المبادئ مجمعة بهوية أو مؤسسة فكرية واحدة. إن الحق في الكلام هو بدوره حق نادر.

للخبراء والسياسيين الحق في الإقناع. ولكل منا الحق في المشاركة. ولعائلات الشهداء الحق بدون منازعة في الكلام. ولكل منا لحظات يكون ما نكتبه أو نقوله ذا قيمة. ولكن الحق في الكلام هو شرف خاص، قد يكون هذا سبب الدور الفاصل الذي لعبته الصور في كيفية إعطاء أحياء هذه الثورة الصوت للأموات. من شاهد منكم ثورتنا من خلال عدسات وسائل الإعلام العالميـة، فليعرف أنه في أغلب الظن لم يسمع عن أم أو أب شهيد، لم يسمع عن أخوه أو أخته أو زوجته أو خطيبته.

تطلق العائلات الزغاريد في جنازة الشهيد. هو صوت غير كل الأصوات في الجنازة، فالزغاريد مكانها الطبيعي هو الأعراس. إذا فهمت هذا الصوت، تفهم ثورتنا.

الإحتفال

شهد العالم إحتفالاً يوم الحادي عشر من فبراير 2011. منذ هذا الحين قرر إهمال هذا الحلم وكتب في القصة عملية تحول فاشلة للديموقراطية، سطى الإخوان المسلمون عليها وبكل بساطة. كتبت هذه القصة نهاية نفسها، آخذة معها الأيام التي كان الناس يتحدثون فيها عن مصر بسعادة، مستبدلة هذا الشعور بإحساس غريب كلما أتت سيرة الموضوع في فضول محرج معتذر.

ولكن عيناك لم تخدعك في هذا اليوم. ومثل كل مصري كان سعيداً بسقوط مبارك، تسرعت أنت بدورك وكتبت النهاية. رأينا هذه اللحظة مرة تلو الأخرى، لحظة يأخذ إحساس زائف بالنهاية قوة النبوءة.

في الواقع، إن الوقت لا يزال مبكراً كي نحكم أين سنكون بعد حتى عام واحد من الآن. فلقد تعاملت الثورة في قرابة العامين مع عواصف عنيفة من أكثر ثلاث قوى منَظمة في مصر: الدولة البوليسية والجيش والإخوان المسلمون. حاولت كل من هذه القوى فرض سلطتها دون أن تنجح إحداهم، لهذا فإن قصة فضح دولة مبارك لازالت قائمة، بإرادة الشعب.

من السهل نسيان أن أهم خصائص الديموقراطية هي مشاركة تتعدى صندوق الإقتراع. هذه هي حال الديموقراطيات الراسخة في الأماكن التي تعمل من أجل دولة الشعب، فنحن ننسى أن أعمدة الدولة التي تستحق الحماية ليست النظام

خالد عبد الله

ممثل وناشط و وأحد مؤسسي مجموعة مُصِرِّين

شهادة

إن الثورة هي عملية إبصار. شيء أشبه بالمعجزة. فهي تكشف عما كان قبل ذلك وراء الأفق وتلقي الضوء على بنيان السلطة وتعيد تشكيل ما كان يبدو راسخاً. إن الثورة في حد ذاتها هي صراع مع الزمن. ولكن، ما هو الوقت المطلوب لكي تتطور الأحداث وتصل لما رأيته؟ لقد تحولت المعجزة الآن إلى مجموعة من القصص ومن المعروف أنه من السهل التلاعب بالقصص. ومع مرور الوقت تزيد القصص وتتحول المعجزة، من معجزة إلى وهم، وتتحول البصيرة إلى إظلام. ومع كل خطوة في هذه الرحلة العجيبة لم يكن هناك مفر من العنف. عندما يقف الشعب في مواجهة السلطة، تتشابك رؤيتان في صراع للبقاء. تصطدم مزاعم امتلاك الماضي والحاضر مع المطالب ومع كل منعطف يخط الدم الطريق.

على كل من شهد هذه المعجزة واجب اتجاه الآخرين. إن قصة ما نراه ليست ملكنا وحدنا لأنها تغير كل شيء. في الثورة يكون هذا التغيير واقع سياسي كامل يستحق أن يضحي المرء بحياته من أجله، ليس لأن الموت هدف ولكن لأن طبيعة الحياة تحولت بشكل لا يسمح بحياة كريمة للآخرين دون أن يخاطر المرء بحياته. هذه هي ثقافة الأكاذيب المتخللة للنظام القديم، تقتلك ثم تزعم أن أحداً لم يمت. معجزة أخرى غامضة.

إن الراوي الحقيقي لهذا التاريخ، هو الأجساد التي اشتبكت في هذه المعركة والعائلات التي أتت منها دماؤهم. للقلب الذي يحرك الجبال حكاية يحكيها لنا. بيد أن أغلب هذه القلوب قد أخمِد. يصبح فعل السرد هو أقرب شيء للشهادة.

شيء ما من هذا العالم يكون حاضراً في اللحظة التي تدخل فيها غرفة، تشغل الكاميرا لتواجه شخصاً يريد التحدث من خلالك. وفي اللحظة التي يحكون فيها عمّا مرّوا به، يكونون قد أظهروا أصدق أنواع الإيمان بجمهورهم. تقول كلماتهم أنك إن استمعت إليّ بصدق، سوف ترى عالم لم تكن تبصره من قبل. أصبحت طريقتهم في الكلام مزدوجة: تقديم الدليل على قصتهم والتأثير. يكتفون بالتأثير في بعض الأحيان لأنه أصدق شهادة، حتى وإن نزلت على آذان صمّاء.

تخلق الإيديولوجيات العفنة مجتمعات تعتمد على ثقافة الكذب. تكون هذه الأكاذيب في بعض الأحيان مطمئنة. وغالباً ما تخدم مصالح السلطة. عندما تكذب السلطة يتوجب إسقاطها. لفعل ذلك يتوجب أولاً دحض هذه الأكاذيب. وهذا يتطلب وقتاً. فإن عملية تقديم الدلائل تأخذ وقتاً أطول من الكذب، بالذات إن كانت الكذبة مطمئنة وغير مرئية مثل النوم.

عندما يقول أحد ما يجول بخاطرك دون أن تقوله، فهو يتملك منك. إن تطابقت حكايته ومخاوفك، تبدأ عملية من الثقة في خطاب معين. إن الثورة هي فترة من الزمن تفسح مجالاً لتغير إجتماعي هائل في وقت قصير جداً. تلك اللحظة التي يؤمن فيها عدد كبير من الناس بنفس الشيء إيماناً جماعياً دون الحاجة إلى النطق بكلمة واحدة، هذه هي اللحظة التي يبدأ فيها التغير في هيكل السلطة. يحتاج الناس في هذه اللحظة للإيمان في نفس الوقت بالذات إن كانوا دون قائد. ولهذا يكون للتوقيت أهمية كبيرة، إذا أردت الإمساك بهذه اللحظة سريعة الزوال. إن إيقاع قصتنا هو إيقاع السرد وعملية الشهادة. فهي تحمينا كما تحمي سردنا. قصة من أين أتينا وأين نحن ذاهبون.

إن كلماتنا وعيوننا وكاميراتنا وحبر أقلامنا هو شهادة لحقيقة أعمق لهذا التغير في هيكل السلطة. هذا لا يعني أننا دائماً على حق ولكن يعني أننا دائماً نحاول الوصول لشيء حقيقي أكثر من مجرد أدلة. نحن نبحث عن أدلة للمستقبل كما رأيناه عندما انهار أفق فوق آخر. لن تتمكن من الوصول إلى هذه الأدلة إلا إذا واظبت على البحث.

فلتأخذوا حذركم إذاً مِن مَن يريدون إسكات الثورة ومطالبها. عندما يحدث شيء له هذا الكم من الأصداء الإنسانية، ينظر الجميع وينصت، في آخر الأمر.

إضطراب

إن الاستقرار كذبة. وفكرة أن الاستقرار هو ما يحمينا هي خدعة. إن ما يحمينا هو قدرتنا على التكيف بلا حدود. فالتغير أثمن من أي شعور بالنوستالجيا. وإذا كانت اللحظات الجميلة تتكرر مثلها مثل القبيحة، فإنها تتكرر كل مرة بشكل مختلف. إن التجديد أفضل من الإعادة، وأجرأ.

في الثورة تتجرأ وتخاطر بالفشل لأنك تيقنت بأن الشيء المسمى بالاستقرار هو مصيبة محققة. ولكن الجرأة متعبة والكسل هو حق لكل إنسان. كيف تجد توازنك إذاً؟ سوف تظل فترة طويلة من الزمن غير قادراً على إيجاد هذا التوازن.

فالوصول إلى حد الإجهاد ثم السقوط في قبضة الكسل هو إيقاع ضروري. يلعب الإيقاع دوراً هاماً في الأعمال الجماعية والاعتراف بوجوده أفضل من التصرف وكأنه ليس موجوداً.

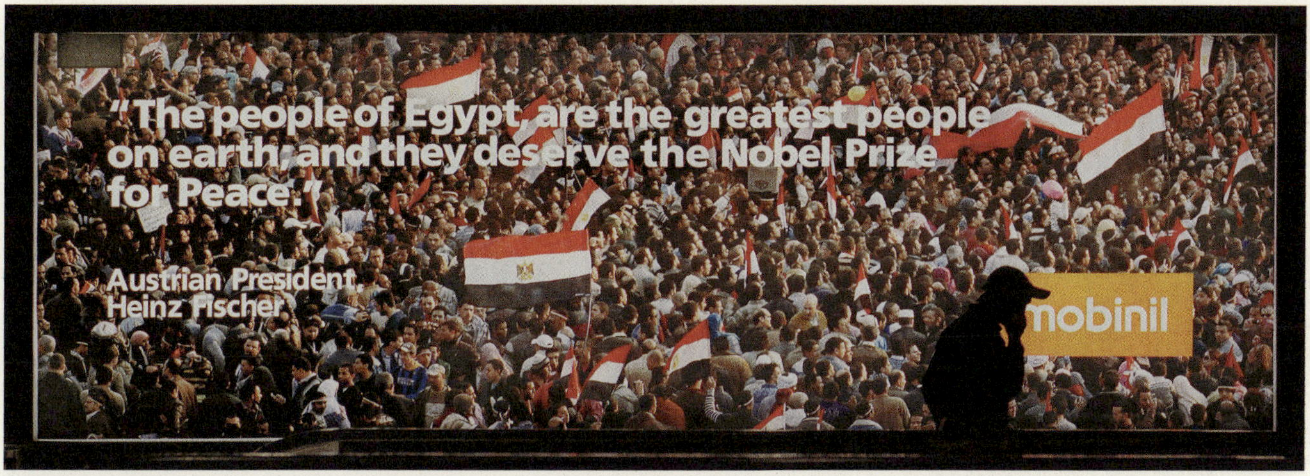

Seen at Cairo International Airport / aufgenommen am Internationalen Flughafen Kairo, Dec. 2011 / أخذت في مطار القاهرة الدولي ديسمبر 2011

Visitors to Cairo are greeted at the airport by huge illuminated advertisements from the Egyptian mobile phone company Mobinil. In its advertising the company uses images from the beginning of the Egyptian Revolution on January 25, 2011, and praise from international politicians for the courage of young Egyptians. Yet, the company did not support the political protests against the regime of Hosni Mubarak. Instead, it succumbed to the demands of the government and suspended its service on January 28, 2011. The shutdown in telecommunications and Internet connections did not, however, cause the protests to diminish; in fact, many more people took to the streets.

Am Kairoer Flughafen empfangen große Leuchtreklamen des ägyptischen Mobilfunkunternehmens Mobinil die Besucher der Hauptstadt.

Für seine Werbekampagnen nutzt das Unternehmen Fotomaterial aus der Anfangszeit der ägyptischen Revolution sowie Äußerungen internationaler Politiker, die die ägyptische Jugend für ihren Mut lobten. Das Unternehmen unterstützte die politischen Proteste gegen das Regime von Husni Mubarak nicht – es folgte vielmehr den Aufforderungen der Staatsmacht und schaltete sein Netz am 28. Januar 2011 ab. Durch den Zusammenbruch der Internet- und Telekommunikationsverbindungen ließen die Proteste jedoch nicht nach, im Gegenteil, noch mehr Menschen gingen auf die Straße.

تستقبل الإعلانات المضيئة التابعة لشركة الإتصالات موبينيل زوار العاصمة في مطار القاهرة.

تستخدم الشركة صوراً من الفترات الأولى للثورة المصرية لحملاتها الإعلانية، بالإضافة إلى عرض عبارات مديح القادة الدوليين لشجاعة الشباب المصري. ولكن الشركة لم تدعم الإحتجاجات ضد نظام حسني مبارك، بل ثابرت على إتباع توجيهات سلطات الدولة وقامت بقطع خدمات الإنترنت والإتصالات في 28 يناير 2011. لم يخفف إنهيار خدمات الإنترنت والإتصالات من حدة الإحتجاجات، بل أدى ذلك إلى زيادة الحضور إلى الشوارع.

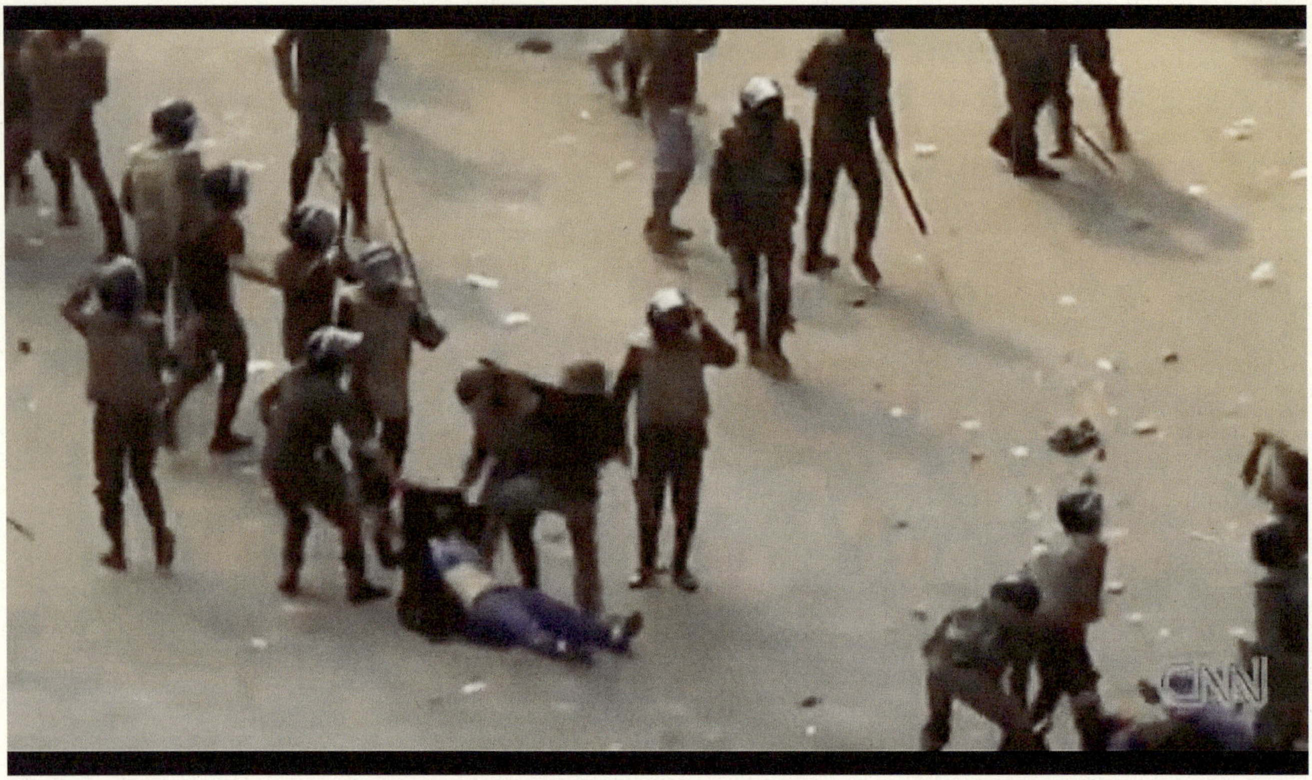

Screenshot from CNN report, taken from Internet. / Bildschirmfoto von CNN-Ausstrahlung, im Internet gefunden, Dec. 2011 /
لقطة من تقرير السي إن إن، مأخوذة من الإنترنت.

December 17, 2011. The video of the woman being stripped and beaten by soldiers in the middle of Tahrir Square in broad daylight shook the world. The image appeared on the front page of newspapers locally and internationally, sparking an international debate on military rule. It went on to appear in artworks, and continues to be proof of the brutality of the military regime. This image was also the main catalyst for the biggest women's march in Egyptian history.

(Documents collected by Rowan El Shimi)

17. Dezember 2011. Das Video der am hellichten Tag mitten auf dem Tahrir-Platz von Soldaten entblößten und geschlagenen Frau erschütterte die Welt. Es erschien als Titelbild nationaler und internationaler Zeitungen, entfachte international die Debatte um die Militärherrschaft und ist Zeugnis der Brutalität der Armee. Auch war es der Auslöser für die größte Frauendemonstration in der Geschichte Ägyptens.

(Dokumente gesammelt von Rowan El Shimi)

السابع عشر من ديسمبر 2011. اهتز العالم لصورة السيدة العارية، التي ضُربت من قِبَل الجنود في وضح النهار وسط ميدان التحرير. ظهرت تلك الصورة كصورة غلاف للعديد من الصحف المحلية والعالمية، وأثارت جدلاً حول سلطة العسكر وأضحت شاهداً على همجية الجيش. أصبحت تلك الصورة مصدر إلهامٍ لإقامة أكبر مظاهرة نسائيّة في تاريخ مصر.

(تجميع الوثائق روان الشيمي)

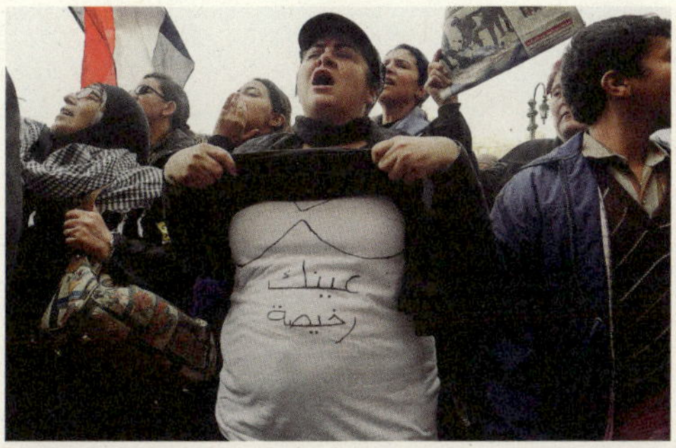

1

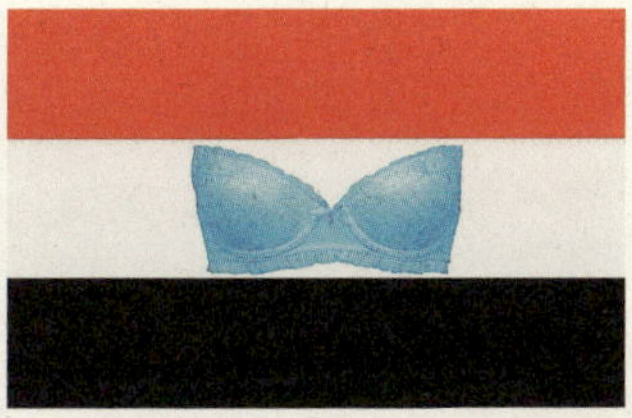

2

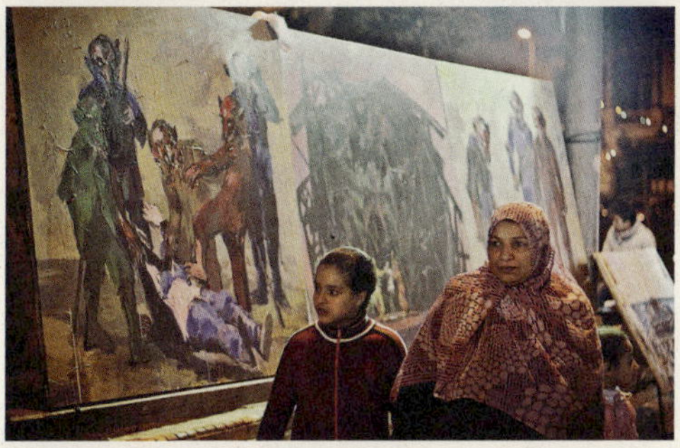

3

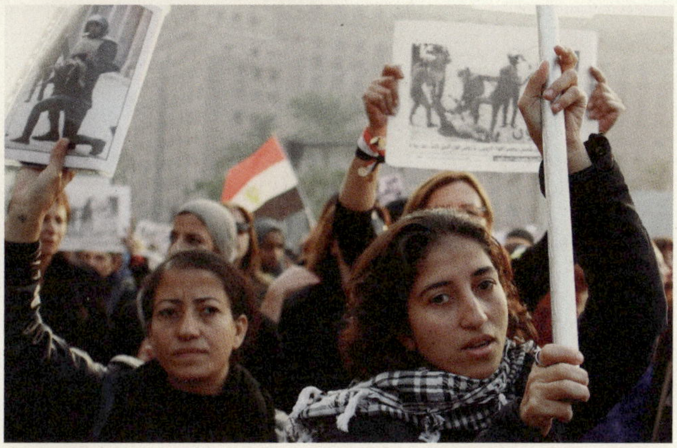

4

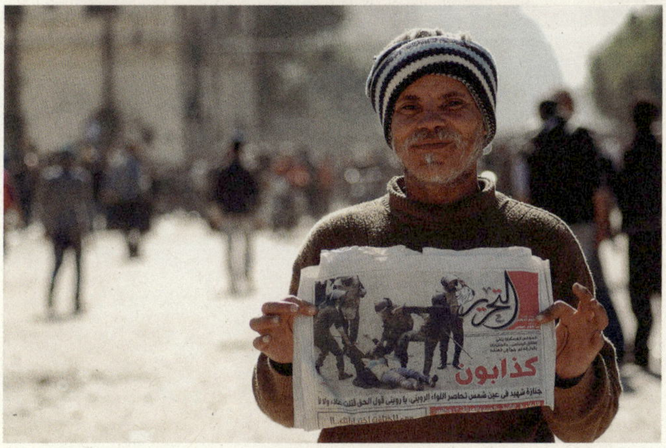

5

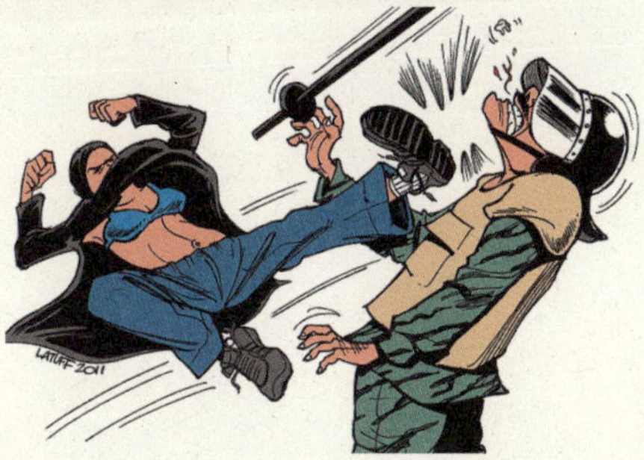

6

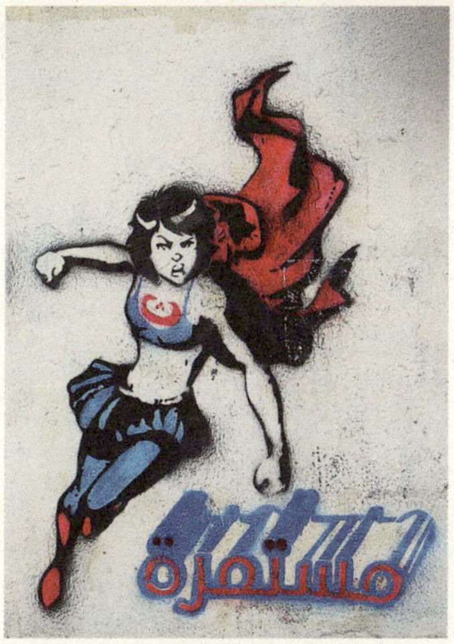

7

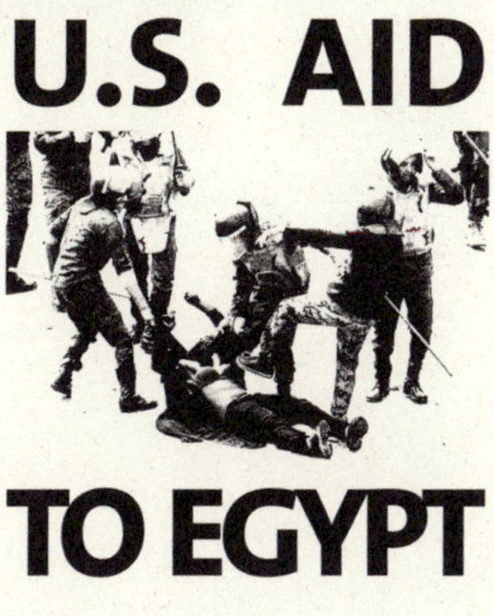

8

1 *"Your eye is cheap" [for looking]*
(Photo/Foto/صورة: Sarah Carr/سارة كار, from the Flickr album/aus dem Flickr-Album/من ألبوم على موقع فليكر تحت عنوان *Women March*, Dec. 20, 2011)

2 Egyptian flag with the blue bra/Ägyptische Flagge mit blauen BH/العلم المصري بمشد الصدر الأزرق (bluebra.files.wordpress.com/2011/12/bra-flag.jpg)

3 *El-Fan Midan*
(Photo/Foto/صورة: Mosa'ab Elshamy/مصعب الشامي from the Flickr album/aus dem Flickr-Album/من ألبوم على موقع فليكر تحت عنوان *El-Fan Midan*, Jan. 7, 2012)

4 *Cairo, Dec. 20, 2011.* Women's march to the Press Syndicate/Protestmarsch von Frauen zum Pressesyndikat/القاهرة، 20 ديسمبر 2011. سيدات في مسيرة إلى نقابة الصحفيين (Photo/Foto/صورة: Aly Hazza'a/علي هزاع)

5 *Tahrir Newspaper: Liars*
(Photo/Foto/صورة: Rowan El Shimi/روان الشيمي from the Flickr album/aus dem Flickr-Album/من ألبوم على موقع فليكر تحت عنوان *Kasr El Einy Street Street Battle*, Dec. 18, 2011)

6 "*Masked Avenger*"
(by Brazilian cartoonist Carlos Latuff, posted on Twitter/von dem brasilianischen Cartoonist Carlos Latuff, auf Twitter geteilt/لرسام الكاريكاتير البرازيلي كارلوس لطوف, Jan. 11, 2012)

7 Graffiti by/von El Teneen/جرافيتي التنين
Tahrir Square, Feb. 10, 2012

8 *U.S. Aid to Egypt*
(posted by Ganzeer on his blog/gepostet von Ganzeer auf seinem Blog/نشرها جنزير في مدونته Dec. 20, 2011)

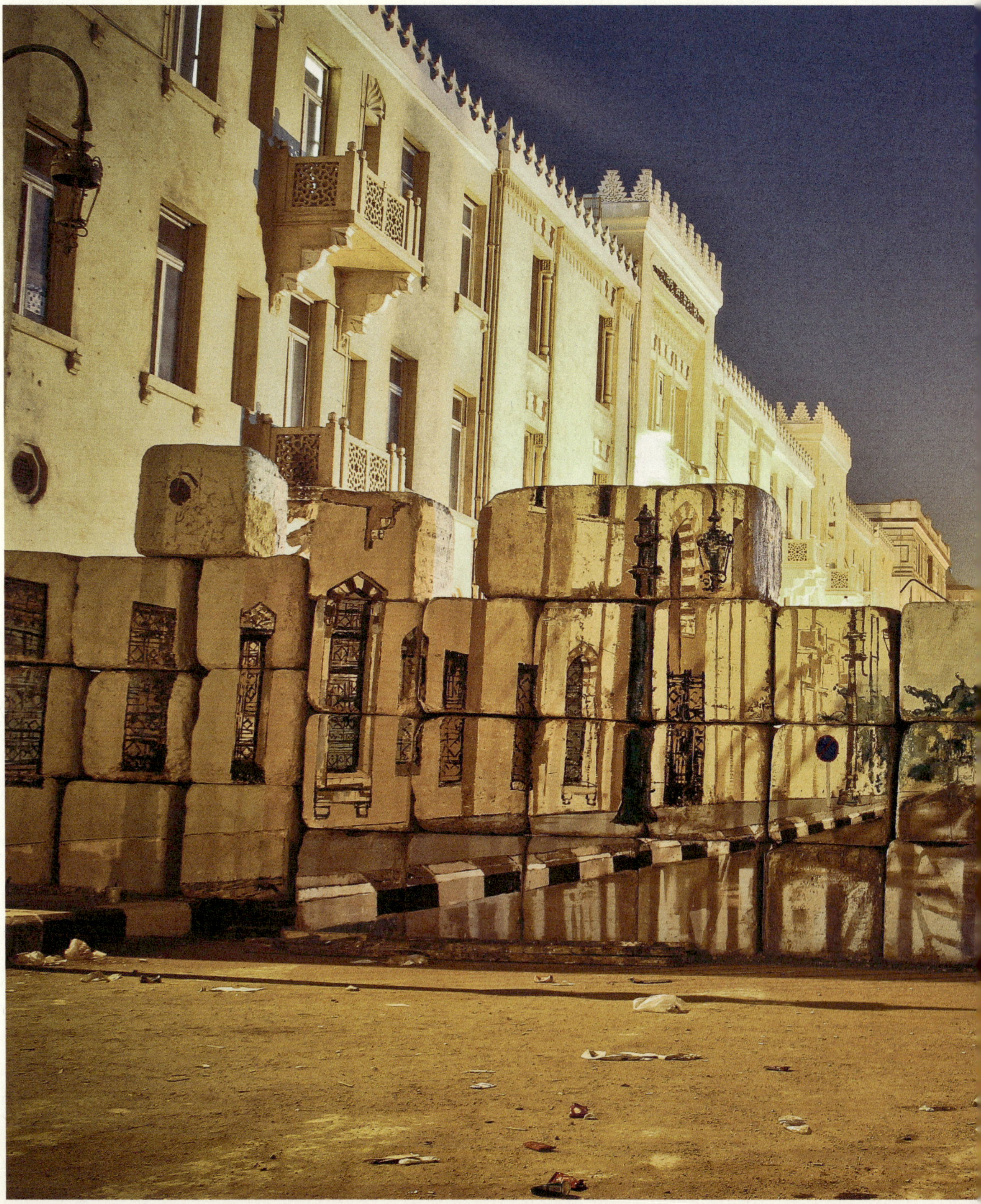

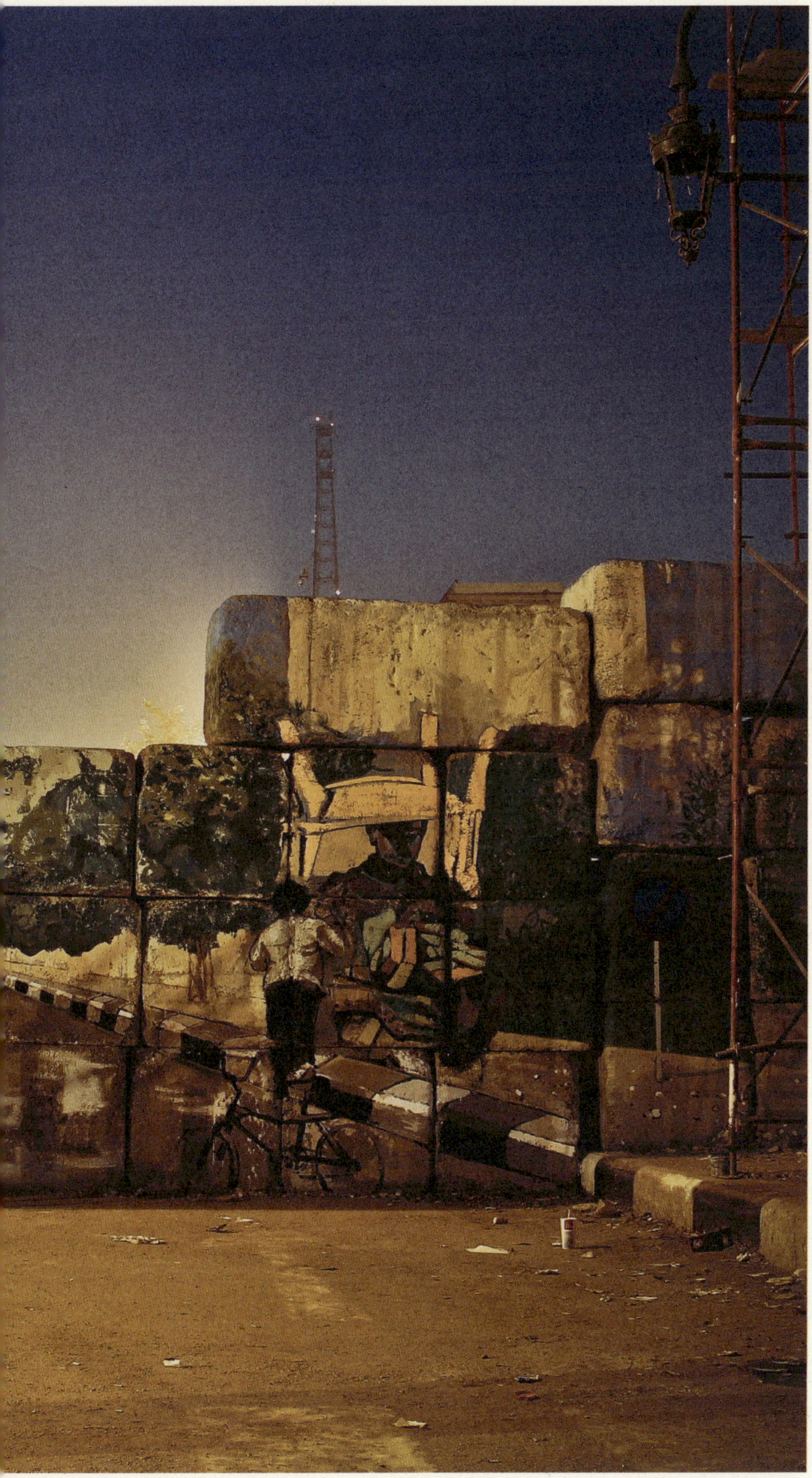

In December 2011, following clashes between the police and protesters on different occasions, various walls were erected in downtown Cairo around Tahrir Square to keep protesters out of the Ministry of the Interior, Parliament, and Cabinet buildings (some popular protest sites). Reactions to these walls varied, but protesters continued to overcome them. Two walls were taken down, stone by stone, by the protesters, while others were painted over by artists to look like open streets, to remind passers-by of the real meaning of these concrete structures.

(Rowan El Shimi)

Nach Zusammenstößen zwischen der Polizei und Demonstranten wurden Ende Dezember 2011 in der Kairoer Innenstadt nahe des Tahrir-Platzes mehrere Mauern errichtet, um die Protestierenden vom Innenministerium, dem Parlament und den Kabinettsgebäuden – beliebten Protestorten – fernzuhalten. Die Demonstranten gingen ganz unterschiedlich mit den Mauern um, haben sie aber immer wieder überwunden. Zwei der Mauern haben sie Stein für Stein abgetragen, andere wiederum haben Künstler so bemalt, dass eine Illusion des Straßenverlaufs dahinter erzeugt wird. Mithilfe der Perspektivmalerei hat man die Betonkonstruktion durchbrochen – eine symbolische Form des Widerstands.

(Rowan El Shimi)

أُنشئت في نهاية ديسمبر 2011 بالقرب من ميدان التحرير في وسط القاهرة العديد من الأسوار الجدارية حول وزارة الداخلية والبرلمان ومجلس الوزراء، بعد تكرر المصادمات بين الشرطة والمحتجين، أملاً بإبقاء المحتجين بعيدين عن أماكنهم المفضلة للتظاهر. اختلف تعامل المتظاهرين مع الجدران، حيث قاموا في كثير من الأحيان بتحطيمها. كما قاموا بتفكيك إثنين منهم حجراً حجراً، بينما قام فنانون بالرسم على جدران أخرى لتبدو وكأنها إمتدادٌ للشارع ذاته. استخدم الفنانون تقنية الرسم المنظوري للتغلب على الجدران الإسمنتية كوسيلة احتجاج رمزية.

(روان الشيمي)

Photo / Foto / صورة: Mosa'ab Elshamy / مصعب الشامي
from the flickr album / aus dem Flickr-Album / من ألبوم
Downtown Walls على موقع فليكر تحت عنوان, Mar. 12, 2012

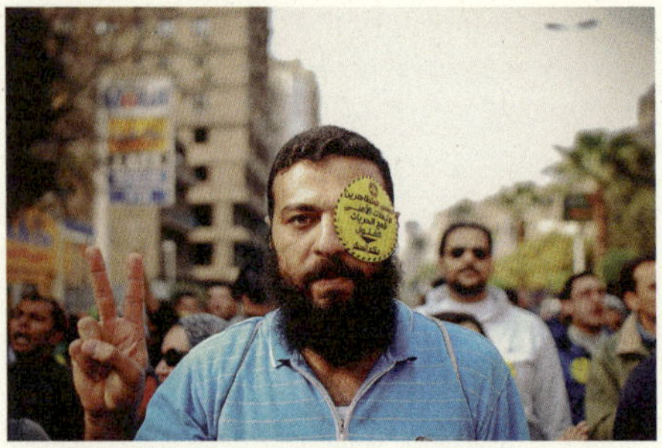

DSC_3946.jpg
A salafi protester covers one of his eyes with a replica eye patch in solidarity with the many protesters who lost their eyes during the clashes.
Taken on November 25, 2011, with a Nikon D80
Der Biege added this photo to his favorites.
(7 months ago)

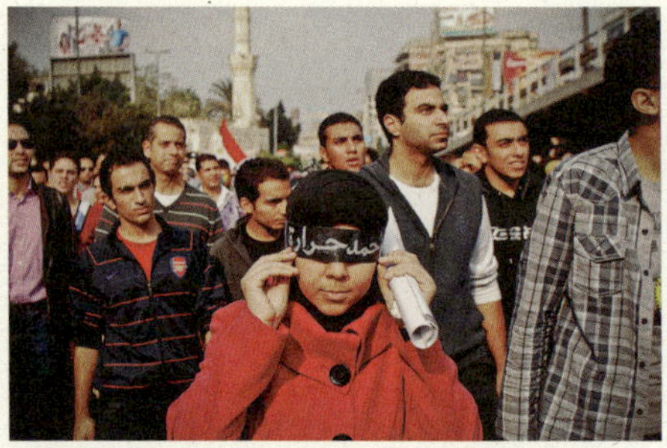

DSC_4011.jpg
A protester covers her eyes with a blindfold that claims the name of Ahmed Harara, a protester who lost an eye on January 28 during the early days of revolution, and the other eye on November 19 after the recent clashes; thus becoming a symbol and hero to many.
Taken on November 25, 2011, with a Nikon D80
owise abu-zaid, kaylangeiger, Muiz_, and 1 other people added this photo to their favorites.

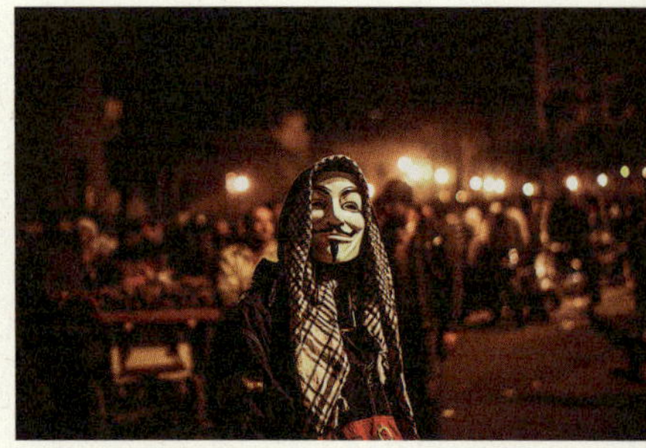

IMG_9120.jpg
A protester wears an Anonymous mask, echoing the popular uprisings in Wall Street and around the world
Taken on November 21, 2011, with a Canon EOS 550D
gordon_ladds, ABajooka, and 144 other people added this photo to their favorites.

EJ Images (20 months ago)
Very dramatic shot.

Sven Loach (20 months ago)
Terrible to hear about the deaths and injuries. Be safe.

PittmanMinnie (20 months ago | reply)
my co-worker's mom makes $75/hr on the laptop. She has been fired for 9 months but last month her income was $7774 just working on the laptop for a few hours. Read about it on this web site CalmCash. com

leogets_Miami (20 months ago)
great photo !!!!

napitip (20 months ago | reply)
Pin 25fc025b

Alan Artemio (20 months ago | reply)
Nice!!

Strong image!

PUAROT (20 months ago | reply)
Una toma espectacular !

Rich Byham (20 months ago | reply)
Great capture!

__Tristan__ (20 months ago | reply)
Zeitgeist.... Zeitgeist. A wonderful pieture of the time being.

4:01a.m Productions (20 months ago)
While you were sleeping, Halliburton poisoned water for millions of people...
This is probably the biggest crime against humanity...
www.youtube.com/watch?v=4xIyhx-zl0U

sho3333 (20 months ago | reply)
a strange picture!

orange hill (20 months ago | reply)
I like this pic so much – great photo!!
We do not forgive, we do not forget...

Alexei Solha (20 months ago | reply)
Congrats on the photo!

New .Trev (20 months ago | reply)
great shot! Check me out: blog / tumblr / twitter

Alex Muller (20 months ago | reply)
Que siniestro... me ha sacado una sonrisa :). Fantástico.

54StorminWillyGJ54 (20 months ago | reply)
Interesting capture

itsthecolleenlife (19 months ago)
Damn, that's a good shot.

Tetley T (17 months ago | reply)
Great shot!

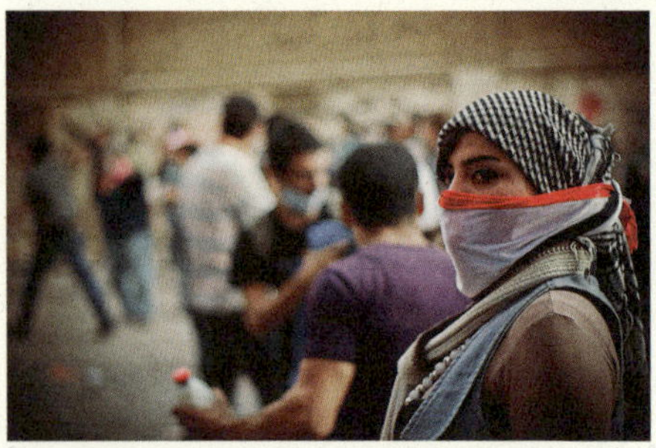

IMG_7922.jpg
Muiz_, Yann Beauson, cheri lucas., and 19 other people added this photo to their favorites.
Taken on November 22, 2011, with a Canon EOS 550D

Tetley T (17 months ago)
Great shot!

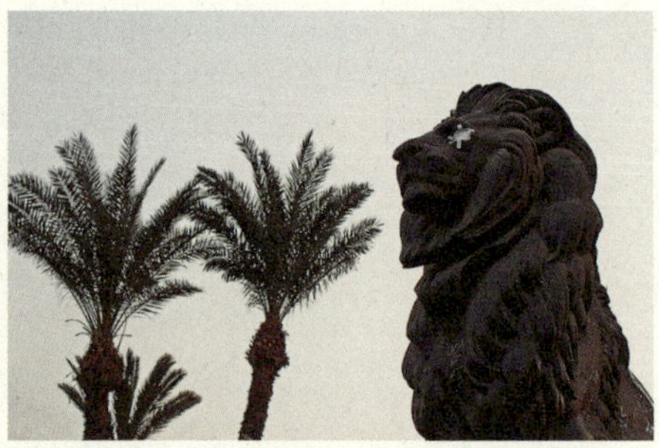

Ahmed Harara the Lionheart
In reference to the many protesters who lost their eyes to rubber bullets aimed directly at their eyes, protest supporters gave the famous Tahrir lion statue a solidarity eye-patch.
Taken on November 25, 2011, with a Canon EOS 550D
RuqayaIzzidien, moftasa, yasminef, and 14 other people added this photo to their favorites.

Éothain (20 months ago)
Wow

Khaled.Galal (19 months ago)
Fantastic :)

BlueisCoool (19 months ago)
Very nice work – congrats on being explored !

MarkoRey (19 months ago | reply)
Nice picture! Congrats on explore, you do deserve it!

M.A.J Photography (19 months ago | reply)
Lovely shot ~! I enjoyed it !

Chocolate Lens Boy (17 months ago | reply)
A very powerful and important photograph in history.
Mabrook wa shukran

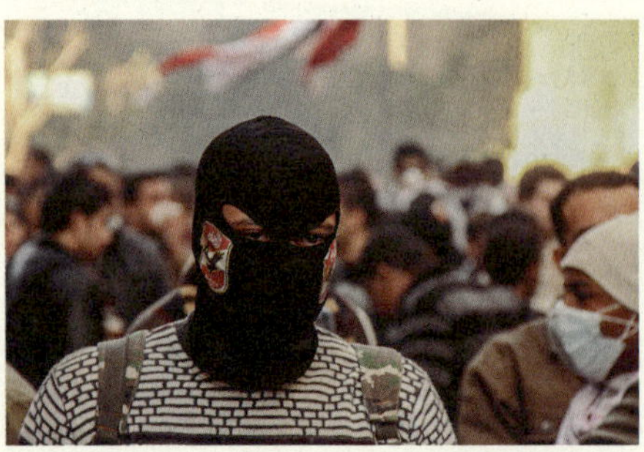

IMG_9914.jpg
Taken on January 26, 2013, with a Canon EOS 60D

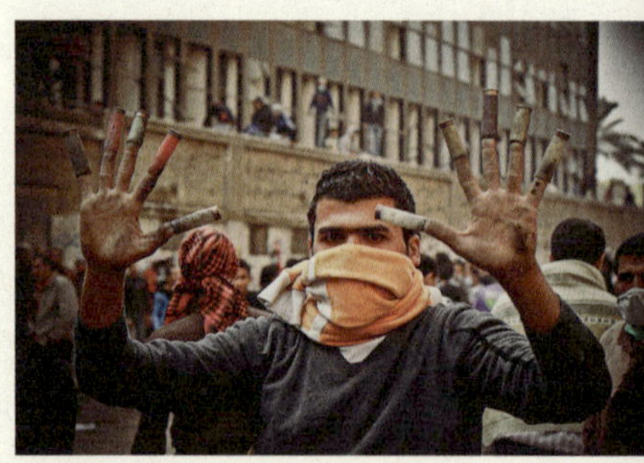

IMG_9139.jpg
Taken on November 21, 2011, with a Canon EOS 550D
HH nsani Yardım Vakfı/TURKEY, and 4 other people added this photo to their favorites.

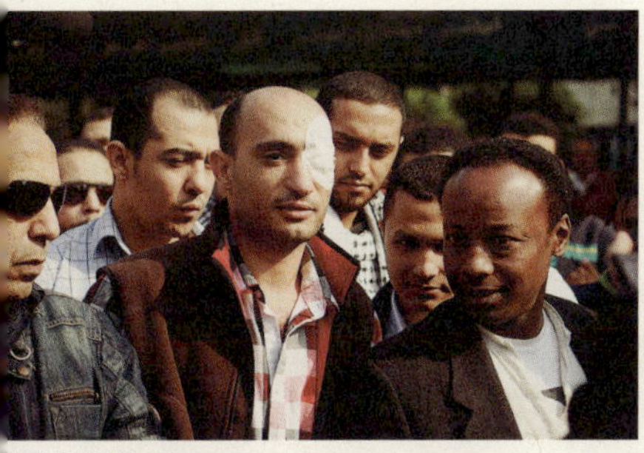

MG_8227.jpg
hmed Harara who lost each eye on Jan28 and Nov19
espectively participates in the march.
aken on November 25, 2011, with a Canon EOS 550D
agliardo_, eimannosho, Muiz_, and 1 other people
dded this photo to their favorites.

uiz_ (20 months ago)
habibi a5e Harara

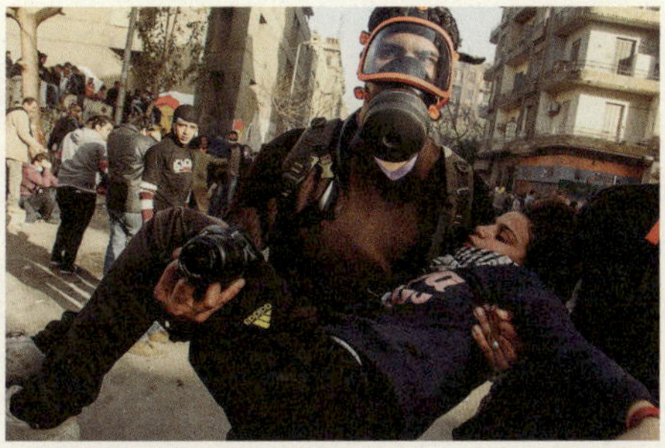

IMG_9858.jpg
Taken on January 26, 2013, with a Canon EOS 60D
eimannosho, HebaTography, and maged.gabra added
this photo to their favorites.

torontolimousineservices (6 months ago)
Nice to see the man saving the woman, instead of beating her, raping her,
or beheading her because she is a woman.
More power to Morsi's opposition. I hope you guys kick Morsi out.
Good Luck

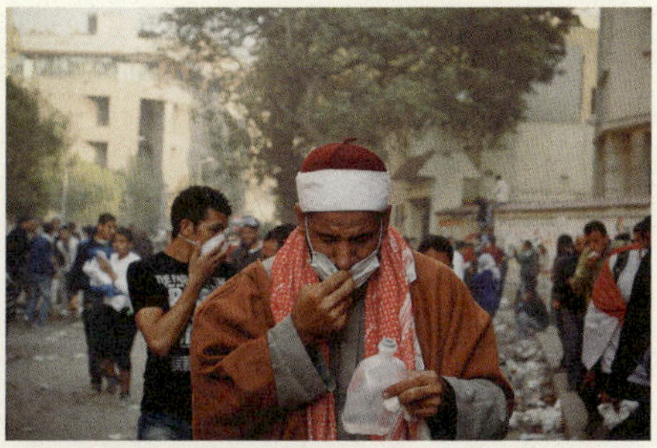

IMG_9380.jpg
Azhar sheikh trying to breathe after a tear gas attack
launched on protesters in Mohamed Mahmoud street.
Taken on November 21, 2011, with a Canon EOS 550D
Muiz_ and Wild_atHeart added this photo to their
favorites.

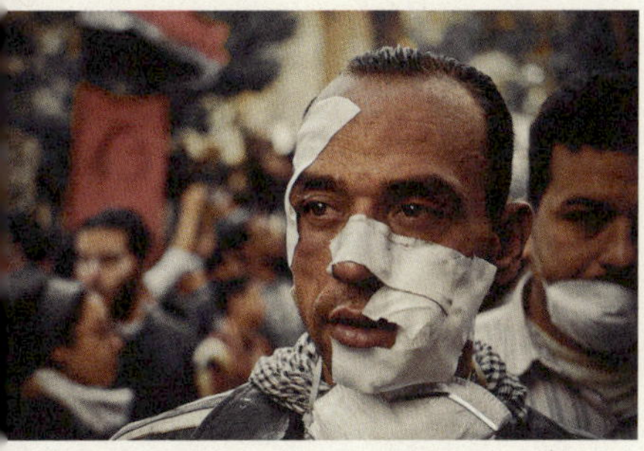

SC_3086.jpg
aken on November 21, 2011, with a Nikon D80
H nsani Yard m Vakf/TURKEY, and 3 other people
dded this photo to their favorites.

Lion ♫ (20 months ago | reply)
ng

tley T (17 months ago)
eat shot!

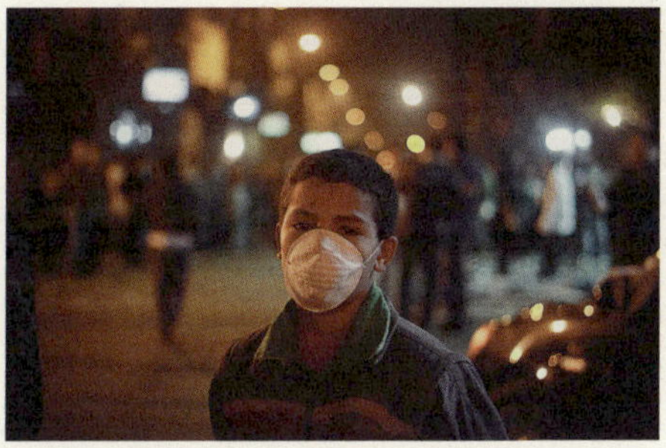

IMG_8148.jpg
A young boy stands vigilant on one of the entrances to
Tahrir square, as he helps in committees that check
people's IDs and bags to ensure everyone's safety.
Taken on November 23, 2011, with a Canon EOS 550D
Muiz_, Sherif Hosni, AviioTM, and 2 other people added
this photo to their favorites.

Corr@do (20 months ago)
molto bella!

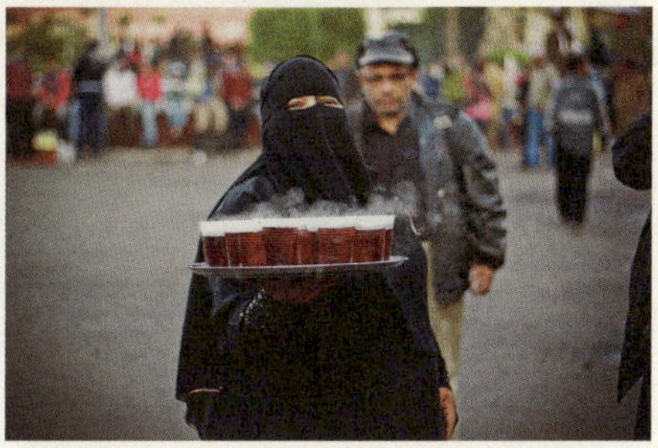

IMG_8866.jpg
A woman sells tea in Tahrir Square
Taken on November 20, 2011, with a Canon EOS 550D
AviioTM, hs64, med mtl, Muiz_, and 22 other people
added this photo to their favorites.

nofrills (20 months ago)
Exactly looks like this Japanese ASCII art.
(^-^)_旦~~ (Here's your tea.)
Or rather:
(^-^)_旦旦旦旦旦旦~~~
Stay strong, safe and warm.

Muiz_ (20 months ago)
7elwe! – walah miss this red shay ;(
Endless Love Photography (20 months ago)
Congrats on Explore (20-11-2011) !!!!!
Very interesting and Well deserved shot !!
Thanks for sharing,
Abdul. :)

NikiC55 [deleted] (20 months ago)
Interesting ...

Paulgil (20 months ago)
Great Shot!

Wild_atHeart (11 months ago)
Epic :D

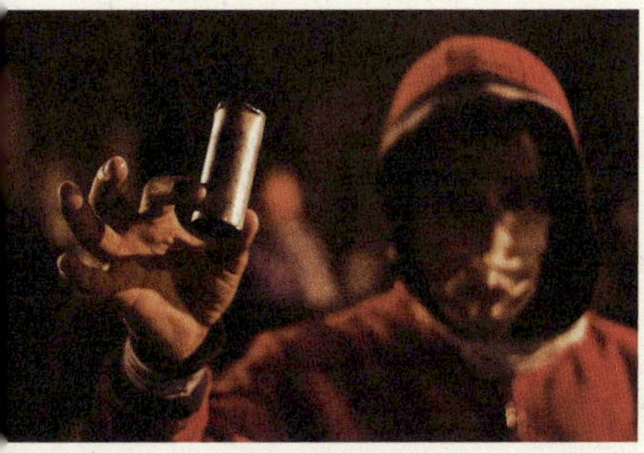

MG_8282.jpg
aken on November 19, 2011, with a Canon EOS 550D
uqayaIzzidien, R.Meyer-Brede, stahran, and 5 other
eople added this photo to their favorites.

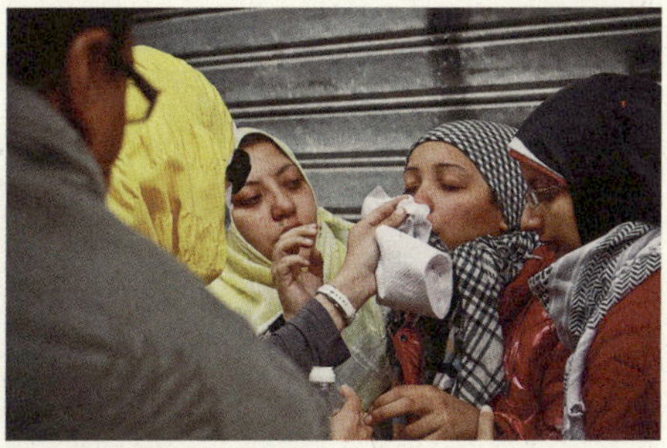

IMG_9257.jpg
Taken on November 21, 2011, with a Canon EOS 550D
Muiz_ added this photo to their favorites.
(20 months ago)

www.flickr.com/photos/mosaaberising/sets/72157628158693001/

٧٧ Lilian Wagdy, *Friday of Anger... Streets and Memories*, 2011
Photographs Collected via Facebook

Lilian Wagdy, *Friday of Anger... Streets and Memories*, 2011
Fotografien, gesammelt auf Facebook

ليليان وجدي، جمعة الغضب... شوارع وذكريات،
2011 صور من على موقع فيسبوك

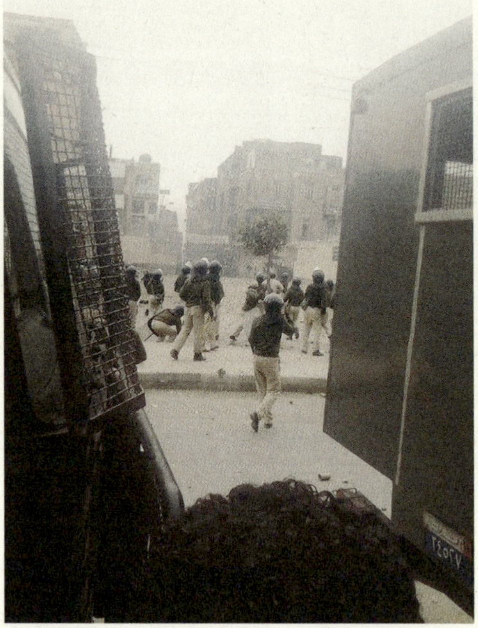

Kafr Al Sheikh. Heavy CSF presence near the railway station on January 28/Große Präsenz der Central Security Forces (CSF) nahe des Bahnhofes am 28. Januar (Photo/Foto: Mustafa Gafaar)/
كفر الشيخ. حضور مكثف لقوات الأمن المركزي بالقرب من محطة القطار، 28 يناير.
(مصطفى جعفر)

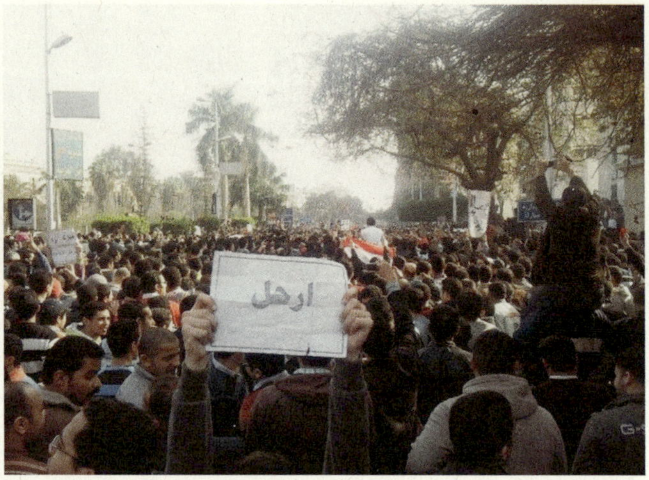

Tanta (Gharbeia). Protesters carrying a banner that reads “Leave” as people march towards Tanta’s First Police Station/Demonstranten halten ein Transparent mit der Aufschrift “Verschwinde” während ihres Marsches zur Polizeihauptwache von Tanta (Photo/Foto: Mohammad Abul Azm)/
طنطا (الغربية). متظاهر يحمل لافتة مكتوب عليها "إرحل" في أثناء تحرك الجموع في مسيرة متجهة إلى قسم أول طنطا
(محمد أبو العزم)

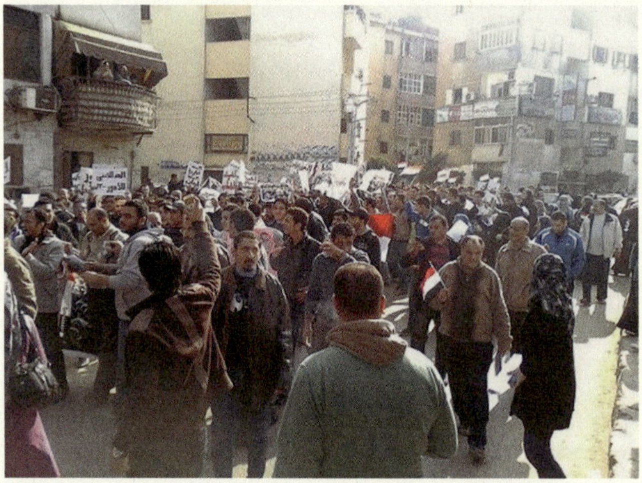

Mansoura (Daqahliya). A march passing by Al Nasr Mosque and the City Hall in Mansoura on the Friday of Anger/Eine Demonstration entlang der Al-Nasr-Moschee und dem Rathaus in Mansoura am Freitag des Zorns (Source unknown/Quelle unbekannt)/
المنصورة (الدقهلية). مسيرة تمر بمسجد النصر والمحافظة في المنصورة يوم جمعة الغضب.

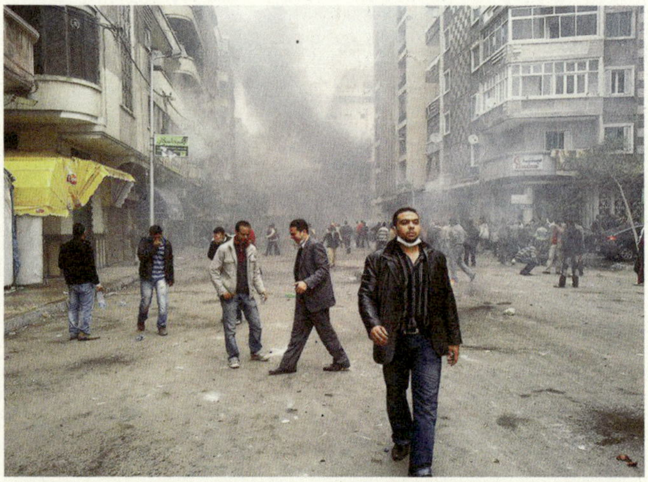

Alexandria. Protesters on January 28 near Al Qaed Ibrahim Mosque/Demonstranten am 28. Januar nahe der Al-Qaed-Ibrahim-Moschee (Photo/Foto: Mohammed Samir Shabaan)/
الإسكندرية. متظاهرون يوم 28 يناير بالقرب من القائد إبراهيم. (محمد سمير شعبان)

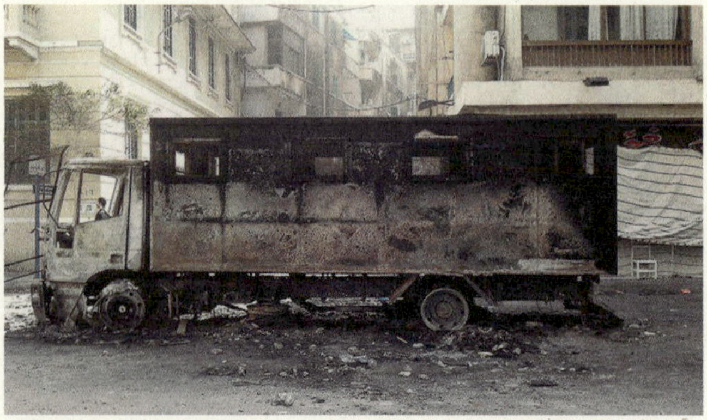

Alexandria. CSF truck burnt by protesters on January 28 near Al Qaed Ibrahim Mosque/Lastwagen der CSF von Demonstranten am 28. Januar in der Nähe der Al-Qaed-Ibrahim-Moschee in Brand gesetzt (Photo/Foto: Mohammed Samir Shabaan)/
الإسكندرية. عربات الأمن المركزي التي حرقها المتظاهرون يوم 28 يناير بالقرب من القائد إبراهيم. (محمد سمير شعبان)

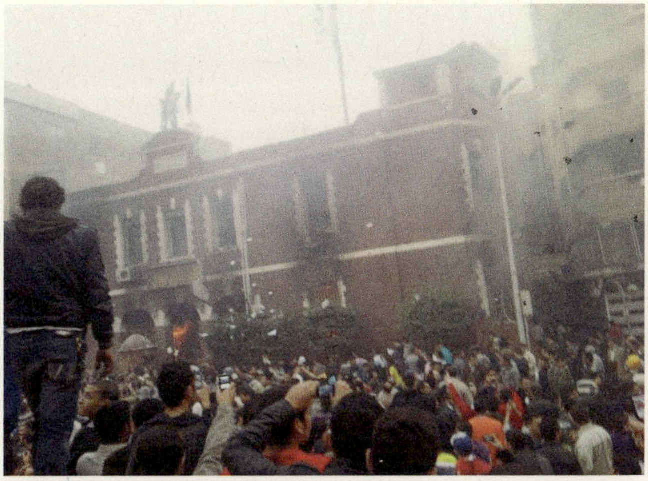

Tanta (Gharbeia). Protester carrying a banner that reads "Leave" as people march towards Tanta's First Police Station. / Demonstranten halten ein Transparent mit der Aufschrift "Verschwinde" während ihres Marsches zur Polizeihauptwache von Tanta (Photo / Foto: Mohammad Abul Azm) /
طنطا (الغربية). متظاهر يحمل لافتة مكتوب عليها "إرحل" في أثناء تحرك الجموع في مسيرة متجهة إلى قسم أول طنطا. (محمد أبو العزم)

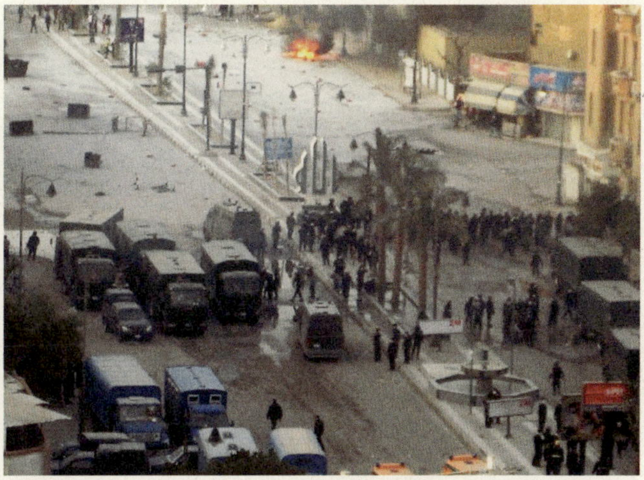

Suez. Protesters clashing with police @ Arba'een Square / Zusammenstöße von Demonstranten und Polizei @ Arba'een-Platz (Source unknown / Quelle unbekannt) /
السويس. اشتباكات بين المتظاهرين والشرطة في ميدان الأربعين. (المصدر غير معروف)

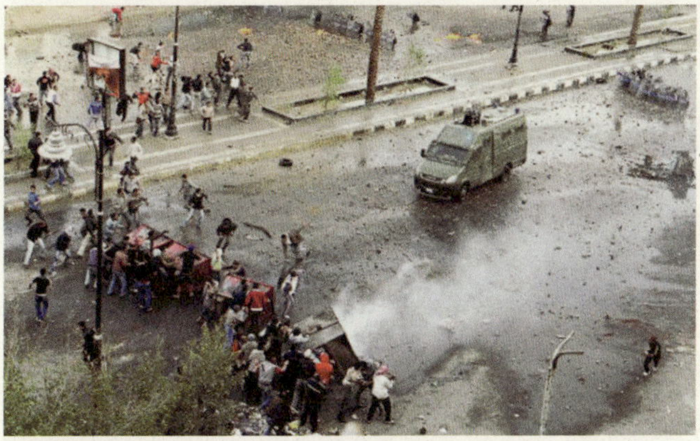

Suez. Protesters clashing with police @ Arba'een Square / Zusammenstöße von Demonstranten und Polizei @ Arba'een-Platz (Source unknown / Quelle unbekannt) /
السويس. اشتباكات بين المتظاهرين والشرطة في ميدان الأربعين. (المصدر غير معروف)

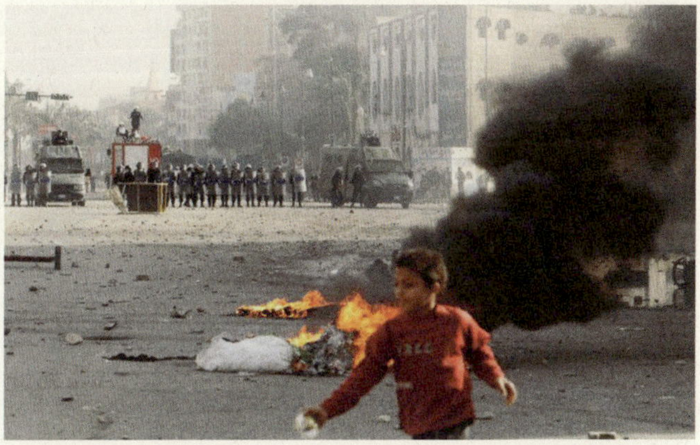

Suez. Protesters clashing with police @ Arba'een Square / Zusammenstöße von Demonstranten und Polizei @ Arba'een-Platz (Source unknown / Quelle unbekannt) /
السويس. اشتباكات بين المتظاهرين والشرطة في ميدان الأربعين. (المصدر غير معروف)

"January 28, 2011 is a pivotal day in the chronicles of the Egyptian Revolution. Millions of Egyptians flood the streets to bring down a regime that has suppressed them for over three decades. *Friday of Anger . . . Streets and Memories* is a project that seeks to pay tribute to this great day and to the citizens who contributed to the documentation of its events: not just in Cairo, but everywhere; not just in Tahrir Square, but in the streets and alleyways as well. In short, it is a publication that celebrates the role citizen journalists played in writing the history of this decisive day in the revolution."

(Lilian Wagdy)

(Produced within the framework of the Alternative News Agency II workshop, Contemporary Image Collective, Cairo)

„Der 28. Januar 2011 ist ein Wendepunkt in den Ereignissen der ägyptischen Revolution. Millionen von Ägyptern überschwemmten die Straßen, um ein Regime zu stürzen, von dem sie mehr als drei Jahrzehnte unterdrückt worden waren. Das Projekt *Friday of Anger.. Streets and Memories* sucht diesen großen Tag und die Bürger, die an der Dokumentation der Ereignisse beteiligt waren, zu würdigen: Bürger nicht nur in Kairo, sondern überall; ... nicht nur auf dem Tahrir-Platz, sondern auch in den Straßen und Gassen. Kurz, es ist ein Projekt, das die Rolle des partizipativen Journalismus an der Geschichtsschreibung dieses historischen Tages der Revolution feiert."

(Lilian Wagdy)

(Entstand im Rahmen des Alternative News Agency II Workshops, Contemporary Image Collective, Kairo)

"إن يوم 28 يناير 2011 هو نقطة تحول في أحداث الثورة المصرية. فلقد خرج ملايين المصريين إلى الشارع لكي يسقطوا نظاماً، عانوا منه لمدة تعدت الثلاثين عام. يهدف مشروع جمعة الغضب، شوارع وذكريات إلى توثيق هذا اليوم التاريخي وتكريم المواطنين الذين شاركوا في توثيق هذا اليوم: ليس فقط في القاهرة ولكن في كل مكان... ليس فقط في ميدان التحرير ولكن في الشوراع والحواري. باختصار، فإن هذا المشروع يهدف إلى الإحتفاء بدور الصحافة الشعبية في كتابة تاريخ هذا اليوم المصيري في الثورة."

(ليليان وجدي)

(أنتج هذا العمل لـ CIC project Alternative News Agency II القاهرة)

Tags: Activism | Egypt | labor | Left | Photography | Visualizing Dissent | workers

Ma3lesh, I'll go back again to the issue of photography . . .

I gave recently some talks about the Mahalla Uprising, among labor and progressive circles in the Bay Area, as part of the effort (tremendously helped by friends in California and NYC I'm grateful for) to spread the word about what's going on back in Egypt among the activist circles here.. I always request from the organizers of the event to bring a projector if possible, so as to play a slideshow of pix from the Mahalla Uprising as well as other photos of demos and strikes in Egypt to accompany my presentation. Why? Because again spreading the image I believe is just as important as spreading the word.. I may sound like a broken record since I already posted few times about this before, but I'll keep stressing it.. Whatever event you are holding, whatever protest you are staging, please take a digital camera with you and snap a pic or two of the event.

(If you can take videos too that would be even greater). It's important for other people around the world to "see" what you are doing with their own eyes, instead of just "hearing" or "reading" about it. People need to see with their own eyes both police brutality and social resistance . . . Struggles spread by the domino effect, as Mahalla proved since December 2006, and as the Palestinian intifada proved in 2000.. When a revolution (or what the Imperialists and the Arab regimes call "instability") breaks out in one country, it hardly stays within its boundaries—and surely the coming Egyptian revolution won't defy what has almost become a natural law in politics as proven in every single uprising in the last century. Spreading the image contributes tremendously as a catalyst in this process. A victory for the workers in one sector will inspire others within the same sector and outside to follow suit. Showing photos and videos of those victories helps in get-ting the message across to the workers: "They have done it over there.. You can do it over here!" Spending hours trying to convince someone with the ability of workers to self organize and bring about a smashing defeat against the state if they act collectively, could just be narrowed down to few minutes if they saw for example Nasser Nouri's photos of the Mahalla Dec 2006 strike . . .

You can talk for hours about the revolutionary potential of the masses in the urban towns to overthrow their shackles of fear and confront the Mubarak's dictatorship at times of rising social struggle, without the help of the American tanks . . . or you can simply show whoever you are talking with these photos from Mahalla, also taken by the brave Nasser Nouri last April . . .

Revolutionary activists involved in consciousness raising efforts, propaganda or agitation among the workers anywhere HAVE to do their best to visualize what they are talking about or arguing for. At the same time, there is an immense need for these images to reach millions of other workers and activists around the world.. That could be very inspiring for the latter, as well as a catalyst to generate more support for those facing the onslaught . . . If you have photos of demos, strikes, factory occupations, or whatever theme that is directly related to the social struggle in your country, please go ahead and upload them online . . . don't leave them on your hard drive.. This is the memory of the class, and we shouldn't lose it coz the ruling classes always do their best to distort or delete it . . .

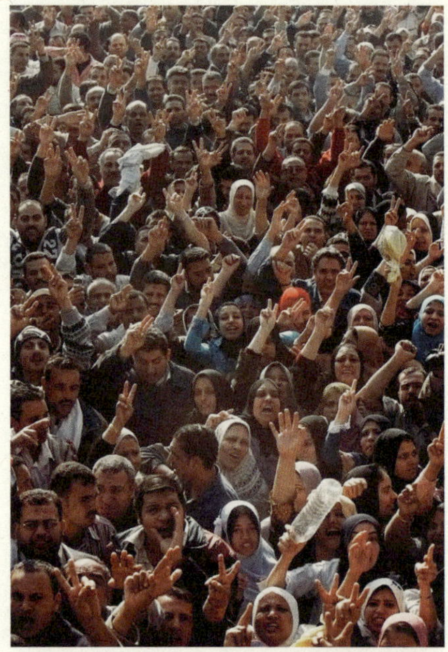

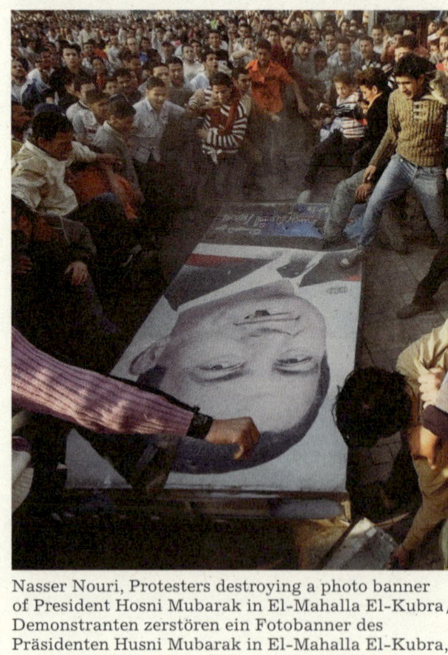

Nasser Nouri, Protesters destroying a photo banner of President Hosni Mubarak in El-Mahalla El-Kubra / Demonstranten zerstören ein Fotobanner des Präsidenten Husni Mubarak in El-Mahalla El-Kubra, Apr. 7, 2008 /
ناصـر نوري، متظاهرون يمزقون صـورة للرئيس حسني مبـارك في المحلـة الكبرى، ٧ أبريـل 2008

www.arabawy.org/2008/05/08/the-revolution-will-be-flickrized

Ma3lesh, gut, ich komme auf die Frage der Fotografie zurück...

Als Teil der Bemühungen (mit enormer Hilfe von Freunden in Kalifornien und NYC, für die ich sehr dankbar bin), unter den Aktivisten hier zu verbreiten, was in Ägypten vor sich geht, habe ich in letzter Zeit einige Vorträge zum Aufstand in Malhalla vor Arbeitern und progressiven Kreisen der Bay Area gehalten. Ich bitte die Organisatoren der Veranstaltungen immer darum, wenn möglich einen Projektor bereitzustellen, damit ich eine Vorführung der Bilder vom Aufstand in Malhalla geben und auch Fotos anderer Demos und Streiks in Ägypten begleitend zu meinem Vortrag zeigen kann. Warum? Noch einmal, darum: Das Bild weiterzutragen ist, davon bin ich überzeugt, ebenso wichtig wie das Wort weiterzutragen. Vielleicht klinge ich wie eine gesprungene Schallplatte, da ich dazu ja schon ein paar Mal gepostet habe, aber ich will es doch weiterhin betonen. Was auch immer für eine Veranstaltung ihr abhaltet, welchen Protest auch immer ihr inszeniert, bitte nehmt eine Digitalkamera mit und schießt ein paar Bilder von der Veranstaltung. (Wenn ihr zusätzlich Videos machen könntet, wäre es sogar noch besser.) Es ist für andere Leute auf der ganzen Welt wichtig, mit eigenen Augen „sehen" zu können, was ihr unternehmt; nicht nur davon zu „hören" oder zu „lesen". Die Menschen müssen mit eigenen Augen sowohl die Polizeigewalt als auch den gesellschaftlichen Widerstand sehen... Kämpfe verbreiten sich durch den Dominoeffekt, wie Malhalla seit Dezember 2006 beweist und wie es die palästinensische Intifada im Jahr 2000 bewiesen hat. Wenn eine Revolution (oder das, was die Imperialisten und das arabische Regime „Instabilität" nennen) in einem Land ausbricht, bleibt sie selten innerhalb dessen Grenzen – und sicherlich wird die bevorstehende ägyptische Revolution nicht dem trotzen, was schon fast ein von jedem einzelnen Aufstand des letzten Jahrhunderts bewiesenes politisches Naturgesetz geworden ist. Das Bild weiterzutragen befördert diesen Prozess als Katalysator gewaltig. Ein Sieg für die Arbeiter in einer Branche wird andere in derselben oder einer anderen Branche anregen, dem Beispiel zu folgen. Bilder und Videos von diesen Siegen zu zeigen hilft, die Botschaft unter die Arbeitern zu bringen: „Die haben es dort geschafft... Ihr könnt es hier schaffen!" Die Stunden, die aufgewendet werden müssen, um jemanden von der Fähigkeit der Arbeiter zur Selbstorganisation zu überzeugen und dazu, eine gewaltige Niederwerfung des Staates zu bewerkstelligen, wenn sie nur zusammen agieren, könnten zu ein paar Minuten schrumpfen, wenn zum Beispiel Nasser Nouris Fotos vom Streik 2006 in Malhalla gezeigt würden.

Man kann stundenlang über dieses revolutionäre Potenzial der Massen in den Städten reden, ihre Fesseln aus Angst abwerfen und Mubaraks Diktatur in den Zeiten des wachsenden sozialen Kampfes die Stirn bieten zu können – ohne die Hilfe amerikanischer Panzer... Oder man kann einfach jenem, mit dem man gerade spricht, diese Bilder aus Malhalla zeigen, ebenso vom tapferen Nasser Nouri im letzten April fotografiert...

Aktivisten der Revolution, die beteiligt daran sind, das Bewusstsein der Arbeiter überall zu schärfen, die Propaganda und Agitation unter ihnen verbreiten, MÜSSEN ihr Bestes geben, um zu visualisieren, worüber sie reden oder wofür sie eintreten. Zugleich gibt es einen großen Bedarf an diesen Bildern, um unzählige andere Arbeiter und Aktivisten auf der ganzen Welt zu erreichen. Für Letztere könnten sie sehr inspirierend sein und zugleich als Katalysator dienen, um für jene, die den Angriffen ausgesetzt sind, mehr Unterstützung hervorzubringen. Wenn ihr Fotos von Demos, Streiks, Werksbesetzungen oder von anderen Motiven und Themen habt, die in direkter Verbindung zu den gesellschaftlichen Auseinandersetzungen in eurem Land stehen, dann, bitte, ladet sie hoch, stellt sie ins Netz... Lasst sie nicht auf eurer Festplatte... Sie sind das Gedächtnis der Klasse, und wir sollten es nicht verlieren, denn die herrschenden Klassen geben immer ihr Bestes, es zu verzerren oder zu löschen.

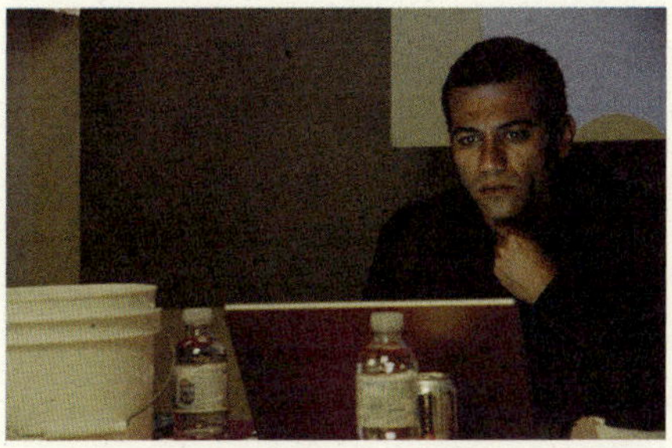

عذراً، سوف أعود لموضوع الفوتوغرافيا مرة أخرى...

كنت تكلمت في الماضي عن الاحتجاجات في المحلة في الدوائر التقدمية المهتمة بأمور العمال في سان فرانسيسكو والمناطق المحيطة بها، وهذا في إطار محاولة العمل على نشر ما يحدث في مصر في دوائر النشطاء (ولقد حصلت على دعم ومساعدة من أصدقائي في كاليفورنيا ونيويورك وأنا ممتن لذلك). دائماً أطلب من المنظمين إحضار جهاز بروجيكتور إن أمكن الأمر، لكي أعرض مجموعة صور من احتجاجات المحلة بالإضافة إلى صور أخرى لمظاهرات وإضرابات في مصر، تصاحب كلمتي. لماذا؟ لأن نشر الصورة هو مهم كنشر الخبر أو الكلمة. لن أتوقف عن التأكيد على أهمية هذا الأمر حتى وإن كان في كلامي تكرار لأنني كتبت أكثر من مرة عن هذا الموضوع. حاول دائماً أن تأخذ كاميرا رقمية معك سواء كنت منظم لحدث أو ذاهب لمظاهرة، والتقط صورة أو اثنين للحدث. (إن استطعت تصوير مقاطع فيديو يكون هذا أفضل). فمن المهم أن "يرى" الآخرين حول العالم ما تفعله، يروه بأعينهم، فضلاً عن "سماعه" فحسب أو "القراءة" عنه. يحتاج الناس أن يرو بأعينهم وحشية الشرطة والمقاومة المجتمعية. فالنضال ينتشر مفعوله مثل قطع الدومينو المتساقطة، هذا ما أثبتته المحلة عام 2006 والانتفاضة الفلسطينية عام 2000. عندما تنطلق ثورة (أو موجة عدم استقرار كما يسميها الإمبرياليون والنظم العربية) في بلد ما، قلما تبقى محصورة داخل حدود هذه الدولة، ولن تشذ الثورة المصرية القادمة عن هذه القاعدة الطبيعية في السياسة، فلقد أثبت كل احتجاج حدث في القرن المنصرم هذه القاعدة. ونشر الصورة يساهم بشكل كبير كمحفز في هذه العملية. فانتصار العمال في قطاع ما سيُلهم عمال نفس القطاع في مكان آخر للسير على نفس الخطى. فنشر الصور ومقاطع الفيديو التي تعرض هذه الانتصارات، يساعد على توصيل الرسالة إلى العمال: "إذا كانوا قد نجحوا هناك، فنحن قادرون على النجاح هنا". ففضلاً عن إهدار ساعات في محاولة إقناع شخص ما بقدرة العمال على تنظيم أنفسهم بأنفسهم محققين بذلك نجاح ساحق في التغلب على الدولة في حالة تصرفهم بشكل جماعي، يمكنك توضيح هذه الفكرة في بضعة دقائق إذا رأى الناس مثلاً صور ناصر نوري من اعتصام المحلة عام 2006.

يمكنك التحدث لساعات عن القدرة الثورية الجمعية في المدن على تكسير قيود الخوف ليواجهوا ديكتاتورية مبارك في أوقات زيادة المقاومة المجتمعية، دون الحاجة إلى مساعدة الدبابات الأمريكية؛ أو يمكنك أن تعرض ببساطة لجمهورك هذه الصور من المحلة، من تصوير الشجاع ناصر نوري أيضاً في أبريل المنصرم.

على النشطاء الثوريين المهتمين بالتوعية أو الدعاية أو الحشد بين العمال في كل مكان، أن يبذلوا قصارى جهدهم على تحويل ما يتحدثون أو يدافعون عنه لمادة بصرية. وفي نفس الوقت هناك حاجة ماسّة لأن تصل هذه الصورة إلى الملايين من العمال والنشطاء حول العالم. قد يكون هذا ملهماً للنشطاء كما يساعد على الحشد لدعم من هم في المواجهة. إذا كان لديك صور لمظاهرات، اعتصامات، احتلال للمصانع أو أي حدث مرتبط بالنضال المجتمعي في بلدك، فأنا أطلب منك أن ترفعها على الإنترنت، لا تتركهم على جهازك. إنها ذكرى لهذه الطبقة، وعلينا أن لا نفقدها لأن الطبقات الحاكمة تبذل قصارى جهدها لتشويهها أو مسحها.

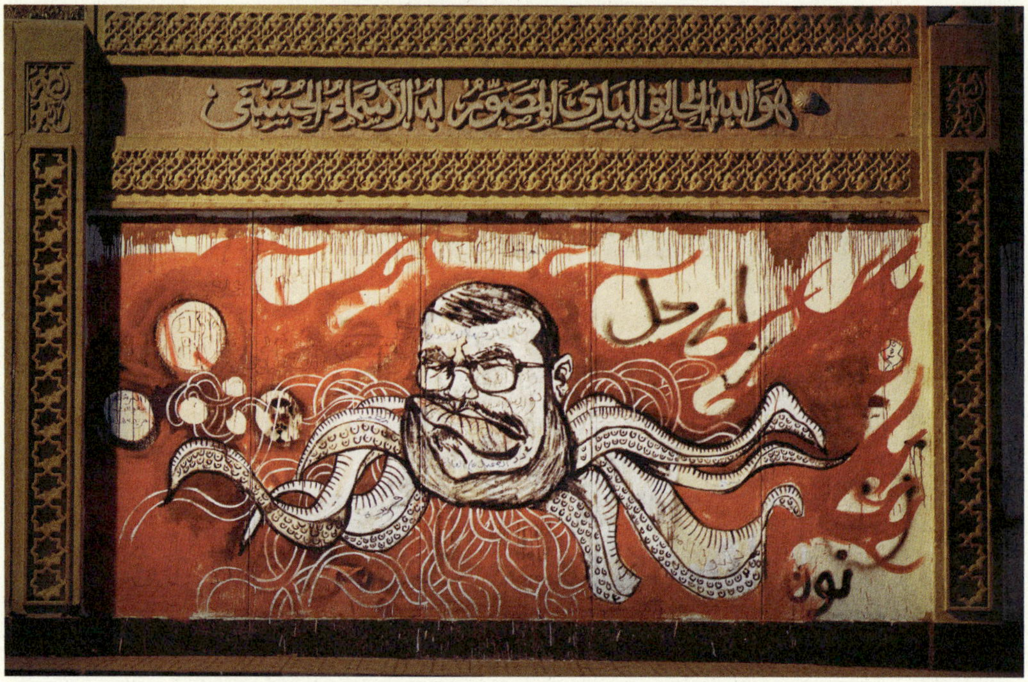

1

The streets of Cairo were turned into "familiar faces" by the revolution. From all sides, passers-by were visually confronted with graffiti, stickers, banners, and photos of faces.

Before the revolution, Mubarak's face had dominated the public space as an oversized symbol of power, but once the system had been called into question, it increasingly became a target for protesters and an object of ridicule. Now the portraits of the "martyrs" of the revolution and its major activists can be found on every wall. Thousands lost their lives on the street or were imprisoned—all represented vicariously by the faces of Khalid Said and Abdel Fattah. The eye patch, which is worn by so many of those blinded by the rubber bullets of the security forces, has become an iconic image of the revolution.

Mit der Revolution haben die Straßen in Kairo Gesichter bekommen. Von überall blicken Graffiti, Aufkleber, Transparente und Fotos von Gesichtern die Passanten an.

Vor der Revolution beherrschte das Gesicht Mubaraks als überdimensionierte Ikone der Macht den öffentlichen Raum, mit der Infragestellung des Systems jedoch wurde es immer mehr zur Zielscheibe des Protests und des Spotts. Jetzt finden sich die Konterfeis der „Märtyrer" der Revolution sowie der wichtigsten Aktivisten an allen Mauern wieder. Tausende verloren auf der Straße ihr Leben oder wurden inhaftiert – die Gesichter von Khalid Said und Abdel Fattah stehen stellvertretend für sie alle. Die Augenklappe, die so viele durch die Gummigeschosse der Sicherheitskräfte erblindete Menschen tragen, ist zu einem ikonischen Motiv dieser Revolution geworden.

أصبحت لشوارع القاهرة أوجه مع قيام الثورة. فمن كل مكان، ترى كعابر سبيل، رسومات الجرافيتي والملصقات واللافتات وصور لوجوه. كان وجه مبارك هو الصورة الطاغية في الأماكن العامة، حيث كان يطل كأيقونة ضخمة في كل مكان. وبعد أن أصبح مصير النظام غير معروف، تحولت صور مبارك إلى هدف للمتظاهرين وواجهة لسخريتهم. أما الآن فقد إنتشرت صور "شهداء" الثورة وصور أهم النشطاء على كل الجدران. خسر الكثير أرواحهم أو تم إعتقالهم في الشوارع، وأضحت صور خالد سيد وعبدالفتاح تذكاراً لهم. إنتشرت مظاهر أناس يحملون عصابة للعين، بسبب تعرضهم لرصاصات قوات الأمن المطاطية وفقدانهم لأعينهم، وأصبح ذلك المنظر موضوع رئيسي لكثير من صور ورسومات هذه الثورة.

---

1 *Anti-Morsi Graffiti Outside Presidential Palace* (Photo / Foto / صورة: Jonathan Rashad / جوناثان رشاد / from the Flickr album / aus dem Flickr-Album / من ألبوم على موقع فليكر تحت عنوان *Presidential Palace Sit-In*, Dec. 10, 2012)

2 *Mubarak = Tantawi* (Photo / Foto / صورة: Gigi Ibrahim, جيجي إبراهيم from the Flickr album / aus dem Flickr-Album *25 Jan 2012: Revolution Continues*, Jan. 25, 2011)

3 *Anti-Mubarak stencil in Nasr City* Text: Go! The people demand the removal of the regime. / Geh! Das Volk verlangt die Absetzung des Regimes. (Photo / Foto / صورة: Hossam el-Hamalawy / حسام الحملاوي, from the Flickr album / aus dem Flickr-Album / من ألبوم على موقع فليكر *Egyptian Street Art*, Feb. 27, 2011)

4 *Prosecute Mubarak* Text: He never went to court, July 8. / Er war nicht vor Gericht, 8. Juli (Photo / Foto / صورة: Gigi Ibrahim / جيجي إبراهيم, from the Flickr album / aus dem Flickr-Album / من ألبوم على موقع فليكر *Egypt Graffiti: Street Art*, July 10, 2011)

5 *Prosecute Tantawi* (Photo / Foto / صورة: Gigi Ibrahim / جيجي إبراهيم cf. / vgl. / #4 انظر, July 10, 2011)

6 *View On Black* Text: Wait a second. I'm in a sit-down strike. I'll be back in a little while. / Sekunde, ich bin kurz im Sitzstreik, dann komme ich zurück. (Photo / Foto / صورة: Hossam el-Hamalawy / حسام الحملاوي, cf. / vgl. / #3 انظر, Oct. 29, 2011)

7 *Kill Tantawi* Text: Cheat/Traitor / Betrüger/Verräter (Photo / Foto / صورة: Gigi Ibrahim / جيجي إبراهيم cf. / vgl. / #4 انظر, Apr. 29, 2012)

8 *Mohamed Mahmoud Street* (Photo / Foto / صورة: Hossam el-Hamalawy / حسام الحملاوي, cf. / vgl. / #3 انظر, Apr. 29, 2012)

9 Text: He never went to court. / Er war nicht vor Gericht. (Photo / Foto / صورة: Mosa'ab Elshamy / مصعب الشامي, from the Flickr album / aus dem Flickr-Album / من ألبوم على موقع فليكر تحت عنوان *Revolution Graffiti*, July 15, 2011)

10 *Mohamed Mahmoud Street* Text: Down with military rule! / Nieder mit der Militärherrschaft! (Photo / Foto / صورة: Hossam el-Hamalawy / حسام الحملاوي, cf. / vgl. / #3 انظر May 1, 2012)

11 *Anti-SCAF Graffiti*, Anti-army graffiti in Mohamed Mahmoud Street, depicting Mubarak with a military police beret . . . / Anti-Militärgraffiti in der Mohamed-Mahmoud-Straße, Mubarak mit Barett ... (Photo / Foto / صورة: Hossam el-Hamalawy / حسام الحملاوي cf. / vgl. / #3 انظر, July 23, 2011)

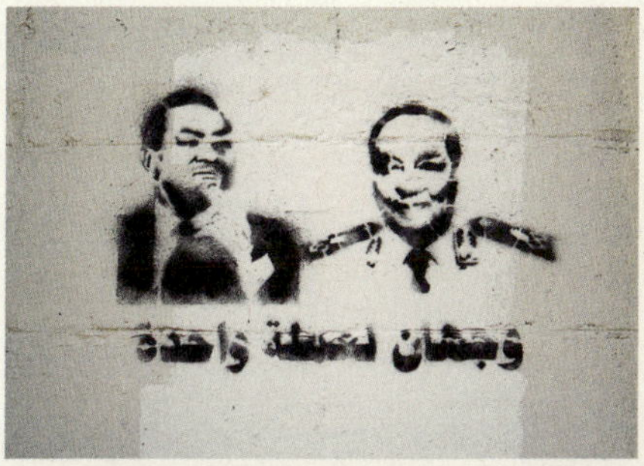

2

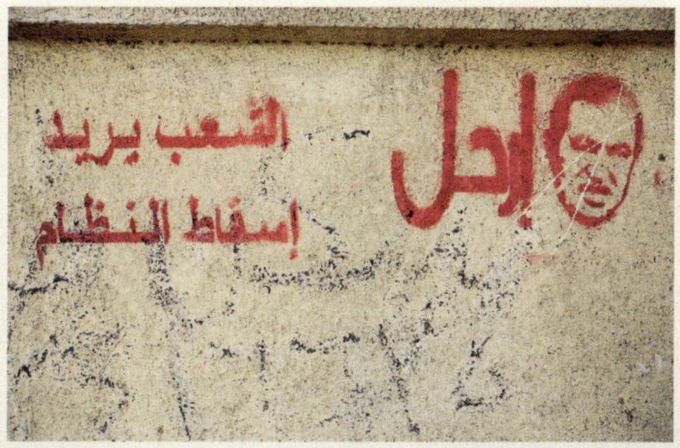

3

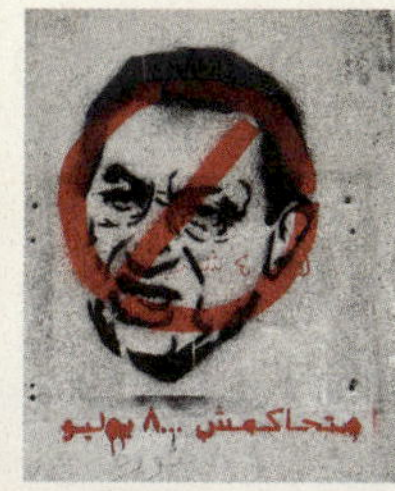

4

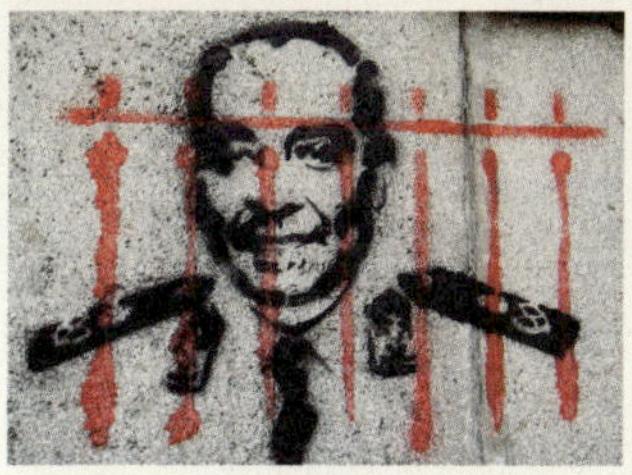
5

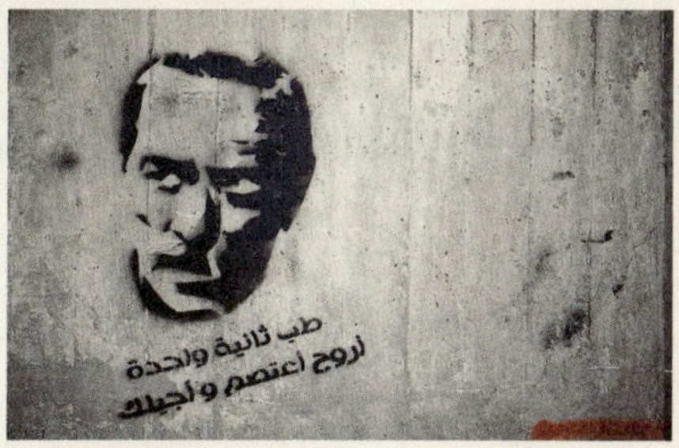

6

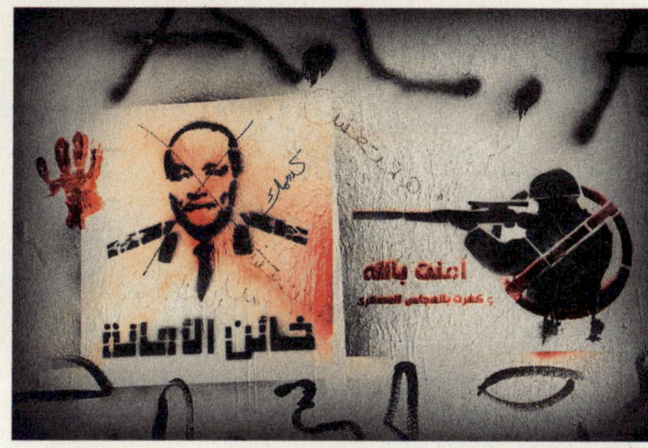

7

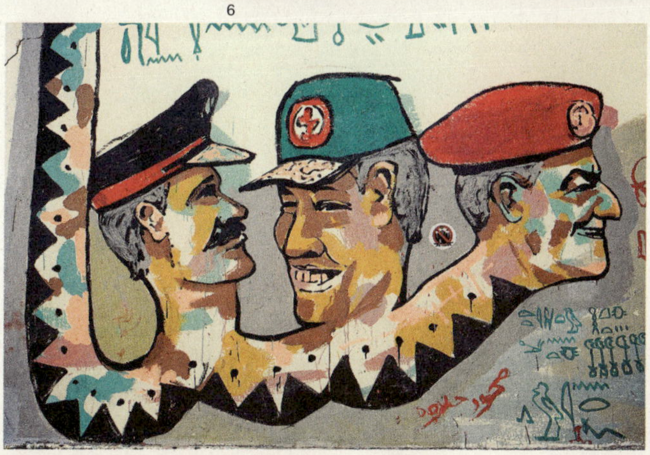
8

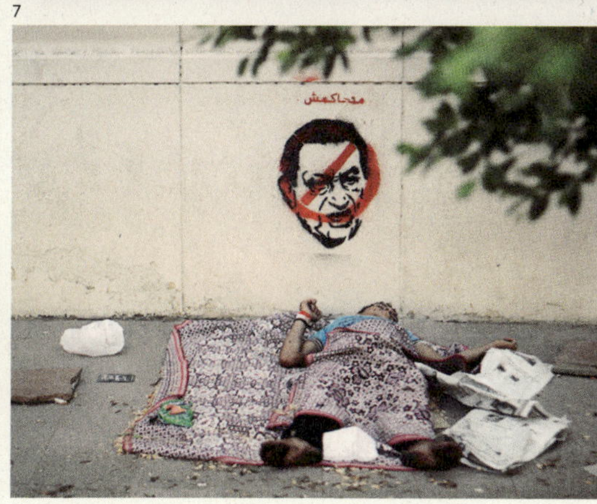

9

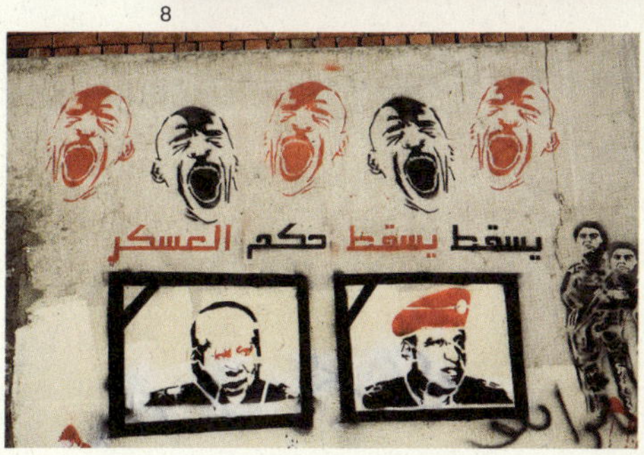

10

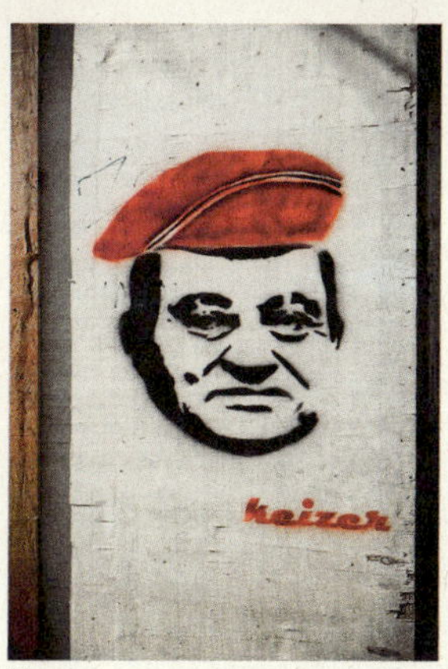

11

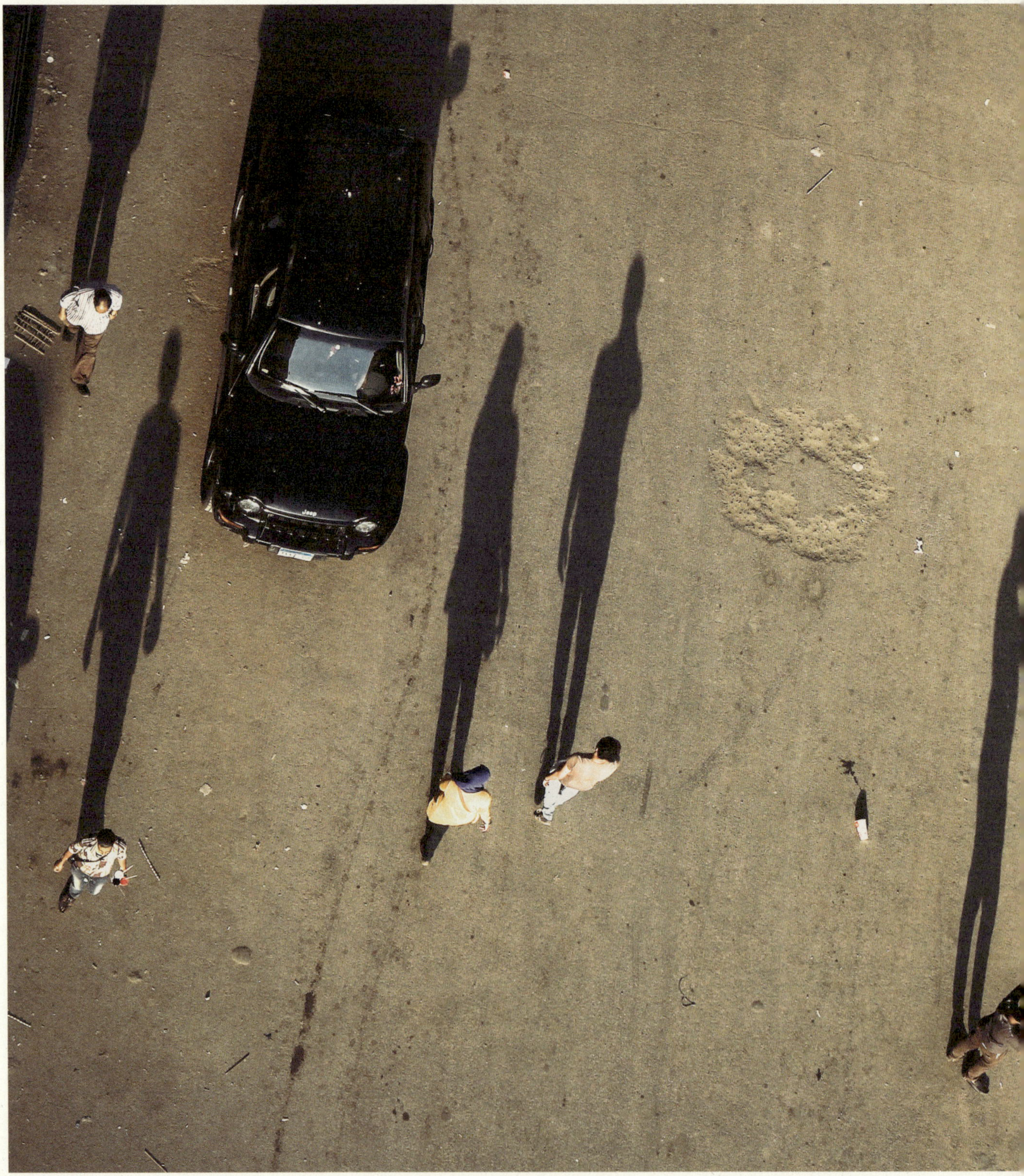

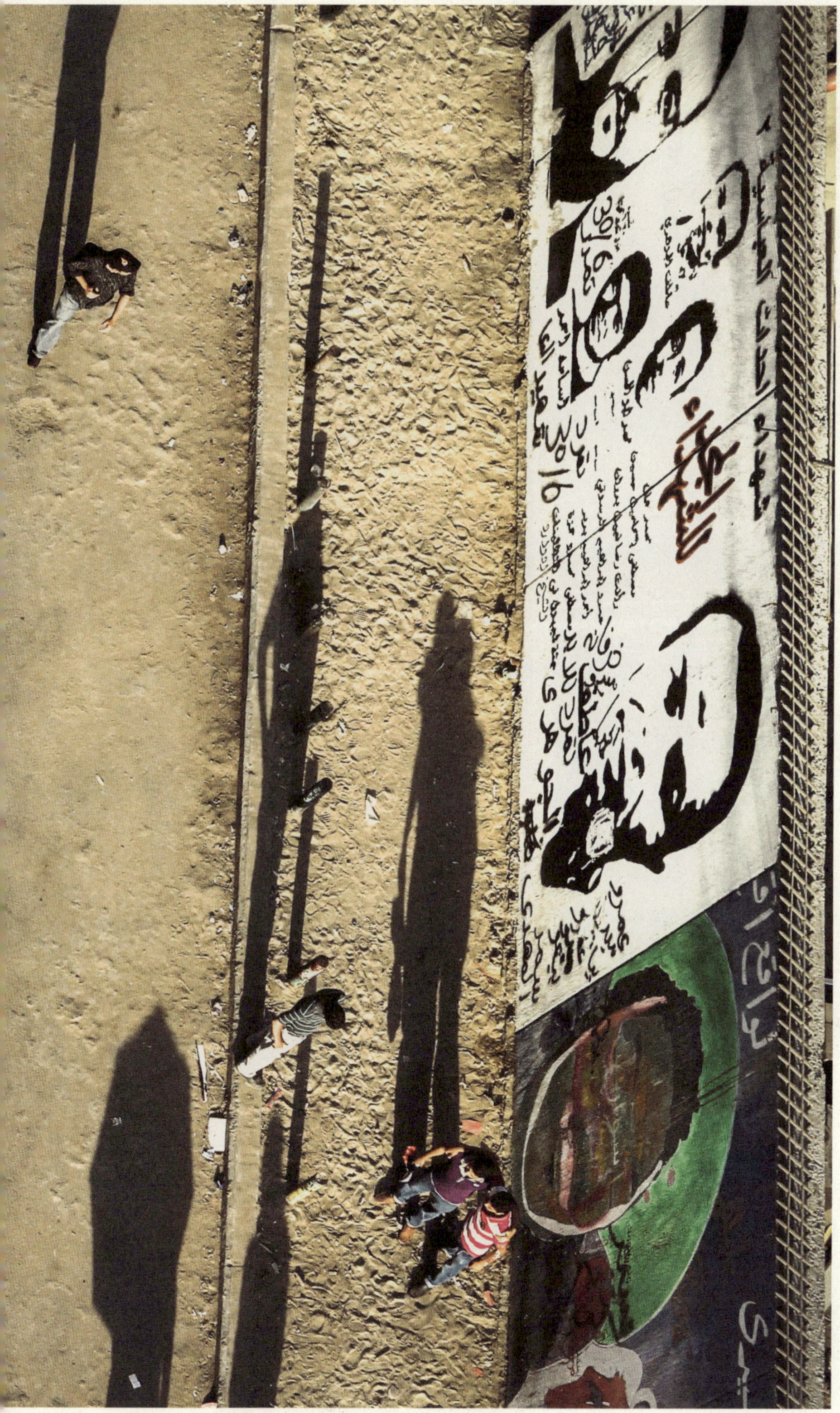

Photo / Foto / صورة: Mosa'ab Elshamy / مصعب الشامي
from the Flickr album / aus dem Flickr-Album / من ألبوم
Most Popular, July 4, 2013 على موقع فليكر

Mohamed Mahmoud street, off Tahrir Square, is, postrevolution, one of the best-known and most cherished streets in the city. A site of some of the deadliest clashes between revolutionaries and security forces that left dozens dead, the street quickly became a hub of incredible graffiti and murals attracting citizens, tourists, and fans of street art. /
Die Mohamed-Mahmoud-Straße beim Tahrir-Platz ist eine der bekanntesten und am meisten aufgesuchten Straßen des postrevolutionären Kairo. Als Ort der mitunter tödlichsten Zusammenstöße von Demonstranten und Sicherheitskräften, mit Dutzenden Toten, wurde die Straße bald schon zu einem zentralen Schauplatz unglaublicher Graffitis und Wandmalereien, die Bürger, Touristen und Fans der Street Art anziehen. /
محمد محمود، الشارع المتفرع من ميدان التحرير هو واحد من أشهر شوارع ما بعد الثورة. مكان لبعض من أبشع الاشتباكات بين المتظاهرين وقوات الأمن، مات بسببها الكثيرون. تحول الشارع بعد ذلك إلى مزار وبيت للكثير من الجرافيتي والجداريات التي اجتذبت المواطنين والسائحين ومحبي فن الشارع.

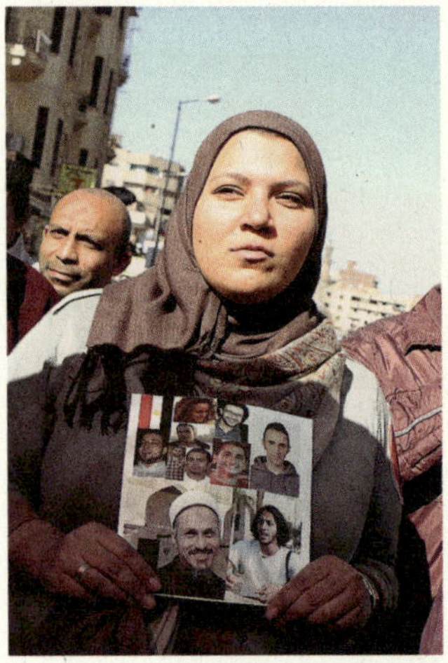
1

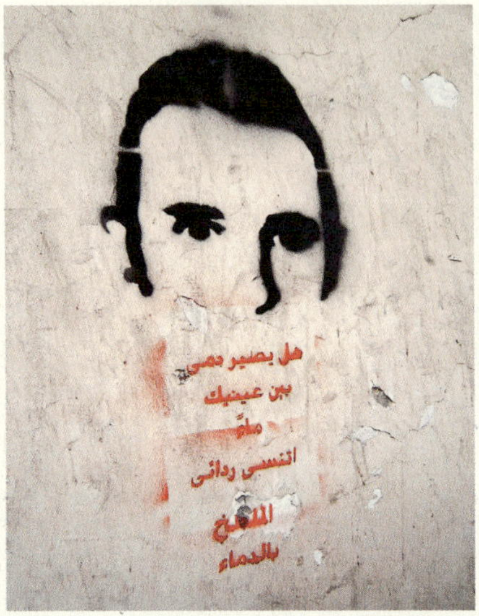
هل بصير دمي
بين عينيك
ماءً
أتنسى ردائي
الملطخ
بالدماء
2

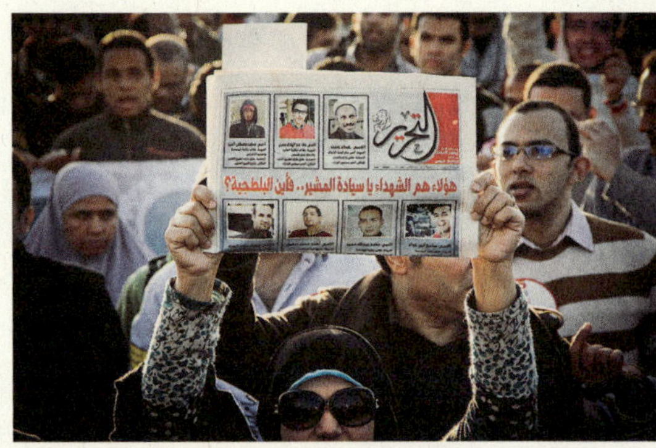
التحرير
هؤلاء هم الشهداء يا سيادة المشير.. فأين البلطجية؟
3

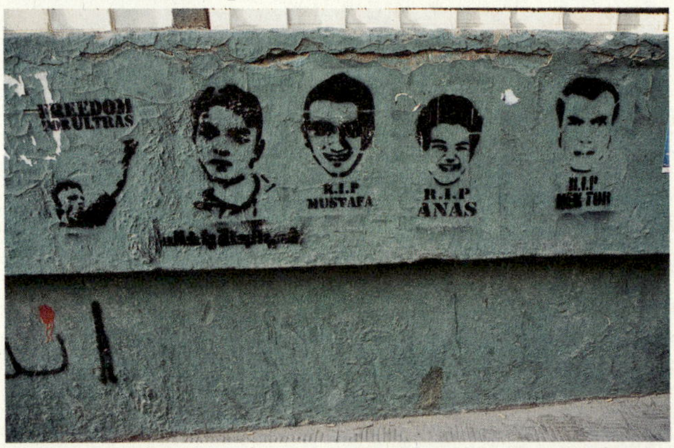
FREEDOM FOR ULTRAS
R.I.P MUSTAFA
R.I.P ANAS
4

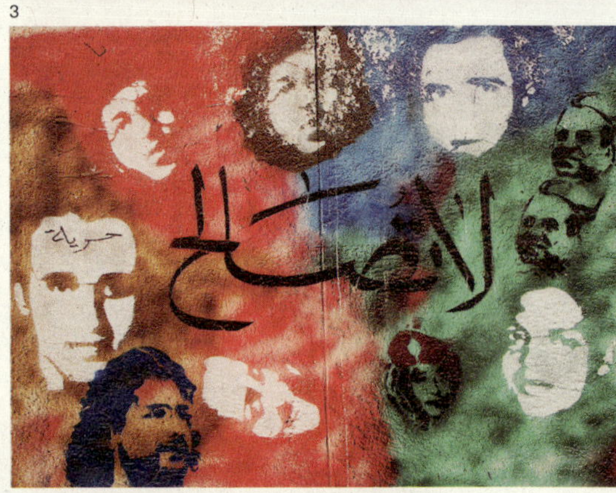
لا تصالح
5

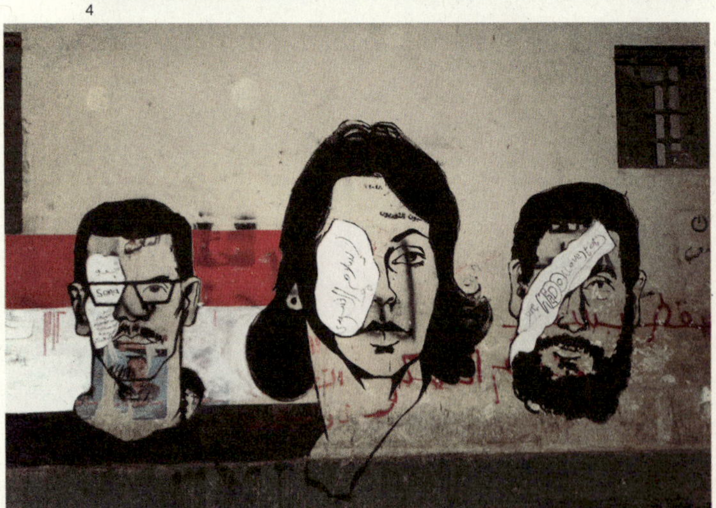
6

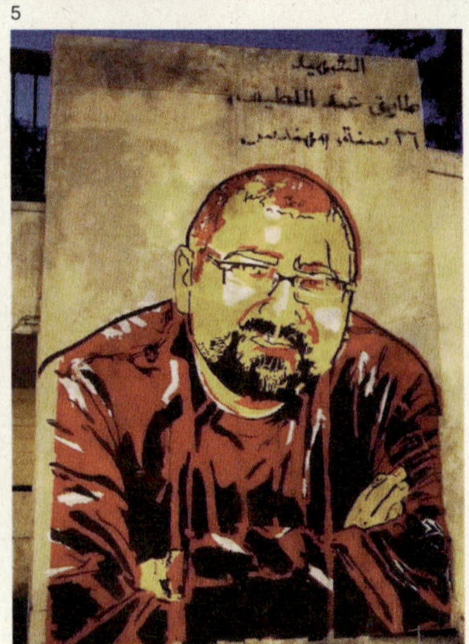
الشهيد
7

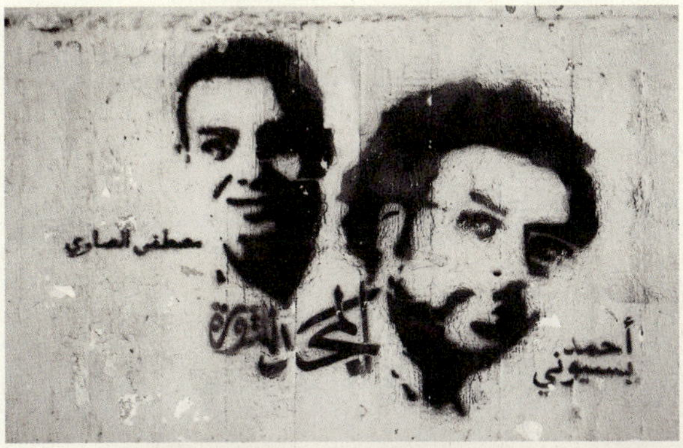

8

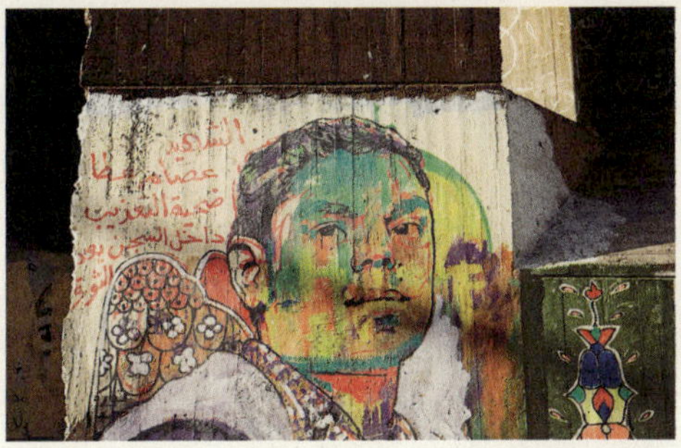

9

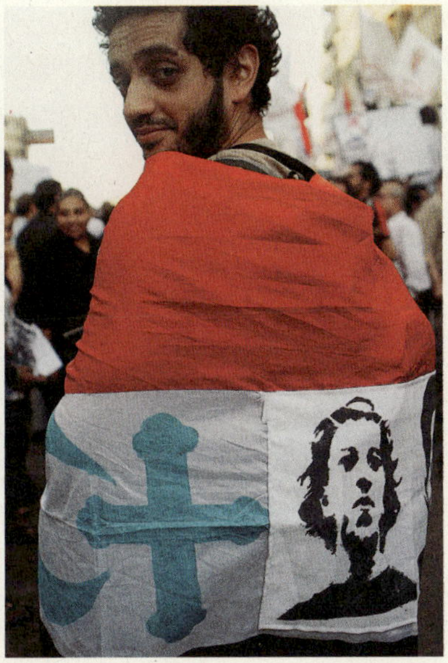

10

1 *Glory to All Martyrs, Martyr Sally Zahran March*
Sally Zahran, 24 years old, an English literature student at Sohag University, she was killed on the Friday of Anger, January 28, 2011, after being hit on the head by security forces. After her death, some conservatives wanted to change or remove her picture because she was not veiled. / Sally Zahran, 24 Jahre, Studentin der Englischen Literatur an der Sohag Universität, wurde am 28. Januar 2011, dem Tag des Zorns, von Sicherheitskräften durch einen Schlag auf den Kopf getötet. Nach ihrem Tod wollten einige konservative Ägypter ihr Bild austauschen oder entfernen, da sie auf diesem nicht verschleiert war. /
سالي زهران مواليد 16 أكتوبر 1987 طالبة بكلية الآداب قسم اللغة الإنجليزية في جامعة سوهاج، وقتلت يوم جمعة الغضب 28 يناير 2011، بتعرضها للضرب على رأسها من قبل قوات الأمن. بعد وفاتها، أراد بعض الناس المحافظين تغيير أو إزالة صورتها زعماً أنها لم تكن محجبة، فأصبحت بمثابة التي قتلت مرتين. أولاً من جانب الشرطة وثانياً من جانب التابوهات المحافظة.
(Photo / Foto / صورة: Sally Zohney / سالي زهني)

2 *Khaled Said*
Khaled Said, 28 years old, was killed on the street on June 6, 2010, by two policemen in Alexandria. The "We are all Khaled Said" page on Facebook was an important driving force for the anti-Mubarak protests. /
Khaled Said, 28 Jahre, wurde am 6. Juni 2010 in Alexandria auf offener Straße von zwei Polizisten zu Tode gefoltert. Die Gründer der Facebook-Gruppe „Wir sind alle Khalid Said" gelten als treibende Kraft hinter den Anti-Mubarak-Protesten. /
خالد سعيد، 28 سنة، قُتل في 6 يونيو 2010 فى الأسكندرية في الشارع على يد شرطيين. وأصبحت صفحة "كلنا خالد سعيد" على الفيسبوك من أهم المحركات التى دعت للثورة على نظام مبارك.
(Photo / Foto / صورة: Gigi Ibrahim / جيجي إبراهيم)

3 *Tahrir Newspaper*
Martyrs of Mohamed Mahmoud street clashes on the front page of Tahrir daily newspaper. /
Auf der Titelseite der Tageszeitung Tahrir: Märtyrer der Auseinandersetzungen auf der Mohamed-Mahmoud-Straße. /
شهداء اشتباكات شارع محمد محمود على الصفحة الأولى من صحيفة التحرير اليومية.
(Photo / Foto / صورة: Mosa'ab Elshamy / مصعب الشامي)

4 *Ultras Martyrs*
A massive riot occurred at Port Said Stadium on Wednesday, February 1, 2012 (the first anniversary of the Camel Attack) after a football match between Al-Masry and Al Ahly. At least seventy-nine people were killed and more than one thousand were injured. Many described it as a 'massacre,' pointing out that it could not have been a normal riot when there were so many victims, and that it must have been planned. /
Am Mittwoch, dem 1. Februar 2012 (der erste Jahrestag der Kamelschlacht) eskalierte die Lage nach einem Fußballspiel zwischen Al-Masry und Al Ahly im Stadium von Port Said. 79 Menschen wurden getötet, weit mehr als 1000 verletzt. Viele bezeichneten es als Massaker, denn ein gewöhnlicher Aufstand hätte nicht mit so vielen Opfern enden dürfen, es deute eher auf ein gezieltes Vorgehen hin. /
وقعت داخل ستاد بورسعيد مساء الأربعاء 1 فبراير 2012 (الذكرى الأولى لموقعة الجمل) عقب مباراة كرة قدم بين المصري والأهلي، وراح ضحيتها أكثر من 79 قتيلا ومئات المصابين. وهي أكبر كارثة في تاريخ الرياضة المصرية. وصفها كثيرون بالـ"مذبحة" أو الـ"مجزرة" مشيرين إلى استبعادهم وقوع هذا العدد من الضحايا في أعمال شغب "طبيعية" وتخطيط طرف ما لها. ويجري التحقيق فيها من أطراف عدّة.
(Photo / Foto / صورة: Hossam el-Hamalawy / حسام الحملاوي)

5 *No Compromise*
(Photo / Foto / صورة: Sally Zohney / سالي زهني)

6 *The Injured Murals*
Graffiti in Mohamed Mahmoud Street, representing the eyes of protesters that were injured by the police. / Graffiti auf der Mohamed-Mahmoud-Straße zeigt erblindete Demonstranten, die von den Sicherheitskräften verletzt wurden. /
جرافيتى فى شارع محمد محمود، يمثل أعين المتظاهرين التى أصيبت على يد الشرطة.
(Photo / Foto / صورة: Gigi Ibrahim / جيجي إبراهيم)

7 *Martyr Tarek Abdel Latif*
Martyr Tarek Abdel Latif, a petroleum engineer, 36 years old, killed on the Friday of Anger, January 28, 2011. His family kept searching for him for 40 days. /
Märtyrer Tarek Abdel Latif, ein Erdölingenieur, 36 Jahre, wurde am 28. Januar 2011, dem Tag des Zorns, getötet. Seine Familie suchte vierzig Tage nach ihm. /
الشهيد طارق عبد اللطيف هو مهندس البترول، 36 سنة قتل يوم جمعة الغضب 28 يناير 2011. ظلت عائلته تبحث عنه لمدة 40 يوماً.
(Photo / Foto / صورة: Gigi Ibrahim / جيجي إبراهيم)

8 *Mustafa al-Sawy, Ahmed Basiony*
(Photo / Foto / صورة: Thomas Hartwell / توماس هارتويل)

9 *Martyr Essam Atta*
Essam Atta, 25 years old, is a young Egyptian man who died while being tortured at the Department of Tora prison in on October 25, 2011, while he was serving a two-year prison sentence for his involvement in a brawl on February 25, 2011 in the area of Mokattam. /
Eassam Atta, 25 Jahre, war ein junger Ägypter, der am 25. Oktober 2011 im Gefängnis von Tora den Verletzungen der Folter erlag. Dort saß er eine zweijährige Haftstrafe ab, zu der ihn ein Militärgericht wegen einer Schlägerei (am 25. Februar 2011 in der Nähe von Mokattam) verurteilt hatte. /
عصام عطا (25 سنة)، هو شاب مصري قتل بسبب التعذيب من قِبَل إدارة سجن طرة في يوم 25 أكتوبر 2011 بينما كان يقضي هناك عقوبة الحبس لمدة سنتين لتورطه في مشاجرة يوم 52 فبراير 2011 في منطقة المقطم، حكمت عليه بعدها المحكمة العسكرية بالحبس سنتين؛ بينما نفت وزارة الداخلية المصرية أنه توفي بسبب التعذيب وقالت أن ما تعرض له كان وعكة صحية، بينما أكدت مصادر حقوقية بالإضافة إلى والد عصام أنه قد عذب من قِبَل ضباط بالسجن بخراطيم المياه حتى الموت.
(Photo / Foto / صورة: Hossam el-Hamalawy / حسام الحملاوي)

10 *Maspero March*
Maspero Demonstrations were staged in October 2011 by a group dominated by Egyptian Copts in reaction to the demolition of a church in Upper Egypt claimed to have been built without proper permission license. The peaceful protesters who intended to stage a sit-in in front of the Maspero television building were attacked by security forces and the army, resulting in twenty-eight deaths, mostly among the Coptic protestors. /
Eine Gruppe von Kopten initiierte die Maspero-Demonstrationen Anfang Oktober 2011 als Reaktion auf die Zerstörung einer Kirche in Oberägypten, welche angeblich ohne Baugenehmigung errichtet worden war. Die friedlichen Demonstranten organisierten einen Sitzstreik vor dem staatlichen Fernsehgebäude Maspero. Sie wurden von Sicherheitskräften und der Armee attackiert – 28 Tote unter den koptischen Demonstranten. /
مظاهرة ماسبيرو وهى عبارة عن تظاهرة انطلقت من شبرا باتجاه مبنى الإذاعة والتلفزيون المعروف باسم "ماسبيرو" فى أكتوبر 2011 ضمن فعاليات يوم الغضب القبطي، رداً على قيام سكان من قرية المريناب بمحافظة أسوان بهدم كنيسة قالوا أنها غير مرخصة، وتصريحات لمحافظ أسوان اعتبرت مسيئة بحق الأقباط. المتظاهرون السلميون الذين كانوا ينوون الإعتصام، تم الإعتداء عليهم من قبل الأمن المركزي وأفراد الجيش، وأفضت الإعتداءات إلى مقتل 28 شخصاً .أغلبهم من الأقباط.
(Photo / Foto / صورة: Sarah Carr / سارة كار)

A Revolutionary Case: Forty-Three Days of Worry

This is the story of an Egyptian family who kept searching for their son for forty-three days.

Ziad Bakir was a distinguished graphic designer working with the Cairo Opera House, who decided to participate in the ongoing action of the January 25 Revolution. Despite being ill with a fever, Ziad was determined to take part in the Friday of Anger, the anti-Mubarak protests on January 28, 2011. He left his home at noon and never returned.

Born on November 9, 1973, Ziad graduated from the High Institute of Fine Arts at Zamalek, obtaining a BA in interior design in 1995 with a "very good" grade for his graduation project on the movie Midaq Alley, based on the novel *Zuqaq al-Midaq* by the famous Egyptian writer Naguib Mahfouz, and for his scenery and costume designs, and studio engineering. In 1997, he started working on his master's degree on "Neorealist Cinema in Egypt: Visual Concepts." His professional experience includes work as a stage designer and an interior and graphic designer. For the last few years before the start of the revolution in 2011, he was best known for his remarkable work in the design department of the Cairo Opera House, where he supervised a team of graphic designers, working on all the printed material related to the opera. Ziad had the ability to see music in colors and translate it into designs, which is why working at the opera house became a passion for him.

Ziad belonged to the intellectual class, in which parents raised their children with a love for their country and its history, His mother, Sawsan Fouad, is an interior designer, and his father, Mohamed Bakir, who used to work as a diplomat and was a high-ranking official, considers caricature art as his main hobby. Ziad inherited his talent from them. Having been raised in a house with thousands of books and many other intellectual elements, Ziad was aware that Egypt deserved a better fate, and he had the feeling that the country was collapsing (especially after the disastrous bombing of the Two Saints Church in Alexandria on January 1, 2011). He was unhappy with the dictatorship of Mubarak's system, the violence of the police, and the lack of human rights, justice, etc. . . . Even though he wasn't personally or directly affected, it was his patriotic feelings and a sense of duty towards his country that moved him.

For forty-three days, his family kept searching for him, hoping to find him alive. During all those weeks, the family contacted practically all the Egyptian and international media to help them in their search, got through to all the crucial institutions and officials asking for support, and searched every hospital and mortuary. There was no trace of Ziad.

Every now and then the family received an anonymous call telling them not to worry, that Ziad was alive and was being detained in a certain place. They then went there with high hopes of finding him. But it was all for nothing. This happened several times.

It was obvious that the government and the people in power during that period were very disturbed by the huge "Search for Ziad Bakir" campaign. The family received many threats on the phone warning them to stop the campaign if they didn't want Ziad to come to harm.

Unfortunately, after all the ups and downs, on March 10, on another visit to the Zenhom mortuary, Ziad's body was finally discovered among other unidentified people, shot by a sniper in the chest. Identifying him required a DNA analysis.

Ziad Bakir will always be remembered as being right at the heart of the Egyptian revolution.

Glory to the Martyrs!

Mirette Bakir, Ziad's sister
Edited by Mohamed Bakir and Sawsan Fouad, Ziad's parents

Ein revolutionäres Schicksal: 43 Tage voller Sorge

Dies ist die Geschichte einer ägyptischen Familie, die 43 Tage lang nach ihrem Sohn suchte.

Ziad Bakir war ein angesehener Grafikdesigner. Er hatte sich entschieden, die Revolution vom 25. Januar zu unterstützen. Obgleich er an jenem Tag krank war, beschloss Ziad, an den Anti-Mubarak-Protesten am 28. Januar 2011, am „Freitag des Zorns", teilzunehmen. Er verließ das Haus um die Mittagszeit. Und kehrte nie zurück.

Ziad wurde am 9. November 1973 geboren. 1995 erhielt er seinen Bachelor of Arts am High Institute of Fine Arts in Zamalak mit der Note „sehr gut". Sein Abschlussarbeit war ein Projekt zum Film *Zoqaq el-Maddaq*, der auf dem Roman des berühmten ägyptischen Schriftstellers Nagib Mahfuz beruht: Er entwarf Settings, Kostüme und Studiotechnik. 1997 begann er an seiner Masterthesis über das visuelle Konzept des neorealistischen Kinos in Ägypten zu arbeiten. Seine berufliche Erfahrung umfasste Tätigkeiten als Bühnenbildner, Innenarchitekt und Grafikdesigner. In den letzten Jahren vor dem Ausbruch der Revolution 2011 war er bekannt für seine bemerkenswerte Arbeit in der Gestaltungsabteilung des Kairoer Opernhauses, wo er einem Team von Grafikdesignern voranstand. Ziad hatte die Fähigkeit, Musik in Farben zu sehen und dies in Entwürfe umzusetzen, daher wurde die Arbeit am Opernhaus für ihn zur Leidenschaft.

Ziad gehörte zur gebildeten Gesellschaftsschicht, die Eltern erzogen ihre Kinder in der Liebe zu ihrem Land und seiner Geschichte. Die Mutter Sawsan Fouad ist selbst Innenarchitektin. Das größte Hobby des Vaters Mohamed Bakir, Diplomat und hochrangiger Funktionär, ist das Zeichnen von Karikaturen. Von seinen Eltern hatte Ziad sein Talent geerbt. Aufgewachsen in einem Haus mit Tausenden von Büchern und vielen anderen Objekten intellektueller Anregung, war Ziad sich bewusst, dass Ägypten ein besseres Schicksal verdiente. Er spürte, dass es mit dem Land abwärts ging (vor allem nach den schrecklichen Bombenanschlägen auf die Two Saints Church in Alexandria am Neujahrsabend 2011). Er war

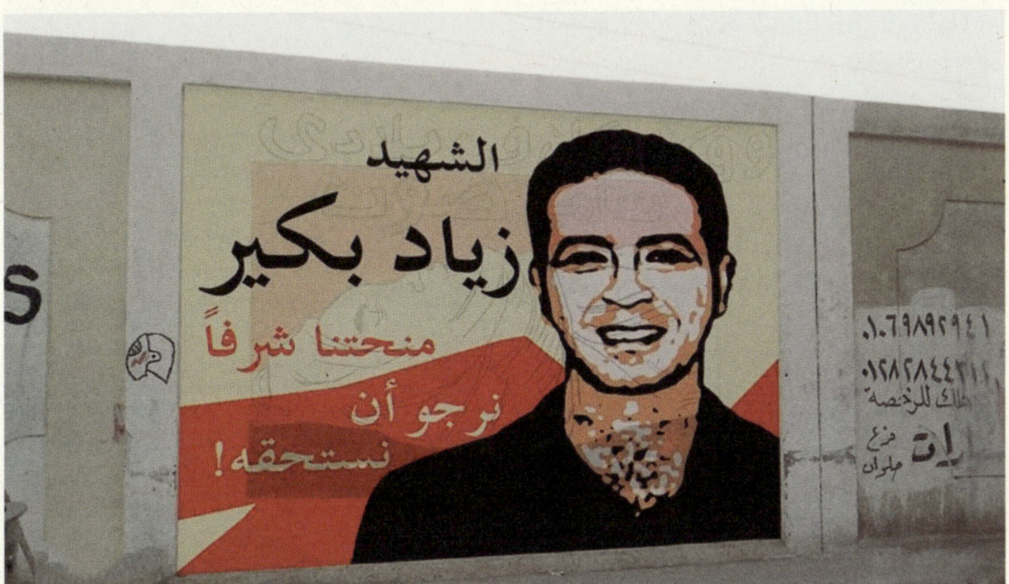

Ziad Bakir Mural, Hadaeq Helwan (Photo / Foto / صورة: Mirette Bakir / ميريت بكير)

unzufrieden mit Mubaraks Diktatur, mit der Gewalt der Polizei, dem Fehlen von Menschenrechten, Gerechtigkeit usw. Auch wenn er nicht persönlich oder direkt davon betroffen war, so empfand er doch patriotisch und fühlte sich gegenüber seinem Land in der Pflicht.

Über 43 Tage suchte seine Familie nach ihm in der Hoffnung, ihn lebend zu finden. Während all der Wochen kontaktierte die Familie beinahe alle ägyptischen und internationalen Medien, damit sie ihnen bei der Suche halfen, setzte sich mit zentralen Institutionen in Verbindung und bat wichtige Funktionäre um Unterstützung. In jedem Krankenhaus und in jeder Leichenhalle suchten sie nach ihm. Aber es fand sich keine Spur.

Hin und wieder erhielten sie einen anonymen Anruf, der ihnen mitteilte, sie sollten sich keine Sorgen machen, Ziad sei am Leben und werde an einem bestimmten Ort festgehalten. Voller Hoffnung suchte die Familie diese Orte auf, aber vergeblich. Dies wiederholte sich einige Male.

Es war offensichtlich, dass die Regierung und die Leute, die in jener Zeit an der Macht waren, angesichts der großen Suchaktion für Ziad Bakir irritiert waren. Die Familie erhielt viele Drohungen, man drängte sie, die Kampagne zu beenden, wenn sie nicht wollten, dass Ziad etwas zustoße.

Tragischerweise entdeckten sie, nach all diesen Höhen und Tiefen, Ziads Körper bei einem erneuten Besuch in der Zenhom-Leichenhalle unter anderen nicht identifizierten Leichen. Heckenschützen hatten ihm in die Brust geschossen, für eine eindeutige Identifizierung war eine DNA-Analyse erforderlich.

Die Erinnerung an Ziad Bakir wird wachgehalten – er ist Teil des Innersten der Revolution.

Ruhm den Märtyrern!

Mirette Bakir, Ziads Schwester
Redigiert von Mohamed Bakir und Sawsan Fouad, den Eltern

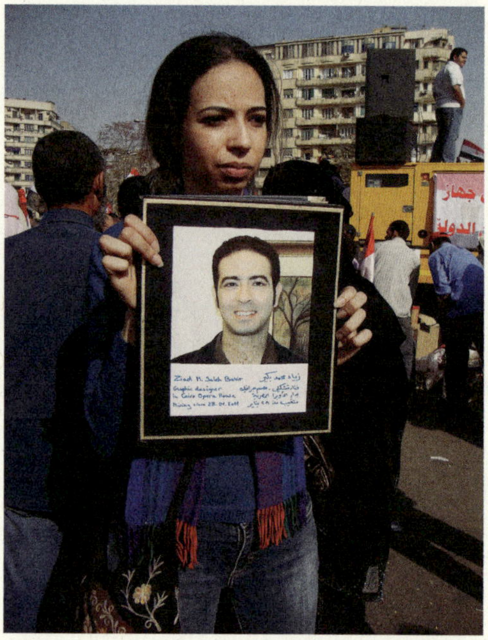

The sister of Ziad Bakir while searching for him, Tahrir Square / Die Schwester von Ziad Bakir auf der Suche nach ihrem Bruder, Tahrir-Platz / أخت زياد بكير وهي تبحث عنه فى ميدان التحرير

حالة ثورية وموعد مع القدر - 43 يوماً من القلق

هى قصة أسرة مصرية ظلت تبحث عن ولدها على مدار 43 يوماً.

زياد بكير، مصمم الجرافيك المتميز الذي يعمل في دار الأوبرا المصرية، والذي قرر يوماً أن يشارك فى الأحداث المتصاعدة لثورة 25 يناير.

بالرغم من نوبة الحمى التي يعانى منها، فقد قرر زياد أن يشارك فى (جمعة الغضب) وهي الإحتجاجات ضد مبارك في 28 يناير 2011، ترك زياد المنزل فى الظهيرة ولكنه لم يرجع أبداً.

ولد زياد في 9 نوفمبر 1973 وتخرج من كل الفنون الجميلة بالزمالك حاصلاً على درجة البكالوريوس فى التصميم الداخلي عام 1995 بتقدير جيد جداً عن مشروع التخرج لتصميم مناظر وملابس وهندسة الاستوديو لفيلم (زقاق المدق) عن رواية الأديب المصري العالمي (نجيب محفوظ).

وفى عام 1997 بدأ العمل فى رسالة الماجستير بعنوان (الواقعية الجديدة فى السينما المصرية، رؤية بصرية) وكانت خبراته المهنية تشمل: العمل فى هندسة المسرح والتصميم الداخلي وأعمال الجرافيك.

وعلى مدار السنين التالية وقبل أن تبدأ ثورة 2011 ذاع صيته عن أعماله فى تصميم مطبوعات دار الأوبرا المصاحبة للعروض المختلفة وأصبح يشرف على فريق من المصممين، ويباشر جميع الأعمال المطبوعة للدار.

كانت لدى زياد القدرة على رؤية الموسيقى بالألوان وترجمتها إلى تصميمات وهذا يفسر كيف كان العمل فى دار الأوبرا يمثل عشقاً بالنسبة له.

ومن نشأته في مستوىً ثقافي عالٍ، حيث ربى الوالدان أبناءهم على حب الوطن والولع بتاريخه، الأم (سوسن فؤاد) مصممة الديكور الداخلي، الوالد (محمد بكير) وكان يعمل دبلوماسياً ومسؤولاً رفيع المستوى ويهوى رسم الكاريكاتير. لقد أخذ زياد موهبته منهما. وبما أنه نشأ فى بيت يحوي الآلاف من الكتب وعناصر الثقافة المتعددة. أصبح زياد على يقين من أن مصر تستحق أكثر مما هي عليه. كان يشعر بأن مصر تسقط، خصوصاً بعد التفجير المفجع لكنيسة القديسين بالأسكندرية عشية رأس سنة 2011، كان لا يخفي غضبه من ديكتاتورية نظام مبارك وعنف الشرطة وتدني حقوق الإنسان وغياب العدالة، وبالرغم من أنه لم يكن متأثراً بشكل مباشر بهذه الأمور، ولكن كان الشعور الوطني والواجب هو الذى جعله يتحرك.

وعلى مدار 43 يوماً ظلت أسرته تبحث عنه على أمل العثور عليه حياً. وخلال كل تلك الأسابيع. خاطبت الأسرة كافة وسائل الإعلام المصرية والعالمية طلباً للعون في البحث عن زياد، ومخاطبة كافة الجهات الرسمية لدعم عملية البحث في المستشفيات والمشارح. ولكن لم يكن هناك أي أثر لزياد.

صاحب هذا من حين لآخر مكالمات مجهولة تنصح الأسرة بألا تقلق وأن زياد مازال حياً وأنه محتجز فى مكان ما. وذهبت الأسرة إلى هذا المكان بدافع الأمل ولكنها لم تعثر عليه. وتكرر ذلك عدة مرات.

كان واضحاً أن الحكومة وهؤلاء الذين في السلطة خلال هذه الفترة كانوا في حرج شديد من حملة البحث عن زياد الواسعة حيث تلقت الأسرة العديد من التهديدات على الهاتف لإيقاف هذه الحملة، وإلا أصاب زياد الأذى.

ولسوء الحظ وبعد كل هذه التقلبات والمعاناة النفسية للأسرة، وفى يوم 10 مارس عند زيارة مجددة لمشرحة (زينهم) تم الكشف عن جثمان زياد بين آخرين مجهولين كانوا هناك، مضروباً برصاصة قناص في الصدر. وتطلب التعرف عليه إجراء تحليلاً للحمض النووي.

سوف تبقى ذكرى زياد في قلب الثورة المصرية والمجد للشهداء.

ميريت بكير، أخت الشهيد
مراجعة محمد بكير وسوسن فؤاد، والدا الشهيد

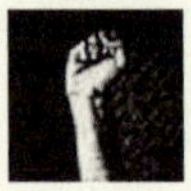

JanoCharbel Jano Charbel
Truly disappointed with the passing of constitutional amendments. Especially because #Mubarak 's NDP & Muslim Brotherhood have most to gain.
20:49 Mar 20, 2011

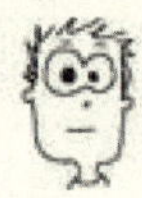

beleidy Amr El Beleidy
Even if this whole thing is a play,
I'm glad we forced them to act it #MubarakTrial
09:23 Aug 3, 2011

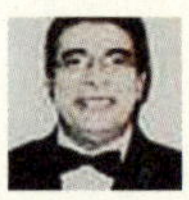

Sarahcarr أبو كار
Army vehicles deliberately crushed protesters using APCs, shot at them at random as they drove at them. This is what happened tonight.
22:05 Oct 9, 2011

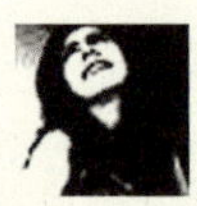

Egyptocracy Egyptocracy
Can you imagine the amount of bravery and strength it takes for unarmed civilians to hold grounds for 3 days against armed police forces?
12:52 Nov 21, 2011

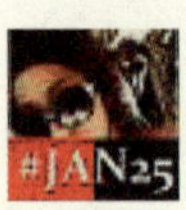

Gsquare86 Gigi Ibrahim جيييييج
MORSI WON #Egypt Thank YOU!
Down with Morsi
16:30 Jun 24, 2012

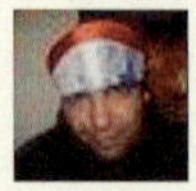

Sandmonkey السيد مانكي
President Morsy just declared himself ruler and dictator. Egypt's last stand against the Islamists begins tomorrow.
21:08 Nov 22, 2012

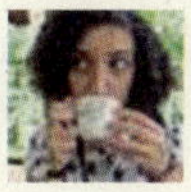

ManarMohsen Manar Mohsen
Morsi seems to believe we overthrew a dictator who thought himself a pharaoh for a dictator who thinks himself God.
الثورة مستمرة! #Egypt
01:18 Nov 24, 2012

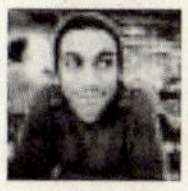

3arabawy Hossam عمو حسام
Morsi is using the same language as Mubarak. The symmetry is amazing. #Egypt
22:20 Dec 6, 2012

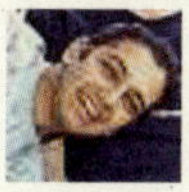

MohammedY Mohammed Yahia
Referendums and elections in #Egypt have grown progressively more depressing. First referendum has festive atmosphere. Today is gloomy
11:16 Dec 15, 2012

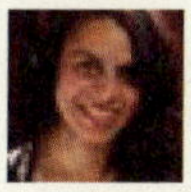

pakinamamer Pakinam and Voice
Morsi is out. It's official. I can hear fireworks. الله أكبر.
21:08 Jul 3, 2013

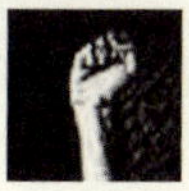

JanoCharbel Jano Charbel
Ecstatic to hear #Morsi's dictatorship is over! Yet I have not an iota of faith in #Egypt's counter-revolutionary generals & judges. #June30
21:25 Jul 3, 2013

ORHamilton Omar Robert Hamilton
We've swapped one hierarchical, secretive, armed, patriarchal, capitalist, violent organisation for another. Again. The revolution continues
23:18 Jul 3, 2013

٦١ After the Port Said Stadium Riot against Al Ahly Supporters, Feb.1–6, 2012

Nach den Ausschreitungen gegen Al-Ahly-Anhänger im Stadion von Port Said, 1.–6. Feb. 2012

بعد أحداث ملعب بورسعيد، 1-6 فبراير 2012

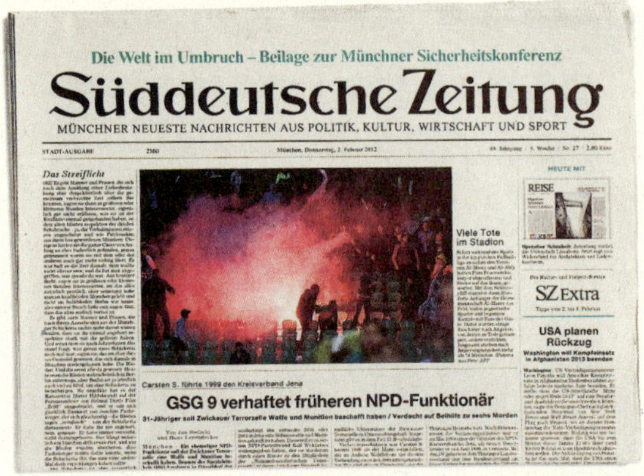

Die Welt im Umbruch – Beilage zur Münchner Sicherheitskonferenz

Süddeutsche Zeitung

MÜNCHNER NEUESTE NACHRICHTEN AUS POLITIK, KULTUR, WIRTSCHAFT UND SPORT

Viele Tote im Stadion

SZ Extra

USA planen Rückzug

Carsten S. führte 1999 den Kreisverband Jena

GSG 9 verhaftet früheren NPD-Funktionär

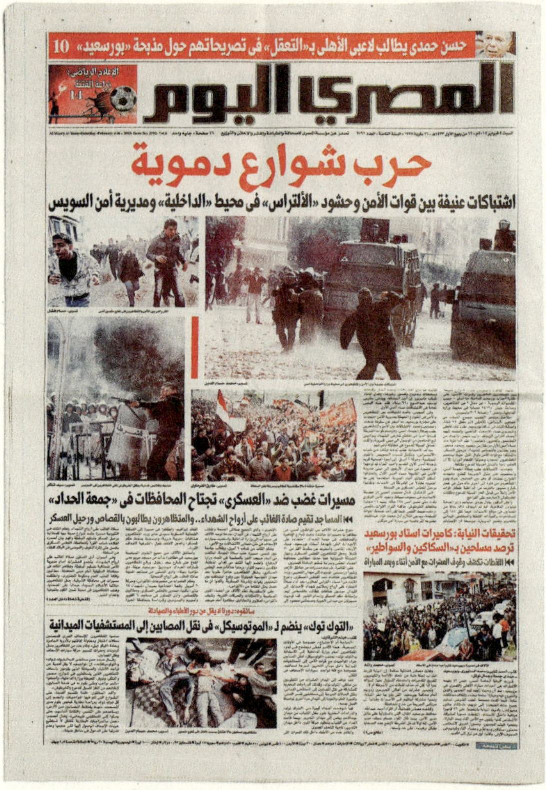

حسن حمدي يطالب لاعبي الأهلي بـ«التعقل» في تصريحاتهم حول مذبحة «بورسعيد»

المصري اليوم

حرب شوارع دموية

اشتباكات عنيفة بين قوات الأمن وحشود «الألتراس» في محيط «الداخلية» ومديرية أمن السويس

مسيرات غضب ضد «العسكري» تجتاح المحافظات في «جمعة الحداد»

تحقيقات النيابة: كاميرات استاد بورسعيد ترصد مسلحين بـ«السكاكين والسواطير»

«التوك توك» ينضم لـ«الموتوسيكل» في نقل المصابين إلى المستشفيات الميدانية

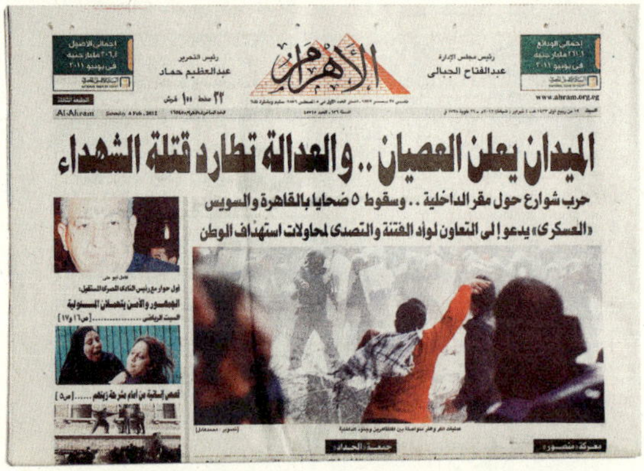

الأهرام

الميدان يعلن العصيان .. والعدالة تطارد قتلة الشهداء

حرب شوارع حول مقر الداخلية .. وسقوط ٥ ضحايا بالقاهرة والسويس

«العسكري» يدعو إلى التعاون لوأد الفتنة والتصدي لمحاولات استهداف الوطن

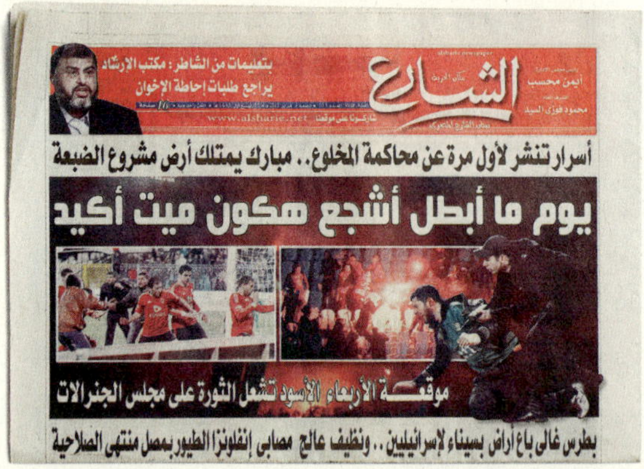

الشارع

أسرار تنشر لأول مرة عن محاكمة المخلوع .. مبارك يمتلك أرض مشروع الضبعة

يوم ما أبطل أشجع هكون ميت أكيد

موقعة الأربعاء الأسود تشعل الثورة على مجلس الجنرالات

بطرس غالي باع أراض بسيناء لإسرائيليين .. ونظيف عالج مصابي إنفلونزا الطيور بمصل منتهى الصلاحية

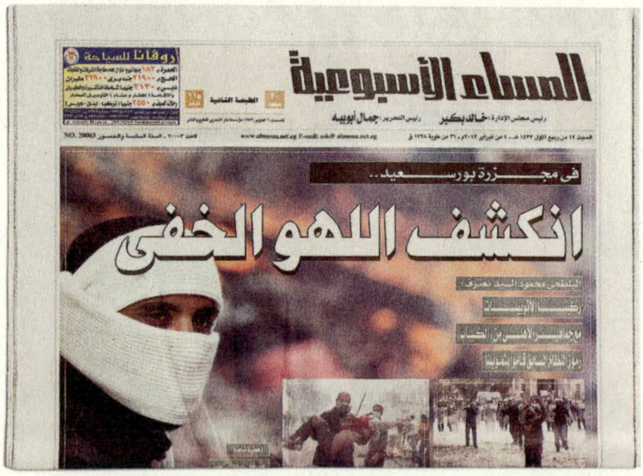

المساء الأسبوعية

في مجزرة بورسعيد..

انكشف اللهو الخفي

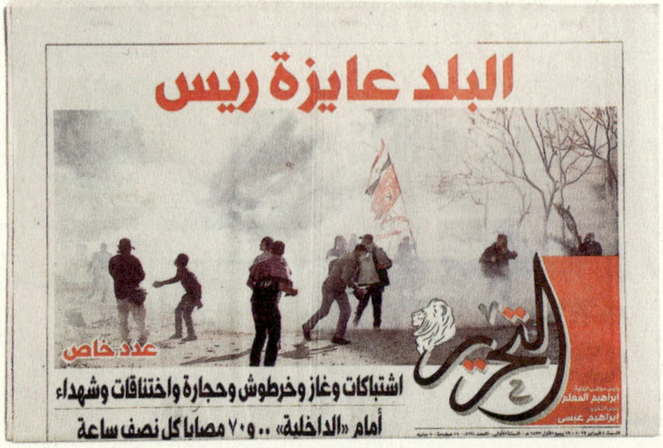

البلد عايزة ريس

التحرير

عدد خاص

اشتباكات وغاز وخرطوش وحجارة واختناقات وشهداء

أمام «الداخلية» .. ٧٠٥ مصابا كل نصف ساعة

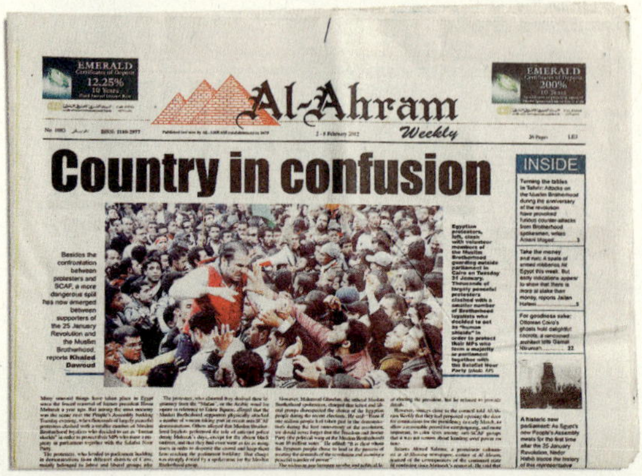

Al-Ahram Weekly

Country in confusion

INSIDE

الطبعة الثانية

الثورة تصحو على دم «الألتراس»

■ راحوا مشجّعين.. رجعوا مشيّعين.. الآلاف يودِّعون أبناءهم لمثواهم الأخير

■ للمرة الرابعة.. «الداخلية» ساحة حرب.. و«التحرير» يستقبل مليونية «الشهيد» اليوم

الشروق الجديد
الجمعة
السنة الرابعة - العدد ١٠٩٨ - ٣ من فبراير ٢٠١٢ م - ١١ من ربيع الأول ١٤٣٣
www.shorouknews.com
١٦ صفحة - جنيه واحد

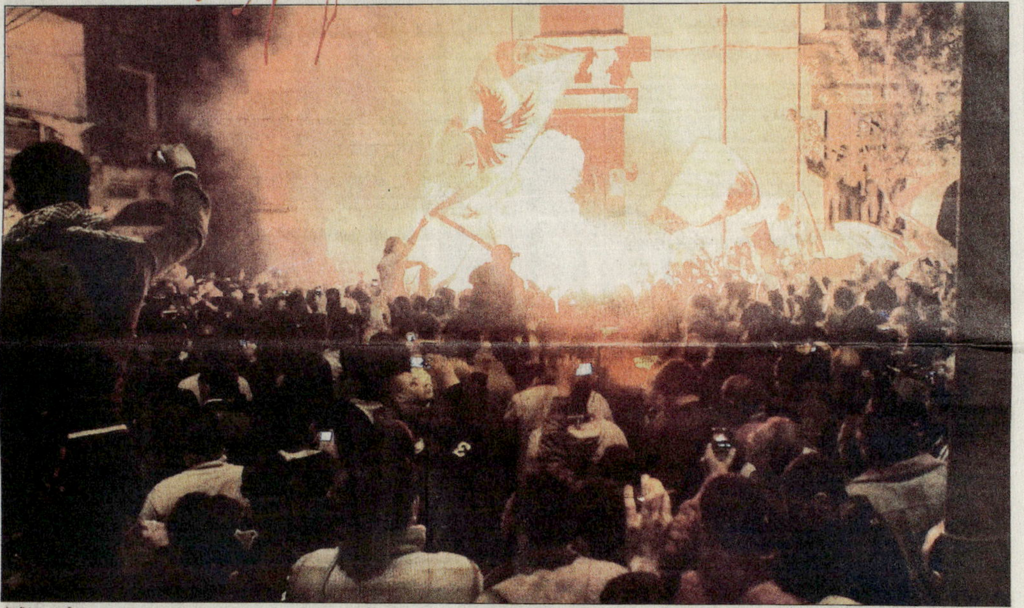

اشتباكات فى محيط وزارة الداخلية — تصوير - محمد الميمونى

الميادين تهتف ضد «العسكر».. و«سقف البرلمان» يتوقف عند وزير الداخلية

■ المجلس يتجاهل طلبات إقالة الحكومة ومساءلة العسكرى.. ويكتفى ببدء إجراءات اتهام محمد إبراهيم

■ نائب إخوانى يدعو لمساءلة المشير.. والكتاتنى: نحن نحاسب الحكومة

النائب العام يعاين الاستاد.. الداخلية تعلن الطوارئ.. ومصدر: تعاملنا مع «شعب بورسعيد» بحكمة

كروفر وقنابل وخرطوش وحجارة ومصابون فى الشوارع المحيطة بالداخلية

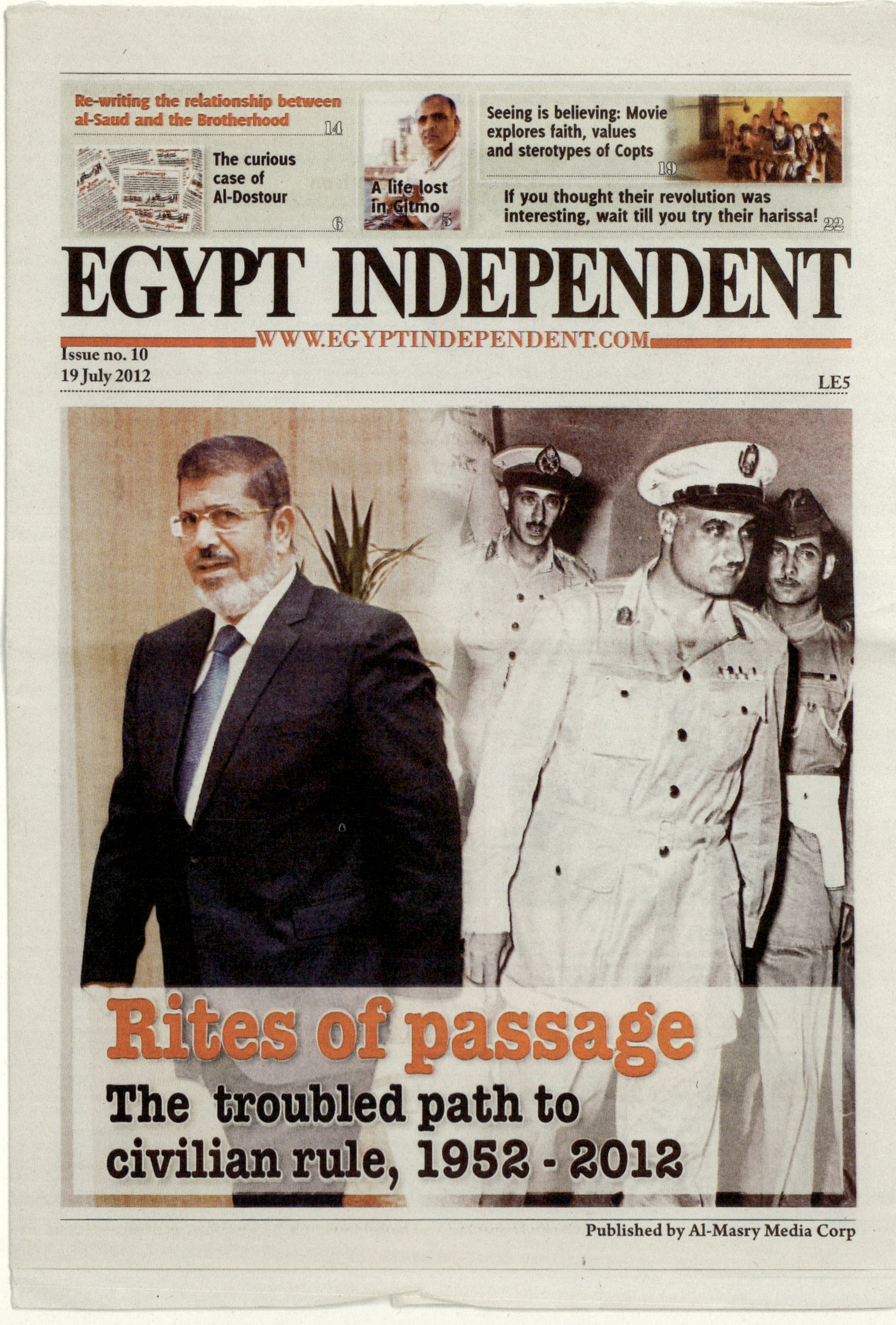

Re-writing the relationship between al-Saud and the Brotherhood 14

The curious case of Al-Dostour 6

A life lost in Gitmo 5

Seeing is believing: Movie explores faith, values and sterotypes of Copts 19

If you thought their revolution was interesting, wait till you try their harissa! 22

EGYPT INDEPENDENT

WWW.EGYPTINDEPENDENT.COM

Issue no. 10
19 July 2012

LE5

Rites of passage

The troubled path to civilian rule, 1952 - 2012

Published by Al-Masry Media Corp

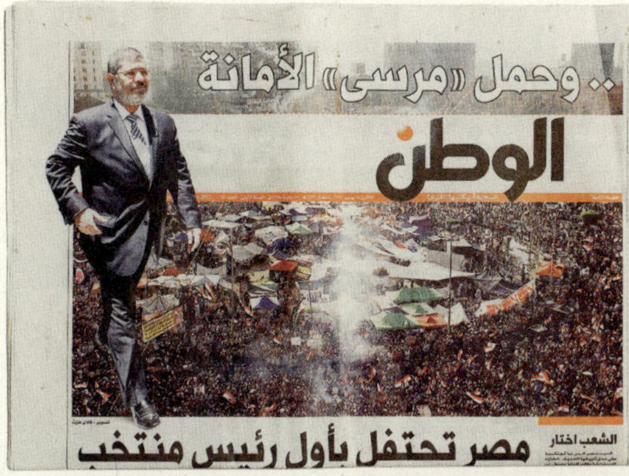
.. وحمل «مرسى» الأمانة

الوطن

الشعب اختار

مصر تحتفل بأول رئيس منتخب

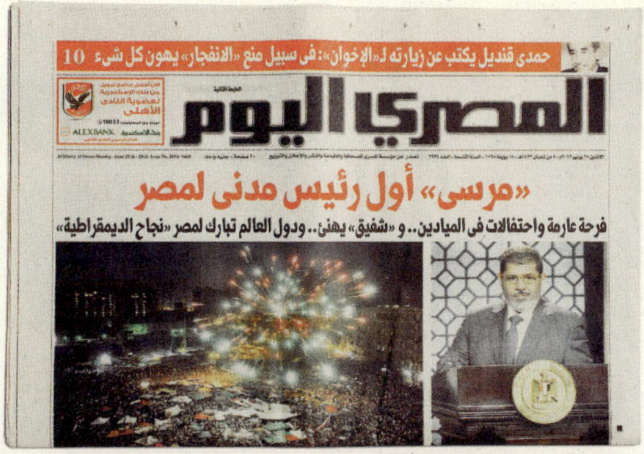
حمدى قنديل يكتب عن زيارته لـ«الإخوان»: فى سبيل منع «الانفجار» يهون كل شىء 10

المصري اليوم

«مرسى» أول رئيس مدنى لمصر

فرحة عارمة واحتفالات فى الميادين.. و«شفيق» يهنئ.. ودول العالم تبارك لمصر «نجاح الديمقراطية»

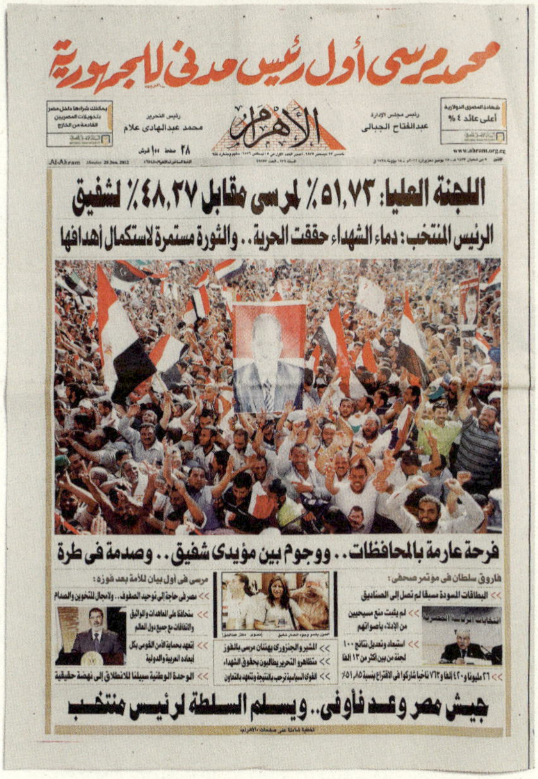
محمد مرسى أول رئيس مدنى للجمهورية

الأهرام

اللجنة العليا: ٥١٫٧٣٪ لمرسى مقابل ٤٨٫٣٧٪ لشفيق

الرئيس المنتخب: دماء الشهداء حققت الحرية.. والثورة مستمرة لاستكمال أهدافها

فرحة عارمة بالمحافظات.. ووجوم بين مؤيدى شفيق.. وصدمة فى طرة

جيش مصر وعد فأوفى.. ويسلم السلطة لرئيس منتخب

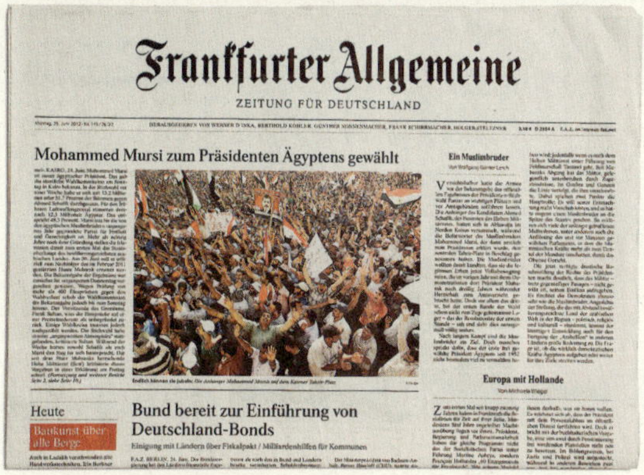
Frankfurter Allgemeine

ZEITUNG FÜR DEUTSCHLAND

Mohammed Mursi zum Präsidenten Ägyptens gewählt

Ein Muslimbruder

Europa mit Hollande

Heute

Bund bereit zur Einführung von Deutschland-Bonds

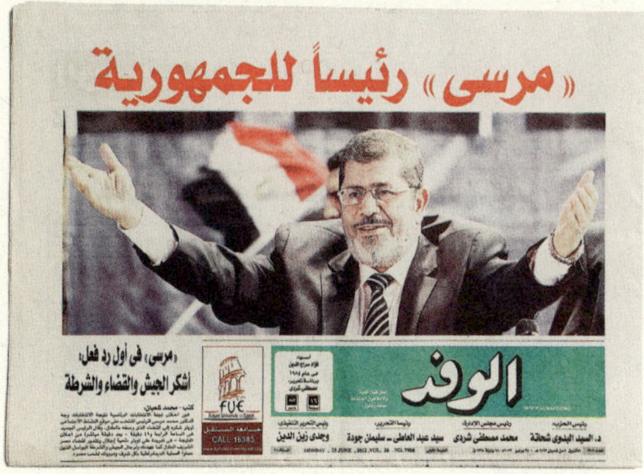
«مرسى» رئيساً للجمهورية

«مرسى» فى أول رد فعل: أشكر الجيش والقضاء والشرطة

الوفد

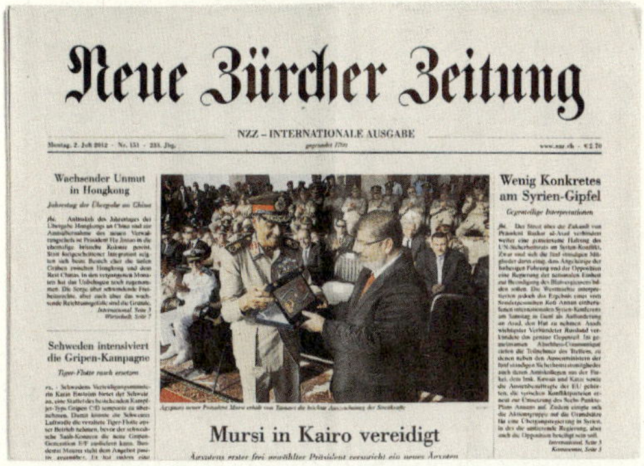
Neue Zürcher Zeitung

NZZ – INTERNATIONALE AUSGABE

Wachsender Unmut in Hongkong

Wenig Konkretes am Syrien-Gipfel

Schweden intensiviert die Gripen-Kampagne

Mursi in Kairo vereidigt

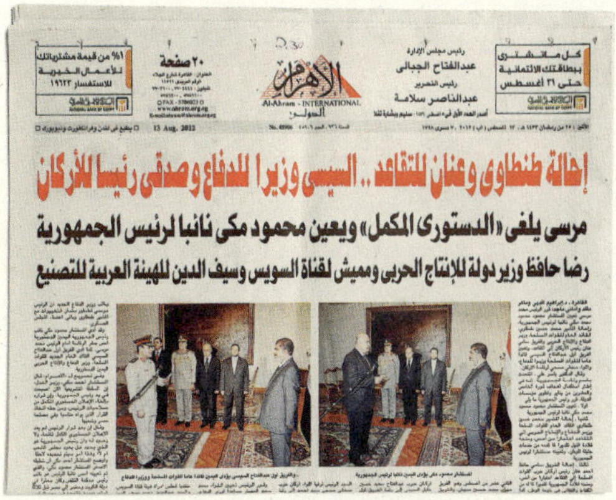
الأهرام

٢٠ صفحة

إحالة طنطاوى وعنان للتقاعد.. السيسى وزيرا للدفاع وصدقى رئيسا للأركان

مرسى يلغى «الدستورى المكمل» ويعين محمود مكى نائبا لرئيس الجمهورية

رضا حافظ وزير دولة للإنتاج الحربى ومميش لقناة السويس وسيف الدين للهيئة العربية للتصنيع

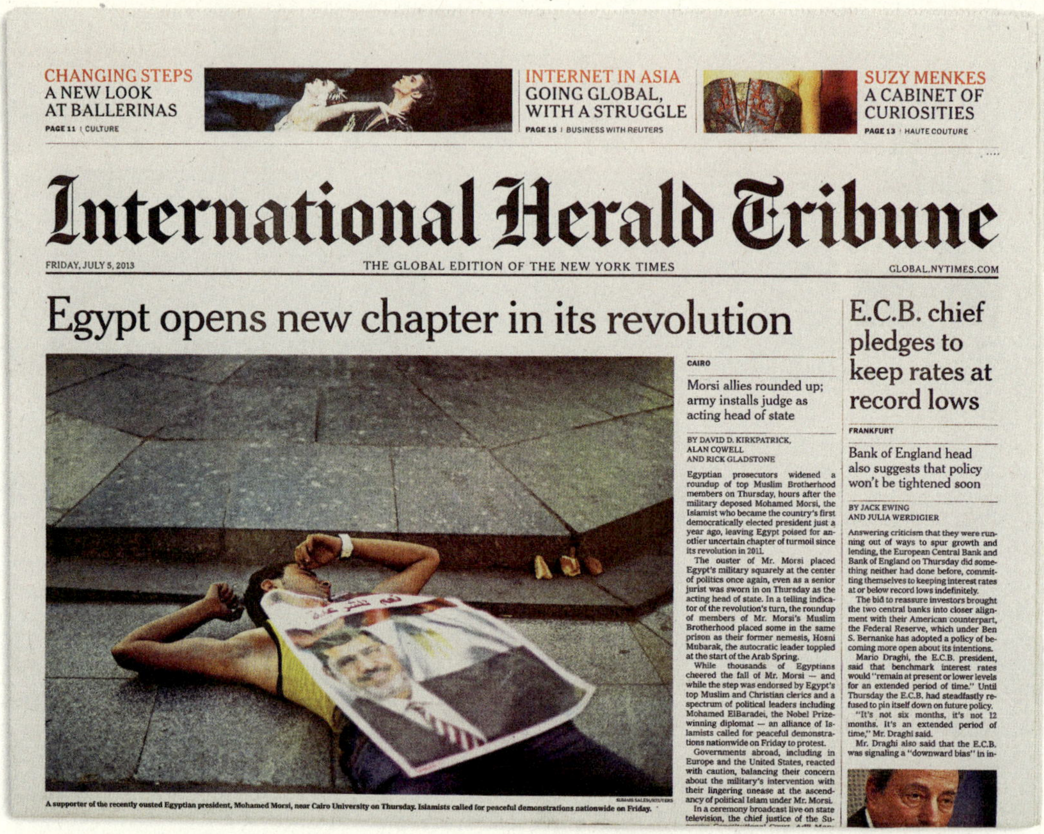

CHANGING STEPS
A NEW LOOK AT BALLERINAS
PAGE 11 | CULTURE

INTERNET IN ASIA
GOING GLOBAL, WITH A STRUGGLE
PAGE 15 | BUSINESS WITH REUTERS

SUZY MENKES
A CABINET OF CURIOSITIES
PAGE 13 | HAUTE COUTURE

International Herald Tribune

FRIDAY, JULY 5, 2013 | THE GLOBAL EDITION OF THE NEW YORK TIMES | GLOBAL.NYTIMES.COM

Egypt opens new chapter in its revolution

A supporter of the recently ousted Egyptian president, Mohamed Morsi, near Cairo University on Thursday. Islamists called for peaceful demonstrations nationwide on Friday.

CAIRO

Morsi allies rounded up; army installs judge as acting head of state

BY DAVID D. KIRKPATRICK, ALAN COWELL AND RICK GLADSTONE

Egyptian prosecutors widened a roundup of top Muslim Brotherhood members on Thursday, hours after the military deposed Mohamed Morsi, the Islamist who became the country's first democratically elected president just a year ago, leaving Egypt poised for another uncertain chapter of turmoil since its revolution in 2011.

The ouster of Mr. Morsi placed Egypt's military squarely at the center of politics once again, even as a senior jurist was sworn in on Thursday as the acting head of state. In a telling indicator of the revolution's turn, the roundup of members of Mr. Morsi's Muslim Brotherhood placed some in the same prison as their former nemesis, Hosni Mubarak, the autocratic leader toppled at the start of the Arab Spring.

While thousands of Egyptians cheered the fall of Mr. Morsi — and while the step was endorsed by Egypt's top Muslim and Christian clerics and a spectrum of political leaders including Mohamed ElBaradei, the Nobel Prize-winning diplomat — an alliance of Islamists called for peaceful demonstrations nationwide on Friday to protest.

Governments abroad, including in Europe and the United States, reacted with caution, balancing their concern about the military's intervention with their lingering unease at the ascendancy of political Islam under Mr. Morsi.

In a ceremony broadcast live on state television, the chief justice of the Su-

E.C.B. chief pledges to keep rates at record lows

FRANKFURT

Bank of England head also suggests that policy won't be tightened soon

BY JACK EWING AND JULIA WERDIGIER

Answering criticism that they were running out of ways to spur growth and lending, the European Central Bank and Bank of England on Thursday did something neither had done before, committing themselves to keeping interest rates at or below record lows indefinitely.

The bid to reassure investors brought the two central banks into closer alignment with their American counterpart, the Federal Reserve, which under Ben S. Bernanke has adopted a policy of becoming more open about its intentions.

Mario Draghi, the E.C.B. president, said that benchmark interest rates would "remain at present or lower levels for an extended period of time." Until Thursday the E.C.B. had steadfastly refused to pin itself down on future policy.

"It's not six months, it's not 12 months. It's an extended period of time," Mr. Draghi said.

Mr. Draghi also said that the E.C.B. was signaling a "downward bias" in in-

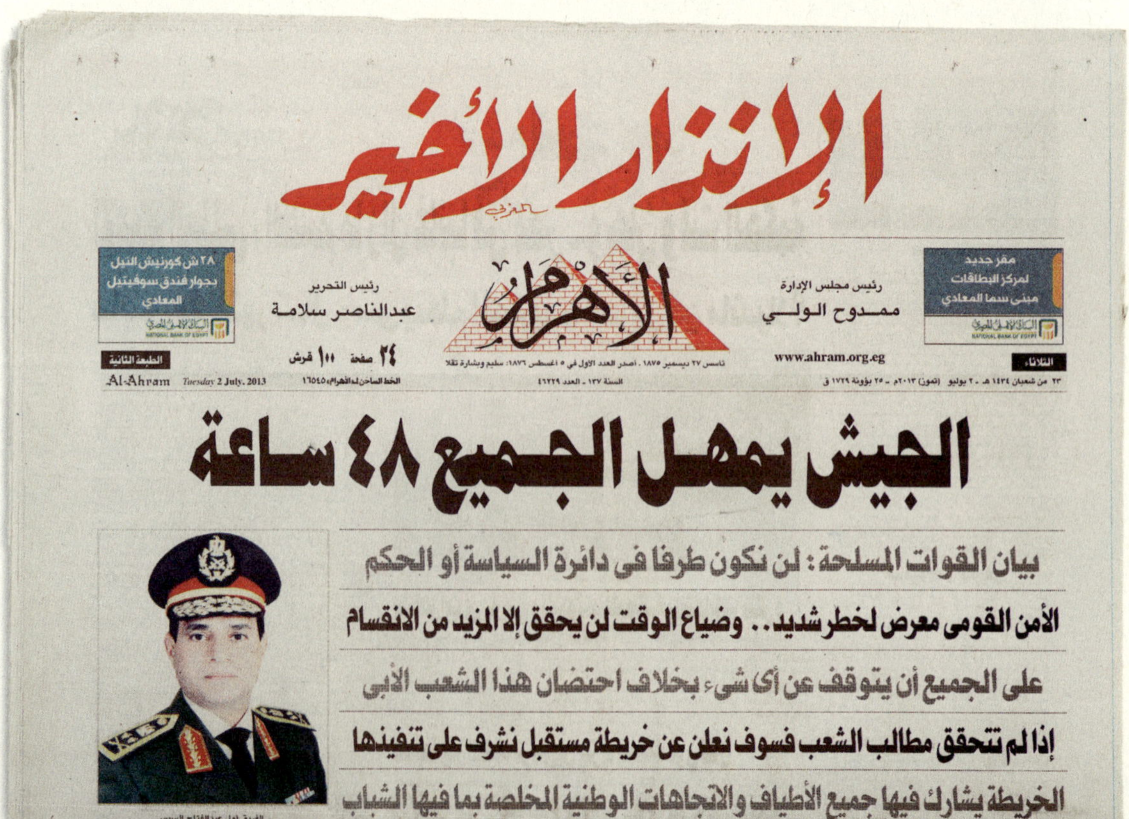

الإنذار الأخير

رئيس مجلس الإدارة
ممدوح الولي

الأهرام

رئيس التحرير
عبدالناصر سلامة

مقر جديد لمركز البطاقات مبنى سما المعادي
البنك الأهلي المصري NATIONAL BANK OF EGYPT

٢٨ ش كورنيش النيل بجوار فندق سوفيتيل المعادي
البنك الأهلي المصري NATIONAL BANK OF EGYPT

الثلاثاء
www.ahram.org.eg
تأسس ٢٧ ديسمبر ١٨٧٥ . أصدر العدد الأول في ٥ أغسطس ١٨٧٦: سليم وبشارة تقلا
٢٤ صفحة ١٠٠ قرش
الطبعة الثانية

٢٣ من شعبان ١٤٣٤ هـ - ٢ يوليو (تموز) ٢٠١٣م - ٢٥ بؤونة ١٧٢٩ ق
السنة ١٣٧ - العدد ٤٦٢٢٩
الخط الساخن لـ الأهرام: ١٦٥٤٥
Al-Ahram Tuesday 2 July. 2013

الجيش يمهل الجميع ٤٨ ساعة

بيان القوات المسلحة: لن نكون طرفا فى دائرة السياسة أو الحكم

الأمن القومى معرض لخطر شديد.. وضياع الوقت لن يحقق إلا المزيد من الانقسام

على الجميع أن يتوقف عن أى شىء بخلاف احتضان هذا الشعب الأبى

إذا لم تتحقق مطالب الشعب فسوف نعلن عن خريطة مستقبل نشرف على تنفيذها

الخريطة يشارك فيها جميع الأطياف والاتجاهات الوطنية المخلصة بما فيها الشباب

الفريق أول عبدالفتاح السيسى

أوسطية وتعمل مع الشروق منذ بدايتها في 2008
⟵ صورة 43
لبنى طارق درست الإعلام وتعمل مع الشروق منذ 2010
⟵ صورة 51
أحمد عبد اللطيف درس الإعلام ويعمل مع الشروق منذ 2008
⟵ صورة 50
فادي عزت
⟵ صورة 12، 48
جورج محسن درس التجارة ويعمل مع الشروق منذ 2012
⟵ صورة 41
صامويل محسن درس التجارة ويعمل مع الشروق منذ 2012
⟵ صورة 37
أميرة مرتضى درست الإعلام وتعمل مع الشروق منذ 2010
⟵ صورة 53
جيهان نصر درست علم الإجتماع وتعمل مع الشروق منذ 2009
⟵ صورة 49
توماس هارتويل
⟵ صورة 52، صفحة ٦٨، ١١٤
علي هزاع درس الهندسة ويعمل مع الشروق منذ 2011
⟵ صورة 54، صفحة ٨٢
⟵ صورة الغلاف، صورة 11، 36
إيمان هلال
⟵ صورة 39

يعبر الخط الأحمر عن القوانين غير المكتوبة، والتي شلّت مصر لأكثر من ثلاثين عاماً. كان هذا الخط الأحمر وقت مبارك هو ما يمكن أن يقال ويفعل أو الأهم ما الذي يمكن نشره للعامة وماذا لا. كان الفرد يملك الاختيار بين الرقابة الشخصية أو العقاب. سنوات من قانون الطوارئ والتطبيق الإنتقائي للقوانين، ساعدت على السيطرة على الآراء المخالفة. هذا الضغط ولد الإنفجار الذي حدث في 25 يناير.
كان المصورون الشباب من جريدة الشروق هم أول من وجد جمهور لصورهم التي لم يكن مسموحاً لها أن تنشر في أي مكان آخر. ذهب خوف مواجهة السلطة في لحظة. رفع الشعب صوته وبدأ في رسم خط أحمر للمجتمع والحكام. أخذ مصوري الشروق على عاتقهم نقل التغيير في حين تستمر مصر في الاحتجاج والنقاش والتعبير وهي تبحث عن نظام جديد.

وُلِد توماس هارتويل عام 1955 في تكساس. درس في جامعة تكساس دراسات الشرق الأوسط والصحافة المصورة. عاش هارتويل فوق الثلاثين عاماً في الشرق الأوسط وصور لوكالات أنباء وإعلام دولية مختلفة. عرضت صوره في مصر والجزائر والبحرين وسويسرا والولايات الأمريكية المتحدة. يعمل حالياً كمحرر للصور في قسم الشرق الأوسط في الأسوشييتد برس بالقاهرة.

رندا شعث

ميدان التحرير في أول يوم لغزو أمريكا للعراق، 21 مارس 2003، من سلسلة القاهرة تحت نفس الشمس: القاهرة، 2003، طباعة بالجيلاتين الفضي 20×25 سم.
⟵ صورة 4+5

"أقيمت في الـ 21 من مارس 2003، أول يوم للإجتياح الأمريكي للعراق، أكبر مظاهرة عرفتها مصر خلال العقود التي سبقت ذلك اليوم. حتى ذلك اليوم كانت الشرطة تعلم دائماً متى ستقوم مظاهرة، وكانت تمركز القوات الأمنية في موقع المظاهرة لتحجيم عدد المتظاهرين. كانت الأجهزة الأمنية تحيط المجموعات المتكونة من أقل من مئة متظاهر بمئات من الشرطة وتتبع سياسة إستخدام العنف والإعتقالات لمنع آخرين عن المشاركة خوفاً. ولكن الغضب المستشري بسبب الحرب في العراق كان أقوى، كما أن الدعوة للإحتجاج قد نُشرت من قِبَل أكثر من مجموعة، وإستجاب لها المصريون من مختلف طبقات المجتمع.
اشتركْتُ في المظاهرة وكنت ألتقط الصور أثناء سيري، وكلما أجش صوتي وأحسست بالتعب كنت أبحث عن موقع مرتفع لأقوم بإلتقاط الصور من هناك. وفر لي المنظور من مرتفع صورة معبرة لجموع المتظاهرين الضخمة. وبعد إنتهاء تلك المظاهرة تم إنشاء حواجز على جوانب أرصفة الشوارع تحجم الحركة فى الميدان. وإبتداءً من 25 من يناير 2011 أصبح ميدان التحرير مكاناً لتجمع المحتجين مجدداً."

ولدت رندا شعث عام 1962 في فيلادلفيا لأب فلسطيني وأم مصرية. درست في الجامعة الأمريكية بالقاهرة وحصلت على درجة الماجستير في مجال الاتصال الجماهيري المرئي في جامعة مينيسوتا. عملت شعث كمصورة لعدة جرائد ومجلات ووكالات للصور. عرضت صورها في جميع أنحاء العالم، مصر ولبنان والبرازيل وأسبانيا وألمانيا والولايات الأمريكية المتحدة. وهي تعمل حالياً كمحررة للصور في جريدة الشروق بالقاهرة.

سارة كار

من ألبوم على موقع فليكر تحت عنوان
ألبوم التحرير، اليوم السابع عشر، 11 فبراير 2011
⟶ صورة 11
خالد سعيد، بعد مرور عام ، 6 يونيو 2011
⟶ صورة 6
ألبوم 23 نوفمبر، 23 نوفمبر 2011
⟶ صورة 46
الهجوم على إعتصام مجلس الوزراء، 18 ديسمبر 2011 ⟶ صورة 43
الذكرى الأولى للثورة، 25 يناير 2012
⟶ صورة 9
إشتباكات بورسعيد، اليوم الثاني، 3 فبراير 2012
⟶ صورة 44+45
المحكمة الدستورية العليا SCC، يونيو 2012
⟶ صورة 13، 42
المسيرة النسائية، 20 ديسمبر 2011
⟶ صفحة ٨٢
مسيرة ماسبيرو، 9 أكتوبر 2012
⟶ صفحة ٦٨

"نصف مصرية. هذه بلدي أيها الأوغاد"
يتقدم هذا الشعار الجريء مدونة الصحفية الإنجليزية-المصرية سارة كار. فهي تعلق في مدونتها على الوضع الإجتماعي في مصر بالإضافة إلى المقالات التي تكتبها لجريدة إيجيبت إنديبندد. تحتوي نصوصها على ملاحظات يومية مخلوطة بتحليل سياسي تصاحبها عادة تعليقات ساخرة. هذا هو أيضاً حال صورها المتروكة بدون تعليق.

سارة كار مصورة إنجليزية-مصرية من القاهرة. تعمل كصحفية لجريدة إيجيبت إنديبندد وآخرين وتكتب في مدونتها www.inanities.org

أحمد كامل

Hypothetical Society, 2009
رسومات على ورق، 49.5×56سم، 32×50سم
⟶ صفحة ١٦٤ - ١٦٥

"أقصد بالمجتمع المنافق، هذه الجماعة من 'الأصدقاء' في الإنترنت بغض النظر عما إذا كانوا يعرفون بعضهم البعض خارج الإنترنت أم لا- فهم يسمحون لبعضهم البعض برؤية الصورة الشخصية. يتمتع المشاركين بحس يعي تماماً شكلهم، يقفون بشكل معين ويلبسون بشكل معين من أجل اللقطة. تحمل الصور الخاصة إلى الإنترنت وتصبح عامة ويحصل على انتباه كإسقاط، يمكن التعليق عليه وضغط زر 'أعجبني'.
تترجم الصور بمساعدة بروجكتور في رسمة غير معبرة، حيث يتم استبدال الخلفية بلون رمادي محايد. وبهذا تتحول نقطة التركيز. تختفي ملامح الوجه، والمحيط المعين، يتم تقليل تفاصيل الملابس والأكسسوارات. تتحول الصورة إلى رسمة على الحائط، ويتحول الأشخاص إلى رسمة أيقونية في مكان مجرد."

ولد أحمد كامل عام 1981 في القاهرة. درس في قسم التصوير بكلية الفنون الجميلة بجامعة حلوان بالقاهرة وحصل على البكالوريوس عام 2003. شارك كامل في العديد من المعارض الفردية والجماعية في الشرق الأوسط وأوروبا، في مركز الصورة المعاصرة وجاليري تاون هاوس على سبيل المثال وأيضاً في معرض فن التصوير الضوئي في الدنمارك وفي الكونستراوم في مدينة دوسلدورف. يعيش كامل ويعمل في القاهرة وبرلين والتحق في 2012 بدفعة المتخصصين مع تينا بارا في كلية الجرافيك وفن الكتاب بمدينة لايبزغ.

أليكس ماجولي

أليكس ماجولي، مصر، القاهرة، 5 فبراير 2011. بعد أسبوعين من بدء الإحتجاجات، يعود المتظاهرون إلى ميدان التحرير.
⟶ صورة 48+49

ولد أليكس ماجولي عام 1971 وهو مصور إيطالي. التحق في سن الخامسة عشر باستوديو F45 في مدينة رافينا وتخرج في أكاديمية الفنون الجميلة عام 1991. بعد أن حصل على عضوية كاملة في وكالة ماجنوم للصور في عام 2001، وجه اهتمامه إلى إسقاط نظام طالبان في أفغانستان وبعد عامين غزو العراق. وثق العديد من الأزمات الدولية للنيوزويك، مجلة نيويورك تايمز، جرانتا والناشيونال جيوغرافيك. حصل في 2003 على جائزة الإنفينيتي للصحافة المصورة من المركز الدولي للتصوير بنيويورك. يعمل ويعيش ماجولي حالياً في نيويورك وميلانو.

مها مأمون

Night Visitor: The Night of Counting the Years, 2011
دقيقة فيديو عالي الجودة 8:00 دقيقة
⟶ صفحة ١٧٨ - ١٧٩

"عندما تشاهد المادة الفيلمية الموجودة على اليوتيوب التي قام بتصويرها الرجال والنساء الذين اقتحموا مبنى أمن الدولة يوم 5 مارس 2011، ترى طرق الكلام المختلفة لهذه اللحظة السياسية والمكان المشحونان. تتيح اللقطات من هذه الهواتف ما هو أكثر من صور لأفعال ودوافع أسياد هذا المبنى، فهي تكشف عن أبعاد سيكولوجية للناشطين ولمن هم في السلطة."

تعيش مها مأمون وتعمل في القاهرة. عرضت أعمالها في الكثير من المعارض حول العالم، منها مركز فيته دي فيت للفن المعاصر في روتردام، في متحف الفن المعاصر بنيويورك ومتحف فيلاديلفيا للفن. شاركت مأمون في إعداد معارض مختلفة ومشاريع فنية منها فوتو كايرو 3 في القاهرة، ميتينج بوينتس 5 وهو معرض للفن المعاصر يجوب أنحاء الشرق الأوسط، وأيضاً مشروع كتاب "ذي ميدل إير". إن مأمون هي عضوة مؤسسة لمركز الصورة المعاصرة، وهو مبادرة مستقلة عامة تخدم الفنانين، أسس في 2004 بالقاهرة.

ياسمينا متولي

Play Time, 2012
عمل فني من مجمع من عرض فيديو (5:00 دقائق) و عروض صور سلايد (20 صورة ثابتة من الفيديو منقولة إلى صور سلايد)
⟶ صفحة ١٧٤ - ١٧٥

ولدت ياسمينا متولي عام 1982 في مدينة وارسو، ونشأت بين وارسو والقاهرة. حصلت على الماجستير عام 2006 من أكاديمية الفنون الجميلة بمدينة بوزنان، بولندا، أعقبتها بدبلوم من كلية الفنون بايم شو في سينترال سانت مارتينز، لندن. انتقلت متولي في 2009 إلى القاهرة وعرضت أعمالها في معرض في جاليري تاون هاوس. كون ياسمينا متولي وفيليب رزق في 2011 فريق يصور مقاطع فيديو وأصدروا سلسلة من الأفلام القصيرة عن الأحداث أثناء وحول ثورة 25 يناير، تحت عنوان إعادة صنع 25 يناير: سلسلة من ستة.

كريس ميشالسكي و سيباستيان شتومف

We didn't see it, but we heard about it, 2012
عمل مركب فيديو وصوت، 11:50 دقيقة
⟶ صفحة ١٥٠ - ١٥١

"نحن لم نرى شيئاً ولكننا سمعنا عنه، عمل فني بالصوت والصورة يعكس آراء وإنطباعات الأطفال والناشئة، الذين يعيشون في حي المقطم في أقصى الجنوب الشرقي من القاهرة. لم يكن هؤلاء الصغار مشاركين في أو شهود عيان على الثورة. أدركوا الثورة عبر التلفاز أو أحاديث أقاربهم أو أقرانهم أو جيرانهم. إنهم لا يعيشون بعيداً عن بؤر المواجهات، ولدى الكثير منهم أقرباء أو أصدقاء شاركوا في المظاهرات. ولكنهم يواجهون كماً هائلاً من المعلومات المتضاربة أحياناً. تبين أقوال هؤلاء محاولاتهم لفهم التغيرات الجذرية للوصول إلى شروحات لوصف ما حدث. إنها محاولات فردية لفهم الأحداث المعقدة ونتائجها المتوقعة. ترافق أقوال الأطفال المسموعة مقاطع فيديو لطفل منهمك في لعبه في وسط شوارع المقطم المليئة بالحركة اليومية".

ولد كريس ميشالسكي عام 1976 في نيويورك وهو يعيش في لايبزغ، ونوفوسيبيرسك، روسيا. كاتب وفنان ومترجم.

ولد سيباستيان شتومف عام 1980 في مدينة فورتسبورج، يعمل بالتصوير الضوئي والتركيبات البصرية. بعد إنهاء الدراسة في كلية الجرافيك وفن الكتاب في مدينة لايبزغ كطالب متميز تحت يد تيم راوتر، حصل في 2010 على جائزة ماريون إيرمر وفي 2010/2011 حصل على منحة المؤسسة الثقافية الإتحادية. تعرض أعماله في معارض مثل مركز الفن والتقنية الوسائطية في كارلسروهه، متحف الصور في فينترتور وفي متحف الفنون الجميلة في لايبزغ.

أليكس نانس

أليكس نانس، ثورة في تغريدات، 2011-2013
⟶ صفحة ٦٢ - ٦٣، ١١٨ - ١١٩

"عندما بدأت الاحتجاجات في مصر، أطلق بعض المعلقين الأجانب على هذه الاحتجاجات اسم ثورة التويتر. ولكنهم كانوا مخطئين. إن الثورات لا تبدأ من العدم وبالتأكيد لا تبدأ في العالم الافتراضي. وان كان تويتر أتاح فرصة نقل أخبار الثورة أول بأول، مبينا بذلك تميزها. وثق كتاب تويتات من التحرير، ما كتب على التويتر في أثناء الثمانية عشر يوماً الأولى للثورة، والتي أنتهت بإسقاط حسني مبارك. لم تنتهي الثورة عند هذا الحد بالطبع. قام معرض القاهرة مدينة مفتوحة، صور جديدة من ثورة مستمرة بأخذ هذا المبدأ مع مد الفترة إلى الحاضر، لكي تتحول الأحداث إلى إطار إخباري. يظهر في الكتابين نفس مستخدمي التويتر، ومع تعقد الموقف السياسي ظهر الخلاف بين الأصوات المختلفة. إن تشتت الأخبار يعكس واقع فترة ما بعد مبارك، التي كانت فترة يصعب إدارتها بالمقارنة بالثماني عشر يوماً الأولى. هذه المجموعة من مستخدمي التويتر لا تمثل الشعب المصري بأكمله على التويتر أو الثوريين أو النظام السياسي الممتد. ولكن تعتبر هذه الشهادات نظرة مبهرة على الثورة المصرية المستمرة.

أليكس نانس، كاتب وناشط سياسي وموسيقي من لندن. كان أحد من أصدروا الكتاب الأول الذي يحكي عن هذا الحدث التاريخي بمساعدة التويتر: تويتات من التحرير: اندلاع الثورة المصرية، بكلمات من أشعلوها. أنتجت قناة الجزيرة بعد ذلك فيلم وثائقي بنفس العنوان. درس نانس التاريخ في جامعة كامبريدج.

نرمين همام

من سلسلة: Upekkha، 2011
طباعة بحبر سائل، 60×90سم، 50×90 سم
⟶ صفحة ١٦٠ - ١٦١

"علمنا أثناء أحداث الثورة المصرية في يناير بأن هناك تحرك من الجيش وخشينا ذلك. لقد تركت تلك القوة الأسطورية ثكناتها في الصحراء لتتصادم مع المدنيين المصريين المتواجدين في ميدان التحرير. تحركت الدبابات ببطء تحت أزيز الجنازير عبر شوارع القاهرة الخالية. وعندما فُتحت كواتها لم تظهر الأوجه الغاضبة النمطية لجبروت السلطة ورمز الرجولة، بل ظهرت أوجه فتية ذات أحداق واسعة لشباب نحيف البنية ببدلة عسكرية لا تتناسب مع أحجامهم. أدهشتني هزالة الجنود وصغر سنهم، في تلك اللحظة تأكد لي بأن السلطة عبارة عن أسطورة تحاك، ليست إلا هيكل، غير متواجد على أرض الواقع ولكن في أذهاننا. كان جبروت العسكر عبارة عن تهيآت متبادلة يتقاسمها كل من المدنيين والجنود. السلطة في نفس الوقت عبارة عن رقصة منسقة بدقة تتضمن ديكورات حولت هؤلاء الشباب إلى رموز لقوة عسكرية رادعة. خلال الأيام الثمانية عشر للثورة لم يتدخل الجيش وظهر الجيش أثناءها في موقف المشاهد للأحداث في مواجهة الآلاف من المتظاهرين. كانت لدي رغبة في السخرية من إعلانات ظهرت في الخمسينات والستينات تعرض رجالاً ونساءاً في مظاهر قوة ورمزية. تُبرز خلفيات الإعلانات في أعمالي التناقض الواضح في تواجد الرجال المسلحين وسط المدنيين في ميدان التحرير: رجال الحرب في الجنة."

ولدت نيرمين همام عام 1967 في القاهرة. درست في معهد السينما التابع لمدرسة تيش للفن في نيويورك. تتضافر في صورها الرمزية المكثفة الصور الفوتوغرافية مع الرسم. عرضت أعمالها في العديد من الأماكن وهي جزء من العديد من المقتنيات في جميع أنحاء العالم.

المصورون الصحفيون بجريدة الشروق

مجدي إبراهيم درس الإعلام ويعمل مع الشروق منذ بدايتها في 2008
⟶ صورة 40
هبه الخولي درست الفنون الجميلة وتعمل مع الشروق منذ 2012
⟶ صورة 13
محمد الميموني درس التجارة ويعمل مع الشروق منذ 2008
⟶ صورة 44
روجر أنيس درس الفنون الجميلة ويعمل مع الشروق منذ 2010
⟶ صورة 15 ⟶ صورة 34، 35، 42
صبري خالد درس طب الأسنان ويعمل مع الشروق منذ نهاية 2012
⟶ صورة 45
هبه خليفة درست الفنون الجميلة وتعمل مع الشروق منذ 2009
⟶ صورة 47
رافي شاكر درس الحقوق ويعمل مع الشروق منذ 2010
⟶ صورة 38
رندا شعث درست الإعلام والدراسات الشرق

يوهانا دومكه و مروان عمارة

CROP, 2013
فيديـو عالـي الجودة، 45:09 دقيقة
⟵ صفحة ١٤٤ - ١٤٥

CROP فيلـم وثائقي يعكس معنى الصـور في الثـورة المصريـة. لا يعـرض الفيلـم مناظـر من الإنتفاضات، لكنه يظهر كيفية عمل صحيفة الأهرام المصرية أكبر صحف الدولة تأثيـراً. يجعلنا الفيلم شهود عيان لعرض متسلسل منسق لصور ثابتـة، تظهر خطوات عمل هذه الصحيفة من الداخل، من مكتب المدير إلى خطوات عمل كل موظف. وكمرافقة صوتيـة نستمع إلى قصة وهميـة لمصور صحفي فاتته الثورة بسبب إقامتـه في المستشفى. تعكس حكايتـه تقييماً شخصياً للإستراتيجيات الإعلامية للنظام القديـم.

ولدت يوهانا دومكه عام 1978 في مدينـة كيـل نشأت في ألمانيـا والأرجنتيـن. درست الفـن في أكاديميـة الفن الملكية الدنماركية في كوبنهاجن، وفي أكاديمية مالمو للفن في السويد. تخصص دومكه هو الأفلام، الفيديو والتصوير. عرضت أعمالها في معارض جماعية دوليـة وفرديـة، آخرها في قاعة شيدهالّة بزيورخ، جاليـري برليـن، قاعـة الفـن نيقولاي في كوبنهاجن وكازينو في لوكسمبورج. تعيش حالياً بين برلين، إسطنبول وكوبنهاجن، تنتج أعمالاً تنتمي إلى الخط الفاصل بين الفن والسينما.

ولد مروان عمارة عام 1987 وهو صانع أفلام من القاهرة. درس التصوير الفوتوغرافي في كلية الفنون التطبيقية وبدأ في 2006 الدراسة في أكاديميـة السينمـا والفن والتكنولوجيـا. عمل كمصور حـر، وعرضت أعماله داخل وخارج مصر. صور العديد من الأفلام الوثائقية وعمل في مشاريـع مختلفة. اشترك في برنامج "آربيبا أوف سكرين" و"دوربان تالنت كامبوس" لصانعـي الأفلام الشبـاب. سوف يتم إنتاج أول فيلم له في 2013 "وقوف متكرر".

فيليب رزق

Sturm: Ahmonseto, 2010
فيديـو عالي الجودة، 6:09 دقيقة
⟵ صفحة ١٤٣
Sturm: Fayoum, 2010
فيديـو عالي الجودة، 4:53 دقيقة
⟵ صفحة ١٤٢

عاصفة: الفيـوم
"إنخفض منسوب مياه نهر النيل المـار عبر قريـة أبو كساة في مركز الفيـوم عن ذي قبـل. جفت الكثير من حقول الفيوم المعروفة بإنتاجها للفواكه والخضروات، وأحد أسباب ذلك هو قلة وصول المياه للأراضي مقارنـة بالمـاضي، الناتـج عن تصرفات المسؤوليـن عن توزيـع الميـاه، حيـث يتصرفـون لمنفعتهم الشخصية: فهم مرتشون ويأخذون أكثر مما يستحقون ويحابـون أصدقـائهم ومعـارفهم. تحولت هذه الجرائم الصغيـرة في بعض المناطق إلى فساد على مستوى عالٍ. يحتـاج قطاع الزراعة الصناعيـة، الذي توسع في السنوات الماضية حول مدينة الفيوم، إلى كميات ضخمة من الميـاه. يقوم ملاك قطاع الزراعـة الصناعيـة بتصديـر معظم المحاصيل الزراعية إلى الخارج لجني ربـح أكبر. تعود ملكية الكثير من المؤسسات الزراعية إلى أعضاء سابقون في البرلمان أو أعضـاء من الجهاز الأمني للحكومة، بالإضافة إلى ذلك تقوم الدولة بدعم سياسة التصدير، عملاً بأن رفع مستوى التصديـر 'يقوي اقتصاد الدولة'. أما المصريون فقد عانـوا من زيـادة أسعار المـواد الغذائيـة في عـام 2011 بنسبة ثمانية عشر في المئة."

عاصفة: أمونسيتو
"في عـام 2002 حاول محمد خميس، أحد كبار ملاك المصانع المقرب من نظام مبـارك، أن يصبح شريكاً في شركة أمونسيتو. وبعـد رفض المـالك عادل آغا إشراك خميس تـم إتهامـه بالإختـلاس ووُضع في السجن. بعد إطلاق سراحه بعد ثلاثـة أعـوام تورط آغا في مشكلة ديـن مع بنـك مصر الحكومي وتم الحكم عليه بالسجن لمدة ثلاثة أعوام أخرى وهرب من مصر. تقدم عمال مصنع النسيج البالغ عددهم الألفيـن بطلب إلى المحكمة لتأميـن أماكن عملهم، وطالبوا بنقل مسؤولية إدارة المصنع أثنـاء غيـاب آغـا إليهم. وبعد سنوات من الجمود إرتأت لجنة حكومية بأن المصنع غير صالح للعمل حيث وُكل محمد خميس بمهمة تقييـم المصنـع وصياغة تقريـر حوله. يكافح العمال منذ إيقـاف العمل في المصنـع للحصـول على تعويـض، ولو بسيـط، عن خسارتـهم لوظائفهم من قبل بنـك مصر، الذي إنتقلت إليه ملكيـة المصنع."

ولد فيليـب رزق عام 1982 في ليماسول، قبرص، يعيش كصانع لمقاطع الفيديو وكاتب في القاهرة. درس الفلسفة والأنثروبولوجيا في الجامعة الأمريكية بالقاهرة. أخرج أول فيلـم وثـائـقي له في عـام 2008 تحت عنوان الحيـاة الفلسطينية وسافر الفيلـم إلى مهرجان لندن للأفلام الوثائقية واحتفل بأول عرض له هنـاك. كون فيليب رزق وياسمينـا متـولي في 2011 فريـق يصور مقـاطـع الفيديـو وأصدرا سلسلة من الأفلام القصيـرة عن الأحداث أثناء وحول ثورة 25 يناير، تحت عنوان إعـادة صنع 25 ينايـر: سلسلة من ستة. إن فيليـب هو أيضاً عضـو في مجموعة مُصرِّيـن التي توثق أحداث الثـورة.

جوناثان رشاد

من ألبومات فليكر
إشتباكات مصر - 2012
⟵ صورة 36-38
إقتحام مقر الإخوان
⟵ صورة 39-41
إعتصام قصر الرئاسة
⟵ صفحة ٧٣

جوناثان رشاد صحفي مصـور شاب من القاهرة. بـدأ يعمل كمصور في 2008 وركز اهتمامـه في 2010 على الصحافـة. استخدمـت صـور رشـاد كصورة لغلاف كتاب "تويتات من التحرير" وأيضاً "في مصـر" هذا فضلاً عن المئات من المقـالات في الإنترنت والمجلات المختلفة. عرضت صوره داخل وخارج مصـر مثـل الولايـات المتحدة الأمريكيـة وإنجلتـرا وتونس وفرنسا. حاز رشاد على جائـزة مسابقة IFES للتصوير في مارس 2011.

إبراهيم سعد

The House of the Republic, 2012
عمل فني مكون من مونتاج صور مكبرة وعرض فيديو ثنـائي القنوات على شاشات 10:06 دقائق
⟵ صفحة ١٧٢ - ١٧٣

"بيـت الجمهوريـة مشروع مقارنـة بيـن الثـورة المصرية والثورة الرومانية والبحث عن أوجه التشابه بينهما. فعلى سبيل المثال يُطرح السؤال لماذا قامت هاتان الثورتان وكيف بدأتا وكيف انتهتا."

إبراهيـم سعد، فنـان تشكيلي يعيـش ويعمل في القاهرة، درس في كليـة الفنون الجميلـة بجامعـة حلوان. عرضت مشاريعه الفنية في مصر وأوروبا وآسيـا. شارك سعـد في العديـد من ورش العمـل وبرامج الإقامة في مصر والصين وهولندا وسويسرا. تبحث أعمالـه أعمـاق النفس البشريـة، يحـاول توصيل الأحاسيس البشرية بمساعدة طرق مبتكرة. يستخدم نفسه كموديل في فقراته الأدائية وصوره والفيديو.

مريم عبد العزيز

من سلسلة الثورة المصرية، 2011
⟵ صورة 46+47
من سلسلة حكايات المحمول، 2012
⟵ صورة 16، ⟵ صورة 14

يجمع منظر الجموع الغفيـرة معظم الصور التي التقطت في أثنـاء فترة الثمانيـة عشر يوماً الأولى للثورة. تمتلك مصورة البورتريه مريم عبد العزيز، التي ولـدت في القاهـرة وتعيش بيـن نيويـورك والقاهرة، المنظورين: الداخلي والخارجي. فهي تركز على الفرد، على الشخص الواحـد، على تفاصيـل والحركات التي تحمل أهمية أكبر من المنظور البعيد، ثم تفكر وتتدبر، ليس فقط في التصوير.

مريـم عبد العزيـز مصورة فرنسيـة من أصل مصري. بدأت حياتها العملية بقضاء سبع سنوات في التسويق، بعد أن أتمت دراسة العلوم السياسية، الصحافة والتسويق. ثم قررت أن تعمل بالتصوير الفوتوغرافي، درست في المركز الدولي للصوري في نيويـورك وأنهـت الدراسـة في 2006. منـذ هذا الوقت تنشر أعمالها في مجلات كبيرة مثل لوموند، نيووزويـك، مجلة التايـم، كوريـر إنترناشيونال وأيمازينج، كما تعرض أعمالـهـا في معارض حول العالم. عبد العزيز عضو المجموعة الفنية "ميدل ايسترن وومان فوتوجرافر: راويـة". تعمل بشكل أساسي على ريبورتـاجـات من الشـرق الأوسـط وأفريقيـا.

محمد عز

Vinegar .. Soldier .. Coke, 2011
طباعة زرقاء على ورق قطني، 120×60سم
⟵ صفحة ١٦٢ - ١٦٣

"...لقد جربنـا ذلك في تونـس، حتى أصبحت قنابلهم من غيـر فائـدة... فليكن اللّه في عـون الشعب المصري." إنتشرت مثل تلك الأخبار في الليلة الأولى للثورة المصرية، عندما نجحت قوات الشرطة بتفريـق المظاهرات. كان السبب في ذلك هي قنابـل الغاز المسيـل للدمـوع وعدم معرفـة المتظاهرين بكيفية حماية أنفسهم منها. وفي اليوم التالي توالت إفادات النشطاء التونسيين حول كيفية التعامل مع الغاز. وفي يـوم جمعـة الغضب حمل المصريون قوارير الخل والكولا معهم، واستطاعوا مقاومة الجنود، وتجددت الإحتجاجات التي قادت إلى إطاحة النظام القائم منذ ثلاثين عاماً.

محمد عز، مصور ومهندس، ولد عام 1985 في القاهرة، حيث يعمل ويعيش الآن. يصور مشاهد وأحداث في بيئته المباشرة وبهذا يحول الانتباه إلى الإنسان في حياته اليومية وإلى تفاصيل مختلفة من حيـاة المجتمع المصري. منذ 2005 يشارك في معارض وأحداث فنية. حصل على جائزة اللجنة لمسابقـة الصـورة الأولـى للبعثـة الأوروبيـة في 2008، والجائـزة الذهبيـة في مسابقـة الشارقـة للصـورة العربية 2011.

هبة فريد

ألبومات لعائلات ينتمي أفرادها للجيش أوائل عشرينات وحتى أواخر سبعينيات القرن العشرين
⟵ صورة 1، صفحة ١٥٦ - ١٥٩
هبة فريد، شهادات، المظاهرات والصحافة المصورة؛ شرح الصورة: هبة فريد، أمجد نجيب، منة خليل، من مقتنيات: أمجد نجيب.
⟵ صورة 2+3، ⟵ صورة 2-4

هبة فريد- صناعة الأبطال- ألبومات صور عائلات ضباط الجيش والشرطة
نُسَخ (صور مجلدة) من 8 ألبومات صور قديمة، ورق وبلاستيك، طباعة بالجيلاتين الفضي، وطباعة بالألوان، بعضها معدل/ملون يدوياً. يرجع تاريخ الألبومات والصور إلى أوائل العشرينات من القرن المنصرم وحتى أواخر السبعينات.

إن ألبومات الصور المُجهزة من قِبَل ذوي ضباط الجيش ورجال الشرطة وعمال الحراسة هي أعمال فنية مجمعة تساعد المتفرج على تكوين صورة لنفسه. ففي ألبوم "الجنرال" لويس إبراهيم تظهر شخصيـة المايسترو غريب الطباع، الحائز على العديـد من النياشيـن، وهـو يقـود الأوركستـرا العسكري المصري من منتصف الستينات وحتى أوائل السبعينات. وهو يفصح عن ميوله المسرحية وحب الظهور وحبه لزوجتـه.

ألبوم الجنرال لويس إبراهيم
⟵ صورة 1، صفحة ١٥٨ - ١٥٩
صور جيب (14×10×1 سم) تحتوي على كارنيهات وبورتريهات للويس إبراهيم وزوجته، من الستينات؛ بلاستيك، من الألبومات المتاحة في المَحَل، أربعـة جيوب بلاستيكية للصور (1 قابلة للفتح، ثلاثة أعمدة)، أربعة صور مطبوعة بالجيلاتين الفضي، 8×11 سم، ثلاثـة بطاقـات تحقيق شخصيـة بها صورة، بقايا (آدمية)، تذكار (القدس) على كرتون، نسخة ملونة لأيقونة، 7×10.5 سم.

ألبوم أكاديمية الشرطة
⟵ صفحة ١٥٦ - ١٥٧
نسخة يعتقد أنها بروفـه للشكل النهائي. توثـق زيارة رسميـة وتؤكد على الهوية المعاصرة لقوات الأمـن في مصر بعـد ثـورة 1952 وروح الدولـة المؤسساتيـة التي تروج لنفسها.
ألبوم يحتوي على صور تذكاريـة من أكاديميـة الشرطة، في فترة الستينيات؛ جلد، ألبوم صور من المتوفرين في السوق، محفور باللون الذهبي كلمة "ألبوم"، مجلد؛ الغلاف مبطن بقماش من الداخل، الصفحـات الداخلية من الورق؛ 16 صفحـة، 15 صورة، طبـاعة بالجيلاتين الفضي، 13.5×18.5 سم؛ 24 صورة: 9×14 سم، مادة لزجـة، فواصل مـن ورق شفـاف؛ فتحـة الغـلاف إلى اليسار 24.5×30.5×2 سم.

ولدت هبـة فريـد عام 1966 في القاهرة، وهي فنانة تعمل في مجالات مختلفة من الفن، درست هندسـة عمارة البيئـة والفنون الجميلـة. وكانت بالإضافة لأنشطتها الفنيـة، عضو مؤسس لمركز الصورة المعاصرة (CIC) وهو مبادرة مستقلة عامـة تخدم الفنانيـن، أُسست في 2004. تعمل هبة فريد منذ 2006 في تنظيـم برنامج لذاكرة الفوتوغرافيـا لمركز توثيق التراث الحضاري والطبيعي، وهو مبادرة قائمة على البحـث، وتركز على تاريـخ التصويـر الضوئي وممارستها في مصر. حاليـاً تعيش فريد وتعمل في القاهرة.

طه بلال

The Death of Pope Shenouda, 2012
ورق جرائد ملصق على ورق، 29,7×42 سم
⟵ صفحة ١٦٦ - ١٦٧

"توفى البابا شنودة الثالث بطريرك معظم الأقباط المصريين والذي يقدر عددهم بـ 12 مليون مسيحي في مصر، في يوم السبت 17 مارس، 2012 بسبب الشيخوخة. لقد قرعت الأجراس مع انتشار الأخبار في حي العباسية في القاهرة، موقع الكاتدرائية القبطية الرئيسية في مصر. أصبح شنودة 88 عاماً، البابا ال 117 للإسكندرية في نوفمبر عام 1971، وكان محبوباً بين المسيحيين والمسلمين في مصر على حد سواء خلال حياته أربعة عقود في السلطة."

ولد طه بلال عام 1984 بالقاهرة. ذهب للدراسة في الولايات المتحدة الأمريكية عام 2001، حصل في 2008 على الماجستير من كلية كاليفورنيا للفنون في سان فرانسيسكو. حصل بلال على إقامة في مركز هيدلاندس للفنون وتم ترشيحه لجائزة متحف سان فرانسيسكو للفن الحديث. عرضت أعماله في معارض مختلفة. وهو يعيش ويعمل الآن في القاهرة.

لارا بلدي

Alone, Together... In Media Res, 2012
تركيب مرئي لثلاثة قنوات تليفزيونية / 42 دقيقة
بحث: لارا بلدي
أرشيف (فيديو، مقالات، صور)
لارا بلدي وأمينة دياب
برمجة: ميشيل كارتر
⟵ صفحة ١٨٠ - ١٨٢

"في يناير 2011، عندما بدأ فيديو (ميدان تيانانمن – القاهرة، شجاعة في القاهرة) بالإنتشار على اليوتيوب بسرعة فائقة، وضع صديق لي على الفيسبوك خطبة ألقاها جان بول سارتر قبل 40 عاماً على عمال صناعة السيارات الفرنسيين المضربين آنذاك. وعندما إشتدت حدة التوترات السياسية، كثرت صور ومقاطع فيديو ميدان التحرير المزدحم في الإنترنت. تشابهت تلك المواد مع صور إنتفاضات أخرى إنطلقت في مناطق مختلفة في الشرق الأوسط وشمال أفريقيا كما تشابهت الأصوات المرافقة للصور مع مظاهر حركات مدنية ولت. كان الوضع وكأن سارتر يحتج معنا في التحرير أيضاً.

بدأت آنذاك بإنشاء مشروع أرشفة حية أسميته "صوت الشعب". جمعت لذلك مقاطع الفيديو والمقالات والصور المتصلة بتلك الأحداث، بالإضافة إلى مواد حول أحداث مهمة حدثت في العالم بعد الـ 25 من يناير. بحثت عن مقاطع مصورة جعلت من ميدان التحرير موضوعاً وكل شيء يتعلق بذلك من أفلام تاريخية حول خطب فلسفية وحتى الكاريكاتورات المحظورة وأشياء أخرى كثيرة.

"فرادأ أو معاً، ...في المعمعة" هو أول عمل قمت بتطويره بإستخدام مواد ذلك الأرشيف. إنه حكاية حبكت من العديد من مقاطع الفيديو تدعو للتفكير في أسئلة كثيرة طرحت أثناء الإنتفاضات العربية. تعتبر الثورة نقطة بداية إنهيار مرحلة تاريخية، وأنا في وسطها كـ أليس في بلاد العجائب أسقط في حفرة اسمها اليوتيوب."

ولدت الفنانة المصرية اللبنانية لارا بلدي في بيروت، قضت سنوات طفولتها وشبابها في القاهرة وباريس ودرست في لندن. تعيش منذ عام 1997 في مصر. عرضت ونشرت أعمال بلدي في العديد من الدول. تتكون أعمالها من صور، فيديو، كولاج/مونتاج بصري، تركيبات، تصاميم هندسية، سجاد وحتى عطور. أثناء إشتعال الاحتجاجات في 2011 ساعدت بلدي في تأسيس مبادرتين إعلاميتين: راديو التحرير وسينما التحرير. يهدف المشروعين إلى خلق أرشيف عن الثورة ومنها ومشاركتها مع الآخرين. كما أن بلدي عضوة في المؤسسة العربية للصورة منذ تأسيسها في 1997. يمثلها في القاهرة جاليري التاون هاوس وفي دبي جاليري ISVDE.

مصطفى بهجت

مقاطع فيديو من الاشتباكات وحرب الشوارع في الفترة الزمنية من نوفمبر 2011 وحتى فبراير 2012
⟵ صفحة ٨٩ - ٩٢

يتمتع صحفي الفيديو مصطفى بهجت في دوائر الناشطين الشباب بسمعة أسطورية. فهو دائماً في الصفوف الأمامية. ويقال أنه قادر على التنسيق بين سرعته في الركض والبعد البؤري لعدسة الزووم الخاصة به. وهو يعيش حياة مزدوجة كمراسل. يعمل بالأساس كمصور لقناة "ONtv"، ويأخذ اللقطات العنيفة واللقطات التي يصورها لأهداف معينة ليستعملها في أفلامه الخاصة.

كايا بهكلام

Excursions in the Dark, 2011
19:40 دقيقة فيديو عالي الجودة
⟵ صفحة ١٣٨ - ١٣٩

"القاهرة في فبراير 2011. تمت الإطاحة بالدكتاتور حسني مبارك وعاد الهدوء إلى الشوارع. لكن الأزقة المظلمة وميادين المدينة تبدو خالية من المارة. حيث أحال حظر التجول الليلي مناطق الثورة إلى عالم مجهول الزمان، إلى مسرح ينتظر أن تبدأ العروض عليه بعد إنسدال الستار وقبل رفعه. يا تُرى ما هو العرض الذي سيُقدم؟ مقاطع حوارات مع نساء ورجال يتذكرون أحلامهم، يتحدثون عن خوف من مجهول وصور مبهمة، يتباين ذلك مع لقطات من كاميرا ثابتة ترى المدينة وكأنها تحقيق للآمال وأصداء لعصور مضت.

وبإستعارة لكلمات والتر بنيامين (نزهة في الظلام يحاكي -اللحظة- التي يتقمص بها حتى المؤرخ نفسه مهمة مفسر الأحلام)، وينتهي العرض بنقل الصورة إلى نقطة التلاشي حيث تتلاقى هندسة المدينة المعمارية والأحلام المشتركة والمراجع السياسية."

ولد كايا بهكلام عام 1978 في برلين. هو فنان وكتب العديد من الكتب منها: A Spectre Haunting Europe: The Middle Eastern Migrant and the German Angst (أوروبا يطاردها شبح: المهاجر الشرق أوسطي والهموم الألمانية). يمتلك بهكلام مصنع في مدينة أضنة بتركيا، تنتج تشكيلات فنية بالطلب. يشغل منصب مدير مساعد في متحف ريلودينج إيمدجز إيماتيريال. يعيش حالياً بالقاهرة ويُدرس في كلية الفنون بالجامعة الأمريكية.

إيفا بيرترام

High Seats, 2008-2012
صور طباعة ألوان، 20×30 سم
⟵ صفحة ١٦٨ - ١٧١

"نرى في العمل الفني كراسي مرتفعة أبراج مراقبة تحتوي على 'حراس' أو لا تحتوي على شيء، كتلك التي نعرفها في محيط المنشآت العسكرية والمؤسسات الحكومية والمرافق ذات الأهمية الإستراتيجية أو العملية. إنها صور تم إلتقاطها بسرعة وفي سرّية وأحياناً من مسافات بعيدة ومن منظور المراقب العادي الذي قد يكون هو أيضاً تحت المراقبة. يظهر في الغالب أن المنطقة المراد مراقبتها لا تفي الغرض الإستراتيجي للمراقبة مما يؤدي إلى مصادفات غريبة. فالأبراج المكشوفة تتحول لآثار وضعت في المكان الخاطىء معلنة عن ضعف القوى.

ولدت إيفا بيرترام عام 1964، درست تصميم الجرافيك / فن الاتصال البصري في جامعة فولكفانج بمدينة إيسّن، تخصصت في التصوير الفني عند يورجن كلاوكه. شاركت في معارض داخل وخارج ألمانيا منذ 1993. أصبحت أعمالها جزء من مقتنيات متاحف مختلفة مثل المتحف في فولكفانج وإيسّن والمركز القومي للصوتيات والمرئيات في لوكسمبورج. تدرس بيرترام منذ عام 2007 في المدرسة الجديدة للتصوير الفوتوغرافي في برلين، ومنذ عام 2012 تدرس في جامعة الفنون في برلين. تعيش وتعمل في برلين.

طارق حفني

you two faced whore!, 2008
طباعة أبيض وأسود على ورق جرائد
⟵ صفحة ١٤٠ - ١٤١

"خلت الكثير من عارضات الإعلانات المنتشرة على الطرق السريعة في مصر وأضحت فارغة منذ الأزمة المالية 2008. تطوق عارضات الإعلانات الطريق الواصل بين القاهرة والإسكندرية وتبرزها وسط الطبيعة المتوحشة المحيطة بالطريق. صور حفني، التي تعتبر إمتداداً لتقليد الصور التوبوغرافية، توثق التغييرات التي تطرأ على الطبيعة بفعل الإنسان، التي تعكس التمدد الحضري بشكل واضح."

يعمل طارق حفني كمصور. حصل في 2005 على البكالوريوس بامتياز، قسم التصوير الزيتي من كلية الفنون الجميلة بجامعة حلوان بالقاهرة. شارك حفني في العديد من المعارض الجماعية والفردية بأعماله من تصوير زيتي وتصوير ضوئي. من أكثر الموضوعات التي تهمه هي الحياة العصرية في المدينة وتبعاتها. وأثرت فيه حياته في القاهرة حيث وجه اهتمامه إلى العلاقة بين الأشخاص والأماكن التي يعيشون فيها.

نادين خان و مريم مكيوي

I Will Speak of the Revolution, 2011
فيديو عالي الجودة، 1:07 دقيقة
⟵ صفحة ١٧٦ - ١٧٥

درست صانعة الأفلام نادين خان في معهد السينما العالي بالقاهرة وحصلت على البكالوريوس في الإخراج. من خلال عملها كمساعد للمخرج ومنتجة عملت مع العديد من المخرجين، منهم والدها، محمد خان ويسري نصرالله ونبيل عيوش.

تعمل مريم مكيوي أيضاً كمخرجة. درست في الجامعة الأمريكية بالقاهرة وهي حالياً طالبة ماجستير في مجال الفيلم/الفيديو والتصوير الفوتوغرافي الفني في كلية الفنون الجميلة بمدينة هامبورج. تعمل مكيوي منذ 2008 كمخرجة ومونتيرة حرة.

أسامة داوود

ماسبيرو، 2012
⟵ صفحة ١١٦ - ١١٧
El Tawheed & El Nour, 2013
فيديو عالي الجودة، 2:30 دقيقة
⟵ صفحة ١٥٢ - ١٥٣

في فيديو أسامة داوود نشاهد عمال ومستخدمين يغادرون بنايات تحتوي على مؤسسات تعود ملكيتها للإخوان المسلمين. يشير الفيديو إلى إحدى أوائل الأعمال السينمائية –فيلم لوي وأوغسطة لوميير المعنون بـ "عمال يغادرون مصانع لوميير"، من العام 1895–، كما تعطيك المقاطع القصيرة إنطباعاً عن التنظيم الصارم للإخوان.

ولد أسامة داوود عام 1980 في الإسماعيلية، مصر. درس التصميم والجرافيك حتى عام 2003 في كلية الفنون الجميلة بجامعة حلوان القاهرة، ثم قام بعمل الماجستير في معهد سان فرانسيسكو للفنون في كاليفورنيا. شارك داوود في العديد من المعارض في مصر وأوروبا وآسيا، منها معارض فردية في جاليري تاون هاوس وآرتلوه. وهو حالياً يدرس التصوير بالجامعة الأمريكية بالقاهرة ويعيش بين القاهرة الإسماعيلية.

دينيس دايّو

Memories of a Revolution, 2012
حبر سائل طباعة، 30×30سم، 60×60سم
⟵ صفحة ١٤٦ - ١٤٩

"القاهرة، الخامس من أبريل 2008. اتصل بي أحد أصدقائي الفرنسيين وقال لي: "لا تخرج غداً فإن هناك دعوة للإضراب على شبكات التواصل الإجتماعية." على الرغم من ذلك خرجت في السادس من أبريل للذهاب إلى ميدان التحرير. لم يكن هناك مظاهرات، وكانت الشرطة متواجدة بالمئات، كانت توقف المصريين الخارجين من مترو الأنفاق بشكل تعسفي، الأمر الذي نشر الرعب بينهم. كانت الشرطة في ذلك اليوم متأهبة لمواجهة الإنتفاضة التي لم تحدث. ولكنني قلت لنفسي ذلك اليوم، يجب أن تكون لدى المصريين الشجاعة للموت من أجل الثورة. ذهبت في الثامن والعشرين من يناير 2011، في حوالي الساعة الرابعة مساءً، برفقة صديق لي إلى ميدان التحرير. وفي طريقنا لفتت أنظارنا آثار المعركة: حواجز منتزعة وأرض مليئة بالأنقاض ورائحة الغاز المسيل للدموع في الهواء. وعند وصولنا إلى كوبري قصر النيل، كانت جموع الشباب تفر إلى كل الإتجاهات، كان البعض منهم يحمل جرحاهم. رأيت مجموعة شباب في عمر الزهور تصرخ لبث الشجاعة في نفسها لمواجهة شرطة مدججة بالسلاح. حمل البعض منهم حجارة فقط والبعض الآخر لم يتسلح إلا بالغضب. في تلك اللحظات لم نكن نعرف أن الثورة قد عمّت القاهرة كلها في ذات الوقت. هرع الشباب من كل صوب للتعبير عن غضبهم تجاه الشرطة. لم يكونوا نشطاء سياسيين ولكنهم مواطنين بسطاء. قتلت الشرطة الكثير منهم قنصاً من أعلى أسطح المنازل. وبعد يومين كانت صور الشهداء في كل مكان في الميدان، حيث قام أصدقاؤهم بنشرها. وفي تلك اللحظة بالذات قررت أن أعبر عن إحترامي لهم يوماً ما بتصوير ذويهم ومحيط معيشتهم حتى لا يطويهم النسيان".

ولد دينيس دايّو عام 1958 في مدينة أنجير بفرنسا. يعيش ويعمل في باريس والقاهرة ويشتغل بالأساس منذ 20 عاماً بالتصوير. دايّو عضو آجنس فو وهي وكالة للمصورين.

بيتر فان أجتميل

بيتر فان أجتميل، مصر، القاهرة، 3 فبراير 2011. مؤيدو مبارك يهربون على كوبري 6 أكتوبر، بعد تفوق معارضي مبارك في التغلب عليهم بعد حرب شوارع استمرت لمدة 24 ساعة.
← صورة 55
بيتر فون أجتميل، مصر، القاهرة، 3 فبراير 2011. تستمر المعركة بين مؤيدي ومعارضي مبارك. الأسلحة المستخدمة بدائية، أحجار، عصي ومولوتوف.
← صفحة 56

"أخذت هذه الصور يوم 2 و3 فبراير من شرفة في فندق هيلتون رمسيس. كنت قد بدأت تصوير ومتابعة أحداث الثورة قبلها بأسبوع، وحاولت دون جدوى أن أنقل حجم وقوة الحدث. وفي يوم 2 فبراير انتهى بي الحال كضحية في يد مؤيدي مبارك حيث أنهم تهجموا عليّ بالضرب، كل هذا بسبب سوء تقدير مني. وبمساعدة بعض المصريين الذين تدخلوا لإنقاذي، تمكنت من العودة إلى الفندق، ولم تسمح لي إصاباتي ولا أعصابي المشدودة بالنزول إلى الشارع مرة أخرى. كان معي في الغرفة كاميرا احتياطية بعدسة زووم رخيصة، فبدأت في تصوير إيقاع العنف أثناء الليل واليوم الذي تلاه، حتى استسلم مؤيدو مبارك وهربوا من على كوبري أكتوبر والخوف يملؤهم."

ولد بيتر فون أجتميل عام 1981 في واشنطن العاصمة. درس التاريخ في جامعة ييل وأنهى دراسته في عام 2003 بامتياز. اشترك في عام 2008 في تنظيم معرض Battlespace معرض استرجاعي لأعمال أكثرها غير معروفة من العراق وأفغانستان. حاز في عام 2011 على جائزة ICP Infinity Award للمصورين الشباب، وفي عام 2012 على جائزة Lumix Freelens كما حصل على جوائز من World Press Photo، American Photography Annual، Photo District News. تم ترشيح أجتميل في عام 2008 ليكون عضواً بوكالة ماجنوم وهو عضو فيها منذ 2011. يعمل بشكل مكثف في العراق وأفغانستان والولايات المتحدة الأمريكية.

أميرة الأهل

مقابلة مع صحفي الفيديو مصطفى بهجت، 2012
← صفحة ٨٩ - ٩٢

ولدت أميرة سيد الأهل لأب مصري وأم ألمانية، تعرفت على الثقافة العربية منذ نعومة أظفارها. بعد إتمامها دراسة الصحافة عملت لمدة عامين كمراسلة دولية لمجلة دير شبيغل من القاهرة، تعمل حالياً كمراسلة حرة وخبيرة في شؤون الشرق الأوسط. سافرت إلى لبنان والجزائر والأردن وسوريا والإمارات العربية المتحدة وأيضاً والولايات الأمريكية المتحدة وجنوب أفريقيا وتقريباً كل دول أوروبا الغربية. فتحت لها إمكانياتها اللغوية وخلفيتها أفق ومدخل إلى الدول العربية بشكل يختلف عن باقي الصحفيين الأجانب. وهي تهدف دائماً إلى الكتابة عن الناس وعاداتهم وطريقة عيشتهم بشكل عادل وصادق، بعيداً عن الكليشات والنمطية.

حسام الحملاوي

ستعرض الثورة على فليكر، 8 مايو 2008
← صفحة ٧٤
من ألبوم فليكر: فن الشارع المصري
← صفحة ٦٨ - ٦٩

كتب المدون والصحفي حسام الحملاوي في عام 2008 عن القوة الثورية للصورة. كان السبب هو لقطات المصور المصري ناصر نوري لاحتجاجات العمال في المحلة الكبرى. لم يكن انتشار الصور فقط هو السبب في اندلاع الاحتجاجات في تونس في يناير 2011، تلتها مصر ومناطق أخرى من الوطن العربي، وإن كانت القنوات الرقمية قد قامت بدور مهم.

حسام الحملاوي، صحفي مصري ومصور ومدون، ولد عام 1977. حصل على البكالوريوس من الجامعة الأمريكية بالقاهرة في التجارة وحصل على درجة الماجستير من نفس الجامعة في مجال العلوم السياسية. التحق أثناء الدراسة بالإشتراكيين الثوريين، منظمة تروتسكية في مصر، تعمل حالياً على إنشاء حزب ديموقراطي للعمال. كان الحملاوي من أول المشاركين والمنظمين للثورة المصرية ويكتب عن كل هذا في مدونته. www.arabawy.org

مصعب الشامي

من ألبوم على موقع فليكر تحت عنوان الذكرى الثانية للثورة، 25 يناير 2013
← صورة 14
أقنعة التحرير، 13-2011
← صفحة ٧٨ - ٧٩
الفن ميدان، 7 يناير 2012
← صفحة ٨٢
أسوار وسط المدينة، 12 مارس 2012
← صفحة ٨٠ - ٨١
ثورة الجرافيتي، 15 يوليو 2011
← صفحة ٧٢
الأكثر شعبية 2013
← صفحة ٧٠ - ٧١
الذكرى الأولى لثورة 25 و 27 يناير 2012
← صفحة ٦٩
مصعب الشامي، متظاهرون أثناء خطاب، ميدان التحرير، 8 أبريل 2011
← صورة 50

أقنعة التحرير
"التحرير يشعرك أحياناً وكأنه حفل تنكري غير مقصود. ويمكن رؤية تنوع الناس الذين حضروا المظاهرات منذ اليوم الأول من خلال الملابس التي يرتدوها. في المشروع، لقد ركزت على وجوههم".

ولد مصعب الشامي عام 1990 وهو مصور حر، يعيش ويعمل بالقاهرة. عرضت صوره وألبوماته عن الثورة المصرية في مجلة تايم، ذي إيكونوميست، فورين بوليسي، الجزيرة والأخبار النسخة الإنجليزية، كما ظهر في مطبوعات وصفحات على الإنترنت.

روان الشيمي

جرافيتي ضد قوة وسائل الإعلام الحكومية
← صفحة ١١٤ - ١١٥
الفتاة ذات حمالة الصدر الزرقاء
← صفحة ٨٢ - ٨٣
من ألبوم فليكر - معركة شارع القصر العيني شارع. 18، ديسمبر 2011
← صفحة ٨٣
أسوار في وسط المدينة، القاهرة
← صفحة ٨٠ - ٨١

روان الشيمي، صحفية تكتب عن الأحداث الثقافية في تأثيرها. هي عضوة في الحركات الشعبية. تهتم بالتصوير وشاركت في العديد من المبادرات منها في عام 2012 ورشة عمل "وكالة الأنباء البديلة" في مركز الصورة المعاصرة، ومركز للفنون الجميلة بالقاهرة. ظهرت صورها للثورة المصرية المستمرة داخل وخارج مصر. تتطوع في أعمال مختلفة وتجد هذا ملهماً.

هالة القوصي

The Myths & Legends Room – The Mural, 2010
48 مطبوعة - ملونة صور، 300×900 سم
← صفحة ١٥٤ - ١٥٥

"يتكون هذا العمل الفني لهالة القوصي من قصص مصورة تستند على حقائق تاريخية وإشاعات وتخيلات دينية وتقاليد وأساطير وخرافات. إنها حكايات تستحضر الواقع الذي ينكشف عبرها: حقيقة الحياة في القاهرة، تلك المدينة التي تكاد تكون منطلق كل أعمال القوصي. وفنياً فإن القوصي تستكشف في هذه اللوحة الجدارية مبادئ مونتاج الصور وتستخدمها بأسلوب كبير وبألوان بهيجة، فهي تدمج صور لاستوديوهات تجارية وصور من الحياة اليومية وصور قديمة إكتشفتها ورسومات والرسومات المنتجة على الكمبيوتر بالإضافة إلى مكونات تصميمية في هذا العمل الفني. تشير القوصي بهذا العمل إلى الرسومات الجدارية التي تعرض مشاهد حربية من تاريخ مصر أو الأعمال البطولية للجيش كتلك التي تعرض في المتحف العسكري الوطني ودعم الشعب لهم."

ولدت هالة القوصي عام 1974 في القاهرة. درست في الجامعة الأمريكية قبل حصولها على درجة الماجستير في الصورة وعلوم الاتصالات بكلية جولدسميث في لندن. حاضرت بين عامي 2002 و2003 في موضوع التصوير الفوتوغرافي. وفي 2004 كانت من إحدى مؤسسي مركز الصورة المعاصرة (CIC) بالقاهرة، في 2006 أنهت إقامة دامت لمدة عامين في أكاديمية رايكس للفنون الجميلة بأمستردام. حصلت في 2010 على جائزة Abraaj Capital Art. حصلت على دعم لفيلمها زهرة الصبار من مؤسسة هوبرت بالد التابعة لمهرجان روتردام.

كيم بدوي

متفرجون على لقطات الفيسبوك في ميدان التحرير، القاهرة، 6 ديسمبر 2011.
← صورة 59

"جذبت العروض الليلية ومقاطع الفيديو التي تم تحميلها على الفيسبوك وغيرها من مواقع التواصل الإجتماعي، جموع المصريين من مختلف الطبقات الإجتماعية والمادية والقناعات والاتجاهات. إن الحياة في المجتمع المصري عادة ما تخضع لمفتاح لغوي صارم. الشكل، البنية، السلوك، نوع المحادثة والجنس، كل هذه العوامل تأثر في شكل و"سمعة" الشخص. ولكن لم يكن ذلك هو الحال في الثمانية عشر يوماً الأوائل في ميدان التحرير. لقد وقف المصريون كتفاً إلى كتف. هذا في حد ذاته كان أمراً مقلقاً ولافتاً. أعطى هذا فرصة للتقارب وأعطى الجموع قوة للإستمرار والمواصلة. كان النور المتاح ضعيفاً ولذلك قررت وضع إطار للصورة عن طريق نور البروجكتور لأبين بذلك مدى تنوع الحضور."

ولد كيم بدوي عام 1980 في باريس. مصور وثائقي أميريكي من أصول فرنسية، مصرية، سلوفينية. يعيش بدوي منذ الأيام الأولى للثورة في مصر، وثّق بدوي تطور الثورة وتبعاتها من زاوية مميزة. إفتُتح أول معرض استرجاعي لبدوي في جاليري راوخفيلد، نوفمبر 2012 في باريس، ضمن إطار مهرجان "الصورة الدولي" و"باريس فوتو".

إيفور بريكت

من سلسة أيام الغضب، 2011
هذه الصور تم إلتقاطها في الفترة ما بين 28 يناير و 12 فبراير توثق المشاهد التي رأيتها في شوارع وسط القاهرة.
← صورة 57 + 58

ولد إيفور بيركت عام 1983 في إيرلندا وهو مصور وثائقي ويهتم بمواقف البلاد بعد الحروب. قضى عامين في الشرق الأوسط، حيث وثق الاحتجاجات في مصر وليبيا في 2011. يعمل لعدة مجلات منها صانداي تايمز والنيوزويك. عرضت صوره أكثر من مرة في فوم، متحف الصور في أمستردام، فوتو 8 في لندن وفي جاليري التصوير في دبلن. يعيش حالياً في اسطنبول ولندن.

أحمد بسيوني

26 يناير 2011
فيديو عالي الجودة، 2:30 دقيقة
← صورة 33

كان أحمد بسيوني من أهم فناني العمل الصوتي المعاصر والفن التشكيلي في مصر. ولد في القاهرة عام 1978 ودرس في كلية التربية الفنية بجامعة حلوان، حيث عمل بعد ذلك كمدرس مساعد في قسم الرسم والتصوير. حصل على درجة الماجستير في فلسفة الفن ودرس أيضاً الفن الصوت - رقمي. كان مهتماً بالبحث عن تركيبات وعلاقات مادية بين الصوتي والمرئي، سواء في النظم الهيكلية أو في تكوين البيئة، وكيفية تطبيق هذه الصلات وصياغتها في مصطلحات أيديولوجية. لقد بحث بسيوني هذه الروابط في مشروعاته المبتكرة مثل: كوبيا، نظام متماثل، مدينة، 30 يوم جري في المكان وأوسكي لا تقرأ اللغة العربية، تضمنت هذه المشاريع والعروض على مقاطع فيديو، أداء، تركيبات صوتية تفاعلية وصوت حي.

توفي أحمد بسيوني يوم 28 يناير 2011، يوم جمعة الغضب، على يد أحد القناصين في ميدان التحرير، عن عمر يناهز 32 عاماً. تحول بسيوني فوراً إلى رمز للأمل للملايين من المصريين، الذين قرروا أن يضحوا بحياتهم للخروج ببلدهم من أمة مقموعة لأمة حرة. تحول بسيوني إلى أسطورة بين أصدقائه وزملائه وطلابه، كرجل مات في سبيل بلده واحترموه لشجاعته وحبه، افتخر الجميع بمعرفته والتعلم من حياته وفهم المبدأ الذي وقف بسيوني ليدافع عنه في هذا اليوم. وحتى وإن كانت الشرطة قد قتلت بسيوني بطريقة وحشية إلا أن آخر رسالة كتبها بسيوني على الفيسبوك قبل موته بيومين، أنه عازم على إكمال الثورة بشكل سلمي.

"لو سمحت، يا أب، يا أم، يا شاب، يا طالب، يا مواطن، يا راجل يا كل الناس. إنتو عارفين إن دي آخر فرصة ليكوا للكرامة، فرصتكوا الأخيرة تغيروا الحكومة اللي قاعدة بقالها 30 سنة. انزلوا الشارع وثوروا، هاتوا أكل ولبس وميه وماسكات ومناديل وإزازة خل وصدقوني دي خطوة صغيرة. لو عايزين حرب إحنا عايزين سلام، وأنا هافضل ماسك نفسي لحد ما ترجعلنا كرامة بلدنا." (كتب النبذة صديق بسيوني، شادي النشوقاتي).

عين الطائر. كانت حركة الناس حول الخيــام المنصوبة في وسط الميدان أحيــاناً تشبه طواف الحجاج حول الكعبة في مكة. وفي العامين المنصرمين أصبح التحرير مقصد الكثير من حجاج الثورة الأجانب.

إن أقدم نقاش في التصوير هو علاقته بالموت: "التصويــر هو طريقة لسجن الواقع... قد لا يتمكن للمرء من امتلاك الواقع ولكنه يمكن أن يمتلك صوراً..." هكذا كتبت سوزان زونتاج في كتابها عن التصوير، "لا يمكن للمرء امتلاك الحاضر ولكن يمكنه امتلاك الماضي". قد يكون الخوف من الموت والخوف من أن يضيع حلم التحرير بعد مرور الثمانيــة عشر يومــاً، هو ما دفع الناس لالتقاط الصور بشكل مستمر. في نهايــة الأمر قد يكون التصوير في التحرير كان فعلاً نابع من إيمان. على أن يكون تسجيل الواقع الحاضر المبهج، تذكرة لنا في المستقبل، بوعد الميدان المثالي وليساعدنا على التمسك بالأمل عند بدء المعركة الحقيقية.

لقد كتب هذا النص لهذا الكتاب في مارس 2013

1 في صفحة الويكيبيديا الخاصة بحرب الخليج، تجد في الجملة الثانية: للمزيد عن عملية عاصفة الصحراء اضغط هنا. وللعبة الفيديو، انظر عملية: عاصفة الصحراء (لعبة فيديو).

في هذه اللحظة كان هناك العديد من الأشخاص العاديين الذين اقتنعوا بقوة الصورة، لدرجة أن وسائل الإعلام باتت غير قادرة على ملاحقة الأخبار في الشارع ولذلك لجأت إلى الإنترنت للحصول على المعلومات، لتذيع مقاطع مصورة على يد هواة أو نشطاء انتشرت بالفعل في الإنترنت. لم يحظى أي حدث تاريخي منذ اختراع الكاميرات بمثل هذه التغطية الواسعة من مقاطع مرئية وصور عددها يفوق عدد المتظاهرين في الميدان.

غيّر التصوير الرقمي الناحية الاقتصادية للتصوير عموماً (كل من يمتلك كاميرا رقمية يمكنه أن ينتج عدد لا حصر له من الصور) وهذا أدى إلى زيادة عدد الصور المنتجة ذات الجودة العالية، حمل هذا التطور في طياته وعد وتهديد. فالصور يتم توزيعها بسرعة كبيرة، الشيء الذي لا يعطي المساحة المطلوبة للقراءة الناقدة- وفي هذا السياق على سبيل المثال فإن الصور المعدلة ببرنامج الفوتوشوب تتسلل بين الصور الحقيقية دون أن تنكشف. وبسبب انعدام المبدأ والأخلاق الذي تتطلبه نشر هذه المواد، تنتشر حالة من فقدان الإحساس بالواقعية. ولقد كان فيلام فلوسر محقاً في تحذيره لنا في مقاله "نحو فلسفة التصوير الفوتوغرافي"، من هذه الديموقراطية المبالغ فيها في عالم التصوير: يجب أن يلتزم المصور بتعليمات الاستخدام -التي أصبحت سهلة بالتدرج- الموضوعة للتحكم في ما تخرجه الكاميرا. هذه هي الديموقراطية في المجتمع ما بعد الصناعي. ولهذا فلقد أصبح الناس غير قادرين على فك شفرة الصور: فهم يعتقدون أن الصور هي انعكاس تلقائي للعالم. في أثناء الثورات العربية تم تحميل عدد مهول من المقاطع المرئية الغير واضحة والمهتزة على الإنترنت، صَوَرَتْها هواتف محمولة في سوريا وليبيا والبحرين يتعذر "فك شفرتها". مشاهد من معارك دموية مصورة بجودة رديئة، تشبه بعضها البعض، يتعذر تفريقها أو التعرف على محتواها بشكل قاطع، تكون في أفضل الحالات مربكة وفي أسوئها مضللة. بهذا انصرف المشاهد عن متابعة الأحداث أو حتى محاولة فهم تطور هذه الثورات وإن حاول فهم ما يحدث، عاد إلى الاعتماد على الإعلام المؤسسي وبهذا أعاد المشاهد القوة إلى الإعلام المؤسسي.

هناك سؤال آخر مُلح فيما يخص هذه الديموقراطية الرقمية للتصوير ألا وهو: إلى متى سيبقى أكبر توثيق متعدد المصادر، هذا البورتريه المتميز دون رتوش عن ميدان التحرير، على قيد الحياة في الأرشيف الافتراضي في الإنترنت؟ كتب إيلي ادواردز في مقاله "من الزائل للباقي: أرشيف الإنترنت ودوره في الحفاظ على الميديا الرقمية": "إن ما يميز الإنترنت وبالأخص الشبكة العنكبوتية العالمية هو القدرة الاستيعاب الآخذة في التوسع وتنوعه وهو في نفس الوقت موصوم بعدم دواميته." عندما تهوي صور الثمانية عشر يوم إلى قاع قاعدة جوجل لترتيب الصفحات (Page Rank) العميق، هل سيموت حلم العالم الجديد الذي آمن به الشعب في الميدان مع هذا السقوط؟

حتى وإن كان هذا الكم الهائل من الصور التي خرجت من التحرير قد خرجت للاستخدام الداخلي وليس لجمهور غربي، فلقد تحولت صور الميدان إلى كليشيه راسخ عن مصر في رؤوسهم. لقد تحول الإرهابي العربي الغاضب إلى محارب سلمي. "ساعدينا يا مصر. عالم واحد، ألم واحد" حملت اللافتات المحمولة في مظاهرة في ولاية ويسكونسين الأمريكية بعد مرور ثلاثة أسابيع على الثورة المصرية، هذه الكلمات. فلقد تحول ما كان يُرى كعربي قذر إلى مواطن مثالي سياسياً واجتماعياً. أعلن الرئيس الأمريكي باراك أوباما في كلمة متلفزة له ألقاها بعد موقعة الجمل أثناء الثمانية عشر يوماً أنه: "علينا تربية أبناءنا ليصبحوا مثل الشباب المصري".

أما أكبر كليشيه استشراقي عن مصر، صورة أهرامات الجيزة التي عاشت في الضمير الجمعي منذ بداية التاريخ، فلقد تفوقت عليها صورة المليون متظاهر في ميدان التحرير من

تجلى معنى هذه الجملة في ميدان التحرير. فلقد تحول التصوير هنا وفي المنطقة العربية في أثناء الثورات، ليس فقط إلى وسيلة للرؤيا والتسجيل ولكنها أصبحت جزءاً من الحدث. ففي قلب الثورة المصرية بات التصوير عملاً سياسياً، أهميته تساوي أهمية التظاهر، العصيان المدني وتحدي النظام. ففي عصر المبارك كان التصوير ممنوعاً في عدة أماكن مختلفة، ولقد أُلقي القبض عليّ سبع مرات بالتمام والكمال على مدار خمسة عشر عاماً، بسبب قيامي بالتقاط الصور في أماكن متفرقة من مصر. نجحت بروباجاندة الترويج للخوف في خلق مواطنين مصابين بالوسوسة نتج عنها خوف منتشر عام من الشك في الكاميرا وبالتالي الخوف من الآخر.

في وسط كل هذه المواقف الطارئة، فقدت كل نظريات ذاتية التصوير معناها. لقد لجأ الناس إلى التصوير في الميدان أثناء الثمانية عشر يوم لإحساساهم بمسؤلية اجتماعية تدفعهم لذلك. تحول التصوير إلى شيء موضوعي؛ عَرَض التصوير الحقيقة- أجل، حقيقة ناتجة عن مجموع حقائق بعدد المتظاهرين المجتمعين في الميدان، ولكنها حقيقة باتت من الضروري كشفها في هذه النقطة الفاصلة في التاريخ. تحولت الكاميرا إلى سلاح سلمي موجه إلى الدولة ليفضحها. بالتالي أصبح دور التصوير هو الوقوف أمام الدولة، هو الطريق لاستعادة المكان ثم الدولة. أصبح التصوير هو الانتماء.

يقول لنا جون بيرجير في برنامجه التلفزيوني الشهير "سبل الرؤيا" أن: "الصور هي التي تأتي لنا ولا نذهب نحن إليها. لقد ولت أيام الحَج". واليوم في العصر الرقمي يضيف سلافوي زيزك: "أظن أن الفكرة الأكثر أهمية الآن والتي يجب أن نفهمها هي ليست ماهية (الواقع الافتراضي) ولكن هي ماهية (واقعية الافتراض). لقد بدأت أيضاً ثورة في الميديا حينما تقابل هذا الواقع مع الواقع الموجود في الشارع. لم تعد الصور فقط تخرج علينا من الشاشة ولكنها تحولت إلى (واقع)".

باستثناء الصين التي أوقفت إمكانية البحث عن كلمة مصر في محرك جوجل، انتشرت صور الميدان في كل الأجهزة التي تحيط بالأشخاص، من شاشات الحاسبات والتلفاز وكل الوسائل المرئية الأخرى، فارضةُ بذلك روح الميدان على جميع أنحاء العالم. قال زيزك في حوار له عن الثورات العربية: "لقد كان حدثاً عالمياً بالفعل، فهمه الناس في جميع أنحاء العالم على الفور... إنها العالمية الحقيقية، عالمية النضال". وبخلاف الأزمات السابقة مثل حرب الخليج والحادي عشر من سبتمبر التي شكلت نقلة في وسائل الإعلام، فلقد شعر الجميع بالتوحد مع المتظاهرين في ميدان التحرير. تحول التحرير إلى ثورة الجميع. وبدأت سلسلة من حركات الأوكيوباي (Occupy) التي أثبتت لتاريخ التصوير أن صناعة الصورة من الممكن أن تغير العالم.

تحرك الآلاف وبدأوا في التصوير، وقفوا جنباً إلى جنب في تضامن ضد الحكم الشمولي. أمسك المتظاهرون بلافتات تحمل شعارات أثناء النهار وأثناء الليل لمع اللون الأزرق الخاص بالأجهزة الاكترونية من هواتف محمولة وأجهزة آيباد وحاسبات محمولة. لم يكن هذا الوميض هو ما تبقى من أمل من ألسنة النيران الراقصة أثناء التظاهرات في الستينات فحسب، فقلد امتص هذا الوميض الضوء المحيط به ليسجل من كل زاوية ممكنة، مع تنوع الجودة ونوع المنتج النهائي، مباشرةً من ميدان التحرير.

ركزت وسائل الإعلام المؤسسية على الحدث واستخرجت منه كل ما يمكن استخراجه. وكان هذا الدعم للجماهير في التحرير هو أيضاً دعماً مدمراً، قضى على زخم الثورة عندما بدأوا بالإشارة إليها باستخدام الفعل الماضي بعد مرور الثماني عشر يوماً والإلتفات إلى أخبار أخرى، وبهذا أكدوا نظرية ماك لوهان عن أنه: "يمكنك تبديد أي موقف بإعطاءه أكبر قدر من التغطية."

ظهرت صورة انفجار طائرة داخل برجين على تلفاز المحل الصغير على الناصية. سألت صاحبة المحل الجالسة تحت الشاشة عن ما يحدث. رمقت الشاشة بنظرة سريعة إلى الخلف وقالت دون اهتمام، "من الواضح أنه فيلم". لم تنجح السينما في تاريخها أن تصور مشهداً بهذا الحجم. ولقد حاولت أفلام الأكشن منذ هذا الحين دون جدوى أن تواكب هذا المستوى، فلقد تفوق الواقع على الخيال.

إن كانت حرب الخليج قد حولت الحرب إلى لعبة فيديو،[1] فلقد أعاد المصورين الهواة على الأرض بتسجيلهم لإنهيار العقار ذو ال110 طابق، الإنسانية للواقع.

إن أول خطوة في اتجاه تحقيق الديموقراطية في الفوتوغرافيا هي لحظة خروج كوداك علينا باختراع الكاميرا البراوني. فلقد جعل جورج أيستمان في عام 1888 من العملية المعقدة المكلفة، التي لم يكن يقدر على تحمل نفقاتها سوى الأغنياء، إلى شيء سهل التعامل معه والحصول عليه، وهذا تحت شعار "أنت تضغط على الزر ونحن نقوم بالباقي". وأصبح التصوير متداول بشكل أوسع عندما خرج علينا مهندس آخر من كوداك إيستمان، ستيفين ساسون في عام 1975 باختراع آخر ضخم وهو الكاميرا الرقمية. وحتى عام 2001 كان أغلب من يعيش في الغرب يمتلك واحدة من هذه الكاميرات. لم يعد التصوير هواية تقتصر على عدد محدود من المهتمين ولكنه أصبح جزءاً لا يتجزأ من الحياة اليومية.

وبعد مرور عقد آخر ومع حُمّى الإنترنت، والهواتف المحمولة ذات الكاميرات (ذكية أو غير ذكية)، وكاميرات الإنترنت ومواقع التواصل الاجتماعي، أخذت عملية تحقيق الديموقراطية في التصوير بُعد جديد بكونه مُتعولِم. وأخذت وسائل الإعلام المؤسسية في الخسارة فيما يخص نشر المعلومات مع ظهور مواقع التواصل الاجتماعي. ففي مواقع التواصل الاجتماعي يشترك المستخدم في عملية إنتقاء ونشر المعلومات وأخذ الصور وإتاحتها بشكل فوري على شبكة الإنترنت، حلت هذه الصور محل الوسائل المرئية وبهذا تقاسم المستخدم القوة مع اليد الممسكة بالكاميرا، وبات متحكماً في اتجاهها. في الشرق الأوسط، عندما هاجمت إسرائيل جنوب لبنان في 2006، نجح المدونون والناشطون اللبنانيون في جذب انتباه العالم، لإحداث ضغط دولي لوقف الحرب. كانت حرباً قصيرة ولكن مدمرة، وكانت المدة كافية لكي تطلق شرارة النشاط السياسي في الانترنت، في الوطن العربي بأكمله. علّق بيتر فايبل في مقاله الحديث بعنوان: "قوة الشعب: صور من الشعب"، عن هذه الظاهرة بقوله: "ينتشر تأثير الحروف والصور في مواقع التواصل الاجتماعي وتتوحد معها، وبهذا تتاح الفرصة للجميع ليكونوا فاعلين بدلاً من أن يكتفوا فقط بكونهم مُمَثلين".

كنت في يوم الخامس والعشرين من يناير 2011 في منزلي مع أصدقاء. لم نكن لنتصور ما وراء هذا الصمت الرهيب في الشارع من مظاهرات لم يسبق لها مثيل. لكي نلهي أنفسنا عن التوتر قررنا لعب لعبة ميموري بصور مرسومة بالأبيض والأسود من أرشيف الصورة العربي (FIA). لم أكن أعلم و أنا ألعب بهذه الصور القديمة من الوطن العربي، أن تاريخ المنطقة وتاريخ التصوير العربي والتصوير بشكل عام، على وشك أن يقفز قفزة نوعية.

وكحال الشعوب المقموعة التي تتحول لشريكة في الجريمة، فقلد اعتاد الشعب المصري واستسلم لإهانة الشرطة لهم بشكل منهجي في وضح النهار وتحملوا ما هو أسوأ في حجرات التعذيب المظلمة. لم ترى صور هذه الجرائم النور. ولكن عادت فكرة حق الشعب في المعرفة بعد قيام الاحتجاجات في المحلة في 2008. حينها كتب المدون المصري عرباوي «سوف تنقل الثورة على فليكر»، مشيراً بذلك إلى الحاجة إلى توثيق وكشف منهج التعذيب المتبع من النظام، فالرؤية في هذا الموقف تعني الإيمان والثورة من أجل من أعمتهم وسائل الإعلام الحكومية، التي أخفت حقيقة القوة الحاكمة مدة ثلاثون عاماً، مع سبق الإصرار.

لارا بلدي

عندما تكون الرؤية انتماء فوتوغرافيا التحرير

حملت الصور المأخوذة من جمعة النصر الوعد بغدٍ أفضل وأصبحت رمز لولادة مصر من جديد، بعد مرور أسبوع على تخلي مبارك عن منصبه، إثر انتفاضة شعبية أجبرته على ذلك. يظهر ميدان التحرير في هذه الصور، كواحة للسلام والعدل، كجنة مستعادة، كرمز للحرية ولهوية مصرية جديدة. وفي الوقت الذي تعني فيه كلمة "كليشيه" في الفرنسية الصورة، فهي لجميع الدول الأخرى تعني تصور جاهز يغطي حقائق أكثر من التي يفصح عنها، حتى وإن كنا نعرف هذه الحقائق جميعاً. هل أخذت هذه الصور من ميدان التحرير، مكان صور الأهرامات، الإكليشية الأكثر شهرة عن مصر؟

خاطب نابوليون بونابارت جيشه قبل معركة الأهرام قائلا: "أيها الجنود، إن أربعين قرناً تتطلع إليكم." وفي أغسطس عام 1990 فرت جموع الكويتين إلى مصر. هؤلاء السائحين رغم أنفهم، راحوا جماعات لزيارة الأهرامات يومياً. كانت بدايتي مع التصوير تصادفت مع الغزو الأول للكويت، وكنت أنا أيضاً هناك على هضبة الجيزة، أصور الأهرامات.

في شتاء هذا العام، كانت عملية عاصفة الصحراء، هي أول حرب تبث بثاً مباشراً على التلفاز. وأكد جموح طريقة عرض الأشياء مرة أخرى على أن نظرية جاي ديبور "مجتمع الفرجة" (La Société du Spectacle) أكثر من مجرد نظرية. ظهرت في الصورة السوداء على الشاشة المحدبة بعض الانفجارات في سماء ليل مدينة مبهمة وشعار السي إن إن، ثابتاً أسفل الشاشة ناحية اليسار. نُقِلت هذه الحرب "النظيفة"، "الخالية من الدماء" مباشرة، دقيقة بدقيقة للعالم أجمع، وتعرضت موضوعات سرعة تطور الأحداث ورد الفعل الأمريكي العسكري العنيف وتكنولوجيا المراقبة الجديدة ذات المستوى الرفيع، للنقد والتحليل بشكل مكثف. وقد ذهب جان بودريار، في كتابه المختَلف عليه عن هذه الفترة والذي استشهد به الكثيرون، إلى القول بأن "حرب الخليج لم تحدث". وبالفعل فإن الصور التي ملأت شاشات التلفاز الخاصة بنا، كانت مصدر إلهام خلق سوق جديد إلى صناعة ألعاب الفيديو، حيث يزحف الجنود في وسط الليل وضوء الأشعة تحت الحمراء الأخضر عليهم.

بعد مرور عقد، انقلبت صورة حرب الخليج "الخالية من الضحايا" التي بثتها قناة السي إن إن في عام 1991 رأساً على عقب على يد جيل جديد من المصورين الموثقين وصناع الأفلام، فلقد ولدت الصحافة الشعبية. وكان 11 سبتمبر أول حدث ضخم تاريخي في القرن الواحد والعشرين توثقه مئات الكاميرات بمنتهى الدقة والفعالية في لحظة حدوثه بشكل أفضل من وسائل الإعلام المؤسسية. وبعيداً عن توثيق المشاهد الرهيبة من قيام أشخاص بالقفز من النوافذ وآخرين مغطون في الرماد يجرون في الحطام والبعض يحمل المصابين والآخر يحاول الهرب من الجحيم، فالذين شهدوا وصوروا الهجوم على المركز التجاري العالمي في نيويورك، شاركوا في إنهاء احتكار وسائل الإعلام لحق تقديم الواقع.

بحُرية أكبر. تضمنت هذه العملية تخفيض العمالة التقليدية، مما أدى إلى اضطرار الطمح في ما يطلق عليه القطاع غير الرسمي، وهذا يعني العمل بدون عقود أو ضمانات أو حماية اجتماعية لتصبح الحالة المتزعزعة الظرف الذي تعمل تحته الطبقة العاملة التقليدية. هؤلاء المقموعين، المستغلين والقانطين في ظل نظام مبارك كانوا هم الطبقة الدنيا دون امتلاك فرصة في التعليم ودون وظائف ثابتة ولذلك كانوا عرضة إلى واقع كون ضباط الشرطة والعاملين بها فوق القانون.

يضطر العمال المؤقتون إلى العمل بمهنتين أو ثلاث لكي يتمكنوا من تغطية المصاريف الأساسية. مقارنة بهم، فالعاملون التقليديون يعيشون في ظروف أكثر أماناً. بالرغم من الأجر الزهيد وساعات العمل الطويلة في القطاع الخاص وظروف العمل السيئة مع أقل المنافع، تمتلك الطبقة العاملة التقليدية عقود ودخول ثابتة مما يعطيهم ميزة الوجود في محيط الطبقة العاملة مع بعض الضمانات. بالتالي تبدأ الطبقة العاملة في تقليد طريقة عيش الطبقة المتوسطة الحذرة لكي لا يعرضون عملهم للخطر. وفي حين أن الطبقة العاملة ستستمر في النضال من أجل ظروف عمل أفضل عن طريق الاحتجاج ضد الفساد والاستغلال في مكان العمل، سيبقى نضالهم محدود لأنهم غير مستعدين -وهذا مفهوم- أن يقوموا بمد نضالهم إلى خارج حدود مكان العمل. فالإشتراك في اشتباكات الثورة في الشارع تعني نزولهم إلى الشارع والمخاطرة بإعطاء رؤسائهم سبب لفصلهم لكونهم من "مثيري شغب"، فصفوف العاطلين المستعدين لشغل وظيفتهم إذا تم فصلهم هي التي حالت دون مشاركاتهم في الثورة والعمال الثابتون لا يريدون المجازفة برفاهية العمل.

ساعد تطبيق النماذج الاقتصادية الجديدة منذ 1968 على تركيز رأس المال في أيدي الأغنياء، مما يخفض مكاسب معيشة لآخرين. حددت هذه السياسات ظروف حياة الطبقة المحرومة. في حين أصبحت العمالة المؤقتة المارقة هي العامل الأساسي في النضال الثوري بعد أن أثبتوا بأنفسهم أنهم قوة يعتمد عليها. إستفز تجذر الفجوة الإقتصادية العميقة في هذه المرحلة النيوليبرالية أشكال جديدة من المقاومة؛ وهذه الحالة هي التي دفعت بالمصريين إلى شفا الثورة، وهذه هي الحالة التي ستظل تحدد خطوط الإحتجاج المستقبلية.

في يوم 19 يونيو 2012، تجمع مؤيدو مبارك أمام المستشفى العسكري على ضفاف النيل بعد انتشار أنباء عن موت الديكتاتور. حمل أحد المتظاهرين لافتة مكتوب عليها: "ثورة 25 يناير: سوف يحكم التاريخ."

عليك أن تقرر كيف ستدخل ثورة 25 يناير التاريخ. هل هي 1968 أخرى؟ ثورة بصورة محببة؟ أم هي حركة أكبر من المعنى الذي أعطيته لها عن طريق بعض الصور التي رأيتها وقد تواجهها في يوم من الأيام أمام دارك؟

لقد كتب هذا النص لهذا الكتاب في أغسطس 2012

فيليب رزق، صانع أفلام وكاتب يعيش في القاهرة. فيليب رزق عضو في مجموعة مُصرِّين. (mosireen.org).

في مقابلة الدولة النيوليبرالية بين الاستدامة الذاتية والتدمير الذاتي. بالإضافة إلى ذلك، ساعدت هذه الاحتجاجات الخالية من الأيديولوجية المجهزة مسبقاً،على خروج أفكار تحت الإنشاء، لمقاومة تحت الإنشاء لاتزال في بدايتها.

العمال والثورة

من اللحظات الفارقة التي جعلت ثورة 25 يناير ممكنة كانت موجات إنتفاضة العمال التي بدأت في عام 2006. كان إضراب الـ27 ألف عامل بالمحلة الكبرى، ديسمبر 2006، هو ما أعطى المصريين فرصة لرؤية هذا العمل العظيم، أو أفسح الطريق للاحتجاجات العديدة التي تبعته، ولذلك فكرة الثورة أصبحت ممكنة. كان من الطبيعي أن تنتشر الإعتصامات والمظاهرات في أنحاء البلاد. دعا القادة المستقلون للعمال يوم 6 أبريل 2008 من نفس الشركة (مصر للغزل و النسيج) لإضراب آخر ولكن هذه المرة نجحت الحكومة في ردع الخطة عن طريق التسوية مع مجموعة مختارة من العمال قبل ميعاد الإضراب. كان طلب رفع الأجور مرتبط بارتفاع أسعار الغذاء وبسبب وجود عامل في الشركة من كل بيت في المحلة، لم يقتصر توقع الإضراب على العمال فقط بل توقع سكان المحلة أيضاً مواجهات. بدأت المواجهات بسبب إهانة ضابط لسيدة مسنة.

كانت أهمية 6 أبريل هي انتقال التظاهرات من المصنع إلى نطاق المجتمع خارج حدود المصنع. كسر العمال في عام 2006 قواعد المنهج الاجتماعي من خلال التظاهر في الأماكن العامة. وفي عام 2008 توسعت مساحة المقاومة الممكنة خارج النطاق الذي حددته الطبقة الحاكمة. استخدمت الحكومة كل ما لديها من دهاء وقوة لمنع حراك 6 أبريل 2008 من التحول إلى ما شاهدناه في 25 يناير 2011. نجحت الحكومة في الإحالة دون انتشار الاحتجاجات من مدينة صناعية واحدة لباقي المدن أو للمنطقة بأكملها بالأمر بتدخل قوات الأمن من ستة محافظات مختلفة إلى المدينة. لم تكن الظروف في أبريل 2008 مناسبة لما حدث بعد أقل من ثلاث سنوات. وفي 28 يناير 2011 انطلق المتظاهرون في جميع أنحاء البلاد وانتصروا على قوات الأمن في بضعة ساعات. وفيما يخص هذه النقطة يجب التأكيد مرة أخرى على أن 2011 ليست 1968 .لم تكن 1968 لتتم دون موجات إضرابات العمال واحتلال المصانع بالتوازي مع الاحتجاجات الطلابية. وفي حالة ثورة 25 يناير، حتى باشتراك جميع الطبقات ومنها الطبقة المتوسطة والعاطلة والعمال والفلاحين، فلقد كان العامل الأساسي في الثورة هو دور العمال المؤقتين وليس الطبقة العاملة. قد تبدو هذه التفصيلة عابرة ولكنها هي صلب الفرق بين 2011 و1968.

من عام 2006 حتى 25 يناير 2011 وإلى هذا الحين، لم يتوقف العمال في المؤسسات المنظمة عن التظاهر من أجل زيادة الأجور وضد الخصخصة والفساد والظلم. جدير بالتوضيح أن موجة الاحتجاجات التي بدأت في25 يناير ضمت عدد كبير من العمّال المؤقتين وخاصة من العشوائيات. منذ 2006 تظاهر العمال ضد آثار عملية النيوليبرالية المكثفة التي خضعت لها حكومة مبارك الأخيرة. أتى رد فعل العمال مباشرة - وإن قلما ما تم التعبير عنها بهذه الكلمات- على تطبيق النموذج الاقتصادي النيوليبرالي الغربي وهذا يعني تسهيل دخول مستثمرين أجانب إلى الصناعة المصرية وخصخصة مصانع وشركات القطاع العام، أو تخفيض الدعم مع تشجيع الإنتاج بهدف التصدير. وبمساندة المؤسسات المالية الدولية، سمح هذا النظام للمستثمرين الأجانب باستغلال مصادر مصر الطبيعية بقيود أقل، واستغلال الطبقة العاملة

الراديكالية بسبب الواقع الإجتماعي والسياسي للحظة. بعد أكثر من أربعين عاماً، استفزت آثار الإمبريالية الناس من خلال غطاء ما بعد الإستعمار ودفعتهم مرة أخرى للتظاهر، تحت هذه الظروف، كما أصاب فرانتس فانون في قوله، نجحت القوى الإستعمارية القديمة في إخفاء إهتماماتها الإقتصادية خلف شراكات مع النخب الحاكمة في دول ما بعد الإستعمار.

ولهذا فإن 2011 ليست 1968. إن ما حدث في 2011 هو إنتفاضة بسبب عدم الرضى عن الواقع السياسي في وجود الإستعمارية الجديدة. 2011 لم تكن ثورة المثقفين، لم يكن فيها تطور للأفكار، لم يَسِر الشعب فيها راديكالياً، ولم تشتبك فيها البلاد في أزمة في خارج الحدود. لم تكن هناك أيديولوجية سوى أيديولوجية اليأس، ثِقَل النفاق وحدود شعب يعيش في إنكار لها. تصاعدت المقاومة بين العمال، والمعارضة الآخذة في النمو بين جنبات الطبقة المتوسطة الصغيرة مثل حركة كفاية وحركة شباب 6 أبريل، بالإضافة إلى صفحات المجموعات على الفيسبوك مثل كلنا خالد سعيد التي جاءت كرد فعل على القمع الممارس من قبل الطبقة السياسية الحاكمة لشعب كامل. مع حلول عام 1968 كان النزاع قد انتشر في كل مكان، ولكن حتى حلول عام 2011 لم يكن هناك سوى بذور ثورية جاهزة للإنبات.

لم تكن في مصر حركة بعينها، بل كان فيها حراك، كما كان هناك زخم، قوة غير محددة أقوى من أي تنظيم أياً كان. أدى القمع تحت نظام مبارك إلى القضاء على أي بذرة تنظيم للمعارضة مما يعني أنه كان هناك بالكاد أي "يسار" يمكن الحديث عنه. كانت الجامعات ولازالت أماكن لاختلاس الأموال العامة وليست أماكن للفكر النقدي.

شهد عام 2011 تسارع في الراديكالية السياسية في مواجهة تسارع النيوليبرالي في السنوات السابقة. كان الشارع هو الأكاديمية، تبادلنا الحجارة بطلقات قوات الأمن وأفراد الجيش، في الوقت الذي تبادلنا فيه الأفكار فيما بيننا.هكذا حدثت عملية التسيس الراديكالي بين المصريين الذين قاموا بالثورة. شارك في الاحتجاجات في الأيام الأولى من عام 2011 أعداداً غير متوقعة. كما كان الحال في الأرجنتين عام 2001، تميزت الاحتجاجات في الشوارع المصرية بالمشاركة من جميع الطبقات، الأعمار والجنس. وكما كان الحال في 1968 شارك بالاحتجاجات الطلاب والعمال، ولكن في مصر لم يشاركوا بصفتهم عمال وطلبة بل شاركوا كجزء من حركة شعبية. ظلت الاحتجاجات دون قائد يذكر؛ واجهنا جهاز دولة قامع وتراتبي ومسيطر، باستخدام أسلوب أفقي. فلقد كانت ضخامة أعداد المتظاهرين هي التي، حتى ولو لوقت قصير، جعلت الدولة المركزية تركع.

تباينت وتنوعت طلبات المتظاهرين، لم يكن هناك سبب واحد فقط هو الذي دفع بالناس إلى الشوارع والميادين في جميع أنحاء مصر يوم 28 يناير، رفض الناس باختلافهم أوجه مختلفة لنفس النظام الذي سيطر على حياتنا اليومية. أما المشاهد، فسيطرت عليه رغبة لفهم هذه الاحتجاجات التي باتت هي سبب وجود صناعة الإعلام، والتي سعت إلى أن تشبع هذه الرغبة. ومن وجهة النظر الغربية المسيطرة، وجّهَت نظرته العلاقة إلى الشائع، للمألوف، لما كان يعرفه مسبقاً، وجعل 2011 تبدو وكأنها 1968.

2011 ليست 1968 .لم تكن الثورة في 2011 هي الثورة "التقليدية" للإشتراكيين: الطلاب والعمال يخرجون إلى الشوارع لكي يستبدلوا النظام القائم بنظامهم. ومهما حاول الناس جاهدين، لم تمتلك الأحزاب أي خطة مبدئية للثورة، لا قبل 25 يناير ولم يتغير هذا الوضع منذ هذا الحين. أصوات متحدة عَلَت بوضوح من البداية، "الشعب يريد إسقاط النظام"، خرجت من مجموع أصوات معارضة، تبلورت في الرغبة في إنهاء الوضع الراهن: بات التغيير ضرورياً، نوع من أنواع التغيير، ولكن شكل التغيير كان غير معروف. لم تكن هذه نقطة ضعف الاحتجاجات ولكنها شاهد على أزمة عالمية في تَخيُل أشكال بديلة للتنظيم المجتمعي

ما طمأنك وأشعرك بذلك. إعتمدت علينا بعدها صناعات أخرى مثل الصحافة الشعبية والأكاديميا والفيلم والفن والمنظمات غير الحكومية في أن نلعب دور المترجم لهذا الحدث الاستثنائي. وأخيراً قاموا بدعم تمجيد الفرد، الناشط، قضية الشباب، الفنان الثائر، المرأة، المتظاهر السلمي، مستخدم الإنترنت. كل هذا حدث تلقائياً في إطار الحاجة الماسة لتحديد وتثبيت وتمجيد دور من هو مألوف. وبالتالي صار من المستحيل تخيل وجود الثورة بدون وجود صورة المتظاهر المثالي الذي قام بحمايتك من مواجهة المجهول: إنتفاضة جماعية ضد نظام عالمي مهيمن لا مكان فيه لمتفرج.

ساعد الإنترنت في خلق هالة تؤكد أن كل هذا كان مألوف بعرض غضب الشارع من خلال وسيط تعرفه، قامت الرواية المعروضة على محطات الأخبار بتخفيف حدة الغموض المخيم على الأحداث وربطت خيالك بالمألوف. وقامت طبقات التحليل المخطوطة فوق الصورة بتبديد مخاوفك من المجهول. "هذه ليست إلا حركة ضد الديكتاتورية". "هذه صرخة الفرد من أجل الحرية". "هذه مظاهرة من أجل الديمقراطية". "الثورة سلمية". الإنترنت قد حل محل الكلاشينكوف. هذا الحديث أسكت الكلام عن الأبعاد التركيبية للظلم وأخفى دور السياسات النيوليبرالية التي تمارسها جهات مثل البنك الدولي والإتحاد الأوروبي والولايات المتحدة الأمريكية في تعميق الفجوة بين الأغنياء والفقراء. جعلوك تنسى أن الرغبة في العدالة الإجتماعية قد ولدت بالأساس من هذه التركيبات الظالمة. هذه الخطابات المسيطرة -خطابات الهيمنة- قامت بتحديد مساحة الإشكالية على سبيل المثال في هذه الديكتاتورية محلية المنشأ. ساعدت هذه الشهادات عن طريق عزل الجريمة والتركيز على فساد الأشخاص، على تجهيز الساحة الإستعمارية الجديدة وشرانق النظام التي باتت خاوية ليتم إستبدالها بآخر يحافظ على نفس المنطق في الحكم.

ليس مفاجئاً أن يكون أصحاب هذه الصور هم الوكالات الإخبارية التجارية التي تديرها مؤسسات تَدعم وتُدعم من نفس أنظمة الهيمنة التي ثرنا ضدها. أصبحت الصور التي سجلتها كاميرات قنوات مثل بي بي سي أو سي إن إن ملكية خاصة لهذه المؤسسات ليستخدموها في خطابهم الخاص فيحتفون بما يريدون الترويج له ويُسكتون ما يريدون تهميشه. إن وضع الصورة في كادر ثم إذاعتها هو في حد ذاته ممارسة للقوة. الحقيقة أن هذه الصور يتم تداولها باسم الحرية، ولكن استخدام الصور هو مشروع هادف للربح.

لم يكن النشطاء الشباب بأية حال هم ممثلي هذه الاحتجاجات، ولكنهم كانوا الصوت المهيمن الذي يتم تقديمه. لم نكن سوى حفنة من الأصوات من بين صرخات كثيرة متفاوتة تطالب بالتغيير. كل فرد بتخوفاته وشكواه ورغباته ودوافعه وأسبابه للإنتقام. في أثناء إشتعال الإحتجاجات مالت الحركة إلى الأفقية، لم يكن صنع القرار مركزياً، كانت حركة بلا قيادة ولا يمكن تمثيلها بجهاز إعلامي يتمحور حول فرد ما، أو مقال مكتوب أو خطبة ملقاة أو كتابات فنية أو فيلم وثائقي عن شخصية بعينها. هذه الطريقة في التمثيل تزيف الواقع. في هذا الجواب أقع أنا أيضا في نفس المنطق الخاطئ.

2011 ليست 1968

كانت الستينيات مُحملة بالعديد من الأحداث السياسية: معارك المساواة العرقية، فيتنام، الحرب الباردة، اللفظات الأخيرة للإمبريالية الصريحة. من هذه اللحظة خرجت مرحلة 1968 بجيل شاب يواجه مشاهد بعيدة عن الإحتلال والإستعمار، جيل من الطلبة مفعم بالأيديولوجيا

فيليب رزق

2011 ليست 1968
جواب مفتوح لمن يشاهد

خرج المصريون في الثامن والعشرون من يناير 2011 إلى الشوارع في مسيرات إحتجاجية قوية، وجلس المشاهد بتركيز شديد أمام شاشات التلفزيون ليتابع هذا الحدث المذاع على العديد من القنوات الدولية .وأدى انبهاره بالصور المتتابعة القادمة من ميدان التحرير إلى تحفيز خياله، ثم شطح هذا الخيـال. لقد ألهمت تونس المصريين، بل وأشعرتهم بالخزي، فشجعتهم على التحرك كما ساعدت ثورتنا في إلهام حركات من جميع أنحاء العالم، من حركة إحتلوا الميادين في أوربا لإعتصام مدينة ماديسون في ولاية ويسكونسن حتى حركات "إحتلوا". هذا بالإضافة إلى العديد من الثورات التي لاتزال مستمرة حتى اليوم ومنها البحرين وسوريا والسودان.

وفي محاولتها لفهم هذه المشاهد، لجأت جميع وسائل الإعلام إلى مجموعة أفراد أصبحت هي من تمثل الثـورة. حاورت هذه الوكالات الإخبارية معلقين سياسيين أو نشطاء -أخذت شهرتهم في التزايد- من أجل فك شفرة ما وراء الصور المعروضة. وأدى إلحاق تفسير ومعنى بالصور إلى تحريف واضح لما يحدث بالفعل خلف الكواليس. لقد اعتمدت وسائل الإعلام غير الناطقة بالعربية بالأساس على النشطاء الناطقين بالإنجليزية -أغلبنا من أبناء الطبقة الوسطى وأغلبنا مُسَيّسون من قبل الخامس والعشرين من يناير. بنفس الطريقة لجأت أيضاً المحطات الإخبارية الناطقة بالعربية إلى نشطاء من الطبقة الوسطى ليتحدثوا بإسم الثورة. ما حدث أن كل فرد فيهم قد فسر كل لحظة بشكل يتفق مع إتجاهه الأيديولوجي وبهذا أصبحنا بمثابة مترجمين لثـورة جماعية نحن أبعد ما يكون عن تمثيـلها. لقد ظهر انعكاس وجوهكم على وجوهنا، أصواتنا صارت مفهومة. لقد ساعدنا في تفسير الثورة وأعطى كلامنا معنى لما كان غامضاً لكم. الحقيقة أن تحليلنا للأحداث قد أرضى المتطلبات العملية ومعايير صناعة وسائل الإعلام لجمورها الذي اعتاد أن يرى متحدثين ذوي شكل محدد وطريقة معينة في النقاش. والحقيقة أن هذه العملية قد طغت على أصوات الأغلبية. بغض النظر عن المجهود الذي بذلناه لإثبات عكس ذلك فالحقيقة أننا نستوفي شروط الدور المطلوب: شباب، طبقة وسطي، مُلِمين بخصائص بالإنترنت، وبالتالي ثوريون.

هل سمعت الأصوات الآتية من الطبقات الشعبيـة؟ هل رأيت عائلات الشهداء وهم متشحين السواد حداداً في بيوتهم؟ هل رأيت صور للمدنيين المجهوليـن الذين أصابهم رصاص القناصة من فوق أسطح أقسام الشرطة؟ هل رأيت ضباط الشرطة وهم يفتحون أبواب السجون لتبديد اللحظة الثورية وإحداث الخراب في المجتمعات المجاورة؟ هل رأيت المتظاهريـن وهم يقتحمون أقسام الشرطة في الثامن والعشرين من يناير للانتقام من سنوات قضوها في عذاب غير مبرر من العنف والتعذيـب والقهر النفسي؟ هل رأيت السيـدات وهن يقُمْن بتحضيـر المولوتوف وإنزاله من شرفات البيـوت للإنتقام ممن شوهوا حيـاة أبنائهم وجيرانهم؟ هذا كله لا يمت للسلميـة بصلة، ولكن عدسة الكاميرا المثبتة على ميـدان التحرير وحده في وضح النهار هي

قد يتيح عرض هذه الصور جنباً إلى جنب في هذا الكتاب فرصة مراجعة نظرية زونتاج التي تحولت إلى نموذج بلاغي منهار. حتى وإن كان على حسب هذا النموذج، أننا نستخدم الصور لأغراض إقتصادية ودعائية، حتى وإن كانت الصور المتجاورة على فيسبوك وفليكر ويوتيوب مليئة بالضوضاء والقمامة، لايزال لهذه الصور مفعول مشترك، الشيء الذي اختفى في سنوات النقد الطويلة: و هو التعاطف. كل صورة تدفع بالفرد للنزول إلى الشارع؛ كل صورة تُرفع في الشارع لساعات طويلة في شكل رسالة. بذلك لا تعزلنا الصور عن الحدث أو تبعدنا عنه، وهي لا تنقل فقط، بل تتحول بالفعل إلى جزء من العملية السياسية والتَدَخُل. هذا لا يعني أننا نؤمن بسذاجة في طيبة الصور، أو أنها تأخذ مكان الجدل السياسي، ولكنها تعتبر أداة مشاركة سياسية مهمة بسبب قدرتها على نقل الإحساس والتعاطف.

مجتمع الصور

عندما تلتقي المدينة الرقمية الجديدة والشارع الفعلي وعندما يتفاعل الإنسان مع الصور، تنشأ صور جديدة. عندما ضرب وركل الضباط إمرأة شابة يوم 17 ديسمبر في القاهرة بشكل وحشي، حتى صارت ملقاة شبه عارية في الشارع، تحولت من متظاهرة إلى المرأة ذات مشد الصدر الأزرق، استفزت فظاعة هذه الصورة ليس العالم أجمع فحسب ولكنها كانت السبب في خروج أكبر مسيرة نسائية في تاريخ الوطن العربي، وبذلك تتحول هذه اللحظة أيضاً إلى لحظة إتهام.

ظهر هذا المشهد الذي ملأه الذل والمهانة والتي التقطته الكاميرا في الصحف ورفعته أيادي ليس لها حصر لمتظاهرات ومتظاهرين، ظهرت في رسومات فناني الشارع وظهرت في شكل الفتاة الخارقة في الثقافة الشعبية للجرافيتي على حوائط المدن أو كبطلة على اللافتات المحمولة في مسيرات التضامن. وبهذا يكون مشهد المرأة الشابة ذات مشد الصدر الأزرق المحاطة بالضباط قد مر بالعديد من المراحل، حتى أصبح له وجود كرمز، شكل مرئي يتم التعرف عليه بسهولة وفي نفس الوقت يكون ذا طبيعة مجردة.

يبدو أن وظيفة الأعمال الفنية المنشورة في هذا الكتاب بشكل خاص، هي إبراز الترحال الدائم للصور. ويلعب تشكيل الهوية الإجتماعية فيها دور كبير. يطل علينا مجتمع افتراضي من رسومات أحمد كامل، التي خرجت إلى النور من الصور الجماعية الموجودة على صفحات الفيس بوك المصرية وتحتوي على شخصيات نمطية، تُعبَر عن وعد الهوية غير الواضح من وسيلة تواصل شابة. ومن ناحية أخرى تركزت نظرة الفنانة هبة فريد على أسلاف الفيسبوك، ألبومات الصور، حافظات وأساليب حكي فوتوغرافية أوشكت على الإندثار. كيف صور أعضاء الجيش المرفهين أنفسهم في الألبومات، ما هي أهمية الجيش لهوية الجمهورية المصرية الشابة في القرن العشرين. في ثلاثيات دينيس دايّو من ناحية أخرى تظهر العائلات وبيوت الشهداء، الذين توفوا أثناء الثورة. أخذت صورهم مكان صور الأبناء المفقودين في البيوت. وأخيراً وليس آخراً تعرض لارا بلدي في أرشيف In media res مجتمع الصور، تجَانُب وتجَاور اللقطات والفيديوهات والشهادات في الإنترنت. يخرج لنا الإنترنت بشكل مباشر بالمطابقة المرئية والمرجع التاريخي. فيصبح الرجل الذي يقف وحده أمام المدرعة من نفس عائلة رجل الدبابة الذي وقف في ميدان تيانانمن في بكين عام 1989، والوسيط يتحول إلى متحف تخيلي للأيقونات الثورية.

صور متداخلة

بجانب عملها الفني، شاركت لارا بلدي في هذا الكتاب أيضاً بمقالة تحت عنوان "عندما تكون الرؤيا إنتماء"، تسأل في نهايته عن وظيفة الصور، التي التقطها الأشخاص في ميدان التحرير. وجدت في خلاصة هذا الكم من الصور خوف الناس من الموت. تشير في مقالها إلى كتاب سوزان زونتاج عن التصوير وتذكر بذلك الكاتبة التي نجحت في التعبير عن نوع من أنواع الإنزعاج من الفوتوغرافيا كما لم ينجح أحد، الشيء الذي أثر في نقد الفوتوغرافيا لمدة ثلاثون عاماً. تقول أن الفوتوغرافيا تزيد الرغبة الموجودة تجاه العالم في التلصص، حيث أخذ التسجيل وحده مكان التدخل.

تسمح هذه المجموعة من الصور أيضاً بوضع سياق رسمي -أين وكيف أُخذت هذه الصورة- وبهذا تعطينا فرصة استنتاج الأماكن المختلفة لهذه الصور، نعرف عن مكان نشرها، عن وجودها الافتراضي في المدونات، المواقع ومواقع الصور، أو أنها في مكانها التقليدي في الصحف والمجلات. كما أنها تجعل تَنَقُل الصور المرئية، من الموقع وحتى اللافتات والبوستر والجرافيتي في فضاء المدينة. قد تكون هذه لحظة فارقة في تاريخ كاميرات التصوير، تعايش الأنواع المختلفة من الصور، أنالوج وديجيتال، عامة وخاصة، يرتبط وجودهم ببعضهم البعض، كما في مصر، حيث تصطدم دفعات التحديث والرفض المجتمعي بشكل دموي.

لهذه الصور العديد من الوظائف: فهي تحث على المقاومة، تسجل الأحداث، تبرر استخدام العنف للأشخاص ضد النظام، تحلل استخدام الصور لأغراض التأثير، تُخَلد الضحايا وتكون صور للذكرى؛ ولكن هناك كلمة تجمع كل هذه الكلمات، المصطلح الإنجليزي Testimony والذي يترجم بالعربية لشهادة دون أن تحتوي على نفس المعنى باللغة الإنجليزية. فكلمة Testimony تحمل الكثير من المعاني بين طياتها، تبدأ من الفيديوهات التي تعرض وجوه تحكي ما رأت، مروراً بتغريدات التويتر التي كتبها شهود العيان في الشارع وحتى الشخص الذي يقف وحده في غرفة وهو ممسك لصورة أو رسالة مكتوبة يرفعها إلى أعلى.

المدينة الرقمية الجديدة والشارع الثوري القديم

في وسط الإنبهار بثورة الفيسبوك و التويتر، نسينا أهمية المكان الفعلي والعام للمدينة. بدا الأمر وكأننا لم نعد نهتم إلا بالمدينة الجديدة غير المرئية، تحول اليوتيوب لسوق عكاظ الإفتراضي، الجزء المقابل المكمل للصور المذاعة على التليفزيون التي عرضت لنا في الثمانية عشر يوماً للثورة صورة الجموع في ميدان التحرير من منظور عين الطائر من على أسقف الفنادق وأدخلتها بيوتنا. تُظهر أغلبية الصور في هذا الكتاب التصوير كنوع من أنواع الإحتجاج في مكان المدينة الفعلي.

تبرز من بين هذه التوثيقات صورة صارت بمثابة تقليد (الصور: → 6 – 14 ,→6 – 16)، تمت إعادة نشرها بشكل مكثف: تجمعات بشرية في ميدان التحرير وميادين وشوارع أخرى في القاهرة، يحملون صور أو لافتات مخطوطة بخط اليد تخاطب المارة، السيارات العابرة أو كاميرات الشهود والمراسلين الحاضرين بكثافة. يقفون في سكون وغضب يملأهم التصميم والكبرياء، وهم ممسكون بلافتات مطبوعة بالليزر بالحجم الكبير أو قطعة من الكرتون المخطوط.

تغيرت الرسائل في العامين والنصف المنصرمين، بعد السخرية من مبارك أتت الإحتجاجات ضد المجلس العسكري، ثم الثورة على محمد مرسي. ومنذ إسقاط الإخوان المسلمين تنوعت أشكال الإحتجاج المرئي، من صور الأبناء المتوفيين التي ترفعها الأمهات اللواتي ارتدين السواد، مروراً بشباب الشهداء ووصولاً إلى المشاهد المتاحة في الإنترنت، مثل صورة الفتاة ذات مشد الصدر الأزرق "ست البنات" المُهانة. هذه الصور تعبر بامتياز عن موقف سياسي، لهذا السبب وأسباب أخرى تتحول هذه الصور هي وحاملوها إلى أبطال أغلبية التقارير: "في صورة الصورة المحمولة يحكي التصوير حكاية من صنعه لها وظيفة ويخلق اختلاف -كصورة إخبارية- عن الصورة المرفوعة: صورة فوق صورة، ميتا-صورة. قد يكون سبب نجاح هذا النوع من الصور أيضاً، أنه يوثق بشكل موثوق فيه مدى تأثير الصور على الأفراد أو بمعنى آخر: كيف يتفاعل الإنسان مع الصور."

الثقافة الرقمية، إنها فكرة إعلامية في طور بداية التصوير وستتواصل في القنوات الرقمية ووسائل الاتصالات. كيف تبدو الصور والأخبار التي تملأ القنوات في جميع أنحاء العالم؟ وما هي وظيفتها وأهدافها، ومن هم مؤلفوها؟ هذه هي أول الأسئلة التي نطرحها، ولكن مشروع "القاهرة، مدينة مفتوحة: صور لثورة مستمرة" يطرح أكثر بكثير من تلك الأسئلة على المحطات المختلفة ويحاول هذا الكتاب توثيقها.

نحن بالطبع من "المتلصصين" الإعلاميين، الذين كتب لهم فيليب رزق خطابه المنشور في هذا الكتاب قبل أن نسافر إلى القاهرة للمرة الأولى في آخر صيف 2011، لمعرفة المزيد عن صور الثورة وفهم خلفياتها على أرض الواقع. كنا بطبيعة الحال جزءاً من المراقبين الأجانب الذين تخطف أعينهم لأول وهلة الأبطال الوهميين لهذه الإنتفاضة الذين يشبهوننا، جيل الإنترنت، واستخدامهم لكاميراتهم وهواتفهم المحمولة مثل الأسلحة "الكلاشينكوف" كما يصور ذلك العديد من رسامي الجرافيتي في الشوارع.

وبعد الإقامة في القاهرة والحوارات "معكم"، أنتم المصورون والفنانون، النشطاء والصحفيون، المخرجون والأمناء، تغير المنظور، لم يعد العرض أهم من الحقيقة، والصور تستطيع أن تقلب منظورها ومدلولاتها، وأن الوقت لم يحن إلى الآن لطرح هذه الأسئلة، فكل هذه أمور فهمناها في موقع الحدث. وإن كان منظور الصور صحيحاً فسيعني ذلك أن ثقافة الصورة في هذه الثورة أكثر من مجرد "توثيق" جديد يحل محل صحافة الصور التقليدية. إن هذا الكتاب رد فعل على ما أظهرتموه لنا وما أشرتم إليه. إنه مجموعة من الرؤى والمواقف التي قمتم "أنتم" باختيارها.

ليس هذا الكتاب بشرى مبكرة للاحتفال بالثورة، على غرار الكثير من الكتب الأخرى، كما أنه ليس كتاب تاريخ يوثق الأحداث أو يقدم تحليلاً تفصيلياً عن دور الصورة، بل إنه نظرة تقسيمية من خلال إنتاج صور هذه الثورة، عملية رسم خريطة تحدد الطرق المختلفة لاستخدام الصورة، إنه ألبوم لهذه الإنتفاضة السياسية والإجتماعية المعقدة، والتي لا تزال في بدايتها ولم تظهر نهايتها في الأفق إلى الآن. إنها تتعلق بصور التقطها صحفي مصري شاب وصور وكالات الأنباء التي يرسلها الصحفيون الأجانب، الأشكال المرئية المتعددة لما يسمى بالصحافة الشعبية، مصوري ميدان التحرير الشباب، الذين ينشرون صورهم على موقع فليكر، فيديوهات النشطاء ومواقعهم، التي تقوم بدور الصحافة البديلة لما تنشره وتذيعه نشرات الأخبار الرسمية، فن الشارع من شباب مُعَولم وآخرين تابعين لحركات سياسية حضرية، مبادرات الفنانات والفنانين الذين يتفادون أن يكونوا ممثلي الأحداث بشكل مباشر، وأخيراً وليس آخراً التسجيلات التاريخية والأعمال الفنية، التي سبقت الحدث والتي تعطي مثالاً على أن الصحافة المصورة والتصوير في تطور وتغير.

الكادر موقف

إن منهج هذا الكتاب هو النظرة المقارنة، فهو يكشف عن طريق المقارنة السهلة تطور الصور، التي تظهر من الوهلة الأولى عن طريق تغير المادة. تتدرب العين عن طريق هذا العرض على تقدير جودة التصوير المختلفة، إذا ما كانت اللقطة صحفية، تحاول تلخيص قلب الحدث من خلال اللقطة. أو أنها صورة من هاتف محمول لا تتمتع بطابع احترافي ولكنها تحمل الكثير من الدراما وتحمل الكثير من المؤثرات الطبيعية. تساعد هذه المقارنة أيضاً على استنتاج موقف المصور من الحدث. هل هي نظرة مشاركة من الداخل أم أنها زاوية بعيدة "من الخارج"؟

فلوريان إيبنر
كونستانزة فيكه

صور متداخلة
خريطة لصور من ثورة

شاهد على البداية

إن النظر لصور الثورة المصرية يسقط لأول وهلة على وجه واحد، فمقطع فيديو "سياستي سياسة عيش" (← 31 صورة) الذي تم تحميله من قِبَل مُصرِّين على موقع يوتيوب في الأول من ديسمبر 2011 يروي حكاية اعتقال واستجواب وتعذيب العامل الأجير محمد منير محمد حسنين. وصَوّر الشاب الدوافع التي قادته لنزول الشارع للتظاهر، فهو ليس من المهتمين بالسياسة، السياسة بالنسبة له هي سياسة لقمة العيش. لقد أثارت غضبه - مثله مثل الكثيرين غيره - مقاطع الفيديو التي نشرها النشطاء على الإنترنت قبل أن تذاع بعد ذلك في التلفاز. إنه مشهد لجثة ألقى بها الجنود في صندوق المهملات بعد شجار وقع على مقربة من ميدان التحرير (← 32 صورة). حتى هو نفسه قد ألقي القبض عليه في إحدى المظاهرات وضرب حتى فقد وعيه. وتم استجوابه بعدما عاد إلى وعيه، ويبدو أن ضابطاً صور المشهد بأحد الهواتف، حيث تخرج قوات الأمن نقوداً من حقيبته كانت قد خُبأت فيها من قبل، ثم قاموا بنشر هذا المقطع المصور على الإنترنت ليكون دليلاً لاتهام محمد بأنه عميل محرض وتشويه شكل الاحتجاجات.

يتكون فيديو "سياستي سياسة عيش" من مستويين، الأول حديث مع محمد والكاميرا المتعاطفة مع وجهه، أما الثاني فيتمثل في مقاطع الفيديو المذكورة للنشطاء الذين سجلوا الإعتداءات الوحشية لرجال الأمن وتتابع الاستجوابات على الوجه المعذب وحملوه من شبكة الإنترنت وقاموا بتركيبه. وبذلك يظهر الفيديو الوظائف والمستويات المختلفة للصور وشهادة إنسان، وكذلك الوظائف الدعائية التوجيهية من خلال الصور، والتي يتطلب كل منها حقيقة أخرى. إن سياسة الخبز ليست مجرد شكوى ضد التعذيب وسوء المعاملة، بل إنه فيلم يلفت النظر إلى طرق استخدام الصور.

من التعاطف إلى التجربة

تظهر بداية الفيديو في هذا المشروع تعاطفاً يبدو ساذجاً، إنه إعجاب اقترب من كثير من التقارير والمقالات الثقافية التي أوردت أن الشباب في مصر وتونس نجح في عمل ثورة الإنترنت أو ثورة الفيسبوك في ربيع عام 2011 باستخدام الوسائل الرقمية وشبكات التواصل الإجتماعي. وقد تمحورت أبعاد الديمقراطية في الربيع العربي، والتي يرجع الفضل فيها إلى

شكل اندلاع الثورات العربية تحدياً للمؤسسات الثقافية الدوليـة، أدى بهذه المؤسسات إلى إعادة النظر في طبيعة عمليـة التبادل الثقـافي الدولي حتى الآن. منذ هذا الحيـن أصبحنا نتحمل مسؤوليـة أكبر من التعاون مع شركائنا في الدولة المضيفـة لنا فحسب وصرنا نلعب دور الوسيـط بين هذه المجتمعات في الوطن العربي وأوروبـا و ألمانيـا، ننقل لهم ما يشغل هذه المجتمعات ويحركها.

عندما بدأت عملية البحث لمعرض "القاهرة. مدينة مفتوحة. صور جديـدة من ثـورة مستمرة." في القاهرة، كان الدافع والهدف واضحاً: على الشباب الفاعل الإمساك بزمام الأمور. قام منسقا المعرض فلوريان إيبنر وكونستانزة فيكه أثنـاء إقامتهمـا في القـاهرة بالعمـل على شراكة المعرض بروح جماعيـة حِرفية مما أدى إلى اكتسابهم احترام وثقة الساحة الثقافيـة في مصر.

كانت النتيجة هي عرض لصور وأفلام وأعمال مركبة في متاحف ألمانية. تجذب علاقة هذه الأعمال بالحاضر ومرئيتها واحتوائـها على هذا الكم من المشاعر المركزة، المشاهد إليـها وتأسره. ففي التبادل الثقافي بالذات تلعب الصور دوراً أكبر من أي كلمات. وبهذا يفتح هذا المعرض طرقاً جديدة للتعرف على هذه المنطقة الكبيرة المجاورة لأوروبا- العالم العربي اليوم.

جابرييلا بيكر وجونتر هازنكامب
معهد جوتة، القاهرة

إن مشروع "القاهرة مدينة مفتوحة. صور جديدة من ثورة مستمرة" هو مشروع قريب من الأحداث السياسية في مصر الآن وهو في نفس الوقت يبعد ثلاثة آلاف كيلومتراً عن الحدث بوجوده في متحف براونشفايج للتصوير، المكان الذي انطلقت منه فكرة المشروع، وفي متحف فولكفانخ في مدينة إيسّن، المكان الذي ستُنقل وتُحدث وتكتمل فيه الصور، وهذا لنقل عملية سياسية مستمرة لم تكتب نهايتها بعد.

هناك فراغ بين التطابق الزمني للمعرض مع الأحداث وبين البعد الجغرافي لمكانه عن مكان الأحداث؛ فراغ قد يملؤه سوء الفهم. فالكثير من التصورات عن ما أسمته وسائل الإعلام الغربية "بالربيع العربي"، هي نتيجة تبسيط قاسٍ في بعض الأحيان ومبالغات خاطئة أو نقص في المصادر في أحيان أخرى. ولذلك فإن واحدة من أهداف هذا المشروع هو مراجعة صورة الثورة في مصر واستكمالها.

قد تبدو فكرة تولي متحف لهذا المشروع للوهلة الأولى صادمة، فلا شيء في هذا الموضوع قديم أو أثري. إن الأمر يتعلق حقيقةً بالعمل: العمل بمساعدة الرؤية والتفكير للوصول إلى طريقة لفهم الثورة، من يدفعها ومن يمثلها وطبيعة دور التصوير في هذا كله. وكما يبرز النص المصاحب لهذه التركيبة من الأعمال، فالذي أمامنا هنا من أعمال يشكل بلا أدنى شك "فصل جديد في التصوير الفوتوغرافي في العالم العربي". وفي نفس الوقت "فصل جديد في تاريخ الصور".

إن التاريخ السياسي وتاريخ الصور مرتبطان ببعضهما البعض، بل أكثر من ذلك: إن الأحداث السياسية هي التي تخلق طرق جديدة في استخدام التصوير الفوتوغرافي، مثل الشهادات السياسية الرقمية التي تُسجل وتُنشر في ثوان معدودة، لتتحول إلى أدلة فورية تتداخل في العملية السياسية وعملية تكوين الرأي العام.

وتُشكل سرعة النقل، مع قدرة كل شخص يمتلك هاتف محمول على التحول إلى صحفي شعبي متصل بشبكة كبيرة من الأشخاص، نقلة نوعية في تأثير التصوير الفوتوغرافي في المجتمع. ولهذا فهو من الطبيعي تسليط الأضواء على "فاعلي الصورة"، الذين أنتجوا المادة المرئية لهذه الثورة (الفوتوغرافية) في القاهرة. وهم ليسوا فقط "السفراء" الذين يتحدثون الإنجليزية، هؤلاء من فَضّل المراسلين الأجانب الإستعانة بهم أمام الكاميرا والميكروفون، ولكن أيضاً صانعي الأفلام والمدونين والفنانين والصحفيين المحترفين والمصورين، الذين تحولوا إلى موثقي التحولات السياسية بكاميراتهم أو هواتفهم المحمولة.

ما يميز هذا المعرض هو وجود فرصة للتعرف على الأشخاص الناشطين خارج نطاق ميدان التحرير، الذين بدأوا منذ سنوات عديدة، قبل اندلاع "الربيع العربي" في التعامل مع، وتحليل الأوضاع الاجتماعية في مصر في أعمالهم. كما توضح تركيبة الصور المختلفة اختلاف أدوار ونوايا هؤلاء الأشخاص من شاهد إلى حارس إلى مُذكِّر.

إنه ليسعد المؤسسة الثقافية الإتحادية تمويل هذا المشروع، نتقدم بالشكر إلى فلوريان إيبنر وكونستانزه فيكّه على فكرة هذا المعرض وعلى دعوتهم لمصورين وفنانين وناشطين وصحفيين مصريين للمشاركة في المعرض ولكي يساهموا في تنسيق أجزاء منه. نتقدم أيضاً بالشكر إلى لارا بلدي، أسامة داود، روان الشيمي، هبة فريد، توماس هارتويل، أحمد كامل، ياسمينا متولي، أليكس نانس، فيليب رزق وطارق حفني؛ فكل منهم يحكي الثورة من وجهة نظره.

أليكسندر فارينهولتز، مجلس الإدارة/مدير الإدارة
هورتسينا فولكرس، مجلس الإدارة / الإدارة الفنية

ألبوم للتاريخ

هيئة التحرير

شاهد عيان على الثورة

شاهد عيان على الثورة

ألبوم للتاريخ

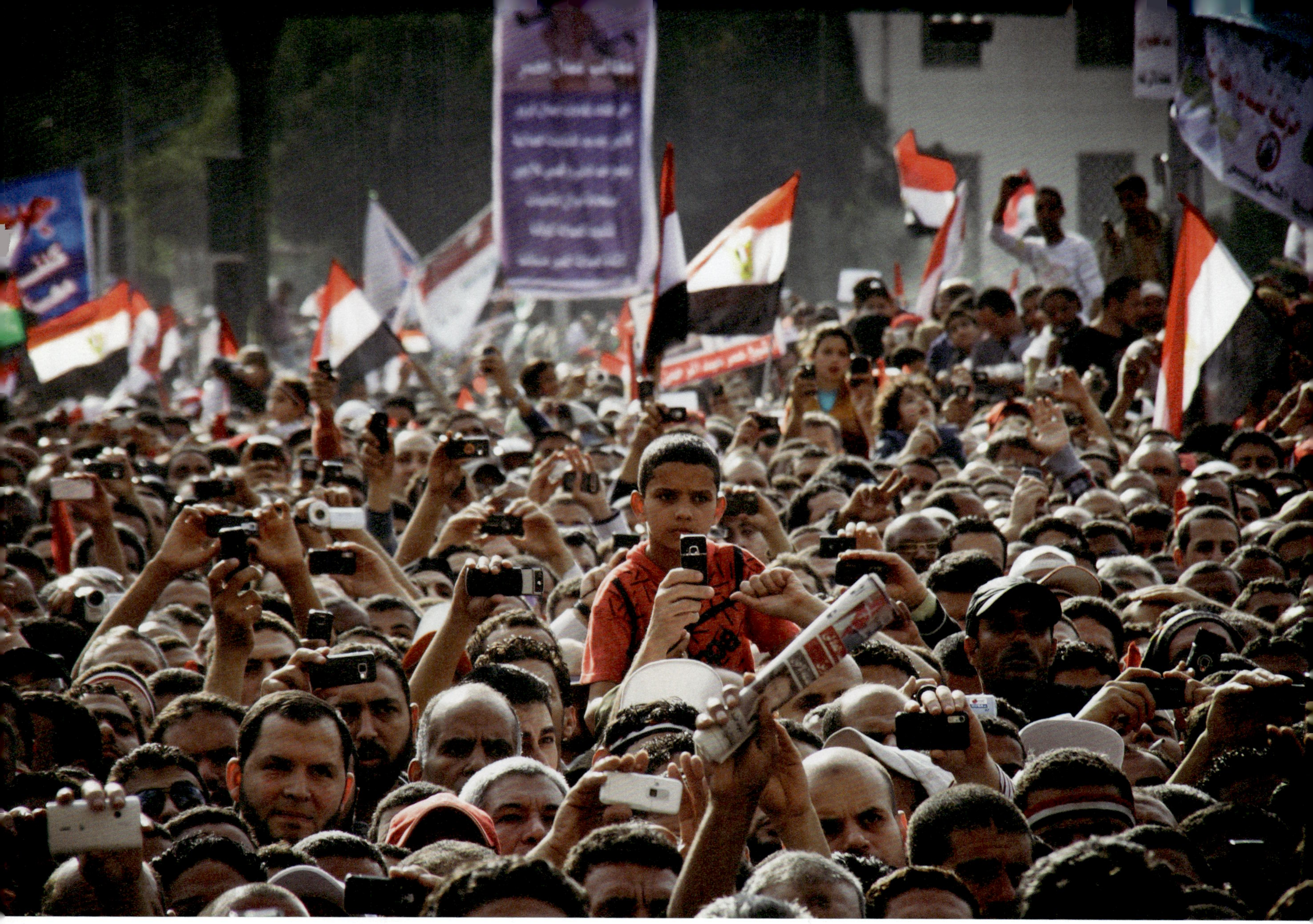

Mosa'ab Elshamy, Protesters during a speech, Tahrir Square / Demonstranten während einer 50
Rede, Tahrir-Platz, Apr. 8, 2011 / 2011 مصعب الشامي، مظاهرات أثناء خطاب، ميدان التحرير، 8 أبريل

From the Flickr album / Aus dem Flickr-Album *Documenting the Revolution* / من ألبوم توثيق الثورة على موقع فليكر

Alex Majoli, *Egypt. Cairo. Feb. 5, 2011* 49 + 48
أليكس ماجولي، مصر، القاهرة، *5* فبراير *2011*

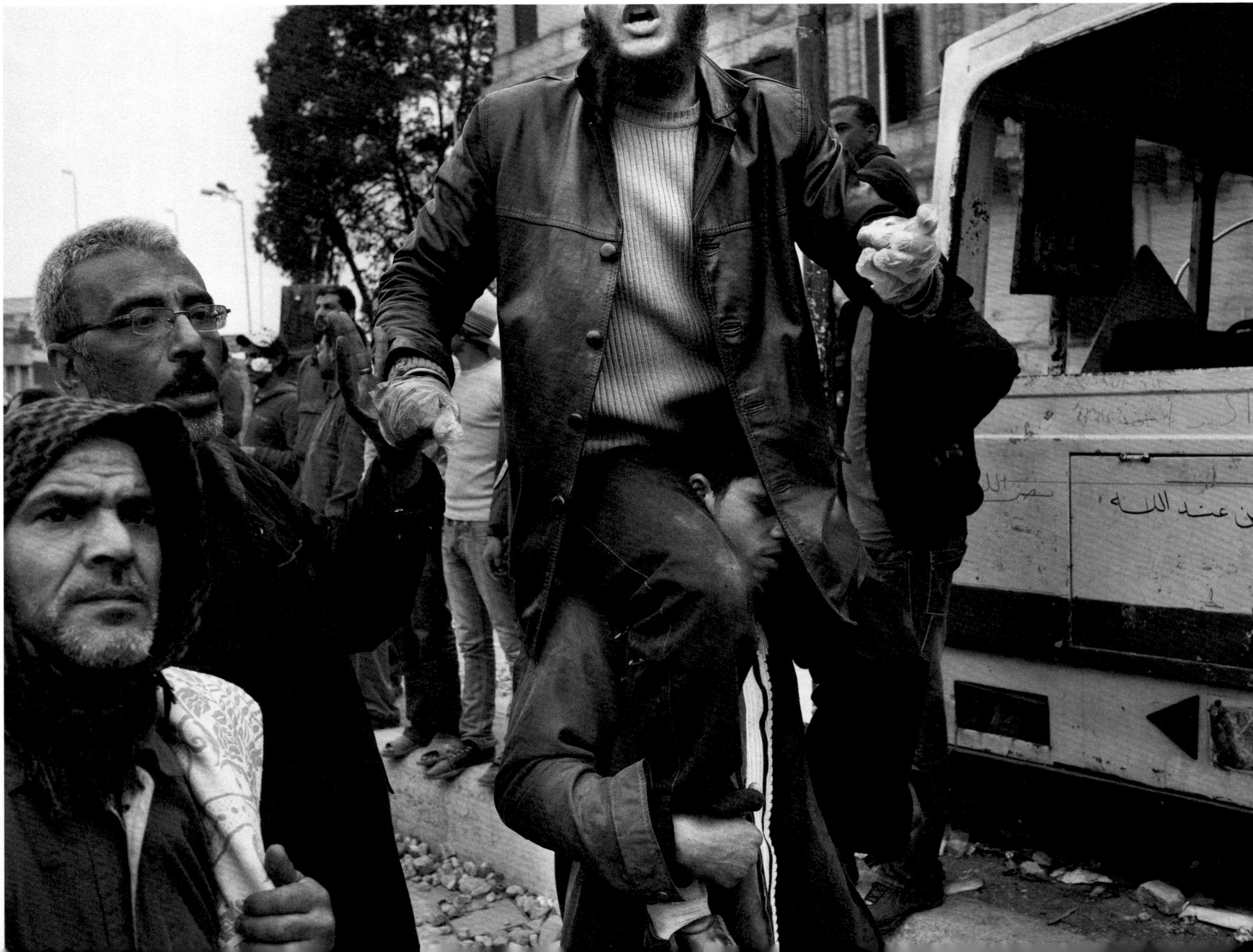

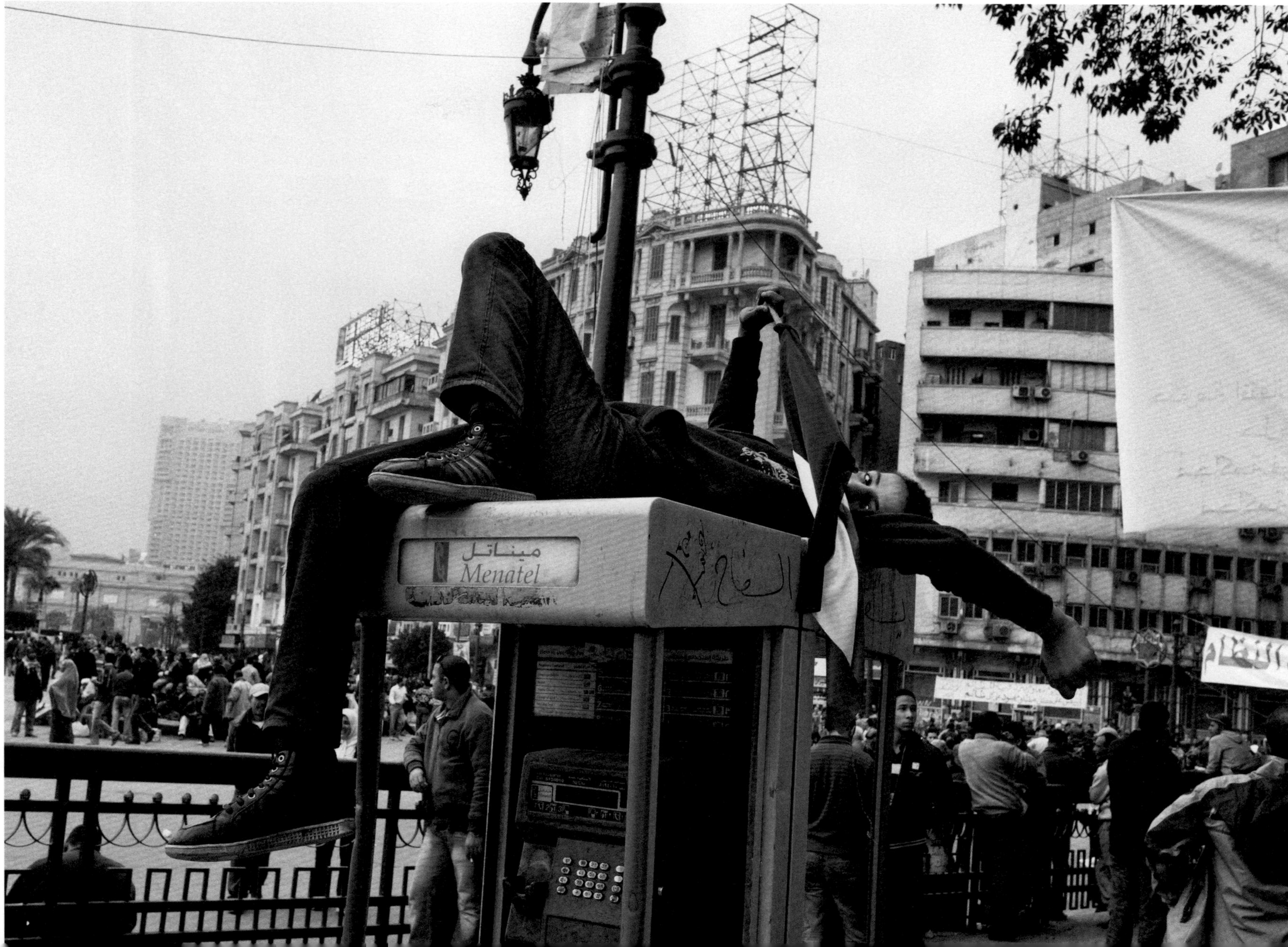
ميناتل
Menatel

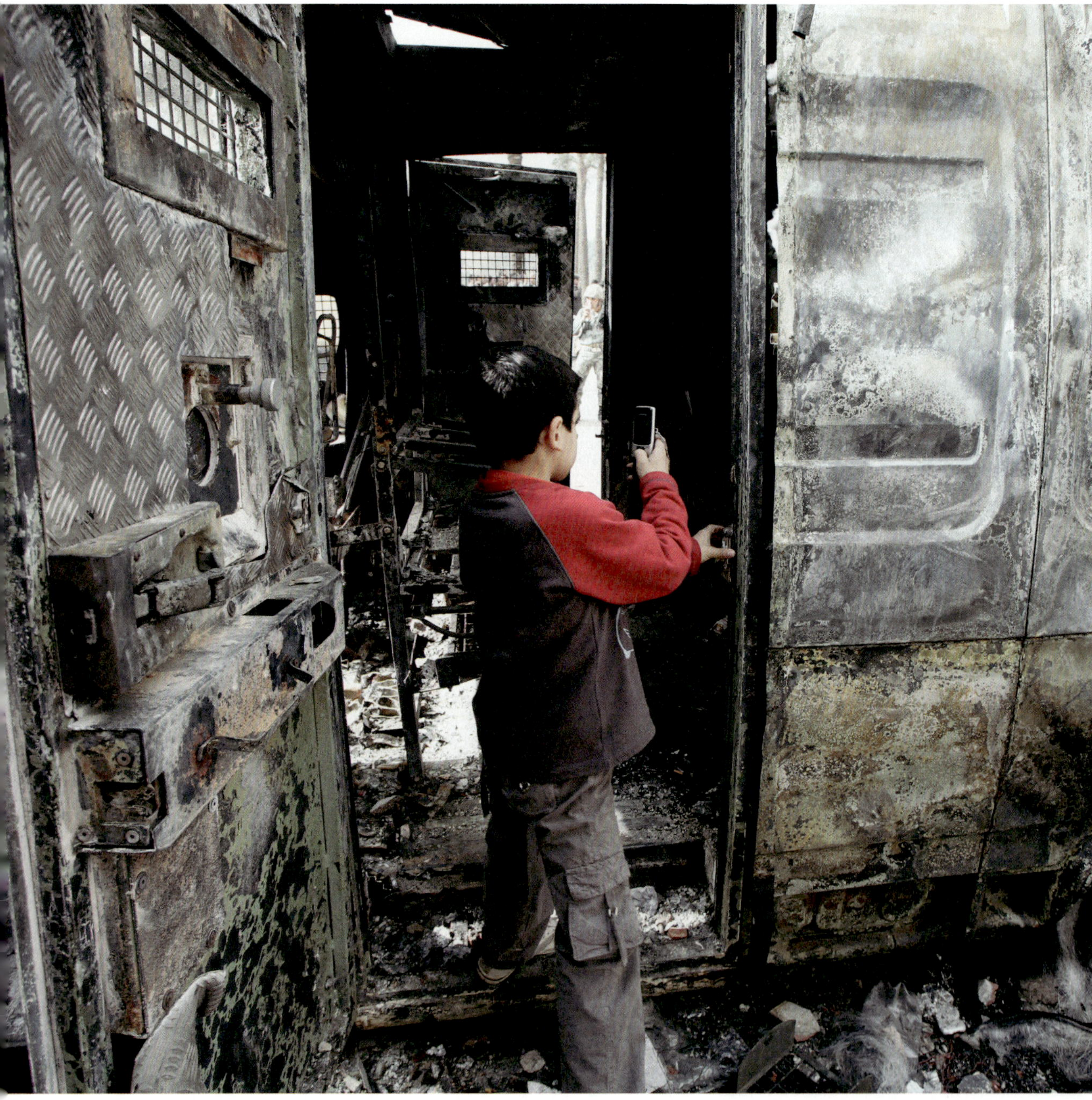

Myriam Abdelaziz, from the series / aus der Serie *Egyptian Revolt*, 2011 47 + 46
مريم عبد العزيز، من سلسلة الصورة المصرية، 2011

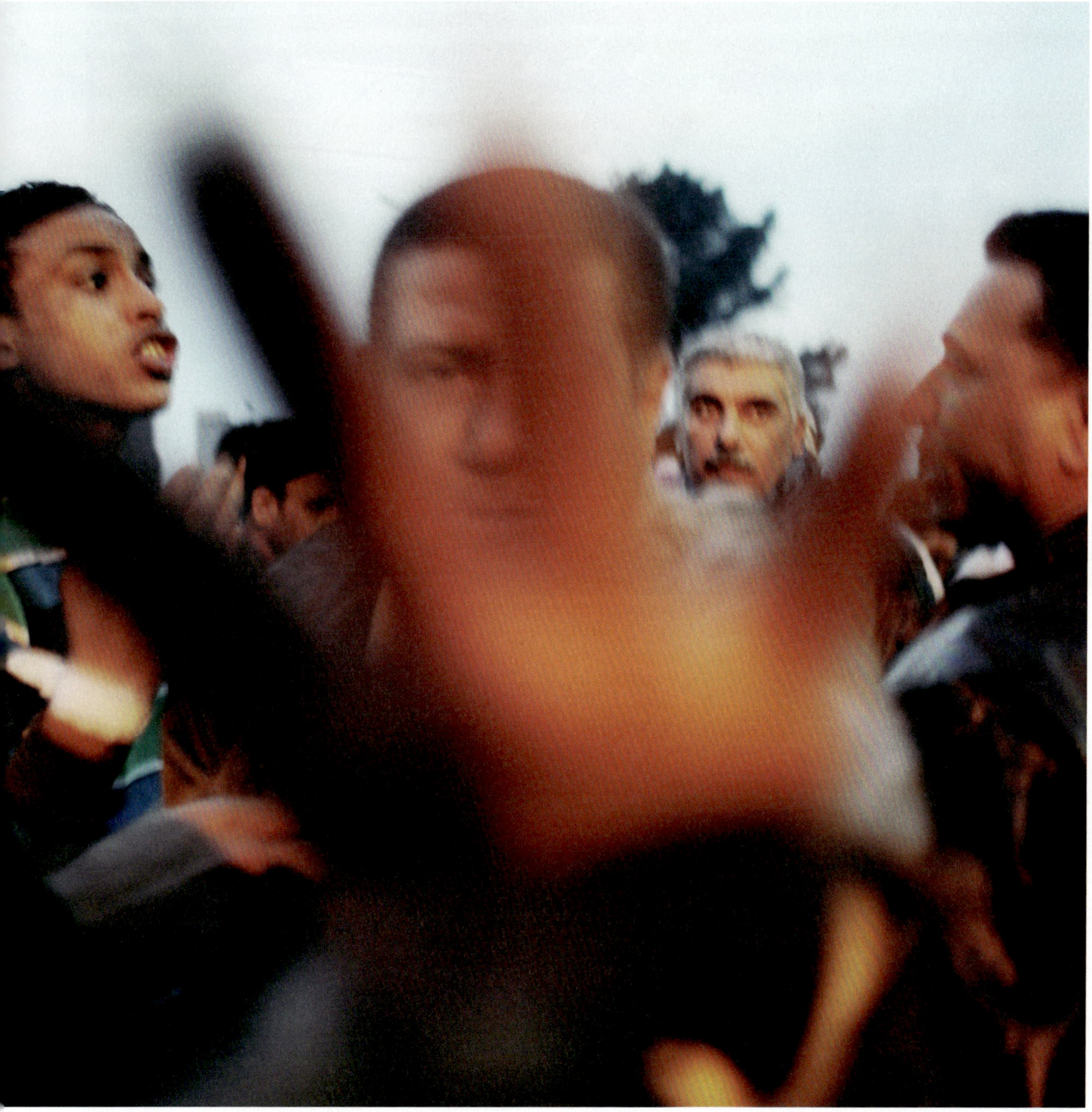

View of an Egyptian Photographer Living Abroad / Blick einer im Ausland lebenden ägyptischen Fotografin / رؤية مصورة مصرية مقيمة في الخارج

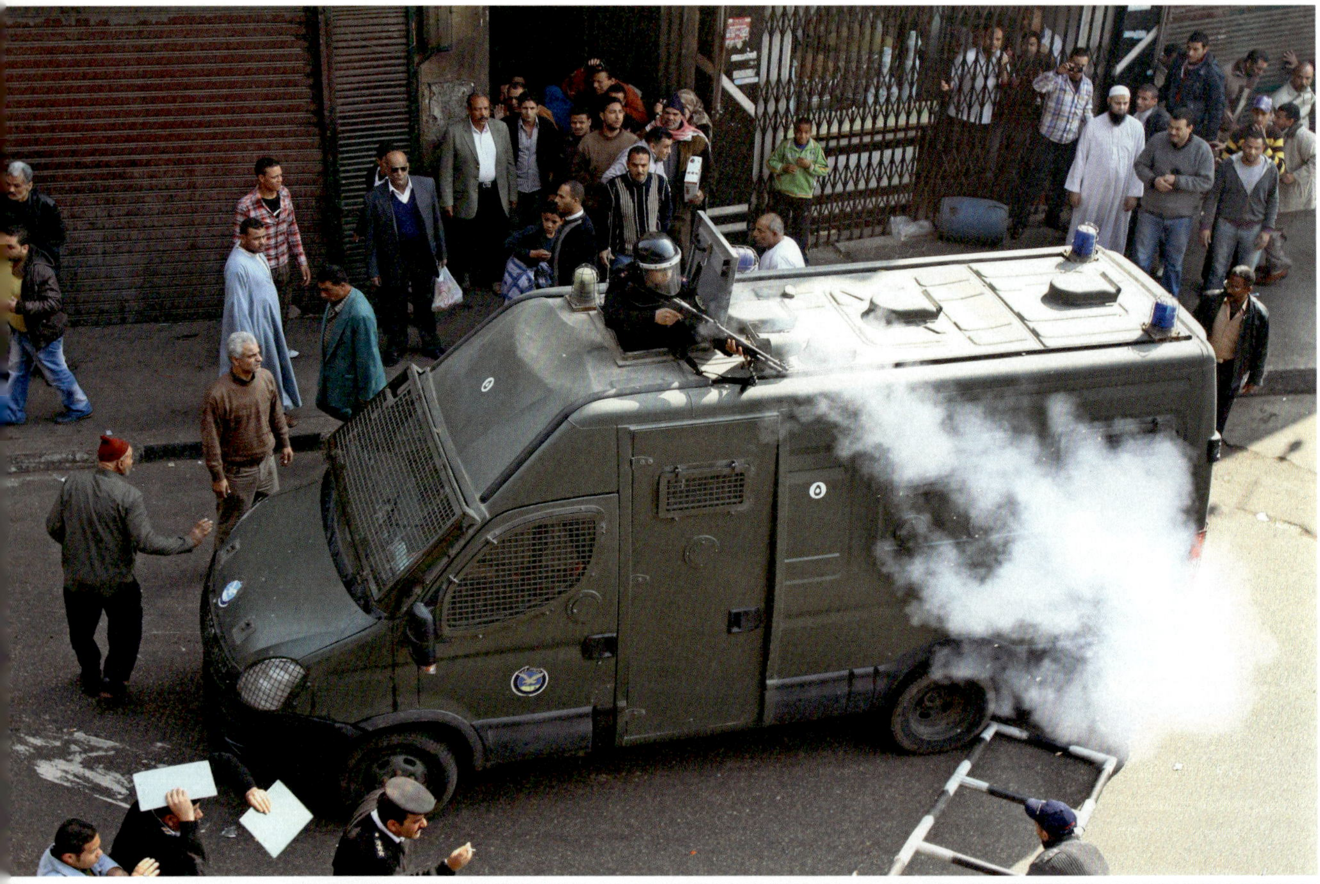

44 Mohammed el Maymouny, *Azhar St., Cairo, Jan. 28, 2011* / محمد الميموني، الأزهر، القاهرة، 28 يناير 2011

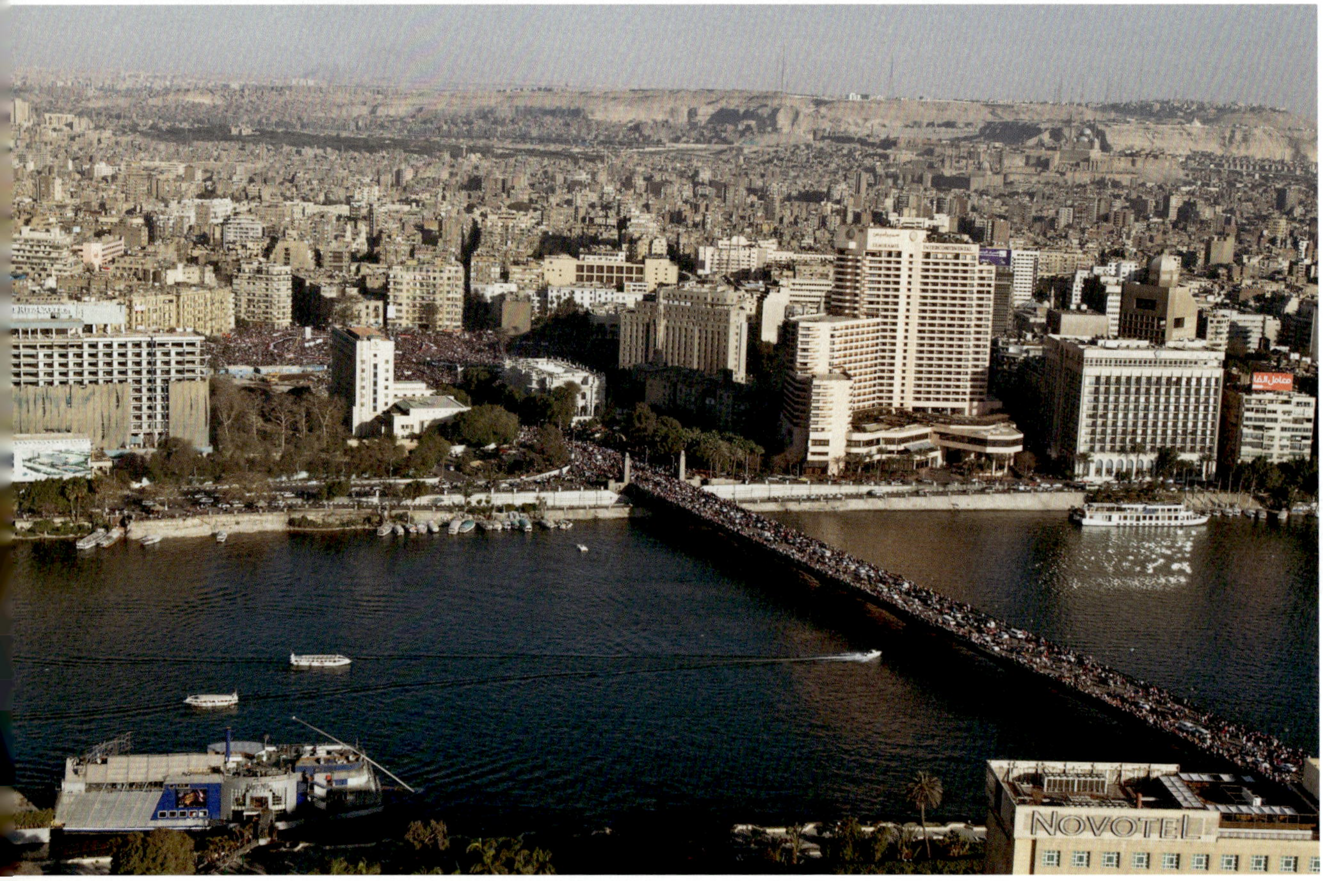

45 Sabry Khaled, *Kasr el Nil Bridge, Cairo, Feb. 18, 2011* / صبري خالد، قصر النيل، 18 فبراير 2011

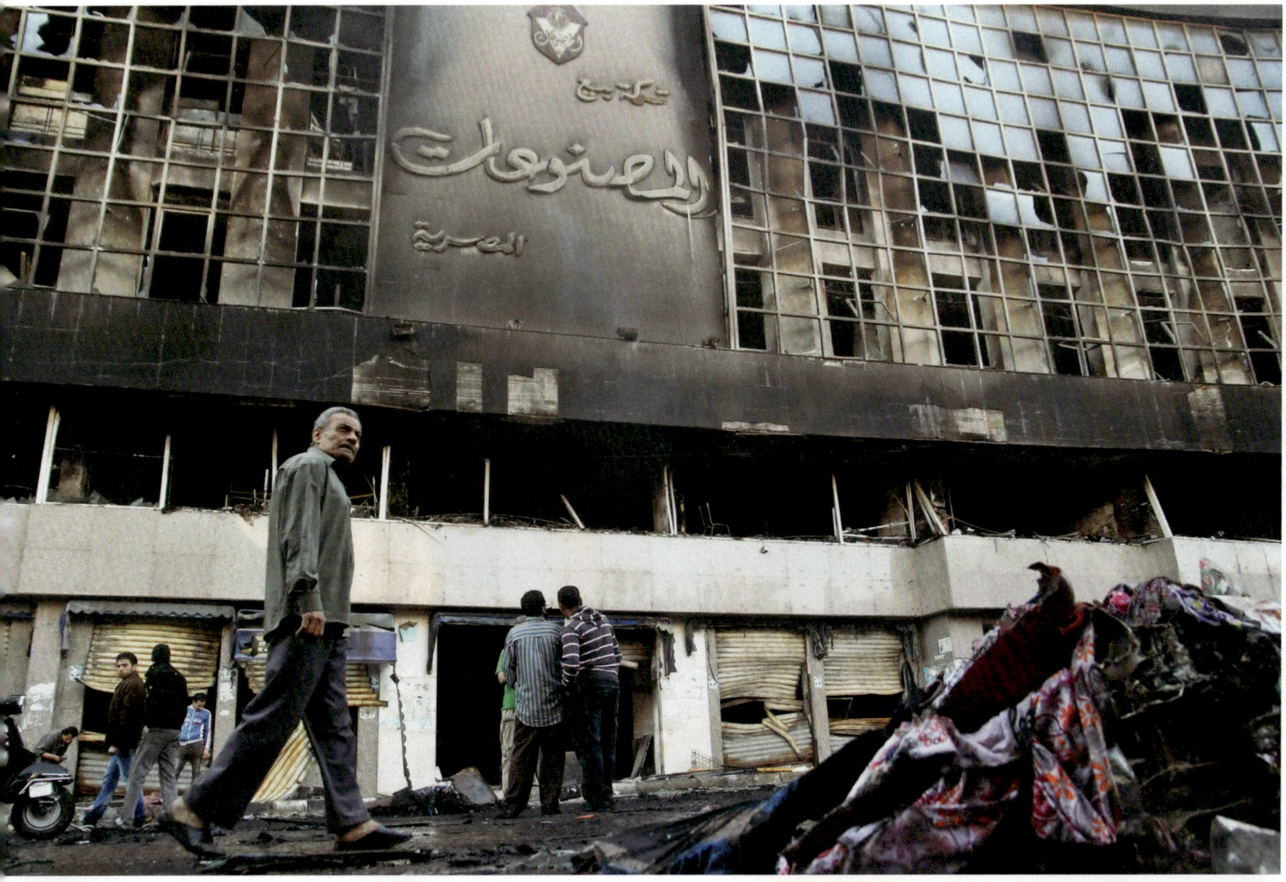

42 روجر أنيس، طنطا، 23 أبريل 2012 / Roger Anis, *Tanta*, Apr. 23, 2012 / 2012

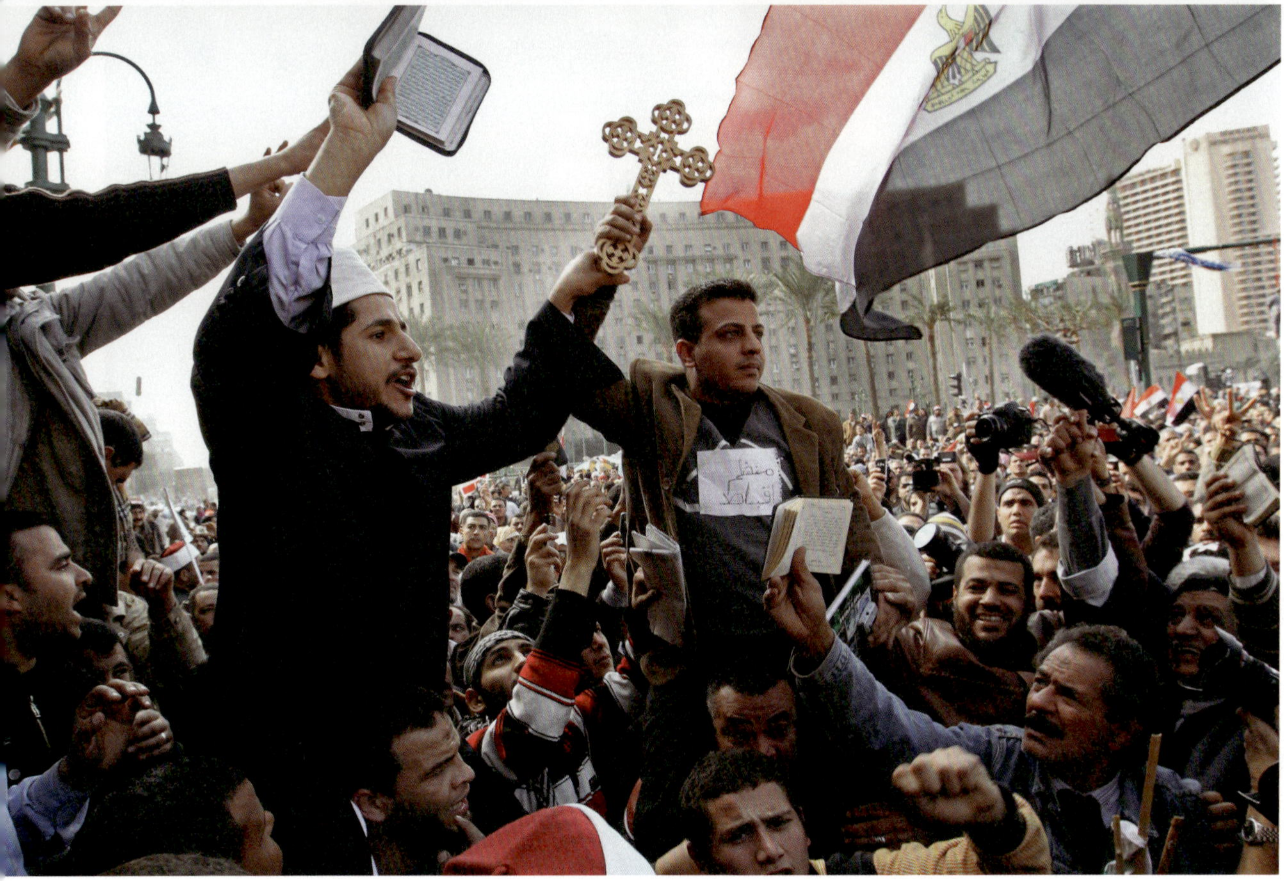

43 رندا شعث، التحرير القاهرة، 6 فبراير 2012 / Randa Shaath, *Tahrir, Cairo*, Feb. 6, 2012 / 2012

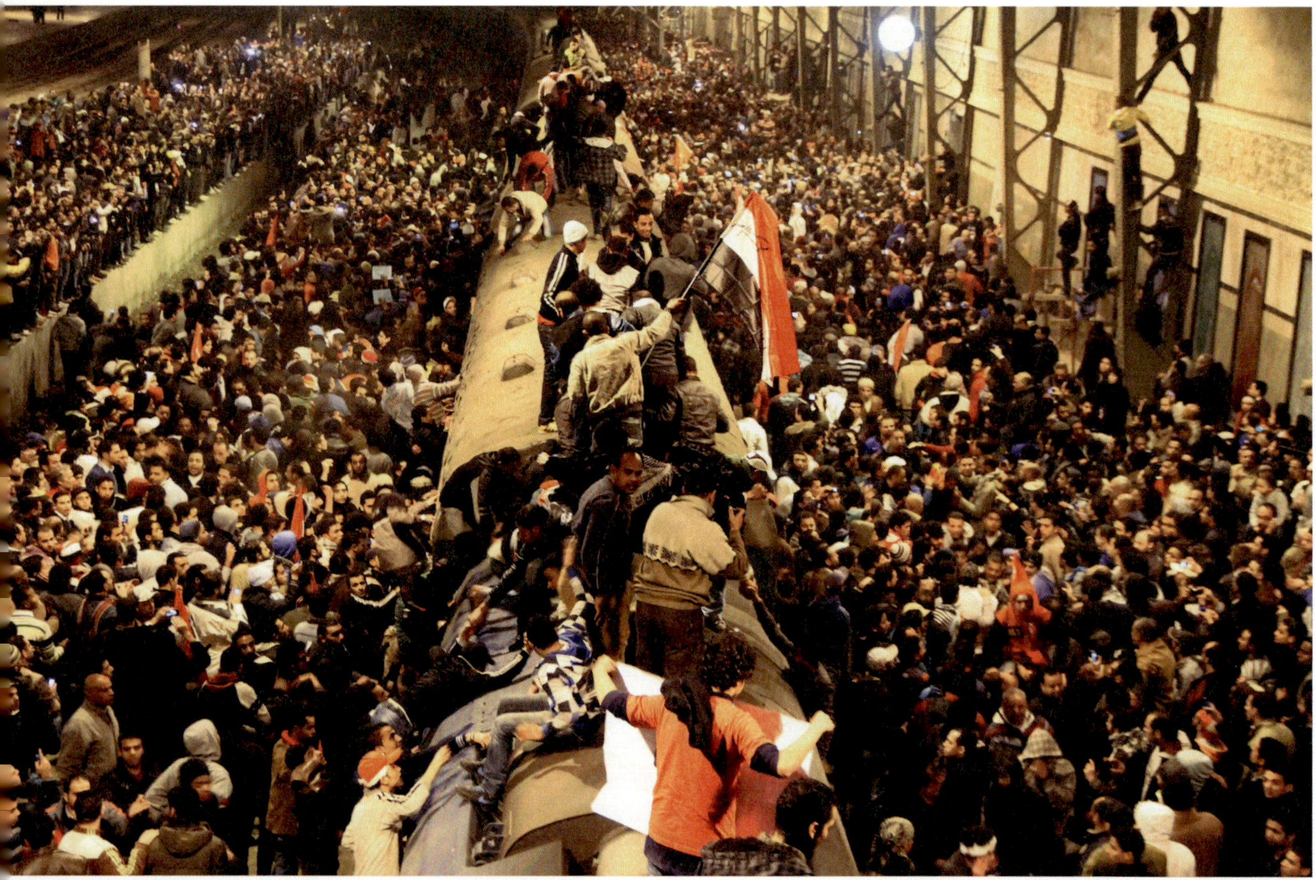

Magdy Ibrahim, *Ramses Station, Cairo, Feb. 2, 2012* / 2012 مجدي ابراهيم، محطة رمسيس، القاهرة، 2 فبراير

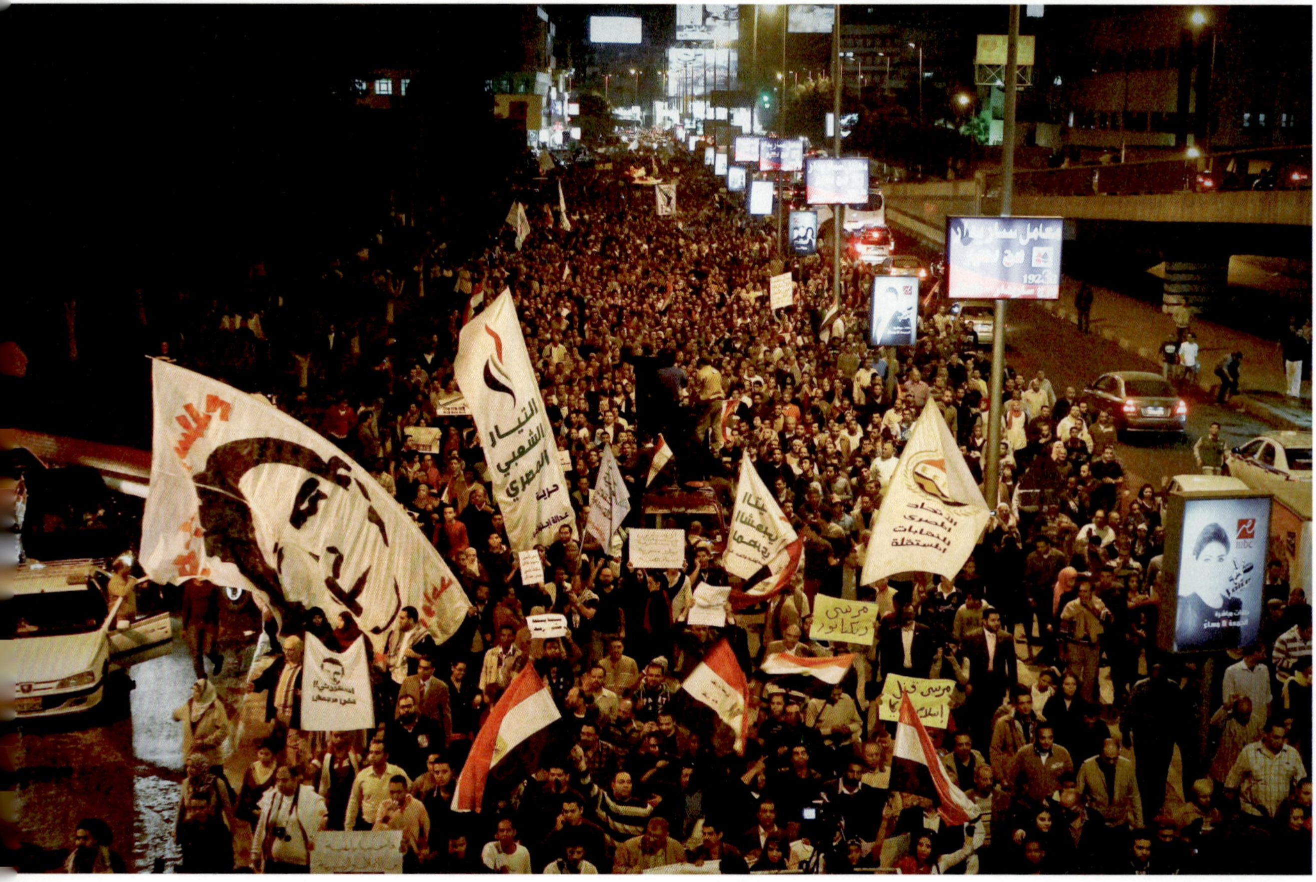

George Mohsen, *Mostafa Mahmoud, Nov. 27, 2011* / 2011 جورج محسن، مصطفى محمود، 27 نوفمبر

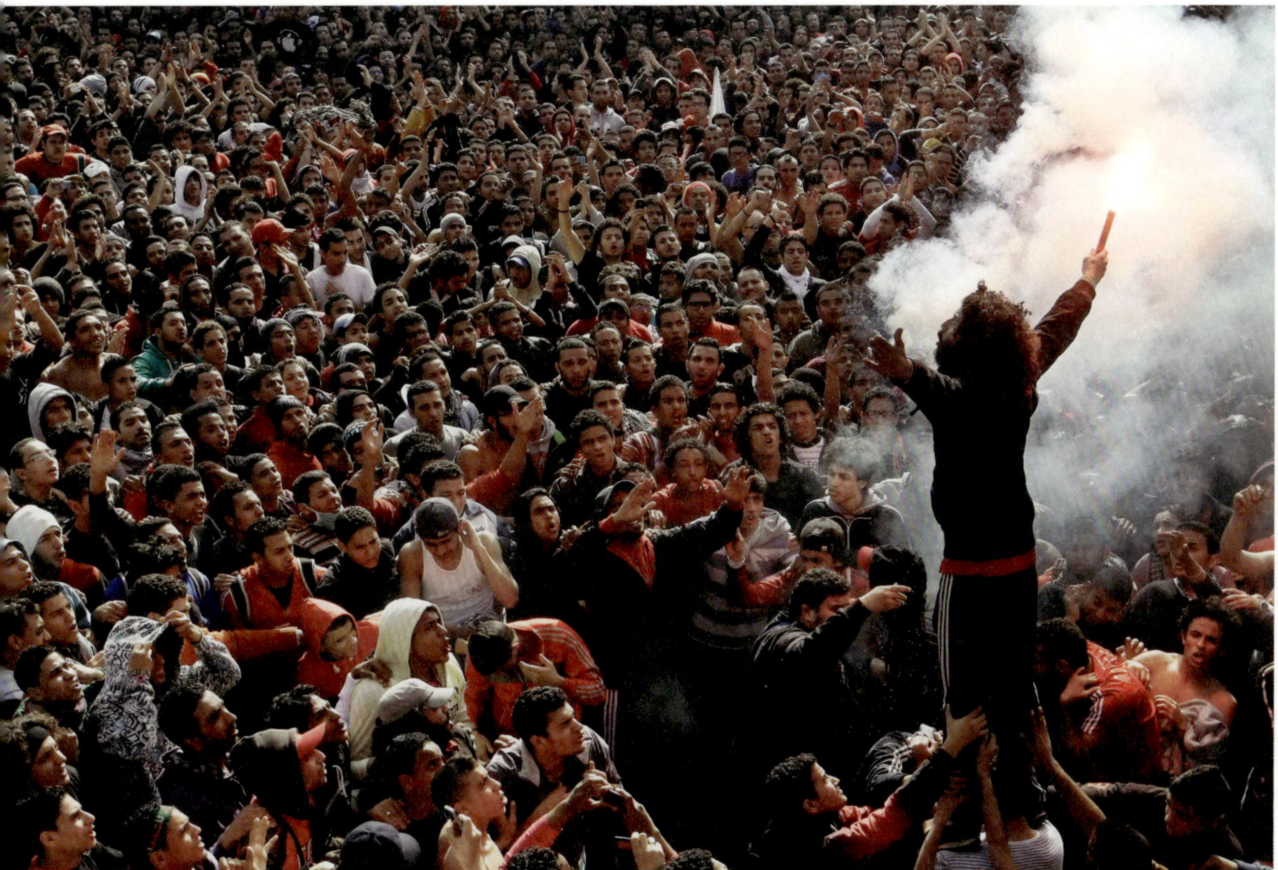

38 رافي شاكر، ألتراس. محاكمة بور سعيد-النادي الأهلي / Rafi Shaker, *Ultras. Port Said Trial Ahli Club*

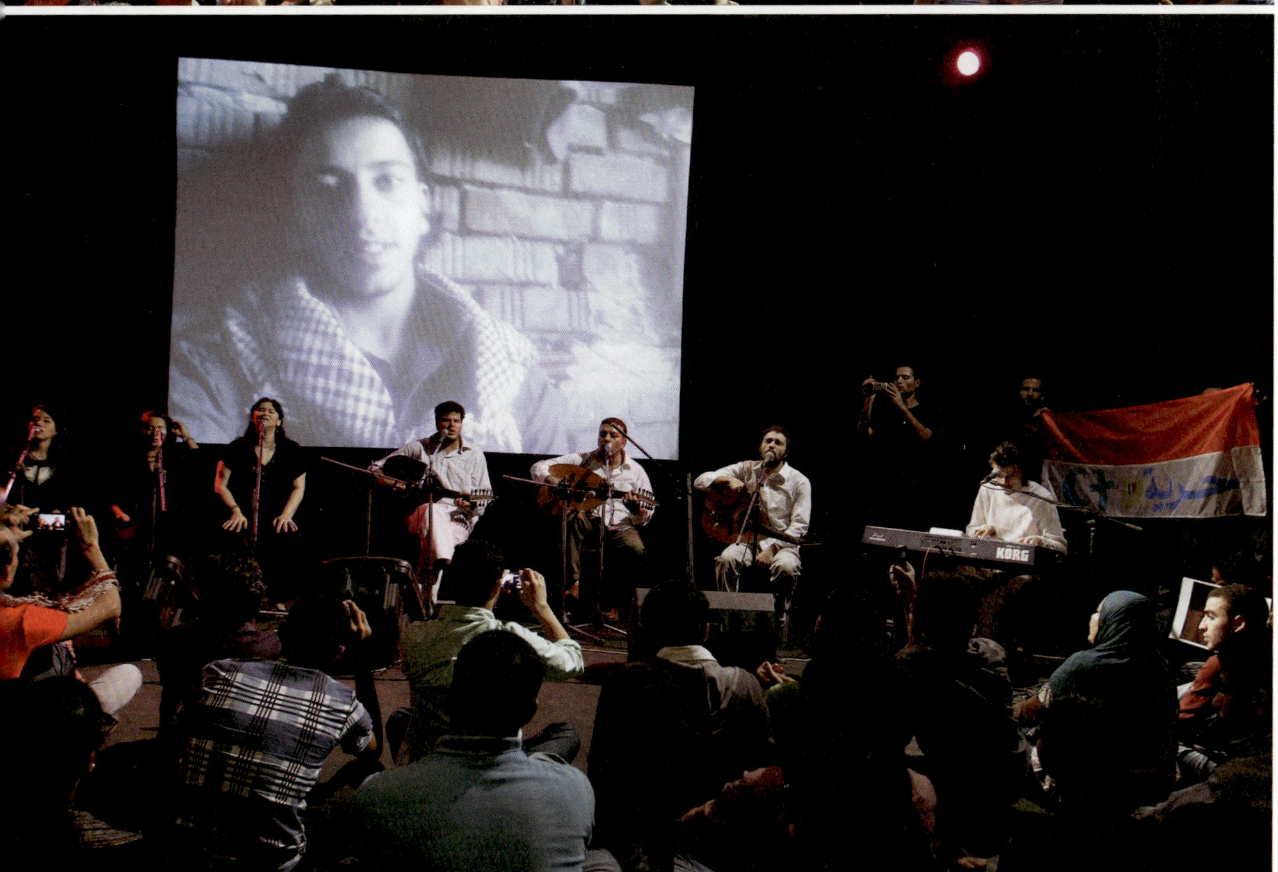

39 إيمان هلال، القاهرة، 19 أكتوبر 2011 / Eman Helal, *Cairo, Oct. 19, 2011*

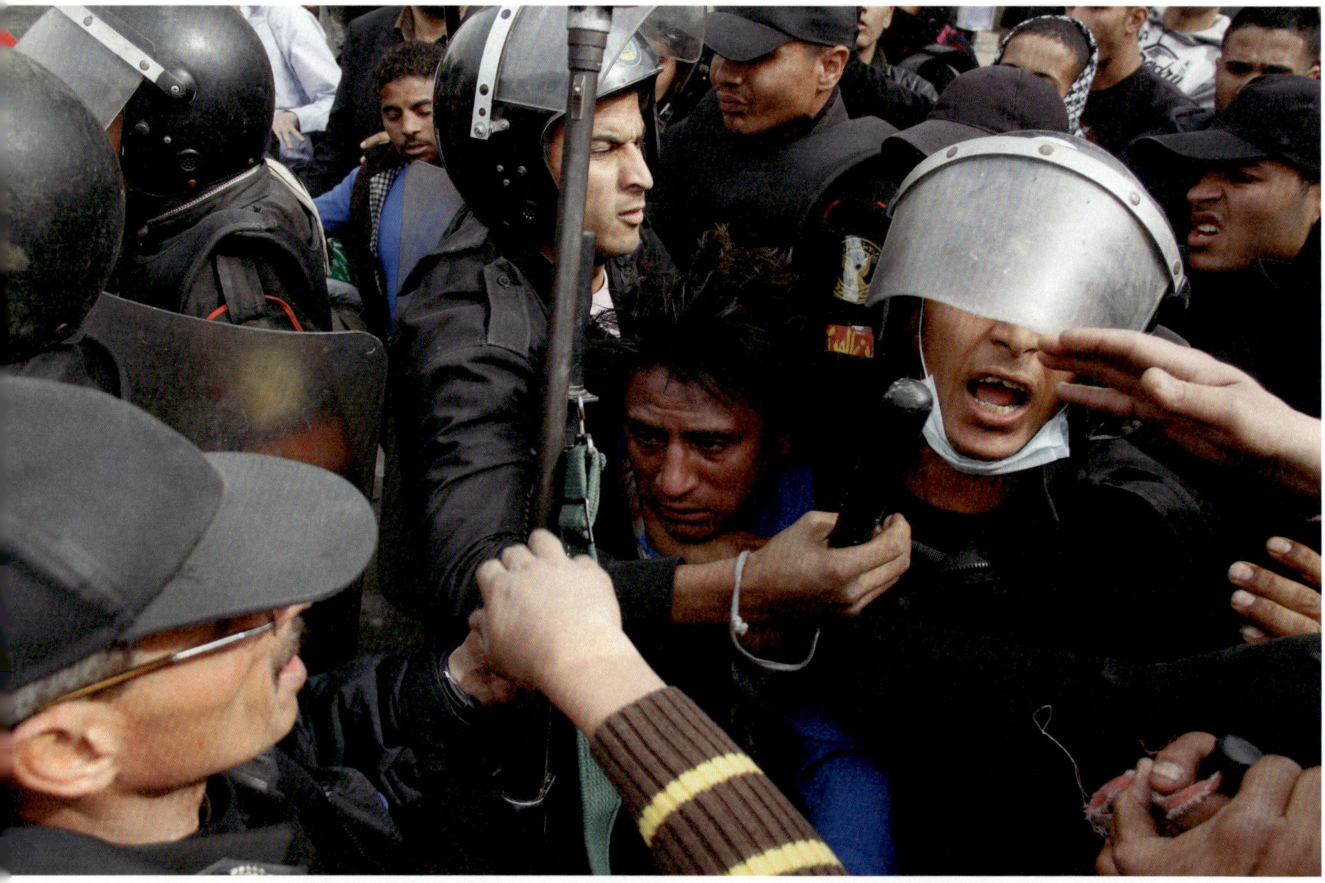

 Aly Hazza'a, *Kasr el Nil, Jan. 27, 2013* / علي هزاع، قصر النيل، 27 يناير 2013

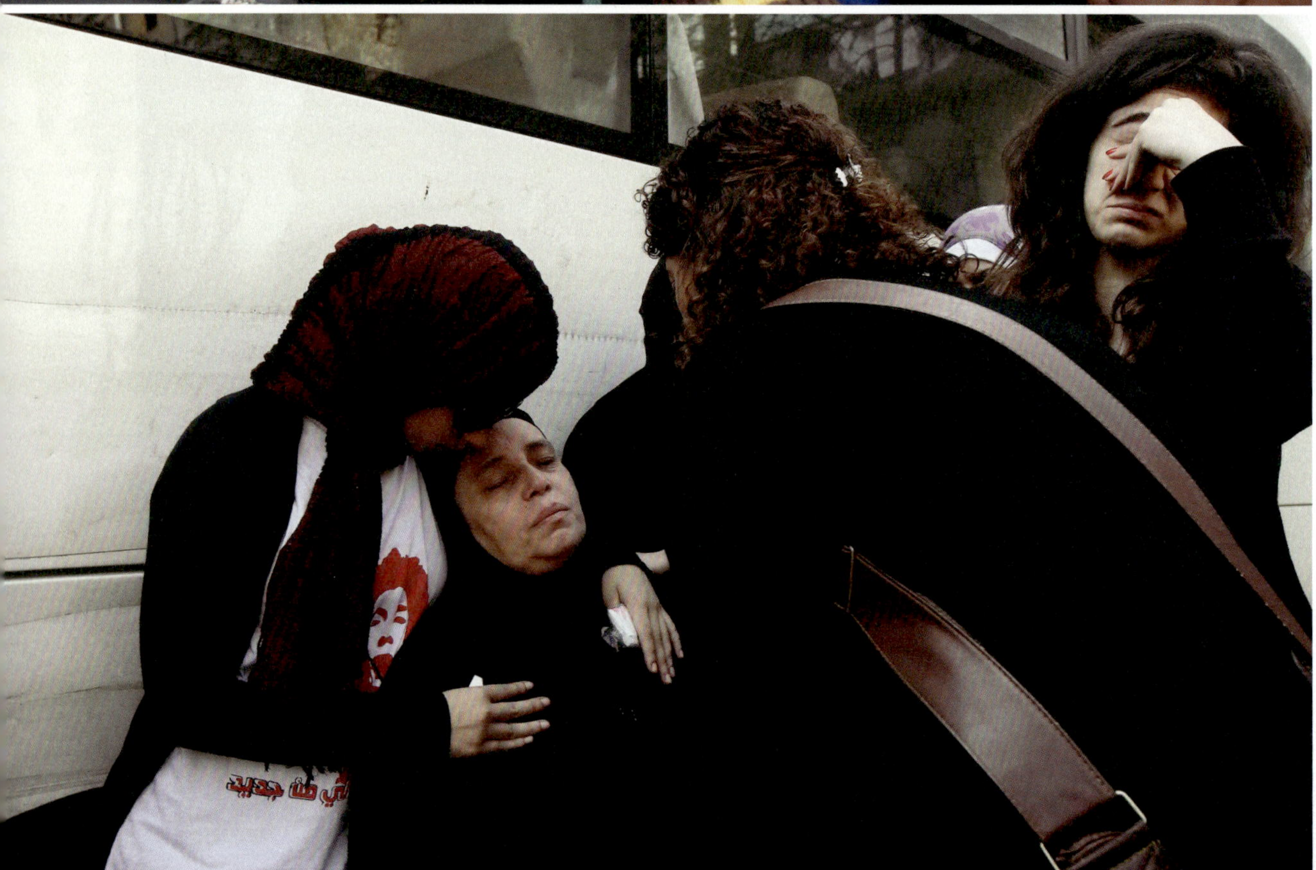

 Samuel Mohsen, *El Kasr El Aini, Nov. 26, 2012* / صامويل محسن، القصر العيني، 26 نوفمبر 2012

34 Roger Anis, *Abdin, Cairo, May 20, 2012* / روجر أنيس، عابدين، القاهرة، *20 مايو 2012*

35 Roger Anis, *Talaat Harb, Feb. 11, 2013* / روجر أنيس، طلعت حرب، *11 فبراير 2013*

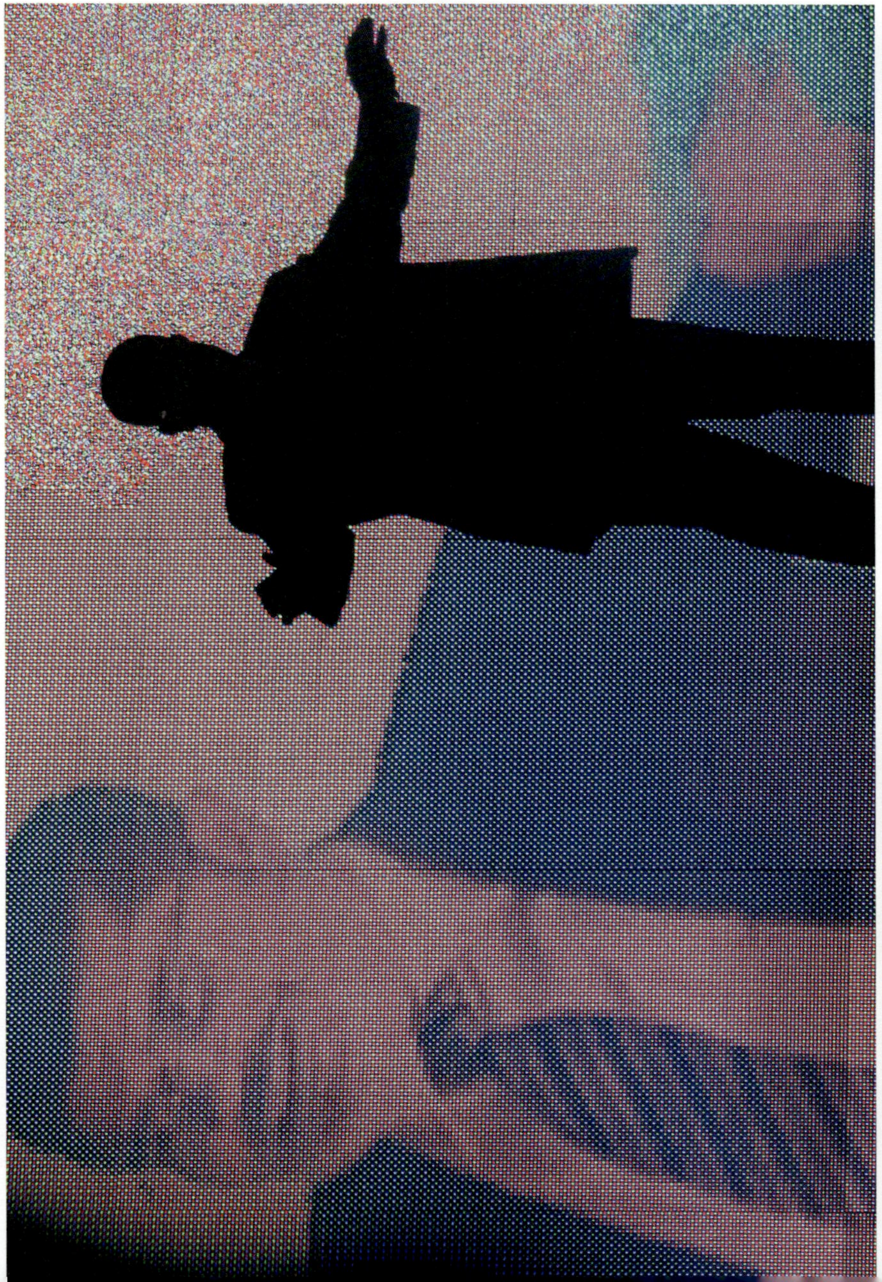

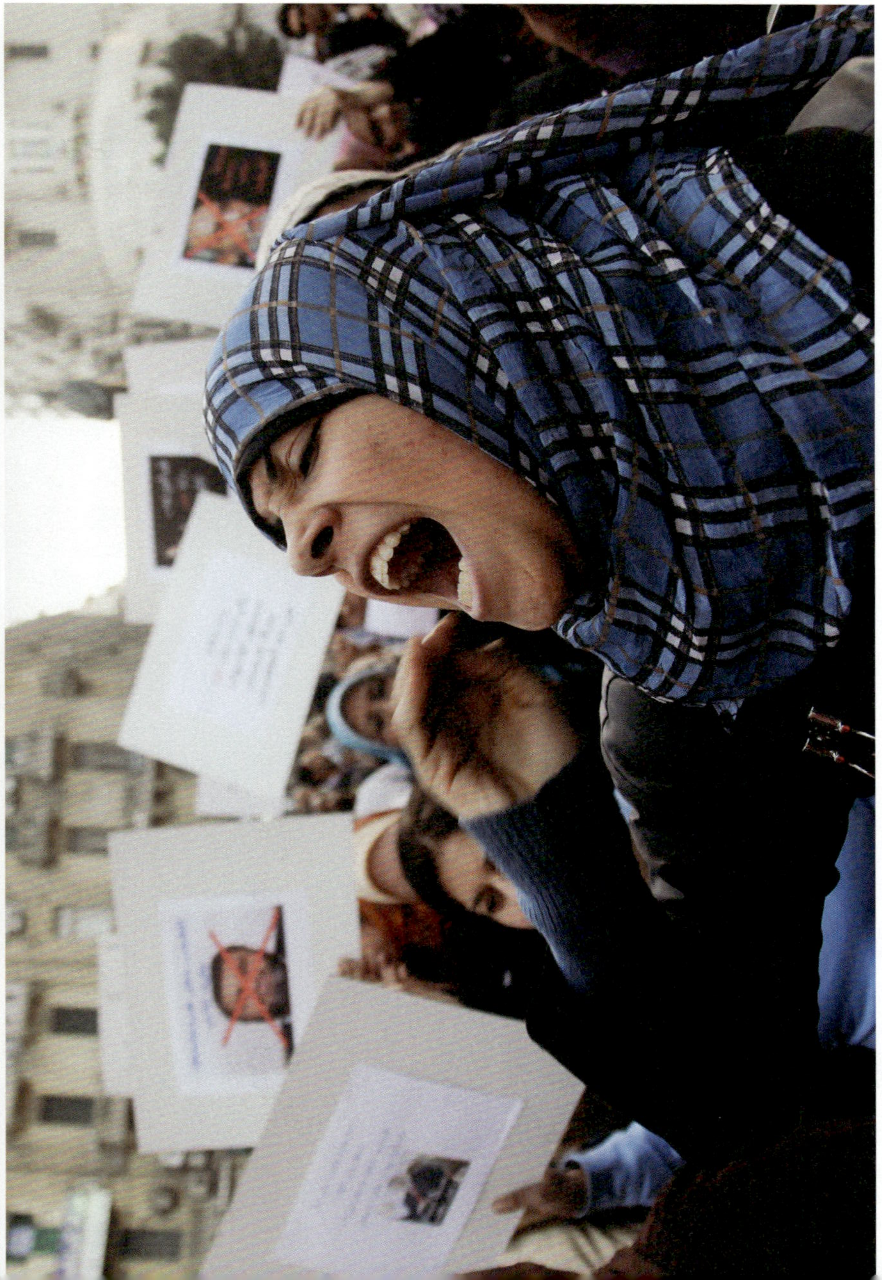

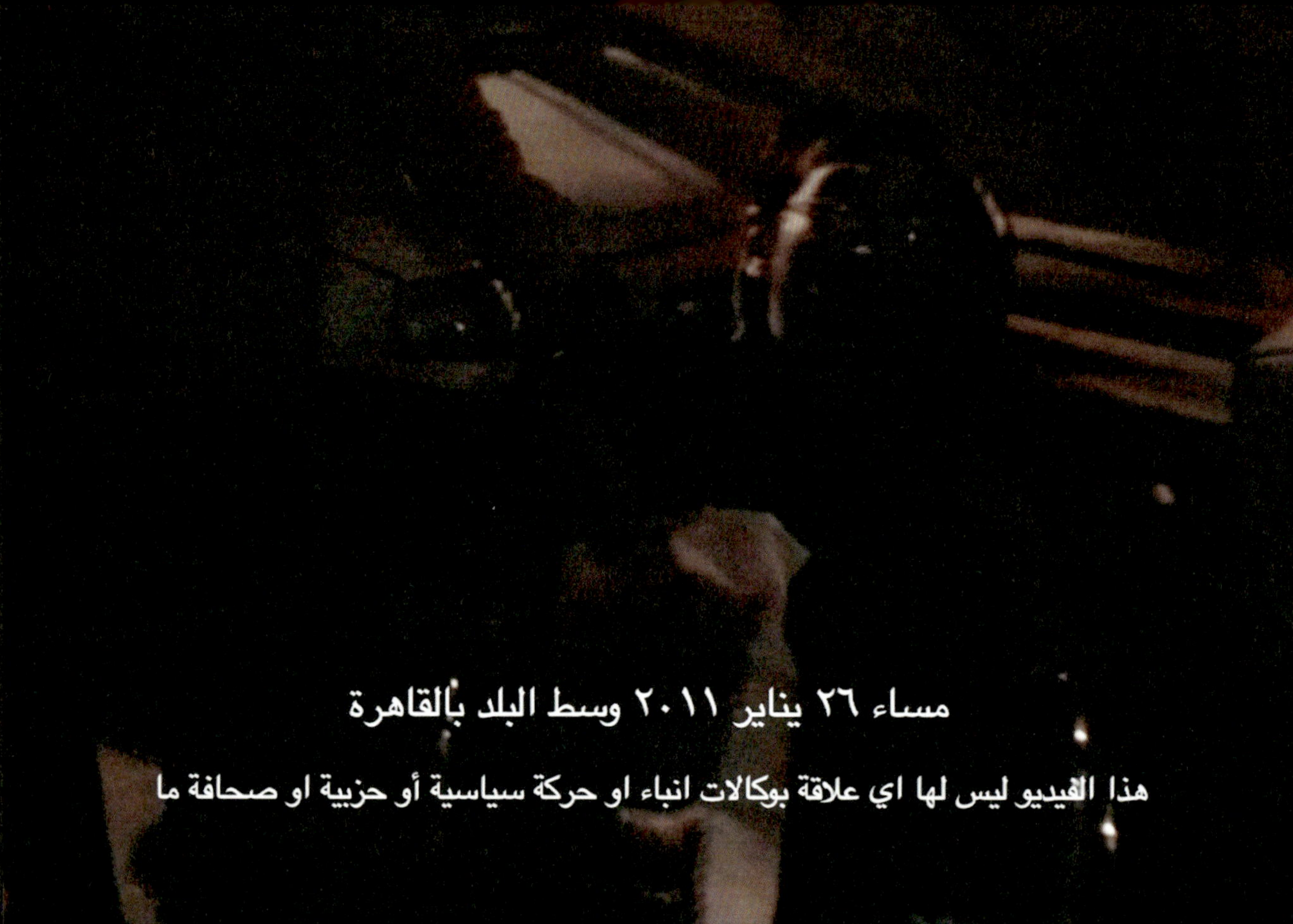
مساء ٢٦ يناير ٢٠١١ وسط البلد بالقاهرة
هذا الفيديو ليس لها اي علاقة بوكالات انباء او حركة سياسية أو حزبية او صحافة ما

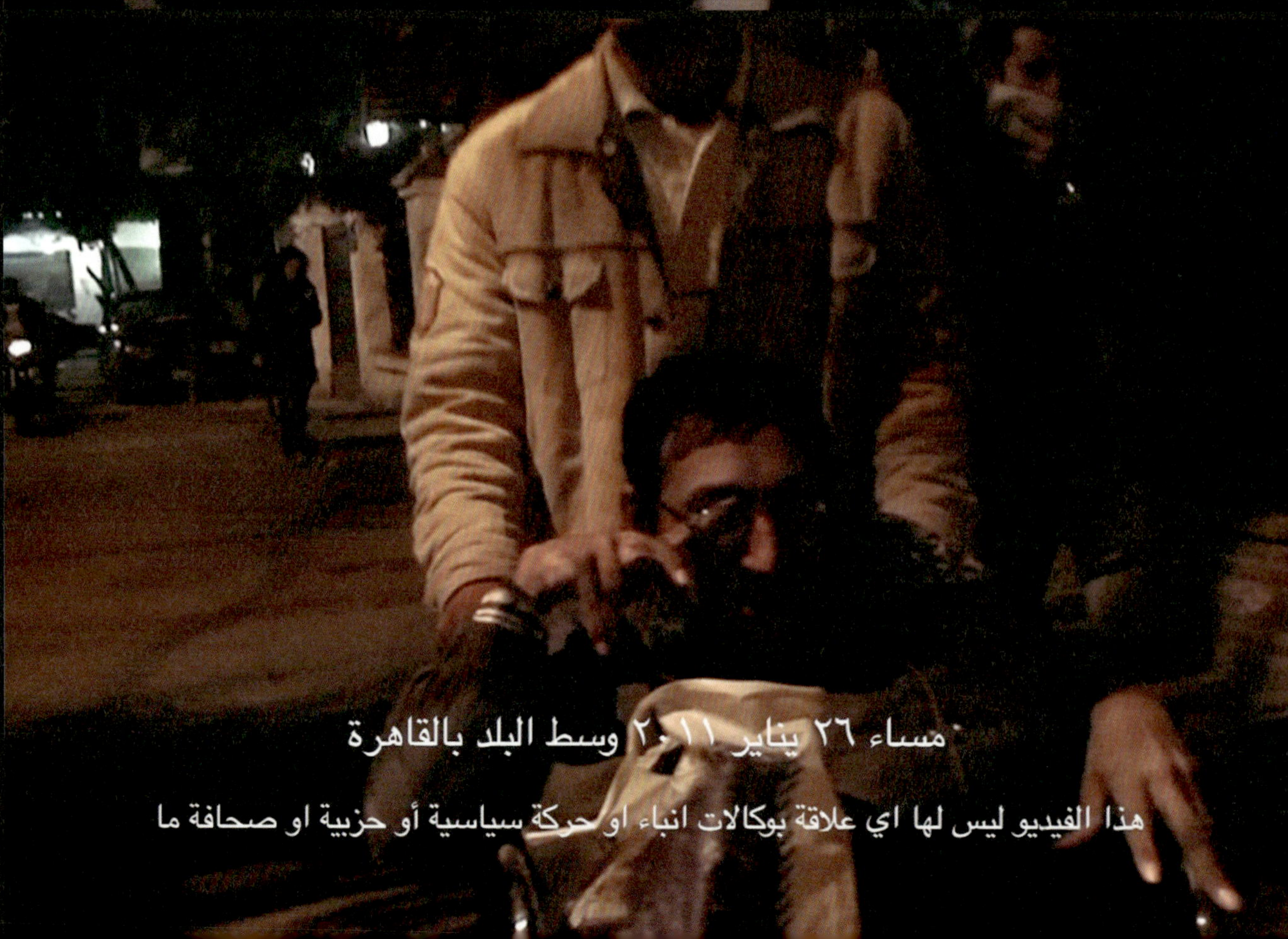
مساء ٢٦ يناير ٢٠١١ وسط البلد بالقاهرة
هذا الفيديو ليس لها اي علاقة بوكالات انباء او حركة سياسية أو حزبية او صحافة ما

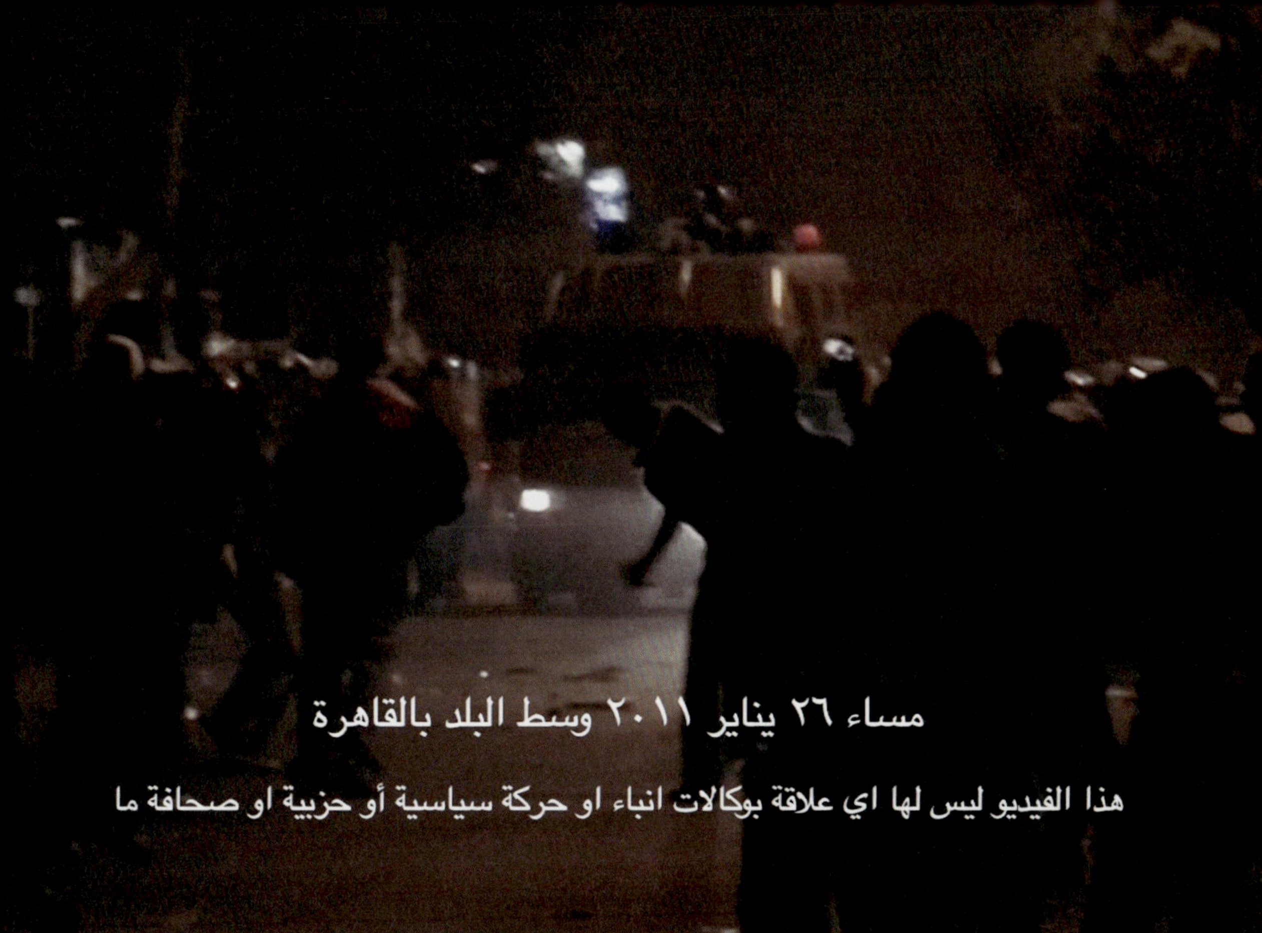
مساء ٢٦ يناير ٢٠١١ وسط البلد بالقاهرة
هذا الفيديو ليس لها اي علاقة بوكالات انباء او حركة سياسية أو حزبية او صحافة ما

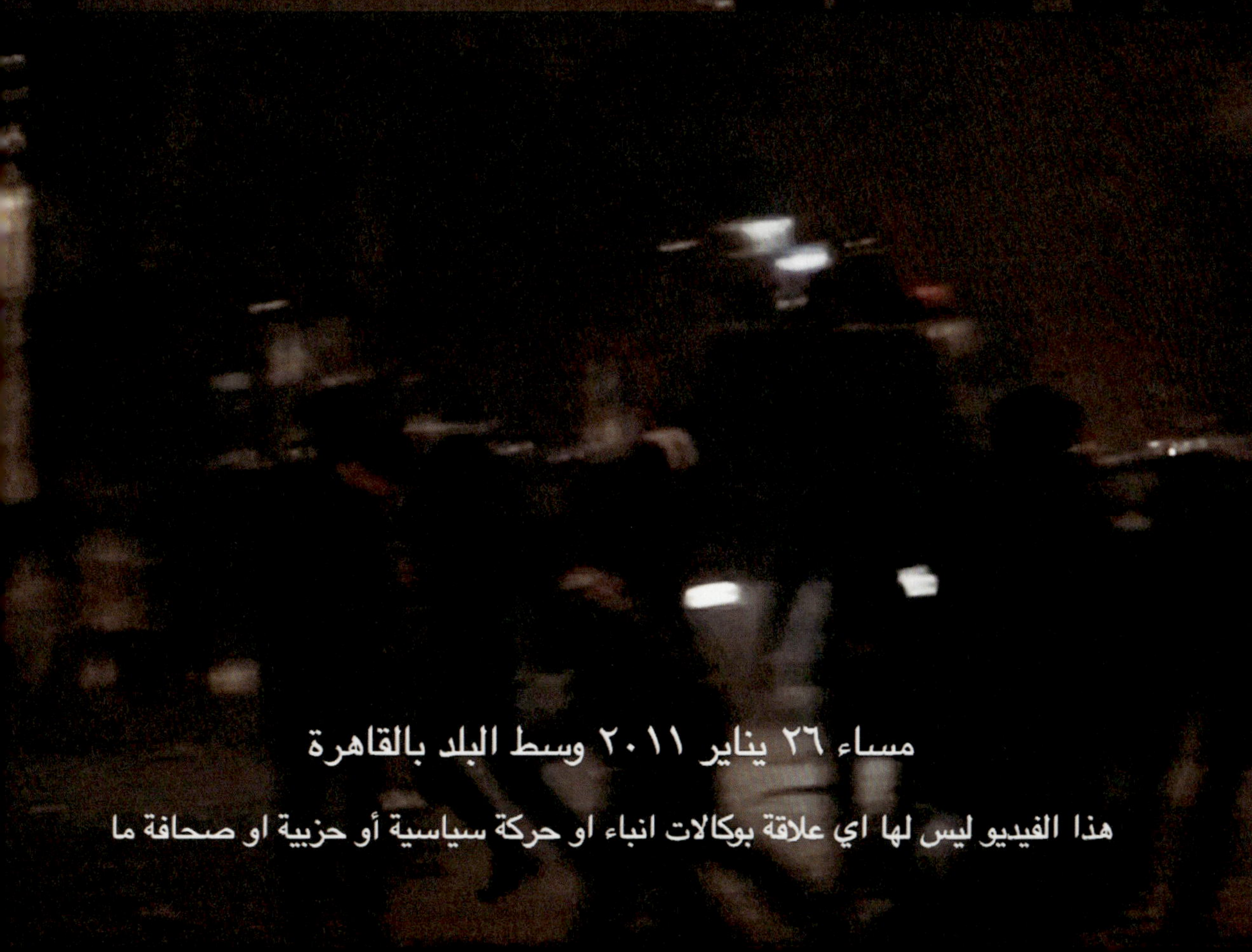
مساء ٢٦ يناير ٢٠١١ وسط البلد بالقاهرة
هذا الفيديو ليس لها اي علاقة بوكالات انباء او حركة سياسية أو حزبية او صحافة ما

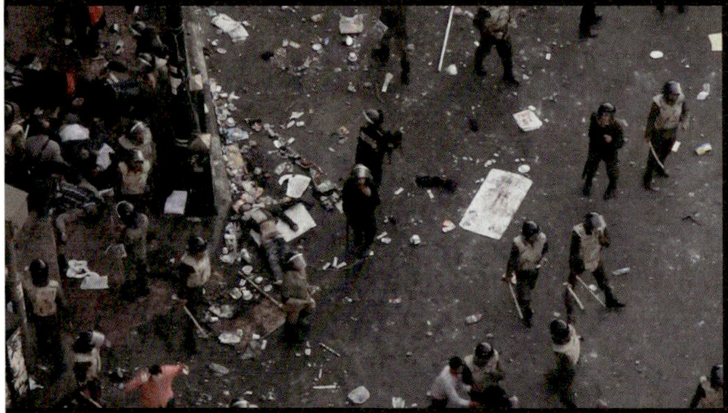

The Martyrs / Die Märtyrer: Toussi / آخرتنا الزبالة؟ قصة توسي
Uploaded on Jan. 21, 2012

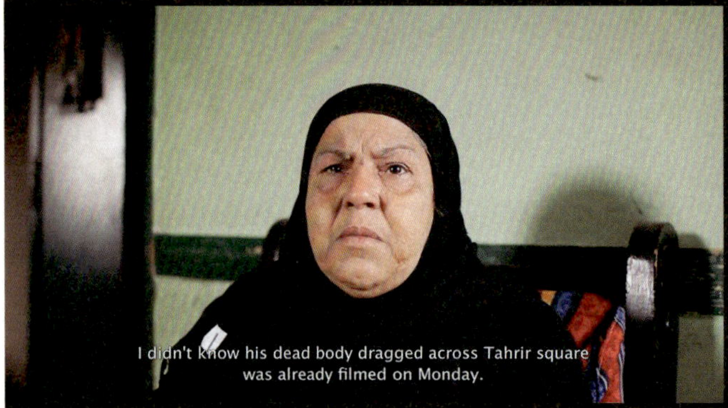

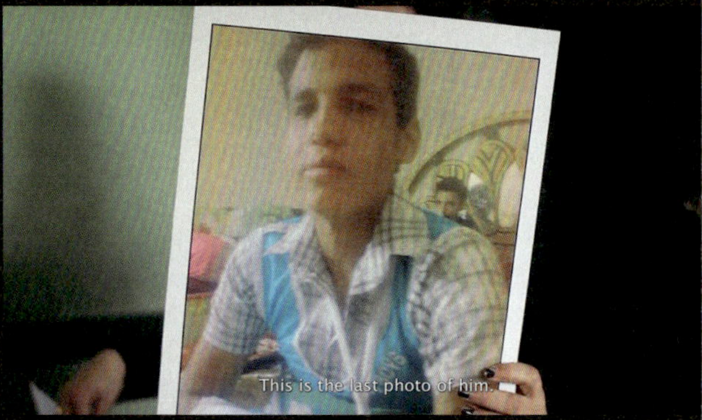

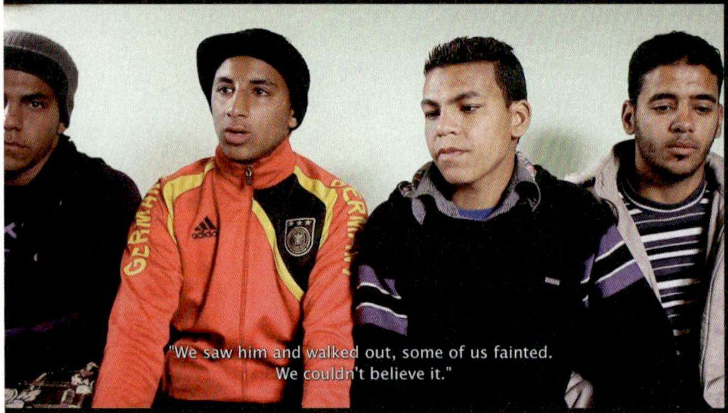

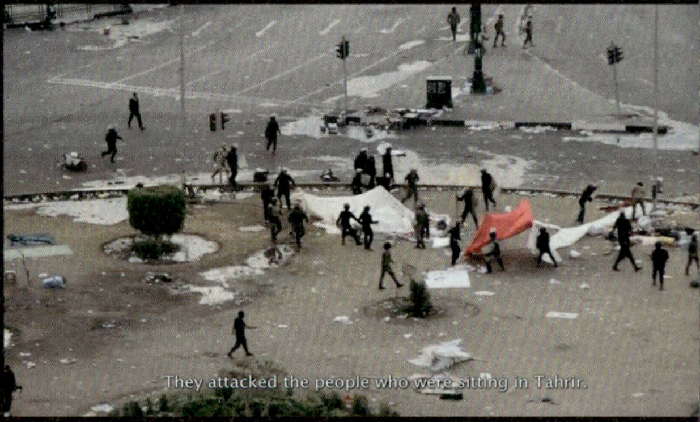

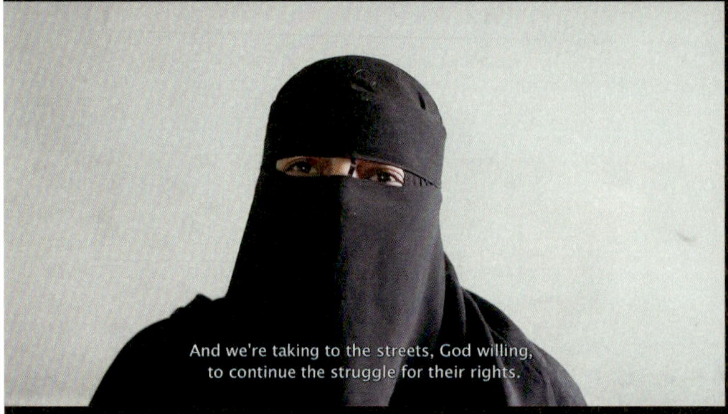

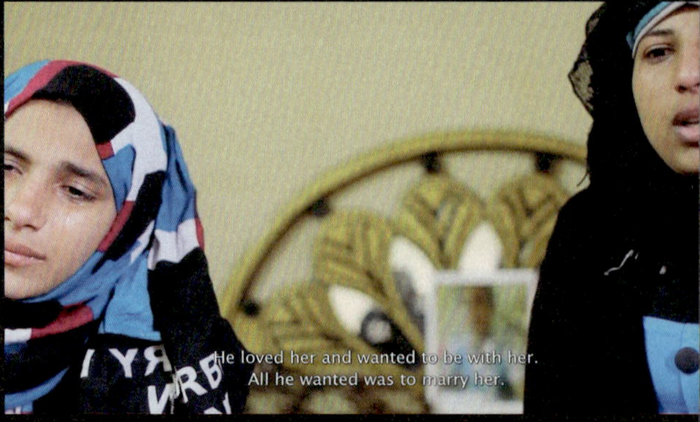

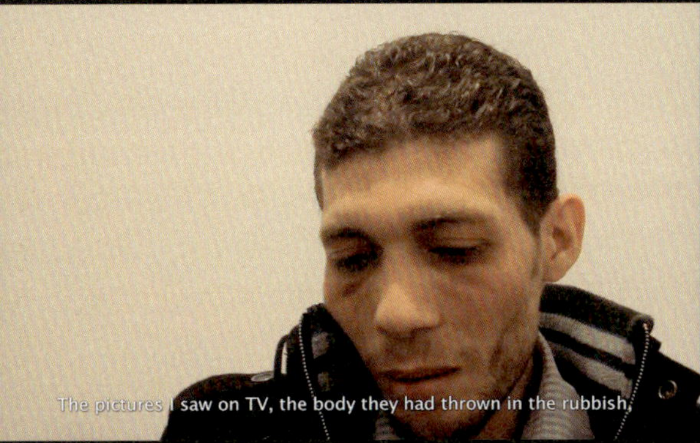

The Politics of Bread / Die Politik des Brotes / سياستي سياسة العيش
Uploaded on Dec. 1, 2011

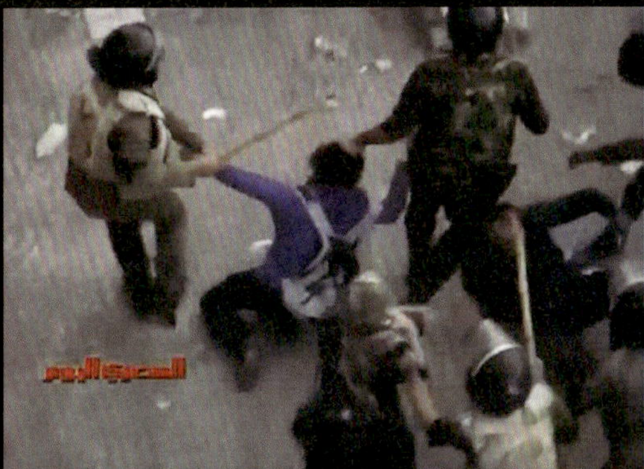

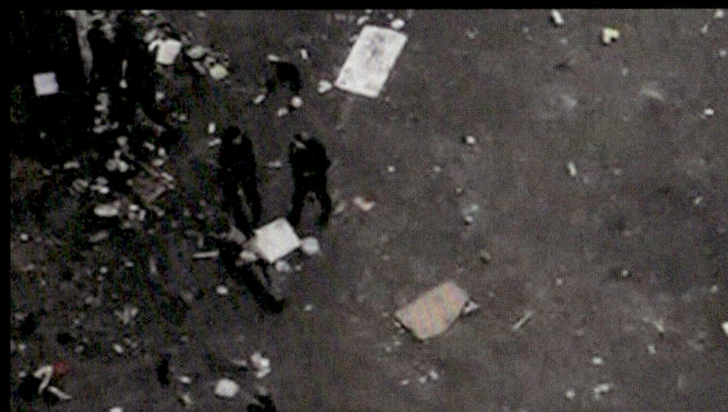

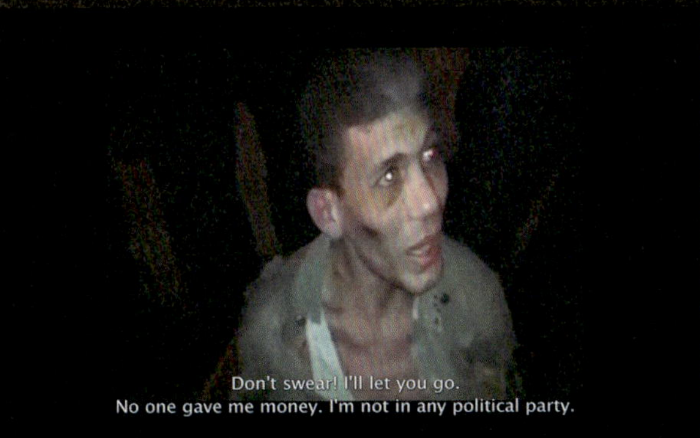

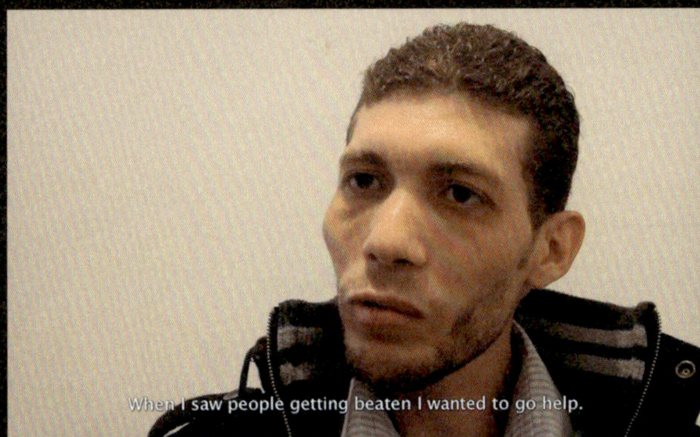

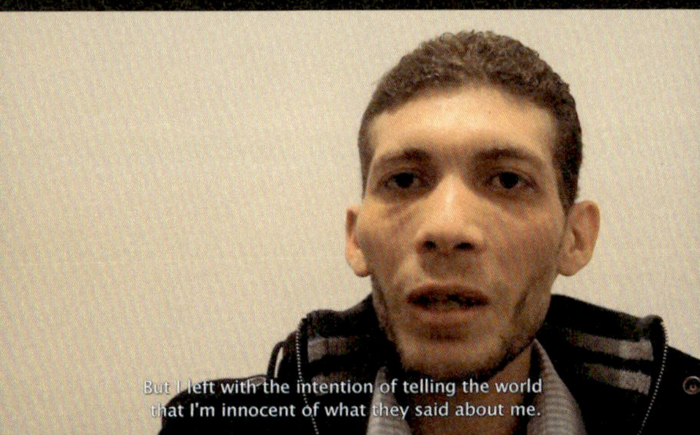

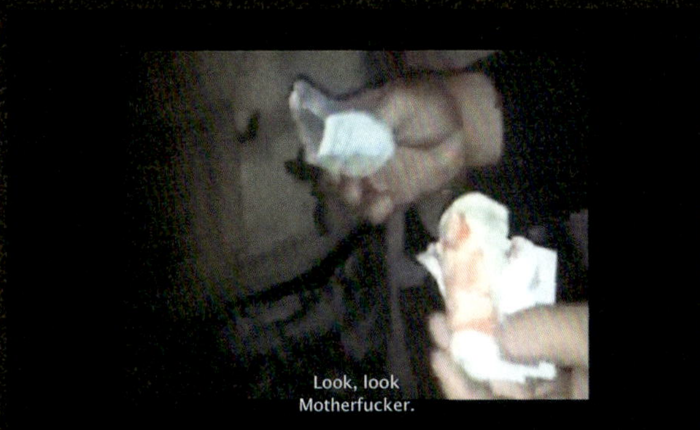

29

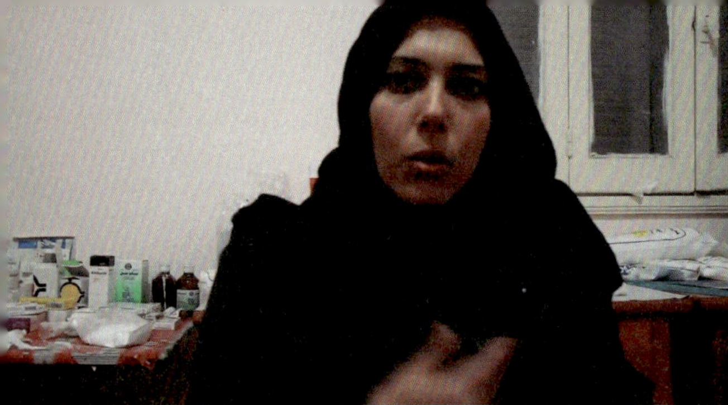

Al-Mansoura: Everybody Shares a Piece of His Name / Jeder passt zu seinem Namen / المنصورة: لكل شخص من اسمه نصيب
Uploaded on Mar. 8, 2013

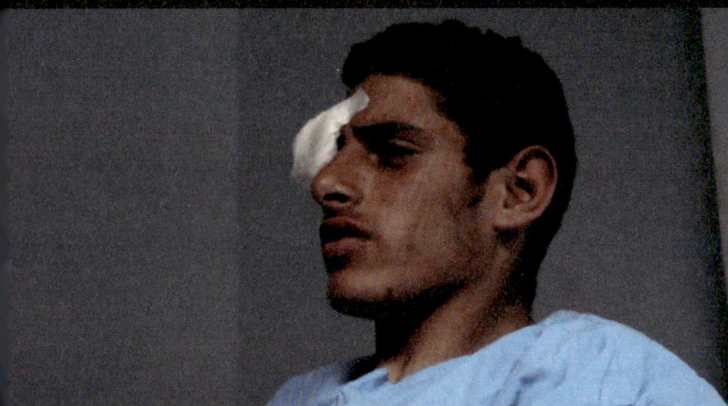

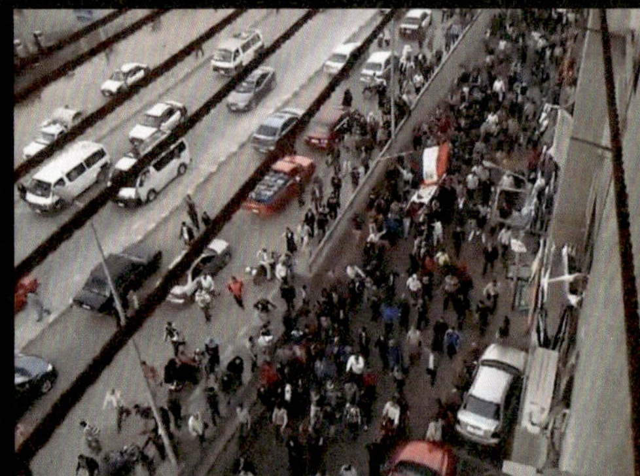

30

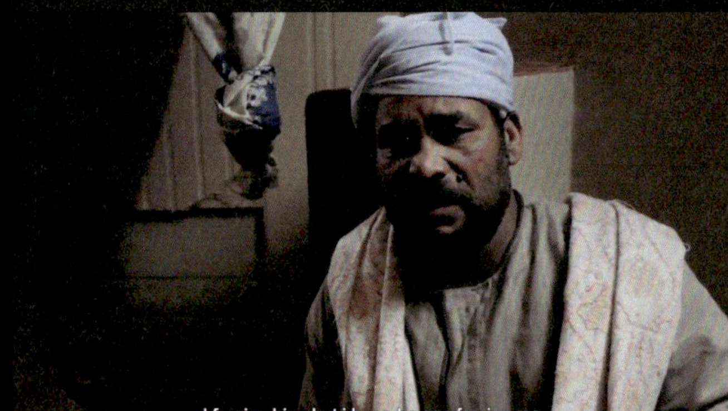

The Martyrs / Die Märtyrer: Omar Salah / الشهيد عمر صلاح: قهر أفضى إلى الموت
Uploaded on Feb. 23, 2013

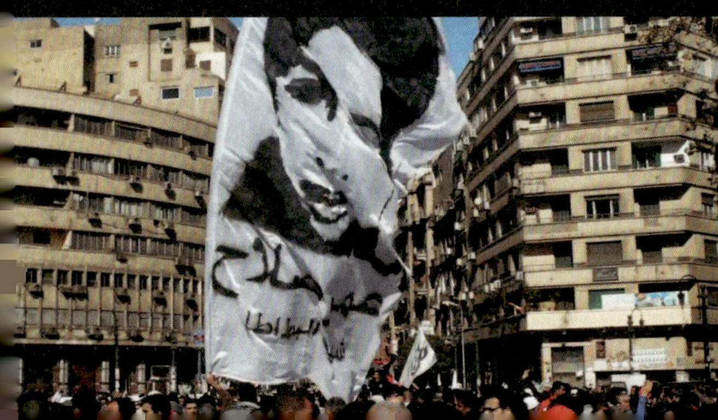

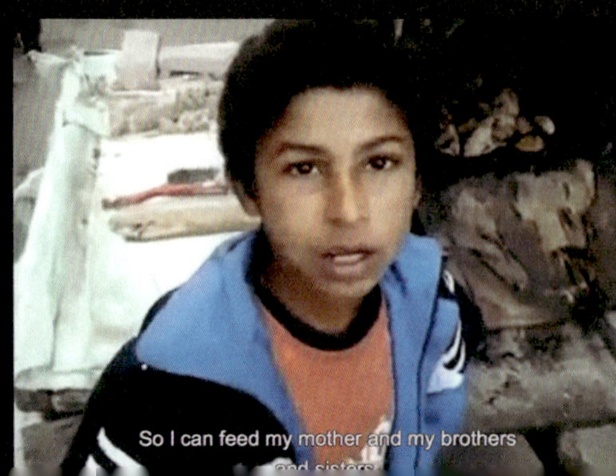

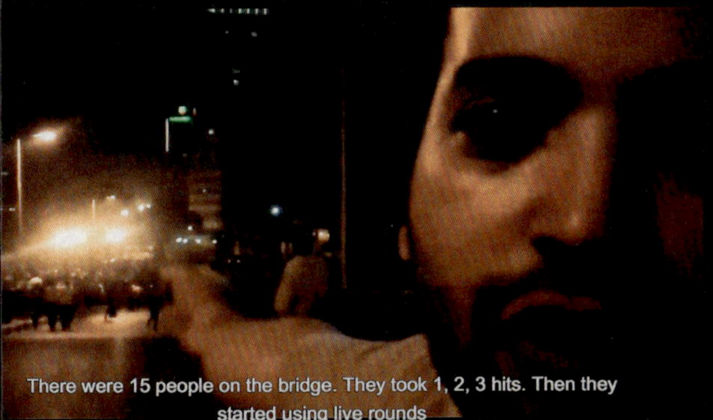

Blood at Night, Grief by Day, Maspero / Blutvergießen in der Nacht, Trauer am Tag, Maspero, Oct. 9 / الدماء و الأسى - ماسبيرو
Uploaded on Oct. 11, 2011

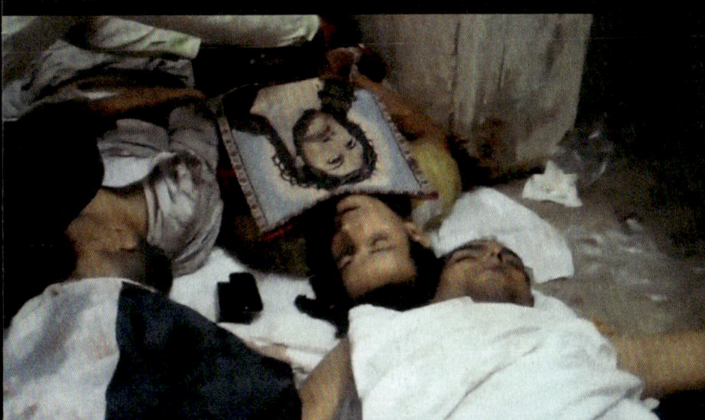

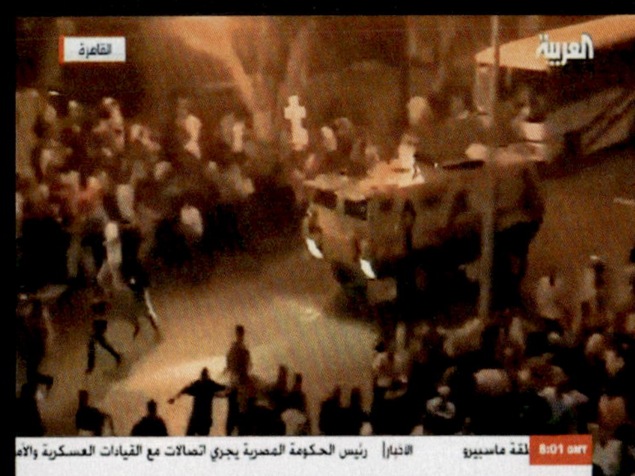

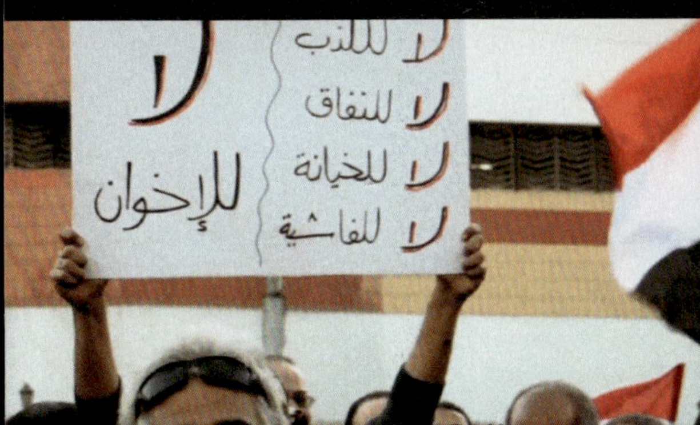

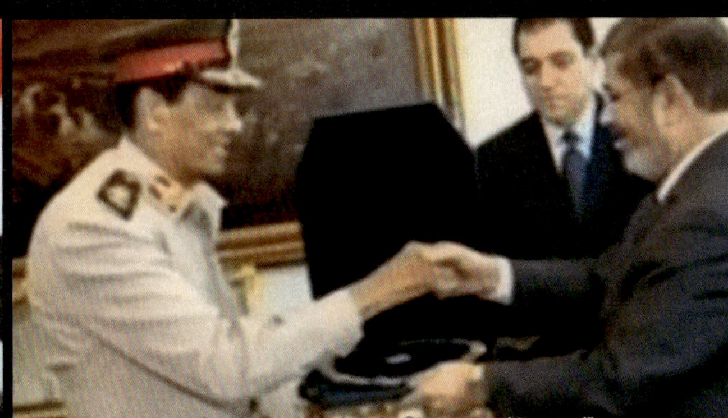

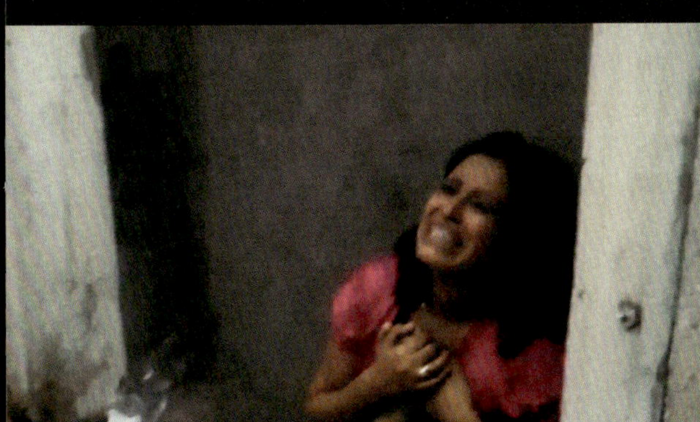

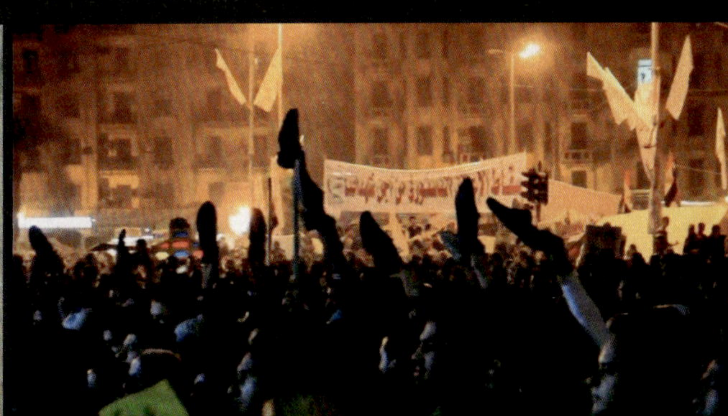

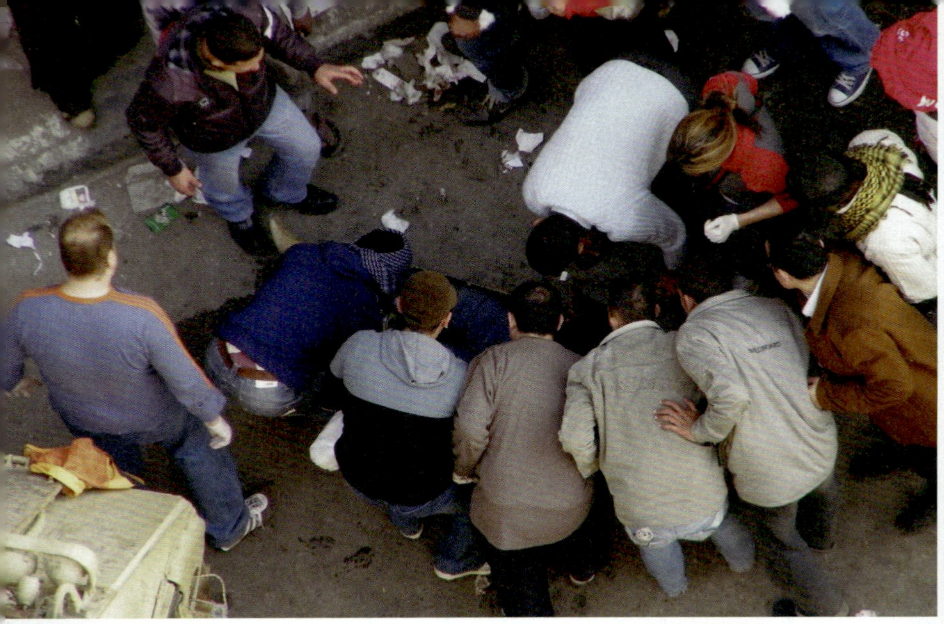

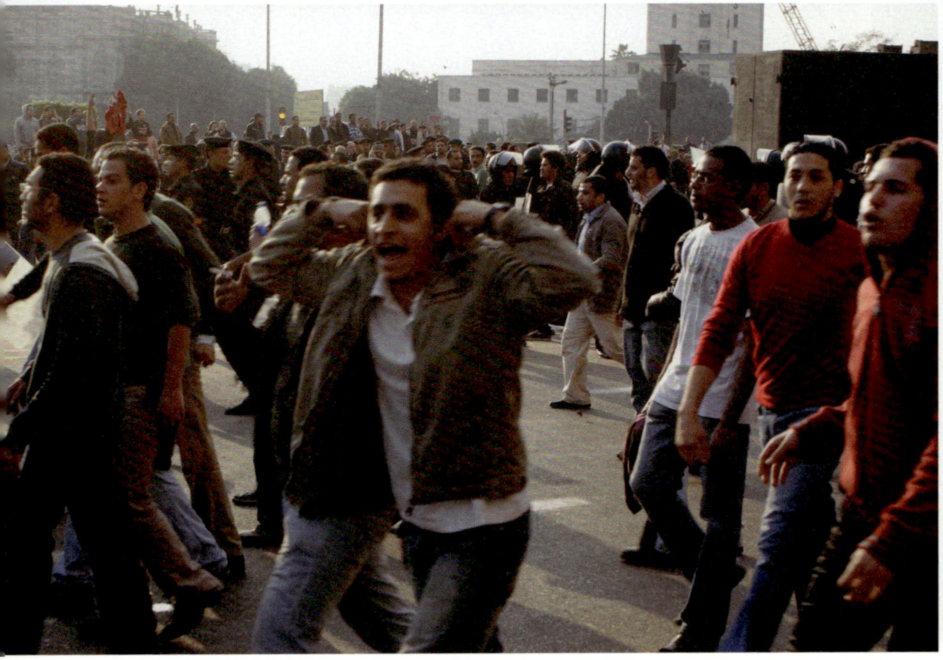

25 المستخدم 2.204 فبراير 2011 / User204, Feb. 2, 2011
26 المستخدم 24.203 يناير 2011 / User203, Jan. 24, 2011

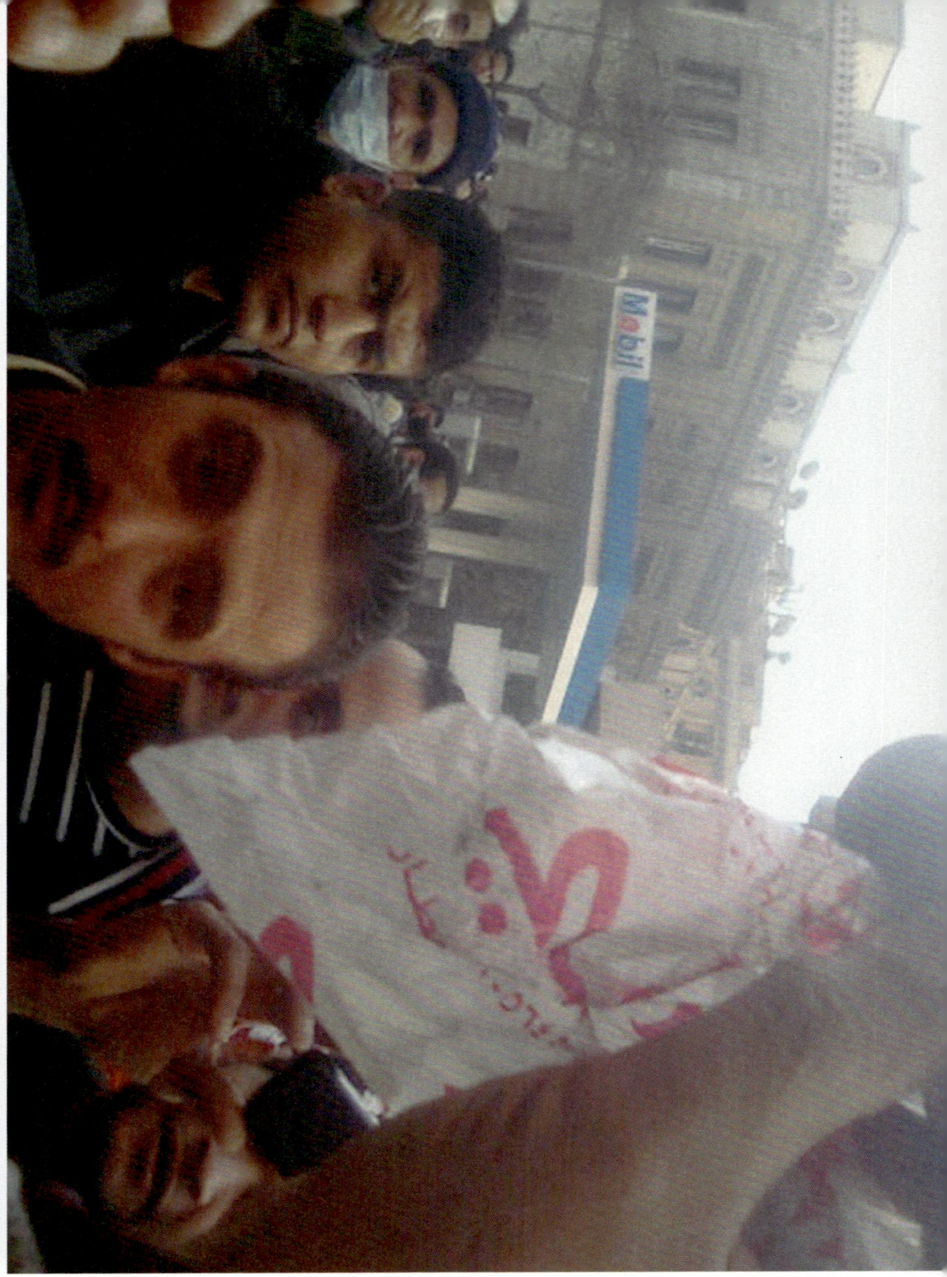

27 المستخدم 28.19 يناير 2011 / User19, Jan 28, 2011

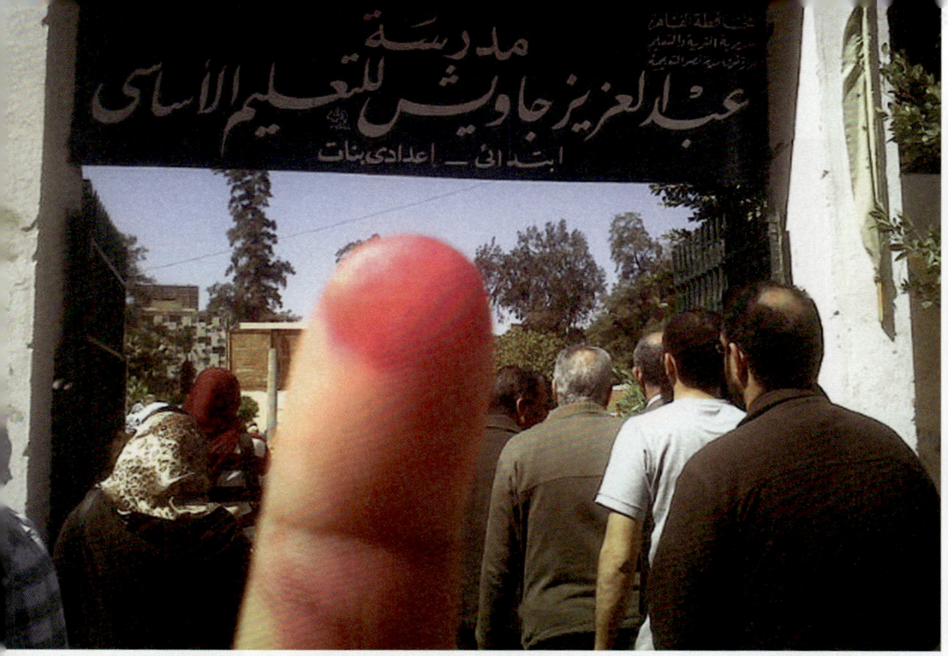

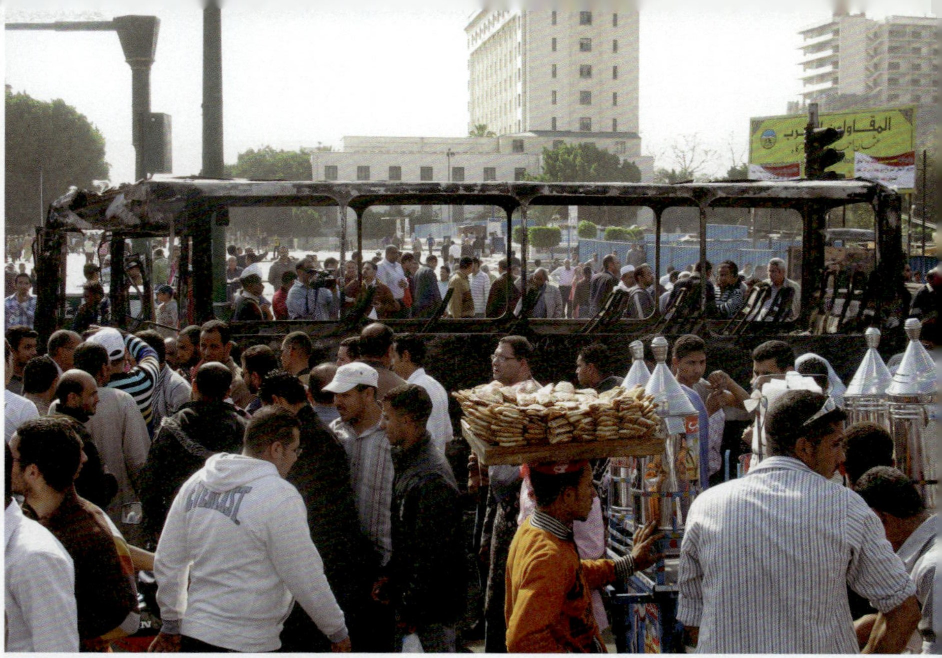

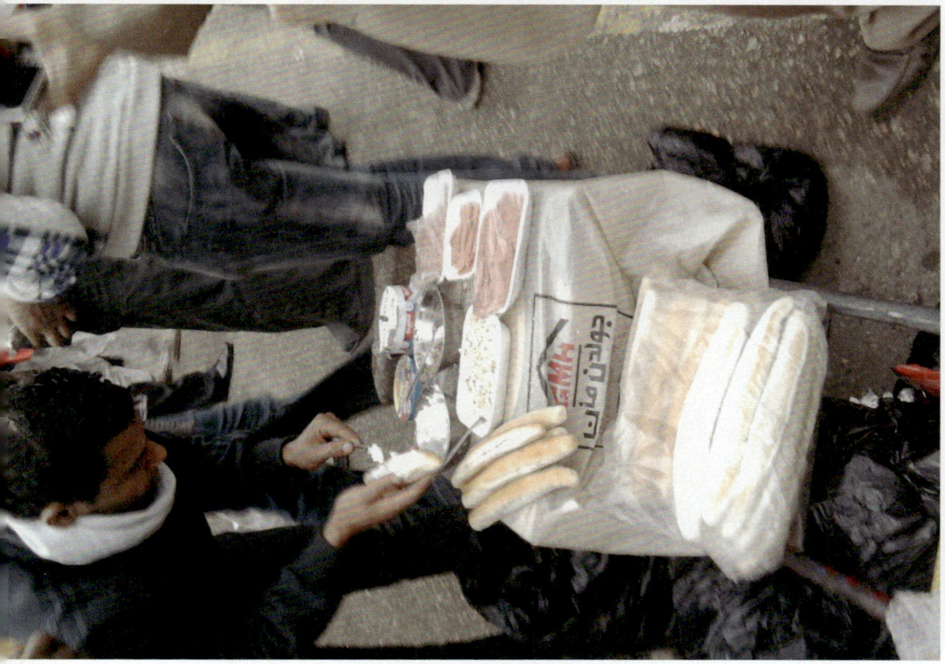

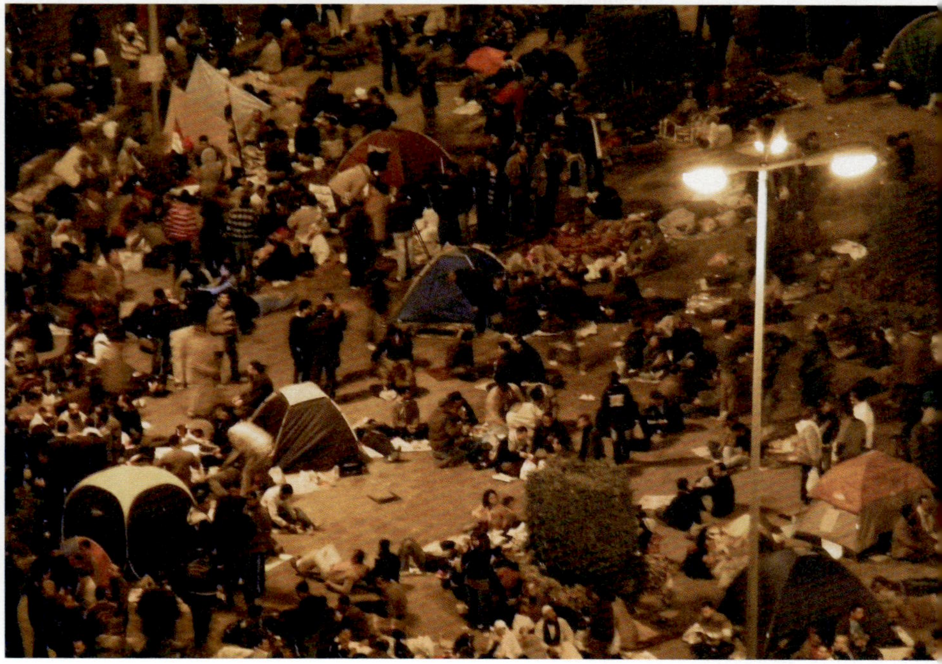

21 المستخدم 19.509 مارس 2011 / User509, Mar. 19, 2011
22 المستخدم 204 / User204

23 المستخدم 9.533 أبريل 2011 / User533, Apr. 9, 2011
24 المستخدم 31.204 يناير 2011 / User204, Jan. 31, 2011

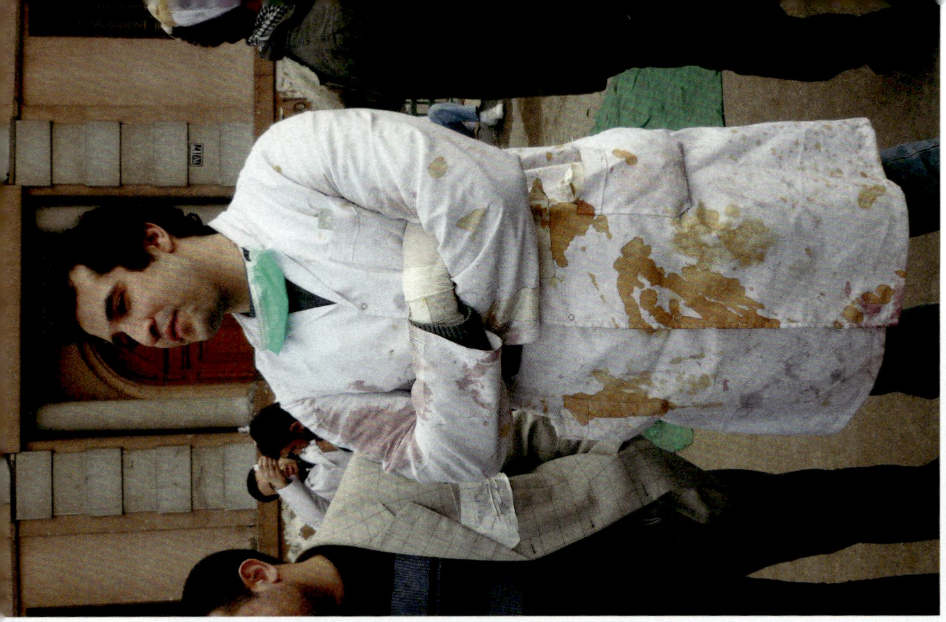

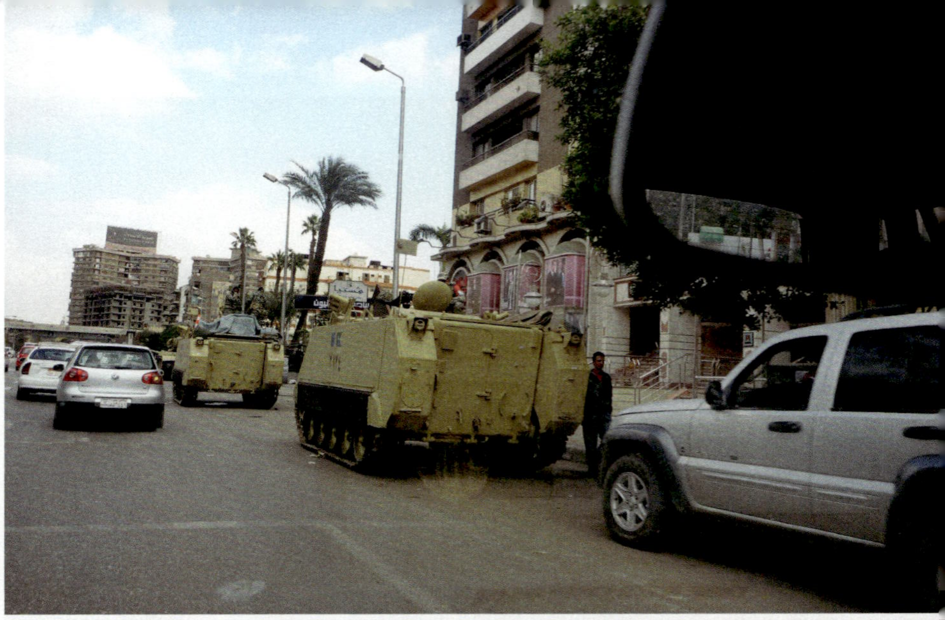

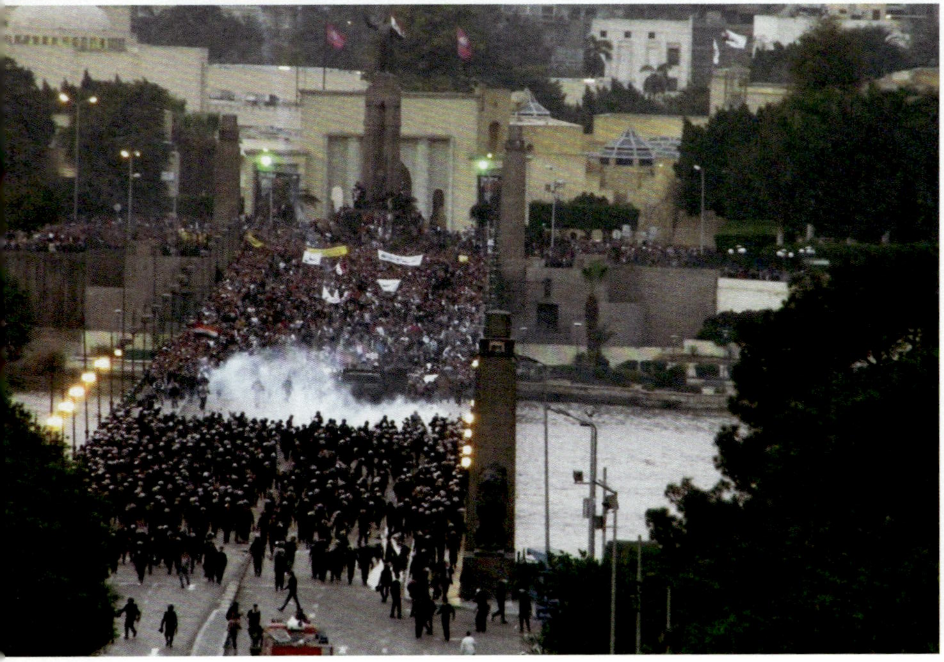

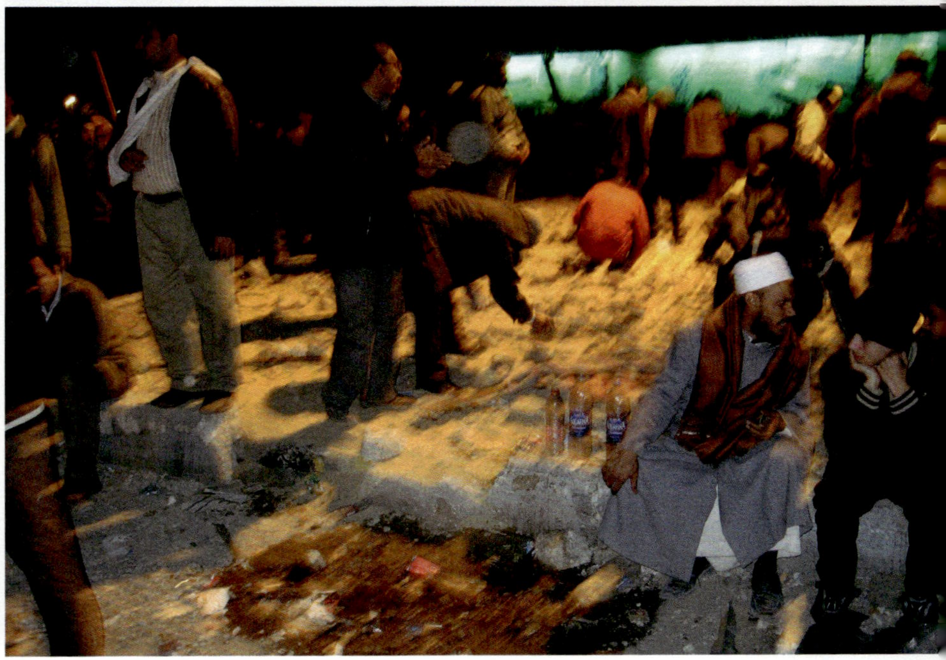

17 User218, Feb. 3, 2011 / 2011 المستخدم 218.3 فبراير
18 User204, Jan. 28, 2011 / 2011 المستخدم 204.28 يناير

19 User217, Feb. 2, 2011 / 2011 المستخدم 217.2 فبراير
20 User20, Feb. 2, 2011 / 2011 المستخدم 20.2 فبراير

ThawraMedia – Internet Archive by Citizen Journalists / Internetarchiv von Bürgerjournalisten / ثـورة ميديـا- مبادرة لبناء أرشيف إلكتروني أسسه صحفيون من مجال الصحافة الشعبية

15 User533, Jan. 25, 2011 / 2011 المستخدم 533، 25 يناير

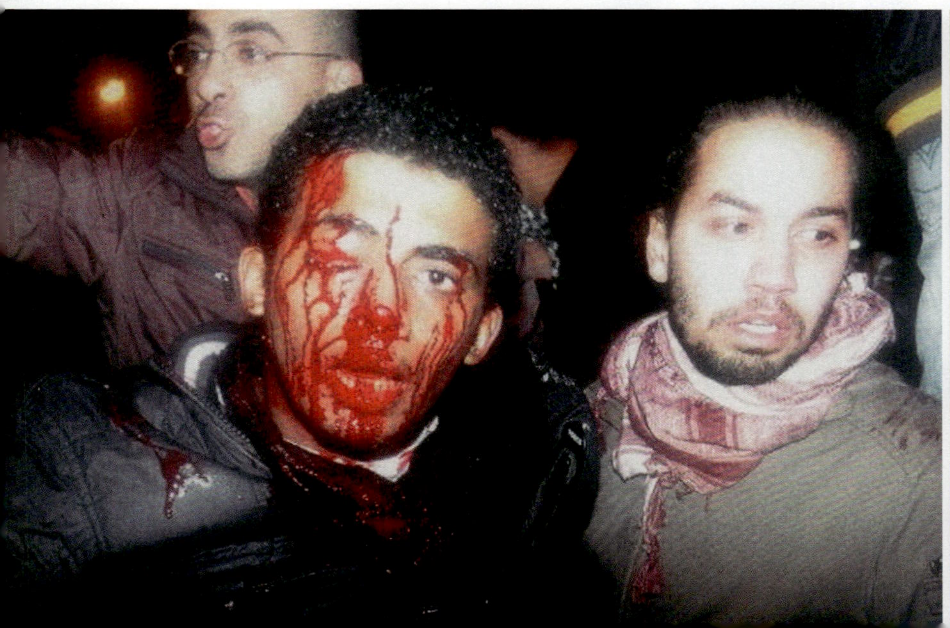

16 User204 / 204 المستخدم

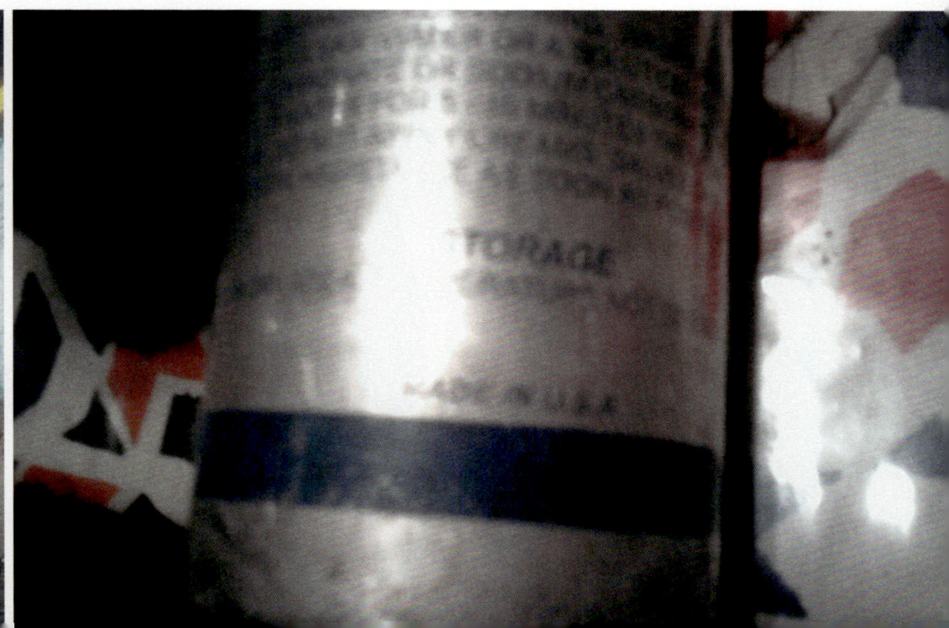

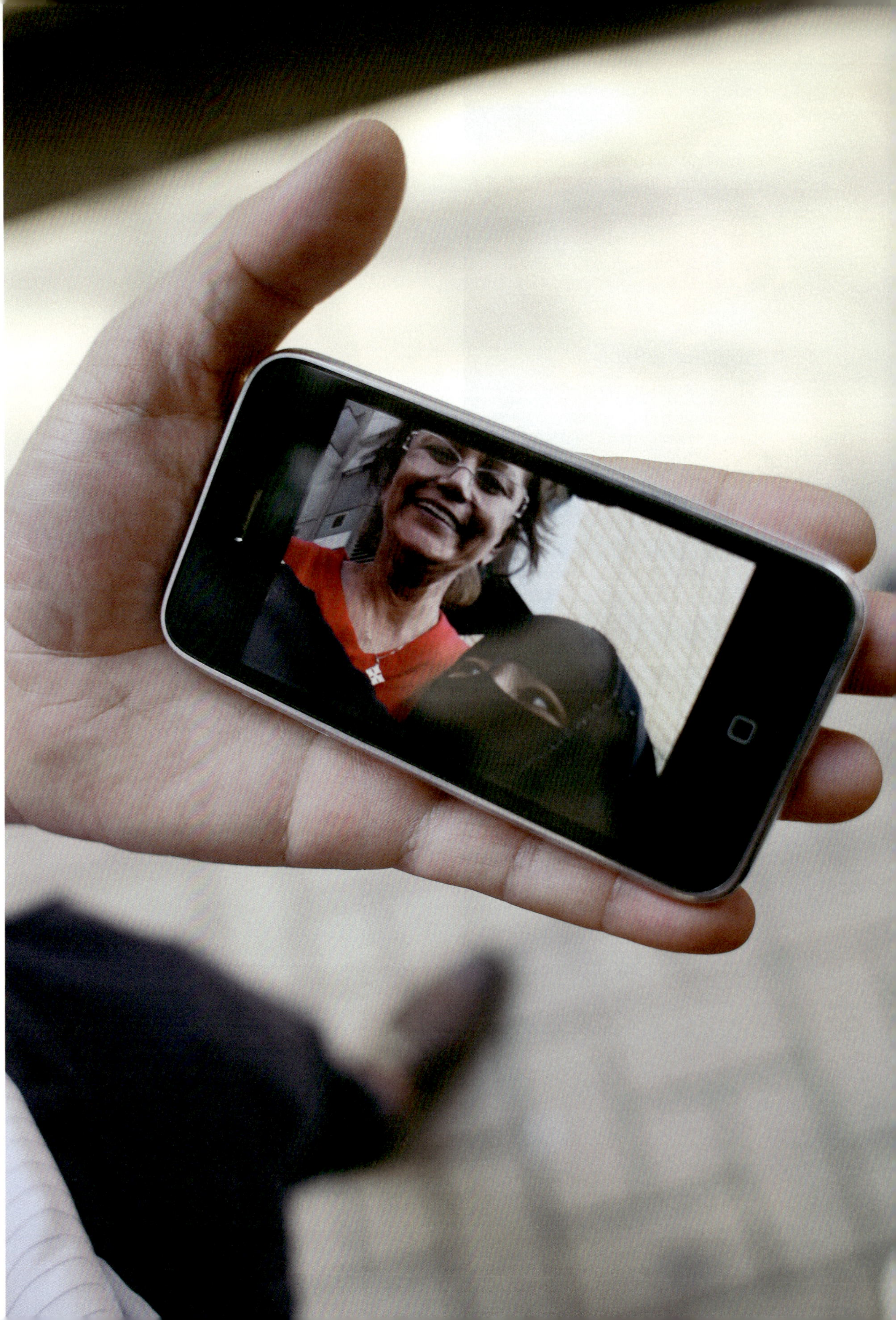

Myriam Abdelaziz, from the series/aus der Serie *Cell Phone Stories*, 2012
مريم عبدالعزيز، من سلسلة حكايات المحمول، 2012

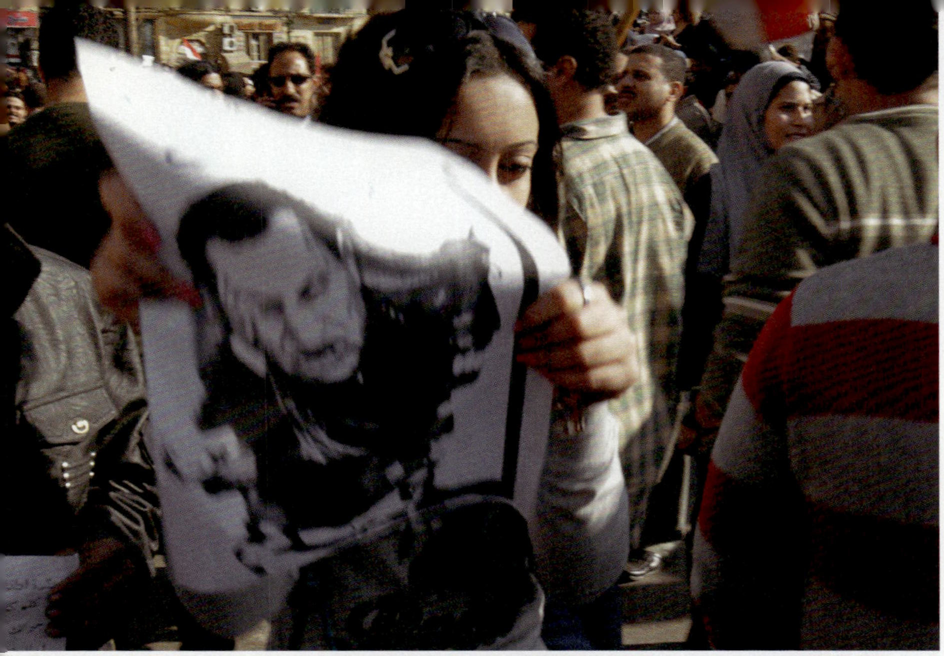

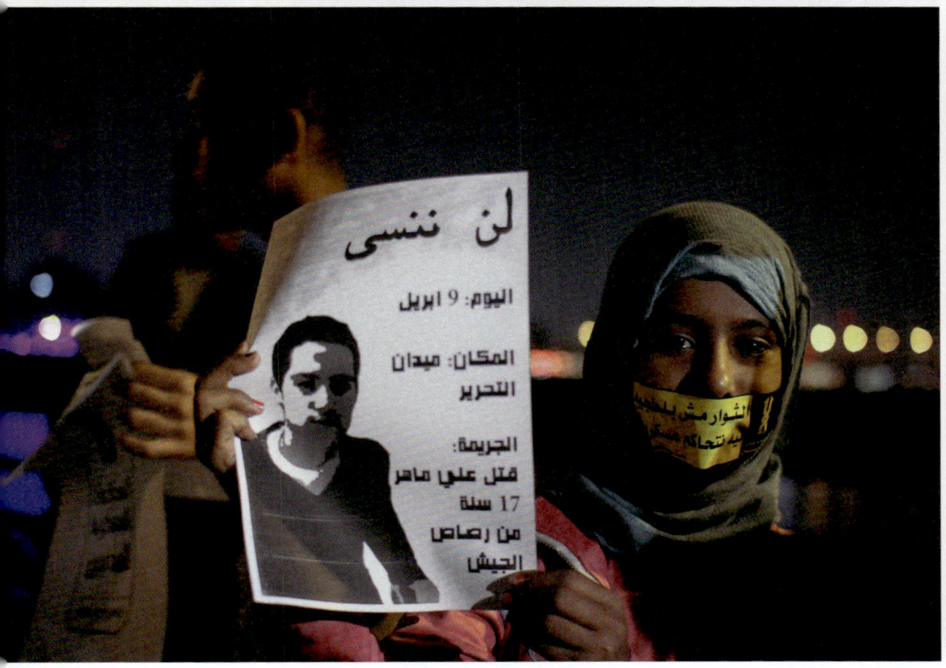

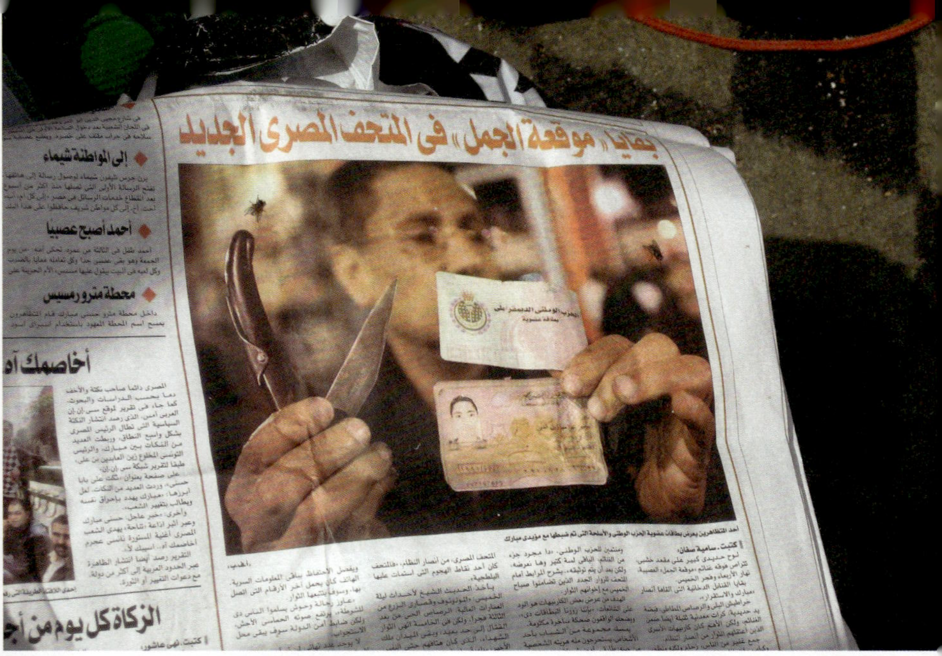

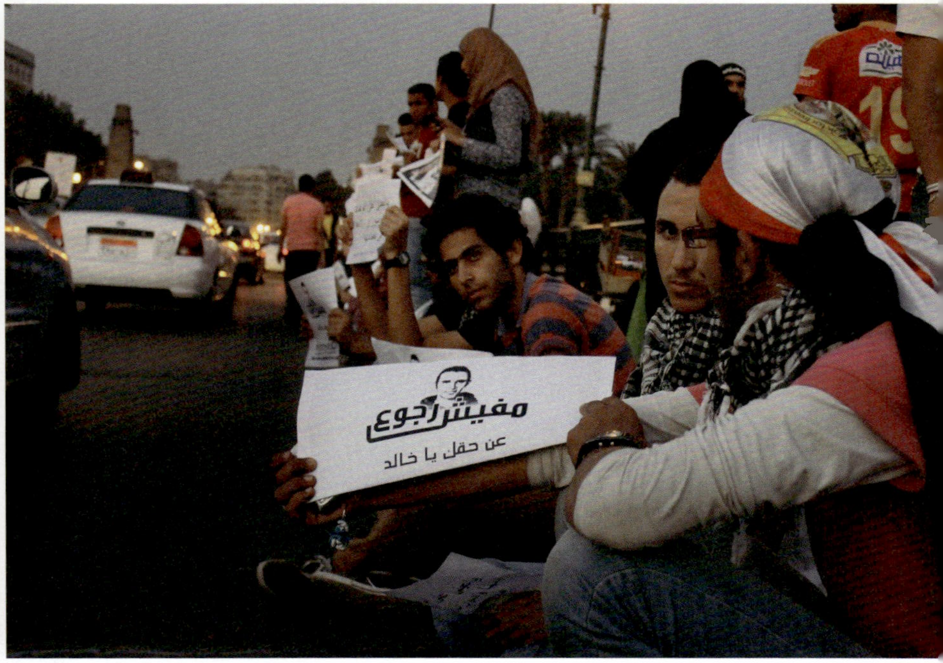

10 المستخدم 208 (ثورة ميديا)، 31 يناير 2011 / User208 (ThawraMedia), Jan. 31, 2011

11 علي هزاع، كوبري قصر النيل، القاهرة، 13 نوفمبر 2011 / Aly Hazza'a, *Kasr el Nil Bridge, Cairo, Nov. 13, 2011*

12 المستخدم 217 (ثورة ميديا)، 3 فبراير 2011 / User217 (ThawraMedia), Feb. 3, 2011

13 هبة خولي، كوبري قصر النيل، القاهرة، 7 يونيو 2012 / Heba el Kholy, *Kasr el Nil Bridge, Cairo, June 7, 2012*

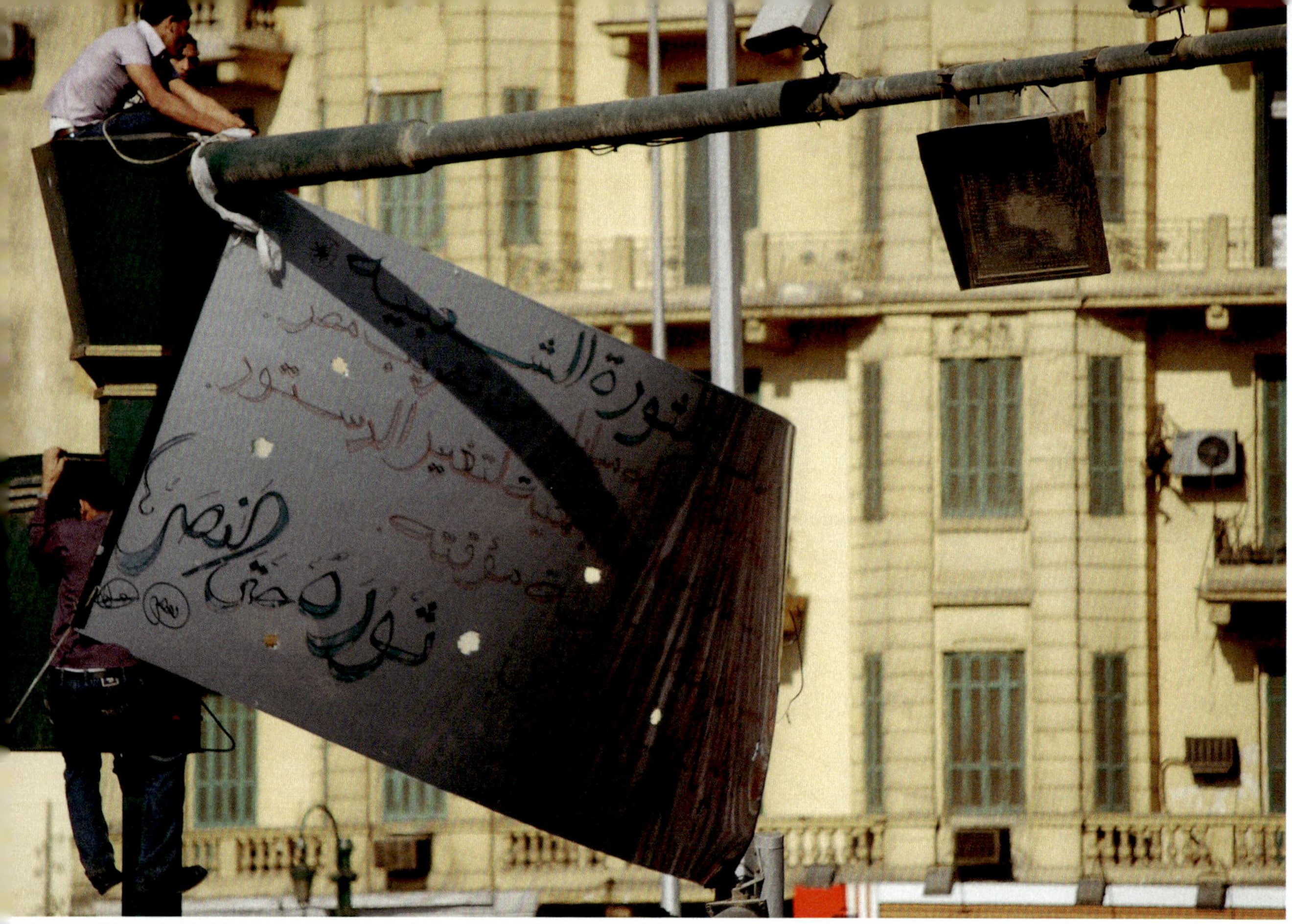

7 User543 (ThawraMedia), Jan. 29, 2011 / 2011 المستخدم 543 (ثورة ميديا)، 29 يناير

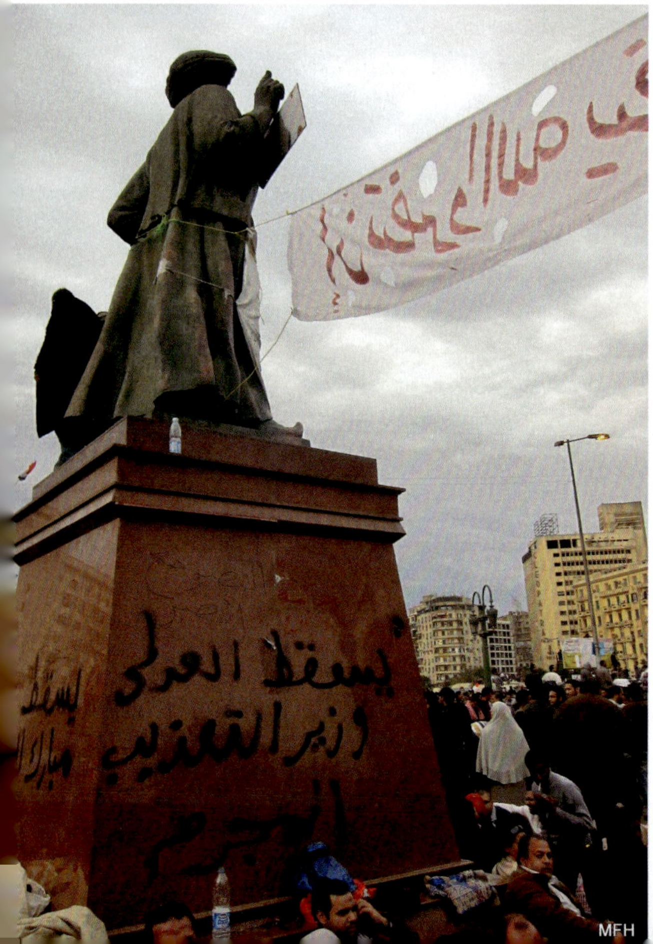

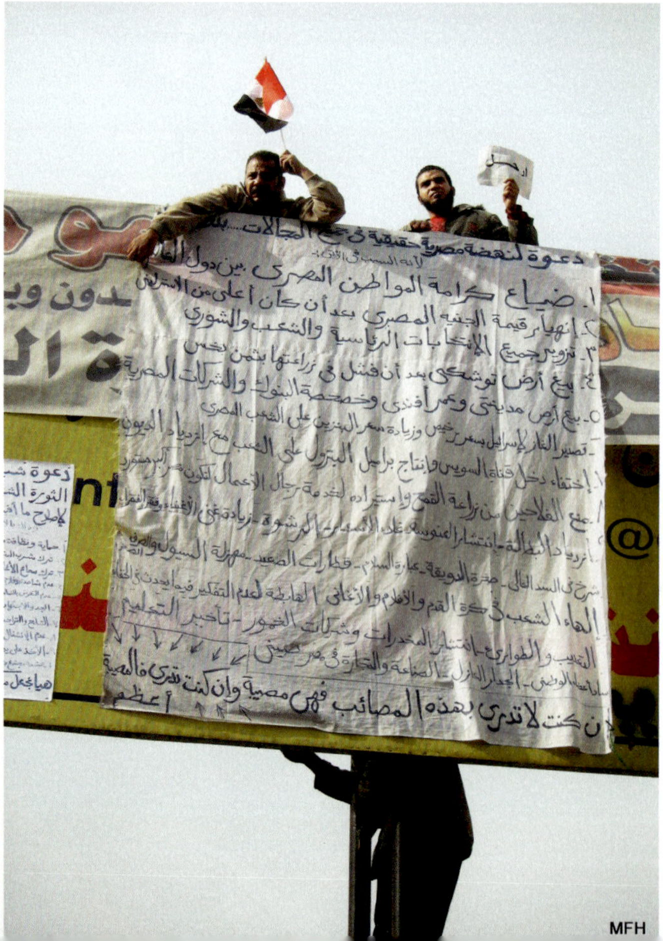

8 User205 (ThawraMedia), May 4, 2011 / 2011 المستخدم 205 (ثورة ميديا)، 4 مايو

9 User205 (ThawraMedia), Feb. 4, 2011 / 2011 المستخدم 205 (ثورة ميديا)، 4 فبراير

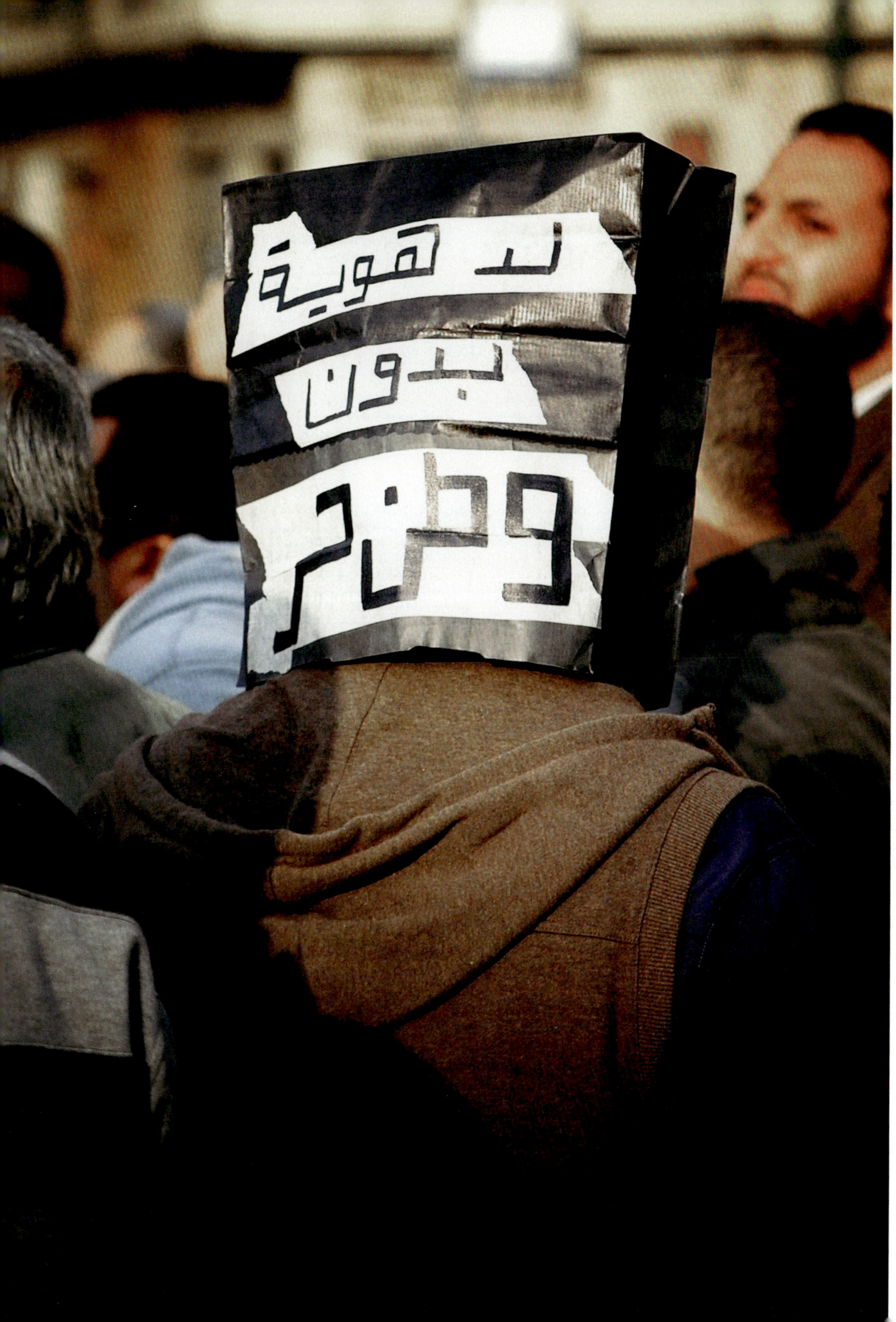

Messages from the People / Botschaften von der Straße / رسائل من الشارع

User543 (ThawraMedia), Jan. 30, 2011 / المستخدم 543 (ثورة ميديا) 30 يناير 2011

"القاهرة. مدينة مفتوحة." صور جديدة من ثورة مستمرة، هو تجربة، مشروع في نهر لا يلبث أن يتحول؛ هو حوار في هذا المكان وعبر آلاف الكيلومترات. يأخذ المشروع شكل واضح في لحظة تحوله لمعرض، تتغير الأشكال على حسب الموقف والسياق السياسي. ونحن نتمنى أن نرى هذا المعرض في يوم من الأيام، في القاهرة.

المعرض

منسقا المعرض:
فلوريان إيبنر، كونستانزه فيكه
بالتعاون مع:
لارا بلدي، أسامة داوود، روان الشيمي، هبة فريد، توماس هارتويل، طارق حفني، أحمد كامل، ياسمينا متولي، أليكس نانس، فيليب رزق

28 سبتمبر إلى 23 ديسمبر 2012
متحف براونشفايج للتصوير
267 كوارتيره للفن المعاصر والفوتوغرافيا
شارع هامبورجر، 267
38114 براونشفايج
ألمانيا

الإنتاج التقني للمعرض: مانويل راينرتس
التنسيق الهندسي: بيرنهارد تاتّر، مهندسي دينكين باوين فونين
فريق البناء: جونتر كوسمان، شتيفان داو، دانيلا فريبل، سيمون كراوس، ماتياس لودت، دافيد جاوبّ-ماير، ياسمين ماينولد، ماكس نويمان، أولريكه وديتر ريكسه
المتدربون في براونشفايج: كيرا هولنكريمر، سابينة نيمشيك، شتيفان زالمولر

إدارة المشروع والعلاقات العامة: سفيا كيلنر
الإدارة: أندريا هيرمان

المجلس التنفيذي
رئيس مجلس الإدارة: ميشائيل شفارتس
نائب رئيس مجلس الإدارة: أوفه برودمان
نائب رئيس مجلس الإدارة:كارل-كريستيان أمّه
السكرتارية: هاوكه هاجينا
الإدارة المالية: أندريا يانسن

2 مارس إلى 5 مايو 2013
متحف فولكفانج
موزيومز بلاتس 1
45128 إيسّن
ألمانيا

المدير: توبيا بيزولا

المقتنيات الفوتوغرافية
المسؤول الإداري: فلوريان إيبنر
إدراة المقتنيات: بيترا شتاينهارت
الإدارة: كريستينا بوشمان، أنجريت كوبرس
التصميم التقني والإنتاج: ماونيل راينارتس، أوليفر زيبر
التنسيق الهندسي: بيرنهارد تاتّر، مهندسي دينكين باوين فونين
الترميم: كريستيانه شنايدر
المتدربات: دنيا ناصري، باربره فيرّ

إدراة المتحف
المدير: هولجر بيترس
الإدارة المالية: فابيان كليمت، ميشائيل كلينرت
تنظيم البناء: أليكسندرا كلاين، دانييل فيمّر
فريق البناء: راينر بالداو، دانييلا فريبل، سيمون كراوس، دافيد جاوبّ-ماير، أناتولي مارتشين، ياسمين ماينولد، ماكس نويمان، ميشائيل بيترز، كلاوس شلوتر، فرانك شتيرنبيرج، جيرد أوفر، تيلّ فيلنر، شتيفان تسمودتسينسكي

التعليم والتواصل: هايكه كروبف
الصحافة والتسويق: دورته رامين
مستشارة الصحافة: أنّـا صوفي ليتمان
مساعدة العلاقات العامة: إينيكه كلوستركيمبر

19 أكتوبر إلى 25 نوفمبر 2012
الدروة الخامسة لشهر التصوير الضوئي في برلين، في متحف كينيدي سابقاً
باريزر بلاتس 4A
10117 برلين
ألمانيا

منسقة شهر التصوير الضوئي: كاتيا رايش
مدير المشروع: أوليفر باتس
مساعدة المشروع: مارته كريهر
فريق دعم المشروع: شارلوته فينكه، جابريليه تسولنر، بيرته هوفمان، آناكاترين مولر
العمل الإعلامي: آخيم كلاب
التصميم التقني والإنتاج: ماونيل راينارتس
تركيب: RT أوسشتيلونجنس تيشنيك برلين

16 أغسطس إلى 17 نوفمبر 2013
متحف هامبورج للفن والحرف
شتاينتور بلاتس
20099 هامبورج

المديرة: سابينه شولتسه
مدير الإدارة: أودو جوركه

مديرة قسم الفوتوغرافي والميديا الجديدة: إستر رولفس
مصمم المعرض: رينيه هيلابراند، هامبورج
إدارة مشاريع المعارض: فرانك هيلدابراند
المتدربات: أنيكا زيلمان، أريانه باتو-تو فان، فيكتوريا هازلير، ناتالي كلينك

رئيس الخدمات التقنية: توماس فراي
الإنتاج التقني: مانويل راينارتس
فريق البناء: ألبيرتو بولو-بالاراس، إيجون بوش، داميان كوفالتسيك، جريجوري ميدفيديف، مايك ماير

إدارة المقتنيات: هارالد دوباو
سجل المقتنيات: أنيكا بول-أوزاوا

التسويق: زيلكه أولدنبورج، أولريكه بلاوت
العلاقات العامة: ميشائيلا هيله
تنفيذ الفن والتصميم: زيلكه أولدنبورج، مانويلا فان روسيم، فريدريكه فانكهينل

كاتالوج

الناشرون: فلوريان إيبنر، كونستانزه فيكّه
محررو الصور: فلوريان إيبنر، أحمد كامل
المحررون: فلوريان إيبنر، كونستانزه فيكّه
تحرير الطباعة للنصوص الألمانية: تانيا ميلفسكي
تحرير الطباعة للنصوص الإنجليزية: سيمون كوبر
تحرير الطباعة للنصوص العربية: دونا عبود، ميريت بكير

فكرة التصميم وتصميم: أحمد كامل، أندريه لول، نيكولا رايتر
صف ومعالجة الحرف العربي: دونا عبود
معالجة الصور: مانويل راينارتس، سيلفيا دوبلت
تجميع وطباعة: مطبعة تسو ألتينبيرج ش.ذ.م.م.

الترجمة

من الألمانية إلى العربية: ابتهال شديد
من الألمانية إلى الإنجليزية: سيمون كوبر
من الإنجليزية إلى الألمانية: دانييلا فريبل، هايكه جايسلر، باربره فير

الطبعة الأولى 2013

ISBN 978-3-940064-70-7

سبيكتور بوكس
10 هاركورت شتراسه
04107 لايبزغ
ألمانيا
www.spectorbooks.com

التوزيع في ألمانيا، النمسا:
GVA جيمانزامه فيرلاجس أوسليفارونج جوتينجن ش.ذ.م.م. & Co. KG
www.gva-verlage.de

التوزيع في سويسرا:
AVA فيرلاجس أوسليفارونج شركة مساهمة
www.ava.ch

التوزيع في المملكة المتحدة، فرنسا، اليابان
أناجرام بوكس ذ.م.م.
www.anagrambooks.com

التوزيع في الولايات المتحدة
RAM للنشر والتوزيع ذ.م.م.
www.rampub.com

شكر وعرفان

نود أن نتوجه بالشكر لكل من شارك في هذا المشروع. فلقد تمكنا بفضل عملهم واقتراحاتهم ونقدهم أن نعطي هذا المشروع-المعرض الشكل الذي خرج به.

نريد أن نخص بالشكر:
لارا بلدي، أسامة داود، روان الشيمي، هبة فريد، توماس هارتويل، طارق حفني، أحمد كامل، ياسمينا متولي، أليكس نانس، فيليب رزق

كما نتوجه بالشكر للكتاب والمنسقين المشاركين والمنتجين الثقافيين في القاهرة:
خالد عبد الله، إيدجر بلومه
جونتر هازينكامب (معهد جوته بالقاهرة)
غادة الشربيني (معهد جوته بالقاهرة)
دينا كفافي (جاليري التاون هاوس، القاهرة)
ميا يانكوفيتش (مركزالصورة المعاصرة CIC)
سيلفيا موليتشي (CIC)
يارا صلاح (معهد جوته بالقاهرة)
تامر السعيد، أميرة الأهل
أليكسندرا شتوك (جاليري تاون هاوس، القاهرة)
ويليام ويلز (جاليري التاون هاوس، القاهرة)

كما نود التوجه بالشكر للفنانين لتعاونهم وثقتهم

مريم عبد العزيز، أحمد عبد اللطيف، بيتر فون أجتميل، روجر أنيس، كيم بدوي، مصطفى بهجت، كايا بهكلام، طه بلال، إيفا بيرترام، سارة كار، دينيس دايو، يوهانا دومكه ومروان عمارة، هبة خليفة، هبة الخولي، هالة القوصي، حسام الحملاوي، محمد الميموني، شادي النشوقاتي، مصعب الشامي، محمد الشتاوي، فادي عزت، محمد عز، نرمين حمام، علي هزاع، إيمان هلال، جيجي إبراهيم، مجدي إبراهيم، صبري خالد، نادين خان ومريم مكيوي، مها مأمون، أليكس ماجولي، كريس ميكالسكي وسيباستيان شتومف، جورج محسن، صامويل محسن، أسامة عبد المنعم، أميرة مرتضى، جيهان نصر، محمد نوهان، ناصر نوري، ماجي أسامة، سوزانه بومرين، إيفور بريكيت، جوناثان رشاد، إبراهيم سعد، رندا شعث، رافي شاكر، لبنى طارق، ليليان وجدي، سالي ذهني، ميريت بكير.

مشتركات و مشتركو ورشة العمل

هشام أمين، سابرينا آشه، بريجيتا باور، جان-مارك سيرينو، كاي بيرينت، هاوكه بورجارت، بولين شابيه، ليزا دومين، دورته آيسفيلد، ماريو فام، آرنولد فؤاد، كولين ج.، موزجان جيل، صوفيا هامان، سابيحا كيف، مانويل كلوتس، مارسيلينا كفياتكوفسكي، بتينا لوكمان، إيناس القمصان، دايفيد ماهر، نادية منير ت.، أمنية نجيب، دورين شفارتس، لورين سكوت، روبرت شتورتسل، سارة فيال

بالتعاون مع

MUSEUM FÜR PHOTOGRAPHIE BRAUNSCHWEIG
Museum Folkwang
MK&G MUSEUM FÜR KUNST UND GEWERBE HAMBURG
Townhouse

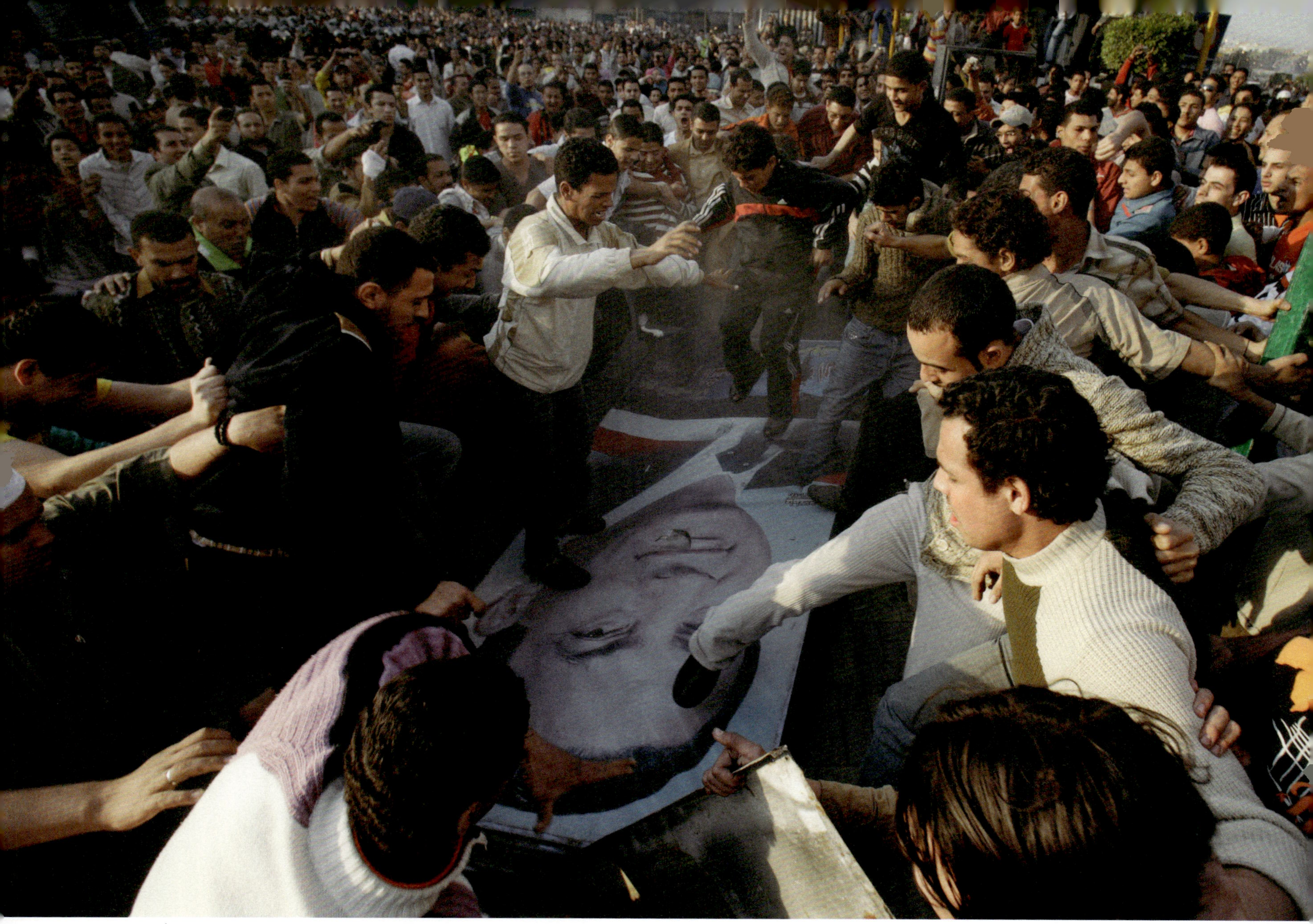

Nasser Nouri, Protesters destroying a photo banner of President Hosni Mubarak in El-Mahalla El-Kubra / Demonstranten zerstören ein Fotobanner des Präsidenten Husni Mubarak in El-Mahalla El-Kubra, Apr. 7, 2008 /

5 ناصر نوري، متظاهرون يمزقون صورة للرئيس حسني مبارك في المحلة الكبرى، 7 أبريل 2008

القاهرة. مدينة مفتوحة

صور جديدة
من ثورة مستمرة

صور وفيديوهات ورسومات ونصوص ووثائق مختارة مقدمة من

جيجي إبراهيم، مجدي إبراهيم، بيتر فون أجتميل، أميرة الأهل، حسام الحملاوي، هبة الخولي، مصعب الشامي، روان الشيمي، هالة القوصي، محمد الميموني، شادي النشوقاتي، ناصر النوري، روجر أنيس، كيم بدوي، إيفور بريكيت، أحمد بسيوني، ميريت بكير، طه بلال، لارا بلدي، مصطفى بهجت، كايا بهكلام، إيفا بيرترام، طارق حفني، صبري خالد، نادين خان و مريم مكيوي، هبة خليفة، أسامة داوود، دينيس دايو، يوهانا دومكه و مروان عمارة، فيليب رزق، جوناثان رشاد، سالي زهني، إبراهيم سعد، رافي شاكر، رندا شعث، لبنى طارق، مريم عبدالعزيز، أحمد عبداللطيف، خالد عبدالله، محمد عز، فادي عزت، هبة فريد، سارة كار، أحمد كامل، أليكس ماجولي، مها مأمون، ياسمينا متولي، جورج محسن، صامويل محسن، أميرة مرتضى، كريس ميشالسكي و سباستيان شتومف، أليكس نانس، جيهان نصر، توماس هارتويل، علي هزاع، إيمان هلال، نرمين همام، ليليان وجدي و بعض المصورين المجهولين.

يقدم هذا الكتاب تركيبة من الصور والنصوص والوثائق، ترتيب ثابت في نهر من الأخبار والتغيرات السياسية. يخرج هذا الكتاب نتيجة عملية تبادلية وحوارية، بعد الكثير من المشاهدة والاستماع.
انتهى العمل التحريري لهذا الكتاب في منتصف شهر يوليو 2013، كان قد اتضح في هذه اللحظة أن التغيير السياسي والاجتماعي في مصر سيكون عملية مؤلمة. ونحن على يقين أن مجموعة الصور المختارة سيتم قراءتها في يوم من الأيام بشكل مختلف عن الشكل الذي نقرأها به الآن.

حُرِّر من قِبَل فلوريان إيبنر وكونستانسه فيكّه

بدعم من

Stiftung Presse-Haus NRZ

GOETHE INSTITUT

KULTURSTIFTUNG DES BUNDES

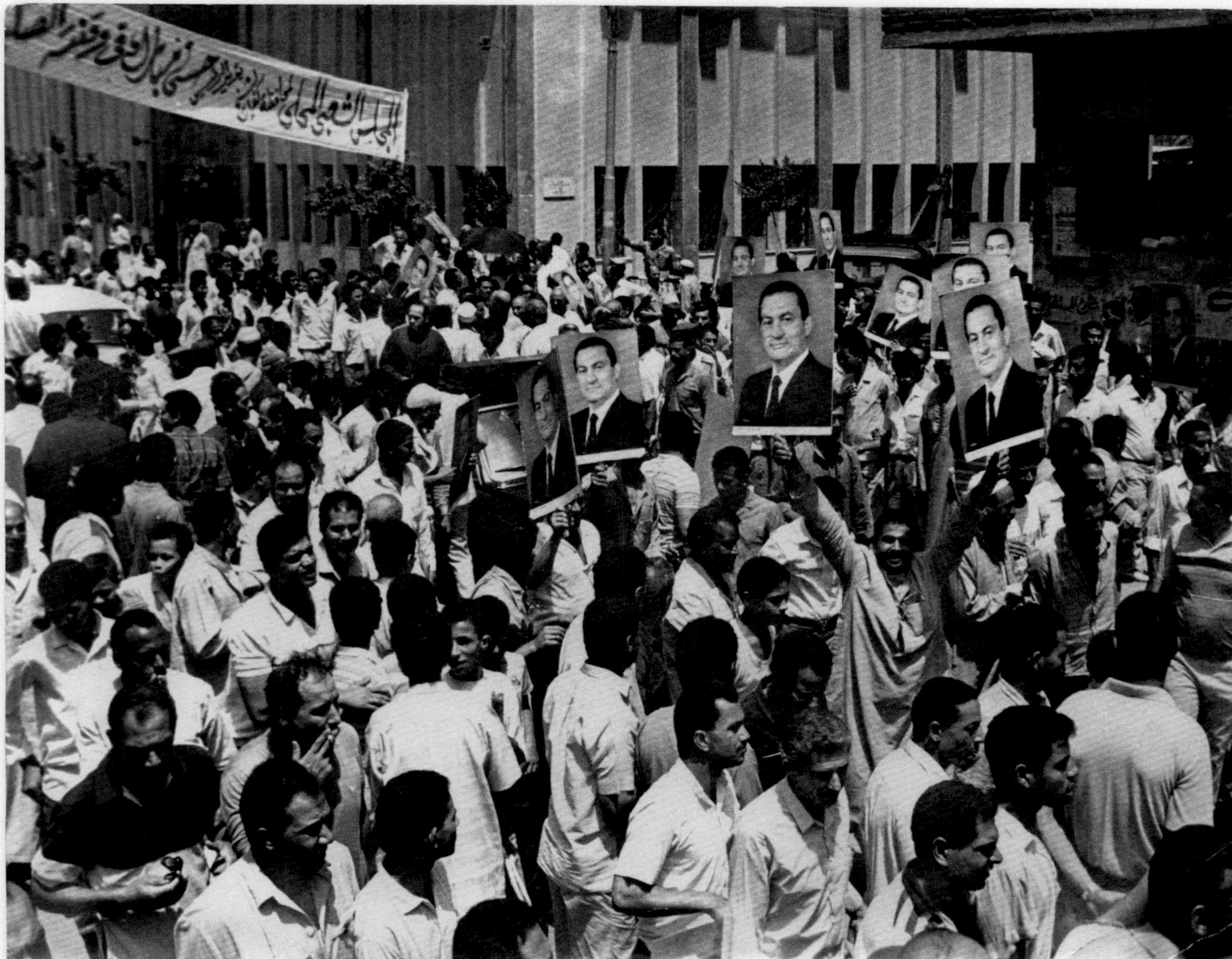

Heba Farid, from the series / aus der Serie *Testimonies, Protests, and Photojournalism*, from the collection of / aus der Sammlung von Amgad Naguib / هبة فريد، شهادات المظاهرات و الصحافة المصورة. من مقتنيات أمجد نجيب

4

Mubarak supporters, Aug. 15, 1990, Kafr El Sheikh governorate / Mubarak-Unterstützer, 15. August 1990, Kafr El Sheikh Gouvernement, photographer / Fotograf: Mahmoud Sho'ayb / مؤيدي مبارك، 15 أغسطس 1990 محافظة كفر الشيخ / المصور: محمود شعيب

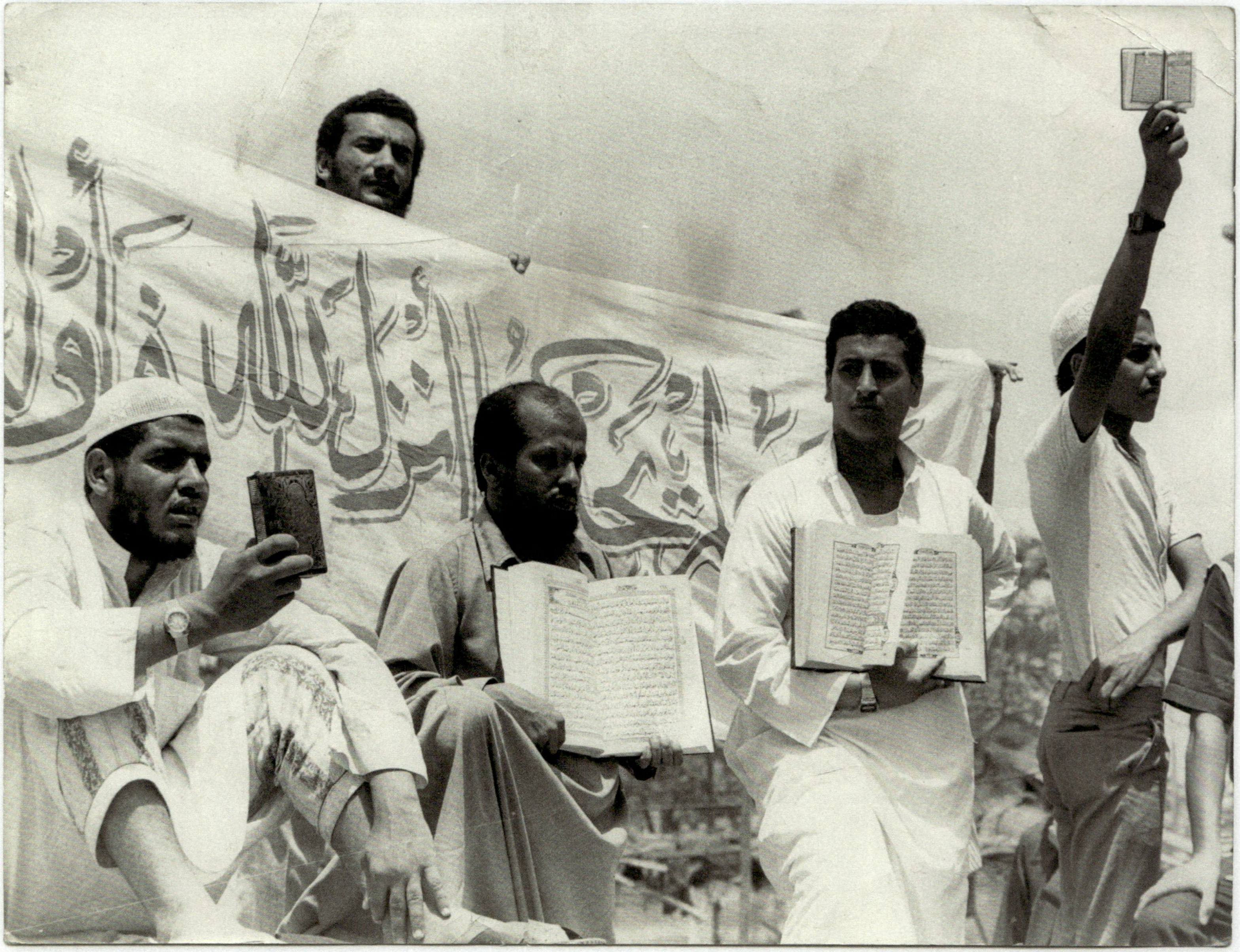

Islamist protest, 1990s, unknown location, photographer unknown / Islamistische Proteste, 1990er, Ort unbekannt, Fotograf unbekannt / مظاهرات إسلامية، في التسعينات، المكان غير معروف، المصور غير معروف

Heba Farid, from the series / aus der Serie *Testimonies, Protests, and Photojournalism*, from the collection of / aus der Sammlung von Amgad Naguib / هبة فريد، شهادات، المظاهرات و الصحافة المصورة. من مقتنيات أمجد نجيب

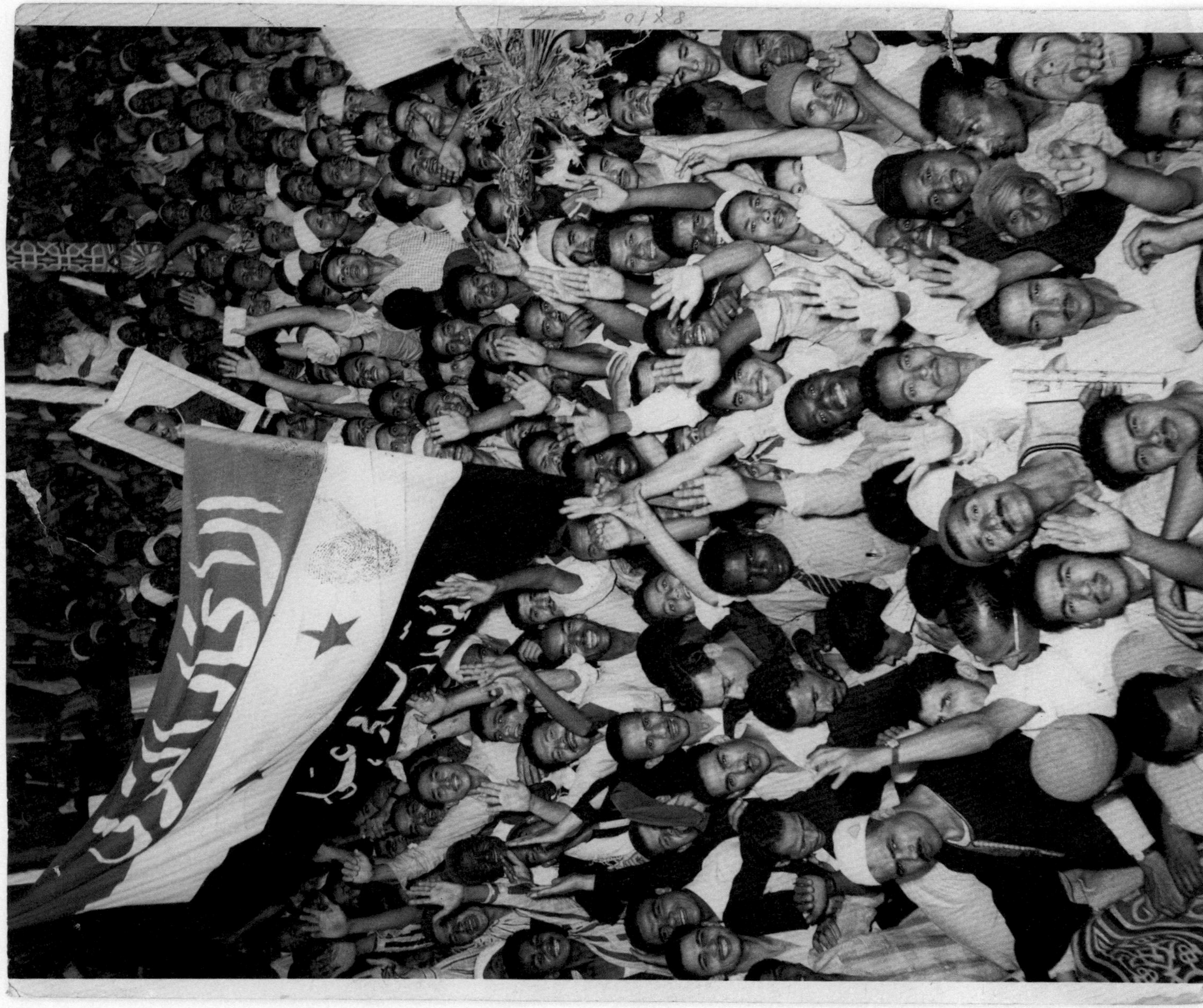

2 Heba Farid, from the series / aus der Serie *Testimonies, Protests, and Photojournalism*, from the collection of / aus der Sammlung von Amgad Naguib / هبة فريد، شهادات المظاهرات و الصحافة المصورة. من مقتنيات أمجد نجيب

Student protest, May 16, 1958, unknown location / Studentenproteste, 16. Mai 1958, Ort unbekannt, photographer / Fotograf: Sa'id Al Nary (possibly / evtl. Sayed Al Nady) / مظاهرات طلابية، 16 مايو 1958 / المصور: سعيد الناري (أو سعيد النادي)

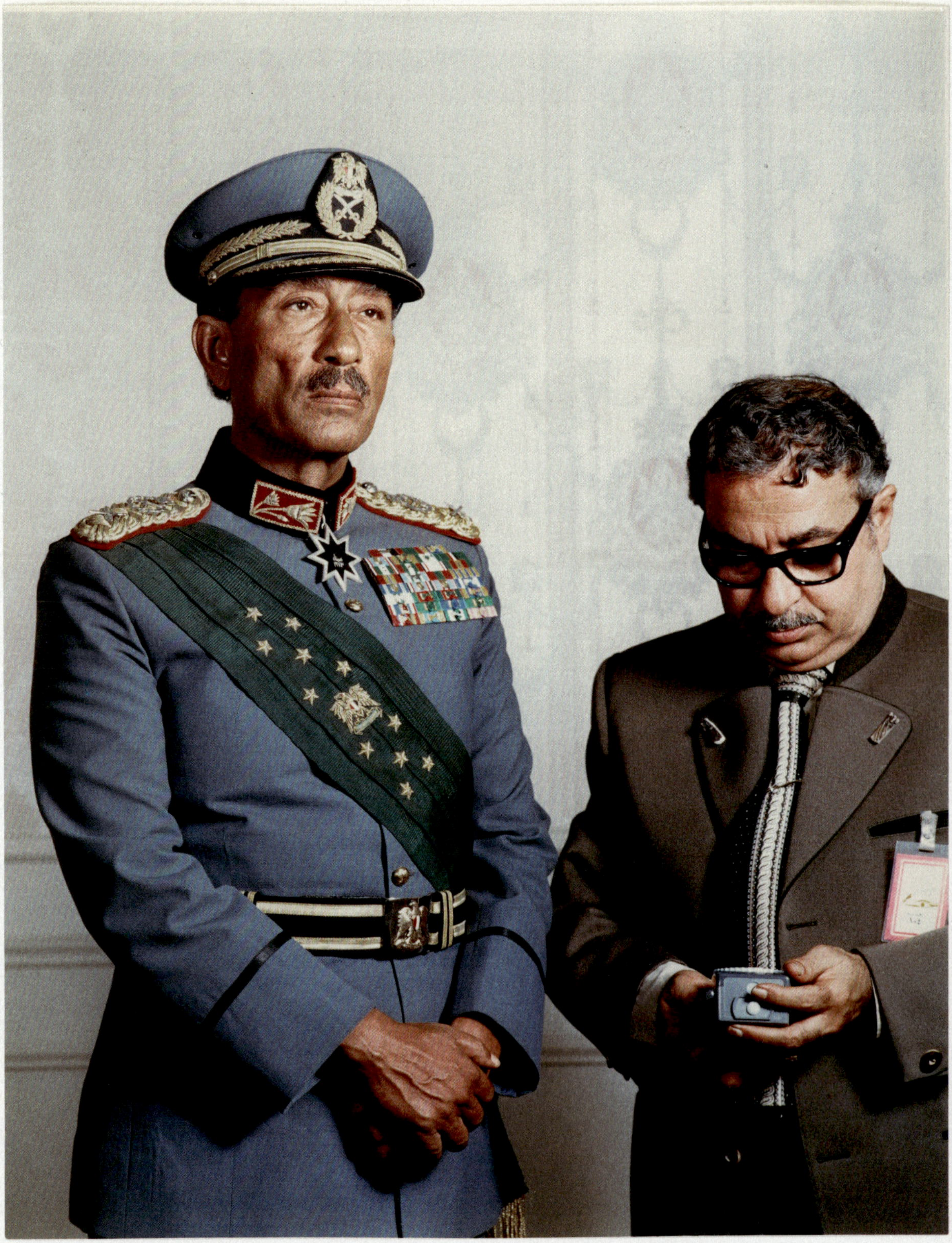

1 Antro, Photographing President Anwar As-Sadat / Präsident Answar As-Sadat wird fotografiert, Oct. 6. 1979 / 1979 أنترو، تصوير الرئيس أنور السادات في السادس من أكتوبر